M000014780

OREGON HIKING

SEAN PATRICK HILL

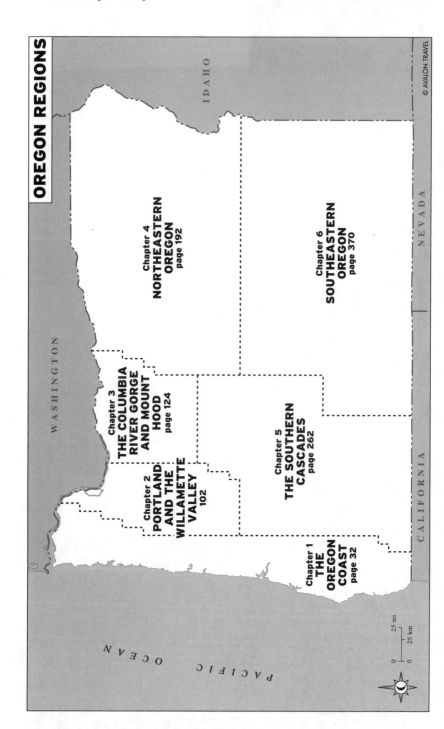

Contents

How to Use This Book 6

Introduction 11

Author's Note 12

Best Hikes 13

(Best Beach and Coastal Walks   **(** Best Self-Guided Nature Walks
(Best for Bird-Watching   **(** Best Short Backpacking Trips
(Best Desert Hiking   **(** Best Non-Technical Summit Hikes
(Best Hikes for Kids   **(** Best Waterfall Hikes
(Best Hikes for Views   **(** Best Wheelchair-Accessible Trails
(Best Hikes Through Old-Growth Forests

Hiking Tips 17

Hiking Essentials 17

Hiking Gear 20

Climate and Weather Protection 20

Safety. 21

Hiking Ethics. 25

Chapter 1
The Oregon Coast. 29

Chapter 2
Portland and the Willamette Valley. 99

Chapter 3
**The Columbia River Gorge
and Mount Hood**. 121

Chapter 4
Northeastern Oregon 189

Chapter 5
The Southern Cascades 259

Chapter 6
Southeastern Oregon 367

Resources 397

Index 405

How to Use This Book

ABOUT THE TRAIL PROFILES

Each hike in this book is listed in a consistent, easy-to-read format to help you choose the ideal hike. From a general overview of the setting to detailed driving directions, the profile will provide all the information you need. Here is a sample profile:

Map number and hike number →

1 SOMEWHERE USA HIKE

Round-trip mileage → **9.0 mi/5.0 hrs**
(unless otherwise noted) and the approximate amount of time needed to complete the hike (actual times can vary widely, especially on longer hikes)

Difficulty and quality ratings

🚶3 ⛰8 ←

at the mouth of the Somewhere River ←

General location of the trail, named by its proximity to the nearest major town or landmark

Map 1.2, page 24   **BEST (**

Map on which the trailhead can be found and page number on which the map can be found

Each hike in this book begins with a brief overview of its setting. The description typically covers what kind of terrain to expect, what might be seen, and any conditions that may make the hike difficult to navigate. Side trips, such as to waterfalls or panoramic vistas, in addition to ways to combine the trail with others nearby for a longer outing, are also noted here. In many cases, mile-by-mile trail directions are included.

Symbol indicating that the hike is listed among the author's top picks

User Groups: This section notes the types of users that are permitted on the trail, including hikers, mountain bikers, horseback riders, and dogs. Wheelchair access is also noted here.

Permits: This section notes whether a permit is required for hiking, or, if the hike spans more than one day, whether one is required for camping. Any fees, such as for parking, day use, or entrance, are also noted here.

Maps: This section provides information on how to obtain detailed trail maps of the hike and its environs. Whenever applicable, names of U.S. Geologic Survey (USGS) topographic maps and national forest maps are also included; contact information for these and other map sources are noted in the Resources section at the back of this book.

Directions: This section provides mile-by-mile driving directions to the trail head from the nearest major town.

Contact: This section provides an address and phone number for each hike. The contact is usually the agency maintaining the trail but may also be a trail club or other organization.

ABOUT THE ICONS

The icons in this book are designed to provide at-a-glance information on the difficulty and quality of each hike.

The **difficulty rating** (rated **1–5** with **1** being the lowest and **5** the highest) is based on the steepness of the trail and how difficult it is to traverse

The **quality rating** (rated **1–10** with **1** being the lowest and **10** the highest) is based largely on scenic beauty, but also takes into account how crowded the trail is and whether noise of nearby civilization is audible

ABOUT THE DIFFICULTY RATINGS

Trails rated 1 are very easy and suitable for hikers of all abilities, including young children.

Trails rated 2 are easy-to-moderate and suitable for most hikers, including families with active children 6 and older.

Trails rated 3 are moderately challenging and suitable for reasonably fit adults and older children who are very active.

Trails rated 4 are very challenging and suitable for physically fit hikers who are seeking a workout.

Trails rated 5 are extremely challenging and suitable only for experienced hikers who are in top physical condition.

MAP SYMBOLS

═══ Expressway	(80) Interstate Freeway	✗ Airfield
┈┈ Primary Road	(101) U.S. Highway	✗ Airport
┈┈ Secondary Road	(21) State Highway	○ City/Town
┈┈ Unpaved Road	(66) County Highway	▲ Mountain
┈┈ Ferry	Lake	▲ Park
━ · ━ National Border	Dry Lake	⁾(Pass
━ ·· ━ State Border	Seasonal Lake	◉ State Capital

ABOUT THE MAPS

This book is divided into chapters based on major regions in the state; an overview map of these regions precedes the table of contents. Each chapter begins with a map of the region, which is further broken down into detail maps. Trailheads are noted on the detail maps by number.

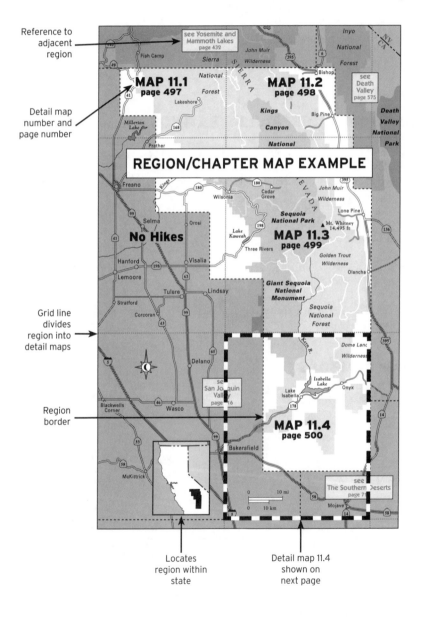

Reference to adjacent region

Detail map number and page number

REGION/CHAPTER MAP EXAMPLE

Grid line divides region into detail maps

Region border

Locates region within state

Detail map 11.4 shown on next page

Indicates adjacent detail maps within region

Locates detail map within region

Map number → **Map 11.4**

Sites shown on detail map and the page range where those sites are listed → **Hikes 105-117**
Pages 564-570

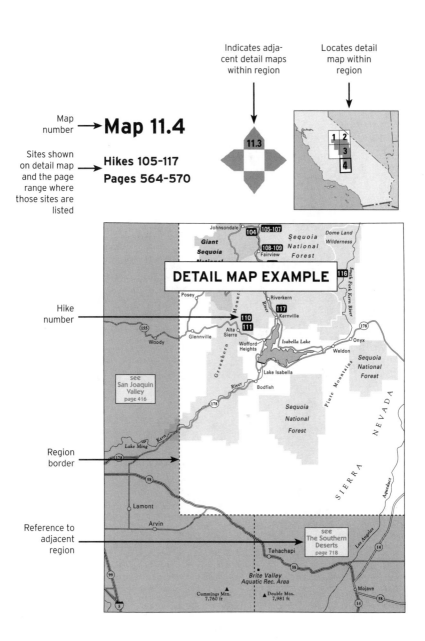

INTRODUCTION

Author's Note

Encompassing landscapes as diverse as Pacific seashore, white oak valleys, volcanic mountain ranges, and sagebrush deserts, no state has quite the span of geography of Oregon. Of all the Pacific Northwestern states, it provides the widest array of potential adventures, many within a few hours driving distance of each other. No wonder it is a popular destination—and home—for so many people.

Oregon can feel as populous as California or as wild as Idaho. A day-trip on Mount Hood, a Cape Falcon exploration, or a survey of waterfalls in the Columbia River Gorge can bring a hiker in contact with many urbanites from nearby Portland. On the other hand, wandering the Siskiyous, or the extensive gorges whittled away from Steens Mountain, or even into the depths of Hell's Canyon can be an experiment in solitude. This is a landscape that quickly changes from cities housing thousands to an occasional lonesome ranch.

Oregon is divided into distinct regions, each with its various opportunities for hiking. The maritime region, known simply as "the coast," offers rocky capes, towering sand dunes, and forests thick with Sitka spruce. The Willamette Valley is home to its namesake river, a rolling countryside of fish-laden creeks, wetlands, and steep buttes. The Columbia River Gorge, a National Scenic Area, is rich with waterfalls, wildflowers, and wild mushrooms. Towering above the Gorge is Mount Hood, Oregon's tallest peak, girdled by the famous Timberline Trail and part of the Cascade Mountains, where old-growth forests and rivers are born. To the southeast lies the high desert, and to the northeast, the pine and larch forests of the Blue Mountains and the awesome chasm of the Snake River.

Oregon is a destination for skiers, kayakers, mountain bikers, and Olympic athletes in training—and, of course, hikers. In Oregon, you can climb to the peak of the Tillamook Head and stand exactly where explorers Lewis and Clark overlooked the Pacific Ocean. You can visit stone shelters built by the Civilian Conservation Corps on Mount Hood and Cape Perpetua, or poke around miners' cabins along the upper reaches of the John Day River. With the right determination, you can even climb South Sister—Oregon's third-highest peak—and see nearly half the state of Oregon around you. No wonder old license plates here read "Pacific Wonderland."

In this book are the best hikes in the state of Oregon. From abandoned cabins to mountain lookouts to decrepit mines, there is plenty of history to see. From mountain lakes to lazy rivers, there are plenty of holes to swim. Bring your camera and pack your gear; with places carrying names like the Painted Hills, the Big Obsidian Flow, and the Devil's Punchbowl, you know you're in for the most memorable of experiences.

Best Hikes

Short on time and in the mood for the spectacular? Here are my picks for the best hikes in Oregon in 11 categories.

◖ Best Beach and Coastal Walks

Cannon Beach to Hug Point, The Oregon Coast, page 41.
Cape Falcon, The Oregon Coast, page 41.
Cape Lookout, The Oregon Coast, page 48.
Heceta Head, The Oregon Coast, page 63.
Baker Beach, The Oregon Coast, page 65.
Umpqua Dunes, The Oregon Coast, page 73.
Sunset Bay to Cape Arago, The Oregon Coast, page 74.
Bullards Beach State Park, The Oregon Coast, page 77.

◖ Best for Bird-Watching

Nehalem Bay, The Oregon Coast, page 42.
Siltcoos River, The Oregon Coast, page 69.
South Slough Estuary, The Oregon Coast, page 75.
Oak Island, Portland and the Willamette Valley, page 105.
Oaks Bottom, Portland and the Willamette Valley, page 108.
Baskett Slough Refuge, Portland and the Willamette Valley, page 112.
Finley Wildlife Refuge, Portland and the Willamette Valley, page 115.
Summer Lake Wildlife Refuge, Southeastern Oregon, page 383.

© SEAN PATRICK HILL

Umpqua Dunes in the Oregon Dunes National Recreation Area

© SEAN PATRICK HILL

Painted Hills in the John Day Fossil Beds

⟨ Best Desert Hiking

Cove Palisades State Park, The Columbia River Gorge and Mount Hood, page 187.
Hells Canyon Reservoir, Northeastern Oregon, page 232.
Painted Hills, Northeastern Oregon, page 233.
Smith Rock State Park, The Southern Cascades, page 288.
Newberry Lava Tubes, The Southern Cascades, page 333.
Leslie Gulch, Southeastern Oregon, page 381.
Petroglyph Lake, Southeastern Oregon, page 387.
Steens Mountain Summit and Wildhorse Lake, Southeastern Oregon, page 393.

⟨ Best Hikes for Kids

Roads End Wayside, The Oregon Coast, page 53.
Willamette Mission State Park, Portland and the Willamette Valley, page 111.
McDowell Creek Falls, Portland and the Willamette Valley, page 116.
Cascadia State Park, Portland and the Willamette Valley, page 116.
Latourell Falls, The Columbia River Gorge and Mount Hood, page 130.
Oxbow Park, The Columbia River Gorge and Mount Hood, page 133.
Wildwood Recreation Site, The Columbia River Gorge and Mount Hood, page 157.
Timothy Lake, The Columbia River Gorge and Mount Hood, page 170.
Shevlin Park, The Southern Cascades, page 301.

⟨ Best Hikes for Views

Saddle Mountain, The Oregon Coast, page 40.
Larch Mountain Crater, The Columbia River Gorge and Mount Hood, page 134.
McNeil Point, The Columbia River Gorge and Mount Hood, page 152.

Zigzag Canyon and Paradise Park, The Columbia River Gorge and Mount Hood, page 159.

Jefferson Park, The Columbia River Gorge and Mount Hood, page 184.

The Obsidian Trail, The Southern Cascades, page 293.

Green Lakes via Fall Creek, The Southern Cascades, page 297.

Mount Thielsen, The Southern Cascades, page 326.

Mount Scott, The Southern Cascades, page 349.

Pilot Rock, The Southern Cascades, page 364.

Steens Mountain Summit and Wildhorse Lake, Southeastern Oregon, page 393.

❰ Best Hikes Through Old-Growth Forests

Valley of the Giants, The Oregon Coast, page 54.

Shrader Old-Growth Trail, The Oregon Coast, page 86.

Redwood Nature Trail, The Oregon Coast, page 96.

Opal Creek, The Columbia River Gorge and Mount Hood, page 177.

Lookout Creek Old-Growth Trail, The Southern Cascades, page 277.

❰ Best Self-Guided Nature Walks

Cascade Head Nature Conservancy Trail, The Oregon Coast, page 52.

Big Pine Interpretive Loop, The Oregon Coast, page 87.

Tryon Creek State Park, Portland and the Willamette Valley, page 110.

Champoeg State Park, Portland and the Willamette Valley, page 111.

McDonald Research Forest, Portland and the Willamette Valley, page 114.

Lewis and Clark Nature Trail, The Columbia River Gorge and Mount Hood, page 130.

Oregon Trail Interpretive Center, Northeastern Oregon, page 257.

Lava Cast Forest, The Southern Cascades, page 335.

❰ Best Short Backpacking Trips

Tillamook Head, The Oregon Coast, page 39.

Vulcan Lake, The Oregon Coast, page 94.

Eagle Creek, The Columbia River Gorge and Mount Hood, page 141.

Mazama Trail to Cairn Basin, The Columbia River Gorge and Mount Hood, page 153.

North Fork John Day River, Northeastern Oregon, page 240.

Strawberry Lake and Little Strawberry Lake, Northeastern Oregon, page 253.

Patjens Lakes, The Southern Cascades, page 286.

Pacific Crest Trail to Matthieu Lakes, The Southern Cascades, page 290.

Divide Lake, The Southern Cascades, page 314.

Big Indian Gorge, Southeastern Oregon, page 392.

❰ Best Non-Technical Summit Hikes

Mirror Lake and Eagle Cap, Northeastern Oregon, page 214.

Onion Creek to Strawberry Mountain, Northeastern Oregon, page 254.

Black Crater, The Southern Cascades, page 290.

South Sister Summit, The Southern Cascades, page 298.

Mount Bailey, The Southern Cascades, page 327.

Mount McLoughlin, The Southern Cascades, page 357.

◖ Best Waterfall Hikes

Kentucky Falls and North Fork Smith River, The Oregon Coast, page 67.

Silver Falls State Park, Portland and the Willamette Valley, page 112.

Wahkeena Falls Loop, The Columbia River Gorge and Mount Hood, page 131.

Multnomaha Falls, The Columbia River Gorge and Mount Hood, page 132.

Oneonta Gorge and Horsetail Falls, The Columbia River Gorge and Mount Hood, page 132.

Ramona Falls, The Columbia River Gorge and Mount Hood, page 151.

Sahalie and Koosah Falls, The Southern Cascades, page 276.

Proxy Falls/Linton Lake, The Southern Cascades, page 294.

Tumalo Falls, The Southern Cascades, page 300.

Salt Creek Falls and Vivian Lake, The Southern Cascades, page 311.

Deschutes River Trail/Dillon and Benham Falls, The Southern Cascades, page 332.

Middle North Falls in Silver Falls State Park

© SEAN PATRICK HILL

◖ Best Wheelchair-Accessible Trails

Fort Stevens State Park, The Oregon Coast, page 38.

Banks-Vernonia Linear Park, The Oregon Coast, page 43.

Powell Butte, Portland and the Willamette Valley, page 108.

Mosier Twin Tunnels, The Columbia Gorge and Mount Hood, page 146.

Timothy Lake, The Columbia Gorge and Mount Hood, page 170.

Natural Bridge and the Rogue Gorge, The Southern Cascades, page 347.

OC&E Woods Line Linear State Park, The Southern Cascades, page 365.

Hiking Tips

HIKING ESSENTIALS

In Oregon, there are those days when you get off work and want to head out for a couple hours of hiking. A day hike is a day hike, and you certainly don't need to lug 30 pounds of tents, stoves, and sleeping bags on your back. But this is absolutely no excuse not to be prepared. The forests resound with stories of people who got lost wandering off the trail, getting hurt or worse. The number one Boy Scout rule for the mountains, shorelines, and deserts of Oregon is *be prepared.* Here's a standard list any good outdoors person should adhere to.

Food and Water

Be sure to carry enough food on even the shortest hike, the reason being you never know if you'll get caught in the woods longer than anticipated. Outdoor stores, even grocery stores, carry a great abundance of high-energy trail food that is lightweight and easy to pack. As far as food goes, suit your tastes but also consider what your body needs. Salty foods replenish much needed sodium lost in sweat. Sugary foods maintain, well, your sugar levels, and they also give good bursts of energy (there are all sorts of great sugar-syrups in little packets for the big burst you need to make it up that final hill). Carbohydrates and proteins are a necessity, as your body will need them for energy and a little muscle repair. In general, bring more food than you think you'll need.

Though food is important, not to mention a great thing to have while you're sitting beside that mountain lake you've been walking for hours to get to, it is water that is far and away the real necessity. What will get you in the woods, even kill you, is not starvation but dehydration. Heat sickness, which can quickly degenerate into hyperthermia, can be damaging if not deadly. On a shorter, easier hike, play it safe and bring at least two quarts of water in your pack. An easy and novel solution is the CamelBak and other such products—small backpacks perfect for day hiking, with plenty of room for food, water, and the rest of the essentials. I swear by it, as does everyone I know who uses one. When I'm properly equipped, I'm carrying upwards of six quarts of water.

If you plan on backpacking and need to carry less weight, be sure to invest in a water filter or some other method of purifying. Never drink straight from the creek! Backcountry water has, unfortunately, largely been infected with *Giardia lamblia* and *Cryptosporidium,* two microscopic organisms that cause a plethora of terrible gastrointestinal problems, the likes of which hardly need to be discussed here. Iodine is still a staple for many backpackers, and there are all sorts of newfangled ways to purify water, including ultraviolet light.

Trail Map and Compass

You'd be surprised how empowering a map can be, especially when you can read it well. Never go on a hike without a map. Despite trail signs, getting confused in the backcountry is more common an occurrence than you'd think. Signs can disappear or get blown down. Trails, too, have a way of sometimes getting lost in certain areas, especially in places with many so-called "user trails" (made by people walking off the designated trail). The best maps are topographic, which can be used in conjunction with a compass to easily pinpoint your position. Plus, they give a good sense of the lay of the land—the more detailed the better. You can find nearby trails and even start adventuring cross-country into areas without trails. But it is imperative to know what you're doing first; one wrong adjustment of the compass can land you miles off track.

You can easily obtain maps from outdoors stores and from the management agencies of the area you are visiting. See the *Resources* chapter for names and contact information for those agencies and for USGS topographical maps, National Forest maps, and maps from commercial services.

A compass is an essential tool for keeping you on track. Take a class from an outdoor group, or a store like REI, and learn to use it correctly and effectively. Many people use GPS devices, but they may not work in some areas. A dense forest canopy may run you the risk of losing a signal, so why depend on it? Knowledge is power, and the compass and map make use of that knowledge.

SOCKS

You cannot underestimate the value of good socks, your cushion against blisters, moisture, and soreness. Hiking socks should be thick enough to fit snugly and cushion your feet all around. Buy plenty, especially for extended backpacking trips, or plan to wash the ones you do have. Dirty, damp, and worn-out socks will not do what they are meant to do. Never wear cotton socks!

Wool blend socks help to wick away moisture from your skin. They run around $15 a pair. Believe me, they're worth it. They are also, I have found, wonderfully warm for when you finally get your boots off at camp.

Extra Clothing

Oregon has a classic saying: Don't like the weather? Wait five minutes, it'll change. Those who say this aren't lying. Conditions fluctuate rapidly, so the right clothing is essential. Being wet and cold is not only uncomfortable, but also downright dangerous. Cotton is the worst clothing to wear: When it gets wet, it stays wet. Wool, the old standby, gets wet and heavy. Today's hiking clothes are manufactured to be waterproof and quick-drying, and even to wick moisture away from the skin. Many clothes are also UV resistant. And they're lightweight, to boot.

You should always carry a lightweight jacket that is both waterproof and wind-resistant. Breathable jackets control your heat, as well. Think ahead if your hike will change in altitude: the higher you go, the colder it may get, so bring a hat and gloves, too. And an extra pair of socks can't hurt, either, particularly ones that keep your feet warm and dry.

Flashlight

You know how sometimes in winter you find yourself saying, "Wow, how'd it get so dark so early?" Well, the *last* place you want to say that is on the trail. It happens.

There is some great and lightweight gear you can use. Headlamps are all the rage, and can cast quite a powerful beam; plus, they keep your hands free. No matter what kind of light source you use, make sure you have extra batteries and an extra bulb. You'll find them very handy around the campsite, as well.

Sunglasses and Sunscreen

One of the trickiest things about hiking near or on a mountain peak is that the air is thinner and therefore—don't ask me how it works—the sun gets stronger. Thus, the mountains are a great place to get sunburned, even on a cold day. Bring both sunscreen with a high SPF and sunglasses with good UV resistance. Put on that sunscreen liberally, and at least 30 minutes before you hike. Later, put on more. Other good accessories to have on hand: a wide-brimmed hat and SPF lip balm.

Insect Repellent

Oregon is famous for its mosquitoes. I mean it. Some of the best destinations, like the mountain wildflower meadows or the lakes and rivers, are overrun with mosquitoes in late spring and early summer. There are many ways to avoid this. One, of course, is to just stay home and wait for fall. The other is to equip yourself with one of the many brands of "bug dope" available in any decent store. The most powerful ones contain a toxic chemical called DEET, which some people prefer to avoid. DEET should not be used on children, and adults should use safe levels. There are also handy mosquito nets that can be pulled over the face, and these are available in outdoors stores.

Long sleeves and long pants will help protect you from the other pest: ticks. Ticks are known to carry nasty diseases like Rocky Mountain Spotted Fever, so it's best to tuck those long pants into your socks and check yourself often. The high desert of Oregon, especially along rivers, is one place ticks frequent.

First-Aid Kit

You really only need a few things here, so frugality is okay when you're dealing with minor cuts, blisters, and sore muscles. A little antibiotic ointment, some bandages, and an anti-inflammatory medication like ibuprofen or acetaminophen can be invaluable. Also be aware of who in your party may be allergic to bee stings, as Oregon has a local ground wasp that can be nasty. Be sure to bring an epinephrine pen or other medication for those with allergies.

It never hurts to learn a little CPR, or even have some Wilderness First-Aid training. When you've gained experience hiking among the rocks, cliffs, and swift rivers, you will quickly see how many potential disasters lurk a little too close for comfort. Be prepared!

Swiss Army-Style Pocket Knife

In Oregon, say "Leatherman" and everyone will know what you're talking about. The Leatherman is a modern equivalent of the famous Swiss Army knife, and a good one has the essentials: a few blades, a can opener, scissors, and tweezers. Whether removing splinters or ticks, or cutting moleskin for that blister, this is a must-have tool.

Firestarter

At night, cold can come on quick in the Oregon mountains, and especially the desert. Starting a fire may be the ultimate necessity in an emergency, for warmth as well as a distress signal, and no hiker should be without either a butane lighter or waterproof matches—and in a state as rainy as Oregon, they should be carried in a waterproof container.

HIKING GEAR

Having the right clothing makes for a comfortable hike. Long gone are the days of climbing mountains in wool pants and hiking to the lake in a pair of cut-off jeans. Today's hiking clothes are made from largely synthetic materials designed to do breathe, meaning to release heat away from the body, and stay dry: that is, they both wick moisture away from the body and dry quickly.

Then, too, there are the feet, which are of course the most heavily used body part while hiking. Caring for your feet is the single most important thing you can do, since nothing makes for a more miserable walk than wet, cold feet or blisters. Take care when choosing footwear and don't worry about frugality: A good pair of hiking shoes or boots is one of the best investments you'll make.

Clothing

Synthetic material, as mentioned above, is what it's all about. So what to bring? With a visit to a good outdoors store, you should walk away with ten articles: synthetic T-shirts, both long sleeve and short sleeve; synthetic hiking shorts and pants (and many companies, like Columbia Sportswear, make those wonderful pants with removable leggings—instant shorts!); a fleece pullover, lightweight and medium-weight; lightweight thermal underwear; synthetic-blend socks that wick away moisture and stay dry; rain jacket and pants; lightweight fleece gloves; waterproof gloves; wide-brimmed sun hat; a warm pullover hat. Snug clothes are better than loose, so make sure they fit properly.

Footwear

In general, you should consider three things when looking for good hiking footwear. For one, there is **support:** a good shoe or boot needs to offer both the foot and ankle ideal support, so as to make those rocky crossings safer and less strenuous. The **weight** of footwear is as important; heavy footwear means tiresome walking, especially if you are considering a long-distance jaunt. Talk about dragging your feet! **Flexibility** will save you from that painful culprit: the blister. Flexibility must balance itself with overall boot fit, since slippage is what generally exacerbates the formation of blisters.

You should fit boots in relation to socks: the combination of the two, once mastered, will save you from sitting around the campfire at night, cutting moleskin for those welts.

There are many options for footwear, from trail running shoes and lightweight hiking boots to sturdier backpacking boots. Consider the tread on the boot, the ankle support, and whether the material is waterproof or water-resistant. Once you purchase new footwear, be sure to take a few test runs and break them in before that big backpacking trip. Your feet will applaud you.

CLIMATE AND WEATHER PROTECTION

Weather in Oregon is diverse and unpredictable. Wind, pouring rain, snow and ice, blazing sun, high and low humidity, all of these are part of the Oregon experience. It is essential to be prepared. Weather reports, especially those from the National Weather Service, help greatly, but be ready for sudden changes—especially along the coast, in the high desert, and in the mountains.

THE PACIFIC CREST TRAIL

The most famous long-distance trail through Oregon is the Pacific Crest Trail (PCT), part of the 2,650-mile trail that passes through three states between Canada and Mexico. The Beaver State has its fair share of this historic and well-used National Scenic Trail, and its 430-mile stretch is usually snow-free between July and September. There's a lot to see: the Siskiyou Mountains, Crater Lake National Park, the Oregon Cascades with its long line of volcanic peaks, and the Columbia Gorge National Scenic Area.

The PCT accounts for a number of popular day hikes, especially in Oregon's famed wilderness areas: Mount Hood, Three Sisters, and Sky Lakes to name a few. Along the way, the trail passes everything from errant graves to lava fields to the incredible Timberline Lodge.

Seasons

Oregon has roughly four seasons, and each region reflects those seasons differently. Everywhere in the state, summer, the peak season, tends to have higher temperatures (though the people of Bend, Oregon, still talk about the time it snowed on the Fourth of July). As late summer approaches, so does the occasional rain and sleet.

Autumn, too, makes for beautiful days, and is my favorite time to hike. The color displays are at a height, and days can be significantly cooler, thus making for a sweat-free ramble.

As winter approaches, so does the wind, rain, and snow. For the most part, a significant number of Oregon's mountains are snowed-in and inaccessible all winter long: check with local agencies before trying a hike in an unfamiliar place. Roads, too, tend to be snowed in, and access to trailheads can be nonexistent. Winter in Oregon, at least in the mountains (including the Cascades, the Blues, the Wallowas, and the high elevations of the Siskiyous), can stretch from November to July.

Spring brings mud and more rain, but also increasing wildflower shows.

Rain Gear

What more needs to be said? Oregonians aren't said to have webbed feet for nothing. Rain gear is crucial, and this is largely why Oregonians tend to not care if it's raining. It's not like hikers are the little kids in front of the window, glumly watching the rain, wishing they could go out. On the contrary, nothing stops hikers in Oregon.

Durable, breathable rain gear (along with waterproof or water-resistant footwear) is an investment that will allow access to many places in Oregon year-round. For the most part, the Oregon coast, the foothills of the Cascades, most of the Columbia River Gorge, and low-elevation valleys are open year-round. Take advantage of it! Much of Oregon's beauty is due to the rains. What else keeps Oregon so green?

SAFETY

Like many Western U.S. states, it is possible to run into rattlesnakes, mountain lions, and bears—not to mention poison oak and biting bugs. Here's a little information about the locals.

NON-TECHNICAL SUMMIT HIKES

Oregon is a mountain climber's dream. With numerous peaks exceeding the 10,000-foot elevation range, there are plenty of opportunities to get on top of the world and enjoy the stunning views that come with them. That being said, it is important to differentiate the kind of mountain climbs featured in this book as available to the common hiker.

A "technical" summit climb requires not just skill but equipment such as ropes, harnesses, protection gear, and other specialized tools like ice axes and crampons. Mount Hood is the most popular of all technical climbs in Oregon, and a summit climb of this kind should never be done without experienced partners and a great deal of training and conditioning. It is a sport unto itself.

Hikes recommended in this book are "non-technical" summits, meaning climbing gear is not required. The mountain hikes covered in this book are those that can be summited on trails recognized by management agencies and detailed on maps. They are generally a long, steep climb, but far safer than climbing extremely steep slopes and crossing glaciers. Think of a non-technical climb, also known as "scrambling," as a really tough hike, where the path may get arduous and you may have to cross some snow now and again.

No matter the climb – whether it be South Sister, Mount McLoughlin, or Eagle Cap – always be prepared as you would for any other hike, if not more so. Be sure to carry more than enough food, water, and clothing, and remember that any change in weather can prove disastrous. Also, pace yourself; any non-technical climb can be especially taxing if you are out-of-shape or tired. Practice on smaller climbs before attempting to bag the big peaks.

Wildlife

RATTLESNAKES

Of the 15 species of snakes in Oregon, only *Crotalus viridis,* the Western Pacific Rattlesnake, is poisonous. They are most active in the spring, summer, and early fall and can be found in parts of the Willamette Valley, the Cascade Mountain foothills, the Siskiyou Mountains, and parts of Eastern Oregon. Their most easily identifiable characteristic, of course, is that heart-stopping rattle. And it's good to stop, because once it has warned you, a rattlesnake is going to try to retreat from you. Stand still; rattlers rarely attack a nonmoving object.

Although rattlesnake bites are certainly painful, they are rarely lethal. Not all rattlesnake bites contain venom, either. If you are bitten, the best thing you can do is call 911 and drive to a hospital. Remove any restrictive clothing and don't attempt to apply a tight tourniquet. Remain calm and avoid running, which can speed venom through the body.

MOUNTAIN LIONS

Cougars, also known as mountain lions, are the largest of the big cats in Oregon. They range pretty much anywhere, and have even passed through towns and cities in the state, especially when following migrating prey such as elk. However, in all likelihood, you will never see one. Cougars will usually avoid humans at all cost. In fact, many people have been near one and never realized it.

In mountain lion country, keep children and pets close. Should you encounter a cougar, don't turn away and don't run. Instead, make yourself appear as large as possible by raising your arms, waving a stick, and opening your coat. Back away slowly, maintaining your pose and speaking loudly.

BLACK BEARS

Like cougars, black bears range widely and try to steer clear of humans. Be alert and make a little noise in bear country to let them know you're coming. If you do see one—which is unlikely, but not impossible—you'll know what it is, since black bears are the only species of bear in Oregon.

If you do encounter a bear, don't run and don't look it in the eye: bears interpret this as a sign of aggression. Instead, back away slowly. If a bear does happen to charge you, stay calm and be prepared to fight back. You can make yourself look bigger by waving your arms and opening your coat. If you have a dog, keep it leashed; an over-protective dog can put a bear on the defensive. One of the worst-case scenarios is to come between a mother bear and her cubs.

A more common way to run into a bear is at camp. Bears are attracted by not only food, and sweet food at that, but by fragrances like toothpaste and perfume. Really. If bears know, or think, that there's something tasty in your tent or your bag, like that honey-almond granola you brought, they'll have at it. Though Oregon doesn't have the same issues with bears as, say, Yosemite National Park in California, it's still wise to hide your food. Backpackers should use a bear-proof canister for overnight trips. You can also make use of a food-hang, where you hang your food by rope from a tree limb, a minimum of 20 feet off the ground and 10 feet from the tree trunk. Tie your rope to a rock and throw it over a branch at least one inch in diameter and four inches at the trunk to accomplish this.

Insects and Plants

Aside from the large mammals and reptiles, it's the little things that get you: mosquitoes, ticks, poison oak, and stinging nettles. Here's how to avoid them.

MOSQUITOES

Mosquitoes in Oregon are by far the peskiest pest of all. Come spring and summer, the valleys and mountains—even the deserts—bloom with the obnoxious buzzing and incessant biting. All this can make for a thoroughly annoying outdoor experience spent swatting and slapping.

Mosquitoes are not merely annoying; they may even be dangerous. As with other states, Oregon has had its first few experiences with West Nile Virus, though it has mostly been confined to a few infections in people, birds, and horses. Better safe than sorry. Know before you go: As snows melt in the mountains, mosquitoes are born, and this typically happens from June to August. Visiting a marshy wildlife refuge in spring? Expect skeeters. Even in deserts, you can expect hordes of them along rivers.

The worst of the worst is the Asian tiger mosquito, a non-native species thought to have been brought to America in automobile tires that contained stagnant water. You'll know them when you see them by their stripes. It's best to carry repellent and netting, or even to avoid certain areas in the peak hatching season.

TICKS

You'll want to corral a friend into a good old "tick check." Ticks find their way into the weirdest of places in an effort to lock in and draw from your blood. The frontline defense is long pants and long sleeves, and to check both your skin and your clothing after hiking. If you find a tick burrowed in, pull it straight out carefully with tweezers, grasping it firmly from the surface of the skin. It's important to get the body and head out, or you can risk infection.

Ticks are most active in spring and summer, in areas of tall grasses and shrubs. Of the four varieties of ticks in Oregon, only the Western black-legged tick is a carrier of Lyme disease. This little tick is mostly black; the larger brown ones are harmless. It's generally said that if you can save a removed tick and take it to a doctor for testing, that's a safe bet. If within a few days or a few weeks you begin to experience flu-like symptoms, see a doctor post-haste.

Dogs, too, are susceptible to ticks, so make sure to check them carefully when you've been hiking in susceptible areas.

POISON OAK

It's been said many times before, but let's say it again: "Leaves of three, let them be." Once you learn to recognize *Toxicodendron diversilobum,* it will become very familiar to you, especially in areas like southern Oregon, the Willamette Valley, and the Columbia Gorge. Otherwise, the brutal rash that can itch for weeks will teach you the hard way to remember. Even as the leaves dry, they still contain the chemical that affects us. Should you come into contact with poison oak, or think you may have, wash thoroughly with warm water and soap as soon as possible. There are several products and soap available that can deal with exposure to poison oak on the trail. As I've learned from experience, dogs pick it up on their fur. Rather than petting, offer your pooch a nice, hot bath.

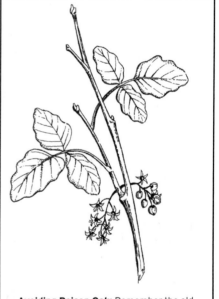

Avoiding Poison Oak: Remember the old Boy Scout saying: "Leaves of three, let them be."

STINGING NETTLES

This member of the nettle family likes to grow in clumps in the Coast Range and in the desert. Heart-shaped, coarse-toothed leaves on a stem bristling with little white hairs gives it away. If you come in contact with those hairs, the resulting sting will let you know immediately that your identification is successful. You'll have to ride out the sting for 24 hours, wondering all the while how it is possible—and delectable—to boil and eat nettles safely!

Safety on the Trail

Stories abound of unfortunate mishaps where people get lost in the wilderness for days on end, and every year seems to bring a new tale of woe. Most of these stories involve two kinds of hikers: the one who hikes alone, and the one who gets separated from a larger group. One wrong turn off a trail, or simply not paying attention in the midst of a huge mountain meadow, can have dire consequences. Weather, too, can have an impact on your safety—for example, getting caught on a ridgeline in a lightning storm (and this one comes from experience!) calls for quick thinking.

Should you find yourself lost, your first priority is to remain calm. Know that it's far better to stay put where you are than to try to keep moving; rescuers will be looking for where you were last known to be (this is why it's so important to fill out wilderness permits at trailheads). Emergency gear, especially a whistle and signaling device, will come in handy here, since rescuers will be listening and looking for signs.

What's the best way to avoid trouble? Simply this: Always tell someone where you'll be. Tell someone at home your travel plans and register with a local ranger station, especially if your plan is to hike into a remote wilderness area. Be specific and detail the area you're visiting, the times you intend to travel, and how long you think you'll be out. It's the responsible thing to do, and it saves searchers much time and effort should you become lost.

Driving Safely

If you think weather can wreak havoc on a trail, try a road. Many of the approaches to trailheads in Oregon require driving on dirt roads that can quickly turn to mud or, worse, can result in a washout. Always check road conditions before you go by calling the Oregon Department of Transportation at 511 or checking www.tripcheck.com. Detailed weather reports and forecasts are available through the National Weather Service online at www.nws.noaa.gov.

Make sure that your car is properly equipped. Fuel up often, check the oil and the brakes, and make sure you've got a spare tire. Have emergency road equipment like snow chains, flashers, and a cell phone.

Make sure your directions are accurate (even mine!). Carry a good atlas of Oregon, like the DeLorme or Benchmark, and don't rely exclusively on Internet maps or GPS devices. If all else fails, ask directions.

Check snow levels. Every year in recent memory has seen individuals or families getting trapped in the snow in the mountains. Just because it's raining in Portland doesn't mean it is at Mount Hood; most likely, it's piling up snow quick. Avoid roads closed in winter or otherwise impassable. Forest Service roads are not shortcuts; stick to main routes and get there safely.

HIKING ETHICS

Trail Etiquette

As wonderful as it is to think like Henry David Thoreau and head for the woods for a little soul-searching solitude, don't expect to find it all the time. Expect instead a lot of other intrepid hikers looking for their own Walden Pond, too. Here are some simple rules to follow to assure a good time for everyone.

WILDERNESS ETHICS

Congressionally designated Wilderness Areas are unique, and are preserved under certain criteria. It's important to maintain the wilderness experience for everyone by limiting human impact. Here are some basic guidelines:

Campfires: Gone are the days of singing around the campfire. For the most part, campfires are discouraged – if not outright prohibited – due to catastrophic forest fires rampant in the Western United States. Land management agencies have decreed that cooking is best done on a backpacking stove. Lighting can be provided by a variety of devices, from flashlights to headlamps.

Water sources: It is imperative to keep Oregon's waters clean. When camping near any lake, stream, or river, give yourself at least 100 feet distance from the waterline before pitching that tent. Likewise, wash all your cooking gear, socks, and hands by carrying water at least 100 feet away from the water source.

Campsites: When you pitch a tent, be aware of where you are plopping down. A misplaced tent can crush sensitive flowers and damage an area for years. You should always camp on a durable surface, such as rock, or even on sand or dead and dry organic matter – never on live vegetation. This helps maintain the environment for all and prevents area closures for rehabilitation.

Garbage: No one is impressed by a trashed campsite. Who wants to see another campfire ring filled with broken glass and blackened cans, or a campsite ringed by toilet paper wads? No matter what you bring, pack out your garbage. Neither burn nor bury it. That goes for human waste, too.

Maintain the silence. You and everyone else come to the wilderness to get away from the usual hustle and bustle of civilization. Be courteous to all the other hikers by refraining from undue noise. Avoid loud conversations, shouting, and above all, cell phones. This way, too, you're more likely to encounter wildlife and hear the falling water and wind in the trees.

Yield to other users accordingly. Standard rules on yielding apply for the three main user groups—hikers, horses, and bikers. In general, bikes must yield to everyone, and hikers should yield to horses.

Stay on maintained trails. Evidence of breaking this rule is everywhere. Degraded switchbacks and the ubiquitous "user trail" show for certain that people are taking shortcuts and wandering off-trail. Don't use closed trails or enter closed areas; often, they have been closed for restoration or because of overuse. Wandering off-trail tramples vegetation and in the end may force management agencies to limit access for everyone.

Hiking with Children

Always keep children close, especially in areas with cliffs and fast-moving water. Consider the trail carefully before taking children, as many routes are too difficult for them. By choosing appropriate trails, you'll make trips memorable and enjoyable for everyone.

Hiking with Dogs

It's possible that there's no more dog-friendly state than Oregon. That being so, you're sure to run into dogs on the trail or to want to bring your own. And what could be more charming than a dog carrying its own pack with little mitts on its paws?

Regardless, dogs open a whole new can of worms in the outdoors. For one thing, chasing wildlife is a leading reason why dogs get lost in the wilderness. A dog on a leash is a dog that goes home again.

Because of conflicts between hikers and pets, dogs are no longer allowed on many trails in Oregon, or are restricted to a leash on others. Some trails, like the Deschutes River Trail in Central Oregon, no longer allow dogs off-leash, but this may not be obvious at the trailhead. It's best to call the area's managing agency for up-to-date rules. If a posted sign says that dogs must be on a leash, follow it strictly. Otherwise, you could well end up with a ticket.

If a dog is allowed off-leash, as in many forest and wilderness areas, take care that your dog responds appropriately to verbal commands, for the dog's own safety. Why worry? Carry a leash or get good dog training and just enjoy the trip for you and your dog both.

Avoiding Crowds

On the one hand, you can hike into a place like Big Indian Gorge on a summer weekend and not see a soul but for a few deer. On the other hand, you can go to Multnomah Falls, trying to get to the top to hike on up to Larch Mountain and fight your way through throngs of tourists, day-trippers, kids with ice cream cones, and parents in flip-flops pushing strollers. What to do? With a little foresight, you can find a bit of solitude after all.

Avoid the weekends. Weekends are notorious for the so-called "weekend warrior" out for a Saturday afternoon. If you get the chance, take your hike when everyone else is at work. From Tuesday through Thursday seems to be the best, and quietest, time.

Be the first one at the trailhead. If you arrive at a trailhead at around 10 or 11 A.M. like most people do, you'll have trouble finding a parking spot and staying out of the parade. But get there at 6 A.M.? Now you're talking. More than likely, you'll be the only one there.

Hike more than just summer. For most of Oregon, the on-season is summer. Memorial Day (which can be horrendous) and Labor Day (even worse) and everything in between means everyone is out for that brief respite between rains. But once the kids are in school and everyone is secure in the usual routine, *now* is the time to get out.

Avoid the popular hikes. If you have a need for peace and quiet on an August weekend afternoon, then maybe Crater Lake is not your best bet. But then nearby Mount Bailey might be. Choose off-the-beaten-path journeys and you're less likely to see the casual tourist.

Hike in the rain. Any bad weather will do, and if you have good gear you can be out looking at wildflowers in the spring rain while the rest of the world is home keeping their feet warm. Oregon is a place of many moods: gale-force winds, fog, clouds, and rain. These make life more interesting—and memorable.

Leave No Trace

As Henry David Thoreau once said, "In wilderness is the preservation of the world." So how do we preserve our wilderness? The Center for Outdoor Ethics offers these simple dictums to "Leave only footprints and take only pictures":

Plan ahead and prepare. Know the special regulations of the area you are visiting. Be prepared. Schedule your trips to avoid high-use times. Visit in small groups. Repackage your food to minimize waste.

Travel and camp on durable surfaces. Use established trails and campsites. Keep campsites small. In pristine areas, disperse use to prevent the creation of camps or trails.

Dispose of waste properly. Pack it in, pack it out. Deposit human waste in a "cathole" dug 6–8 inches at least 200 feet from water, camp, and trails; cover and disguise when finished. Pack out toilet paper and hygiene products. To wash yourself or dishes, carry water 200 feet away from streams and lakes. If you must use soap, make sure it's biodegradable. Scatter the water when done.

Leave what you find. Examine, but do not touch or remove, cultural or historic structures and artifacts. Leave rocks, plants, and natural objects as you find them. Avoid introducing non-native species. Do not build structures or furniture or dig trenches.

Minimize campfire impacts. Use a stove for cooking, a candle for lighting. Where fires are permitted, use established fire rings, pans, or mounds. Keep fires small and use only ground material to burn. Burn wood and coals to ash, douse completely, and scatter the cool ashes.

Respect wildlife. Remember that you are only a visitor in the wilderness, but it is home to animals. Observe wildlife from a distance, and do not approach or follow. Never feed animals. Store your food securely and control your pets. Avoid wildlife during times of mating, nesting, and raising young.

Be considerate of other visitors. Respect others and protect the quality of their experience. Be courteous. Camp away from other people. Let nature's sounds prevail.

This copyrighted information has been reprinted with permission from the Leave No Trace Center for Outdoor Ethics. For more information or materials, please visit www.lnt.org or call 303/442-8222 or 800/332-4100.

Permits and Land Use

There are different permits you'll need for each of Oregon's 115 state parks, 13 national forest, and five state forests. Many trails on National Forest land, but not all, require the Northwest Forest Pass to park within a quarter-mile of a posted trailhead. These cost $5 a day or $30 for a yearly pass.

Most wilderness areas on National Forest land require a free wilderness permit (available at trailheads) to enter. There are exceptions, such as the Obsidian Trail or the Pamelia Lake area, which require a free special permit beforehand, secured simply by calling the ranger station.

Oregon State Parks vary widely. Some require a day-use fee, while others are free. Many of the more popular parks require a day-use fee, but the waysides—especially along beaches—tend to be free.

The Bureau of Land Management, National Forest Service, and National Park Service manage Oregon's national monuments, national recreation areas, Crater Lake National Park, and the Columbia Gorge National Scenic Area. In addition to the information provided in this book, be sure to contact the appropriate agency for up-to-date information on fees and permits.

THE OREGON COAST

© SEAN PATRICK HILL

BEST HIKES

❰ Coastal Hikes
Cannon Beach to Hug Point, page 41.
Cape Falcon, page 41.
Cape Lookout, page 48.
Heceta Head, page 63.
Baker Beach, page 65.
Umpqua Dunes, page 73.
Sunset Bay to Cape Arago, page 74.
Bullards Beach State Park, page 77.

❰ Bird-Watching
Nehalem Bay, page 42.
Siltcoos River, page 69.
South Slough Estuary, page 75.

❰ Hikes for Kids
Roads End Wayside, page 53.

❰ Hikes for Views
Saddle Mountain, page 40.

❰ Hikes Through Old-Growth Forests
Valley of the Giants, page 54.
Shrader Old-Growth Trail, page 86.
Redwood Nature Trail, page 96.

❰ Self-Guided Nature Walks
Cascade Head Nature Conservancy Trail, page 52.
Big Pine Interpretive Loop, page 87.

❰ Short Backpacking Trips
Tillamook Head, page 39.
Vulcan Lake, page 94.

❰ Waterfall Hikes
Kentucky Falls and North Fork Smith River, page 67.

❰ Wheelchair-Accessible Trails
Fort Stevens State Park, page 38.
Banks-Vernonia Railroad, page 43.

Oregonians go to "the coast," but never to

"the beach." Sure, there are beaches here, but forget your image of the West Coast. This is not your ordinary Los Angeles beach with surfers riding the waves — though you'll see them, too. Oregon's coastline is 363 miles of rugged, awe-inspiring, and unforgettable landscape. From enormous, cliff-lined capes to windswept sand dunes, from rhododendron-sheltered coves to forested mountains, from sandy spits to towering sea stacks teeming with wildlife, Oregon's coast runs the gamut. You can see ancient Sitka spruce and redwoods, climb lava flow headlands, explore tidal pools, or just sit on a beach watching the brown pelicans skirt the surf, making Oregon's coastline by far some of the most dramatic in the country.

The Oregon state parks on the coast are among the best in the state, and many are free. There are also scores of "waysides," simple turnouts with a picnic table or two that are often the site of amazing trailheads. Many parks offer camping, swimming, and historical sites in addition to trails and beaches. You will also find National Forest land with dense forests of Douglas fir, Western red cedar, Western hemlock, and Sitka spruce. Wildlife is plentiful, from elk to deer to shorebirds. Among the parks and forestlands is the Oregon Dunes National Recreation Area, a must-see for anyone, with its stupendous dunes rising hundreds of feet and covering nearly 36 miles of coastline.

But there is more than just ocean and sand; what Oregonians know of the coast also includes the Coast Range, mountains that separate the coastline proper from the Willamette Valley. In the Coast Range, you'll find incredible mountain hikes, flowering rhododendrons, and waterfall after waterfall. The southern portion of the Coast Range gives way to the Klamath and Siskiyou Mountains, a granite landscape that geographically is one of the oldest parts of the state. The sweeping forest fire known as the Biscuit Fire, among the largest in Oregon's history, swept through here in 2002, but the area is recovering nicely. Flowers bloom and many trees were spared. Cutting through these mountains are the Rogue and Illinois Rivers, destinations for river rats and wilderness aficionados.

Many of the trails in this area follow the 360-mile Oregon Coast Trail, extending from Brookings in the south to Astoria in the north. Following this trail, you'll cross rivers, follow rocky headlands, and pass through quaint towns. As with the more well-known Pacific Crest Trail, this path can be followed for the entire distance, backpacked for shorter sequences, or just make for some great day-tripping.

In the coastal area, towering, inaccessible cliffs often hem in beaches, so be sure to check tide charts and go at low tide. Be extra careful when atop the cliffs themselves, too. Though the many capes and cliffs make for great vistas, they can also be dangerous. Make sure you don't step on anything living around sea stacks and tidepools. Many areas, like Haystack Rock on Cannon Beach, are federally protected wildlife preserves, and it is against the law to intrude on these important nesting and breeding sites. When in doubt, check with local agencies and land management.

So don't go thinking "coast" means bathing suits and sand castles, though you'll see your share of those. Instead, think of it as a real wilderness. In this regard, it is valuable to not only check the weather before you go (Oregon weather anywhere, let alone the finicky coast, can change abruptly; believe me, I know), but check the tide charts. Oregon is famous for its "sneaker waves" that come up quite unexpectedly with little fore-warning. Be safe on your adventures on the Oregon coast, and you'll remember it as the rugged adventure it has always been.

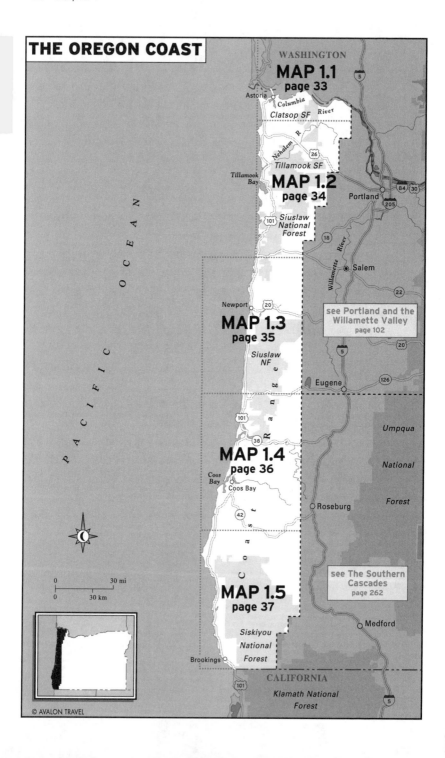

THE OREGON COAST

WASHINGTON
MAP 1.1
page 33

Astoria
Columbia River
Clatsop SF

Nehalem R.
26
Tillamook SF

Tillamook Bay
MAP 1.2
page 34

Portland
84 30
205

101
Siuslaw National Forest

18
Willamette River

Salem
22

Newport
20
MAP 1.3
page 35

Siuslaw NF

Coast Range

Eugene
126
5
20

see Portland and the Willamette Valley
page 102

101
38
MAP 1.4
page 36

Coos Bay
Coos Bay
42
Roseburg

Umpqua

National

Forest

PACIFIC OCEAN

Coast Range

101
MAP 1.5
page 37

see The Southern Cascades
page 262

Medford

0   30 mi
0   30 km

Siskiyou National Forest

Brookings

CALIFORNIA
101
Klamath National Forest

5

© AVALON TRAVEL

Map 1.1

Hikes 1-2
Pages 38-39

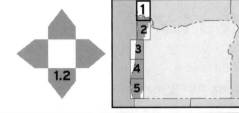

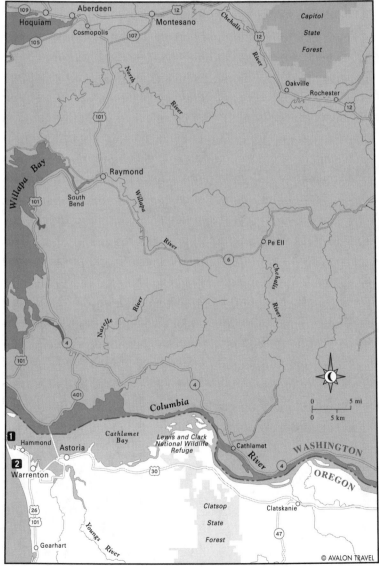

Map 1.2

Hikes 3-24
Pages 39-53

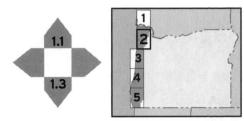

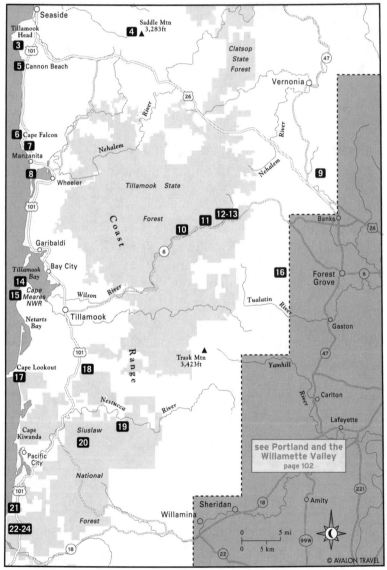

Map 1.3

Hikes 25-48
Pages 53-67

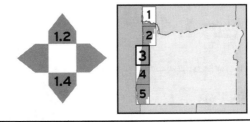

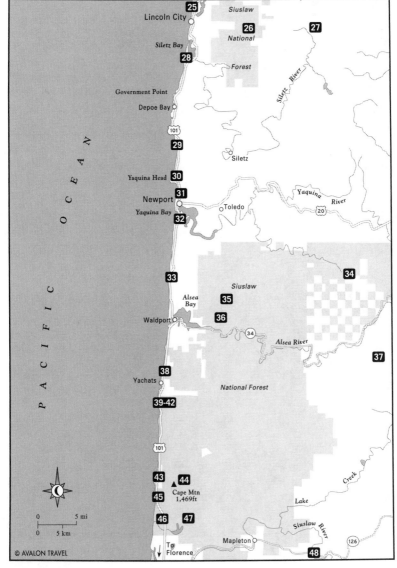

Map 1.4

Hikes 49-66
Pages 67-77

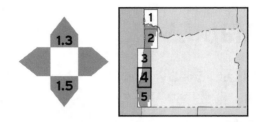

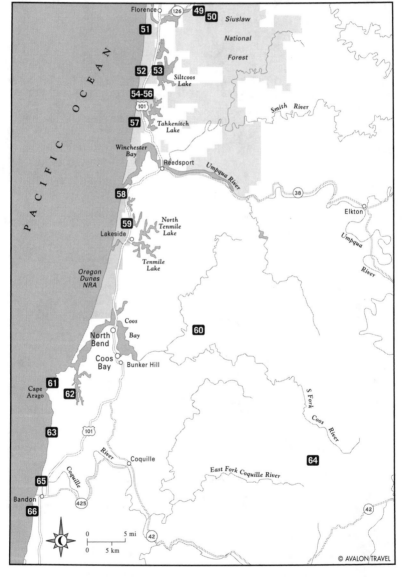

Map 1.5

**Hikes 67-98
Pages 78-97**

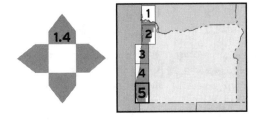

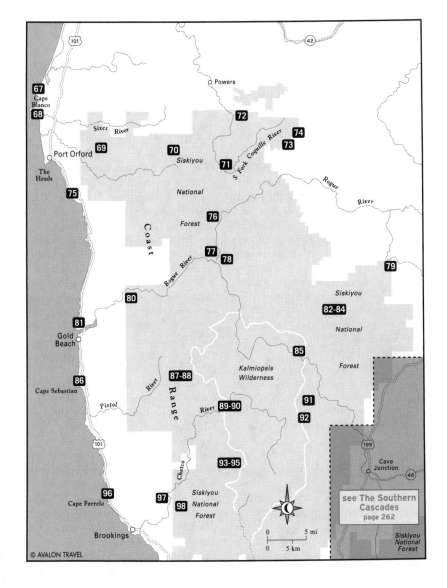

❶ CLATSOP SPIT
4.5 mi/2.0 hr   🏃₁ ⛰₇

on the Columbia River in Fort Stevens State Park

Map 1.1, page 33

The Oregon coast begins at Clatsop Spit, where the Columbia River meets the Pacific Ocean. Here the fishing boats and towering barges butt their way inland, reckoning with the Columbia Bar and crazy tides. With all this water comes a lot of wildlife, too, and the Spit offers an easy way to see famous shorebirds. An easy hike begins in Area D of Fort Stevens State Park, with opportunities to get in a bit of both bird-watching and barge-watching, as enormous freighters and marine birds push against the tides and winds.

This easy exploration of the spit and the South Jetty begins at the Area D lot, with a short boardwalk leading to a bird blind overlooking Trestle Bay, an excellent place to spot coastal birds, and a trail leading through the dunes to the beach on the Columbia River. Follow the beach to the left for 2.3 miles to the massive jetty, then go left another 0.5 mile to a viewing platform. Continuing south along the top of the jetty 0.3 mile brings you to an X-junction; turn left here another 0.3 mile to the paved road, and follow it to the left, going 1.1 mile back to Area D.

User Groups: Hikers and dogs on leashes. No horses or mountain bikes. No wheelchair facilities.

Permits: Permits are not required. If you use the day-use area only, parking and access are free. Otherwise, a $3 day-use fee is collected at the camping entrance, or you can get an annual Oregon Parks and Recreation pass for $25; contact Oregon Parks and Recreation, 800/551-6949.

Maps: For a free park brochure, call Oregon Parks and Recreation, 800/551-6949, or download a free map at www.oregonstateparks.org. For a topographic map, ask the USGS for Clatsop Spit.

Directions: Drive south of Astoria on U.S. 101 for four miles and turn west at a sign for Fort Stevens State Park. Follow park signs for 4.9 miles, turning left at the day-use entrance. Drive at total of 3.9 miles, passing Battery Russell, to a fork. Go right to Area D.

Contact: Oregon Parks and Recreation Department, 1115 Commercial Street NE, Salem, OR, 97301, 800/551-6949, www.oregonstateparks.org.

❷ FORT STEVENS STATE PARK
5.3 mi/2.5 hr   🏃₁ ⛰₆

northwest of Astoria in Fort Stevens State Park

Map 1.1, page 33   **BEST (**

The tip of the Oregon coast lies between the Pacific Ocean and the Columbia River, the "Gateway to the West," at least for ships. Explorers had been trying for years to find the elusive mouth of the Columbia, which more often than not was shrouded in fog. As you can imagine, this area was heavily guarded during World War II by no less than three military installations. Fort Stevens was in use for a total of 84 years, from the Civil War to the close of World War II. Today it is an 11-square-mile state park with campgrounds, miles of bike paths, a swimmable lake, and even the rusting remains of the *Peter Iredale,* a historic 1906 shipwreck. The network of paved trails makes it that much more accessible for everyone.

To begin your exploration, park in the loop lot for Battery Russell. Behind an exhibit board, climb a stairway and walk along the concrete bunkers, site of a battery that guarded the Columbia's mouth for 40 years. When you reach a sandy trail, follow it 1.3 miles, staying right at all junctions, to Picnic Area A and the loop trail around Coffenbury Lake. At the end of the loop, and to try a different way back, head to the nearby campground to the start of the Nature Trail behind campsite B5T. This 1.4-mile trail follows a creek and joins with a paved bike path, going left 0.2 mile back to the Battery Russell lot.

User Groups: Hikers and dogs on leashes.

Bikes on designated paths only. Paved paths are wheelchair accessible.

Permits: Permits are not required. If you use the day-use area only, parking and access are free. Otherwise, a $3 day-use fee is collected at the camping entrance, or you can get an annual Oregon Parks and Recreation pass for $25; contact Oregon Parks and Recreation, 800/551-6949.

Maps: For a free park brochure, call Oregon Parks and Recreation, 800/551-6949, or download a free map at www.oregonstateparks. org. For a topographic map, ask the USGS for Warrenton.

Directions: Drive south of Astoria on U.S. 101 for four miles and turn west at a sign for Fort Stevens State Park. Follow park signs for 4.9 miles, turning left at the day-use entrance. Drive one mile to Battery Russell.

Contact: Oregon Parks and Recreation Department, 1115 Commercial Street NE, Salem, OR, 97301, 800/551-6949, www.oregonstateparks.org.

3 TILLAMOOK HEAD
6.1 mi one-way/3.0 hr   🏃2 ⛰8

north of Cannon Beach in Ecola State Park

Map 1.2, page 34   **BEST (**

The Oregon coast has some of the best state parks in Oregon, and this is by far one of the most scenic. The Tillamook Head, a remnant of a 15-billion-year-old Columbia River basaltic lava flow, rises over 1,000 feet above the Pacific Ocean, and it was on this headland that Lewis and Clark stood on their famous cross-country journey, their mission to find an overland route to the Pacific successful. In fact, they were crossing this head in 1806 to make their way down to nearby Cannon Beach to buy some blubber from a beached whale from some local Native Americans. No one said exploration was easy. You can re-create this journey, seeing things they never saw, like the abandoned military bunker and an unbelievable lighthouse on the island of Tillamook Rock, which operated from 1881 to 1957. The only reason it is unmanned today is that winter storms tended to throw waves right over the top of the lighthouse. Today, it houses cremated remains taken ashore by helicopters. Consider bringing a backpack for this one—there's a handy camping area in a nook atop the head.

You can tour the entire head or take it in pieces. Start at the Ecola Point Picnic Area lot, where you can take a short walk out to the point to see a sea lion-populated rock. The hike begins in the trees at the edge of the lot, heading north on the Oregon Coast Trail. The first 1.5 miles breezes through some woods before dramatically following the cliffs over the ocean and dropping down to secluded Indian Beach, usually rife with surfers, which is a good turnaround for a short hike. If you continue on, the hike gets more difficult as it climbs 1.6 mile to a primitive campground (either on the road to the right or the trail to the left), complete with sheltered bunkhouses. From this camping area, follow a short trail toward the ocean for a look at the mossed-over bunkers. If you're up for more, you can continue as far as you like up the headland, but be ready to climb. The trail gains 200 feet in the next half-mile, then eases off for the next 2.1 miles to the summit. The remaining 1.7 miles of this stretch of the OCT descends to the beach at Seaside.

User Groups: Hikers and dogs on leashes only. No horses or mountain bikes permitted. No wheelchair facilities.

Permits: Permits are not required. A $3 day-use fee is collected at the camping entrance, or you can get an annual Oregon Parks and Recreation pass for $25; contact Oregon Parks and Recreation, 800/551-6949.

Maps: For a free park brochure, call Oregon Parks and Recreation, 800/551-6949 or download a free map at www.oregonstateparks.org. For a topographic map, ask the USGS for Tillamook Head.

Directions: From U.S. 101, take the north exit for Cannon Beach and follow Ecola State Park signs, keeping right for two miles to the entrance booth. To shuttle, drive north from the north exit to Cannon Beach on U.S. 101 toward Seaside for 5.8 miles. Turn left on Avenue U for 0.2 mile and take the first left on Edgewood Street for 0.4 mile. Continue on Edgewood Street until becomes Ocean Vista Drive, and follow it for 0.2 mile. Ocean Vista Drive turns into Sunset Boulevard. Follow Sunset Boulevard for 0.7 mile to its end at the trailhead.

Contact: Oregon Parks and Recreation Department, 1115 Commercial Street NE, Salem, OR, 97301, 800/551-6949, www.oregonstateparks.org.

4 SADDLE MOUNTAIN

5.0 mi/3.0 hr 　　　　🥾3　⛰9

east of Seaside in Saddle Mountain State Natural Area

Map 1.2, page 34 　　　BEST (

© SEAN PATRICK HILL

Saddle Mountain

Aptly named for its dipping peak, Saddle Mountain is the highest point in northwestern Oregon. It has a commanding 360-degree view reaching from the Pacific to five Cascade peaks ranging from Rainier to Jefferson. To earn that view, you must endure the difficult hike up a steep trail, though it is comforting to know that the trail has been drastically improved of late. On the other hand, the flower show here is famous: trilliums, bleeding hearts, goatsbeard, chocolate lily, candyflower, larkspur, Indian paintbrush, fawn lily, purple iris, and phlox are some of the 300-odd blooms you'll see along the trail, particularly in spring, and the peak offers refuge to the rare crucifer and Saddle Mountain bittercress, a mustard-family flower found virtually nowhere else on earth.

The first 0.2-mile portion of the Saddle Mountain Trail passes through an alder forest, passing a short side trail to the right that climbs 0.2 mile to a rocky viewpoint of the mountain itself—a worthy side trip. The next 1.1 miles climbs steeply up a series of switchbacks to the long wall of a basalt dike formed from lava poured into cracks in the ground and cooled, the ground having slowly eroded away around it leaving a wall that resembles stacked wood. The next 0.9 mile crosses the wild-flowered meadows populated by Ice Age species (stay on the trail) before reaching the saddle itself. The remaining 0.4 mile is a steep pitch lined with cables that ascends to an awe-inspiring viewpoint at the 3,283-foot peak, with vistas reaching as far as the Pacific Ocean, Cape Disappointment, the Columbia River, and the Cascades.

User Groups: Hikers and dogs on leash only. No horses or mountain bikes allowed. No wheelchair facilities.

Permits: Permits are not required. Parking and access are free.

Maps: For a topographic map, ask the USGS for Saddle Mountain.

Directions: From Portland, take U.S 26 west of Portland 66 miles and turn north at a state park sign. This winding, paved road seven miles to its end at a picnic area ...pground.

... Oregon Parks and Recreation ...nt, 1115 Commercial Street NE, Salem, ... 97301, 800/551-6949, www.or-egonstateparks.org.

5 CANNON BEACH TO HUG POINT
8.6 mi/4.0 hr   🚶1 ⛰7

in the Tolovana Beach State Recreation Site in Cannon Beach on the Pacific Ocean

Map 1.2, page 34   **BEST (**

If you wonder why the town of Cannon Beach is so named, it dates back to 1846 when a Navy ship broke up crossing the infamous Columbia River bar. An entire piece of the deck, with the cannon mounted to it, washed ashore. The town is known especially for Haystack Rock, the 235-foot sea stack that ends up on quite a few calendars.

This stretch of beach was, for the longest time, the main travel route for motorists. Getting around Hug Point during even low tide required motorists to "hug" the cliff; they decided the easiest way around it was over it, and so they dynamited their own road into the sandstone. An easy beachside stroll visits all these points, plus other sea stacks, tidepools, and a waterfall pouring right onto the beach.

Start at the Haystack Rock Parking Area, within view of Haystack Rock. Head south along the sandstone cliffs for 1.2 miles to the Tovana Beach Wayside. For the next 1.8 miles, watch for a number of sea stacks, including Silver Point, Jockey Cap, and Lion Rock. Round Humbug Point, aptly named because it is not the fabled Hug Point, and arrive at the Arcadia Wayside. Continuing another 1.3 miles brings you to Hug Point itself, with its powder-blasted road, a cave, the falls of Fall Creek, and the Hug Point Wayside.

User Groups: Hikers, dogs, and horses. No wheelchair facilities.

Permits: Permits are not required. Parking and access are free.

Maps: For a topographic map, ask the USGS for Arch Cape.

Directions: From U.S. 101 take the southern Cannon Beach exit, heading west on East Sunset Boulevard 0.2 mile to Hemlock Street. Go right on Hemlock to the Haystack Rock parking area.

Contact: Oregon Parks and Recreation Department, 1115 Commercial Street NE, Salem, OR, 97301, 800/551-6949, www.or-egonstateparks.org.

6 CAPE FALCON
5.0 mi/2.5 hr   🚶2 ⛰8

south of Cannon Beach in Oswald West State Park

Map 1.2, page 34   **BEST (**

Oswald West is a certain kind of hero in Oregon. As the 14th governor of Oregon, his lasting contribution was to designate the entire length of the Oregon coast as a public highway, thus forever protecting it from development. His legacy shows, in particular at the state park named for him. Dense with old-growth Sitka spruce forests, with Neahkahnie Mountain and Cape Falcon cupping the wide Smuggler Cove and a sandy beach, Oswald West State Park brings a hiker close to a coastal wilderness area. The Oregon Coast Trail goes either direction from Short Sands Beach: to the south, it climbs the cliffs and continues on to Neahkahnie Mountain (see *Neahkahnie Mountain* listing in this chapter), and to the north it climbs to raptor-shaped Cape Falcon.

For an easy exploration, follow Short Sand Creek from the parking area to the coast for 0.4 paved miles. If the view here isn't staggering enough, just wait. A moderate 2.1-mile trail following the OCT route leads up from the beach and into groves of Sitkas that rival the fabled redwoods. The trail skirts a cliff above the cove with views to lofty Neahkahnie Mountain. Watch for the side trail to the left traveling 0.2 mile out the headland of rocky Cape Falcon, the peak a dense cover of leathery salal. This makes a good turnaround point, but to add another 2.4 miles on for more rewarding views, keep going up the OCT to three astonishing viewpoints of the wave-pounded inlets. When the trail begins to steeply ascend away from the ocean, turn back.

User Groups: Hikers, dogs, horses. No mountain bikes allowed. The paved trail to Short Sands Beach is wheelchair accessible.

Permits: Permits are not required. Parking and access are free.

Maps: For a free park brochure, call Oregon Parks and Recreation, 800/551-6949, or download a free map at www.oregonstateparks.org. For a topographic map, ask the USGS for Arch Cape.

Directions: Drive 10 miles south of Cannon Beach on U.S. 101. Park in the lot on the east side of the highway a bit south of milepost 39.

Contact: Oregon Parks and Recreation Department, 1115 Commercial Street NE, Salem, OR, 97301, 800/551-6949, www.oregonstateparks.org.

7 NEAHKAHNIE MOUNTAIN
3.0 mi/2.0 hr   🏃3 ⛰️8

south of Cannon Beach in Oswald West State Park

Map 1.2, page 34

Rising above the surf and breezy ocean air, Neahkahnie Mountain in Oswald West State Park is a panoramic dream. As far as climbing mountains goes, this one is fairly easy, at 1,600 feet above sea level, but enough of a haul to get your heart going. It was a coastal Indian tribe, probably the Tillamook, who named this peak to mean, roughly, "place of the gods." The hike can be extended, too, out onto a ridge with red huckleberry bushes that fan out overhead like green umbrellas, and if you're really daring, a descent down the west slope leads to Highway 101 and farther to an oceanic cliff-edge view of the Devil's Cauldron.

The hike follows the Oregon Coast Trail, an easy, single trail, that steeply switchbacks up the first 0.9 mile before leveling out on the wooded peak for 0.6 mile, arriving at the summit meadows and an easy view down to the town of Manzanita. Turning around here makes for a three-mile round-trip, though the trail continues down another two miles to Highway 101, where it crosses the roadway and continues about 100 yards to two good viewpoints over the rugged cliffs to the Pacific.

User Groups: Hikers and dogs. No mountain bikes or horses. No wheelchair facilities.

Permits: Permits are not required. Parking and access are free.

Maps: For a free park brochure, call Oregon Parks and Recreation, 800/551-6949, or download a free map at www.oregonstateparks.org. For a topographic map, ask the USGS for Nehalem.

Directions: Drive south of Cannon Beach on U.S. 101 about 13 miles to a brown hiker symbol between mileposts 41 and 42. Turn east onto a gravel road for 0.4 mile to a Trailhead Parking sign. The trail begins at a post.

Contact: Oregon Parks and Recreation Department, 1115 Commercial Street NE, Salem, OR, 97301, 800/551-6949, www.oregonstateparks.org.

8 NEHALEM BAY
5.2 mi/2.5 hr   🏃1 ⛰️6

south of Manzanita in Nehalem Bay State Park

Map 1.2, page 34   **BEST (**

The beach that lies between Neahkahnie Mountain and Nehalem Spit has seen its share of bad luck: In 1913, a drunk captain steered the British *Glenesslin,* with an astoundingly inexperienced crew, into the nearby cliffs, and rumors still abound of a wrecked Spanish galleon heavy with treasure, most of which is believed to have been buried by survivors somewhere in the area. Needless to say, people are still looking for it. There's other treasure to be found here today in a trove of seals and seabirds along the Nehalem Spit. Formed by tidal patterns, the Oregon spits make for ideal wildlife-viewing, especially of seabirds. This hike visits two distinct zones: the beach and the bay, seemingly worlds apart.

From the Nehalem Bay State Park picnic area, head out along the ocean 2.3 miles to the North Jetty, and turn right for 0.5 mile to a beach where harbor seals tend to lay around and sun themselves. It's illegal to harass them, though they'll quickly disperse if you approach at all. Return along the bay for a 2.2-mile walk, turning left at the boat ramp for a quick 0.2-mile return to the picnic area.

User Groups: Hikers, dogs, and horses. Mountain bikes allowed on loop path only. A 1.5-mile loop is wheelchair accessible.

Permits: Permits are not required. A $3 day-use fee is collected at the entrance, or you can get an annual Oregon Parks and Recreation pass for $25; contact Oregon Parks and Recreation, 800/551-6949.

Maps: For a free park brochure, call Oregon Parks and Recreation, 800/551-6949, or download a free map at www.oregonstateparks.org. For a topographic map, ask the USGS for Nehalem.

Directions: From Manzanita, follow U.S 101 to milepost 44. Turn right on Necarney City Road and follow signs for two miles to Nehalem Bay State Park. Park at the picnic area after the fee booth

Contact: Oregon Parks and Recreation Department, 1115 Commercial Street NE, Salem, OR, 97301, 800/551-6949, www.oregonstateparks.org.

9 BANKS-VERNONIA RAILROAD

5.3 mi one-way/2.5 hr   🏃1   ⛰7

northwest of Portland in Banks Vernonia Linear Park

| Map 1.2, page 34 | BEST (|

Oregon has many fine examples of "rails-to-trails" paths, and this is certainly one of them. Totaling 21 miles in all, the former grade of this 1920s Burlington-Northern Railroad Line used primarily for lumber and, later, excursion trains, has been converted to a great pathway through the Coast Range foothills. Though there are plenty of options for journeys along the old route, a good day trip can be made by going between two old wooden trestles, either as a longer hike or with a car shuttle. The trail can accommodate just about anyone on foot, horses, bikes, and wheelchair users.

Start at the Buxton Trestle just outside the town of Buxton. An easy loop explores the area around the trestle spanning Mendenhall Creek, which is now open to trail use. From there the trail stretches north 5.3 miles to a second trailhead beneath Horseshoe Trestle, which is not to be crossed—but is a good place for a shuttle. Along the way, you'll cross Logging and Williams Creeks and stay largely out of sight of Highway 43.

User Groups: Hikers, dogs, mountain bikes, and horses. Parts of the paved path are wheelchair accessible.

Permits: Permits are not required. Parking and access are free.

Maps: For a free park brochure, call Oregon Parks and Recreation, 800/551-6949, or download a free map at www.oregonstateparks.org. For a topographic map, ask the USGS for Buxton.

Directions: From Portland, drive 28 miles west on U.S. 26 and turn right on Fisher Road. In 0.7 mile, the road becomes Baconia Road and leads to the Buxton Trailhead on the right. To shuttle to the Horseshoe Trestle, return to Highway 47 and drive 5.5 miles north to the Tophill Trailhead on the left.

Contact: Oregon Parks and Recreation Department, 1115 Commercial Street NE, Salem, OR, 97301, 800/551-6949, www.oregonstateparks.org.

🔟 KINGS MOUNTAIN
5.4 mi/3.5 hr   🚶4 ⛰8

east of Tillamook in the Tillamook State Forest

Map 1.2, page 34

Between 1933 and 1951, four massive fires swept through this area of the Coast Range in what is known as the Tillamook Burn. With the help of determined locals, an equally massive campaign was waged to replant the area into what is now the Tillamook State Forest. Kings Mountain bears both the scars of the fire (those emblematic snags testify to that) and also the regrowth capable with the help of humans and nature. This hike passes through that history and ultimately rises above it to views of the Wilson River Valley and the Cascade Mountains. Granted, this hike is difficult: You'll have to climb more than 2,500 feet in 2.5 miles, but because of the burned trees—known as "gray ghosts"—it makes for good views. You'll even pass a picnic table before the last pitch, and you can leave your name in a summit registry at the top. A 1.3-mile extension connects to nearby Elk Mountain, potentially making this a daunting day.

The first mile of the Kings Mountain Trail threads through red alder and maple woods and wildflowers and then steepens dramatically for the next 1.4 miles. At the top of the 2.7-mile climb is the 3,226-foot peak of Kings Mountain, having passed through meadows of summer beargrass plumes (a type of lily). This hike can be stretched to nearby pinnacles and Elk Mountain (see *Elk Mountain* listing in this chapter) but only for the exceptionally hardy. Otherwise, return as you came.

User Groups: Hikers and dogs only. No wheelchair facilities.

Permits: Permits are not required. Parking and access are free.

Maps: For a Tillamook Forest Visitor Map & Guide, contact the Forest Grove District Office, 503/357-2191, egov.oregon.gov/ODF/TSF/about_us.shtml. For a topographic map, ask the USGS for Rogers Peak.

Directions: From Portland, drive U.S. 26 west 20 miles to Highway 6. Go west on Highway 6 for 22 miles to the trailhead and parking area near milepost 25, on the north side of the road.

Contact: Tillamook State Forest, Forest Grove District Office, 801 Gales Creek Road, Forest Grove, OR, 97116, 503/357-2191, egov. oregon.gov/ODF/TSF/about_us.shtml.

1️⃣1️⃣ ELK MOUNTAIN
3.0 mi/2.5 hr   🚶3 ⛰8

east of Tillamook in the Tillamook State Forest

Map 1.2, page 34

Because the route to loop this hike with Kings Mountain can prove arduous, it is easiest to climb Elk Mountain by its own trail. Did I say "easy"? This is also a strenuous hike, but ultimately a rewarding one, with views on a clear day as far as the Pacific Ocean and Mounts Adams, Hood, and Jefferson, due in part to the massive Tillamook Burn that swept much of this mountain clear of living trees, leaving the ghostly white snags behind. This trail is narrower than Kings Mountain, gaining 1,900 feet in 1.5 miles.

Starting from the Elk Creek Campground, the Wilson River Trail heads 0.1 mile to the junction with the Elk Mountain Trail, which climbs steeply through alder forests and onto the rocky trail for 1.4 miles to the 2,788 peak. Be sure to watch your footing and wear good boots, as much of the trail can be loose scree. Crossing four saddles, as well as vaunting a false summit, you'll arrive at the peak, which bears white Washington lilies in spring.

User Groups: Hikers and dogs only. No wheelchair facilities.

Permits: Permits are not required. Parking and access are free.

Maps: For a Tillamook Forest Visitor Map & Guide, contact the Forest Grove District Office, 503/357-2191, egov.oregon.gov/ODF/TSF/about_us.shtml. For a topographic map, ask the USGS for Cochran.

Directions: From Portland, drive U.S. 26 west

20 miles to Highway 6. Go west on Highway 6 for 19 miles to the Elk Creek Campground near milepost 28, on the north side of the road. Turn right into the campground, driving 0.6 mile to the far end of the campground and crossing a bridge. The trailhead is behind the information board.

Contact: Tillamook State Forest, Forest Grove District Office, 801 Gales Creek Road, Forest Grove, OR, 97116, 503/357-2191, egov. oregon.gov/ODF/TSF/about_us.shtml.

12 GALES CREEK
3.6 mi/1.5 hr   🏃1 ⛰7

east of Tillamook in the Tillamook State Forest

Map 1.2, page 34

In the deep green forests of the Coast Range, Gales Creek glides swiftly in its bed. To find this creek from the highway, visiting two picturesque fern-draped creeks, begin at the Summit Trailhead and descend sharply on the Gales Creek Trail, following Low Divide Creek 1.9 miles along an old 1930s railroad grade to the Gales Creek Campground (which is suitable for picnics, as there are plenty of tables amidst the trees). Near the end of the trail, a spur trail to the left leads to the parking area and the Gales Creek Trail. Granted, the return trip to the highway will be uphill, a little more than 600 feet elevation gain, but either way this trail is remarkably wild in comparison to much of the devastation resulting from decades of forest fires.

Gales Creek, too, is entirely explorable, with a trail leading out of the campground and following Gales Creek up into the hills. Beginning from the junction with the Low Divide Creek Trail, head upstream 0.8 mile, staying right at a junction with the Storey Burn Trail. The remaining trail follows Gales Creek through forest for 5.2 miles farther, meeting Bell Camp Road; this section may be closed due to storm damage. Once open, you will be able to continue on another 3.4 miles from Bell Camp Road to the terminal trailhead at Reehers Camp.

User Groups: Hikers, dogs, and mountain bikes. Horses allowed on parts of Gales Creek Trail north of the campground. No wheelchair facilities.

Permits: Permits are not required. Parking and access are free.

Maps: For a Tillamook Forest Visitor Map & Guide, contact the Forest Grove District Office, 503/357-2191, egov.oregon.gov/ODF/ TSF/about_us.shtml. For a topographic map, ask the USGS for Cochran and Timber.

Directions: From Portland, drive U.S. 26 west 20 miles to Highway 6. Go west on Highway 6 for 21 miles to milepost 33 at the Coast Range Summit. The parking area for Low Divide Creek and the Summit Trailhead is on the north side of the highway. To enter the Gales Creek Campground parking area, open mid-May through October, follow Highway 6 west of Portland 39 miles to a sign near milepost 35 reading "Gales Creek CG" and turn north through a yellow gate. If the gate is locked, park to the side and walk in 0.7 mile.

Contact: Tillamook State Forest, Forest Grove District Office, 801 Gales Creek Road, Forest Grove, OR, 97116, 503/357-2191, egov. oregon.gov/ODF/TSF/about_us.shtml.

13 UNIVERSITY FALLS
8.6 mi/4.5 hr   🏃2 ⛰7

east of Tillamook in the Tillamook State Forest

Map 1.2, page 34

Despite the massive Tillamook Fires—particularly the 1933 fire, which torched 240,000 acres—the forest has been reborn. Now there's second-growth Douglas fir, western hemlock, red alder, and red cedar, with a sturdy undergrowth of sword ferns, Oregon grape—the state flower—and leathery salal. Wildlife has returned; you can hear grouse on occasion in the underbrush. This loop, sometimes following an old wagon road, tours the reborn forest with University Falls as the destination high in the headwaters of the Wilson River. The 65-foot falls on Elliott Creek just southwest of the Coast Range summit suffers from off-road vehicle use, particularly the motorcycles whining in the distance. You'll leave them behind eventually on this small epic tour of the rain forest.

From the Rogers Camp RV parking area, briefly follow the Fire Break 1 road uphill to the Nels Rogers Trail. The first 1.3 miles crosses two roads and reaches a junction on the Devils Lake Fork of the Wilson River. Turn left over a footbridge, cross the creek, and turn left again, staying on Nels Rogers, which ends in 0.3 mile at the Beaver Dam Road and continues as the Wilson River Wagon Road Trail on the opposite side. This trail wanders three miles, crossing roads, ducking under power lines, crossing clear-cuts and Deyoe Creek, where you'll find a bench near a footbridge, before ending at University Falls Road and another trailhead. From here follow the Gravelle Brothers Trail, arriving in 0.4 mile at the wispy University Falls, where a left-hand junction comes to a viewpoint. To complete the loop, follow the Gravelle Trail two miles to an old road, going right toward Rogers Camp. Follow a gravel road to the right to the top of the hill and a maintenance shed. Go behind the cement barriers on the Elliott Creek OHV Trail, then follow Beaver Dam Road 0.2 miles back to the trailhead.

User Groups: Hikers, dogs, mountain bikes, horses. No wheelchair facilities.

Permits: Permits are not required. Parking and access are free.

Maps: For a Tillamook Forest Visitor Map & Guide, contact the Forest Grove District Office, 503/357-2191, egov.oregon.gov/ODF/TSF/about_us.shtml. For a topographic map, ask the USGS for Woods Point.

Directions: From Portland, drive U.S. 26 west 20 miles to Highway 6. Go west on Highway 6 for 21 miles to milepost 33 at the Coast Range Summit. Watching for signs to Rogers Camp, turn left on Beaver Dam Road and go 250 feet to a T-junction. Turn left 0.1 mile to the trailhead.

Contact: Tillamook State Forest, Forest Grove

District Office, 801 Gales Creek Road, Forest Grove, OR, 97116, 503/357-2191, egov.oregon.gov/ODF/TSF/about_us.shtml.

14 BAYOCEAN SPIT

8.1 mi/4.0 hr

west of Tillamook in Cape Meares State Park

Map 1.2, page 34

Cradling Tillamook Bay like a mother's arm, the Bayocean Spit is the site of a ghost town that is more ghost than town. The town formerly known as Bayocean, the "Atlantic City of the West," sold some 600 lots for excited resort types, in addition to having a bowling alley, hotel, dance hall, and grocery store. The developer apparently went mad one fateful night and disappeared. And that, as they say, was that. But what really did the town in was the construction of the South Jetty, which altered currents so that the town slowly eroded into the sea. Now it's a great place to spot wading birds in Tillamook Bay. Being a spit, you'll be able to enjoy both bird-watching and beach-strolling, and there is even the opportunity for camping. In the center of the spit, a large forested rock formation makes for a short cut and exploration, and makes a good turnaround point if you want to cut this hike in half.

Start out by following the old road for 1.6 miles. About halfway out, a well-marked trail cuts 0.5 mile through a forested bluff to the left. Follow this route to the beach, and head left 1.9 miles to the South Jetty. Watch for tufted puffins and brown pelicans. Continuing onward toward the bay for another 2.8 miles will bring you past Crab Harbor, a primitive campsite, and back to the beginning of the loop. Follow the road back 1.6 miles to your car.

User Groups: Hikers, dogs, horses. Bikes allowed on the old road. No wheelchair facilities.

Permits: Permits are not required. Parking and access are free.

Maps: For a topographic map, ask the USGS for Garibaldi.

Directions: From U.S 101 in downtown Tillamook, follow signs for Three Capes Scenic Route for seven miles. On the right, near a large wooden sign about Bayocean Spit, turn right on a gravel road along the dike for 0.9 mile to a parking area.

Contact: Oregon Parks and Recreation Department, 1115 Commercial Street NE, Salem, OR, 97301, 800/551-6949, www.oregonstateparks.org.

15 CAPE MEARES
0.6–4.0 mi/0.5–3.0 hr

west of Tillamook in Cape Meares State Park

Map 1.2, page 34

Cape Meares is a great place to take the grandparents when they come for a visit. There are a number of short trails, making it easy to experience wonders like the historic lighthouse or the Octopus Tree, a giant Sitka spruce that has to be seen to be believed. But it is also a fine place to take a longer hike over a magnificent Oregon cape, visiting a 400-year-old, 16-foot-thick spruce and descending to a pleasant cove on the Pacific. Keep an eye on those cliffs, which are home to peregrine falcons. There's also the Three Arch Rocks, an offshore wildlife refuge home to common murres, black oystercatchers, Leach's storm-petrels, and pigeon guillemots.

For two easy hikes to the lighthouse and the Octopus Tree, start at the main parking lot on Cape Meares. The 0.4-mile round-trip to the lighthouse is paved and easy, and the 0.2-mile round-trip to the Octopus Tree is mostly level dirt but just as easy. For a more challenging hike on the Big Spruce Tree Trail, park at a small lot just before the entrance to the park off Three Capes Loop Drive. From here the trail quickly splits; 0.2 mile to the left is the giant spruce, and to the right a 0.9-mile descent, dropping 500 feet, to a cove on the ocean only passable at low tide. It's a good way to get down to the beach and watch for seabirds, and provides views out to Bayocean Spit.

User Groups: Hikers and dogs only. No horses or mountain bikes allowed. Paved portions of the park are wheelchair accessible.

Permits: Permits are not required. Parking and access are free.

Maps: For a free park brochure, call Oregon Parks and Recreation, 800/551-6949, or download a free map at www.oregonstateparks.org. For a topographic map, ask the USGS for Netarts.

Directions: From U.S 101 in downtown Tillamook follow signs for Three Capes Scenic Route for 10 miles. The park entrance is on the right. Follow the paved road 0.6 mile to a parking lot turnaround.

Contact: Oregon Parks and Recreation Department, 1115 Commercial Street NE, Salem, OR, 97301, 800/551-6949, www.oregonstateparks.org.

16 HAGG LAKE
13.1 mi/6.5 hr

southwest of Forest Grove in Scoggins Valley Park

Map 1.2, page 34

Hagg Lake has been a destination for boaters and fishermen since 1975, when the Scoggins Valley Dam was built. Now hikers can get in on Hagg's unique landscape and spend anywhere from an hour to an entire day exploring the lake's weaving inlets and meadows from a plethora of access points. There are a number of creeks tumbling over smooth rock beds, and a variety of forest types from Douglas fir to white oak. Watch for poison oak along some trails. Also be aware that at times the trail joins the road for short intervals. All trails are marked by posts and along the way there are opportunities to stop at picnic areas and explore side creeks in shaded coves.

Should you decide to have a go at the entire 13.1-mile loop, you can start from the "free parking" lot by climbing the earth dam to the road, and following it to the left for 0.8 mile past a fishing dock to a lot where the official shoreline trail begins. The first 3.6 miles to Boat Ramp "C" crosses long span footbridges and scenic picnic areas. The next 1.3 miles follows the lake well past the "buoy line," thus moving away from the motorized boats and into the quieter areas of the park. The trail follows the road 0.6 mile over Scoggins Creek and another picnic area, then follows the lake 3.7 miles through grasslands and forest, over Tanner Creek and out to a grassy promontory on the lake. The remaining 3.1 miles returns along the north shore to the dam, passing more picnic areas and Boat Ramp "A."

User Groups: Hikers, dogs, and mountain bikes. Horses are not allowed. There is wheelchair access on some trails, boat ramps, and picnic areas.

Permits: Permits are not required. A $5 day-use fee is collected at the park entrance unless parking at the free parking lot beside the fee booth.

Maps: For a map, contact Washington County Facilities Management, 169 North 1st Avenue, MS 42, Hillsboro, OR, 97124, 503/846-8715. For a topographic map, ask the USGS for Gaston.

Directions: From Portland, drive U.S. 26 west 20 miles to Highway 6. Go west on Highway 6 for 2.3 miles and take the ramp for NW OR-47, following this highway south for 12.2 miles. Turn right at SW Scoggins Valley Road for 3.2 miles to the park.

Contact: Washington County Facilities Management, 169 North 1st Avenue, MS 42, Hillsboro, OR, 97124, 503/846-8715.

🄱🄳 CAPE LOOKOUT
5.0 mi/2.5 hr

south of Tillamook in Cape Lookout State Park

Map 1.2, page 34   **BEST (**

Of all the capes on the Oregon coast, this one stands out by sheer length: it extends two full miles to sea like an accusing finger, making it one of the best places to whale-watch and, of course, hike. Numerous viewpoints scan north, south, and west, including one viewpoint over the spot where a patrolling B-17 bomber crashed into the cliffs on a foggy 1943 day. You'll see Cape Kiwanda, Cape Foulweather, the Cascade Head, and Cape Meares from this promontory—all on a single trail that boasts enormous trees and boggy microclimates. The destination is a sheer cliff viewpoint where the shoreline tidal sounds are a distant echo.

Beginning at the main parking area, take the left-hand Cape Lookout Trail (the right descends 2.3 miles to the day-use area on Netarts Spit) and just ahead stay straight at a second junction (this left-hand trail descends two miles to a beach) and continue 2.5 miles overland, descending into a hollow and back up and crossing several wooden bridges. The trail can be muddy. At the tip of the cape, the ocean hovers 400 feet below, and the surf against the mainland is a distant white noise. Each year, 20,000 gray whales migrate around this cape between December and June. Return as you came.

User Groups: Hikers and dogs. No mountain bikes or horses allowed. No wheelchair facilities.

Permits: Permits are not required. A $3 day-use fee is collected at the camping entrance, or you can get an annual Oregon Parks and Recreation pass for $25; contact Oregon Parks and Recreation, 800/551-6949.

Maps: For a free park brochure, call Oregon Parks and Recreation, 800/551-6949, or download a free map at www.oregonstateparks.org. For a topographic map, ask the USGS for Sand Lake.

Directions: From Tillamook, drive 3rd Street west following signs for Cape Lookout State Park for 13 miles. Head 2.7 miles past the campground turnoff to the trailhead lot on the right.

Contact: Oregon Parks and Recreation Department, 1115 Commercial Street NE, Salem, OR, 97301, 800/551-6949, www.oregonstateparks.org.

18 MUNSON CREEK FALLS
0.6 mi/0.25 hr   🏃₁ ⛰₇

south of Tillamook in Munson Creek State Natural Site

Map 1.2, page 34

At 366 feet, the five-tiered Munson Creek Falls, named for early pioneer Goran Munson, is the tallest in the Coast Range. Munson settled near here, coming all the way from Michigan in 1889. Today, visitors have easy access and a short walk through old-growth Western red cedars and Sitka spruce to see the falls, and even eat from a picnic table viewpoint. At the right time of year, you may see salmon spawning here. In fact, these trails are good any time of year, even winter when ice crystallizes around the falls.

The 0.3-mile trail begins in Munson Creek State Natural Site and follows an easy path to the falls. Along the way, the trail is shaded by a variety of trees, hung heavy with mosses and lichens. The gravel path makes this one good for a good family trip.

User Groups: Hikers and dogs. No wheelchair facilities.

Permits: Permits are not required. Parking and access are free.

Maps: For a topographic map, ask the USGS for Beaver.

Directions: Drive south of Tillamook eight miles on U.S. 101. Just before milepost 73, turn left at a sign for Munson Creek Falls, following a paved road for one mile and forking right on a 0.4-mile gravel road to a small turnaround lot.

Contact: Oregon Parks and Recreation Department, 1115 Commercial Street NE, Salem, OR, 97301, 800/551-6949, www.oregonstateparks.org.

19 NIAGARA FALLS
2.0 mi/1.0 hr   🏃₁ ⛰₇

southeast of Tillamook in the Siuslaw National Forest

Map 1.2, page 34

Well, it may not be as grand as *the* Niagara Falls we all know, but then *those* Niagara Falls don't plunge 107 feet over a magnificent lava wall into a lush box canyon of vine maples and yellow monkeyflower, either. Sometimes, smaller is better. This trail also passes shimmering Pheasant Creek Falls, another 112-foot cascade, along the way. This easy one-mile trail crosses a gurgling creek several times to a picnic table overlooking the amphitheatre wall over which the falls pour. The trail makes use of four wooden bridges and an observation deck overlooking the lush creeks.

User Groups: Hikers and dogs. No wheelchair facilities.

Permits: Permits are not required. Parking and access are free.

Maps: For a map of the Siuslaw National Forest, contact the Siuslaw National Forest headquarters, 4077 SW Research Way, P.O. Box 1148, Corvallis, OR, 97339, 541/750-7000. For a topographic map, ask the USGS for Niagara Creek.

Directions: Drive U.S. 101 south of Tillamook 15 miles to the village of Beaver near milepost 80. Turn east on Blaine Road for 6.7 miles. At Blaine Junction, turn right on Upper Nestucca River Road for 5.8 miles to Forest Service Road 8533. Go south on this road 4.3 miles to FS 8533-131. Turn right at the junction and continue 0.7 mile to the trailhead.

Contact: Siuslaw National Forest, Hebo Ranger District, 31525 Highway 22, Hebo, OR, 97122, 503/392-5100.

20 MOUNT HEBO

6.5 mi/4.0 hr   🏃2 ⛰7

east of Pacific City in the Siuslaw
National Forest

Map 1.2, page 34

The Pioneer-Indian Trail is so named because
this trail, if you can believe it, was the first
developed route between the Willamette Valley and the Tillamook Valley. Why wouldn't
you believe it? Because this is a mountain, and
one tall enough to be buried in snow, a rarity
for these elevations so close to the ocean and
sea level. Native Americans first used it, likely
figuring it easier to cross this meadow plateau
rather than fighting through the deep forests.
Later, Hiram Smith and some Tillamook settlers improved the trail in 1854. This route
remained the main thoroughfare over the
Coast Range until a new wagon road was built
in 1882. The trail went forgotten until the
Forest Service reopened it as an 8-mile trail
over Mount Hebo. This 3,174-foot summit
commands a view of the Coast Range, extending to the Cascade volcanoes from Rainier to
Jefferson. And, of course, the Pacific Ocean.
Locals say the best time to see the view is late
summer, though even the valleys may be bot-
tomed out in fog. All this is likely what helps
designate the area as the Mount Hebo Special
Interest Area.

Starting at a signboard at Hebo Lake, the
Pioneer-Indian Trail climbs 2.9 miles, crossing
both a gravel road and a meadow of bracken
fern, which can grow to five feet tall, before
reaching a saddle and Road 14. Cross the
road and take a side trail on an abandoned
road to the right leading 0.3 mile up to the
peak. Here there was once a Cold War–era
radar station, but now only a bulldozed site
surrounded by steep meadows of edible thimbleberry. For those in the mood for a 16-mile
day, the Pioneer-Indian Trail continues along
the plateau, paralleling Road 14 to a primitive
campground before descending to North and
South Lakes.

User Groups: Hikers, dogs, and horses.

Mountain bikes not allowed. The trail around
Hebo Lake is wheelchair accessible.

Permits: Permits are not required. A federal
Northwest Forest Pass is required to park here;
the cost is $5 a day or $30 for an annual pass.
You can buy a day pass at the trailhead, at
ranger stations, or through private vendors.

Maps: For a map of the Siuslaw National
Forest, contact the Siuslaw National Forest
headquarters, 4077 SW Research Way, P.O.
Box 1148, Corvallis, OR, 97339, 541/750-
7000. For a topographic map, ask the USGS
for Niagara Creek and Hebo.

Directions: Drive U.S. 101 south of
Tillamook 19 miles to Hebo and turn east on
Highway 22 for 0.3 mile. Turn left at a sign
for Hebo Lake just before the Hebo Ranger
Station. Follow Road 14 for 4.7 miles, taking
the right-hand fork at the Hebo Lake campground entrance. Keep right for 0.2 mile to
the trailhead parking area. From November to mid-April, the campground is gated
closed, so you'll need to walk in 0.2 mile to
the trailhead.

Contact: Siuslaw National Forest, Hebo
Ranger District, 31525 Highway 22, Hebo,
OR, 97122, 503/392-5100.

21 KIWANDA BEACH AND PORTER POINT

9.2 mi/3.5 hr   🏃3 ⛰7

at Neskowin on the Pacific Ocean

Map 1.2, page 34

It's always interesting to see the estuaries where
a coastal river flows into the ocean; sometimes
they argue, each pushing against the other,
creating a unique landscape amenable to
birds and other wildlife. This lovely beach
trek heads up Kiwanda Beach to the mouth
of the Nestucca River. Along the way it passes
climbable Proposal Rock, where an 1800s sea
captain was said to have rowed his beloved
to ask her hand, and continues to the cliffs
of Porter Point and the river mouth opposite
the Nestucca Spit.

From the Neskowin Wayside, hike 0.3 mile along Neskowin Creek to Proposal Rock. To the south, the Cascade Head looms up. Hike 3.3 miles along a sandy beach to the base of Winema Road and Camp Winema. From there, it is one mile to the mouth of the Nestucca. Return as you came.

User Groups: Hikers, dogs, and horses. No wheelchair facilities.

Permits: Permits are not required. Parking and access are free.

Maps: For a topographic map, ask the USGS for Neskowin.

Directions: Drive south of Tillamook on U.S. 101 for 33 miles and turn west at a "Neskowin" pointer. Head straight about 100 yards to the Neskowin Wayside.

Contact: Oregon Parks and Recreation Department, 1115 Commercial Street NE, Salem, OR, 97301, 800/551-6949, www.oregonstateparks.org.

22 HARTS COVE
5.4 mi/2.5 hr

on Cascade Head in the Siuslaw National Forest

Map 1.2, page 34

The Cascade Head is a unique landform, a massive headland rising above the ocean like a fortress, capped with forests and swaths of meadow. Harts Cove is a trek that requires you to climb down 900 feet, and then back up, to see the spectacle. It's worth it: With views of the Cascade Head's jaggy cliffs, the Chitwood Creek waterfall plunging into a towering ocean cove, and a Sitka spruce and western hemlock forest, you'll see what the fuss is about. But note that the road to the trailhead is closed from January 1 to July 15 to protect endangered butterflies and rare wildflowers that thrive here. This area is part of the Cascade Head Scenic Research Area for just this reason.

Harts Cove Trail begins from the road on a series of switchbacks dropping 0.7 mile to Cliff Creek then meanders through the forest of giants another 1.4 miles before reaching a bench looking down to Harts Cove's head. Continue on the main trail 0.5 mile to Chitwood Creek, then another 0.6 mile to a former homestead meadow. A path on the left overlooks Harts Cove and its waterfall. Like many places on the coast, you can sometimes hear the sea lions barking below.

User Groups: Hikers and dogs. No horses or mountain bikes allowed. No wheelchair facilities.

Permits: Permits are not required. Parking and access are free.

Maps: For a map of the Siuslaw National Forest, contact the Siuslaw National Forest headquarters, 4077 SW Research Way, P.O. Box 1148, Corvallis, OR, 97339, 541/750-7000. For a topographic map, ask the USGS for Neskowin.

Directions: From the junction of U.S. 101 and Highway 18 north of Lincoln City, drive north on 101 for 4 miles. Just before the crest, turn left on Cascade Head Road (Road 1861) and follow Hart's Cove signs down this 4.1-mile gravel road to road's end.

Contact: Siuslaw National Forest, Hebo Ranger District, 31525 Highway 22, Hebo, OR, 97122, 503/392-5100.

23 CASCADE HEAD INLAND TRAIL
6.0 mi one-way/3.0 hr 🥾2 ⛰6

north of Lincoln City in Cascade Head Experimental Forest

Map 1.2, page 34

The Cascade Head is a veritable museum, preserved and protected from development because of its unique ecosystem and importance to education and study. The inland trail over the head does not visit the ocean, but certainly does tour the rainforests of coastal Oregon. A path leads into the Cascade Head Experimental Forest, an area studied by foresters since 1934. It shelters a grove of six-foot-thick Sitka spruce on the headwater springs of Calkins Creek, but it's a less-traveled trail because of its lack of views. Check with the Siuslaw National Forest before heading out, as this trail may be closed due to tree hazards.

From the trailhead at Three Rocks Road, the path switchbacks up a hill of elderberry, salmonberry, and thimbleberry. The Sitka grove is 2.9 miles along the trail where a boardwalk path crosses a marsh of skunk cabbage. In another 0.7 mile the trail meets Road 1861. Go right 100 yards to find the remainder of the trail, a 2.4-mile stretch that ends at U.S. 101.

User Groups: Hikers and dogs. No horses or mountain bikes allowed. No wheelchair facilities.

Permits: Permits are not required. Parking and access are free.

Maps: For a map of the Siuslaw National Forest, contact the Siuslaw National Forest headquarters, 4077 SW Research Way, P.O. Box 1148, Corvallis, OR, 97339, 541/750-7000. For a topographic map, ask the USGS for Neskowin.

Directions: From the junction of U.S. 101 and Highway 18 north of Lincoln City, drive north on U.S. 101 for one mile and turn left on Three Rocks Road and immediately park on the right by a trail sign. To shuttle, continue north on U.S. 101 toward Neskowin for about five miles and park at a trailhead sign on the left, one mile south of Neskowin on U.S. 101.

Contact: Siuslaw National Forest, Hebo Ranger District, 31525 Highway 22, Hebo, OR, 97122, 503/392-5100.

24 CASCADE HEAD NATURE CONSERVANCY TRAIL

3.4 mi/1.5 hr   👫2 ⛰8

north of Lincoln City in Cascade Head Preserve

Map 1.2, page 34

The steep and undulating meadows atop Cascade Head are the home of a rare

© SEAN PATRICK HILL

the Pacific Ocean from Cascade Head

checkermallow and an equally rare caterpillar of the Oregon silverspot butterfly. Because of this, this trail is considered a delicate area, and with the support of locals, the area was purchased by the non-profit Nature Conservancy. The road to the upper trailhead is closed from January 1 to July 15 to protect this fragile habitat, but the lower trailhead is open year-round. Be sure to stay on the trail and respect nature, and pay attention to seasonal closure signs. The trail is steep at times, but the expansive views are rewarding beyond belief—the ocean surges forth hundreds of feet below, and the coastline stretches out to the south as far as the eye can see.

From the boat ramp trailhead, follow the trail along the Three Rocks Road then uphill along Savage Road for 0.6 mile, passing the Sitka Arts Center. From this road, the well-marked trail climbs steadily through old-growth spruce and over several creeks for 1.1 miles to the first viewpoint down to the Salmon River estuary and Cape Foulweather. The next 0.6 mile to the top is breathtaking—both for its views and for its steepness. A marker points out the actual peak at 1,200 feet; relax and enjoy the view and the play of light on the surf in the distance. From here, the trail continues an easy mile through more woods to the trailhead on the 1861 road.

User Groups: Hikers and horses. Mountain bikes and dogs are not allowed. No wheelchair facilities.

Permits: Permits are not required. Parking and access are free.

Maps: For a map of the Siuslaw National Forest, contact the Siuslaw National Forest headquarters, 4077 SW Research Way, P.O. Box 1148, Corvallis, OR, 97339, 541/750-7000. For a topographic map, ask the USGS for Neskowin.

Directions: From the junction of U.S. 101 and Highway 18 north of Lincoln City, drive north on 101 for one mile and turn left on Three Rocks Road and immediately park on the right by a trail sign.

Contact: Siuslaw National Forest, Hebo Ranger District, 31525 Highway 22, Hebo, OR, 97122, 503/392-5100.

25 ROADS END WAYSIDE
2.8 mi/1.5 hr   🏃1 ⛰7

north of Lincoln City on the Pacific Ocean

Map 1.3, page 35   BEST (

An easy stroll along the beach from the hidden town of Roads End leads 1.4 miles north to rough basalt cliffs and tidepools alive with barnacles, sea stars, and anemones. This is a great hike for kids, who'll enjoy poking around the lakes of seawater in the bowls of black rock. You might even see a few old guys panning for gold. If the tide is low, make your way farther north to a secret cove where stones of just about every color are washed up alongside polished agates on the beach in droves. The entire cove is hemmed in by rugged sea stacks and overhanging cliffs—there's even a cave to

poke around in. Bring the kids; they'll stay entertained for a long time. Just be sure to check the tide charts, since isolated spots like this can quickly become inundated with waves. Go at low tide and be safe.

User Groups: Hikers, dogs, and horses. No wheelchair facilities.

Permits: Permits are not required. Parking and access are free.

Maps: For a topographic map, ask the USGS for Neskowin OE W.

Directions: From Lighthouse Square on U.S. 101 in Lincoln City, turn onto Logan Road and follow it one mile to Roads End Wayside.

Contact: Oregon Parks and Recreation Department, 1115 Commercial Street NE, Salem, OR, 97301, 800/551-6949, www.oregonstateparks.org.

26 DRIFT CREEK FALLS
3.0 mi/1.5 hr   🏃1 ⛰7

east of Lincoln City in the Siuslaw National Forest

Map 1.3, page 35

It's all about the numbers: Here you can overlook a 75-foot horsetail waterfall from a 240-foot-long swaying suspension bridge hung 100 feet over Drift Creek. Sound perilous? It's actually quite easy, a three-mile walk through ferns, salal, red huckleberry, and vine maple. The best time to go is in the spring and fall when the rains have powered the flow, making for a great show in this rain-forested chasm. The bridge itself is one of the more popular features of the trail, and in and of itself is an engineering marvel. Whether you dare to step foot on it is entirely up to you.

The first mile on the Drift Creek Falls Trail is an easy descent through forest to a 20-foot creek crossing. In the next 0.3 mile, the trail briefly traverses an old clear-cut before entering an old-growth grove and reaching the suspension bridge. The last 0.2 mile heads down to the waterfall's misty pool.

User Groups: Hikers and dogs. Part of the gravel trail is wheelchair accessible.

Permits: Permits are not required. A federal Northwest Forest Pass is required to park here; the cost is $5 a day or $30 for an annual pass. You can buy a day pass at the trailhead, at ranger stations, or through private vendors.

Maps: For a map of the Siuslaw National Forest, contact the Siuslaw National Forest headquarters, 4077 SW Research Way, P.O. Box 1148, Corvallis, OR, 97339, 541/750-7000. For a topographic map, ask the USGS for Devils Lake.

Directions: From Lincoln City, follow Highway 101 south of town to milepost 119 and turn east on Drift Creek Road for 1.5 miles, turn right at a T-junction and go 0.3 mile to another fork, heading uphill to the left onto Road 17/Drift Creek Camp Road. After 0.8 mile, turn uphill to the left. Go 9.1 miles to a large parking area on the right.

Contact: Siuslaw National Forest, Hebo Ranger District, 31525 Highway 22, Hebo, OR, 97122, 503/392-5100.

27 VALLEY OF THE GIANTS
4.7 mi/2.0 hr ☒1 ◮7

west of Falls City in the Coast Range

Map 1.3, page 35   **BEST (**

At one point, Oregon was renowned for its old-growth trees. Nowadays finding a trail that really brings out the big guys is not as easy as it was, say, 100 years ago. Though the drive to the Valley of the Giants requires navigating a maze of old logging roads, the end is an easy trail through some of Oregon's oldest and largest trees. This 51-acre forest preserve receives more than 180 inches of rain a year, and it shows. Douglas firs and Western hemlocks dominate the sky here. In spring and early summer, marbled murrelets roost high in these trees but build no nests, instead laying their eggs on flat branches a good 150 feet above the forest floor. They spend the rest of their lives at sea, but stands of trees like this are crucial to the birds' survival. To get here, it is crucial to get the directions right, and it is in your best interest to call the BLM's Salem District Office (503/375-5646). The route is best traveled on weekends to avoid log truck traffic.

Begin your descent into 450-year-old trees following the Valley of the Giants Trail 0.4 mile, crossing the river on a six-foot thick log. The main portion of the trail loops 0.7 mile through the area's biggest and most impressive stand of Oregon-style old-growth and wildflowers. Go right or left, either way you'll miss nothing.

User Groups: Hikers and dogs. No wheelchair facilities.

Permits: Permits are not required. Parking and access are free.

Maps: For a topographic map, ask the USGS for Warnicke Creek.

Directions: From the intersection of U.S. 99 West and OR 22, follow signs for Dallas for four miles. From Dallas, follow signs nine miles to Falls City. At the far end of town, curve left across a bridge onto Bridge Street, which becomes gravel in 0.7 mile, then becomes a one-lane log road. A total of 14.9 miles from Falls City, the road turns left at a locked gate with a Keep Out sign. At another 200 yards past this gate, turn right at a T-junction. Travel 8.2 miles past this gate, keeping right around an old lakebed, until you reach a wooden bridge over the South Fork Siletz River. At 0.2 mile past the bridge, head uphill to the right. In another 0.3 mile, go left at a fork. For the remaining 4.9 rough and potholed miles, keep left at all junctions to a bridge over the North Fork Siletz River. Continue 1.1 miles to a fork, going right 0.5 mile to the trailhead.

Contact: Bureau of Land Management, Salem District Office, 1717 Fabry Road SE, Salem, OR, 97306, 503/375-5646.

28 SALISHAN SPIT
8.0 mi/4.0 hr

north of Gleneden Beach on the Pacific Ocean

Map 1.3, page 35

Of all the sandy peninsulas in Oregon, the "spits" that guard the bays of every coastal river mouth, only the Salishan Spit has been developed for houses. Well, actually it's a resort. Though storms threatened the stability of this community and did indeed do some damage, the land has been stabilized. Why hike here? Because people aren't the only inhabitants: Harbor seals and sea otters frequent the more wild tip of the spit, away from the everyday human world. Views extend to the Cascade Head in the north and up to a gaggle of strange houses lining the ocean.

From the Gleneden Beach Wayside, a short paved trail leads down the sandstone bluffs to the beach. From here head north—that is, to the right—up the beach for a casual four-mile walk to the tip of the Salishan Spit. Be prepared for a moderately difficult hike not only for the distance, but because you'll be walking through sand.

User Groups: Hikers, dogs, and horses. No wheelchair facilities.

Permits: Permits are not required. Parking and access are free.

Maps: For a topographic map, ask the USGS for Lincoln City.

Directions: Head south from Lincoln City on U.S. 101 about 3.8 miles and turn west on Wessler Street at a sign for Gleneden Beach State Park, driving 0.2 mile to the parking lot.

Contact: Oregon Parks and Recreation Department, 1115 Commercial Street NE, Salem, OR, 97301, 800/551-6949, www.oregonstateparks.org.

29 DEVILS PUNCH BOWL
4.1 mi/2.0 hr

north of Newport in Devils Punch Bowl State Natural Area

Map 1.3, page 35

Surfers, tidepools, whale-watching, and thundering tides pounding into a series of sea caves beneath Otter Rock. Need I say more? There's a lot to see at the Devils Punch Bowl, and a number of ways to do it. An easy hike out the headland, a short saunter to its base within view of the Marine Gardens, and a hike down Beverly Beach are all possibilities at this state wayside. Winter storms are a great time to visit, as the ocean becomes vehement as it crashes into the sea-carved bowl, thundering and exploding like the devil himself. From the town of Newport, you can also spend some time on nearby Beverly Beach, going from violent to mellow in the space of a mile.

The first easy hike (0.3 mile round-trip) begins from the day-use lot and heads to a picnic area atop the rock. From a fenced overlook, you can see the churning Punch Bowl, waves pounding against sandstone and basalt. The second hike (0.4 mile one-way) goes down to the Punch Bowl itself and a series of tidepools called the Marine Gardens. To get here, return to the lot and walk C Street for two blocks to a Dead End sign and take the trail to the left to a hidden beach. Be sure to try this one at low tide, when anemones, mussels, and starfish are revealed. At the southern edge of the beach, at low tide you can slip into two caves. To access Beverly Beach, return to the lot and cross the road to a long staircase descending Otter Rock to a 1.5-mile walk along the beach to Spencer Creek.

User Groups: Hikers and dogs. No wheelchair facilities.

Permits: Permits are not required. Parking and access are free.

Maps: For a topographic map, ask the USGS for Newport North.

Directions: Drive north of Newport eight miles on U.S. 101 to the turnoff for the Otter

Crest Loop between mileposts 132 and 133. Follow signs 0.7 mile to the day-use parking area.

Contact: Oregon Parks and Recreation Department, 1115 Commercial Street NE, Salem, OR, 97301, 800/551-6949, www.oregonstateparks.org.

ⓛ YAQUINA HEAD LIGHTHOUSE
0.1-2.6 mi/0.25-1.0 hr   🏃‍♀️₁ ⛰️₇

north of Newport on Yaquina Head

Map 1.3, page 35

With a name like Yaquina Head Outstanding Natural Area, it ought to be good. With a historic 1873 lighthouse, whale-watching opportunities, colonies of seals, and views to seabird-populated Colony Rock, it really is one-of-a-kind. Five trails in all explore the head, with an interpretive center and viewpoints suitable for binoculars and cameras.

The centerpiece, of course, is the 93-foot lighthouse, the tallest in Oregon. The 200-yard paved Yaquina Head Lighthouse Trail

leads to its base. This trail begins at the parking area located at the end of Lighthouse Drive, where the 0.4-mile Salal Hill Trail also begins. From the Quarry Cove parking area, the Quarry Cove Trail dives down 0.5 mile to a series of low-tide tidepools and the 0.5-mile Communications Hill Trails climbs to excellent viewpoints. There's even a stairway leading down to Cobble Beach. Bring a picnic and spend a day here.

User Groups: Hikers and mountain bikes. No dogs or horses allowed. There is wheelchair access to the tidepools.

Permits: Permits are not required. A $7 day-use fee is collected at the camping entrance, or you can get an annual Yaquina Head Vehicle Pass for $15; contact Bureau of Land Management, Salem District Office, 503/375-5646.

Maps: For a brochure and map, contact the Bureau of Land Management, 503/375-5646, or download a free map and brochure at www.blm.gov/or/resources/recreation/picbrochures.php. For a topographic map, ask the USGS for Newport North.

Directions: From Newport, drive two miles north on U.S. 101 to the park entrance. All

© SEAN PATRICK HILL

Yaquina Head Lighthouse

trailheads start from the parking areas and are well labeled.

Contact: Bureau of Land Management, Salem District Office, 1717 Fabry Road SE, Salem, OR, 97306, 503/375-5646.

31 NYE AND AGATE BEACH
4.0 mi one-way/2.0 hr   🏃2 ⛰6

in Newport on the Pacific Ocean

Map 1.3, page 35

The 93-foot Yaquina Head Lighthouse is not the original lighthouse for this area; in fact, it is the Yaquina Bay Lighthouse that originally steered ships into the bay at Newport. This unique lighthouse is actually a lighthouse atop a house, making for an easy workday for past lighthouse keepers. You can visit this lighthouse and explore two beaches divided by an eroded sea stack called Jumpoff Joe; it used to have an arch beneath it, but it's been worn away by the surging tides.

Beginning from the Yaquina Bay Lighthouse picnic area, head down the stone steps to the North Jetty and views of the massive Yaquina Bay Bridge. Head to the right, going as far as you like. After 1.8 miles, you'll reach Jumpoff Joe, a good turnaround point. If you're up for more, continue along the 2.2-mile stretch of Agate Beach, so named for its abundance of agates and jaspers washed up by the tides, especially in winter.

User Groups: Hikers, dogs, and horses. No wheelchair facilities.

Permits: Permits are not required. Parking and access are free.

Maps: For a topographic map, ask the USGS for Newport North.

Directions: From the north end of Newport's Yaquina Bay Bridge (U.S. 101), follow state park signs to a picnic area at the Yaquina Bay Lighthouse. To shuttle from the Agate Beach State Wayside, drive 2.2 miles north of Yaquina Bay State Park on U.S. 101. Turn left on NW 26th Street for 0.2 mile, then right on NW Oceanview Drive for 0.2 mile

to the Agate Beach pullout. From here, you can walk 1.2 miles north along the beach to its end at the Yaquina Head, or south 2.8 miles to Yaquina Bay.

Contact: Oregon Parks and Recreation Department, 1115 Commercial Street NE, Salem, OR, 97301, 800/551-6949, www.oregonstateparks.org.

32 SOUTH JETTY TRAIL
2.1 mi/1.0 hr   🏃1 ⛰6

south of Newport in South Beach State Park

Map 1.3, page 35

If you're looking for the perfect place to let the kids run off their energy without running off yours, South Beach State Park across the Yaquina Bay from Newport is perfect. In the course of a single hour (or more, depending on how much those kids may run in and out of the sand dunes), you'll cross a golden beach, skirting a foredune to a view of an old railroad route, and cross a deflation plain, a lowland area where the winds have stripped the sand down to hard ground.

From the day-use area, cross the foredune to the ocean shore. From here, walk to the right 0.9 mile toward the South Jetty on the Yaquina River. Climb the jetty for a look at the nearby Yaquina Bay Lighthouse and a series of pilings marking the long-lost railroad that brought the rocks here. Follow the jetty road back inland 0.3 mile, watching for a trail sign on the right. Follow the left fork path 0.2 mile to a paved trail. Go left a short distance on the paved path, then go right on a bark dust path across the deflation plain for 0.7 mile back to the day-use lot.

User Groups: Hikers, dogs, and horses. Bicycles on marked trails only. Paved paths are wheelchair accessible.

Permits: Permits are not required. Parking and access are free.

Maps: For a topographic map, ask the USGS for Newport South.

Directions: Drive U.S. 101 south of the

Yaquina Bay Bridge 1.4 miles and turn right at a sign for South Beach State Park. Drive straight on this road 0.5 mile to the day-use parking area.

Contact: Oregon Parks and Recreation Department, 1115 Commercial Street NE, Salem, OR, 97301, 800/551-6949, www.oregonstateparks.org.

33 SEAL ROCK
4.2 mi/2.5 hr 👫1 ⛰6

south of Newport in Ona Beach State Park

Map 1.3, page 35

This rock, recognized in the Chinook language as "seal home," is just that. You can reach Seal Rock, one of the southernmost remnants of a 15-million-year-old lava flow that originated somewhere near Hells Canyon, by car. You could have a sandwich in the neat little picnic area in a grove of spruce and shore pine. There's another way to enjoy it, though: For a more rewarding adventure, try a 2.1-mile beach walk from Ona Beach State Park and twisting Beaver Creek. It will make the sight of those seals, and sea lions, all the more spectacular.

From the Ona Beach State Park turnout, take the large paved trail toward the ocean. Cross the footbridge over Beaver Creek and head south toward Seal Rock. At a small creek, about 0.3 mile short of the cape, take a side trail up the bluff to the highway, and continue south about 300 yards to the Seal Rock Wayside. From there, you can descend another trail to a beach on the other side of the cape.

User Groups: Hikers and dogs. Paved paths are wheelchair accessible.

Permits: Permits are not required. Parking and access are free.

Maps: For a topographic map, ask the USGS for Newport South.

Directions: Follow U.S. 101 south of Newport seven miles to the parking area near milepost 149.

Contact: Oregon Parks and Recreation Department, 1115 Commercial Street NE, Salem, OR, 97301, 800/551-6949, www.oregonstateparks.org.

34 MARY'S PEAK
4.0-10.0 mi/2.0-6.0 hr 👫2 ⛰8

west of Philomath in the Siuslaw National Forest

Map 1.3, page 35

From summer daisy fields to trees bowed down by winter snow, Mary's Peak is accessible all year long to some degree. Even better, it's the highest point in the Coastal Range, with views from the ocean to the Cascade Mountains. The Kalapuya sent their young men here on vision quests, naming the mountain Chateemanwi, the "place where spirits dwell." In fact, native legend has it that an angry coyote dammed up the Willamette, flooding all the world but this sole peak, which he spared as a refuge for all living things.

Mary's Peak is a designated Scenic Botanical Area, boasting a unique noble fir forest that rings many Ice Age flower species (more than 200 in all) dating back an estimated 6,000 years. A number of trails explore this unique vista, fanning out over the North and East Ridges with an easy, hikeable road to the summit.

From the observation point parking lot, an easy hike follows the East Ridge Trail out 1.2 miles, connecting to a 1.1-mile tie trail and returning on a 0.7-mile section of the North Ridge Trail. The East Ridge Trail in all is 2.2 miles, dropping 1,200 feet to a lower trailhead. The North Ridge Trail in its entirety is a more difficult 3.7 miles, switchbacking down nearly 2,000 feet to a trailhead and gate on Woods Creek Road.

The easier trails are the 4,097-foot summit, accessible from the observation point by climbing the gated road 0.6 mile to the top. From the campground, the easy Meadow Edge Trail loops 2.2 miles and connects to the summit as well.

User Groups: Hikers, dogs, mountain bikes,

and horses. The summit is wheelchair accessible.

Permits: Permits are not required. A federal Northwest Forest Pass is required to park here; the cost is $5 a day or $30 for an annual pass. You can buy a day pass at the trailhead, at ranger stations, or through private vendors.

Maps: For a map of the Siuslaw National Forest, contact the Siuslaw National Forest headquarters, 4077 SW Research Way, P.O. Box 1148, Corvallis, OR, 97339, 541/750-7000. For a topographic map, ask the USGS for Mary's Peak.

Directions: Drive U.S. 20 west of Corvallis through Philomath, then follow OR 34 for 8.8 miles and turn right onto Mary's Peak Road for 9.5 miles to its end at the observation point. For the Meadow Edge Trail, drive Mary's Peak Road from OR 34 8.8 miles up to the campground on the right, forking left to a picnic area and the trailhead.

Contact: Siuslaw National Forest, Waldport Ranger District, 1130 Forestry Lane, P.O. Box 400, Waldport, OR, 97122, 541/563-3211.

35 HORSE CREEK TRAIL
8.0 mi/4.0 hr   👫2 ⚠7

northeast of Waldport in Drift Creek Wilderness

Map 1.3, page 35

Welcome to the northernmost and largest wilderness area in the Oregon Coastal Range: the Drift Creek Wilderness. Dropping 1,000 feet to this wilderness's namesake creek, the Horse Creek Trail wanders under moss-draped maples, passing huge and substantially bigger trees along the way, including hemlock, fir, and spruce. In spring, queen's-cup dots the forest floor, and in autumn chanterelle mushrooms poke from the duff.

From the trailhead, the path remains level the first mile or so, then descends 2.6 miles to a ford with a view of the ocean along the way. Turn right and follow the creek downstream one mile to another ford. Take the right hand-path, an unofficial trail to a campsite

and continue uphill 0.4 mile to return to the Horse Creek Trail.

User Groups: Hikers, dogs, and horses. No mountain bikes allowed. No wheelchair facilities.

Permits: Permits are not required. Parking and access are free.

Maps: For a map of the Siuslaw National Forest, contact the Siuslaw National Forest headquarters, 4077 SW Research Way, P.O. Box 1148, Corvallis, OR, 97339, 541/750-7000. For a map of Drift Creek Wilderness, ask the USFS for Drift Creek Wilderness. For a topographic map, ask the USGS for Tidewater.

Directions: Drive seven miles north of Waldport on U.S. 101 to Ona Beach State Park and turn right on North Beaver Creek Road for one mile. At a fork, head left for 2.7 miles to another junction and turn right onto the paved, one-lane North Elkhorn Road/Road 51 for 5.8 miles. At the next junction, turn left on Road 50 for 1.4 miles. Take a right fork onto gravel Road 5087 for 3.4 miles to the trailhead at a gate.

Contact: Siuslaw National Forest, Waldport Ranger District, 1130 Forestry Lane, P.O. Box 400, Waldport, OR, 97122, 541/563-3211.

36 HARRIS RANCH TRAIL
4.4 mi/2.5 hr   👫2 ⚠7

northeast of Waldport in Drift Creek Wilderness

Map 1.3, page 35

Like the hike along Horse Creek Trail (see previous listing), this trail leads down to Drift Creek in its namesake wilderness area, though this trail is shorter and less difficult. To boot, it visits a meadow overgrown with bracken fern and blackberry and the site of an old homestead. For further adventuring, you can easily ford the creek here (especially in summer) and continue on to the Horse Creek Trail and the unmaintained Boulder Ridge Trail. Watch for wildlife in the meadow, including elk and black bear. This is also a good place to watch for bald eagles and the northern spotted owl.

In fall, the creek teems with spawning chinook and coho salmon, as well as steelhead and cutthroat trout.

From the trailhead, descend a whopping 1,200 feet on the Harris Ranch Trail, which is actually an abandoned road, down 2.2 miles to some small meadows and the remains of the pre–World War II ranch along Drift Creek. If the water is low, you can ford the creek 0.3 mile past the meadows and join the Horse Creek Trail, which connects to the Boulder Ridge Trail in one mile.

User Groups: Hikers, dogs, and horses. No mountain bikes allowed. No wheelchair facilities.

Permits: Permits are not required. Parking and access are free.

Maps: For a map of the Siuslaw National Forest, contact the Siuslaw National Forest headquarters, 4077 SW Research Way, P.O. Box 1148, Corvallis, OR, 97339, 541/750-7000. For a map of Drift Creek Wilderness, ask the USFS for Drift Creek Wilderness. For a topographic map, ask the USGS for Tidewater.

Directions: Drive east of Waldport on OR 34 for 6.9 miles to a bridge over the Alsea River. Turn north on Risley Creek Road/Road 3446 for 4.1 miles, staying on the larger road at each junction. Veer left on Road 346 for 0.8 mile to the Harris Ranch Trailhead.

Contact: Siuslaw National Forest, Waldport Ranger District, 1130 Forestry Lane, P.O. Box 400, Waldport, OR, 97122, 541/563-3211.

37 ALSEA FALLS
3.5 mi/1.5 hr   🥾1 ⛰6

east of Waldport on the South Fork Alsea River

Map 1.3, page 35

If you've never seen a fish launch itself into the air to get itself over a waterfall, this is the place to do it. The 20-foot Alsea Falls are a bit off the beaten path on a scenic route over the Coast Range. A Boy Scout–constructed loop trail circles the South Fork Alsea River, while providing access to another span to another nearby waterfall in a lush side canyon. Along the way are the enormous stumps left from old-time logging, though the forest has had a long time to recover.

Starting from the Alsea Falls Recreation Area, take the left-hand trail beginning at a sign behind a maintenance garage. This trail follows the creek through second-growth woods for 0.6 mile to the first look at Alsea Falls and continues 0.3 mile down to the creek and over a logjam and boulder crossing beneath the pool at the base of the falls. Now the old-growth begins, as does the poison oak. At a junction, the right-hand trail continues the loop back one mile upstream and over a footbridge back to the car, but save that for the return; instead, take the left-hand trail, which joins a road to McBee Park. From here it's a short, 0.8-mile walk to Green Peak Falls. Stay on the gravel road until reaching the entrance road; turn right on that road, then take a quick right through a picnic site and follow that path to the 60-foot falls. A steep path can be scrambled down to reach a pool at the base.

User Groups: Hikers, dogs, and mountain bikes. No wheelchair facilities.

Permits: Permits are not required. Day-use fee is $3.

Maps: For a brochure and map, contact the Bureau of Land Management, Salem District Office, 503/375-5646, or go to www.blm.gov/or/resources/recreation/files/brochures/Alsea_Falls_Trail_System.pdf. For a topographic map, ask the USGS for Glenbrook.

Directions: Drive 16 miles south of Corvallis on U.S. 99W and turn west on South Fork Road at a sign for Alpine, and follow Alsea Falls signs to the camping area entrance on the right. Keep left to the trailhead.

Contact: Bureau of Land Management, Salem District Office, 1717 Fabry Road SE, Salem, OR, 97306, 503/375-5646.

38 SMELT SANDS WAYSIDE
1.4 m/0.75 hr

north of Yachats on the Pacific Ocean

Map 1.3, page 35

Smelt are a family of small fish found in many waters, including the Pacific. Just offshore of the quaint town of Yachats, a landowner blocked access to some traditional fishing rocks in the 1970s. Some locals went to the books and discovered a long-forgotten, 19th-century right of way for a road that was never built. A decade-long court battle went all the way to the Oregon Supreme Court and left us the 0.7-mile 804 Trail in a State Park wayside. You'll have the opportunity to see some "spouting horns" (waves crashing upward through cracks in the lava) and a long beach with running creeks and grassy dunes.

From the wayside, strike out on the gravel trail that eventually heads north, passing a motel and crossing a driveway before descending steps to the beach. From here, Tillicum Beach Campground is 2.7 miles ahead and Patterson State Park is 6.3 miles ahead.

User Groups: Hikers and dogs. No wheelchair facilities.

Permits: Permits are not required. Parking and access are free.

Maps: For a topographic map, ask the USGS for Yachats.

Directions: On the north end of Yachats on U.S. 101, turn west onto Lemwick Lane, driving to the end at a turnaround and parking area.

Contact: Oregon Parks and Recreation Department, 1115 Commercial Street NE, Salem, OR, 97301, 800/551-6949, www.oregonstateparks.org.

39 CAPE PERPETUA
1.0–6.8 mi/0.5–3.5 hrs

south of Yachats in Cape Perpetua Scenic Area

Map 1.3, page 35

The Cape Perpetua Scenic Area is one of the jewels of the Oregon coast. A network of trails radiates from the visitors center, offering access to a giant spruce, an ancient Native American midden, the Devil's Churn, Cooks Chasm and a spouting horn, and the centerpiece: a wonderful stone shelter atop 746-foot Cape Perpetua itself, built in 1933 by the Civilian Conservation Corps. It's easy to do three interesting trails in a single day and visit the top spots.

All trails begin at the visitors center lot. For the ocean hike, follow the "Tidepools" pointer on a paved trail, which goes 0.2 mile and under U.S. 101, then forks. The left fork circles 0.2 mile for a view to the spouting horns at Cooks Chasm, named for Captain Cook, who in turn named this cape for St. Perpetua in 1778. You'll also walk over the midden, a staggering mound of white mussel shells left by Native Americans (possibly as long as 6,000 years ago). The right fork heads out 0.5 mile to a loop around the Devil's Churn, a wave-pounded chasm in the lava.

For two inland hikes, return to the lot. First, follow "Giant Spruce" and "Viewpoint" pointers. In 0.2 mile, the trail splits: To see the 15-foot-thick, 600-year-old Sitka spruce, an Oregon Heritage Tree whose roots form a small tunnel, go to the right on the Giant Spruce Trail 0.8 mile. To climb Cape Perpetua, head left at this junction over Cape Creek to cross two paved roads and climb the switchbacks 1.3 miles up the Saint Perpetua Trail to the stone shelter, which affords views 37 miles to sea and 104 miles south to Cape Blanco. It's an excellent place to whale-watch, and you can consider how the CCC men endured winter storms and lugged buckets of sand up from the shore to make the mortar for the shelter.

User Groups: Hikers and dogs. Paved paths are wheelchair accessible.

Permits: Permits are not required. A federal Northwest Forest Pass is required to park here; the cost is $5 a day or $30 for an annual pass. You can buy a day pass at the visitors center, at ranger stations, or through private vendors.

Maps: For a map of the Siuslaw National Forest, contact the Siuslaw National Forest headquarters, 4077 SW Research Way, P.O. Box 1148, Corvallis, OR, 97339, 541/750-7000. For a topographic map, ask the USGS for Yachats.

Directions: Drive U.S. 101 south of Yachats three miles to the Cape Perpetua Visitor Center turnoff between mileposts 168 and 169.

Contact: Cape Perpetua Visitor Center, 2400 Highway 101, Yachats, OR, 97498, 541/547-3289, or Siuslaw National Forest, Waldport Ranger District, 1130 Forestry Lane, P.O. Box 400, Waldport, OR, 97122, 541/563-3211.

🟦40 GWYNN CREEK
6.7 mi/3.5 hr　　　　🧍2 ⛰7

south of Yachats in Cape Perpetua Scenic Area

Map 1.3, page 35

Sitka spruce thrive on the foggy ocean climate and can only survive within three miles of the coastline. It so happens that some of the best spruce forests on the entire coast are in the canyons south of Cape Perpetua. This loop trail spans Cooks Ridge, drops into Gwynn Creek's canyon, and follows the Oregon Coast Trail back to the visitors center. Mushrooms love it here, too, including the delectable chanterelle and the poisonous panther amanita. Parts of the trail follow old logging roads and an 1895 wagon road between Yachats and Florence that ran until about 1910.

From the visitors center upper parking lot, follow signs for the Cooks Ridge Trail. In 0.4 mile, the path forks but rejoins, forming the Discovery Loop. Take either side and continue 0.3 mile to where the paths meet and continue on the Cooks Ridge Trail two

miles to a junction. Turn right on the Gwynn Creek Trail, descending 3.3 miles and 1,000 feet down the canyon. At the Oregon Coast Trail, go right for a 0.7-mile return to the visitors center.

User Groups: Hikers, dogs, and horses. No wheelchair facilities.

Permits: Permits are not required. A federal Northwest Forest Pass is required to park here; the cost is $5 a day or $30 for an annual pass. You can buy a day pass at the visitors center, at ranger stations, or through private vendors.

Maps: For a map of the Siuslaw National Forest, contact the Siuslaw National Forest headquarters, 4077 SW Research Way, P.O. Box 1148, Corvallis, OR, 97339, 541/750-7000. For a topographic map, ask the USGS for Yachats.

Directions: Drive U.S. 101 south of Yachats three miles to the Cape Perpetua Visitor Center turnoff between mileposts 168 and 169.

Contact: Cape Perpetua Visitor Center, 2400 Highway 101, Yachats, OR, 97498, 541/547-3289, or Siuslaw National Forest, Waldport Ranger District, 1130 Forestry Lane, P.O. Box 400, Waldport, OR, 97122, 541/563-3211.

🟦41 CUMMINS CREEK
8.0 mi/4.0 hr　　　　🧍3 ⛰7

south of Yachats in Cape Perpetua Scenic Area

Map 1.3, page 35

Traversing the edge of the Cummins Creek Wilderness and connecting to the network of trails in the Cape Perpetua Scenic Area, this little-known trail itself never comes near the creek, but a small user trail will get you there nonetheless. A moderate-length loop offers a good tour of this area with opportunities for even longer hikes if you wish.

Beginning at the barricade, the initial part of the Cummins Creek Trail is an abandoned road. In the first 300 yards, an unofficial side trail to the right leads to two spots on the canyon, about 1.8 miles out and back. But the main Cummins Creek Trail ascends gradually up a forested ridge 1.4 miles to a junction. The Cummins Creek Loop Trail continues to the left 1.2 miles to the next junction; turn right for 0.5 mile, watching for a short spur trail to the left that offers a view. At the next junction, follow the Cummins Creek Trail to the right 1.4 miles back to the first junction, then stay to the left on the Cummins Creek Trail 1.4 miles back to the barricade.

User Groups: Hikers, dogs, and horses. No wheelchair facilities.

Permits: Permits are not required. A federal Northwest Forest Pass is required to park here; the cost is $5 a day or $30 for an annual pass. You can buy a day pass at the visitors center, at ranger stations, or through private vendors.

Maps: For a map of the Siuslaw National Forest, contact the Siuslaw National Forest headquarters, 4077 SW Research Way, P.O. Box 1148, Corvallis, OR, 97339, 541/750-7000. For a topographic map, ask the USGS for Yachats.

Directions: Drive U.S. 101 south of the Cape Perpetua Visitors Center one mile to a sign for Cummins Creek Trailhead. Turn left and drive gravel road 1050 for 0.3 mile to the barricade.

Contact: Cape Perpetua Visitor Center, 2400 Highway 101, Yachats, OR, 97498, 541/547-3289, or Siuslaw National Forest, Waldport Ranger District, 1130 Forestry Lane, P.O. Box 400, Waldport, OR, 97122, 541/563-3211.

42 CUMMINS RIDGE
12.0 mi/6.0 hr   👥3 ⛰7

south of Yachats in Cummins Creek Wilderness

Map 1.3, page 35

With only 9,173 acres, Cummins Creek Wilderness is not huge. It has, in fact, only one trail. On the other hand, it has the only old-growth Sitka spruce forest in the entire wilderness system of Oregon, so why not visit? You'll find not only Cummins Creek but Bob Creek, both overhung with droopy maple and alder. The Cummins Ridge tops out at 2,200 feet

and bisects the wilderness. Wild salmon and trout spawn in the cold waters, and flowers like yellow monkeyflower, white candyflower, purple aster, and the tall spikes of foxglove thrive here. With 80–100 inches of rain a year here, it's no wonder that spruce in this rainforest sometimes reach nine feet in diameter.

From the barricade on the dirt road, the Cummins Ridge Trail begins at 1,000 foot elevation. Follow the abandoned road up three miles, gaining 750 feet in elevation, to a cairn, then follow the trail to the right another three miles to trail's end on Forest Service Road 5694-515. Return the way you came.

User Groups: Hikers, dogs, and horses. No mountain bikes allowed. No wheelchair facilities.

Permits: Permits are not required. A federal Northwest Forest Pass is required to park here; the cost is $5 a day or $30 for an annual pass. You can buy a day pass at the visitors center, at ranger stations, or through private vendors.

Maps: For a map of the Siuslaw National Forest, contact the Siuslaw National Forest headquarters, 4077 SW Research Way, P.O. Box 1148, Corvallis, OR, 97339, 541/750-7000. For a topographic map, ask the USGS for Yachats.

Directions: From Yachats, drive four miles south on U.S. 101 and turn inland on gravel Road 1051 for 2.2 miles to the end at a barricade.

Contact: Siuslaw National Forest, Waldport Ranger District, 1130 Forestry Ln., P.O. Box 400, Waldport, OR, 97122, 541/563-3211.

43 HECETA HEAD
6.9 mi/3.0 hr   👥2 ⛰8

north of Florence in Carl Washburne State Park

Map 1.3, page 35   BEST (

A plethora of fantastic landscapes nearly assaults the senses in this everything-and-the-kitchen-sink hike. From beaver ponds to a lighthouse on a surf-pounded rock to the strange "Hobbit Trails," there is plenty to discover here. There is even, if you believe in this sort of thing, a supposedly haunted light keeper's house. All in all, you'll get the best of all worlds in this meandering loop.

From the day-use area, follow the beach south 1.2 miles, crossing Blowout Creek, toward the looming Heceta Head, where starfish and mollusks cling in the booming waves. Piles of gravel near the base are a good place to dig around for agates. You'll spot a trail leading into the woods; take this up 0.4 mile through a network of paths called the Hobbit Trails (tunnels of a sort made by hollowed-out sand chutes and arching rhododendrons). At the top of the climb, nearing the highway, go right on the next trail, which climbs 1.3 mile over the Heceta Head itself, coming down to the lighthouse and an overlook. Just offshore, Parrot Rock and other sea stacks are roosting areas for thousands of Brandt's cormorants; it's the largest nesting colony in Oregon. Walk the last 0.5 mile toward the Heceta House, an 1893 Queen Anne–style home for the lighthouse keepers that is supposedly haunted; it's a bed-and-breakfast now, so you can find out for yourself.

To complete the loop, head back over the head to the U.S. 101 Hobbit Trail trailhead and cross the highway to the continuation of the Valley Trail, which in the course of 1.1 miles passes a number of ponds and a beaver lake before forking to the left (though you could hike a bit down China Creek if you head right). This trail returns to the Washburne Campground, where you can follow the entrance road out and across the highway to return to the day-use area.

User Groups: Horses and dogs. No wheelchair facilities.

Permits: Permits are not required. Parking and access are free.

Maps: For a free park brochure, call Oregon Parks and Recreation, 800/551-6949, or download a free map at www.oregonstateparks.org. For a topographic map, ask the USGS for Heceta Head.

Directions: Drive U.S. 101 north of Florence

one mile to milepost 176 and turn left into the Washburne State Park day-use area, parking at the far end of the picnic area. The trail begins past the restrooms.

Contact: Oregon Parks and Recreation Department, 1115 Commercial Street NE, Salem, OR, 97301, 800/551-6949, www.oregonstateparks.org.

44 CAPE MOUNTAIN
2.0 mi/1.0 hr   🏃1 ⛰7

north of Florence in the Siuslaw National Forest

Map 1.3, page 35

In a joint venture between the Forest Service and equestrian club volunteers, a network of trails was built on and around Cape Mountain. The Coast Horse Trail system is open to hikers, too. An easy two-mile loop leads to the peak, the site of a 1932 fire watchtower. Once you've done this easy loop, you can fan out into the wild network of trails going every which way, exploring Nelson and Scurvy Ridge and a number of loops. Much of the forest here was spared by previous wildfires, leaving habitat for old-growth trees and wildlife.

From the Dry Lake Trailhead, head behind the stables for the Princess Tasha Trail, climbing 0.4 mile through old-growth Douglas fir and coastal spruce to a four-way junction. Turn left on the Cape Mountain spur for 0.5 mile, keeping left at all junctions to attain the summit. For a loop option, follow the old road down, keeping left at all junctions to return directly to the car.

User Groups: Hikers, dogs, mountain bikes, and horses. No wheelchair facilities.

Permits: Permits are not required. Parking and access are free.

Maps: For a map of the Siuslaw National Forest, contact the Siuslaw National Forest headquarters, 4077 SW Research Way, P.O. Box 1148, Corvallis, OR, 97339, 541/750-7000. For a topographic map, ask the USGS for Mercer Lake.

Directions: Drive U.S, 101 north of Florence

seven miles and go right on Herman Peak Road for 2.8 miles to the Dry Lake Trailhead on the left.

Contact: Siuslaw National Forest, Mapleton Ranger District, 4480 Highway 101, Building G, Florence, OR, 97439, 541/902-8526.

45 BAKER BEACH
0.5-6.5 mi/0.25-3.5 hr

north of Florence in the Siuslaw National Forest

Map 1.3, page 35   **BEST (**

Baker Beach's windswept dunes sure look a lot like something from *Lawrence of Arabia,* and standing amid such colossal waves it's hard to believe we're still in Oregon. Interspersed with Sutton Creek, grassy hummocks, and perhaps even a little lupine flower or wild strawberry, it doesn't seem like other beaches. Nearby Lily Lake provides an easy 1.4-mile loop, and the beach itself is explorable (with trails and dunes). Hike from the lot 0.4 mile toward the ocean, then strike out in any direction; heading north three miles will land you at the estuary of Sutton Creek, a great place to bird-watch. But you may just want to go striding over the dunes themselves, finding a big one and rolling down the other side. Kids love this area, as do horseback riders.

User Groups: Hikers and horses. Dogs allowed on leash only. Bikes prohibited. No wheelchair facilities.

Permits: Permits are not required. A federal Northwest Forest Pass is required to park here; the cost is $5 a day or $30 for an annual pass. You can buy a day pass at the visitors center, at ranger stations, or through private vendors.

Maps: For a map of the Siuslaw National Forest, contact the Siuslaw National Forest headquarters, 4077 SW Research Way, P.O. Box 1148, Corvallis, OR, 97339, 541/750-7000. For a topographic map, ask the USGS for Mercer Lake.

Directions: Drive U.S. 101 north of Florence seven miles and turn west on gravel Baker Beach Road for 0.5 miles to its end.

Contact: Siuslaw National Forest, Mapleton Ranger District, 4480 Highway 101, Building G, Florence, OR, 97439, 541/902-8526.

46 SUTTON CREEK DUNES
4.4 mi/2.0 hr

north of Florence in the Siuslaw National Forest

Map 1.3, page 35

If you've never seen the famous Oregon rhododendrons, this is the place to do it. In the Sutton Creek Recreation Area, jungles of these sweet flowering trees line the meandering Sutton Creek, easy and warm to wade in the summer. Patches of spiny salal rustle in the wind, and blue herons wade in the water. A loop trail courses through the dunes and follows the creek. If you go to the shore, keep out of designated snowy plover nesting sites, as these birds are endangered and protected. A variety of dunes punctuate the landscape, making for a geographically and biologically diverse area. Look for the rare *Darlingtonia,* the insect-munching cobra lily.

From the Holman Vista lot, start at the trail behind the kitchen shelter in the picnic area. This trail curves 0.8 mile along the creek, passing a number of fords, to a bench and footbridge. Follow a sign upstream to the right for the Sutton Campground, following the Sutton Creek Trail. In 0.5 mile, you'll reach the campground's A Loop. Turn left along the road and cross a footbridge over the creek and stay to the left at the next two junctions (part of a 0.4-mile loop), continuing 1.4 miles out along the dunes (a right-hand trail leads to the Alder Dune Campground) before dropping down to the footbridge to Boldac's Meadow. Turn right along the creek, then left at the next junction to return the half-mile back to Holman Vista.

User Groups: Hikers, dogs on leash only, and horses. No bikes allowed. The Holman Vista Observation Deck is wheelchair accessible.

Permits: Permits are not required. A federal Northwest Forest Pass is required to park here; the cost is $5 a day or $30 for an annual pass. You can buy a day pass at the visitors center, at ranger stations, or through private vendors.

Maps: For a map of the Siuslaw National Forest, contact the Siuslaw National Forest headquarters, 4077 SW Research Way, P.O. Box 1148, Corvallis, OR, 97339, 541/750-7000. For a topographic map, ask the USGS for Mercer Lake.

Directions: From Florence, drive U.S. 101 north for five miles, turning west at the Sutton creek Recreation Area sign. Follow this paved road 2.2 miles to the Holman Vista lot.

Contact: Siuslaw National Forest, Mapleton Ranger District, 4480 Highway 101, Building G, Florence, OR, 97439, 541/902-8526.

47 ENCHANTED VALLEY
5.0 mi/2.5 hr

north of Florence in the Siuslaw National Forest

Map 1.3, page 35

This former dairy farm has been abandoned, and a host of wildlife (including deer and elk) has taken the place of the cows. The bed of Bailey Creek shimmers with bits of iron pyrite and is being restored for native coho salmon, thus making this a place to see both silver salmon and fool's gold: a real treasure. This fairly easy hike follows the creek 2.5 miles from a feeder creek for Mercer Lake along meadows teeming with horsetail and skunk cabbage, visiting an old farmhouse site and an upper homestead meadow, site of an old apple orchard. Following an old road converted to a path, there's really no way to lose your way. Return as you came.

User Groups: Hikers, dogs, and horses. No wheelchair facilities.

Permits: Permits are not required. Parking and access are free.

Maps: For a map of the Siuslaw National Forest, contact the Siuslaw National Forest headquarters, 4077 SW Research Way, P.O. Box 1148, Corvallis, OR, 97339, 541/750-

7000. For a topographic map, ask the USGS for Mercer Lake.

Directions: Drive five miles north of Florence on U.S. 101 and turn right on Mercer Lake Road for 3.7 miles. Fork left on Twin Fawn Drive for 0.3 mile to a parking area at the end of the road.

Contact: Siuslaw National Forest, Mapleton Ranger District, 4480 Highway 101, Building G, Florence, OR, 97439, 541/902-8526.

48 SIUSLAW RIDGE
2.6 mi/1.0 hr

west of Eugene in Whittaker Creek Recreation Site

Map 1.3, page 35

From the campground at the Whittaker Creek Recreation Site deep in the Coastal Range, you can watch the annual salmon run. Chinook, coho, and steelhead all push upstream to their spawning grounds. Just off the road, the Siuslaw River cuts its way through the mountains heading for the sea, and here the Siuslaw Ridge rises above it with a trail leading to a truly large Douglas fir: seven-feet thick and 500-years-old. The trail is just steep enough to give your heart a workout.

From the parking area near a dam, head across a footbridge spanning Whittaker Creek and down the campground road to a sign reading Old Growth Ridge Trail. This one-mile climb rockets up 800 feet to a junction at the peak of the ridge. Take a left for a short 0.1-mile jaunt to the giant fir, and a right for a short 0.2-mile walk to a river viewpoint.

User Groups: Hikers and dogs. No wheelchair facilities.

Permits: Permits are not required. Parking and access are free.

Maps: For a topographic map, ask the USGS for Roman Nose Mountain.

Directions: Drive west of Eugene 33 miles on OR 126 to a junction between mileposts 26 and 27. Turn south on Siuslaw River Road, following signs for "Whittaker Cr. Rec. Area"

for 1.5 miles, turn right for 0.2 mile, then right again into the campground.
Contact: Bureau of Land Management, Eugene District Office, 2890 Chad Dr., Eugene, OR, 97440, 541/683-6600.

49 SWEET CREEK FALLS
5.2 mi/2.5 hr   👥1 ⚠7

east of Florence in the Siuslaw National Forest
Map 1.4, page 36

This hike would be quite epic if not for lack of a bridge spanning the gorge at Sweet Creek Falls. No matter. Two trailheads will do fine to visit not just two different views of Sweet Creek, but Beaver Creek Falls, which is—to my understanding—the only double waterfall in Oregon made of two completely different creeks. One section of the trail follows an old wagon road through the Zarah T. Sweet homestead, the path now pioneered only by red alders, which thrive in disturbed ground. The other fans out toward both sets of waterfalls and stunning views. Rain or shine, it's beautiful. A total of four trailheads break these trails up into easy segments that pass a dozen waterfalls in all. To make it easy and worthwhile, try these two. Part of the trail, by the way, is a dramatic catwalk on a metal walkway hugging the canyon wall.

The Homestead Trailhead sets out into Punchbowl Falls Canyon 0.7 mile, joining up with the trail from the Sweet Creek Falls Trailhead for the final 0.4-mile walk to Sweet Creek Falls. It's easiest to return the way you came, though in very low water a ford is possible over slippery boulders. Instead, proceed by car to the Wagon Road Trailhead, where two trails begin. Directly across the road from the parking area, one 0.8-mile trail, a stretch of the old Sunset Wagon Road, leads down to a viewpoint of Sweet Creek Falls opposite the previous trails. The second route, Beaver Creek Trail, begins over the roadway bridge from the parking area for a 0.6-mile trail to Beaver Creek Falls.

User Groups: Hikers and dogs only. No wheelchair facilities.
Permits: Permits are not required. Parking and access are free.
Maps: For a map of the Siuslaw National Forest, contact the Siuslaw National Forest headquarters, 4077 SW Research Way, P.O. Box 1148, Corvallis, OR, 97339, 541/750-7000. For a topographic map, ask the USGS for Goodwin Peak.
Directions: Drive 15 miles east of Florence on OR 126 to Mapleton to the Siuslaw River Bridge. Cross the bridge and turn right on Sweet Creek Road for 10.2 miles. Take a paved turnoff to the right for the Homestead Trail. To get to the Wagon Road Trailhead, drive 1.3 miles farther to a parking area on the left.
Contact: Siuslaw National Forest, Mapleton Ranger District, 4480 Highway 101, Building G, Florence, OR, 97439, 541/902-8526.

50 KENTUCKY FALLS AND NORTH FORK SMITH RIVER
4.4-17.4 mi/2.0 hr-1 day   👥2 ⚠7

west of Eugene in the Siuslaw National Forest
Map 1.4, page 36   BEST (

Eugenians certainly know about Kentucky Falls. It boasts an upper and lower fall, both dropping 100 feet, and this short trail visits both. The roads here may be twisty, and the hike may require you to climb back out of this rainforest canyon, but it's a must at any time of year. These falls are among the most famous in the entire Coast Range, and among the biggest. Because the drive to get here is so long, it's tempting to extend the hike along the North Fork Smith River, a trail that is only accessible in summer's low water.

From the trailhead, descend the Kentucky Falls Trail 0.8 mile to Upper Kentucky Falls, and continue another 1.4 miles to an observation deck overlooking Lower Kentucky Falls. From here, a newer trail follows the North Fork Smith River 6.5 miles. Head downstream two miles to a switchbacking descent, and in another 1.5 miles the trail fords the river for the first time, and in another 1.5 miles fords a second time. The trail leaves the river and ends at another trailhead after the last 1.5 miles. Note that this trail is accessible in summers only, and as of July 2008, there is an impassable slide about four miles north of the North Fork Smith Trailhead; contact the Mapleton Ranger District (541/902-8526) for up-to-date information.

User Groups: Hikers and dogs. No wheelchair facilities.

Permits: Permits are not required. Parking and access are free.

Maps: For a map of the Siuslaw National Forest, contact the Siuslaw National Forest headquarters, 4077 SW Research Way, P.O. Box 1148, Corvallis, OR, 97339, 541/750-7000. For a topographic map, ask the USGS for Baldy Mountain.

Directions: Drive west of Eugene 33 miles on OR 126 to a junction between mileposts 26 and 27. Turn south on Siuslaw River Road, following signs for "Whittaker Cr. Rec. Area" for 1.5 miles, then turn right over a bridge at another Whittaker sign. Follow this one-lane, paved road back into the hills 1.5 miles and fork left onto Dunn Ridge Road. Follow this fork 6.7 miles uphill to a junction at pavement's end and turn left on Knowles Creek Road for 2.7 miles, then right on Road 23 for 1.6 miles, then right on paved Road 919 for 2.6 miles to trailhead parking on the right. To make this hike an 8.7-mile one-way trip, shuttle a car at the North Fork Smith River Trailhead. From the junction of Forest Service Road 23 and Road 919, go 5.7 miles south on Road 23 to the trailhead.

Contact: Siuslaw National Forest, Mapleton Ranger District, 4480 Highway 101, Building G, Florence, OR, 97439, 541/902-8526.

51 HONEYMAN STATE PARK DUNES

1.6 mi/1.0 hr

south of Florence in Honeyman State Park

Map 1.4, page 36

The Oregon Dunes, the jewel of the Northwest, begin just south of historic Florence. With nearly 40 miles of rippling coastline, this is an otherworldly place of massive sand dunes, tree islands, and quiet estuaries reached only by rugged hikes over sort and shifting sand. Honeyman State Park is the second-largest overnight camp in the state, and with its two freshwater lakes, pink rhododendrons, and fall huckleberries, there is more to the park than just sand. Yet sand is why they come in droves, and an easy loop allows you to get your first glimpse of what wind and weather can do to a landscape.

From the day-use lot, a sand trail leads out along lovely Cleawox Lake. At the edge of the lake, turn left and crest a grassy dune. Looking ahead and to the left of a tree island, you'll spot the biggest of the dunes here at 250 feet. Strike out on the trail-less dunes 0.5 mile toward that big one. Spend some time up top, as the views are extensive. Head down the slope opposite the ocean and head into one of the sandy trails that emerges in a sandy bowl circled by forest. Cross the bowl and head for a gap on the ridge which leads to the campground on the "I" loop. Go left on the paved road and left again on the main campground road, 0.4 mile in all. Just past the campground fee booth, go left on a paved trail for 0.2 mile to return to the day-use area.

User Groups: Hikers, dogs, and horses. Paved areas of the park are wheelchair accessible.

Permits: Permits are not required. A $3 day-use fee is collected at the camping entrance, or you can get an annual Oregon Parks and Recreation pass for $25; contact Oregon Parks and Recreation, 800/551-6949.

Maps: For a free park brochure, call Oregon Parks and Recreation, 800/551-6949, or download a free map at www.oregonstateparks.

org. For a topographic map, ask the USGS for Florence.

Directions: Drive south of Florence three miles on U.S. 101 and turn right into the park entrance, following signs 0.3 mile to the Sand Dunes Picnic Area.

Contact: Oregon Parks and Recreation Department, 1115 Commercial Street NE, Salem, OR, 97301, 800/551-6949, www.oregonstateparks.org.

52 SILTCOOS RIVER
2.6 mi/1.0 hr   🏃1 ⛰6

in the Oregon Dunes National Recreation Area

Map 1.4, page 36   BEST (

A small estuary at the mouth of the Siltcoos River is home to nesting snowy plovers, among other water-loving birds. The Waxmyrtle Beach Trail sets out toward the coastline with views of the estuary along a meandering river where kayakers glide by quietly. Note: The Estuary Trail is closed March 15 through September 15 to protect snowy plover nesting sites.

From the Stagecoach Trailhead, start out on the Waxmyrtle Trail, which runs 0.2 mile between the river and road, then turn right on the campground road over the river. After crossing the bridge, turn right on the trail and follow the river 0.7 mile (if it's snowy plover season, you'll have to instead take a sandy, gated road to the left and follow it 0.8 mile). At a junction, continue toward the ocean 0.3 mile on the sandy old road. Turn right 0.2 mile to the river's mouth.

User Groups: Hikers, dogs on a leash, and horses. No wheelchair facilities.

Permits: Permits are not required. A federal Northwest Forest Pass is required to park here; the cost is $5 a day or $30 for an annual pass. You can buy a day pass at the visitors center, at ranger stations, or through private vendors.

Maps: For a map of the Siuslaw National Forest, contact the Siuslaw National Forest headquarters, 4077 SW Research Way, P.O.

Box 1148, Corvallis, OR, 97339, 541/750-7000. For a topographic map, ask the USGS for Tahkenitch Creek.

Directions: Drive U.S. 101 south of Florence eight miles to the Siltcoos Recreation Area turnoff at milepost 198. Turn west and drive 0.9 mile to the Stagecoach Trailhead on the left.

Contact: Siuslaw National Forest, Mapleton Ranger District, 4480 Highway 101, Building G, Florence, OR, 97439, 541/902-8526, or the Oregon Dunes National Recreation Area, 855 Highway Avenue, Reedsport, OR, 97467, 541/271-6019.

53 SILTCOOS LAKE
4.3 mi/2.0 hr   🏃1 ⛰7

in the Oregon Dunes National Recreation Area

Map 1.4, page 36

At 3,500 acres, Siltcoos Lake is the largest freshwater lake on the Oregon coast. A loop trail visits two isolated campsites on the lake's shore facing forested Booth Island.

From the highway, hike inland and downhill on the Siltcoos Lake Trail 0.8 mile to a junction. Go right 0.7 mile to another junction, then right for 0.2 mile to South Camp on the lake. Head back up this spur trail to the junction, then go right 0.5 mile to access North Camp, which has more spots to pitch a tent. In the jumble of trails, continue on the main one to complete the loop and return 1.1 miles back to the first junction, then right the remaining 0.8 mile to the highway.

User Groups: Hikers, dogs, horses, and mountain bikes. No wheelchair facilities.

Permits: Permits are not required. A federal Northwest Forest Pass is required to park here; the cost is $5 a day or $30 for an annual pass. You can buy a day pass at the visitors center, at ranger stations, or through private vendors.

Maps: For a map of the Siuslaw National Forest, contact the Siuslaw National Forest headquarters, 4077 SW Research Way, P.O. Box 1148, Corvallis, OR, 97339,

541/750-7000. For a topographic map, ask the USGS for Florence.

Directions: Drive U.S. 101 south of Florence eight miles and park on the east side of 101 opposite the Siltcoos Recreation Area turnoff at milepost 198.

Contact: Siuslaw National Forest, Mapleton Ranger District, 4480 Highway 101, Building G, Florence, OR, 97439, 541/902-8526, or the Oregon Dunes National Recreation Area, 855 Highway Avenue, Reedsport, OR, 97467, 541/271-6019.

54 CARTER LAKE DUNES
2.7 mi/1.5 hr　　　　　　🏃2 ⛰7

in the Oregon Dunes National Recreation Area

Map 1.4, page 36

Two lakes, Carter and Taylor, sit atop a forested ridge overlooking the Oregon Dunes. In some spots, the ocean is far away and a slogging walk just to reach the shore. From here, it's pretty easy, actually, and you can walk along beautiful Taylor Lake on your way to the big dunes. You'll have to follow blue-striped posts out over the dunes, over the deflation plain with its shore pine and Scotch broom forest and down to the beach. Just keep an eye on that trail once you reach the beach, so as not to wander off and lose it. Also keep in mind that sand-hiking can be tiring and slow-going.

The first 0.4 mile passes Taylor Lake to two view decks and a bench before dropping 0.5 mile to the dunes to join with the Carter Lake Trail. From here, follow posts 0.5 mile to the ocean. For a loop possibility, you could well follow the Carter Lake Trail back to the road, then head 0.4 mile left along the road to the Taylor Dunes Trailhead.

User Groups: Hikers, dogs, and horses. The first 0.5 mile is wheelchair accessible.

Permits: Permits are not required. A federal Northwest Forest Pass is required to park here; the cost is $5 a day or $30 for an annual pass. You can buy a day pass at the visitors center, at ranger stations, or through private vendors.

Maps: For a map of the Siuslaw National Forest, contact the Siuslaw National Forest headquarters, 4077 SW Research Way, P.O. Box 1148, Corvallis, OR, 97339, 541/750-7000. For a topographic map, ask the USGS for Tahkenitch Creek.

Directions: Drive U.S. 101 south of Florence nine miles, or north of Reedsport 12 miles, and turn west into the Carter Lake Campground entrance. The Taylor Dunes Trailhead is on the left just after the entrance.

Contact: Siuslaw National Forest, Mapleton Ranger District, 4480 Highway 101, Building G, Florence, OR, 97439, 541/902-8526, or the Oregon Dunes National Recreation Area, 855 Highway Avenue, Reedsport, OR, 97467, 541/271-6019.

55 OREGON DUNES OVERLOOK
2.2 mi/1.0 hr　　　　　　🏃1 ⛰7

in the Oregon Dunes National Recreation Area

Map 1.4, page 36

What a great view these overlooks afford: a vast sea of sand, massive tree islands swelling between the dunes, and beyond a shore pine forest, the rolling tides. Want a closer look? Then hike right past those decks and down to the sand, where blue-striped posts lead hikers to a long beach with opportunities to explore the wild-flowered deflation plain, where deer wander and the hummocks of sand cradle deep valleys where kids can play and dogs can run. This is one of the easier, meaning shorter, paths through the dunes to the shoreline.

The main trail begins as a paved path that drops 0.3 mile to the sand, though another trail begins just past the observation decks, briefly passing through the scrubby trees and out onto the peak of a dune. Once you get down to the flatter ground, the posts lead 0.8 mile to the shore.

User Groups: Hikers, dogs, and horses, No mountain bikes allowed. Viewing decks are wheelchair accessible.

Permits: Permits are not required. A federal Northwest Forest Pass is required to park here; the cost is $5 a day or $30 for an annual pass. You can buy a day pass at the visitors center, at ranger stations, or through private vendors.

Maps: For a map of the Siuslaw National Forest, contact the Siuslaw National Forest headquarters, 4077 SW Research Way, P.O. Box 1148, Corvallis, OR, 97339, 541/750-7000. For a topographic map, ask the USGS for Tahkenitch Creek.

Directions: The Oregon Dunes Overlook entrance is on the west side of U.S. 101, 10 miles south of Florence or 11 miles north of Reedsport.

Contact: Siuslaw National Forest, Mapleton Ranger District, 4480 Highway 101, Building G, Florence, OR, 97439, 541/902-8526, or the Oregon Dunes National Recreation Area, 855 Highway Avenue, Reedsport, OR, 97467, 541/271-6019.

Tahkenitch Creek

56 TAHKENITCH CREEK
4.2 mi/2.0 hr

in the Oregon Dunes National Recreation Area

Map 1.4, page 36

The Oregon Dunes are more than just sand, as the Tahkenitch Creek Trail amply demonstrates. This lazy creek, forested with Douglas fir and flowering rhododendrons, drifts toward the sea, meeting the tides at a lonely and largely unvisited estuary frequented by brown pelicans frequent and nesting snowy plovers. Thorny gorse, a particularly nasty invasive bush, grows here as well. Be mindful that winter often brings flooding in certain areas, making some of the loops impossible.

The first 0.3 mile of the Tahkenitch Creek Trail is in a coastal forest, crossing the creek on a long footbridge with views of the creek along the way. At a junction, a short loop is possible by heading to the right, hugging the creek a short distance until the next junction, where a left turn brings you to another left turn: a 1.6-mile loop in all. But continuing on along the creek to another junction, as well as a view of the estuary, taking the same two left turns, then keeping right at the next two junctions represents another loop, 2.6 miles in all. The longest loop follows the creek out a full mile past this first junction, eventually passing a few marshy lakes to a four-way junction with the Tahkenitch Dunes Trail; going hard left here to return to the Tahkenitch Creek Trail and keeping to the right at each consecutive junction makes a 4.2-mile loop. If you feel like you've got a bit more oomph, you could head right on the Tahkenitch Dunes Trail from this last junction an extra 0.3 mile, then take a right for another 0.3 mile to reach the beach; remember, though, that this much sand makes for a tiring hike, so save your energy.

User Groups: Hikers, dogs, and horses. No mountain bikes allowed. No wheelchair facilities.

Permits: Permits are not required. A federal Northwest Forest Pass is required to park here;

the cost is $5 a day or $30 for an annual pass. You can buy a day pass at the visitors center, at ranger stations, or through private vendors.

Maps: For a map of the Siuslaw National Forest, contact the Siuslaw National Forest headquarters, 4077 SW Research Way, P.O. Box 1148, Corvallis, OR, 97339, 541/750-7000. For a topographic map, ask the USGS for Tahkenitch Creek.

Directions: The Tahkenitch Creek Trailhead is located on the west side of U.S. 101 between mileposts 202 and 203, about 12 miles south of Florence or nine miles north of Reedsport.

Contact: Siuslaw National Forest, Mapleton Ranger District, 4480 Highway 101, Building G, Florence, OR, 97439, 541/902-8526, or the Oregon Dunes National Recreation Area, 855 Highway Avenue, Reedsport, OR, 97467, 541/271-6019.

57 TAHKENITCH DUNES
6.5 mi/3.0 hr

in the Oregon Dunes National Recreation Area
Map 1.4, page 36

For those who want to explore the Oregon Dunes on a far more rugged expedition, the Tahkenitch Dunes offer this kind of epic journey in excess. Along the way, you can view the Tahkenitch Creek estuary and a beach along Threemile Lake, and cross over a forested summit above the sand. Be aware that long hikes through sand can be tiring and slow-going, so plan on plenty of time and pack plenty of water.

The first 0.2 mile of the Tahkenitch Dunes Trail climbs into the forest to a junction. Go right for 1.1 miles across the open dunes, eventually entering a brushy forest of shore pine— also known as lodgepole pine. At a junction, go left for 0.3 mile along a marsh, then right for 0.3 mile to the beach. Note that ORV vehicles are allowed on this beach, so don't be surprised by the dune buggies. Heading to the right 0.9 mile will take you to the estuary,

but for a longer hike head to the left instead, going north 1.3 miles along the beach. Watch for a trail sign on the foredune, then head inland 0.4 mile to a viewpoint over a beach on Threemile Lake. Follow the Threemile Lake Trail 2.7 miles up and over a 400-foot summit of second-growth woods back to the first junction, and head right the remaining 0.2 mile back to the campground.

User Groups: Hikers, dogs, and horses, No mountain bikes allowed. No wheelchair facilities.

Permits: Permits are not required. A federal Northwest Forest Pass is required to park here; the cost is $5 a day or $30 for an annual pass. You can buy a day pass at the visitors center, at ranger stations, or through private vendors.

Maps: For a map of the Siuslaw National Forest, contact the Siuslaw National Forest headquarters, 4077 SW Research Way, P.O. Box 1148, Corvallis, OR, 97339, 541/750-7000. For a topographic map, ask the USGS for Tahkenitch Creek.

Directions: The Tahkenitch Dunes Trailhead is located in the Tahkenitch Campground on the west side of U.S. 101 about 13 miles south of Florence or eight miles north of Reedsport. Keep left at the loop and park at a small picnic area.

Contact: Siuslaw National Forest, Mapleton Ranger District, 4480 Highway 101, Building G, Florence, OR, 97439, 541/902-8526, or the Oregon Dunes National Recreation Area, 855 Highway Avenue, Reedsport, OR, 97467, 541/271-6019.

58 LAKE MARIE
1.4 mi/1.0 hr

south of Reedsport in Umpqua Lighthouse State Park
Map 1.4, page 36

High atop a bluff over Winchester Bay and the mouth of the Umpqua River stands the 65-foot lighthouse blinking its read and white warning to boats. Also beneath the fog-piercing light lie the beginning of the seven-mile stretch of the Umpqua Dunes and little Lake Marie. An easy hike around this forested lake begins at a picturesque picnic area, and proceeds to a viewpoint of the dunes themselves, a worthy goal for exploration.

From the shoreline, head on the right-hand trail following the lakeside 0.2 mile. At a junction, follow the right trail 0.2 mile to a view of the Umpqua Dunes. Head back and continue an easy 0.8 mile back to the picnic area.

User Groups: Hikers, dogs, and horses. No wheelchair facilities.

Permits: Permits are not required. Parking and access are free.

Maps: For a free park brochure, call Oregon Parks and Recreation, 800/551-6949, or download a free map at www.oregonstateparks.org. For a topographic map, ask the USGS for Winchester Bay.

Directions: Drive U.S 101 south of Reedsport five miles to milepost 217 and follow signs for Umpqua Lighthouse State Park. Travel one mile west, passing the campground entrance, and park at a picnic area on the left on the shore of Lake Marie.

Contact: Oregon Parks and Recreation Department, 1115 Commercial Street NE, Salem, OR, 97301, 800/551-6949, www.oregonstateparks.org.

59 UMPQUA DUNES
5.0 mi/2.5 hr 🥾3 ⛰9

in the Oregon Dunes National Recreation Area

Map 1.4, page 36 **BEST (**

The sheer enormity of the Umpqua Dunes is staggering. This stretch of sand, nearly unreal in its proportions, makes this one of Oregon's most outstanding and beautiful areas. If you're going to pick any area of the Dunes to hike, make it this one. That being said, reaching the ocean on the John Dellenback Dunes Trail, named for the U.S. congressman who helped establish this recreation area, is one of the most difficult hikes on the coast. These towering

Umpqua Dunes in the Oregon Dunes National Recreation Area

© SEAN PATRICK HILL

dunes south of the Umpqua River are the largest and the broadest, stretching over two miles to the distant ocean. Blue-striped trail posts seem lonely in the vast waves of sand, following a valley between massive oblique dunes, sloping on one side and sharply carved by wind on the other. The otherworldly beauty is so tremendous that it's worth a day's journey just to get here, let alone hike this area.

From Eel Creek Campground, follow the 0.2-mile trail through twisting red-barked madrones to an impressive overlook, the sea a far-off rumble. Head for the long, high dune for a sweeping view to a massive tree island and mile after mile of cascading sand. Look toward the ocean to spot the tiny trail markers marching off into the sand. Follow these posts a total of 2.2-miles to reach the ocean.

User Groups: Hikers, dogs, and horses. No wheelchair facilities.

Permits: Permits are not required. A federal Northwest Forest Pass is required to park here; the cost is $5 a day or $30 for an annual pass.

You can buy a day pass at the visitors center, at ranger stations, or through private vendors.

Maps: For a map of the Siuslaw National Forest, contact the Siuslaw National Forest headquarters, 4077 SW Research Way, P.O. Box 1148, Corvallis, OR, 97339, 541/750-7000. For a topographic map, ask the USGS for Lakeside.

Directions: Drive 11 miles south of Reedsport on U.S. 101. Near milepost 222, turn west into Eel Creek Campground and keep left for 0.3 mile to a parking lot. The trailhead begins at a large signpost.

Contact: Siuslaw National Forest, Mapleton Ranger District, 4480 Highway 101, Building G, Florence, OR, 97439, 541/902-8526, or the Oregon Dunes National Recreation Area, 855 Highway Avenue, Reedsport, OR, 97467, 541/271-6019.

60 GOLDEN AND SILVER FALLS

3.0 mi/1.5 hr   🥾1 ⛰8

east of Coos Bay in Golden and Silver Falls State Park

Map 1.4, page 36

Not to be confused with Silver Falls State Park just outside of the Willamette Valley, this state park has two falls that topple hundreds of feet into two canyons, the creeks joining a short distance below. Three different trails fan out here, following Glenn and Silver Creeks, and it's worth it to take them all, as they afford multiple views of both plunging falls. Along the way you'll see myrtlewood trees, common to this part of the state.

To start, go to the trailhead and take the farthest left-hand trail up 0.3 mile to a view of 160-foot Silver Falls, a good warm-up. Return to the lot and take the right-hand trail, which crosses Silver Creek. Here the trail splits. The left trail goes 0.4 mile up Silver Creek to another breathtaking view of Silver Falls, and continues up the canyon walls on a dizzying climb up 0.5 mile to a couple overlooks

over 200-foot Golden Falls. Return the way you came, and take the last of the trails, the right-hand junction after the footbridge, which heads through groves of myrtlewood along Glenn Creek to a lower view of Golden Falls.

User Groups: Hikers and dogs. No wheelchair facilities.

Permits: Permits are not required. Parking and access are free.

Maps: For a topographic map, ask the USGS for Golden Falls.

Directions: Follow U.S. 101 to the south end of Coos Bay and follow signs for Alleghany, eventually turning east on Coos River Highway. In 13.5 miles, arrive at Alleghany, then follow state park signs 9.4 miles on East Millicoma Road and Glen Creek Road to the end of the road at a picnic area.

Contact: Oregon Parks and Recreation Department, 1115 Commercial Street NE, Salem, OR, 97301, 800/551-6949, www.oregonstateparks.org.

61 SUNSET BAY TO CAPE ARAGO

9.4 mi/4.5 hr   🥾3 ⛰9

west of Coos Bay in Sunset Bay/Shore Acres State Parks

Map 1.4, page 36   **BEST (**

Leave it to the Oregon State Parks to hold onto history. Cape Arago, hovering above a series of reefs, islands, and barking sea lions, was first spotted by Sir Francis Drake in the 1500s. Later, the land in what is now Shore Acres State Park was the estate for lumber baron Louis Simpson, including an unforgettable garden that is still blooming to this day. Today you can see all of this history and migrating whales, too, thanks to a stretch of the Oregon Coast Trail that passes along this rugged and wild coastline. You can pay a fee to enter the main part of the park, or you can hike your way in on a stunning trip along one of Oregon's best seaside trails.

For the full day's walk, start at Sunset Bay State Park parking area and follow an 0.8-mile stretch of the Oregon Coast Trail overlooking Sunset Bay and the Norton Gulch. The path briefly heads to the right along the road, then parallels the road before heading back into the woods for 1.3 miles before arriving in the core of Shore Acres State Park, site of the Botanical Gardens and the 1906 Simpson mansion, with an observation building suitable for whale-watching. Stay right at a sign for Simpson Beach. The next 0.3 mile leads to this beach in Simpson's Cove. In 0.2 mile, continue right on the Oregon Coast Trail one mile, crossing a creek and heads up a gully to an intersection. Go right on the OCT toward the stunning cliff viewpoints. The trail meets the road, follows it for a brief stretch before passing through a coastal forest and rejoining the road at the Sea Lion Viewpoint, where you can look out a quarter-mile to Shell Island where masses of the sea lions congregate. From here, you'll need to follow the paved road 0.7 mile to Cape Arago, where a short 0.3 mile trail leads out to views over North Cove, the Simpson Reef, and Shell Island. It is possible to arrange a shuttle from this point.

User Groups: Hikers only. Dogs are not allowed in Shore Acres State Park. No horses or mountain bikes allowed. Paved paths in Shore Acres State Park are wheelchair accessible.

Permits: Permits are not required. Parking and access are free.

Maps: For a free park brochure, call Oregon Parks and Recreation, 800/551-6949, or download a free map at www.oregonstateparks.org. For a topographic map, ask the USGS for Charleston and Cape Arago.

Directions: From Coos Bay, drive 12 miles south on Cape Arago Highway, following signs to Sunset Bay State Park. Park in the day-use area on the right. The trailhead is marked as the Oregon Coast Trail.

Contact: Oregon Parks and Recreation Department, 1115 Commercial Street NE, Salem, OR, 97301, 800/551-6949, www.oregonstateparks.org.

62 SOUTH SLOUGH ESTUARY
5.0 mi/2.0 hr   🏃1 ⛰7

south of Coos Bay in South Slough Reserve

Map 1.4, page 36   **BEST (**

The South Slough National Estuarine Research Reserve is a 4,800-acre mix of freshwater and tidal wetlands, open-water channels, riparian areas, and coastal forest. Egrets perch in the trees, mudflats are exposed at low tide, and Pacific wax myrtle and Port Orford cedar populate the uplands. Salt marshes, sand flats, the list goes on. So why not visit?

There are a number of trails throughout the park, eight miles altogether. To try a loop trail, begin at the Interpretive Center and follow the 0.5-mile Middle Creek Trail. Cross a road and follow the 1.2-mile Hidden Creek Trail to a boardwalk over a skunk cabbage grove and a tide flats observation deck. From here, the 0.4-mile Tunnel Trail heads out a peninsula between the South Slough and Rhodes Marsh right out to the tip, near some old pilings. Head back from the point to a right-hand junction over the Rhodes Dike to the Bog Loop, continuing straight on the 2.5-mile North Creek Trail (where dogs are not permitted). This trail completes the loop, connecting with the 0.2-mile Ten-Minute Trail loop.

User Groups: Hikers. Leashed dogs are admitted on some trails. Some trails are wheelchair accessible.

Permits: Permits are not required. Parking and access are free.

Maps: A downloadable brochure and map is available at www.oregon.gov/DSL/SSNERR/maps.shtml. For a topographic map, ask the USGS for Charleston.

Directions: From U.S. 101 in Coos Bay, take the Cape Arago Highway nine miles west to Charleston. Turn left on Seven Devils Road and go 4.3 miles, turning left into the South Slough Reserve entrance road. In 0.2 mile, park on the left by the interpretive center.

Contact: South Slough Reserve, P.O. Box 5417, Charleston, OR, 97420, 541/888-5558.

63 SEVEN DEVILS WAYSIDE
3.0 mi/1.5 hr

north of Bandon on the Pacific Ocean

Map 1.4, page 36

Some towns have all the luck—and some don't. One of the ones that didn't was Randolph, a gold-rush town that once sat on Whiskey Run Beach and was all but gone in two years. The nearby town of Bandon was burned twice by fires feeding on spiny gorse, a nasty, thorny shrub that blankets areas of the Oregon coast, including the ravines above Whiskey Run Beach and the Seven Devils Wayside. The beaches, though, are thankfully free of it, and this excursion escapes the bristling bush in favor of a hike beneath sandstone cliffs around Fivemile Point. From the Seven Devils Wayside, strike out south along the ocean for 1.4 miles along Merchants Beach to the headland of Fivemile Point, easily passable if the tide is low. Another 0.8 mile beyond this leads along Whiskey Run Beach to another ravine with a beach access road.

User Groups: Hikers, dogs, and horses. No wheelchair facilities.

Permits: Permits are not required. Parking and access are free.

Maps: For a topographic map, ask the USGS for Bullards.

Directions: From Bandon, go north on U.S. 101 for five miles and turn left on Randolph Road, which becomes Seven Devils Road. Follow signs 4.2 miles to Seven Devils State Park.

Contact: Oregon Parks and Recreation Department, 1115 Commercial Street NE, Salem, OR, 97301, 800/551-6949, www.oregonstateparks.org.

64 THE DOERNER FIR
1.0 mi/0.5 hr

east of Coos Bay in the Coast Range

Map 1.4, page 36

Sometimes when you're passing through an area, or taking a nearby hike, it's worth it to get in a little side trip to see something special. The Doerner Fir is one such spectacle, and at 329 feet tall and 11 feet in diameter, maybe this side trip isn't so "small." It is, in fact, the world's largest Douglas fir—and it's somewhere between 500 and 700 years old. This is an opportunity to see how trees grow; you'll notice that on a true old-growth fir, the limbs don't even begin until hundreds of feet up, having been lost over the course of time as they grew in the darkness of other big trees' crowns. Now its own crown is about 10 stories up in the atmosphere. This easy half-mile hike is also a good tour of a coastal rainforest considered to be pristine, with abundant undergrowth of ferns, salmonberry, and vine maple. The trail begins across the road from the parking area, descending into a drainage only 200 feet to visit the massive fir.

User Groups: Hikers and dogs. No wheelchair facilities.

Permits: Permits are not required. Parking and access are free.

Maps: For a topographic map, ask the USGS for Sitkum.

Directions: From Coos Bay, take U.S. 101 south five miles then go left on OR 42 toward Roseburg 11 miles. Just before Coquille, turn left on West Central Boulevard for one mile and go left toward Fairview for 8.1 miles. At a junction, go right onto the Coos Bay Wagon Road for 3.7 miles and turn left on Middle Creek Road for 6.3 miles. At a fork go left toward the Park Creek Recreation Site for 6.6 miles, then turn to the right heading uphill on Burnt Mountain-Middle Creek Tie Road for 4.4 miles to a junction. Turn left, following a "Burnt Ridge Road" sign for 4.6 miles, then go right on gravel Road 27-9-21.0 for 4.3 miles to the trailhead.

Contact: Bureau of Land Management, Coos Bay District, 1300 Airport Lane, North Bend, OR, 97459, 541/756-0100.

65 BULLARDS BEACH STATE PARK
5.0 mi/2.0 hr   🏃1 ⛰7

north of Bandon on the Pacific Ocean

Map 1.4, page 36   **BEST (**

The scenic tip of the Bullards Beach peninsula passes an 1896 lighthouse, a view of Bandon (the "Storm Watching Capitol of the World"), and the estuary of the Coquille River, with views to the Bandon Marsh Wildlife Refuge. This state park even has a horse camp, so be prepared to see equestrians passing over the sand at sunset. Anglers and crabbers find this to be one of the best places to ply their trade. You'll get plenty of beach exploration here, both along the ocean and the bay.

From the beach parking area, head to the beach and go left 1.7 miles toward the north jetty and the 47-foot lighthouse. An easy 0.6-mile round-trip walk extends to the tip of the jetty. Then head east from the lighthouse along the river 0.4 mile on an old road and follow the beach 1.9 mile farther along the river to the road. Turn left along the road for 0.4 mile to return to the parking area.

User Groups: Hikers, dogs, and horses. The 1.3-mile bike trail is wheelchair accessible.

Permits: Permits are not required. Parking and access are free.

Maps: For a free park brochure, call Oregon Parks and Recreation, 800/551-6949, or download a free map at www.oregonstateparks.org. For a topographic map, ask the USGS for Bullards.

Directions: Drive U.S. 101 north of Bandon three miles and turn west at a Bullards Beach State Park sign. Drive past the campground entrance and picnic areas 1.4 miles to a junction. Turn right into the beach parking area.

Contact: Oregon Parks and Recreation Department, 1115 Commercial Street NE, Salem, OR, 97301, 800/551-6949, www.oregonstateparks.org.

66 FACE ROCK
3.8 mi/2.0 hr   🏃1 ⛰8

in Bandon at Face Rock Wayside

Map 1.4, page 36

A Coquille tribal legend says that a maiden named Ewauna, daughter of Chief Siskiyou, decided to sneak off for a late-night swim. Unfortunately, an evil spirit named Seatka who lived in the ocean grabbed her. But she was bright enough to know that to look into his eyes was to be caught forever; to this day, she looks instead to the sky. Looking at Face Rock, the resemblance is, to say the least, uncanny. This maiden is only one of many sea stacks and rocks jutting from the ocean offshore of Bandon-by-the-Sea, and some easy hiking brings one close to this jumble of tide-worn stone.

A staircase descends down Grave Point from the Face Rock Wayside. Turn right at the beach to view Cat and Kittens Rocks, Face Rock, and Elephant Rock. Continue to jutting Coquille Point; by now you've gone 0.9 mile. The next mile continues to the south jetty, with views to the Coquille River Lighthouse and Table Rock.

User Groups: Hikers and dogs. Overlook is wheelchair accessible.

Permits: Permits are not required. Parking and access are free.

Maps: For a topographic map, ask the USGS for Bandon.

Directions: From U.S. 101 in Bandon, head west on 11th Avenue for 0.9 mile, then go left on Beach Loop Road 0.6 mile to the Face Rock Wayside on the right.

Contact: Oregon Parks and Recreation Department, 1115 Commercial Street NE, Salem, OR, 97301, 800/551-6949, www.oregonstateparks.org.

67 BLACKLOCK POINT

3.8 mi/1.5 hr ☖1 ⛰7

north of Port Orford in Floras Lake State
Natural Area

Map 1.5, page 37

On the way to Blacklock Point, you'll pass through a whole litany of shore shrubbery and coastal trees, including Sitka spruce and Sitka alder, pygmy shore pine, evergreen huckleberry, wax myrtle and juniper, black twinberry, salal, and wild azalea, rhododendron and black crowberry. All this leads to some serious cliffs atop Blacklock Point. In this largely undeveloped natural area, you may find some solitude; being off the beaten path, not many people even know about it. On the grassy headland, you can spot the Cape Blanco Lighthouse, a waterfall, and a number of islands.

The trail begins to the left of the gate on a dirt road that becomes a trail. Follow this 0.8 mile to a creek and trail junction, going left for 0.6 mile. Then fork left again, then right for 0.5 mile to the sheer headland of Blacklock Point. From here, trails fan out into Floras Lake State Natural Area—following the trail north along the coast leads to Floras Lake, and two side trails to the left lead back to the runway. Taking the first left after a waterfall makes for a 4.4-mile loop, and taking the next left at Floras Lake makes a 7.6-mile loop.

User Groups: Hikers, dogs on leash, horses, and mountain bikes. No wheelchair facilities.

Permits: Permits are not required. Parking and access are free.

Maps: For a topographic map, ask the USGS for Floras Lake.

Directions: Go seven miles north of Port Orford on U.S. 101 and between mileposts 293 and 294, turn west at an "Airport" sign. Follow County Road 160 for 2.8 miles to a parking area on the right at the gated entrance to the airport.

Contact: Oregon Parks and Recreation Department, 1115 Commercial Street NE, Salem, OR, 97301, 800/551-6949, www.oregonstateparks.org.

68 CAPE BLANCO

4.0 mi/2.0 mi ☖1 ⛰8

north of Port Orford in Cape Blanco State Park

Map 1.5, page 37

Standing at the tip of Cape Blanco, you are at the westernmost point in the state of Oregon. An 1870 lighthouse still functions here, throwing its light from a cape named on a 1602 Spanish exploration (in which the majority of the ship's crew died of scurvy). There are many trails here to explore, as well as a historic 1898 Victorian house-turned-museum. For a good opening exploratory route, a looping tour of the headland and the North Beach passes within view of islands, the Sixes River, and over the headland.

From the boat ramp, and beyond a gate, take the left-hand path 0.3 mile across a pasture, then fork to the right for 0.4 mile to the beach. Head left 1.2 miles along North Beach toward the lighthouse. Just before the end of the beach, take a trail up a slope 0.3 mile to the parking area for the lighthouse. Head left down the road 0.2 mile, then cut to the left at a trailpost, crossing a meadow 1.3 miles along the cliff's edges to return to the boat ramp.

User Groups: Hikers, dogs, horses, mountain bikes. Paved portions of the park are wheelchair accessible.

Permits: Permits are not required. Parking and access are free.

Maps: For a free park brochure, call Oregon Parks and Recreation, 800/551-6949, or download a free map at www.oregonstateparks.org. For a topographic map, ask the USGS for Bullards.

Directions: Drive U.S 101 north of Port Orford four miles and turn west at a Cape Blanco State Park sign for four miles to a fork. Go right, passing the Hughes House Museum, and park at the Sixes River Boat Ramp.

Contact: Oregon Parks and Recreation Department, 1115 Commercial Street NE, Salem, OR, 97301, 800/551-6949, www.oregonstateparks.org.

69 GRASSY KNOB

2.4 mi/1.0 hr

east of Port Orford in Grassy Knob Wilderness

Map 1.5, page 37

From an old fire watchtower that once stood atop Grassy Knob during World War II, lookouts spotted a Japanese airplane that dropped an incendiary bomb into the forest, hoping to start a fire. The bomb never went off and was never found. The watchtower is now gone, and what remains in this corner of the Siskiyou Mountains is a 17,200-acre Wilderness Area designated by Congress in 1984. The area remains short on trails, but this one trail, actually an old road, leads to a peak overlooking the mountains and the ocean.

From the end of Grassy Knob Road, follow the road behind the gate up 0.4 mile to a side trail on the right leading 0.1 mile up to Grassy Knob's summit. Then continue up the road another 0.7 mile to a gravel turnaround, with views along the way.

User Groups: Hikers and dogs. No wheelchair facilities.

Permits: Permits are not required. Parking and access are free.

Maps: For a map of the Siskiyou National Forest, contact the Rogue River–Siskiyou National Forest headquarters, 3040 Biddle Road, Medford, OR, 97504, 541/618-2200. For a topographic map, ask the USGS for Father Mountain.

Directions: From Port Orford, drive U.S. 101 north four miles and turn east on Grassy Knob Road for 3.9 paved miles and 3.8 more gravel miles to a gate and parking area. The trail begins on the road beyond the gate.

Contact: Siskiyou National Forest, Powers Ranger District, 42861 Highway 242, Powers, OR, 97466, 541/439-6200.

70 BARKLOW MOUNTAIN

2.0 mi/1.0 hr

northeast of Gold Beach in Siskiyou National Forest

Map 1.5, page 37

Due to budget cuts, many of the classic fire watchtowers have been abandoned and unmanned for a long time. Many of the relics of that age remain, including a shelter here atop Barklow Mountain. Of course, many of these sites have "remote" as their middle name. Still, if it's solitude you're looking for, you'll find it here.

The short 0.6-mile Barklow Mountain Trail climbs only 500 feet through a forest to the former lookout site here atop the 3,579-foot peak, with views over the Siskiyou Range; a 0.4-mile spur trail leads to the long-collapsed shelter at Barklow Camp. The Barklow Mountain Trail, in all, is six miles and wanders along the north ridge of the mountain, though this stretch is unmaintained, thus making for more opportunity to explore.

User Groups: Hikers and dogs. No horses or mountain bikes allowed. No wheelchair facilities.

Permits: Permits are not required. Parking and access are free.

Maps: For a map of the Siskiyou National Forest, contact the Rogue River–Siskiyou National Forest headquarters, 3040 Biddle Road, Medford, OR, 97504, 541/618-2200. For a topographic map, ask the USGS for Barklow Mountain.

Directions: From Gold Beach, drive Jerrys Flat Road 32 miles along the Rogue River to a bridge near Agness, and continue on Road 33 to Powers for 15.6 miles. From Powers, drive 11.5 miles south on Road 33 and turn right on Road 3353 for 11 miles to the trailhead just past milepost 11.

Contact: Siskiyou National Forest, Powers Ranger District, 42861 Highway 242, Powers, OR, 97466, 541/439-6200.

71 COQUILLE RIVER FALLS
1.0 mi/0.5 hr 　　　　🏃₁ ⛰₇

northeast of Gold Beach in Siskiyou National
Forest

Map 1.5, page 37

The Coquille River Falls Natural Area was
established in 1945 to provide examples of
the Port Orford cedar, and this rugged mountain canyon also plays host to the Douglas
fir, myrtle, Pacific yew, grand fir, and sugar
pine. Salamanders, voles, and secretive mammals like the bobcat, martin, and ermine all
thrive here. The destination is the double
falls on the Coquille River pouring over a
bedrock edge into a stony bowl scoured into
pockmarked mortars.

From the parking area, the trail abruptly
switchbacks down 0.5 mile to a viewpoint of
the Coquille River Falls and a series of cascades on Drowned Out Creek. It is possible
to scramble around to a higher viewpoint and
around the falls themselves, but it should only
be attempted in the dry season. Mossy stones
and wet leaves on the rocks around the base
of the falls beg disaster—care should be taken
on the slick rock.

User Groups: Hikers and dogs. No wheelchair
facilities.

Permits: Permits are not required. Parking
and access are free.

Maps: For a map of the Siskiyou National Forest, contact the Rogue River–Siskiyou National Forest headquarters, 3040 Biddle Road,
Medford, OR, 97504, 541/618-2200. For a
topographic map, ask the USGS for Illahe.

Directions: From Gold Beach, drive Jerrys
Flat Road 32 miles along the Rogue River to
a bridge near Agness, and continue on Road
33 to Powers for 15.6 miles. From Powers,
travel south on FS 33 for 17 miles to paved FS
3348, turning left. Go 1.5 miles to a pullout
on the left.

Contact: Siskiyou National Forest, Powers
Ranger District, 42861 Highway 242, Powers,
OR, 97466, 541/439-6200.

72 ELK CREEK FALLS
2.4 mi/1.0 hr 　　　　🏃₁ ⛰₇

northeast of Gold Beach in Siskiyou National
Forest

Map 1.5, page 37

By the time you've come this far south into
Oregon, the landscape begins to change
along with the trees. Here, the Port Orford
cedar is impressive, and the trail past 60-
foot Elk Creek Falls goes on to arrive at
the world's largest Port Orford, as well as
other big tree varieties. But you'll realize
you're lucky to see such trees, as logging
and a kind of root fungus have seriously
jeopardized the survival of the handsome
Port Orford.

The trail forks at the trailhead, with the
left-hand fork heading a scant 0.1 mile to Elk
Creek Falls, a lovely cascade in a fern-lined
grotto. Then head up the right-hand fork for
1.2 miles, switchbacking up a steep ridge
through flowering rhododendrons. When
the trail hits an old dirt road at the one-mile
mark, head to the right and watch for the
continuation of the path on the left. Here
you'll see big Douglas firs and bigleaf maples,
and when you turn left at the next junction,
you'll easily spot Big Tree, the 239-foot-tall,
12-foot-thick cedar.

User Groups: Hikers and dogs. No wheelchair
facilities.

Permits: Permits are not required. Parking
and access are free.

Maps: For a map of the Siskiyou National
Forest, contact the Rogue River–Siskiyou
National Forest headquarters, 3040 Biddle
Road, Medford, OR, 97504, 541/618-2200.
For a topographic map, ask the USGS for
China Flat.

Directions: From Gold Beach and U.S. 101,
take Jerrys Flat Road for 32 miles to the bridge
over the Rogue River, then continue on Road
33, which eventually turns to gravel, toward
Powers another 25.6 miles. The trailhead is
between mileposts 57 and 58.

Contact: Siskiyou National Forest, Powers

Ranger District, 42861 Highway 242, Powers, OR, 97466, 541/439-6200.

73 PANTHER RIDGE
4.0 mi–11.2 mi one-way/2.0 hr–1 day
🏃3 ⛰8

northeast of Gold Beach in Wild Rogue Wilderness

Map 1.5, page 37

Here is your introduction to the Siskiyou Mountains: the classic Oregon trees like cedar and Douglas fir augmented by knobcone pine and tanoak, manzanita and chinquapin, and an amazing display of springtime rhododendrons. A wilderness ridge offers unparalleled views over the Rogue River Valley and its associated drainages. Most of this trail traverses the Wild Rogue Wilderness, which cradles the roaring river below. Here is a great opportunity for backpacking, but be sure to bring plenty of water. There's even a rentable lookout at Bald Knob where you may spot early morning elk and black bear. An easy way to start is to visit Hanging Rock, a dizzying edge above the canyon of the Wild Rogue, where the Devil's Backbone descends to Paradise Bar on the Rogue River.

From the Buck Point Trailhead, the Panther Ridge Trail climbs a mile-long ridge to Buck Point, and just around that point is a camping spot around the cedar-shaded spring of Buck Creek. The trail switchbacks up 0.6 mile to a junction. To the left, and 0.4 mile away, is the Hanging Rock. Returning to the trail, you could call it a day or continue on 2.3 miles through what becomes a maze of faint paths—stick to the lowest path to stay on the Panther Ridge Trail. A junction on the right leads 0.3 mile to Panther Camp, another backpacking site. From this junction, the trail continues 1.3 miles to a gravelly spot, where

you'll want to be careful to watch for the right trail. After this, the trail follows an old and overgrown road for 0.2 mile before meeting another road; follow this road to the left 0.2 mile to return to the forest path. In another 0.3 mile pass a spur trail, and enter a denser understory of rhododendron and wildflowers. The next 1.5 miles are a rough descent, then skirts clear-cuts for 1.3 miles. The trail then turns right along an abandoned road for 0.2 mile, then cuts left into the dense forest again. The Panther Ridge Trail ends at Forest Service Road 5520.020 near a gate. Go left on this road for 0.3 mile to arrive at the Bald Knob Lookout, with its expansive views.

User Groups: Hikers, dogs, and horses. No mountain bikes allowed in the wilderness area. No wheelchair facilities.

Permits: Permits are not required. Parking and access are free.

Maps: For a map of the Siskiyou National Forest and the Wild Rogue Wilderness, contact the Rogue River–Siskiyou National Forest headquarters, 3040 Biddle Road, Medford, OR, 97504, 541/618-2200. For a topographic map, ask the USGS for Marial.

Directions: From Gold Beach, drive Jerrys Flat Road 32 miles along the Rogue River to a bridge near Agness, and continue on Road 33 toward Powers for 15.6 miles. Go right on FS Road 3348 for 8.7 miles and turn right on gravel Road 5520 for 1.2 miles, then left on Road 230 to its end at the trailhead. To leave a shuttle at the Bald Knob Lookout, follow Road 3348 for two miles from the junction with Forest Service Road 33, then turn right on Road 5520. Follow this gravel road two miles to the spur road 020 on the right, and take it two miles to the Bald Knob Trailhead.

Contact: Siskiyou National Forest, Powers Ranger District, 42861 Highway 242, Powers, OR, 97466, 541/439-6200.

74 MOUNT BOLIVAR
2.8 mi/2.0 hr

northeast of Gold Beach in Wild Rogue Wilderness

Map 1.5, page 37

For whatever reason, this mountain seems to be named for Simón Bolívar, though his conquests were thousands of miles away in South America. If you are of the conquistador spirit, then you'll spot your goal from the trailhead itself, a steep climb to 4,319-foot Mount Bolivar in the Wild Rogue Wilderness. Though it is a notoriously long drive to get here, it's comforting to know that from the peak you will have the commanding view from the Cascades to the California Siskiyous in a 360-degree panoramic view. The trail switchbacks up through open meadows, a Douglas fir forest, and finally onto the wildflower-covered rocky slopes, and all within 1.4 miles and over the course of 1,200 feet elevation gain. At the top, the site of a former lookout, you'll find a plaque commemorating Bolívar.

From the trailhead, begin on the Mount Bolivar Trail. The first mile meanders easily through dense woods and into a drier, sparser pine-fir forest intermingled with manzanita. The trail circles around the north face of the mountain, then begins to climb in the next 0.5 mile, growing steeper as the summit is neared. Return as you came.

User Groups: Hikers and dogs. No horses or mountain bikes allowed. No wheelchair facilities.

Permits: Permits are not required. Parking and access are free.

Maps: For a map of the Siskiyou National Forest, contact the Rogue River–Siskiyou National Forest headquarters, 3040 Biddle Road, Medford, OR, 97504, 541/618-2200. For a topographic map, ask the USGS for Mount Bolivar.

Directions: From Gold Beach, drive Jerrys Flat Road 32 miles along the Rogue River to a bridge near Agness, and continue on Road 33 to Powers for 15.6 miles. From Powers, turn right on Road 3348 for 18.7 miles to a trailhead on the right, with the final 0.9 mile in BLM land.

Contact: Siskiyou National Forest, Powers Ranger District, 42861 Highway 242, Powers, OR, 97466, 541/439-6200.

75 HUMBUG MOUNTAIN
5.5 mi/3.0 hr

south of Port Orford in Humbug Mountain State Park

Map 1.5, page 37

This trail has been popular ever since settlers arrived in 1851 looking for gold. They were told that if they climbed this mountain, they would see the mountains filled with gold. Instead, what the scouts saw was more ocean, and they named the peak accordingly. On a sunny day, expect to see the hordes still arriving, looking for that as-good-as-gold view. You will earn that gold in a breathtaking 1,700 foot ascent conveniently, if not mockingly, marked every half-mile up the slope from myrtlewood groves to old-growth Douglas fir. Humbug Mountain also holds the last uncut grove of old-growth trees on the southern Oregon coast. You can even, surprisingly, take this trail as a loop.

After a mile, the path forks. The right-hand fork proves shorter but a bit steeper, and climbs 1.4 mile with views to Cape Blanco. Near the top, a short spur leads 0.1 mile to the summit. Descend by taking the opposite fork, this time to the right, descending 1.9 mile back to the first junction. Continue to the right to return to the trailhead.

User Groups: Hikers and dogs. No horses or mountain bikes allowed. No wheelchair facilities.

Permits: Permits are not required. Parking and access are free.

Maps: For a free park brochure, call Oregon Parks and Recreation, 800/551-6949, or download a free map at www.oregonstateparks.org. For a topographic map, ask the USGS for Port Orford.

Directions: Drive U.S. 101 south of Port Orford six miles and park at a large sign for "Humbug Mountain Trail Parking."

Contact: Oregon Parks and Recreation Department, 1115 Commercial Street NE, Salem, OR, 97301, 800/551-6949, www.oregonstateparks.org.

76 ROGUE RIVER TRAIL

40.0 mi one-way/4-5 days 5 ⛰10

northeast of Gold Beach in Wild Rogue Wilderness

Map 1.5, page 37

In the heart of the Wild Rogue Wilderness, this 40-mile National Recreation Trail follows a stretch of the Wild and Scenic Rogue River into some serious canyonlands. Give yourself a week to do the entire length, travel time included. There are numerous opportunities for backpacking camps along the river, usually near creeks and sometimes equipped with toilets; there are even lodges along the way where you can make reservations. You'll pass rapids, waterfalls, and nice areas to relax, like Solitude Bar and the Coffeepot. If you're not up for a 40-mile journey, there are plenty of day-hike options in the first 15-mile wilderness stretch. This first portion can be hot and dry, particularly in summer, so be sure to pack enough water.

From the trailhead at Foster Bar, the first 4.3 miles rounds the river opposite Big Bend and continues to Flora Dell Falls, a good day-hike in itself. In another 1.7 miles you'll reach Clay Hill Lodge just above a series of rapids, with a primitive campsite on Tate Creek 0.8 mile beyond that. The next two miles passes a vista at Solitude Bar and another campground at Brushy Bar, beneath the long ridge of the Devil's Backbone. The next 2.9 miles rounds a bend to the Paradise Lodge and an airstrip and a primitive campsite at Blossom Bar beyond that. Another 1.4 miles climbs to a view at Inspiration Point, and the remaining 0.7 mile before a dirt road trailhead passes over the churning Coffeepot, a boiling cauldron on the river where boaters often face disaster.

Walking along the road to Marial and the Rogue River Ranch for 1.8 miles connects to the remaining 23.2 miles of the Rogue River Trail to its end at Grave Creek, including a cabin at Winkle Bar (5.5 more miles), and campsites at Kelsey Creek (7.6 miles), Meadow Creek (9.4 miles), Copsey Creek (11.1 miles), Russian Creek (17.2 miles), Big Slide (19.3 miles), and Rainie Falls (23 miles). You'll also pass the Tyee Rapids, a narrow stretch appropriately called Slim Pickins, and the Whiskey Creek Cabin museum.

As of April 2009, the Bunker Creek Bridge nine miles downriver from Grave Creek is closed indefinitely, though a detour is in place. A slide in the Dulog area 14 miles downriver from Grave Creek has been deemed difficult to cross or impassable by managing agencies. Contact the Medford office of the BLM (503/808-6001) for updates.

User Groups: Hikers and dogs only. No mountain bikes and horses allowed. No wheelchair facilities.

Permits: Permits are not required. Parking and access are free.

Maps: For a map of the Siskiyou National Forest and the Wild Rogue Wilderness, contact the Rogue River–Siskiyou National Forest headquarters, 3040 Biddle Road, Medford, OR, 97504, 541/618-2200. For a topographic map, ask the USGS for Agness, Marial, Bunker Creek, Quosatana Butte, and Mount Reuben.

Directions: From U.S. 101, at the south end of the Gold Beach Bridge, follow Jerrys Flat Road for 32 miles along the Rogue River; the road becomes Road 33. Just after a river crossing, take a right fork at a sign for Illahe and follow this road for 3.5 paved miles to a trailhead spur on the right. To leave a shuttle at the trailhead, the Grave Creek Trailhead is located north of Galice. From Grants Pass, follow SW G Street/OR 260 west 1.2 miles, then continue on Upper River Road 2.4 miles. Turn right on Azalea Drive Cutoff 0.4 mile, and continue right on Azalea Drive 5.8 miles. Turn left on Galice Road, which becomes Merlin-Galice Road, for 10.7 miles to the town of Galice. Go about 7 miles north of Galice on BLM Road 35-8-13 to the Grave Creek Trailhead.

Contact: Siskiyou National Forest, Gold Beach Ranger District, 29279 Ellensburg Avenue, Gold Beach, OR, 97444, 541/247-3600.

77 COPPER CANYON ON THE ROGUE RIVER

12.6 mi one-way/7.0 hr   🥾4   ⛰9

northeast of Gold Beach in Siskiyou National Forest

Map 1.5, page 37

Though the Lower Rogue River Trail can be dauntingly long and laborious, there are options for taking it easier. Or at least, shorter. For a look at a lower section of the Rogue, crossing creek after creek, dipping down to a beach, passing viewpoints of Copper Canyon and crossing the lower reaches of Adams Prairie and a camping spot on Dog Creek, try this section of trail out of the town of Agness. You'll get the best of this region's dramatic canyon scenery, creek hopping along the way on this designated Scenic and Recreational River. You'll begin the trail with a jog over gravel roads and through gates, bringing you to an access point of a beach on an eddy. From there, despite both the private residences and ruins you'll sometimes pass, things get wilder. A shorter stretch can be made out to the halfway point and back for a good 12-mile day, but the ambitious can tackle the whole canyon and even arrange for a shuttle with the myriad providers who do just that for boaters and hikers.

From the lot, walk the trail to a crossing of Rilea Creek and a junction. Here the trail becomes a road to the left, passing through farm property and several gates. Just after the road climbs, the trail picks up on the right. The next 2.1 miles passes a 400-foot elevation viewpoint of the Rogue's Copper Canyon and

Painted Rock Creek, where you'll climb at the 1.5-mile mark to a dirt road, where the trail heads left, crossing Blue Jay Creek before bearing right. You'll arrive at painted Rock creek at the 3.1-mile mark, followed by Leo, Stonehouse, Spring, and Sundown Creeks. This is a good turnaround point, but if you're up for more, the next 4.8 miles reaches a high point of 750 feet at the Adams Prairie, with a spur trail leading into an exploration of its meadows. You'll reach Auberry Creek at the 8.7-mile mark, the campground on Dog Creek at the 9.1-mile mark, and Slide Creek at the 11-mile point. The trail ends at the trailhead on Road 3533 another 2.5 miles past that.

User Groups: Hikers and dogs only. No mountain bikes or horses allowed. No wheelchair facilities.

Permits: Permits are not required. Parking and access are free.

Maps: For a map of the Siskiyou National Forest, contact the Rogue River–Siskiyou National Forest headquarters, 3040 Biddle Road, Medford, OR, 97504, 541/618-2200. For a topographic map, ask the USGS for Agness.

Directions: From U.S. 101, at the south end of the Gold Beach Bridge, follow Jerrys Flat Road for 32 miles along the Rogue River; the road becomes Road 33. Just after a river crossing, turn left at a sign for Agness. Follow this one-lane paved road three miles to the Agness Store and turn right on Cougar Lane for 0.2 mile. Park in the Agness Community Library gravel lot. Walk straight on the gravel road, following trail signs and passing two gates to the trail's start on the right. To shuttle and do the entire length of this trail, leave a vehicle at the west trailhead. To get there, take Jerrys Flat Road from Gold Beach (the road becomes FS 33) about 9.8 miles to the Lobster Creek Bridge. Cross the bridge and take the first right on FS Road 3533, continuing 3.7 miles to FS Road 340. Follow signs about three miles to the trailhead.

Contact: Siskiyou National Forest, Gold Beach Ranger District, 29279 Ellensburg Avenue, Gold Beach, OR, 97444, 541/247-3600.

78 ILLINOIS RIVER

5.0-17.2 mi/3.0 hr-2 days

northeast of Gold Beach in Siskiyou National Forest

Map 1.5, page 37

A tributary of the Rogue River, the Illinois River is every bit as rugged as the famous waterway, the difference being that this National Recreation Trail never comes close to the river. Instead, this trail traverses into the Kalmiopsis Wilderness and even goes up and over Bald Mountain. The river itself holds a Wild and Scenic River designation, in no small part because of its substantial beauty—and good fishing. If the whole trail is not an option for the day, an easy hike to the Buzzards Roost is a good destination. But if you're in the mood and in tip-top shape, the strenuous hike to Silver Creek will test your endurance. When you've warmed up, then you may be ready to tackle the entire 27-mile length. This trail is located in the area charred by the 2002 Biscuit Fire burn; take caution and proceed knowingly. Along the way, look for recovering madrone, tanoak, myrtlewood, and black huckleberry.

The Illinois River Trail sets out from Oak Flat and climbs the canyon wall for 2.5 miles to Buzzards Roost, hung over 1,000 feet in the air above the river. This makes for a good day trip. Continuing 1.7 miles up the trail, you'll come to Indigo Creek and Indian Flat, with a left-hand spur trail leading into the meadows just before the creek. From there the trail descends slowly for 3.7 miles past the old Fantz Ranch, now USFS property, crossing numerous creeks before arriving at the canyon of Silver Creek.

User Groups: Hikers, dogs, and horses. No mountain bikes allowed. No wheelchair facilities.

Permits: Permits are not required. Parking and access are free.

Maps: For a map of the Siskiyou National Forest and the Kalmiopsis Wilderness, contact the Rogue River–Siskiyou National Forest headquarters, 3040 Biddle Road, Medford, OR, 97504, 541/618-2200. For a topographic map, ask the USGS for Agness.

Directions: From U.S. 101, at the south end of the Gold Beach Bridge, follow Jerrys Flat Road for 28 miles along the Rogue River to the bridge over the Illinois River. On the far side of the crossing, turn right on Oak Flat Road for three miles. The trailhead lot is on the left along a gravel road just beyond the end of the pavement.

Contact: Siskiyou National Forest, Gold Beach Ranger District, 29279 Ellensburg Avenue, Gold Beach, OR, 97444, 541/247-3600.

79 INDIAN MARY PARK

2.8 mi/1.5 hr

west of Grants Pass on the Rogue River

Map 1.5, page 37

This historic park has a long history in an area known for its wars between white settlers and Native Americans. In 1855, one Umpqua Joe warned the white settlers of an impending attack, which they thwarted. For this he was awarded a piece of land from where he operated a ferry. He died in 1886, and his daughter, Indian Mary, kept operating the ferry crossing. Once she left for Grants Pass, the land changed hands several times until 1958, when Josephine County bought it and made it into the park it is today. The sole trail in the park is named for Umpqua Joe and climbs to a viewpoint over the Rogue River.

The trail starts across the highway from the campground and day parking lot. The trail alternates between steep and easy, climbing 0.8 mile to a 0.2-mile viewpoint loop fork to the left. Returning to the main trail, climb 0.5 mile through black oaks to the official trail's end high above the river.

User Groups: Hikers and dogs. No wheelchair facilities.

Permits: Permits are not required. A $2-per-car day-use pass is required, or you can purchase a $25 annual pass.

Maps: For a topographic map, ask the USGS for Galice.

Directions: From I-5, take the Merlin exit 61 north of Grants Pass and follow signs 3.6 miles to Merlin on the Merlin-Galice Road, then go straight seven miles to the park entrance on the right.

Contact: Josephine County Parks, 125 Ringuette Street, Grants Pass, OR, 97527, 541/474-5285.

80 SHRADER OLD-GROWTH TRAIL
0.8 mi/0.5 hr ☒1 ⛰6

northeast of Gold Beach in Siskiyou National Forest

Map 1.5, page 37   BEST (

This easy loop trail is the home of Laddie Gale Douglas fir, 220 feet high and 10 feet thick, named for a legendary University of Oregon basketball player who led the team to a national championship victory way back in 1939. Quite the commemoration. The wide and easy trail is perfect for families. This is a fine trail to take slowly, savoring the forest that a typical hiker may normally move through at a quick clip.

From the parking area, the loop is an easy stroll through not only stately Douglas fir and cedars, but deciduous tanoak. Just inside the forest, the trail splits for the loop. Go left and in 0.2 mile cross a stream on a footbridge. From here, follow the loop through the colossal trees another 0.6 mile, gradually ascending back to the start of the loop. Along the way you'll pass the Laddie Gale commemorative tree.

User Groups: Hikers and dogs only. No wheelchair facilities.

Permits: Permits are not required. Parking and access are free.

Maps: For a map of the Siskiyou National Forest, contact the Rogue River–Siskiyou National Forest headquarters, 3040 Biddle Road, Medford, OR, 97504, 541/618-2200. A

brochure map is available at the trailhead. For a topographic map, ask the USGS for Brushy Bald Mountain.

Directions: From U.S. 101, at the south end of the Gold Beach Bridge, follow Jerrys Flat Road for 11.2 miles. Pass Lobster Creek Campground on the left and turn right at a sign for the Frances Schrader memorial Trail. Follow Road 3300-090 for 2.1 steep miles to a lot on the left.

Contact: Siskiyou National Forest, Gold Beach Ranger District, 29279 Ellensburg Avenue, Gold Beach, OR, 97444, 541/247-3600.

81 OTTER POINT
1.4 mi/0.5 hr ☒1 ⛰7

north of Gold Beach on the Pacific Ocean

Map 1.5, page 37

This seldom-seen series of trails are off the beaten path a bit, though not far from nearby U.S. 101. Wind-sculpted sandstone formations and a long beach laid bare by waves are only a short distance from all the traffic—and are worth a visit. From the parking area at this State Recreation Area, it's a 0.4-mile round-trip to the headland of Otter Point, with its view out over a long southern beach, and a short scramble trail to a hidden beach on the north face. A second trail heads south from the lot, descending to a beach with plenty of room to run.

User Groups: Hikers and dogs. No wheelchair facilities.

Permits: Permits are not required. Parking and access are free.

Maps: For a topographic map, ask the USGS for Gold Beach.

Directions: From Gold Beach, drive north on U.S. 101 for three miles. Near milepost 325, take a right at a sign for "Old Coast Road" and drive west to a T-junction. Turn right for 0.6 mile, then left at a state park sign, driving to the end at a parking area.

Contact: Oregon Parks and Recreation Department, 1115 Commercial Street NE,

Salem, OR, 97301, 800/551-6949, www.oregonstateparks.org.

82 BIG PINE INTERPRETIVE LOOP

2.5 mi/1.0 hr   👥1 ⛰8

west of Grants Pass in Siskiyou National Forest

Map 1.5, page 37   **BEST (**

Along a stretch of Myers Creek, a network of four looping trails goes through a forest centered around "Big Pine," a 250-foot-high, double-topped ponderosa pine tree with a six-foot diameter. It's anyone's guess how many people it would take to get their arms around it. This is a great hike for the family, especially if you're staying at the Big Pine Campground. With wheelchair-friendly paths and more great trails nearby, this makes for a good launch point into the area. A second trail extending from the loop further surveys the old-growth Douglas fir and ponderosa pine in the area.

To walk the Big Pine Interpretive Loop, cross the bridge over Myers Creek and bear right. You'll find Big Pine in the first 0.1 mile. Continue around the loop 0.3 mile to find a marginally maintained spur, the Taylor Camp Trail. This trail is steeper and brushier, but makes for an added exploration of up to a mile one-way, before it ends at an old logging road. Return as you came and continue counterclockwise on the Big Pine Trail to complete the loop.

User Groups: Hikers and dogs. The path is wheelchair accessible.

Permits: Permits are not required. A federal Northwest Forest Pass is required to park here; the cost is $5 a day or $30 for an annual pass. You can buy a day pass at the trailhead, at ranger stations, or through private vendors.

Maps: For a map of the Siskiyou National Forest, contact the Rogue River–Siskiyou National Forest headquarters, 3040 Biddle Road, Medford, OR, 97504, 541/618-2200. For a topographic map, ask the USGS for Chrome Ridge.

Directions: From I-5, take the Merlin exit 61 north of Grants Pass and follow signs 3.6 miles to Merlin on the Merlin-Galice Road, then go straight 8.5 miles toward Galice and turn left on Briggs Valley Road/FS 25 for 12.5 miles. Turn right at the Big Pine Campground entrance and keep right for the day-use parking area.

Contact: Siskiyou National Forest, Wild Rivers Ranger District, 2164 Spalding Avenue, Grants Pass, OR, 97526, 541/471-6500.

83 TAYLOR CREEK

10.1 mi one-way/1–2 days   👥3 ⛰7

west of Grants Pass in Siskiyou National Forest

Map 1.5, page 37

Taylor Creek's watershed in the Siskiyou Mountains offers many opportunities to explore in many directions. Briggs Creek, Minnow Creek, China Creek, Dutchy Creek, and two interpretive trails, including the Big Pine Loop (see *Big Pine Interpretive Loop,* previous listing) and the Burned Timber Nature Trail all extend from Taylor Creek's trail. It is possible to hike the creek in differing lengths, as the trail ducks in an out of the forest, meeting the road. Active claims are still to be found along the way, as this area has a mining legacy going way back.

From the lower trailhead, hike into the forest of red-barked madrone, live oak, and Douglas fir. Watch for miner's claim notices tacked to trees. Within the first 1.8 miles, the path crosses Taylor Creek on a 60-foot-high bridge, passes the Burned Timber Loop, and meets up with another bridge to the Tin Can Campground. After another 1.4 miles, the trail crosses Road 052 and continues another 0.6 mile to the next trailhead. The next 2.6 miles crosses the creek twice and arrives at Lone Tree Pass. The final 3.6 miles leaves the creek and heads into the woods, passing a 0.7-mile spur trail to the Big Pine Campground before reaching the final trailhead.

User Groups: Hikers, dogs, horses, and mountain bikes. No wheelchair facilities.

Permits: Permits are not required. A federal Northwest Forest Pass is required to park here; the cost is $5 a day or $30 for an annual pass. You can buy a day pass at the trailhead, at ranger stations, or through private vendors.

Maps: For a map of the Siskiyou National Forest, contact the Rogue River–Siskiyou National Forest headquarters, 3040 Biddle Road, Medford, OR, 97504, 541/618-2200. For a topographic map, ask the USGS for Chrome Ridge and Galice.

Directions: From I-5, take the Merlin exit 61 north of Grants Pass and follow signs 3.6 miles to Merlin on the Merlin-Galice Road, then go straight 8.5 miles toward Galice and turn left on Briggs Valley Road/FS 25 for 3.1 miles to a pullout on the left marked "Taylor Creek Trailhead." Consider a shuttle at the Big Pine Campground, which connects to the Taylor Creek Trail. To find the campground from the town of Merlin, follow Galice Road 8.5 miles and go left at Road 25, continuing 12.5 miles to the campground on the right.

Contact: Siskiyou National Forest, Wild Rivers Ranger District, 2164 Spalding Avenue, Grants Pass, OR, 97526, 541/471-6500.

84 BRIGGS CREEK

9.5 mi/1 day   👣3 🔺7

west of Grants Pass in Siskiyou National Forest

Map 1.5, page 37

Briggs Creek has mining history to spare, and in this section of the Siskiyous, there are even some modern mining claims continuing today. Though this trail goes on much farther, there is a great option of visiting the abandoned Courier Mine Cabin, making for a great day. This trail is easiest in low water, as several fords are required. It's also popular for its abundance of swimming holes. In the meadow at Sam Brown Campground, once the site of an entire mining town, the only thing left is the grave of Sam Brown himself, one of the first African American men in southern Oregon, shot for allegedly conferencing with the miners' wives in a way the miners didn't appreciate.

The trail sets out, alternately following dirt roads and trail, from clear-cut to forests of fir, yew, and cedar, for 2.4 miles along the creek, passing the Elkhorn Mine, with its rusty machinery still left behind, and reaching the 30-foot-wide creek ford. The trail continues another 1.5 miles past tanoak, madrone, and sugar pine to the abandoned flume of the Courier Mine and finally to the one-room cabin. From here, the trail fords the creek again, continuing on to its end at Soldier Creek.

User Groups: Hikers, dogs, horses, and mountain bikes. No wheelchair facilities.

Permits: Permits are not required. A federal Northwest Forest Pass is required to park here; the cost is $5 a day or $30 for an annual pass. You can buy a day pass at the trailhead, at ranger stations, or through private vendors.

Maps: For a map of the Siskiyou National Forest, contact the Rogue River–Siskiyou National Forest headquarters, 3040 Biddle Road, Medford, OR, 97504, 541/618-2200. For a topographic map, ask the USGS for York Butte.

Directions: From I-5, take the Merlin exit 61 north of Grants Pass and follow signs 3.6 miles to Merlin on the Merlin-Galice Road, then go straight 8.5 miles toward Galice and turn left on Briggs Valley Road/FS 25 for 13.4 miles. One mile after the Big Pine Campground, turn right on FS Road 2512 for 0.3 mile, then turn left into the Sam Brown Campground, keeping left. Park in the large trailhead lot on the right.

Contact: Siskiyou National Forest, Wild Rivers Ranger District, 2164 Spalding Avenue, Grants Pass, OR, 97526, 541/471-6500.

85 ILLINOIS RIVER TRAIL TO BALD MOUNTAIN

20.6 mi/1-2 days

northwest of Cave Junction in Kalmiopsis Wilderness

Map 1.5, page 37

Many hikers think of this trail as one of the best in southern Oregon. This entry into the Kalmiopsis Wilderness, overlooking the Wild and Scenic Illinois River, has plenty to brag about. Pounding rapids, sweet campsites, and an abundance of creeks, all crowned by 3,917-foot Bald Mountain, are enough to suit anyone's taste. Although the 2002 Biscuit Fire started with a lightning strike at Florence Creek near this trail, many of the towering trees survived. In other areas, pine are repopulating the area, slowly but surely, and scrub oak and tanoak have already made their comeback.

The Illinois River Trail begins at a 140-foot steel bridge over Briggs Creek and the site of an old homestead. The first 4.5 miles heads into the wilderness area and crosses several creeks beneath York Butte, with views to the river below. At a junction, a loop trail begins with the goal being Bald Mountain. Go left 0.8 mile on the Pine Flat Trail to get to Pine Flat, a great camping spot overlooking Boat Eater Rapids, a granite island and six-foot drop whose name speaks for itself. Continue 2.6 steep miles to a junction. If you're tired, go to the right on a spur trail for 1.3 miles to connect to and follow the Illinois River Trail to the right four miles back to the junction above Pine Flat. If not, endure another 1.8-mile climb on the Pine Flat Trail to a campsite by a spring, keeping left at a junction with the Illinois River Trail to ascend to a 0.2-mile loop around lofty Bald Mountain's summit. Then descend, following the Illinois River Trail down 5.6 miles to the junction above Pine Flat, going left on the Illinois River Trail to return to the trailhead.

User Groups: Hikers, dogs, and horses. No mountain bikes allowed. No wheelchair facilities.

Permits: Permits are not required. A federal Northwest Forest Pass is required to park here; the cost is $5 a day or $30 for an annual pass. You can buy a day pass at the trailhead, at ranger stations, or through private vendors.

Maps: For a map of the Siskiyou National Forest and the Kalmiopsis Wilderness, contact the Rogue River–Siskiyou National Forest headquarters, 3040 Biddle Road, Medford, OR, 97504, 541/618-2200. For a topographic map, ask the USGS for Agness, York Butte, and Silver Peak.

Directions: From Grants Pass, head south on U.S. 199 toward Crescent City for 20 miles to a flashing yellow light in Selma. Turn right on Illinois River Road 4103 for 18.6 miles to the end of a rough gravel road at the Briggs Creek Trailhead.

Contact: Siskiyou National Forest, Wild Rivers Ranger District, 2164 Spalding Avenue, Grants Pass, OR, 97526, 541/471-6500.

86 CAPE SEBASTIAN

3.8-5.8 mi/2.0-3.0 hr

south of Gold Beach in Cape Sebastian State Park

Map 1.5, page 37

In 1603, the Spanish explorer Sebastian Vizcaino named this cape—not so much for himself as for Saint Sebastian. The views on a clear day extend 43 miles to the north to Humbug Mountain. To the south, a 50-mile view extends all the way to California. The cape itself hosts a dense Sitka spruce forest and overlooks Hunters Cove and Hunters Island, where cormorants hang out.

From the lot, the trail heads out over the cape for 1.4 miles, descending in the last portion to a striking lookout. The next 0.5-mile section follows the headland for more views before descending to the beach. For a longer hike, follow the beach towards the sea stacks for another mile to the Myers Creek pullout, a good turnaround point.

User Groups: Hikers and dogs. Paved trails are wheelchair accessible.

Permits: Permits are not required. Parking and access are free.

Maps: For a topographic map, ask the USGS for Cape Sebastian.

Directions: Drive south of Gold Beach seven miles on U.S. 101 and near milepost 335 turn at a "Cape Sebastian Viewpoint" sign, following this road 0.6 mile up the cape to a parking area.

Contact: Oregon Parks and Recreation Department, 1115 Commercial Street NE, Salem, OR, 97301, 800/551-6949, www.oregonstateparks.org.

87 SNOW CAMP LOOKOUT
7.0 mi/3.5 hr

northeast of Brookings in Kalmiopsis Wilderness

Map 1.5, page 37

One of the losses of the Biscuit Fire was the original Snow Camp Lookout, a 15-by-15-foot lookout that had been restored prior to the fire. The good news is, it's been rebuilt yet again. From the new lookout, rentable for $30 a night, the ocean is visible on clear days—and in fact, this site offers a 360-degree view. The longer trail to the lookout is one of the oldest in the Siskiyou National Forest, dating at least as far back as 1911, and portions of it have been identified as an old Native American trail.

Snow Camp Trail passes through wildflower heaven in the spring and summer, including azalea, beargrass, iris, cat's ear lilies, death camas, and Indian paintbrush. The first 1.7 miles pass the ruins of an old shelter, a rocky knoll, and eventually meeting up with Windy Creek. Take the left-hand turn here, fording the deep and cold Windy Creek and continuing steeply another mile. It is not a difficult ford but is best done in summer. A left-hand junction heads to Panther Lake, but stick to the right another 0.7 mile, climbing Snow Camp Mountain. At the next junction,

go right again 0.6 mile on the Snow Camp Lookout Trail to the lookout road and head for the top.

User Groups: Hikers, dogs, and horses. No mountain bikes allowed. No wheelchair facilities.

Permits: Permits are not required. Parking and access are free.

Maps: For a map of the Siskiyou National Forest, contact the Rogue River–Siskiyou National Forest headquarters, 3040 Biddle Road, Medford, OR, 97504, 541/618-2200. For a topographic map, ask the USGS for Collier Butte.

Directions: From Brookings and the U.S. 101 bridge, take the North Bank Road east eight miles and continue straight on Road 1376 an additional eight miles to a junction after the South Fork Chetco Bridge. Turn left, following "Snow Camp Lookout" signs on Road 1376 another 13 miles to a trailhead on the left a few hundred yards after milepost 21.

Contact: Siskiyou National Forest, Chetco Ranger District, 539 Chetco Lane, Brookings, OR, 97415, 541/412-6000.

88 WINDY VALLEY
4.4 mi/2.5 hr

northeast of Brookings in Siskiyou National Forest

Map 1.5, page 37

The Klamath Mountains rise above the ocean at the southernmost stretch of the Oregon coast, playing host to a wild diversity of trees and wildflowers. The Windy Valley Trail, unfortunately, is located along a stretch burned by the 2002 Biscuit Fire, one of the biggest in Oregon's history. Yet, for a learning experience, trails like this are a great way to see how a forest regenerates itself. One thing that colonizes this area is the Darlingtonia californica, the carnivorous pitcher plant also known as the cobra lily, which makes a meal of local bugs. This strange flower is native to this area and is rarely found anywhere else.

The Windy Valley Trail will pass through wildflower heaven in the spring and summer, including azalea, beargrass, iris, cat's ear lilies, death camas, and Indian paintbrush. The first 1.7 miles pass the ruins of an old shelter, a rocky knoll, and eventually meeting up with Windy Creek. Stay to the right for 0.5 mile to another crossing (there may still be a log there) and continuing into Windy Valley's meadows to the foundations of an old cabin beside a pool and small waterfall. Return as you came.

User Groups: Hikers, dogs, and horses. No mountain bikes allowed. No wheelchair facilities.

Permits: Permits are not required. Parking and access are free.

Maps: For a map of the Siskiyou National Forest, contact the Rogue River-Siskiyou National Forest headquarters, 3040 Biddle Road, Medford, OR, 97504, 541/618-2200. For a topographic map, ask the USGS for Collier Butte.

Directions: From Brookings and the U.S. 101 bridge, take the North Bank Road east 8 miles and continue straight on Road 1376 an additional 8 miles to a junction after the South Fork Chetco Bridge. Turn left, following "Snow Camp Lookout" signs on Road 1376 another 13 miles to a trailhead on the left a few hundred yards after milepost 21.

Contact: Siskiyou National Forest, Chetco Ranger District, 539 Chetco Lane, Brookings, OR, 97415, 541/412-6000.

89 MISLATNAH TRAIL TO MISLATNAH PEAK

9.6 mi/4.5 hr   👫 3   ⛰️ 8

northeast of Brookings in Kalmiopsis Wilderness

Map 1.5, page 37

There is only one route into the Big Craggies Botanical Area deep in the Kalmiopsis Wilderness, and this is it. The Big Craggies is a rocky, densely brushed area requiring cross-country travel. On top of that, this trail also

tops Mislatnah Peak, the site of a former lookout. Access to this trail is somewhat sketchy, as there is a slide on the Tincup Trail, which provides access to this trail about 0.9 mile from the trailhead. Also, you have to watch as you cross the prairies, as the trail has a way of vanishing and reappearing like magic. Check current conditions before you go.

From the parking area, start out on the Tincup Trail, descending 0.9 mile to Mislatnah Creek and the woodsy, grassy bench of Mislatnah Camp. Follow the trail upstream 0.1 mile to a horse crossing and ford the creek. Continue downstream for 0.3 mile and turn left on the Mislatnah Trail. In 0.6 mile, you'll pass a spring and enter the Upper Mislatnah Prairie in 0.2 mile beyond that. Here is where to really watch for the trail as it crosses the prairie 0.3 mile, entering the trees on the far side. The trail continues through a dry tanoak and madrone woodland for 1.4 miles to Jacks Camp, where signs point out a spring. Beyond the camp, the Kalmiopsis Wilderness begins, and the brush grows thicker along this steep ridge. Only 1.0 mile farther, the trail ascends to the 3,124-foot Mislatnah Peak, with views to the Big Craggies.

User Groups: Hikers, dogs, and horses. No mountain bikes allowed. No wheelchair facilities.

Permits: Permits are not required. Parking and access are free.

Maps: For a map of the Siskiyou National Forest and the Kalmiopsis Wilderness, contact the Rogue River–Siskiyou National Forest headquarters, 3040 Biddle Road, Medford, OR, 97504, 541/618-2200. For a topographic map, ask the USGS for Big Craggies.

Directions: From Brookings and the U.S. 101 bridge, take North Bank Road east eight miles and continue straight on Road 1376 an additional eight miles to a junction after the South Fork Chetco Bridge. Turn left, following Road 1376 another 10 miles to milepost 18, then fork right onto Road 360 for 1.5 miles, keeping right at Road 365 for the last 0.8 mile to the Tincup Trailhead.

Contact: Siskiyou National Forest, Chetco Ranger District, 539 Chetco Lane, Brookings, OR, 97415, 541/412-6000.

90 TINCUP TRAIL TO BOULDER CREEK CAMP

7.2 mi/3.0 hr 👣3 ⚠7

northeast of Brookings in Kalmiopsis Wilderness

Map 1.5, page 37

The Tincup Trail makes its way into the Kalmiopsis Wilderness following the Chetco River along an old gold prospectors' trail, heading across Bronson Prairie to the confluence of the Chetco and Boulder Creek, a good turnaround for a 7.2-mile day. Note that fords are necessary and those fords can only be done in late summer. Also, access to this trail is limited due to a slide on the Tincup Trail at Mislatnah Creek 0.9 mile from the trailhead, though there are other options to get to the trail. Check current conditions before you go.

From the parking area, start out on the Tincup Trail, descending 0.9 mile to Mislatnah Creek and the woodsy, grassy bench of Mislatnah Camp. Follow the trail upstream a mile to a horse crossing and ford the creek. Continue downstream for 0.3 mile to a junction with the Mislatnah Trail. Continue 2.3 miles upstream to Boulder Creek Camp, with access to water and campsites—meaning this a great place to cool your heels. Hardy hikers can continue on the nearly 20-mile trail to its end at Darling Creek.

User Groups: Hikers, dogs, and horses. No mountain bikes allowed. No wheelchair facilities.

Permits: Permits are not required. Parking and access are free.

Maps: For a map of the Siskiyou National Forest and the Kalmiopsis Wilderness, contact the Rogue River–Siskiyou National Forest headquarters, 3040 Biddle Road, Medford, OR, 97504, 541/618-2200. For a topographic map, ask the USGS for Big Craggies.

Directions: From Brookings and the U.S. 101 bridge, take North Bank Road east eight miles and continue straight on Road 1376 an additional eight miles to a junction after the South Fork Chetco Bridge. Turn left, following Road 1376 another 10 miles to milepost 18, then fork right onto Road 360 for 1.5 miles, keeping right at Road 365 for the last 0.8 mile to the Tincup Trailhead.

Contact: Siskiyou National Forest, Chetco Ranger District, 539 Chetco Lane, Brookings, OR, 97415, 541/412-6000.

91 ILLINOIS RIVER FALLS

1.2 mi/0.5 hr 👣1 ⚠6

northwest of Cave Junction in Siskiyou National Forest

Map 1.5, page 37

Heavily damaged during the Biscuit Fire, the Fall Creek Trail was closed due to a burned-out bridge; check on the status of this trail with the U.S. Forest Service before attempting it. If you can get there, it's an easy hike across a bridge to the far side of the Illinois River. Go left 0.4 mile, then head cross country along the river about 300 yards to a view of the 10-foot Illinois River Falls. Watch out for poison oak, as it grows back viciously after fires.

User Groups: Hikers, dogs, and horses. No mountain bikes allowed. No wheelchair facilities.

Permits: Permits are not required. Parking and access are free.

Maps: For a map of the Siskiyou National Forest, contact the Rogue River–Siskiyou National Forest headquarters, 3040 Biddle Road, Medford, OR, 97504, 541/618-2200. For a topographic map, ask the USGS for Pearsoll Peak.

Directions: From Grants Pass, head south on U.S. 199 toward Crescent City for 20 miles to a flashing yellow light in Selma. Turn right on Illinois River Road 4103 for 11 miles. At an "End Maintenance" sign, turn left at a gravel pullout onto Road 087, a rough descent 0.5 mile to a bridge.

Contact: Siskiyou National Forest, Wild Rivers Ranger District, 2164 Spalding Avenue, Grants Pass, OR, 97526, 541/471-6500.

92 BABYFOOT LAKE

2.4–5.3 mi/1.0–2.5 hr　　🥾2 ⛰7

west of Cave Junction in Siskiyou National Forest

Map 1.5, page 37

For a firsthand look at the devastation—and survival—of flora in a wildfire, head to Babyfoot Lake. The trail passes through a ghost wilderness of black snags that nevertheless harbor new blooms of beargrass and Oregon grape, feeding on sunlight from the opened canopy. The lake itself is an oasis, and the trail passes through the Babyfoot Lake Botanical Area: Western red cedar, incense cedar, and Port Orford cedar all survived here, as did Jeffrey pine and Brewer's weeping spruce. Tanoak trees along the way simply sprout new trees from their roots. The entire hike is a valuable lesson in fire ecology. The lake itself is a high mountain lake in a glacial cirque.

From the trailhead, enter the burned forest on the Babyfoot Lake Trail, going 0.3 mile to a junction. From there, head to the right, descending gently 0.9 mile to the Kalmiopsis Wilderness border and Babyfoot Lake. For an interesting loop, continue past Babyfoot to Trail 1124, an old road, in 0.5 mile. Go left, following this Kalmiopsis Rim Trail along 1.8 miles to a rock cairn and a burned sign marking the trail to the left. Follow the Ridge Trail for another view down to Babyfoot Lake, keeping right at the next two junctions for 1.8 miles back to the trailhead.

User Groups: Hikers and dogs. No horses or mountain bikes allowed. No wheelchair facilities.

Permits: Permits are not required. A federal Northwest Forest Pass is required to park here; the cost is $5 a day or $30 for an annual pass.

You can buy a day pass at the trailhead, at ranger stations, or through private vendors.

Maps: For a map of the Siskiyou National Forest and the Kalmiopsis Wilderness, contact the Rogue River–Siskiyou National Forest headquarters, 3040 Biddle Road, Medford, OR, 97504, 541/618-2200. For a topographic map, ask the USGS for Josephine Mountain.

Directions: Drive U.S. 199 south of Grants Pass 24 miles and turn west on Eight Dollar Road, following signs for Kalmiopsis Wilderness. The road becomes Road 4201 and crosses the Illinois River in three miles then continues on gravel for 12 more miles. At a fork, follow signs for Babyfoot lake and go left on Road 140 for 0.7 mile to a trailhead spur on the right.

Contact: Siskiyou National Forest, Wild Rivers Ranger District, 2164 Spalding Avenue, Grants Pass, OR, 97526, 541/471-6500.

93 VULCAN PEAK

2.6 mi/2.0 hr　　🥾2 ⛰8

east of Brookings in Kalmiopsis Wilderness

Map 1.5, page 37

Atop Vulcan Peak lie the remains of an old fire watchtower, a few metal pieces, some bits of glass. The view is expansive across, ironically, the massive burn of the 2002 Biscuit Fire. Nonetheless, this is a straightforward climb with views extending down to Vulcan Lake (see *Vulcan Lake,* next listing) and the Chetco River drainage system.

From the trailhead, walk up an abandoned roadbed 0.2 mile to a junction with the Chetco Divide Trail. Fork left and climb 1.1 miles and nearly 1,000 feet to a view encompassing the Siskiyou Mountains, the Kalmiopsis Wilderness, and the Pacific Ocean.

User Groups: Hikers, dogs, and horses. No mountain bikes allowed. No wheelchair facilities.

Permits: A free wilderness permit is required and available at the trailhead. Parking and access are free.

Maps: For a map of the Siskiyou National Forest and the Kalmiopsis Wilderness, contact the Rogue River–Siskiyou National Forest headquarters, 3040 Biddle Road, Medford, OR, 97504, 541/618-2200. For a topographic map, ask the USGS for Chetco Peak.

Directions: From the U.S. 101 bridge in Brookings, head east on North Bank Road for eight miles, continuing straight on Road 1376 another eight miles. At a junction just beyond the South Fork Chetco Bridge, turn right on gravel Road 1909 for 13.4 miles, following signs for Kalmiopsis Wilderness. At a fork, go right into the Vulcan Peak Trailhead.

Contact: Siskiyou National Forest, Chetco Ranger District, 539 Chetco Lane, Brookings, OR, 97415, 541/412-6000.

94 VULCAN LAKE
3.7 mi/2.5 hr

east of Brookings in Kalmiopsis Wilderness

Map 1.5, page 37   **BEST (**

Every good explorer can recount some beautiful mountain lake stumbled upon in the heat of the day, and how refreshing it was to sink down into some cold mountain water and feel all tensions slip away. Vulcan Lake is certainly one of these places, and as a destination it seems fitting: Its loop trail leads over some serious rocky country scarred by the 2002 Biscuit Fire but, all things considered, is recovering nicely. It makes for a hot hike and a cool finish. On the way, the trail passes the remains of the old Gardner Mine, the Sorvaag Bog, and two lovely lakes in the presence of Vulcan Peak. The lakes themselves lie in a prehistoric cirque, when this area was scoured down to bedrock by glaciers. Vulcan Lake is not only great for swimming on a hot day, it's also a great entry point for a backpacking exploration.

From the trailhead at road's end, head to the right on the Vulcan Lake Trail for 1.4 miles, climbing to a pass overlooking not one, but two lakes (a bit farther in the distance is Little

Vulcan Lake) before heading down to Vulcan Lake. Here you'll find a junction; go right to Vulcan Lake, straight to Little Vulcan, and to the left for a challenging loop. This left-hand trail leads 1.1 miles along a barely discernable path, so watch the cairns stacked here. You'll pass the bog and the mine—both good for exploration—before joining the Johnson Butte Trail. Go left 0.8 mile along this old roadbed to return to the trailhead.

User Groups: Hikers, dogs, and horses. No mountain bikes allowed. No wheelchair facilities.

Permits: A free wilderness permit is required and available at the trailhead. Parking and access are free.

Maps: For a map of the Siskiyou National Forest and the Kalmiopsis Wilderness, contact the Rogue River–Siskiyou National Forest headquarters, 3040 Biddle Road, Medford, OR, 97504, 541/618-2200. For a topographic map, ask the USGS for Chetco Peak and Tincup Peak.

Directions: From the U.S. 101 bridge in Brookings, head east on North Bank Road for eight miles, continuing straight on Road 1376 another eight miles. At a junction just beyond the South Fork Chetco Bridge, turn right on gravel Road 1909 for 13.4 miles, following signs for Kalmiopsis Wilderness. At a fork, go left 1.7 miles to road's end at the trailhead.

Contact: Siskiyou National Forest, Chetco Ranger District, 539 Chetco Lane, Brookings, OR, 97415, 541/412-6000.

95 JOHNSON BUTTE
12.6 mi/6.5 hr

northeast of Brookings in Kalmiopsis Wilderness

Map 1.5, page 37

The Kalmiopsis Wilderness is so named for the bug-eating blooms of the *Kalmiopsis* carnivorous plant that grow in profusion along the Johnson Butte Trail. The best times to see the flowers are May and June, about when the snows melt in this remote section of the Klamath Mountains. The trail follows an old mining road, long abandoned. But the ridge it follows offers substantive views, especially in light of the 2002 Biscuit Fire, which did a number on this part of the world. Still, the trail passes accessible, lily-covered Salamander Lake along the way, as well as a rare azalea found in patches in this wilderness area.

From the trailhead, the Johnson Butte Trail is a single run at 6.3 miles one-way. It follows a ridge on an old road for 1.5 miles before turning to trail, then crosses the ridge 0.4 mile later. After four miles, the trail rounds Dry Butte and arrives at a spur trail to Salamander Lake. About 1.1 miles beyond this lake is a spur trail on the right that leads to a spring. From here, it's a 1.2-mile run to a junction with the Upper Chetco Trail in the shadow of Johnson Butte, at a flat good for camping—but there's no water. Return as you came.

User Groups: Hikers, dogs, and horses. No mountain bikes permitted. No wheelchair facilities.

Permits: A free wilderness permit is required and available at the trailhead. Parking and access are free.

Maps: For a map of the Siskiyou National Forest and the Kalmiopsis Wilderness, contact the Rogue River–Siskiyou National Forest headquarters, 3040 Biddle Road, Medford, OR, 97504, 541/618-2200. For a topographic map, ask the USGS for Chetco Peak and Tincup Peak.

Directions: From the U.S. 101 bridge in Brookings, head east on North Bank Road for eight miles, continuing straight on Road 1376 another eight miles. At a junction just beyond the South Fork Chetco Bridge, turn right on gravel Road 1909 for 13.4 miles, following signs for Kalmiopsis Wilderness. At a fork, go left 1.7 miles to road's end at the trailhead.

Contact: Siskiyou National Forest, Chetco Ranger District, 539 Chetco Lane, Brookings, OR, 97415, 541/412-6000.

96 BOARDMAN STATE PARK
12.6 mi one-way/1-2 days 👣5 ⛰10

north of Brookings on the Pacific Ocean

Map 1.5, page 37

Samuel Boardman—a 21-year veteran of the Oregon State Parks, and in fact the first superintendent of that newly created system back in the early 1900s—left Oregon with the firm foundations of a supreme park system as his legacy. No wonder that what is now Boardman State Park is named for him. It's grandiose, epic, and as far as the Oregon coast goes, you can get just about every pleasure out of it you could imagine: 300-year-old Sitka spruce, rock arches and natural bridges, amazing vistas, cove beaches, timbered sea stacks, and old midden mounds left by Native Americans. What's more, this park is easily sampled in short stretches, as the trail itself—part of the Oregon Coast Trail—parallels U.S. 101, with a number of pullouts for easy access. To do the whole trail, or to backpack it, you'll want to have tide charts handy, as some stretches will require some beach portages. Be prepared for wonder at a discount, as all sections are free. But where to start?

The southernmost stretch begins at the Lone Ranch Picnic Area on a nice beach and heads north immediately onto Cape Ferrelo, named for a 1542 Spanish explorer, traversing its grassy and wildflower-strewn meadows 1.2 miles to a viewpoint parking area. The next 1.4 miles provides a side trail down to a beach on the north end of the cape and continues through Sitka spruce forests over House Rock Creek to a viewpoint of the same name. The trail continues over the rocky headlands 1.3 miles then dives down for a 1.2-mile beach crossing before heading up to the Whalehead Beach Picnic Area—the "whalehead" being a sea stack that spouts water out its head when the tide comes in just right. You'll need to follow the entry road up 0.3 mile to connect with the rest of the trail. Continue 1.4 mile for some stunning viewpoints, arriving at the Indian Sands, a series of strange wind-sculpted sandstone formations. Follow the headlands north 1.4 miles to U.S. 101, where the trail briefly joins the highway to cross the highest bridge in Oregon at 345 feet over the canyon of Thomas Creek. The next 1.3 miles follows the cliffs and drops down to China Beach, passable only at low tide. Cross the beach and head back to the highway for 0.6 mile. Then in 1.1 miles, pass over the beautiful Natural Bridges with a viewpoint. The final 1.4-mile stretch again follows the cliffs with views out to Spruce Island and Arch Rock. The trail ends at Arch Rock Picnic Area.

User Groups: Hikers and dogs. The Arch Rock and Cape Ferrelo Viewpoints are wheelchair accessible.

Permits: Permits are not required. Parking and access are free.

Maps: For a free park brochure, call Oregon Parks and Recreation, 800/551-6949, or download a free map at www.oregonstateparks.org. For a topographic map, ask the USGS for Brookings.

Directions: Drive north of Brookings on U.S. 101 about four miles. The southernmost start of the trail is at the Lone Ranch Picnic Area between mileposts 352 and 353. The northernmost start of the trail at Arch Rock Picnic Area is between mileposts 344 and 345.

Contact: Oregon Parks and Recreation Department, 1115 Commercial Street NE, Salem, OR, 97301, 800/551-6949, www.oregonstateparks.org.

97 REDWOOD NATURE TRAIL
2.6 mi/1.0 hr 🥾1 ▲7

east of Brookings in Siskiyou National Forest

| Map 1.5, page 37 | BEST (|

Though California gets all the fame for its redwood trees, Oregon has its own share. They extend, in fact, about this far north into the state, and an easy tour in Loeb State Park visits the *Sequoia sempervirens* on land donated to the state by a group called Save the Myrtlewoods. That's not all they saved:

The park is also a haven for red alder, tanoak, evergreen huckleberries, and salmonberries. The Riverview Trail follows the Chetco River for some grand views of the rocky-bottomed river, as well.

From the picnic area, head out 0.7 mile along the Riverview Trail on the Chetco River, home to river otters and fish-hunting osprey. The trail ends at the North Bank Road, so cross the road to the Redwood Nature Trail parking area and follow this trail along Elk Creek. Head to the left for the 1.2-mile loop uphill into the stately redwood grove. Return along the Riverview Trail.

User Groups: Hikers and dogs. No wheelchair facilities.

Permits: Permits are not required. Parking and access are free.

Maps: A trail guide is available at the trailhead. For a topographic map, ask the USGS for Mount Emily.

Directions: From the U.S. 101 bridge in Brookings, head east on North Bank Road for 7.3 miles and turn right into Loeb State Park and drive to the trailhead parking area.

Contact: Oregon Parks and Recreation Department, 1115 Commercial Street NE, Salem, OR, 97301, 800/551-6949, www.oregonstateparks.org.

98 WHEELER RIDGE
1.6 mi/1.0 hr 🥾1 ▲7

east of Brookings in Wheeler Creek Research Natural Area

| Map 1.5, page 37 |

On September 9, 1942, a Japanese submarine surfaced off the coast of southern Oregon, and a small aircraft was launched by catapult. The pilot, Nobuo Fujita, carrying his family's 400-year-old samurai sword, dropped two incendiary bombs. The plan was to start massive forest fires. The plan failed, as the fires on Wheeler Ridge were quickly put out, and another bomb dropped on Grassy Knob (see *Grassy Knob* listing in this chapter) never went off—and indeed was never found. The pilot got away scot-free. Later, though, the pilot returned, first in 1962 to present his family's samurai sword to the city of Brookings, and then in 1992 as an act of reconciliation when he hiked this ridge and planted a redwood tree.

To find the bomb site, hike from the trailhead 0.8 mile into the Wheeler Creek Research Natural Area. This easy path weaves through big Douglas fir, tanoak, pine, and huge redwoods. The trail ends at an interpretive sign and the redwood seedling planted as a gesture of peace.

User Groups: Hikers and dogs. No wheelchair facilities.

Permits: Permits are not required. Parking and access are free.

Maps: For a map of the Siskiyou National Forest, contact the Rogue River–Siskiyou National Forest headquarters, 3040 Biddle Road, Medford, OR, 97504, 541/618-2200. For a topographic map, ask the USGS for Fourth of July Creek.

Directions: From the south end of the U.S. 101 bridge in Brookings, drive inland on South Bank Road five miles, then turn right on gravel Mount Emily Road, following "Bombsite Trail" signs 13 miles to the trailhead sign. Park along the road.

Contact: Siskiyou National Forest, Chetco Ranger District, 539 Chetco Lane, Brookings, OR, 97415, 541/412-6000.

PORTLAND AND THE WILLAMETTE VALLEY

© SEAN PATRICK HILL

BEST HIKES

❰ Bird-Watching
Oak Island, **page 105.**
Oaks Bottom, **page 108.**
Baskett Slough Refuge, **page 112.**
Finley Wildlife Refuge, **page 115.**

❰ Hikes for Kids
Willamette Mission State Park, **page 111.**
McDowell Creek Falls, **page 116.**
Cascadia State Park, **page 116.**

❰ Self-Guided Nature Walks
Tryon Creek State Park, **page 110.**
Champoeg State Park, **page 111.**
McDonald Research Forest, **page 114.**

❰ Waterfall Hikes
Silver Falls State Park, **page 112.**

❰ Wheelchair-Accessible Trails
Powell Butte, **page 108.**

Though it's home to the majority of Oregon's

population, the Willamette Valley isn't as dense as you might think. A drive up Highway 99 (East or West; there are two) takes you through pioneer towns, vast tracts of farmland, and into the center of Portland, Oregon's biggest city. But "the Valley," as it's known, is also a gateway to some of the best explorations in the state. State parks of cottonwood-lined riverbanks and stunning waterfalls are within easy distance of most cities, including Salem, Corvallis, and Eugene. In the Willamette Valley, you can climb a butte to get above winter fog, find beaver dams in the numerous wetlands, or go bird-watching in the many wildlife refuges. From Silver Falls to Forest Park to Sauvie Island, city folk – and visitors – have a wealth of hiking options.

Even Portland, smack in the middle of an urban area of more than two million people, has a lot of wilderness to offer. For one, there's Forest Park. At more than 5,000 acres, it is one of the largest urban wilderness parks in North America, and it has nearly 70 miles of trails and gravel roads open to hiking. Scattered throughout the city are a host of parks, many of them threaded with trails. Portland also has a series of trail networks; the 40-mile Springwater Corridor, for instance, offers access to some of the hikes in this book, such as Oaks Bottom Refuge and Powell Butte.

It's easy to see why so many people live here. Yet there is that grey-cloud gloomy idea of Oregon being eternally associated with rain. Don't sweat it; first of all, Western Oregon gets a lot of its precipitation in the form of a light misty rainfall – hardly a torrential downpour. Consider what Oregon would look like without the rain, anyway. It's a small price to pay for such a dense green, one that draws comparison to the fabled fields of Ireland. Still, Oregon isn't exactly all green. Western Oregon sustains a far-more interesting mix of landscapes. Much of the valley floor remains in its natural state as a white-oak savanna, a series of rolling grasslands where deer browse in the foggy mornings. The wetlands regions, though certainly marshy, are entirely open to exploring and are home to myriad native and migrating birds. The buttes and foothills of the Cascade Mountains, remnants of ancient volcanoes, offer rocky terrain and the beginnings of the dense conifer forests for which Oregon is famous.

Though the Willamette Valley is home to the majority of Oregon's population, it is somewhat of a blessing for explorers. For one, you don't have to travel far to access the coast, the Columbia River Gorge, or the Cascade Mountains. Secondly, you don't have to drive for hours and hours to get to the hikes listed in this section. These are fun and easy day trips, great for kids and adults alike.

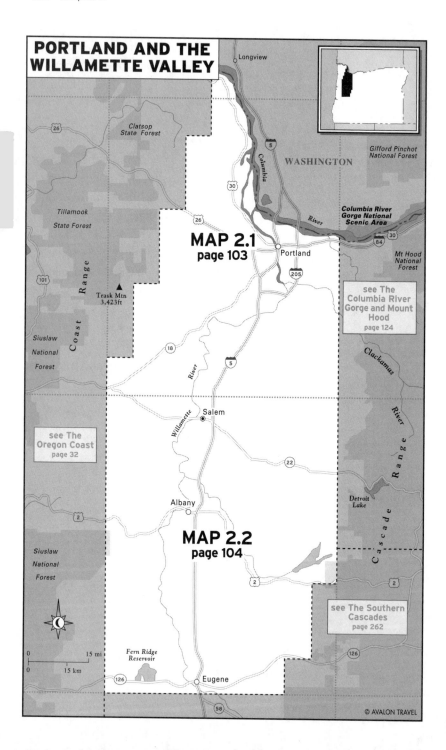

PORTLAND AND THE WILLAMETTE VALLEY

Longview

WASHINGTON

Clatsop State Forest

Gifford Pinchot National Forest

Columbia River Gorge National Scenic Area

Tillamook State Forest

MAP 2.1
page 103

Portland

Mt Hood National Forest

Trask Mtn 3,423ft

see The Columbia River Gorge and Mount Hood
page 124

Siuslaw National Forest

River

Clackamas River

Coast Range

Willamette

Salem

see The Oregon Coast
page 32

Detroit Lake

Albany

MAP 2.2
page 104

Cascade Range

Siuslaw National Forest

see The Southern Cascades
page 262

Fern Ridge Reservoir

0   15 mi
0   15 km

Eugene

© AVALON TRAVEL

Map 2.1

Hikes 1-11
Pages 105-112

2.2

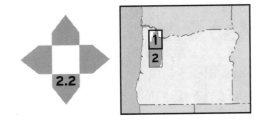

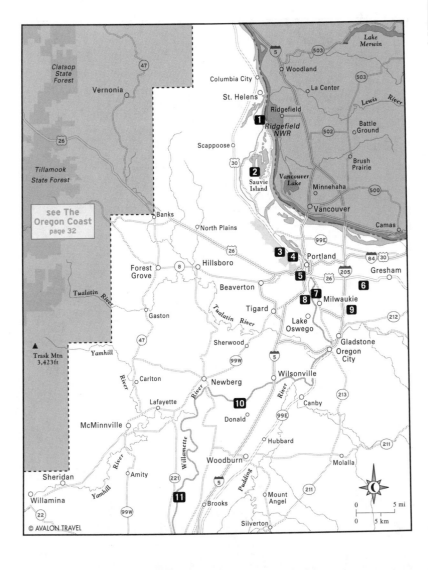

Map 2.2

Hikes 12-25
Pages 112-120

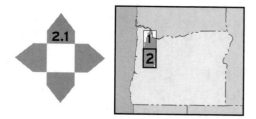

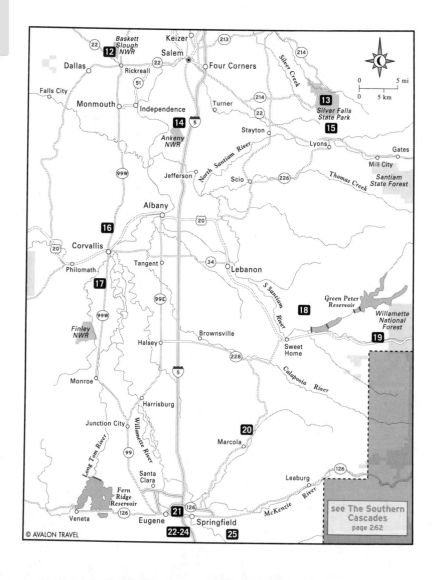

1 WARRIOR ROCK

7.0 mi/3.5 hr　　　　🚶2 ⛰6

on Sauvie Island, northwest of Portland

Map 2.1, page 103

Sauvie Island is Oregon's largest island. Once the home of the Multnomah tribe (who fed Lewis and Clark as the intrepid explorers threaded their way across the continent), in the 1830s it became a giant dairy farm for nearby Fort Vancouver. Though most of it remains farmed land, the island hosts a Wildlife Refuge with an impressive array of birds. The trail to a small lighthouse on Warrior Rock is a great place to start. You'll see some of the classic riverside ecology, with its cottonwoods towering overhead and wild Nootka rosebushes below. Warrior Rock Trail follows the Columbia River right out to the tip of the island, where a lighthouse, originally built in 1889 but replaced by the U.S. Coast Guard, watches over one of the largest rivers in the Western United States.

The unmarked Warrior Rock Trail starts at the edge of the parking lot and follows the massive Columbia River, passing through forests of cottonwoods for three miles, reaching the tip of the island where the white lighthouse perches on solid sandstone. Past the lighthouse, go a half-mile farther up the beach to a view of the town of St. Helens, or just sit and watch the enormous ships passing slowly on the immense river. Watch, too, for the bald eagles that make this island their home.

User Groups: Hikers and dogs on leash. No wheelchair facilities.

Permits: A daily use permit is $3.50 (or $11 a year) and is available from Oregon Department of Fish and Wildlife in Portland or Sam's Grocery on Sauvie Island Road.

Maps: For a topographic map, ask the USGS for St. Helens.

Directions: From downtown Portland, go north on U.S. 30 toward St. Helens. After about 10 miles, turn right across the Sauvie Island Bridge and continue north on Sauvie Island Road. Drive 1.8 miles past the store on Sauvie Island Road and turn right on Ree Road, following this road 12.6 miles to its end at a parking area.

Contact: Oregon Department of Fish and Wildlife/Sauvie Island Wildlife Area, 503/621-3488, www.dfw.state.or.us/resources/visitors/sauvie_island_wildlife_area.asp.

2 OAK ISLAND

2.9 mi/1.5 hr　　　　🚶1 ⛰6

on Sauvie Island, northwest of Portland

Map 2.1, page 103　　　　**BEST (**

If it's possible to imagine an island within an island, then you'll have a fair picture of Oak Island. It's not exactly an "island," but it comes close. Surrounded on three sides by water from Sturgeon Lake, Steelman Lake, the Narrows, and Wagonwheel Hole, it is technically a peninsula, but you'll feel as if you're on an island. This loop circles a dense cottonwood and white oak forest and crosses open fields with views to the timbered ridge above the distant Multnomah Channel and an expansive sky. The best time to come, undoubtedly, is during bird migrations: This is one of the best places to see the spectacular sandhill cranes as they pass through. The trail is only open April 16 through September 30 to protect wildlife. Be sure to watch for bald eagles and explore the edges of an abandoned farm, hemmed in by walls of blackberry brambles.

Starting at the parking lot, cross the gate and go straight on the abandoned road for 0.3 mile to begin the Oak Island Nature Trail. At a junction, go to the left to begin the loop. For 1.1 miles, the trail crosses some woods and enters the vast fields, curving at the Narrows with an occasional side trail to the water. The returning 0.9 mile looks out over Sturgeon Lake toward the Cascade peaks. At a bench, continue to the right on the loop 0.3 mile back to the initial trail, going left to your car.

User Groups: Hikers and dogs on leash. No wheelchair facilities.

Permits: A daily use permit is $3.50 (or $11

from Oregon Depart-
...fe in Portland or Sam's
...nd Road.

...hic map, ask the USGS

Directions: From downtown Portland, go north on U.S. 30 toward St. Helens. After about 10 miles, turn right across the Sauvie Island Bridge and continue north on Sauvie Island Road. Drive 1.8 miles past the store on Sauvie Island Road and turn right on Reeder Road, following this road 1.2 miles. Turn left on Oak Island Road, crossing a dike after 2.7 miles. Continue straight for 0.4 mile to a parking area.

Contact: Oregon Department of Fish and Wildlife/Sauvie Island Wildlife Area, 503/621-3488, www.dfw.state.or.us/resources/visitors/sauvie_island_wildlife_area.asp.

🛈 WILDWOOD TRAIL

30.2 mi one-way/2 days 3 6

in Portland's Washington and Forest Parks

Map 2.1, page 103

If not for the vision of some early Portland residents, the 5,000-acre Forest Park never would have existed. You'll thank them: In a city as large and bustling as Portland, Oregon, it's hard to imagine that such easy, natural respite lies so close at hand. The Wildwood Trail, which spans Forest Park, crosses through a number of city parks, following the long forested ridge of the Tualatin Hills with a variety of side trails branching off the Wildwood Trail, not to mention the gravel Leif Erickson Road, making for nearly 70 miles in all. Here in the hills above the Willamette River and its sprawling industrial area, stands of Western maple, Douglas fir, and even wild cherry trees colonize the steep hills and wide ravines, making it a refuge for deer and birds, as well as wildflowers like the big-leafed trillium. Any time of day or on any day of the week, you're sure to find people on the trail; in order to limit some of the traffic, bikes are not allowed on footpaths (except the old Leif Erickson Road).

There are scores of possibilities for short and long day trips, and numerous access points. Depending on the season, there is ample opportunity to listen to bubbling creeks and songbirds, and to keep count of the many native flowers that bloom here. Trails weave along the steep ridges of Douglas fir and bigleaf maples. The trail officially begins in Washington Park, circling the Vietnam Veterans Memorial before launching into the Hoyt Arboretum. Once it crosses Burnside Road, passing the Pittock Mansion and an Audubon center, the trail enters the forest, continuing all the way to the northern edge of the city.

User Groups: Hikers and dogs only. No horses. Mountain bikes allowed on Leif Erickson Road only. No wheelchair facilities.

Permits: Permits are not required. Parking and access are free.

Maps: For a free trail map contact Portland Parks and Recreation, 503/823-PLAY (503/823-7529). For a topographic map, ask the USGS for Portland and Linnton.

Directions: There are a number of points of access to the Wildwood Trail. To reach the southernmost trailhead from downtown Portland, head west on U.S. 26 to Exit 72/Canyon Road. Drive past the Oregon Zoo and the World Forestry Center to a lot near the Vietnam Veterans Memorial. The trail begins to the right of the Memorial. To reach the northern trailhead, drive north on U.S. 30 to Germantown Road. Drive up the hill to a clearly marked parking area on the left.

Contact: Portland Parks and Recreation, 1120 SW 5th Avenue, Suite 1302, Portland, OR, 97204, 503/823-PLAY (503/823-7529).

4 MACLEAY PARK
5.5 mi/2.5 hr   🧍1 ⛰6

in Northwest Portland

Map 2.1, page 103

If you feel like showing off Portland, bring friends here to the Lower Macleay Trail. As soon as you enter the little canyon of Balch Creek, named for an early settler hanged for murder (the first man legally hanged in Oregon, by the way), you'll quickly understand why Portland is one of the premier "livable" cities in the country. The land for the park was bought by a wealthy Portland merchant named Donald Macleay, who donated it to the city. Generations later, the creek still resounds with the calls of wrens and the wind through the trees. The Wildwood Trail passes over the Lower Macleay Trail, which opens up possibilities to hike as far out as you'd like (see *Wildwood Trail,* previous listing).

Follow the paved path up the creek, which turns into a dirt trail after a viewpoint. Watch for the little sign that designates one of Portland's Heritage Trees: an enormous Douglas fir near the stream. At the intersection with the Wildwood Trail lies an old stone hut, the ruin of an old Works Project Administration effort, which makes a great playhouse for kids. Continue along the creek to a crossing, a good turnaround point for a 1.75-mile hike. Feel like more? Continue uphill to the left and stay on the Wildwood Trail, crossing Cornell Road, and up to the historic Pittock Mansion, which has an amazing view of Portland and the Cascades. When you're ready to head back, and if you're in the mood for a loop, start back down on the Wildwood Trail and take a left on the Upper Macleay Trail, strolling through the woods until it rejoins the Wildwood Trail, returning you to Balch Creek.

User Groups: Hikers and dogs only. Paved path is wheelchair accessible.

Permits: Permits are not required. Parking and access are free.

Maps: For a free trail map contact Portland Parks and Recreation, 503/823-PLAY (503/823-7529). For a topographic map, ask the USGS for Portland and Linnton.

Directions: From downtown Portland, go north on NW 23rd Street to NW Thurman Street. Go left on Thurman and continue to NW 28th, going right. Take the next left on NW Upshur and continue to the small parking area at the end. The trail begins at the lot.

Contact: Portland Parks and Recreation, 1120 SW 5th Avenue, Suite 1302, Portland, OR, 97204, 503/823-PLAY (503/823-7529).

5 COUNCIL CREST VIA MARQUAM GULCH
3.8 mi/2.0 hr   🧍2 ⛰6

south of downtown Portland in Marquam Nature Park

Map 2.1, page 103

Just across a busy freeway from downtown Portland lies the Marquam Nature Park. This network of forested trails climbs a canyon that runs like a cleft between neighborhoods of houses on stilts, rising to a crescendo to Council Crest, with its commanding view of the Cascade Range. From up here, you'd never know that Council Crest was once the site of an amusement park. Now it offers quiet benches and a chance to look over the city of Portland and the Willamette River. It also offers a steady climb, as well as a loop option to further explore this oasis in the midst of a city.

From the lot, follow the right-hand Sunnyside Trail for 0.4 mile up the gulch to an intersection and go right, staying on Sunnyside. From here the trail begins to climb in earnest, crossing several streets along the way. After 1.3 miles, the trail emerges from the woods into the open-air Council Crest Park. The hilltop viewpoint points out views to Mount Rainier, Mount St. Helens, Mount Adams, and Mount Hood. After soaking up the panorama, follow the trail back down 1.3 miles to the junction. From here, instead of returning on the trail you started on, go right for a 0.8-mile diversion on the Marquam Gulch Trail and Goldy Corridor Trail to complete the loop back to the lot, staying left at all junctions.

User Groups: Hikers and dogs only. The overlook at Council Crest is wheelchair accessible, but the trail from the Nature Park is not.

Permits: Permits are not required. Parking and access are free.

Maps: Maps are available at the trailhead. Parking and access are free.

Directions: From downtown Portland, go south on SW 6th Avenue, crossing the I-405 freeway. Follow blue "Hospital" signs for Oregon Health and Sciences University (OHSU) onto Terwilliger Avenue. At the intersection of Terwilliger and Sam Jackson Road, go straight on Sam Jackson. At the next bend in the road, immediately turn right into the parking area.

Contact: Portland Parks and Recreation, 1120 SW 5th Avenue, Suite 1302, Portland, OR, 97204, 503/823-PLAY (503/823-7529).

⑥ POWELL BUTTE
3.1 mi/1.5 hr   🥾2 ⛰7

in Southeast Portland in Powell Butte Nature Park

Map 2.1, page 103	BEST (

Rising above Johnson Creek, this volcanic remnant of an ancient past offers an open meadow at its summit with views to Mount Hood and two other Cascade peaks. Perfect all year long, this loop trail wanders through the open meadows and explores the Douglas fir and red cedar slopes along its flanks. Pileated woodpeckers, deer, and, surprisingly, coyotes are all possibilities for wildlife-spotting here. The peak is the site of an old orchard, and the spiny shrubs around the meadows are hawthorn trees. Both the Mount Hood Trail and the Pioneer Orchard Trail connect to the Springwater Corridor, a marvelous 40-mile loop around the east side of Portland.

Beginning from the lot, follow the paved Mountain View Trail through fields of hawthorn and clover 0.6-mile to the walnut orchard at the summit—a good place for a picnic. Go left on the Orchard Trail Loop, following the loop around the orchard to an astonishing view of Mount Hood and waves of volcanic buttes. Staying to the right at all junctions, circle 0.8 mile almost entirely around back to the Mountain View Trail, but instead turn left on the Mount Hood Trail, diving 0.5 mile into the forest. Cross a creek and go right on the Cedar Grove Trail, staying on it for 0.3 mile, and continuing 0.3 mile on the Cougar Trail. This trail intersects with the Meadowland Trail, which you can take to the left to find the Service Road Trail, going right for 0.6 mile back to your car. Trails radiate out on Powell Butte, so feel free to explore further.

User Groups: Hikers and dogs. Horses and bicycles on designated trails only. Part of the Mountain View Trail is paved and wheelchair accessible.

Permits: No permits are required. Parking and access are free.

Maps: A brochure map is available at the trailhead. For a topographic map, ask the USGS for Gladstone.

Directions: From I-205, take Exit 19 and follow Powell Boulevard east for 3.5 miles. Turn right on 162nd Avenue, driving up to road's end at the parking lot.

Contact: Portland Parks and Recreation, 1120 SW 5th Avenue, Suite 1302, Portland, OR, 97204, 503/823-PLAY (503/823-7529).

⑦ OAKS BOTTOM
2.8 mi/1.5 hr   🥾1 ⛰5

in Southeast Portland in Oaks Bottom Wildlife Refuge

Map 2.1, page 103	BEST (

Nestled between the Willamette River, an amusement park, a mausoleum, and a neighborhood set atop 100-foot cliffs lies Portland's first urban wildlife refuge. If that isn't strange enough, consider the birds one can spot here: bald eagles high in the cottonwoods, great blue

© SEAN PATRICK HILL

view of Mount Hood, Powell Butte Nature Park in Southeast Portland

herons wading in a marsh, numerous geese and ducks, and an assortment of songbirds both year-round and migratory. This easy trail circles a large seasonal lake that shrinks and swells with the rainfall and goes purple with loosestrife (an invasive species) in the summer. An easy loop follows a channel of the Willamette River as it circles a branching island where fish-hunting osprey nest.

From the main Oaks Bottom parking area, a paved trail painted with icons of local animals descends 0.3 mile to a junction. Follow the paved path to the right 0.1 mile to an underpass ducking beneath a set of railroad tracks. From here, follow an excellent bike path to the left, part of the Springwater Corridor. For 0.8 mile, watch to the right for the cottonwood-lined shores of the Willamette, including views to East and Ross Islands, where birds of prey nest. To the left, you'll see the massive lake where waterfowl wade and dive year-round. At the second overpass, duck again beneath the tracks and follow a dirt path along the lake, where you'll disappear into the wooded shoreline. With a good field guide and a pair of binoculars, this trip can be particularly rewarding for spotting wildlife.

User Groups: Hikers. Dogs permitted on leash only. Bikes allowed on paved paths only. Paved paths are wheelchair accessible.

Permits: Permits are not required. Parking and access are free.

Maps: A brochure and map are available at the trailhead. For a topographic map, ask the USGS for Lake Oswego.

Directions: From the east end of the Ross Island Bridge (Highway 26) take the exit for McLaughlin Blvd/Highway 99 E. In one mile, take the exit for Milwaukie Avenue, turn right at the stop sign, and immediately turn right into a parking area for Oaks Bottom Wildlife Refuge.

Contact: Portland Parks and Recreation, 1120 SW 5th Avenue, Suite 1302, Portland, OR, 97204, 503/823-PLAY (503/823-7529).

CREEK STATE PARK

🚶2 ⛰8

in Southwest Portland

Map 2.1, page 103   **BEST (**

Cradled between the cities of Portland and Lake Oswego, this urban state park represents a quiet wilderness. Open all year, the park offers a bit of every season from wildflowers in spring to snow blankets in winter. For an easy introduction to glassy Tryon Creek, start at the nature center, where you can pick up a map. You'll need it: This state park is a weave of wonderful trails fanning out into the forested canyon. The handy map leads you through the many varieties of trees, wildflowers, and birds that are found in the park, and the nature center gives a good introduction to the ecology of the area. The centerpiece, of course, is Tryon Creek, which flows softly through this forest preserve.

Beginning at the nature center, turn right along the paved Old Main Trail 0.3 mile to the Red Fox Trail, which continues 0.2 mile to the Red Fox Bridge. After crossing the bridge, take a 0.3-mile detour to the Iron Mountain Bridge and back—it's worth it just to see this gulch. Then go back and continue left up the Cedar Trail to tour a side canyon for 0.9 mile to another intersection with a bridge. Don't be confused by the horse trails; instead, head left to the High Bridge. Linger a moment on the bridge, then follow signs to the right to the nature center for the 0.6-mile return. Once you get this loop down, you can begin to fan out on the network of trails linking the quiet neighborhoods surrounding the park.

User Groups: Hikers and dogs on six-foot or shorter leashes. Horses allowed only on designated equestrian trails. Bicycles allowed only on designated bike trail. The 0.35-mile Trillium Trail is paved and wheelchair accessible.

Permits: Permits are not required. Parking and access are free.

Maps: For a free park brochure, call Oregon Parks and Recreation, 800/551-6949, or download a free map at www.oregonstateparks.org.

For a topographic map, ask the USGS for Lake Oswego.

Directions: From I-5, take the Terwilliger Exit 297, driving south on Terwilliger Boulevard following Tryon Creek State Park signs. After 2.2 miles, turn right onto the entrance road and park at the end of the loop road.

Contact: Tryon Creek State Park, 11321 SW Terwilliger Blvd., Portland OR, 97219, 503/636-9886, or Oregon Parks and Recreation Department, 1115 Commercial Street NE, Salem, OR, 97301, 800/551-6949, www.oregonstateparks.org.

🔟 MOUNT TALBERT

4.2 mi/2.0 hr

in Clackamas in Mount Talbert Natural Area

Map 2.1, page 103

Within earshot of I-205, and entirely surrounded by new housing and apartment complexes, the 144-acre Mount Talbert Natural Area is a 750-foot green island in an urban sea. It is preserved as such by Metro, whose mission is to preserve jewels like this for future generations. With its Douglas fir and sword ferns, it looks like anywhere you can find in the mountain ranges of Oregon. Its stands of white oaks are home to the white-breasted nuthatch, an increasingly rare bird in this part of the world, but with the right ear you'll hear them easily enough. There are a total of 4.2 miles of trail, so why not do them all? A big signboard at the trailhead clearly labels the trails. A good start is the 2.4-mile Park Loop, which has access trails to the timbered summit.

User Groups: Hikers. Dogs and bikers are not permitted. Paved portions of the park are wheelchair accessible.

Permits: Permits are not required. Parking and access are free.

Maps: A map is available at the trailhead. For a topographic map, ask the USGS for Gladstone.

Directions: From the I-205 in Clackamas, take Exit 14 (Sunnyside Rd./Sunnybrook Blvd.).

Go east on Sunnybrook Boulevard and take a right on SE 97th Avenue, following it one mile (it becomes Mather Road after a curve) to the trailhead lot on the left.

Contact: North Clackamas Parks and Recreation District, 9101 SE Sunnybrook Boulevard, Clackamas, OR, 97015, 503/794-8041.

10 CHAMPOEG STATE PARK
3.2 mi/1.5 hr   🏃🏃1 ⛰6

east of Newberg on the Willamette River

Map 2.1, page 103   **BEST (**

This historic state park (pronounced sham-POO-ey) is the site of an early Oregon town that came to prominence as the home of the first provisional government of the Oregon Country. Founded by 100 white men in 1843, the new town was virtually erased by two floods in 1861 and 1890. The only remaining structure is the 1852 Newell House, situated on high ground. The rest of the town is now a quiet meadow circled by a loop trail, with posts designating the original streets. Try this park for a good dose of early Oregon history, with plenty of markers and signs pointing out what you may find.

Starting from the Riverside Day Use Area, follow signs to the Pavilion, where a monument commemorates the actual site where the 100 men debated. Start the first short loop by walking to the Willamette River and taking a paved 0.5-mile loop through enormous cottonwoods along the high banks of the river. At the end of the loop, continue east along the riverbank past the 1931 log cabin and following the road to the 1.1-mile Champoeg Townsite Trail. From this meadow you'll spot not only the ghost town site but the distant La Butte. The path skims along the Oak Grove Day Use Area and connects with the paved bike path heading right 1.1 mile back to the start of the loop. From there, return the way you came back to Riverside.

User Groups: Hikers and dogs. Bicycles are allowed only on designated bike paths. No horses allowed. Paved portions of the park are wheelchair accessible.

Permits: Permits are not required. A $3 day-use fee is collected at the park entrance, or you can get an annual Oregon Parks and Recreation pass for $25; contact Oregon Parks and Recreation, 800/551-6949.

Maps: For a free park brochure, call Oregon Parks and Recreation, 800/551-6949, or download a free map at www.oregonstateparks.org. For a topographic map, ask the USGS for Newberg.

Directions: From I-5, take Exit 278 to Donald. Turn west, following signs 5.7 miles to the entrance of the Champoeg Heritage Area. Park in the Riverside Day Use Area.

Contact: Oregon Parks and Recreation Department, 1115 Commercial Street NE, Salem, OR, 97301, 800/551-6949, www.oregonstateparks.org.

11 WILLAMETTE MISSION STATE PARK
2.7 mi/1.0 hr   🏃🏃1 ⛰7

north of Salem on the Willamette River

Map 2.1, page 103   **BEST (**

Willamette Mission State Park has plenty to see. It's the site of a historic 1843 Methodist mission, home to the world's largest black cottonwood tree, plus filbert and walnut orchards, and the oldest ferry landing in Oregon, dating back to the 1844 mule-winched log barge. Start with an easy loop around the park's central meadow, hemmed in by Mission Lake—once the original channel of the Willamette River. This hike is great for kids, as most of the paths are easy and paved, and there's ample opportunity for exploration of the riverbank ecosystem.

Beginning in the Filbert Grove Day Use Area, walk 0.2 mile down to the riverbank and turn right on the paved path along the river, heading 1.2 miles to the landing for the Wheatland Ferry, which is free for pedestrians. Heading back to the loop, this time go right to walk along marshy Mission Lake. Here you'll find a monument describing the mission founded in 1834 by Jason Lee. Tired of the floods, he moved on to what is now Salem and founded what is now Willamette University. Follow this trail 0.9 mile to a road and the sign to the 155-foot black cottonwood champion (with a 26-foot circumference). Follow the road back to the Filbert Grove.

User Groups: Hikers, dogs, bikes, and horses. Paved portions of the park are wheelchair accessible.

Permits: Permits are not required. A $3 day-use fee is collected at the park entrance, or you can get an annual Oregon Parks and Recreation pass for $25; contact Oregon Parks and Recreation, 800/551-6949.

Maps: For a free park brochure, call Oregon Parks and Recreation, 800/551-6949, or download a free map at www.oregonstateparks.org. For a topographic map, ask the USGS for Mission Bottom.

Directions: From I-5, take Exit 263 towards Brooks/Gervais. Head west on Brookland Road for 1.7 miles and turn right onto Wheatland Road North for 2.4 miles to the park entrance. Drive to the Filbert Grove Day Use Area.

Contact: Oregon Parks and Recreation Department, 1115 Commercial Street NE, Salem, OR, 97301, 800/551-6949, www.oregonstateparks.org.

12 BASKETT SLOUGH REFUGE
4.7 mi/2.5 hr   🥾1 ⛰6

east of Salem

Map 2.2, page 104	BEST

Each autumn, migrating dusky Canada geese use the Willamette Valley as a winter stomping ground from their yearly passage from Alaska. The Baskett Slough Refuge is the perfect destination if you've ever wanted to hear the sound of 20,000 geese honking and taking off in a flurry. You're likely to see and hear quite a few other birds, too, including swans, buffleheads,

and redwing blackbirds. Though part of the refuge around Morgan Lake is closed between October 1 and March 31 to protect these birds, the Baskett Butte hike is open all year.

From a parking area at the southern edge of the refuge, head in for an easy 1.5-mile loop up the butte. Go straight on the wide grassy path for 0.5 mile and then left at the junction up grass-topped Baskett Butte for a view over the Willamette Valley and out to the Coast Range. If the refuge is open, you can continue straight into the refuge through a white oak forest another 0.4 mile to a junction and an old barn colonized by darting swallows. Going right takes you to the shores of Morgan Lake, a 1.4-mile walk to a gate, where you can return via an old road for another mile back to the barn, passing a small pond of cattails and the nutria, a beaver-like rodent found throughout the Willamette Valley.

User Groups: Hikers only. Dogs are not permitted. No wheelchair facilities.

Permits: Permits are not required. Parking and access are free.

Maps: A downloadable map is available online at www.fws.gov/willamettevalley/baskett. For a topographic map, ask the USGS for Dallas.

Directions: From Salem, follow Highway 22 to Rickreall, turn north on U.S. 99 West for 1.8 miles, and turn left on gravel Colville Road 1.4 miles to the trailhead lot on the right.

Contact: U.S. Fish and Wildlife Service, Baskett Slough National Wildlife Refuge, 10995 Hwy. 22, Dallas, OR, 97338, 503/623-2749.

13 SILVER FALLS STATE PARK
7.1 mi/3.5 hr   🥾3 ⛰8

east of Salem

Map 2.2, page 104	BEST

There are many fine state parks in Oregon, and Silver Falls State Park is in the upper echelon. A rugged river canyon trail passes 10 waterfalls, half of them over 100 feet high;

© SEAN PATRICK HILL

Middle North Falls in Silver Falls State Park

it's one of the best hikes in the state. Though winter can be harsh here, closing and washing out trails, the park is open year-round. Starting from the South Falls parking area and the historic lodge built in 1940 by the Civilian Conservation Corps, head to the paved viewpoint of 177-foot South Falls and continue down the paved Canyon Trail into the canyon. What you'll see is the effect of erosion on soft ground beneath 15-million-year-old basalt, the remnants of a massive lava flow. This is why the falls go over such an overhanging lip. You'll get to see this close-up, seeing as the trail goes behind the falls.

After 0.3 mile, the trail reaches its first junction; stay left on the Canyon Trail, which turns to dirt. Continue on to the first junction past Lower South Falls, a total of 1.5 miles so far. From here, you could go right and ascend out of the canyon on the Ridge Trail another 1.3 miles to return to the lot.

Not quite ready? Then continue on 1.6 miles to viewpoints of Lower North, Double, Drake,

and Middle North Falls. At the 3.2-mile mark, a second cutoff trail to the right leads to a viewpoint of Winter Falls. Continue upstream on the Canyon Trail for some of the best falls, where another 1.5 miles will lead you to Twin Falls and finally to the grand North Falls, which you'll walk behind to continue. If you made it this far, then you may as well take the left-hand junction, which crosses under the road and brings you in only 0.2 mile to Upper North Falls. To complete the loop, head back toward North Falls and stay left this time on the Rim Trail. The remaining 2.5 miles on this trail passes through quiet woods and more views of the spectacular waterfalls before returning to South Falls.

User Groups: Hikers only. No dogs allowed on canyon trails. Paved portions of the park are wheelchair accessible.

Permits: Permits are not required. A $3 day-use fee is collected at the park entrance, or you can get an annual Oregon Parks and Recreation pass for $25; contact Oregon Parks and Recreation, 800/551-6949.

Maps: For a free park brochure, call Oregon Parks and Recreation, 800/551-6949, or download a free map at www.oregonstateparks.org. For a topographic map, ask the USGS for Drake Crossing.

Directions: From I-5, take Salem Exit 253 and drive 10 miles east on OR 22 to Highway 214. Turn left and drive 16 miles to the park entrance, following signs towards South Falls and Parking Area C.

Contact: Oregon Parks and Recreation Department, 1115 Commercial Street NE, Salem, OR, 97301, 800/551-6949, www.oregonstateparks.org.

🔟 ANKENY WILDLIFE REFUGE
2.2 mi/1.0 hr　　🏃1　⛰5

south of Salem

Map 2.2, page 104

One of three large tracts of land in the Willamette Valley set aside as winter habitat for dusky Canada geese, the Ankeny Wildlife

Refuge provides the opportunity to get up close and personal with wild birds using two blinds—of course, a pair of binoculars couldn't hurt, either. Unlike the Baskett Slough trails, this refuge is open all year long. Bird-watching peaks during two migrations in April and September, but the lush network of ponds and marshes provides opportunities to spot a variety of birds any time.

From the Rail Trail lot—named after a type of bird, not a guardrail or the like—head south 0.2 mile, then turn right along a 0.6-mile boardwalk through a boggy maple forest. About halfway out, a spur trail to the right leads to a blind over Wood Duck Pond. At the end of the boardwalk, and if it's dry, go right for 0.9 mile to the sound of bullfrogs and redwing blackbirds to a junction, returning 0.7 mile through the geese's wintering ground along an old road. There are other side trails to explore, including a mile-long dike trail and a half-mile Forest Trail loop, and across Wintel Road is another bird blind to spot pintails and egrets.

User Groups: Hikers only. Dogs and bicycles not allowed. No wheelchair facilities.

Permits: Permits are not required. Parking and access are free.

Maps: A map is available at the trailhead. For a topographic map, ask the USGS for Sidney.

Directions: From Salem, drive 10 miles south on I-5 to Talbot Exit 242, and go west on Talbot Road for 0.4 mile, turning right on Jorgensen Road for 0.6 mile, and then left on Wintel Road for 1.2 miles. Turn left at a sign for "Rail Trail Boardwalk."

Contact: U.S. Fish and Wildlife Service, Ankeny National Wildlife Refuge, 2301 Wintel Road, Jefferson, OR, 97352, 503/588-2701.

15 SHELLBURG FALLS
4.8 mi/2.0 hr   👣1   ⛰7

east of Salem in the Santiam State Forest

Map 2.2, page 104.

Located just outside the more famous Silver Falls State Park, this jewel of a waterfall is

practically unknown. Amid stalks of foxglove and sword ferns, the Shellburg Falls Trail begins on a 1.3-mile road that crosses private land, so stay on the path. You'll cross meadows and woods before crossing Shellburg Creek on a concrete bridge over Lower Shellburg Falls, a 40-foot plummet into a green canyon. Climb the steps to the left and you'll reach Shellburg Falls in about 0.2 mile and pass behind the 100-foot cascades; there's even a bench to sit on. Continue on, switchbacking up a staircase and crossing the creek on the remaining 0.6 mile of this trail, which ends at an upper trailhead and campground. Follow the gravel road to the right, staying to the right at another junction, for a 2.3-mile descent on the August Mountain Trail to the car. Where the road turns sharply right, a 0.2-mile side trail leads to a scramble down to a viewpoint of Stassel Falls and a 200-foot deep canyon. But go no farther: This waterfall is on private land.

User Groups: Hikers and dogs only. No wheelchair facilities.

Permits: Permits are not required. Parking and access are free.

Maps: For a topographic map, ask the USGS for Lyons.

Directions: From I-5, take Salem Exit 253 and go east on OR 22. After 22.4 miles, turn left at the flashing yellow light in Mehama and follow the Fern Ridge Road 1.3 miles and take a sharp turn uphill to a locked yellow gate. The trail begins here.

Contact: Santiam State Forest, 22965 North Fork Road SE, Lyons, OR, 97358, 503/859-4344.

16 MCDONALD RESEARCH FOREST
4.8 mi/2.0 hr   👣1   ⛰7

north of Corvallis off Highway 99 West

Map 2.2, page 104   **BEST (**

There's plenty learn in this 11-square-mile research forest managed by Oregon State University. Six self-guiding nature walks overlap and mingle between th~~e~~ ...oretum and the McDonald Forest..... a lake and an old-growth forest. The:.... en a viewpoint of the Willamette Valley. If you need a place to take the kids for an educational adventure, this is it.

From the trailhead for the Forest Discovery Trail, start into the maple and fir forest. To access the popular Section 36 Loop, take the right-hand fork at the first junction, leaving the Forest Discovery Trail; follow this trail about 0.5 mile, crossing a road and passing several other trails until you arrive at the loop. Take a quick detour to the right and get a trail brochure at the Forestry Club Cabin, then head back the way you came. You'll pass through an experimental ponderosa pine forest before coming to a junction with the Powder House Trail after 1.2 miles. Climb 0.4 mile to the left to reach the 1,285-foot viewpoint across the Willamette Valley to Mount Hood, Mount Jefferson, and the Three Sisters. The trail descends 1.1 mile from here, crossing three gravel roads, passing a dynamite cap storage shed, and finally entering a forest of true old-growth Douglas fir. In another mile you'll reach Cronemiller Lake—the site of an annual logrolling competition. At the far end of the lake, watch for signs for the Forestry Club Cabin to complete the loop.

User Groups: Hikers, dogs, mountain bikes, and horses. (Section 36 Loop/Powder House Trail is for hikers only.) No wheelchair facilities.

Permits: Permits are not required. Parking and access are free.

Maps: A trail map is available at local outdoors vendors like the Oregon State University bookstore in Corvallis. A brochure is available at the Peavy Arboretum offices in the forest, or online at www.cof.orst.edu. For a topographic map, ask the USGS for Airlie South.

Directions: From Corvallis, drive north on Highway 99W for five miles and turn left onto Arboretum Road to the park entrance. Park at the day-use parking area.

Contact: Oregon State University, College of Forestry, 8692 Peavy Arboretum Road, Corvallis, OR, 97330, 541/737-2004, www.cof.orts.edu.

🔟🔟 FINLEY WILDLIFE REFUGE
6.1 mi/3.0 hr 👣1 ⛰6

south of Corvallis

Map 2.2, page 104 **BEST (**

This eight-square-mile former farm was purchased in the 1960s by the U.S. Fish and Wildlife Service to protect wintering grounds for the dusky Canada goose. With its mix of ponds, meadow, and woods, it is both bird and hiker friendly. If you come, why not try all the trails? They're easy, and you could very well see some extraordinary birds. The 1.2-mile Woodpecker Loop crosses a field of wild roses and blackberry to an observation deck with views to Mount Jefferson and the Three Sisters. The next loop starts out from the Finley Refuge Road, passing a lake teeming with birds in season. Follow Mill Hill Loop signs, heading in 0.3 mile to a gravel road, turning right for another 0.2 mile to a junction at a curve. To the right, a 1.9-mile trail circles Mill Hill and follows Gray Creek. At the end of the loop, another loop continues on, though it is closed November 1 to April 30 to protect geese. If it's open, go right 0.4 mile to another junction, then take a right on a 1.2-mile trail past Beaver Pond (which has no beavers, unfortunately) and a cattail swamp back to the road. Turn right for 0.3 mile, then go left on a trail for another 0.3 mile, and finally follow the road back to your car for another 0.3 mile. As long as you're here, head up the road to see the 1855 Fiechter House, a Greek Revival clapboard farmhouse paid for with California Gold Rush money.

User Groups: Hikers only. No wheelchair facilities.

Permits: Permits are not required. Parking and access are free.

Maps: For a topographic map, ask the USGS for Greenberry.

Directions: Drive south of Corvallis 10 miles on Highway 99W to a Finley Refuge sign at milepost 93. Turn west on gravel Bellfountain Road for 0.7 mile, then left on Finley Refuge Road for 1.5 miles to the Fiechter House. Two trailheads are along Finley Refuge Road.

Contact: U.S. Fish and Wildlife Service, Finley National Wildlife Refuge, 26208 Finley Refuge Road, Corvallis, OR, 97333, 541/757-7236.

18 MCDOWELL CREEK FALLS
1.7 mi/0.75 hr   🏃1 ⛰7

east of Lebanon

Map 2.2, page 104	BEST (

Hidden back in the Cascade foothills, this lovely glen with three waterfalls makes a perfect stop on a journey into the Cascades, or a destination unto itself, especially when the mountains are snowed in for winter. This tour of the Cascade foothills makes an ideal hike for kids: It's easy, short, and fascinating.

From the lower lot, this loop traverses up McDowell Creek amid bunches of sword fern, white trilliums, bleeding hearts, and the yellow blooms of Oregon grape, the state flower. In 0.2 mile you'll spot three-tiered Royal Terrace Falls; at 119 feet, it's the largest of the cascades here. Another 0.6 mile crosses under the highway and passes the 20-foot cascade into Crystal Pool before arriving at 39-foot Majestic Falls, a great place to pick your way across the stones to the base of the falls—but beware of wet, slippery rocks. A stairway takes you to a viewpoint at the top, and another stairway to the upper lot. To make a loop of this hike, head to the lot, then follow the road down about 200 yards and take the left-hand paved road 0.2 mile. Opposite the park entrance sign, keep an eye out for the path that descends 0.4 mile back to Royal Terrace Falls.

User Groups: Hikers and dogs. No wheelchair facilities.

Permits: Permits are not required. Parking and access are free.

Maps: For a topographic map, ask the USGS for Sweet Home.

Directions: From Lebanon, go 4.5 miles east on U.S. 20, turning left on Fairview Road for two miles. Watch for signs to McDowell Creek Park, and turn on McDowell Creek Road, going seven miles to the park.

Contact: Linn County Parks and Recreation, 3010 SW Ferry St., Albany, OR, 97322, 541/967-3917.

19 CASCADIA STATE PARK
2.6 mi/1.0 hr   🏃1 ⛰7

east of Sweet Home on the South Santiam River

Map 2.2, page 104	BEST (

Say you're traveling from the Willamette Valley to the Santiam Pass. Consider how long this route, now Highway 20, has been used by people doing exactly as you have done, from the Native Americans to early pioneers. All of them stopped here, at what is now Cascadia State Park. Excavations have shown that nearby Cascadia Cave (on private land) was used by Native Americans. The highway was once a for-profit wagon road between Albany and Sisters. In 1895, George and Jennie Geisendorfer bought this land, with its natural mineral springs and waterfalls, and built a resort with a hotel, store, cabins, a bathhouse, and campgrounds. When they sold it to the state, it became Cascadia State Park. Though the buildings are gone, the mineral springs and waterfall remains, and several easy loops explore Soda Creek, the springs, and the shore of the South Santiam.

For the first easy hike to see the springs, take the Soda Spring Trail from the parking lot down a paved path 100 yards to an open pipe where you'll see the bubbling iron-laden orange water. Following the paved path and keeping right at all junctions for 200 yards will bring you to the gravel beach on the river. From the restroom in the East Picnic Area, an old road becomes a bark-dust trail, making an easy 0.6 mile-loop. To hike to Lower Soda Falls, head toward the road to the East Picnic Area. The broad trail heads off to the left, following Soda Creek 0.7 mile to the falls.

User Groups: Hikers and dogs. Paved paths are wheelchair accessible.

Permits: Permits are not required. Parking and access are free.

Maps: For a free park brochure, call Oregon Parks and Recreation, 800/551-6949, or download a free map at www.oregonstateparks. org. For a topographic map, ask the USGS for Cascadia.

Directions: From Sweet Home go east on U.S. 20 for 14 miles. At a State Park sign between mileposts 41 and 42, turn left over a bridge and follow the road to a parking lot on the left.

Contact: Oregon Parks and Recreation Department, 1115 Commercial Street NE, Salem, OR, 97301, 800/551-6949, www.oregonstateparks.org.

20 SHOTGUN CREEK PARK
3.4 mi/1.5 hr   🏃1 ⛰6

north of Springfield in Shotgun Creek Recreation Site

> **Map 2.2, page 104**

Legend has it that sometime in the 1800s, a young man left his shotgun here. He came back to get it, and named the creek Shotgun. A simple story, unlike the one involving the two engineers and the Hellsgate Construction company, who took two years to build this park—and even then they ran out of the resources to complete it. Nonetheless, the park offers a couple of easy hikes and a great place to swim under moss-draped bigleaf maples. It's usually open from early June through the end of September.

From the trailhead parking area, head toward the creek on a paved path, passing a picnic shelter. Turn onto the loop following Shotgun Creek upstream. Eventually, the trail heads up into second-growth woods, and

begins to loop back. At the 2.1-mile mark, a right turn leads 0.3 mile back to the lot, but you can continue on for a longer loop. If you do, another 0.6 mile brings you to a junction. The trail to the left climbs 1.2 miles up Drury Ridge, and going right brings you back 0.7 mile to the creek and picnic grounds.

User Groups: Hikers and dogs. Paved paths are wheelchair accessible.

Permits: Permits are not required. From June through September, a $3 parking fee is collected at the entrance.

Maps: For a topographic map, ask the USGS for Marcola.

Directions: From Springfield, take Exit 194 off I-5 and drive four miles east on I-105 to the 42nd Street/Marcola exit. Turn left on 42nd Street for 0.6 mile to a junction, turning right on Marcola Road for 13.3 miles. Three miles past the town of Marcola, turn left at a "Shotgun Creek" sign onto Shotgun Creek Road, going 1.6 miles to the park entrance on the right.

Contact: Bureau of Land Management Eugene Office, 2890 Chad Drive, Eugene, OR, 97440, 541/683-6600.

21 RUTH BASCOM RIVERSIDE PATH SYSTEM
1.0-14.0 mi/0.5-7.0 hr   🏃2 ⛰6

in Eugene on the Willamette River

> **Map 2.2, page 104**

This perfectly paved, 14-mile trail system girdles the Willamette River in the city of Eugene. It provides access to many parks—including Alton Baker, Skinner Butte, Maurie Jacobs, and Rasor Parks—and passes the Owen Rose Gardens, the Delta Ponds, and Pre's Trail, where Oregon legend Steve Prefontaine used to practice running. The trail system follows the river up and downstream in the shade of cottonwood trees, where beavers and water birds are active. With so many access points, it's hard to say where to begin, but Alton Baker Park, where Pre's Trail is located, is as good a place as any.

From Alton Baker Park, head to the North Bank path at the DeFazio Pedestrian/Bike Bridge, going right downstream about 1.75 miles to the Greenway Pedestrian/Bike Bridge and crossing the river. On the other side, turn left on the South Bank Trail for a tour of Eugene's wonderful Maurie Jacobs and Skinner Butte Parks, a continuous greenway that features a community garden, the Owen Rose Garden with its 150-year old cherry tree, the towering Skinner Butte, and a bevy of playgrounds and picnic areas. Follow this path back 1.75 miles to the DeFazio Bridge. A longer loop is possible by continuing north past the Greenway Bridge 1.9 miles to the Owosso Bike Bridge, then crossing the river and going left two miles on the West Bank Trail to join the South Bank Trail.

User Groups: Hikers, dogs, and bicycles. Paved portions of the park are wheelchair accessible.

Permits: Permits are not required. Parking and access are free.

Maps: A downloadable map is available from the City of Eugene Willakenzie Parks website, www.eugene-or.gov/portal/server.pt. For a topographic map, ask the USGS for Eugene East.

Directions: From downtown Eugene, drive north over Ferry Street Bridge and turn right on Centennial Boulevard. Turn right at the first light and go a short distance to the large lot at Alton Baker Park.

Contact: City of Eugene Parks, 99 West 10th Avenue, Suite 340, Eugene, OR, 97401, 541/682-5333.

22 MOUNT PISGAH
3.0 mi/1.5 hr

southeast of Eugene in the Howard Buford Recreation Area

Map 2.2, page 104

From the grassy peak of Mount Pisgah, named by pioneers for the biblical hill from which Moses viewed the Promised Land, you'll get

your own grand view. At the peak you'll find a bronze sighting pedestal for the nearby peaks, a memorial to Jed, the son of *One Flew Over the Cuckoo's Nest* author Ken Kesey, who lived in nearby Pleasant Hill. Numbered trails circle this 1,516-foot mound near Eugene and Springfield, and an arboretum at its base lies along the Coast Fork of the Willamette River.

From the visitors center, start uphill at a gate on Trail #1. Without veering from this path, you will arrive at the peak in 1.5 miles. Trails go off in all directions and the possibilities for exploration are numerous.

User Groups: Hikers and dogs. No bikes or horses are allowed.

Permits: Permits are not required. From May through October, a $2 parking fee is collected at the entrance.

Maps: For a free map, contact Lane County Parks, 90064 Coburg Road, Eugene, OR, 97408, 541/682-2000. For a topographic map, ask the USGS for Springfield.

Directions: From the southern end of Eugene, take I-5 south to Exit 189 (30th Street). At the second light, turn left over the freeway, turn left at the next stop sign, and turn right onto Franklin Road. In 0.25 mile, turn left onto Seavey Loop Road. Drive 1.5 miles and turn right at the park entrance. Parking is at the end of the road at the arboretum entrance.

Contact: Lane County Parks, 90064 Coburg Road, Eugene, OR, 97408, 541/682-2000.

23 SPENCER BUTTE
2.0 mi/1.0 hr

south of Eugene in Spencer Butte Park

Map 2.2, page 104

Looming above Eugene is the imposing Spencer Butte, a 2,054-foot knob thick with Douglas fir, ferns, poison oak, and, if one is to believe the signs, rattlesnakes. Nevertheless, there is no better hike in Eugene. A fairly easy hike ascends and descends the rocky knob, but more challenging courses can be arranged

© SEAN PATRICK HILL

peak of Spencer Butte in Eugene

Permits: Permits are not required. Parking and access are free.

Maps: For a topographic map, ask the USGS for Creswell.

Directions: From downtown Eugene, drive five miles south on Willamette Street, going uphill much of the way, and turn left into the parking lot for Spencer Butte Park.

Contact: City of Eugene Parks, 99 West 10th Avenue, Suite 340, Eugene, OR, 97401, 541/682-5333.

24 RIDGELINE NATIONAL RECREATION TRAIL

6.6 mi one-way/3.5 hr 👣1 ⛰7

in the South Hills of Eugene

Map 2.2, page 104

Designated a National Recreation Trail in 2006, Eugene's Ridgeline Trail is a pleasant stroll through patches of Douglas fir woods and out into open grasslands overlooking the city in the valley below. Along the trail, numerous access points offer a variety of options for short or long hikes. At one end lies 1,233-foot Mount Baldy, an easy climb to a view over the city. In the middle, the trail connects to a summit of Spencer Butte (see *Spencer Butte,* previous listing).

off the Ridgeline Trail (see *Ridgeline National Recreation Trail,* next listing) to lengthen your stay on this high, forested ridge. This is the classic hike for Eugenians looking for the perfect sunset and moonrise, with views to the Three Sisters and Fern Ridge Reservoir.

From the main lot, head up the right-hand trail, which begins at a signboard and gently climbs for 0.5 mile to the first junction, a side trail leading to the Ridgeline Trail. Continue to the left; the trail gradually grows steeper as it rises from the woods onto the rocky crest. Watch out for poison oak here! A summit benchmark handily marks the top. For a more challenging hike, start at a gravel lot on Willamette Street just beyond 52nd Street on the left; from here, follow the Ridgeline Trail 1.2 miles to the first junction on the right. Go right 0.5 mile, then right again for the last 0.5-mile climb.

User Groups: Hikers and dogs only, though bikes are allowed on the Ridgeline Trail. No horses.

For an easy excursion in Dillard Skyline Park to Mount Baldy, start from the Dillard North Trailhead off Dillard Road. Climb 0.5 mile to a sweet view of the Willamette Valley. The trail accesses other trailheads and points from along the way. The Fox Hollow Trailhead lies at 0.8 mile, where the path heads to the right along the road before re-entering the forest. At the 1.2-mile mark, after a set of stairs, a left-hand spur connects to the Spencer Butte climbing trail. In another 1.2 miles, the trail crosses Willamette Street and continues 1.5 miles to the 52nd Avenue Trailhead.

User Groups: Hikers and dogs. Bikes on designated paths only.

Permits: Permits are not required. Parking and access are free.

Maps: A downloadable map is available from the City of Eugene Willakenzie Parks website, www.eugene-or.gov/portal/server.pt. For a topographic map, ask the USGS for Creswell.

Directions: From downtown Eugene, drive south on Pearl Street (it becomes Amazon Parkway) to 30th Street and go right on Hilyard Street. At the next light, go left on Amazon Drive East, driving 1.2 miles and turning left on Dillard Road for 1.5 miles to a hiker symbol on the left. To access the western trailhead from downtown Eugene, drive south on Willamette Street to Crest Drive. Go west on Crest Drive 0.6 mile, then left on Storey Boulevard for 0.3 mile, then straight onto Crest Drive for 0.2 mile. Continue onto Blanton Road for 0.5 mile to West 40th Avenue and the trailhead.

Contact: City of Eugene Parks, 99 West 10th Avenue, Suite 340, Eugene, OR, 97401, 541/682-5333.

25 ELIJAH BRISTOW STATE PARK

1.0-10.0 mi/0.5-5.0 hr

southeast of Eugene on Highway 58

Map 2.2, page 104

This state park on the Middle Fork Willamette River is named for Lane County's first settler, Elijah Bristow, who was born in Virginia in 1788 and took up residence in Oregon in 1846 in nearby Pleasant Hill. Here you can hike along a channel lake or slosh your way to Dexter Dam. This park comprises a series of wetlands and so can be quite marshy in winter, but it's nothing a good pair of big boots can't handle. Trekking here, you can see the rare Oregon ash tree (as well as western hemlock, red cedar, Douglas fir, cottonwoods, white oak, and bigleaf maple) and you may even get lucky and spot the threatened Western pond turtle.

For an easy one-mile loop, park on the left before the second bridge about 0.6 mile in from the highway. Follow the Turtle Trail around an ancient channel of the river, keeping right at all junctions. If this gets you warmed up for more, there are plenty of loops and longer hikes available throughout the park, including the 1.5-mile Heron Trail, the two-mile Elk Trail, and the five-mile River Trail.

User Groups: Hikers, dogs, bikes, and horses. No wheelchair facilities.

Permits: Permits are not required. Parking and access are free.

Maps: For a free park brochure, call Oregon Parks and Recreation, 800/551-6949, or download a free map at www.oregonstateparks. org. For a topographic map, ask the USGS for Lowell.

Directions: From Eugene, drive seven miles east on Highway 58 and turn left into the park entrance.

Contact: Oregon Parks and Recreation Department, 1115 Commercial Street NE, Salem, OR, 97301, 800/551-6949, www.oregonstateparks.org.

THE COLUMBIA RIVER GORGE AND MOUNT HOOD

© SEAN PATRICK HILL

BEST HIKES

《 Desert Hiking
Cove Palisades State Park, page 187.

《 Hikes for Kids
Latourell Falls, page 130.
Oxbow Park, page 133.
Wildwood Recreation Site, page 157.
Timothy Lake, page 170.

《 Hikes for Views
Larch Mountain Crater, page 134.
McNeil Point, page 152.
Zigzag Canyon and Paradise Park, page 159.
Jefferson Park, page 184.

《 Hikes Through Old-Growth Forests
Opal Creek, page 177.

《 Self-Guided Nature Walks
Lewis and Clark Nature Trail, page 130.

《 Short Backpacking Trips
Eagle Creek, page 141.
Mazama Trail to Cairn Basin, page 153.

《 Waterfall Hikes
Wahkeena Falls Loop, page 131.
Multnomah Falls, page 132.
Oneonta Gorge and Horsetail Falls, page 132.
Ramona Falls, page 151.

《 Wheelchair-Accessible Hikes
Mosier Twin Tunnels, page 146.
Timothy Lake, page 170.

At 11,249, feet Mount Hood is the tallest

mountain in Oregon and towers over the city of Portland. Circled by the Timberline Trail – built by the Civilian Conservation Corps in the 1930s – the mountain provides easy access to some of the best alpine country in the state. Wildflower-covered meadows, tumbling creeks, massive glaciers, and a series of stone huts make for exciting hiking. It's as if the whole area rises up to meet the mountain, and all trails lead to Hood, including the Pacific Crest Trail, which skirts just behind the famous Timberline Lodge and spans the Columbia River Gorge and the entire Cascade Range.

Then there is the massive Columbia River, which pounded its way through the Cascade Range in a series of prehistoric floods, the grandest canyon by far. What the deluges left behind is not one gorge, but many; the Oregon side of the Columbia is awash with side gorges, waterfalls, and salmon-filled creeks extending deep into the mountains. Because of the sheer walls here, some of the most challenging climbs in Oregon begin from the shores of the Columbia, including the prominent Mount Defiance, a nearly 5,000-foot ascent with stunning views from the Gorge to the Cascades.

Looming above the Gorge, Mount Hood broods with its glacier-clad slopes. But it's not only the mountain that dominates here; the surrounding area is just as stunning. The Sandy, Hood, and Salmon Rivers flow close by, carving out their own canyons. And ridge upon ridge of other glacier-carved mountains provide spectacular vistas and challenging hiking. With a number of wilderness areas in the area, you'll find some pristine outback lands in northwestern Oregon. Lake upon lake dots the basins, where huckleberries bloom on the shores and deer and elk come down to drink.

With the proximity of these mountains and gorges to a major urban area, it's not hard to see why people flock to Oregon to live, work, and play.

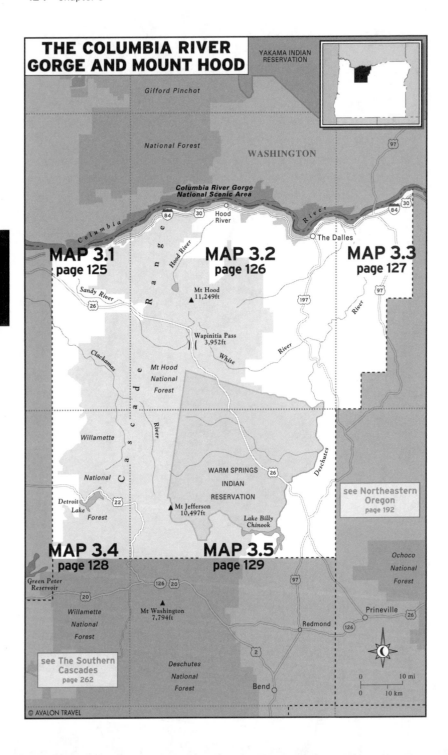

THE COLUMBIA RIVER GORGE AND MOUNT HOOD

YAKAMA INDIAN RESERVATION

Gifford Pinchot

National Forest

WASHINGTON

97

Columbia River Gorge National Scenic Area

84 30 Hood River

30 84

Columbia Range

MAP 3.1
page 125

Hood River

MAP 3.2
page 126

The Dalles

MAP 3.3
page 127

Sandy River

26

Mt Hood
11,249ft

197

97

River

Clackamas

Wapinitia Pass
3,952ft

White River

Mt Hood National Forest

Cascade River

Willamette

River

National

Deschutes

WARM SPRINGS INDIAN RESERVATION

26

see Northeastern Oregon
page 192

Detroit Lake 22

Forest

Mt Jefferson
10,497ft

Lake Billy Chinook

MAP 3.4
page 128

MAP 3.5
page 129

Green Peter Reservoir

Ochoco National Forest

126 20

97

20

see The Southern Cascades
page 262

Willamette

National

Forest

Mt Washington
7,794ft

Redmond

126

Prineville 26

2

Deschutes

National

Forest

Bend

0   10 mi
0   10 km

© AVALON TRAVEL

Map 3.1

Hikes 1-15
Pages 130-139

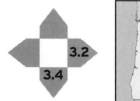

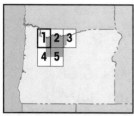

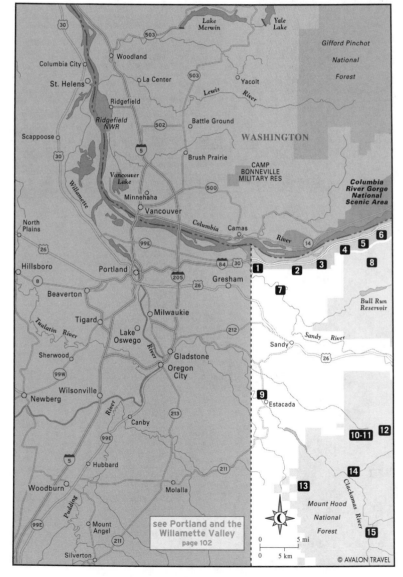

Map 3.2

Hikes 16-68
Pages 139-171

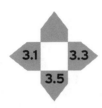

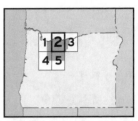

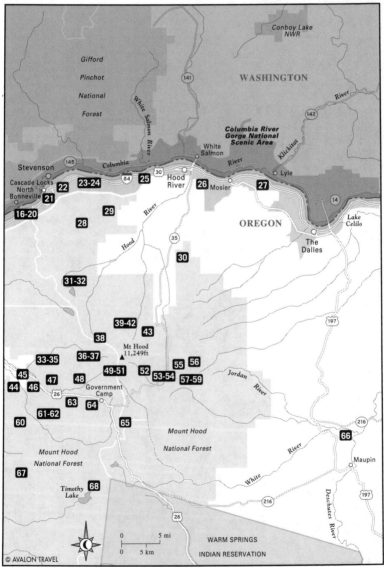

Map 3.3

Hike 69
Page 171

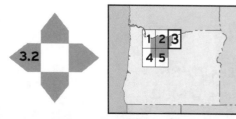

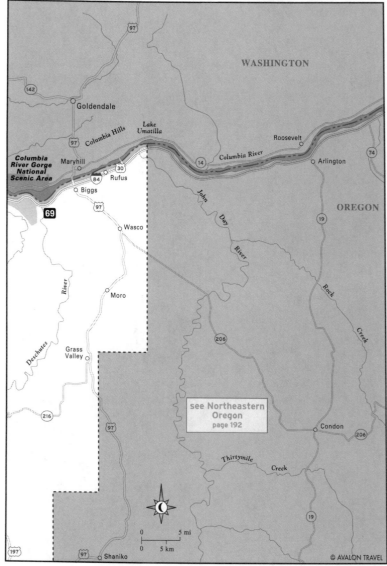

Map 3.4

Hikes 70-86
Pages 171-180

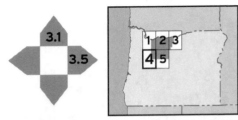

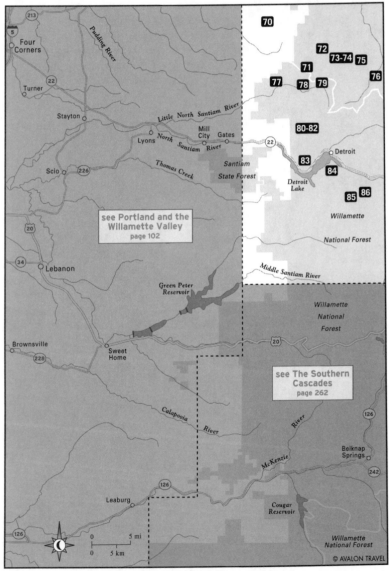

Map 3.5

Hikes 87-98
Pages 181-188

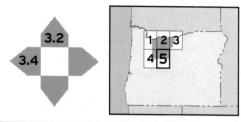

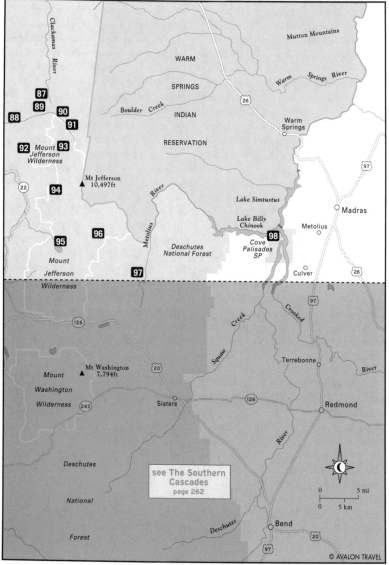

◼ LEWIS AND CLARK NATURE TRAIL
4.0 mi/2.0 hr

in the Columbia Gorge in Lewis and Clark State Park

Map 3.1, page 125 **BEST ☾**

In 1805, Lewis and Clark, nearly to their exploration's goal of the Pacific Ocean and the mouth of the Columbia River, arrived at the banks of Sandy River. They tried to cross it and found themselves sinking, and thus named it the Quicksand River. The name didn't stick, and neither did they—they eventually made it to the Oregon coast and sighted the destination President Jefferson had sent them to. Today you can explore this boundary area between the Cascade Mountains and the Willamette Valley on an easy nature trail that tours white oak, Oregon crabapple, and bigleaf maple woods dotted with flowers like Oregon grape root. A second trail leads to Broughton's Bluff, a popular climbing area, but it's a rocky trail best done on dry days.

The Lewis and Clark Nature Trail begins in the main entrance area. The unnamed, unmaintained Broughton's Bluff climber's trailhead is south from the lot on a gravel path. It switchbacks up to the base of the cliffs.

User Groups: Hikers and dogs. No horses or mountain bikes allowed. No wheelchair facilities.

Permits: Permits are not required. Parking and access are free.

Maps: You can purchase a Trails of the Columbia Gorge Map from Geo-Graphics. For a topographic map, ask the USGS for Camas.

Directions: From Portland, drive east on I-84 to Exit 18 and follow signs less than 0.1 mile to Lewis and Clark State Park.

Contact: Oregon Parks and Recreation Department, 1115 Commercial Street NE, Salem, OR, 97301, 800/551-6949, www.oregonstateparks.org.

◻ LATOURELL FALLS
2.3 mi/1.0 hr

east of Gresham in the Columbia River Gorge

Map 3.1, page 125 **BEST ☾**

For an introduction to the Columbia Gorge, look no further than Guy W. Talbot State Park, a summer estate for the Talbot family until it was donated to the state. What the state—and by extension, you—got was two waterfalls in a beautiful side canyon and a wonderfully green trail along a splashing creek. Of all the waterfalls in the Gorge, this one is closest to Portland and hence the most accessible. And the drive to get there follows the 1922 Columbia River Highway, a historic road that twists and curves along the Columbia. Not to mention it's one of the easiest, and most level hikes of the bunch—bring the whole family.

From the parking area, take the 0.2-mile paved path down for a quick look at 250-foot Latourell Falls, dropping over lichen-encrusted lava cliffs, then go back to the lot and head uphill on the Latourell Falls Trail to the left. This trail climbs 0.3 mile to a viewpoint over the lower falls and continues steadily and easily 0.5 mile to the twisting 100-foot Upper Latourell Falls and a creek crossing. From here, the path follows the opposite shore 0.5 mile, passing a dizzying overlook of the lower falls that is not for the squeamish, and then switchbacks down one final mile to the picnic area of Guy Talbot Park, circling back to the parking area.

User Groups: Hikers and dogs. No horses or mountain bikes allowed. There is a short wheelchair-accessible path to the lower falls.

Permits: Permits are not required. Parking and access are free.

Maps: You can purchase a Trails of the Columbia Gorge Map from Geo-Graphics. For a topographic map, ask the USGS for Bridal Veil.

Directions: From Portland, drive I-84 east to Exit 28 and turn right on the Columbia River Highway, driving 2.8 miles to a lot on the left.

Contact: Oregon Parks and Recreation Department, 1115 Commercial Street NE, Salem, OR, 97301, 800/551-6649, www.oregonstateparks.org.

3 ANGELS REST

4.4 mi/2.5 hr

east of Gresham in the Columbia River Gorge

Map 3.1, page 125

If there's one thing the Columbia Gorge is famous for it's wind. Just driving into the Gorge on a blustery day can be an exercise in wheel-gripping anxiety. Trees, though, have a way of deadening that wind, but not so on the burned slopes leading to the Angels Rest, a magnificent view over the Gorge and a spot that truly buffets with wind. On the hardest-blowing days, you can stand on this lava tongue and lean into the wind. Believe me, it will hold you.

From the parking area, climb on the Angels Rest Trail 0.6 mile on the Bridal Veil Trail to Coopey Falls, hidden somewhat in the underbrush. From there the trail climbs 1.6 miles to the edge of the Angels Rest; follow the cliff out for stunning views. From here, return the way you came for an easy 4.4-mile round-trip.

User Groups: Hikers and dogs. No horses or mountain bikes allowed. No wheelchair facilities.

Permits: Permits are not required. Parking and access are free.

Maps: You can purchase a Trails of the Columbia Gorge Map from Geo-Graphics. For a topographic map, ask the USGS for Bridal Veil.

Directions: From Portland, drive I-84 east to Exit 28 and park a few hundred yards past the exit at the junction with the Columbia River Highway.

Contact: Oregon Parks and Recreation Department, 1115 Commercial Street NE, Salem, OR, 97301, 800/551-6649, www.oregonstateparks.org.

4 WAHKEENA FALLS LOOP

5.0 mi/2.5 hr

east of Gresham in the Columbia River Gorge

Map 3.1, page 125   **BEST (**

The Columbia Gorge offers an amazing network of trails off the beaten path—though it is true that some of those paths are well beaten, particularly on weekends. This trail is one of them, but don't let that dismay you. With fortitude, and an early start, you can beat the crowds and visit five waterfalls, a massive spring, and deep woods with towering Douglas firs and tiny calypso orchids. Wahkeena Creek is almost a continual waterfall itself, and Multnomah Creek hosts not only the famous Multnomah Falls, but two others besides that higher up on the trail.

From the lot, head up the paved Wahkeena Trail 0.2 mile to a stone bridge beneath 242-foot Wahkeena Falls, a triple cascade in a lava slot that comes crashing down with a vengeance. The next 1.4 miles climbs the canyon, passing the base of Fairy Falls and a left-hand spur trail, the 419, continuing to a junction with Trail 415 to Angels Rest. For a short side trip, head right on the 415 trail a short distance to see the massive spring that gives birth to Wahkeena Creek, then head back to the junction. Continue uphill on the Wahkeena Trail 0.3 mile to a four-way junction and stay straight on the Wahkeena Trail. In 0.9 mile, the trail reaches a junction at Multnomah Creek; go left along the creek 1.8 miles to the base of Multnomah Falls and the historic lodge. From here, go to the left on the Gorge Trail paralleling the Columbia Highway for the 0.8-mile return to your car.

User Groups: Hikers and dogs. No horses or mountain bikes allowed. The steep but paved path to Wahkeena Falls provides wheelchair access.

Permits: Permits are not required. Parking and access are free.

Maps: You can purchase a Trails of the Columbia Gorge Map from Geo-Graphics. For a topographic map, ask the USGS for Bridal Veil.

Directions: From Portland, drive I-84 east to Exit 28 and turn left on the Columbia River Highway for 2.6 miles to the Wahkeena Falls Picnic Ground pullout on the left.

Contact: Columbia Gorge National Scenic Area, 902 Wasco Avenue, Suite 200, Hood River, OR, 97031, 541/308-1700.

5 MULTNOMAH FALLS
2.2-3.6 mi/1.0-2.0 hr 🥾1 ⛰8

east of Gresham in the Columbia River Gorge

Map 3.1, page 125 **BEST (**

Most famous of all the falls in Oregon is perhaps Multnomah—it's not only the tallest, at 542 feet, but nothing rivals its unparalleled beauty. The stone bridge just below the first tier is one of the most photographed places in the state. It's also one of the most heavily visited areas in the state; it's not uncommon to find hundreds of people here at a time, many of them making the steep switchback climb to the top of the falls and the observation deck at the water's edge. To escape the crowds, all you need to do is go higher and farther than that for even more waterfalls along the creek.

From the lot, duck under the highway and train tracks through a tunnel and under a bridge to the Multnomah Lodge. Continue past the viewpoint up the paved Multnomah Falls Trail to the stone bridge at the base of the upper falls. By now you've gone 0.5 mile. To continue to the top, follow the paved path up a long series of switchbacks 0.6 mile to a junction; head right and down along the creek on this paved path to the viewpoint high above the lodge. To add another 1.4 miles and two waterfalls to your hike, continue upstream to the junction with the Wahkeena Trail (see *Wahkeena Falls Loop* listing in this chapter).

User Groups: Hikers and dogs. No horses or mountain bikes allowed. The paved path to the stone bridge provides wheelchair access.

the bridge at Multnomah Falls

© SEAN PATRICK HILL

Permits: Permits are not required. Parking and access are free.

Maps: You can purchase a Trails of the Columbia Gorge Map from Geo-Graphics. For a topographic map, ask the USGS for Bridal Veil.

Directions: From Portland, drive I-84 east to the Multnomah Falls turnoff at Exit 31 into the lot.

Contact: Columbia Gorge National Scenic Area, 902 Wasco Avenue, Suite 200, Hood River, OR, 97031, 541/308-1700.

6 ONEONTA GORGE AND HORSETAIL FALLS
2.7 mi/1.5 hr 🥾2 ⛰9

east of Gresham in the Columbia River Gorge

Map 3.1, page 125 **BEST (**

The Columbia Gorge, as impressive as it is, isn't the only gorge around here. Take the Oneonta Gorge, for instance, a narrow slot sliced into sheer volcanic rock extending back more than a mile into the cliffs. On a summer day, with the right clothes and footwear, it's possible to wade back into the gorge to a secret waterfall. The more common way to see this gorge is to climb up and around it, passing numerous falls and crossing a crazily high bridge on your way to a triple waterfall falling on Oneonta Creek.

The hike begins at 176-foot Horsetail Falls, climbing the cliffs to the Gorge Trail. Turn right on the Gorge Trail and continue up to 80-foot Ponytail Falls, which the trail ducks behind, and a viewpoint over the Columbia River. The trail follows the creek and switchbacks down to a steel bridge over two falls, the lower one careening into the Oneonta Gorge. All this takes place in the first 1.3 miles.

At a junction on the far side of the bridge, go left on the Oneonta Trail, climbing steadily up 0.9 mile to 120-foot Triple Falls, pouring over a basalt lip. Just beyond lies a bridge and an area to stop and explore. To make a loop of the trail, head back down to the junction by the high bridge, this time going left to stay on the Oneonta Trail. In the next 0.9 mile, the trail descends to another viewpoint, then gradually returns to the highway. Keep right at a junction with the Gorge Trail, going 0.2 mile back to the highway, then following the highway east toward the mouth of the Oneonta Gorge—a designated botanical area—and a partially renovated tunnel through which the old highway once passed. The walk along the highway is a short 0.5 mile back to the Horsetail lot.

User Groups: Hikers and dogs. No mountain bikes or horses allowed. No wheelchair facilities.

Permits: Permits are not required. Parking and access are free.

Maps: You can purchase a Trails of the Columbia Gorge Map from Geo-Graphics. For a topographic map, ask the USGS for Multnomah Falls.

Directions: From Portland, drive I-84 east to Exit 35 for Ainsworth Park and follow the Columbia Highway to the right 1.5 miles to the Horsetail Falls Trailhead parking area.

Contact: Columbia Gorge National Scenic Area, 902 Wasco Avenue, Suite 200, Hood River, OR, 97031, 541/308-1700.

▇ OXBOW PARK
3.5 mi/2.0 hr   ▓▓₁ ◮₇

southeast of Gresham on the Sandy River

Map 3.1, page 125   **BEST (**

Just a short ways past the bustle of highways and shopping centers that is Gresham lies this jewel of a park along an oxbow on the Sandy River. There are 1,200 acres of quiet woods, browsing deer, an ancient forest, and cobbled beaches on the river curving around Alder Ridge—all awaiting exploration. Along the way, you'll see anglers, campgrounds, and likely an osprey or two hunting fish in the river. A few stretches of trail may be wiped out when you visit due to winter storms; they don't seriously disrupt these hikes, since the network of trails and a few paved roads gives easy portage around the destruction. On top of that, you'll see firsthand what effect massive rains have on this ever-changing landscape. Kids will love it here, as the trails are easy and fun.

There are so many options for hiking, it's hard to say where to begin. The lot at Area C makes as good a spot as any, so start there and follow the trail out of the lot into the woods toward the river. At a junction, head right 0.5 mile through the woods, staying left at all junctions, until you reach the large lot and group picnic area. From here, you'll be able to see the huge washout the river slope suffered, taking many large trees and a half-mile length of trail with it. Head for the road, crossing it and heading up a gravel road. Go uphill to a junction on the left and head down into the woods for 0.8 mile. At the next junction, go right 0.2 mile, then left 0.2 mile toward the river. At a trail junction near a group camping site, and if the trail is mended, you can follow the river 0.6 mile around the oxbow, passing a stone beach and some impressive washouts (if not, pay attention to your map, adjusting as you go). From the junction marked "M," continue along the river 0.4 mile to the boat ramp. At this point, you'll have to use the road for 0.8 mile along the campsites, heading downstream. When you return to the picnic area "A," you can head back into the woods to return to your car.

User Groups: Hikers and dogs. Horses and mountain bikes on designated trails only. Paved portions of the park are wheelchair accessible.

Permits: Permits are not required. A fee of $4 per car is collected at the entrance. An annual pass is $40.

Maps: A brochure and map is available at the entrance gate or online at www.oregonmetro. gov. For a topographic map, ask the USGS for Sandy.

Directions: From I-205, take Exit 19 and go east on Division Street. Cross Burnside Street in Gresham and continue as the road becomes Oxbow Parkway. After 13 miles turn left at a four-way junction and follow park signs 1.4 miles to the entrance. Continue along the river to the first trail parking area, marked "C," on the left.

Contact: Metro Regional Center, 600 NE Grand Avenue, Portland OR, 97232, 503/797-1700.

🖥 LARCH MOUNTAIN CRATER
6.0 mi/3.0 hr   🏃3 ⛰8

above Multnomah Falls in the Columbia River Gorge

Map 3.1, page 125   **BEST (**

Sherrard Point, at 4,055 feet, has a commanding view of the Columbia River Gorge, several Cascade peaks, and the distant city of Portland. It also looks down into the remnants of its volcanic crater, ground out by glaciers and the headwaters of Multnomah Creek. For a firsthand look at the crater, including its

Sherrard Point from Larch Mountain Crater

© SEAN PATRICK HILL

marshy core where bog orchids thrive, you'll have to climb down and into the heart of this ancient mountain.

From the parking lot, the trail to Sherrard Point begins to the left of a signpost. Follow this obvious paved path to a junction and head right and steeply uphill, finally climbing a row of stairs to the impressive overlook. Then head back down, but this time follow the right-hand junction that heads into a picnic area, then head downhill on the Larch Mountain Trail to the right down a cathedral-like wooded ridge. After 1.5 miles, the trail crosses a dirt road, and in another 0.4 mile connects with a spur trail, Multnomah Creek Way. Take this trail to the right for 0.2 mile, then at a junction with the Multnomah Way Trail, go to the right again, following the young Multnomah Creek into the crater. This 2.5-mile section skirts the boggy meadows with views to Sherrard Point's massive volcanic plug. The trail makes use of an old logging road then joins the Oneonta Trail. Go right up the ridge 0.9 mile, where avalanche lilies bloom in spring right out of the snow. When the trail reaches the Larch Mountain Road, head to the right on the paved road 0.3 mile back to the lot.

User Groups: Hikers, dogs, horses, and mountain bikes. No wheelchair facilities.

Permits: Permits are not required. A federal Northwest Forest Pass is required to park here; the cost is $5 a day or $30 for an annual pass. You can buy a day pass at the trailhead, at ranger stations, or through private vendors.

Maps: You can purchase a Trails of the Columbia Gorge Map from Geo-Graphics. For a topographic map, ask the USGS for Multnomah Falls.

Directions: From Portland, drive I-84 east to the Corbett exit (Exit 22), and drive one mile uphill to Corbett. Turn left on the Columbia River Highway for two miles and fork right on Larch Mountain Road for 12 miles to its end.

Contact: Columbia Gorge National Scenic Area, 902 Wasco Avenue, Suite 200, Hood River, OR, 97031, 541/308-1700.

9 MILO MCIVER STATE PARK
6.0 mi/2.0 hr ♟1 ▲7

northwest of Estacada off Highway 211

Map 3.1, page 125

There's more to this state park than Frisbee golf, a fish hatchery, and an annual Civil War re-enactment. A woodsy loop trail sets out from the fish hatchery in the southern day-use area and follows a path along the Clackamas River, shared by equestrians. Because this park receives the national average for rainfall, winter is not the best time to go, unless you like hiking in the mud. The Nature Trail continues past views of the Clackamas River to the northern day-use area, connecting to loops with the Maple Ridge Trail and Cedar Knoll Trail.

User Groups: Hikers, dogs, and horses. No mountain bikes allowed. Paved portions of the trail are wheelchair accessible.

Permits: Permits are not required. A $3 day-

use fee is collected at the camping entrance, or you can get an annual Oregon Parks and Recreation pass for $25; contact Oregon Parks and Recreation, 800/551-6949.

Maps: For a free park brochure, call Oregon Parks and Recreation, 800/551-6949, or download a free map at www.oregonstateparks. org. For a topographic map, ask the USGS for Estacada.

Directions: From Estacada, drive OR 211 south toward Molalla one mile, following signs to McIver Park and the fish hatchery. The trail heads around the hatchery to the right.

Contact: Oregon Parks and Recreation Department, 1115 Commercial Street NE, Salem, OR, 97301, 800/551-6949, www.oregonstateparks.org.

10 OLD BALDY
7.7 mi/4.0 hr ♟3 ▲8

east of Estacada in Mount Hood National Forest

Map 3.1, page 125

In 1999, a group of environmental activists barricaded the access road to Old Baldy, protesting the cutting of old-growth trees here. After a standoff with the Forest Service, the timber sale buyers decided to back out, and all is at peace again. Now you can visit Old Baldy along an ancient route predating the Forest Service through groves of noble fir. Though the peak itself, once the site of a fire lookout, is now largely overgrown and viewless, there is a cliff-edge viewpoint along the way with views to Mount Hood and Mount Adams.

From the Baldy Trailhead, go left on the Baldy Trail and follow it 2.9 miles, rounding Githens Mountain. At a crest, near a rock cairn, head to the right 30 yards to the cliff viewpoint. Returning to the trail, continue 0.9 mile to 4,200-foot Old Baldy.

User Groups: Hikers, dogs, horses, and mountain bikes. No wheelchair facilities.

Permits: Permits are not required. Parking and access are free.

Maps: For a map of the Mount Hood National Forest, contact the Mount Hood National Forest Headquarters, 16400 Champion Way, Sandy, OR, 97055, 503/668-1700. For a topographic map, ask the USGS for Wildcat Mountain.

Directions: From I-205 near Oregon City, take Exit 12 and drive east toward Estacada 18 miles. Drive through town and continue 1.6 miles on Highway 224. Just beyond milepost 25, turn left on Surface Road for 1.1 mile and turn right on Squaw Mountain Road. Follow this paved road, which becomes Road 4614, for 14.4 miles. Park on a pullout on the right, and at the end of a short path find the Old Baldy Trailhead.

Contact: Mount Hood National Forest, Clackamas River Ranger District, 595 NW Industrial Way, Estacada, OR, 97023, 503/630-6861.

11 TUMALA MOUNTAIN
4.4 mi/2.5 hr   👣2 ⛰8

east of Estacada in Mount Hood National Forest

Map 3.1, page 125

Near the headwaters of both the North Fork Clackamas River and the South Fork Eagle Creek, the mountain formerly known as Squaw Mountain rises 4,770 feet above the Salmon-Huckleberry Wilderness. This is the site of an old fire watchtower, of which only an old concrete staircase remains, and the view of Mount Hood and Mount Jefferson is unimpeded, as is the view down to the Tumala Lakes Basin. As of 2001, the Oregon State Legislature called for the removal of the word "Squaw" from all place names, and the Oregon Geographic Names Board has worked to replace that antiquated and derogatory name with the word "Tumala," a Chinook word meaning "tomorrow" or "afterlife."

From the Fanton Trailhead, located in an old clear-cut, climb 0.7 mile through an old-growth forest, passing a marsh and primitive campsite. At the Old Baldy Trail, turn right

for 0.6 mile, then right again at the next junction. Climb to the peak up 0.4 mile of trail and finally along an old service road, going to the left on this rutted track.

User Groups: Hikers, dogs, horses, and mountain bikes. No wheelchair facilities.

Permits: Permits are not required. Parking and access are free.

Maps: For a map of the Mount Hood National Forest, contact the Mount Hood National Forest Headquarters, 16400 Champion Way, Sandy, OR, 97055, 503/668-1700. For a topographic map, ask the USGS for Estacada.

Directions: From I-205 near Oregon City, take Exit 12 and drive east toward Estacada 18 miles. Drive through town and continue 1.6 miles on Highway 224. Just beyond milepost 25, turn left on Surface Road for 1.1 miles and turn right on Squaw Mountain Road. Follow this paved road, which becomes Road 4614, for 13.4 miles. Turn right on a gravel road to the Fanton Trailhead.

Contact: Mount Hood National Forest, Clackamas River Ranger District, 595 NW Industrial Way, Estacada, OR, 97023, 503/630-6861.

12 SHEEPSHEAD ROCK
2.8 mi/1.5 hr   👣1 ⛰7

east of Estacada in Mount Hood National Forest

Map 3.1, page 125

If it wasn't timber thieves and sheepherders threatening these forests in the early 1900s, it was fire. The Forest Service built a guard station atop The Plaza, a wide plateau, in order to thwart the people, and a fire watchtower atop nearby Salmon Mountain to thwart the flames. Now the whole area is within the Salmon-Huckleberry Wilderness, all accessible by the Plaza Trail. An easy destination is Sheepshead Rock, a barren stony outcrop atop mighty cliffs.

From the trailhead, go right for 1.4 miles along the Plaza Trail, which joins an old road at the guard station site, then continues. The trail descends from the plateau, and just before it switchbacks back up, a side trail to the right leads to a scramble up Sheepshead Rock.

User Groups: Hikers, dogs, and horses. No mountain bikes allowed. No wheelchair facilities.

Permits: A free self-issue Wilderness Permit is required and is available at the trailhead. Parking and access are free.

Maps: For a map of the Mount Hood National Forest and the Salmon-Huckleberry Wilderness, contact the Mount Hood National Forest Headquarters, 16400 Champion Way, Sandy, OR, 97055, 503/668-1700. For a topographic map, ask the USGS for Three Lynx.

Directions: From I-205 near Oregon City, take Exit 12 and drive east toward Estacada 18 miles. Drive through town and continue 6.5 miles on Highway 224. Across from Promontory Park, turn left at a sign for Silver Fox RV Park and go left onto Road 4610. Follow this road 18.4 miles, forking left at 7.1 miles, right at eight miles, and left at 17 miles. Watch for a trailhead sign on the left and park at the Twin Springs Campground a hundred yards beyond on the right. Walk back to the trailhead.

Contact: Mount Hood National Forest, Zigzag Ranger District, 70220 East Highway 26, Zigzag, OR, 97049, 503/622-3191.

13 MEMALOOSE LAKE AND SOUTH FORK MOUNTAIN

4.6 mi/2.5 hr 🥾2 ⛰️8

southeast of Estacada in Mount Hood National Forest

Map 3.1, page 125

Less than an hour from Portland, you'll feel as if you're deep in the mountains. Memaloose Lake sits beneath South Fork Mountain in what remains of an ancient cirque from the Ice Age, and now plays home to salamanders and huckleberries. The lake is as family-friendly as it gets, but for a challenge you can continue on to the top of the mountain with views of nine Cascade peaks—a rarity, for sure.

From the trailhead, the Memaloose Lake Trail climbs modestly over 1.3 miles, switchbacking at its end down to the lake. To climb South Fork Mountain on an unmaintained trail, don't confuse it with the spur trails leading to the shores and campsites around the lake, but continue to the left up 700 feet in 1.0 mile.

User Groups: Hikers, dogs, horses, and mountain bikes. No wheelchair facilities.

Permits: Permits are not required. Parking and access are free.

Maps: For a map of the Mount Hood National Forest, contact the Mount Hood National Forest Headquarters, 16400 Champion Way, Sandy, OR, 97055, 503/668-1700. For a topographic map, ask the USGS for Wanderers Peak.

Directions: From I-205 near Oregon City, take Exit 12 and drive east toward Estacada 18 miles. Drive through town and continue 9.2 miles on Highway 224. Between mileposts 33 and 34, go right across a bridge onto Memaloose Road 45 and drive 11.2 miles. Keep right on a gravel road for one more mile to a trailhead on the left.

Contact: Mount Hood National Forest, Clackamas River Ranger District, 595 NW Industrial Way, Estacada, OR, 97023, 503/630-6861.

14 CLACKAMAS RIVER

7.8 mi one-way/4.0 hr 🥾2 ⛰️8

southeast of Estacada in Mount Hood National Forest

Map 3.1, page 125

This breezy trail follows the rough and tumbling Clackamas River on a great day's journey. Along the way, you'll pass a couple of waterfalls, including Pup Creek Falls in a side canyon, and The Narrows, where the river squeezes through a gorge between two pieces of a lava flow, narrowing the river to a thin whitewater rush. Though the trail parallels the highway, the road is on the far shore.

The trailside has some great up-and-down hauls through dense woods and even passes a couple beaches.

From the Fish Creek Trailhead, follow the trail along the river, rounding a bend, for 3.6 miles. At that point, there is a side trail to the right leading in 200 yards to a viewpoint of Pup Creek Falls. Continue on the main trail 1.3 miles to The Narrows. From there, the trail continues on for three miles to an upper trailhead at Indian Henry Campground.

User Groups: Hikers and dogs. Horses and mountain bikes not allowed. No wheelchair facilities.

Permits: Permits are not required. A federal Northwest Forest Pass is required to park here; the cost is $5 a day or $30 for an annual pass. You can buy a day pass at the trailhead, at ranger stations, or through private vendors.

Maps: For a map of the Mount Hood National Forest, contact the Mount Hood National Forest Headquarters, 16400 Champion Way, Sandy, OR, 97055, 503/668-1700. For a topographic map, ask the USGS for Three Lynx.

Directions: From I-205 near Oregon City, take Exit 12 and drive east toward Estacada 18 miles. Drive through town and continue 14.4 miles on Highway 224. Past milepost 39, after crossing the second green bridge, turn right on Fish Creek Road 54. Follow this road 0.2 mile, cross the Clackamas River, then park at a big lot on the right. To reach Indian Henry Campground, stay left on OR 224, following the river seven miles. Follow signs for Indian Henry Campground straight on Road 4620 for 0.6 mile and park in a lot on the right across from the campground entrance.

Contact: Mount Hood National Forest, Clackamas River Ranger District, 595 NW Industrial Way, Estacada, OR, 97023, 503/630-6861.

15 RIVERSIDE NATIONAL RECREATION TRAIL
8.0 mi/3.0 hr

southeast of Estacada in Mount Hood National Forest

Map 3.1, page 125

The Riverside Trail is only one of three in the Mount Hood Forest to be designated a National Recreation Trail. It's outstanding natural beauty is due to thick forests of Douglas fir and red cedar, and the fact that the river provides companionship for the trail's whole length. It's worth it to hike the whole thing in one burst.

From the trailhead, the trail goes in two directions. To the left, it ambles down 1.4 miles to a beach and its terminus at the Riverside Campground. To the right, it extends out 2.6 miles along cliffs, over creeks, down to a beach, down to a nice pool, and to a fine viewpoint over the river, before continuing along the Oak Grove Fork to its end at the Rainbow Campground.

User Groups: Hikers, dogs, and mountain bikes. Horses not allowed. No wheelchair facilities.

Permits: Permits are not required. A federal Northwest Forest Pass is required to park here; the cost is $5 a day or $30 for an annual pass. You can buy a day pass at the trailhead, at ranger stations, or through private vendors.

Maps: For a map of the Mount Hood National Forest, contact the Mount Hood National Forest Headquarters, 16400 Champion Way, Sandy, OR, 97055, 503/668-1700. For a topographic map, ask the USGS for Fish Creek Mountain.

Directions: From I-205 near Oregon City, take Exit 12 and drive east toward Estacada 18 miles. Drive through town and continue 26 miles on Highway 224 to the Ripplebrook Bridge. Turn right onto Road 46 for 1.8 miles to a Riverside Trailhead sign and a parking lot on the right.

Contact: Mount Hood National Forest, Clackamas River Ranger District, 595

NW Industrial Way, Estacada, OR, 97023, 503/630-6861.

🔢 NESMITH POINT AND ELOWAH FALLS
3.0-9.8 mi/1.5-5.0 hr 🥾3 ⛰8

west of Cascade Locks in the Columbia River Gorge

Map 3.2, page 126

Two very different hikes launch from Yeon State Park, named for one of the principal architects of the historic Columbia River Highway. The first views 289-foot Elowah Falls from both the bottom and the top, making use of a unnerving but fenced cliff-ledge trail to climb over Elowah to Upper McCord Creek Falls. The second climbs steeply up a dry gorge to Nesmith Point, almost 4,000 feet above the trailhead, and provides absolutely stunning views to the mountains on the far side of the Columbia River.

To hike to the falls, take the left-hand Trail 400 from the parking lot 0.4 mile to a junction. Two trails lead from here: The first goes 0.4 mile to the left to a footbridge at the base of Elowah Falls; the second heads up the cliff face 0.7 miles to 60-foot Upper McCord Falls, with sweeping views from the dynamite-blasted ledge along the cliff.

To climb to Nesmith Point, take the right-hand junction from Yeon Park on Trail 428. The first 0.9 mile climbs steadily through the forest. At a junction with the Gorge Trail by a creek, head left. From here, the trail climbs 2,300 feet in only 2.4 miles, reaching its crest at a saddle with excellent views. Continue on this ridgeline trail 1.3 miles, passing a spring along the way, turning uphill through a forest of towering trees not unlike being in a massive cathedral. The trail joins an old road, so go right up 0.3 mile to a cliff-edge view and the site of an

Columbia River Gorge from Nesmith Point

old watchtower, with one building's ruins still collapsing into the ground.

User Groups: Hikers and dogs. No mountain bikes or horses allowed. No wheelchair facilities.

Permits: Permits are not required. Parking and access are free.

Maps: You can purchase a Trails of the Columbia Gorge Map from Geo-Graphics. For a topographic map, ask the USGS for Tanner Butte.

Directions: From Portland, drive I-84 east and take Exit 35 for Ainsworth Park, and turn left toward Dodson for 200 feet, then turn right onto Frontage Road. Follow Frontage Road 2.1 miles to a pullout on the right.

Contact: Oregon Parks and Recreation Department, 1115 Commercial Street NE, Salem, OR, 97301, 800/551-6949, www.oregonstateparks.org.

17 WAHCLELLA FALLS

1.8 mi/1.0 hr 👣1 ⛰8

west of Cascade Locks in the Columbia River Gorge

Map 3.2, page 126

Once the stretch of Columbia River Highway ends, it's easy to miss off-the-beaten-path spots like Wahclella Falls. It's unfortunate, because this double-plunge waterfall tumbling into the canyon where massive boulders line Tanner Creek is unique and worth a visit. The Wahclella Falls Trail sets out on an old road that becomes a trail beyond an old dam, heading into the canyon 0.9 mile along Tanner Creek. Watch for a side falls along the way. The trail comes to a junction, the beginning of a short loop. Go left to reach the base of the falls, a pounding cataract, then cross the creek on a footbridge, passing a small cave and the giant boulders left from a landslide decades ago. The trail crosses the creek again on a footbridge and climbs to rejoin the original trail. Head left to return to the lot.

User Groups: Hikers and dogs. No horses or mountain bikes allowed. No wheelchair facilities.

Permits: Permits are not required. A federal Northwest Forest Pass is required to park; the cost is $5 a day or $30 for an annual pass. You can buy a day pass at the trailhead, at ranger stations, or through private vendors.

Maps: You can purchase a Trails of the Columbia Gorge Map from Geo-Graphics. For a topographic map, ask the USGS for Tanner Butte.

Directions: From Portland, drive I-84 east and take Exit 40 for the Bonneville Dam. At the intersection, keep right and then stay to the right again for the parking area.

Contact: Columbia Gorge National Scenic Area, 902 Wasco Avenue, Suite 200, Hood River, OR, 97031, 541/308-1700.

18 WAUNA VIEWPOINT

3.8 mi/2.0 hr 👣2 ⛰8

west of Cascade Locks in the Columbia River Gorge

Map 3.2, page 126

Two sections of the Columbia River Highway are abandoned but open as a State Trail. Paralleling the interstate that eventually made this highway obsolete, the old highway is open to hikers and bikers, and provides access to other trails, including a viewpoint of Wauna Point, a challenging climb. For an easy day, you can hike out the old highway and back, a two-mile walk that hugs Tooth Rock on a parapet-like section of the road. Either way, this stretch of old road accesses the Wauna Viewpoint nicely.

Beginning at the Tooth Rock Trailhead, follow the paved path 0.2 mile to a junction. Stay straight on the old highway another 0.8 mile to the road's end at a stone stairway.

For a different hike from the same trailhead, try Wauna Viewpoint. Follow the old highway from the Tooth Rock Trailhead to the junction and go right 0.4 mile on a poorly marked spur trail toward Wauna. Take the next trail to the right, heading uphill 0.1 mile to an old roadbed that marks the Gorge Trail. Stay left, going uphill to find the continuation of the trail. Follow the trail to the left another 0.4 mile. Then go right at a sign for Wauna Viewpoint, plodding up the switchbacks to the 1,050-foot viewpoint near a powerline base. From here you can spot Mount Adams in Washington. Head back the way you came.

User Groups: Hikers and dogs. Mountain bikes allowed on paved trails only. No horses allowed. Paved portions are wheelchair accessible.

Permits: Permits are not required. Parking and access are free.

Maps: You can purchase a Trails of the Columbia Gorge Map from Geo-Graphics. For a topographic map, ask the USGS for Bonneville Dam.

Directions: From Portland, drive I-84 east and

take Exit 40 for the Bonneville Dam. At the intersection, keep right and then turn left for the parking area.

Contact: Oregon Parks and Recreation Department, 1115 Commercial Street NE, Salem, OR, 97301, 800/551-6949, www.oregon-stateparks.org, and Columbia Gorge National Scenic Area, 902 Wasco Avenue, Suite 200, Hood River, OR, 97031, 541/308-1700.

19 EAGLE CREEK

12.0 mi/7.0 hr   ⛷3 🏔9

west of Cascade Locks in the Columbia River Gorge

Map 3.2, page 126	BEST (

Eagle Creek is surely one of the best hikes in Oregon—and it's one of the oldest, built in the 1910s as part of the Columbia River Highway project. You'll pass six waterfalls in all, and for the finale you'll walk behind Tunnel Falls through a little cave carved out of the cliff wall. The whole route is nothing short of spectacular, and there's ample opportunity to backpack as well, with several woodsy group camping areas along the way. Of course, parts of the trail are perilous, walking alongside sheer cliffs with naught but a cable handrail to ease the anxiety. Almost every year, it seems, someone falls into the canyon and needs to be rescued, or worse. Keep an eye on kids and dogs, and the trip will be one for posterity.

From the trailhead, head upstream on the Eagle Creek Trail. At 1.5 miles, a side trail leads to a viewpoint of Metlako Falls, and at 2.1 miles a side trail leads down to Punchbowl Falls, a great place to spot water ouzels, little grey birds that spend much of their time underwater and darting in and out of waterfalls looking for insects. Returning to the trail, the next 1.2 miles brings you to the first high bridge, crossing not only a creek but a faultline. From here, it's 0.4 mile farther to Tenas Camp, then another mile to Wy-East Camp, and finally another 0.6 mile to Blue Grouse Camp. Once you've passed Blue Grouse

Camp, it's only 0.7 mile to Tunnel Falls, and if you're not yet tired out, head around the bend a short distance to reach another falls and a good lunch spot. Return as you came.

User Groups: Hikers and dogs. No horses or mountain bikes allowed. No wheelchair facilities.

Permits: Permits are not required. A federal Northwest Forest Pass is required to park here; the cost is $5 a day or $30 for an annual pass. You can buy a day pass at the trailhead, at ranger stations, or through private vendors.

Maps: You can purchase a Trails of the Columbia Gorge Map from Geo-Graphics. For a topographic map, ask the USGS for Bonneville Dam.

Directions: From Portland, drive I-84 east and take Exit 41 for Eagle Creek. At the intersection, keep right for one mile to the parking area.

Contact: Columbia Gorge National Scenic Area, 902 Wasco Avenue, Suite 200, Hood River, OR, 97031, 541/308-1700.

20 RUCKEL RIDGE

9.6 mi/5.0 hr   ⛷4 🏔8

west of Cascade Locks in the Columbia River Gorge

Map 3.2, page 126

Ruckel Creek Trail may not be appropriately named, since it provides only two glimpses of Ruckel Creek. But what this trail accomplishes is far more ambitious: a demanding climb to the Benson Plateau, where trails go off in all directions like the strands of a spider's web. Along the way, you'll pass mysterious pits that could be 1,000 years old, most likely vision quest sites for young Native American men. The rest is what my friend used to call a "death march" up the rugged ridge into the Hatfield Wilderness area with views to Table Mountain and Mount Adams.

From the trailhead in the Eagle Creek Campground, follow the Gorge Trail east 0.7 mile east, following the paved old Columbia River Highway for a spell. Cross Ruckel Creek on a picturesque stone bridge and head to the right on the Ruckel Creek Trail, which quickly becomes a thigh-burner. In 0.3 mile, you'll enter a moss-covered rockslide area, where you'll find the pits. Touch nothing and remove nothing; these sites are federally protected. The next 1.5 miles is steep, arriving at a viewpoint at 2,000 feet. After this, the trail affords a break for 1.5 miles through a fairly level, grassy slope before climbing again steeply for the remaining 0.8 mile. Once on top, walk through the woods to a trail fork, and go right to visit Ruckel Creek. Return as you came.

User Groups: Hikers and dogs. No wheelchair facilities.

Permits: Permits are not required. A federal Northwest Forest Pass is required to park here; the cost is $5 a day or $30 for an annual pass. You can buy a day pass at the trailhead, at ranger stations, or through private vendors.

Maps: You can purchase a Trails of the Columbia Gorge Map from Geo-Graphics. For a topographic map, ask the USGS for Bonneville Dam.

Directions: From Portland, drive I-84 east and take Exit 41 for Eagle Creek. At the intersection, keep right and then turn left into the parking area.

Contact: Columbia Gorge National Scenic Area, 902 Wasco Avenue, Suite 200, Hood River, OR, 97031, 541/308-1700.

21 DRY CREEK FALLS
4.8 mi/2.0 hr

south of Cascade Locks in Mount Hood National Forest

Map 3.2, page 126

There's a sign for the Pacific Crest Trail on the Bridge of the Gods, a long steel bridge spanning the Columbia River. How else would through-hikers get over that river? Just off the road here, the beginning of the Oregon stretch of the PCT starts into the forest. Within a few miles is the first footbridge over rushing water, the misnamed Dry Creek. Hikers may not realize that

the old road leading off the PCT and upstream comes to a 50-foot waterfall pouring through a slot in lumpy lava flows. Don't let the early stage of the trail fool you; this is actually a quiet walk through some deep fir woods.

From the trailhead, head south on the PCT, away from the Bridge of the Gods, going under I-84 and briefly up a dirt road, following PCT signs typically nailed to trees (and a telephone pole). The trail spurs to the left off the road. After 1.2 miles, cross an old powerline road and continue into the woods. After 0.9 mile, the trail crosses Dry Creek, but take the road to the right up 0.3 mile to the base of the falls and an abandoned diversion dam that, if anything, adds charm to this spot.

User Groups: Hikers, dogs, and horses. No mountain bikes allowed. No wheelchair facilities.

Permits: Permits are not required. A federal Northwest Forest Pass is required to park here; the cost is $5 a day or $30 for an annual pass. You can buy a day pass at the trailhead, at ranger stations, or through private vendors.

Maps: You can purchase a Trails of the Columbia Gorge Map from Geo-Graphics. For a topographic map, ask the USGS for Bonneville Dam and Carson.

Directions: From Portland, drive I-84 east to the Cascade Locks (Exit 44) and follow signs for the Bridge of the Gods. Just before the tollbooth for the bridge, turn right into a parking area. The trail begins across the road.

Contact: Columbia Gorge National Scenic Area, 902 Wasco Avenue, Suite 200, Hood River, OR, 97031, 541/308-1700.

22 HERMAN CREEK TO INDIAN POINT
8.0-8.4 mi/4.0-4.5 hr

east of Cascade Locks in the Columbia River Gorge

Map 3.2, page 126

Herman Creek Trail is a bit of a misnomer, since you'll have to go 4.2 miles just to get to a point on the water. The destination, though, is a truly lovely and untrammeled spot on the confluence of Casey and Herman Creeks. On the way, you'll pass tiger lilies in summer and a side creek with a nice waterfall. This trail is also the access point for a killer climb to Indian Point, a promontory high above the Columbia River and sweeping views.

For the hike above Herman Creek, begin from the campground, climbing through a boulder field on the Herman Creek Trail 0.6 mile to a junction with the Herman Bridge spur. Go left 0.7 mile, staying on the Herman Creek Trail, where the trail eventually joins an old road. At the next junction, site of Herman Camp, go to the right to stay on Herman Creek, keeping right at the next junction as well, for 2.6 miles. After that, you'll reach a second camp and a junction of trails; an unmarked side trail to the right goes down the canyon 0.3 mile to the confluence.

For the Indian Point climb, begin from the campground, climbing through the boulder field 0.6 mile to a junction with the Herman Bridge spur. Go left 0.7 mile, where the trail eventually joins the old road. At the next junction, site of Herman Camp, go left up the Gorton Creek Trail and climb steadily for 2.6 miles to a junction. Continue 50 yards up the Gorton Creek Trail and take an unmarked side trail to the left 0.1 mile to Indian Point. Return to the junction and go left down the Cutoff Trail 0.6 mile to the Nick Eaton Trail, going right on this trail down a steep ridge for two miles. At the junction with the old road, follow it back to Herman Camp, then return to the right down the road as you came to the Herman Creek campground.

User Groups: Hikers, dogs, and horses. No mountain bikes allowed. No wheelchair facilities.

Permits: A free self-issue Wilderness Permit is required and is available on the trail. A federal Northwest Forest Pass is required to park here; the cost is $5 a day or $30 for an annual pass. You can buy a day pass at the trailhead, at ranger stations, or through private vendors.

Maps: You can purchase a Trails of the Columbia Gorge Map from Geo-Graphics. For a topographic map, ask the USGS for Carson.

Directions: From Portland, drive I-84 east to Cascade Locks (Exit 44), driving through town for two miles. At the next on-ramp for I-84, go straight onto a road marked "To Oxbow Fish Hatchery" and follow this road two miles to a Forest Service complex, and turn right into the Herman Creek Campground entrance to a parking area at the end of the road. In the winter, the gate is closed, but you can park off the road near the gate and walk in to the campground.

Contact: Columbia Gorge National Scenic Area, 902 Wasco Avenue, Suite 200, Hood River, OR, 97031, 541/308-1700.

23 STARVATION CREEK FALLS
2.5 mi/1.0 hr

east of Cascade Locks in the Columbia River Gorge

Map 3.2, page 126

Located just off I-84, nestled in a canyon beneath Starvation Ridge, is a 186-foot waterfall on Starvation Creek. The creek is named for an 1884 disaster; a train was stranded in the snow for weeks here, and the passengers were paid to help dig it out as they waited for food to arrive.

It's easy enough to walk to Starvation Creek Falls from the lot along a paved stretch of the out-of-use section of the Columbia River Highway. But there are more falls back in those hills above the freeway, and a somewhat demanding hike visits them all.

After visiting Starvation Creek Falls, head west on the paved Mount Defiance Trail skirting the highway, following signs for Mount Defiance. At a junction with the Starvation Ridge Cutoff Trail in 0.3 mile, stay to the right for 0.6 mile, passing Cabin Creek Falls and Hole-in-the-Wall Falls. These falls were a bizarre undertaking by highway workers in

1938 to prevent Warren Creek Falls from constantly flooding out the highway. They fixed this by tunneling the creek right through a cliff—quite a feat.

The trail climbs to a junction, and it's worth it to head right on the Mount Defiance Trail a short distance for a peak at Lancaster Falls, which falls right down to the trail. Go back to the junction and head uphill to the right on the Warren Creek Trail. In the course of an unbelievable mile, the trail fords Warren Creek and climbs to high meadows overlooking the Gorge and traces some precarious cliffs. At the Starvation Ridge Cutoff Trail, head to the left and down an incredibly steep 0.3 mile to return to the old highway site, heading to the right to return to the Starvation Creek Falls lot.

User Groups: Hikers and dogs. No mountain bikes or horses allowed. Paved areas of the park are wheelchair accessible.

Permits: Permits are not required. Parking and access are free.

Maps: You can purchase a Trails of the Columbia Gorge Map from Geo-Graphics. For a topographic map, ask the USGS for Mount Defiance.

Directions: From Cascade Locks, drive 10 miles east on I-84 to the Starvation Creek trailhead at Exit 55.

Contact: Oregon Parks and Recreation Department, 1115 Commercial Street NE, Salem, OR, 97301, 800/551-6949, www.oregonstateparks.org, and Columbia Gorge National Scenic Area, 902 Wasco Avenue, Suite 200, Hood River, OR, 97031, 541/308-1700.

MOUNT DEFIANCE AND STARVATION RIDGE

11.4 mi/1 day   🏃5 ⛰8

east of Cascade Locks in the Columbia River Gorge

Map 3.2, page 126

Mount Defiance is one of the most difficult hikes in the entire state of Oregon, so let's just say that right off the bat. Are you ready for a rough-and-tumble challenge in the highest degree? Then climb this monster of a trail—with a nearly 5,000-foot elevation gain—to the peak rising from the Hatfield Wilderness. Talk about views. This being the highest point in the Columbia Gorge, you'll see Cascade peaks ringing you in. For a real day of it, try an exhausting but ultimately rewarding loop trail down Starvation Ridge. Don't let words like "Defiance" and "Starvation" get you down, but give yourself a full day to tackle this one.

Following signs for Mount Defiance, hike along the highway for the first mile on the Mount Defiance Trail, keeping right at junctions and passing two waterfalls. After the second junction with the Warren Creek Trail, continue to the right toward Mount Defiance, passing Lancaster Falls and charging up the mountain 3.9 miles on switchbacks and through the woods to a junction with the Mitchell Point Trail, which will serve as the return route. Go uphill 0.2 mile to the next junction, and take the Mount Defiance Trail to the right, overlooking Bear Lake and the Hatfield Wilderness. In one mile, you'll arrive at the peak.

To head down, pass the tower and look for an old trail sign. Follow this trail down 0.8 mile, crossing a road twice, then go downhill at the next junction 0.2 mile, then head right 0.8 mile along the Mitchell Trail, reaching Warren Lake. Continue forward, watching for a junction and turning left onto the Starvation Ridge Trail, for a total of 3.7 miles. Near the bottom, take the right-hand Starvation Cutoff Trail, steeply switchbacking 0.3 mile, then going right on the Mount Defiance Trail 0.3 mile back to the lot.

User Groups: Hikers and dogs. No mountain bikes or horses allowed. No wheelchair facilities.

Permits: A free self-issue Wilderness Permit is required and is available on the trail. Parking and access are free.

Maps: You can purchase a Trails of the

Columbia Gorge Map from Geo-Graphics. For a topographic map, ask the USGS for Mount Defiance.

Directions: From Cascade Locks, drive 10 miles east on I-84 to the Starvation Creek trailhead at Exit 55.

Contact: Columbia Gorge National Scenic Area, 902 Wasco Avenue, Suite 200, Hood River, OR, 97031, 541/308-1700.

25 WYGANT PEAK
8.5 mi/5.5 hr   👥4 ⛰️8

east of Cascade Locks in the Columbia River Gorge

Map 3.2, page 126

Two prominent points rise above a small rest area on I-84: 1,200-foot Mitchell Point and 2,144-foot Wygant Peak. The trail up 1.1 miles to Mitchell is relatively easy; it's a hardier hike to get to forested Wygant Peak, but along the way there are great views over the Gorge and a loop-trail option along Perham Creek. What makes it hardy is that, for the most part, this trail is not maintained, meaning that you'll be ducking under fallen trees and hopping over some collapsed trail. Use caution. What's most frustrating is how much longer it takes when you have to bushwhack your way along the route.

From the lot, head back down the road to a gated road, following the clearly marked Wygant Trail one mile along both trail and a stretch of the old Columbia River Highway to a junction. Stay straight on the Wygant Trail for 1.6 miles, crossing Perham Creek and topping a viewpoint before climbing to the Chetwood Trail. To climb Wygant, go right 1.7 miles past a few good viewpoints to the peak.

Returning 1.7 miles to the junction, you can either return as you came or try some adventure by going right on the Chetwood Trail for 1.5 mile, crossing Perham Creek higher up in its canyon, before returning to the Wygant Trail via the Perham Loop Trail.

footbridge on the Wygant Trail

When you hit the Wygant, go right to return to the car. Be aware that this extra loop is every bit as unmaintained as the Wygant, and the creek crossing should be done when the water is low.

User Groups: Hikers and dogs. No mountain bikes or horses allowed. Paved areas of the park are wheelchair accessible.

Permits: Permits are not required. Parking and access are free.

Maps: You can purchase a Hood River map from Geo-Graphics. For a topographic map, ask the USGS for Mount Defiance.

Directions: From Cascade Locks, drive 14 miles east on I-84 to Exit 58 to the Lausman State Park rest area.

Contact: Oregon Parks and Recreation Department, 1115 Commercial Street NE, Salem, OR, 97301, 800/551-6949, www.oregonstateparks.org.

© SEAN PATRICK HILL

26 MOSIER TWIN TUNNELS
4.5 mi one-way/2.0 hr   👣1 ⛰8

east of Hood River in the Columbia River Gorge

Map 3.2, page 126   **BEST (**

The old Columbia River Highway sat abandoned for decades—until 1995, when stretches of it were restored to become part of the state trail system. The stretch between the city of Hood River and the town of Mosier is perfect for a long bike ride or an easy hike—excepting, perhaps, the wind, which is famous in the Columbia Gorge.

The real treasures here are a couple of tunnels that took two years to build. For an easy visit to the tunnels, start on the Mosier side and go as far as you'd like: to the County Line Overlook, a viewpoint over Koberg Beach State Wayside, or all the way to the Hood River trailhead. By the time you get east of Hood River you're in a new landscape of basalt rock and oak and ponderosa pine, differing dramatically from the more lush western Gorge.

From the Mosier parking area, follow a paved path to the gated road that marks the trail's entrance. From here it's a 0.7-mile walk to the Mosier Twin Tunnels and their sturdy roof, built to withstand massive rockfall. In another 0.9 mile, you'll reach the County Line Overlook on the border of Wasco and Hood River Counties. Yet another 0.8 mile beyond that is a 0.2-mile side trail out on a cliff to the overlook of Koberg Beach. From here, it's another 1.9 miles to the trail's end.

User Groups: Hikers, dogs, and mountain bikes. No horses allowed. The Historic Columbia Highway Trail is entirely wheelchair accessible, and there is a separate parking area for wheelchair users.

Permits: Permits are not required. A $3 day-use fee is collected at the park entrance, or you can get an annual Oregon Parks and Recreation pass for $25; contact Oregon Parks and Recreation, 800/551-6949.

Maps: For a map of the Historic Columbia River Highway State Trail, contact Oregon Parks and Recreation Department, 800/551-6949, www.oregonstateparks.org. For a topographic map, ask the USGS for White Salmon and Hood River.

Directions: Drive east of Hood River five miles on I-84 to the Mosier exit (Exit 69). Go south from the exit 0.2 mile to Mosier and turn left on Rock Creek Road for 0.7 mile to the Hatfield Trailhead on the left. For the western trailhead, take I-84, exit 64, and follow Government Camp signs for 0.3 mile. At a stop sign, go left on Old Columbia River Drive for 1.3 miles to road's end.

Contact: Oregon Parks and Recreation Department, 1115 Commercial Street NE, Salem, OR, 97301, 800/551-6949, www.oregonstateparks.org.

27 TOM MCCALL PRESERVE
5.6 mi/3.0 hr   👣2 ⛰7

east of Hood River in the Columbia River Gorge

Map 3.2, page 126

More than 300 varieties of plants grow on the dramatic oak grasslands above the Columbia River and Rowena Dell. Thanks to The Nature Conservancy, this fabulous preserve—named for former Oregon Governor McCall, a conservationist—is open to everyone. Spring and early summer mark some of the showiest wildflower shows anywhere, though poison oak has a grip here, too. Lava flows and ash deposits coupled with massive floods have produced this strange mound-and-swale topography that baffles even the experts on that sort of thing. Here you'll find meadowlarks, the Oregon state bird, as well as canyon wrens, Pacific chorus frogs, and mule deer. Flowers include grass widows, prairie stars, lupine, Indian paintbrush, balsamroot, milk vetch, shooting stars, and waterleaf, several of which are found only in the Gorge.

Two trails lead out from the Rowena Crest Viewpoint. Opposite the highway from the parking area, a sign marks the lower plateau trail, an easy 2.2-mile round-trip that visits two ponds and several viewpoints. The upper trail to Tom McCall Point leads uphill for 1.7 miles to the 1,722-foot knob overlooking the eastern Gorge.

User Groups: Hikers only. No dogs, horses, or mountain bikes allowed. No wheelchair facilities.

Permits: Permits are not required. Parking and access are free.

Maps: Brochures are typically available at the trailhead. For a topographic map, ask the USGS for White Salmon.

Directions: Drive east of Hood River five miles on I-84 to the Mosier exit (Exit 69) and follow "Scenic Loop" signs 6.6 miles to the Rowena Crest Viewpoint.

Contact: The Nature Conservancy, 821 SE 14th Street, Portland, OR, 97214, 503/802-8100.

28 WAHTUM LAKE
4.1 mi/2.5 hr

south of Hood River in the Hatfield Wilderness

Map 3.2, page 126

Hiking the entire length of the Eagle Creek Trail (see *Eagle Creek* listing in this chapter) is one way to get to Wahtum Lake, but it requires a backpack and several days. There's an easier way: You can start right from the deep blue lake itself and follow the Pacific Crest Trail to a viewpoint on the rocky bluffs of Chinidere Mountain, looking out to Tanner Butte, the Benson Plateau, and five Cascade peaks.

From the Wahtum Lake Campground, take the Wahtum Express Trail down 0.2 mile to the lake. Turn right on the Pacific Crest Trail, rounding the lake through the Hatfield Wilderness and going 1.6 miles to a junction, going left. Then go right and uphill past a "Chinidere Mountain" sign up a steep 0.4 mile to the former lookout site. To return via the loop, head down to the PCT, go left 100 yards, and continue right 0.9 mile on the Chinidere Mountain Trail. You'll pass campsites and cross a creek, then join the Eagle Creek Trail. Stay to the left at this junction and the PCT

junction, going another 0.4 mile and passing more campsites along the lakeshore. At the final junction, go right on the Wahtum Express to return 0.2 mile to the car.

User Groups: Hikers, dogs, and horses. No mountain bikes allowed. No wheelchair facilities.

Permits: A free self-issue Wilderness Permit is required and is available at the trailhead. A federal Northwest Forest Pass is required to park here; the cost is $5 a day or $30 for an annual pass. You can buy a day pass at the trailhead, at ranger stations, or through private vendors.

Maps: You can purchase a Trails of the Columbia Gorge Map from Geo-Graphics. For a topographic map, ask the USGS for Wahtum Lake.

Directions: Drive I-84 east of Portland to West Hood River at Exit 62, driving 1.1 miles into Hood River. Turn right on 13th Street, and follow signs for Odell for 3.4 miles. Cross the Hood River Bridge and turn right on a fork past Tucker Park for 6.3 miles. Fork right again toward Dee, cross the river, and turn left toward Lost Lake for 4.9 miles. Turn right at a "Wahtum Lake" sign and follow Road 13 for 4.3 miles, then go right on Road 1310 for six miles to the Wahtum Lake Campground.

Contact: Columbia Gorge National Scenic Area, 902 Wasco Avenue, Suite 200, Hood River, OR, 97031, 541/308-1700.

29 BEAR LAKE AND MOUNT DEFIANCE
6.4 mi/ 3.5 hr

south of Hood River in the Hatfield Wilderness

Map 3.2, page 126

The grueling way up Mount Defiance (see *Mount Defiance and Starvation Ridge* listing in this chapter) isn't for everyone; this is a far easier way to the top, and one that visits pretty little Bear Lake along the way. It's so shallow and warm in summer that it's perfect for a quick swim.

Follow the Mount Defiance Trail to a junction and go right for 0.5 mile. A left-hand trail at the next junction leads 0.8 mile to Bear Lake. Continuing on the Mount Defiance Trail 0.9 mile, the path comes to another junction; go right 0.2 mile to the peak. To make a loop of it, with a view down to Bear Lake, walk past the tower and look for an old trail sign for the Mount Defiance Trail. Follow this trail down 0.8 mile, crossing a road twice, then go left on an unmarked trail one mile, rounding the peak. This will bring you back to the Mount Defiance Trail, which you can follow 1.4 miles back to the road.

User Groups: Hikers, dogs, and horses. No mountain bikes allowed. No wheelchair facilities.

Permits: A free self-issue Wilderness Permit is required and is available on the trail. Parking and access are free.

Maps: You can purchase a Trails of the Columbia Gorge Map from Geo-Graphics. For a topographic map, ask the USGS for Mount Defiance.

Directions: Drive I-84 east of Portland to West Hood River at Exit 62, driving 1.1 miles into Hood River. Turn right on 13th Street, and follow signs for Odell for 3.4 miles. Cross the Hood River Bridge and turn right on a fork past Tucker Park for 6.3 miles. Fork right again toward Dee, cross the river, and turn right toward Rainy Lake. Follow paved Punchbowl Road for 1.4 miles and continue on gravel Road 2820 for 10 miles to a sign for Mount Defiance Trail on the right.

Contact: Columbia Gorge National Scenic Area, 902 Wasco Avenue, Suite 200, Hood River, OR, 97031, 541/308-1700.

30 BALD BUTTE
8.2 mi/5.0 hr   🥾4 ⛰8

south of Hood River in Mount Hood National Forest

Map 3.2, page 126

Not to be confused with the plethora of other Bald Buttes out there, this one has the required

old lookout site to provide a sweeping view of the Hood River Valley and nearby Mount Hood, then clear out into the Washington Cascades: St. Helens, Rainier, and Adams. Not bad for a hike that'll make you work for it, gaining 2,300 feet in elevation when all is said and done. Making use of the popular horse-and-bike trail on Surveyor's Ridge, this peak still remains fairly off-the-map.

Take the Oakridge Trail 2.5 miles from the grassy meadow into the fir and oak forest and climb the switchbacks. Turn left on the Surveyor's Ridge Trail for 0.9 mile then stay straight on a dirt road another 0.7 mile to the summit.

User Groups: Hikers, dogs, mountain bikes, and horses. No wheelchair facilities.

Permits: Permits are not required. Parking and access are free.

Maps: For a map of the Mount Hood National Forest, contact Mount Hood National Forest Headquarters, 16400 Champion Way, Sandy, OR, 97055, 503/668-1700. For a topographic map, ask the USGS for Parkdale.

Directions: From I-84 at Hood River, take Exit 64 and follow Highway 35 south for 14.8 miles. Turn left on Smullen Road 0.3 mile, then turn left on a gravel road 0.1 mile to the trailhead.

Contact: Mount Hood National Forest, Hood River Ranger District, 6780 Highway 35, Parkdale, OR, 97041, 541/352-6002.

31 LOST LAKE
3.2 mi/1.5 hr   🥾1 ⛰7

south of Hood River in Mount Hood National Forest

Map 3.2, page 126

Located on the north slope of Mount Hood, this lake has long been a popular destination for travelers. The Hood River tribe knew about it, naming it "Heart of the Mountains." A resort and campground are there now, and the lakeshore has been restored after years of heavy use. In just over three miles, you can treat yourself to stunning views of Mount Hood and Lost Lake Butte, watching for high-elevation birds along the water. The 3.4-mile shoreline loop trail can be taken in either direction, and a junction near a group camp leads to Lost Lake Butte (see *Lost Lake Butte,* next listing).

User Groups: Hikers and dogs. Mountain bikes and horses not allowed. Parts of the trail are wheelchair accessible.

Permits: Permits are not required. There is a day-use fee of $7 collected at the entry booth.

Maps: For a map of the Mount Hood National Forest, contact Mount Hood National Forest Headquarters, 16400 Champion Way, Sandy, OR, 97055, 503/668-1700. For a topographic map, ask the USGS for Bull Run Lake.

Directions: From Exit 62 in Hood River, drive 1.1 miles into town, turn right on 13th Street and follow signs for Odell for five miles. Cross a bridge and fork right past Tucker Park for 6.3 miles, then fork right again toward Dee and follow signs 14 miles to Lost Lake. Drive past the Lost Lake entry booth, go toward the store, and follow the lake to the right to a picnic area at the end of the road.

Contact: Mount Hood National Forest, Hood River Ranger District, 6780 Highway 35, Parkdale, OR, 97041, 541/352-6002.

32 LOST LAKE BUTTE
3.8 mi/2.0 hr 🚶2 ⛰8

south of Hood River in Mount Hood National Forest

Map 3.2, page 126

Rising over a thousand feet above picturesque Lost Lake, this butte of the same name has a character all its own. Hiking its viewless forested slopes will eventually lead to an unimpeded view of Mount Rainier, Mount Adams, and Mount Hood. Along the way, you'll find beargrass blooms in summer and rhododendron blossoms in spring.

This hike begins from Campground Loop

B, climbing 1.9 miles up the forested slope to some easy switchbacks at the top. The best views are from the remains of an old watchtower.

User Groups: Hikers and dogs. Mountain bikes and horses not allowed. Parts of the trail are wheelchair accessible.

Permits: Permits are not required. There is a day-use fee of $7 collected at the entry booth.

Maps: For a map of the Mount Hood National Forest, contact Mount Hood National Forest Headquarters, 16400 Champion Way, Sandy, OR, 97055, 503/668-1700. For a topographic map, ask the USGS for Bull Run Lake.

Directions: From Exit 62 in Hood River, drive 1.1 miles into town, turn right on 13th Street and follow signs for Odell for five miles. Cross a bridge, and fork right past Tucker Park for 6.3 miles, then fork right again toward Dee and follow signs 14 miles to Lost Lake. Drive past the Lost Lake entry booth, go toward the store, and follow the lake to the right to a picnic area at the end of the road.

Contact: Mount Hood National Forest, Hood River Ranger District, 6780 Highway 35, Parkdale, OR, 97041, 541/352-6002.

33 WEST ZIGZAG MOUNTAIN
11.0 mi/8.0 hr 🚶4 ⛰9

north of Zigzag in the Mount Hood Wilderness

Map 3.2, page 126

Just above the town of Zigzag, the border of the Mount Hood Wilderness begins at the base of Zigzag Mountain, so big it becomes two peaks: East and West. Tackling West Zigzag is no mean feat, as the trail climbs nearly 3,000 feet in only 2.3 miles, then heads out over the ridge to a lookout site. Still, this well-graded trail won't totally break you; it'll just strengthen your calves a bit.

The first 1.3 miles of the Zigzag Mountain Trail switchback up steeply. The next 2.3 miles climbs as well, to a high point of 4,300 feet. After that, the next 1.9 miles provides some views over the mountains, coming to the old lookout site atop some rocky cliffs.

User Groups: Hikers, dogs, and horses. No mountain bikes allowed. No wheelchair facilities.

Permits: A free self-issue Wilderness Permit is required and is available at the trailhead. Parking and access are free.

Maps: For a map of the Mount Hood National Forest, contact Mount Hood National Forest Headquarters, 16400 Champion Way, Sandy, OR, 97055, 503/668-1700. A map of the Mount Hood Wilderness is available from Geo-Graphics. For a topographic map, ask the USGS for Rhododendron.

Directions: Drive east of Portland 42 miles on U.S. 26 to Zigzag, turning left onto East Lolo Pass Road for 0.4 mile. Turn right on East Mountain Drive for 0.2 mile, keeping right at a fork. After 0.5 mile, watch for a sign on the left for the Zigzag Mountain Trail and park on the shoulder.

Contact: Mount Hood National Forest, Zigzag Ranger District, 70220 East Highway 26, Zigzag, OR, 97049, 503/622-3191.

34 EAST ZIGZAG MOUNTAIN
8.0 mi/5.0 hr   🥾 3 ⛰️ 9

north of Zigzag in the Mount Hood Wilderness

Map 3.2, page 126

Like West Zigzag Mountain, East Zigzag Mountain provides some immense views over the surrounding country. The difference, though, is that this trail isn't quite as difficult. It's still difficult, just not bone-crushingly so. What you'll find is a ramble through Devil's Meadow, a side trail to Cast Lake, and high-alpine country looking out over the Mount Hood Wilderness.

From the Burnt Lake Trailhead, follow signs for Devil's Meadow. The Burnt Lake Trail follows an old road into this abandoned campground, going 2.6 miles to a junction, the start of the loop. Follow "Burnt Lake" signs to the right, going 1.4 miles to a junction atop a ridge.

Go left one mile, passing the East Zigzag summit at 4,971 feet and arriving at a junction with the Cast Creek Trail, heading to the left. The next junction leads to Cast Lake on the right, which will add 1.2 miles to your round-trip mileage. Continuing on the Zigzag Mountain Trail, you'll reach a junction with the Devil's Tie Trail; take this left-hand turn for 0.4 mile to return to Devil's Meadow, then go right the remaining 2.6 miles back to the trailhead.

User Groups: Hikers and dogs. No horses or mountain bikes. No wheelchair facilities.

Permits: A free self-issue Wilderness Permit is required and is available at the trailhead. Parking and access are free.

Maps: For a map of the Mount Hood National Forest, contact Mount Hood National Forest Headquarters, 16400 Champion Way, Sandy, OR, 97055, 503/668-1700. A map of the Mount Hood Wilderness is available from Geo-Graphics. For a topographic map, ask the USGS for Government Camp.

Directions: Drive east of Portland 47 miles on U.S. 26 to the village of Rhododendron. Turn left on Road 27 for 0.6 mile. Turn left on gravel Road 207 for 4.5 miles until it ends; this road is rough, so cars should take it slow.

Contact: Mount Hood National Forest, Zigzag Ranger District, 70220 East Highway 26, Zigzag, OR, 97049, 503/622-3191.

35 BURNT LAKE
6.8 mi/3.5 hr   🥾 2 ⛰️ 8

northeast of Zigzag in the Mount Hood Wilderness

Map 3.2, page 126

The area around Burnt Lake burned once and left massive hollowed-out cedar stumps. It's a heavily visited spot in the Mount Hood Forest, and rightfully so: It reflects nearby Mount Hood and is ringed in by big trees and a half-mile loop trail. Along the way, the nearly hidden Lost Creek Falls lie a bit off the trail and East Zigzag Mountain looms overhead like a great wall.

From the Burnt Lake Trailhead, follow the trail between two creeks—Burnt Lake Creek and Lost Creek—for 2.4 miles, crossing Burnt Lake Creek and arriving at a side trail to the left leading down to Lost Creek Falls. Continue on the main trail another mile to arrive at the shore of Burnt Lake.

User Groups: Hikers and dogs. No horses or mountain bikes allowed. No wheelchair facilities.

Permits: A free self-issue Wilderness Permit is required and is available at the trailhead. A federal Northwest Forest Pass is required to park here; the cost is $5 a day or $30 for an annual pass. You can buy a day pass at the trailhead, at ranger stations, or through private vendors.

Maps: For a map of the Mount Hood National Forest, contact Mount Hood National Forest Headquarters, 16400 Champion Way, Sandy, OR, 97055, 503/668-1700. A map of the Mount Hood Wilderness is available from Geo-Graphics. For a topographic map, ask the USGS for Government Camp.

Directions: Drive east of Portland 42 miles on U.S. 26 to Zigzag. Turn left on East Lolo Pass Road, following this route 4.2 miles and turn right on Road 1825 for 0.7 mile. Turn right across the Sandy River Bridge and continue on Road 1825 another 2.1 miles to the entrance for Lost Creek Campground. Go left on a gravel road 1.4 miles to its end at a parking area.

Contact: Mount Hood National Forest, Zigzag Ranger District, 70220 East Highway 26, Zigzag, OR, 97049, 503/622-3191.

36 RAMONA FALLS

7.1 mi/3.5 hr   👣2 ⛰8

northeast of Zigzag in the Mount Hood Wilderness

Map 3.2, page 126   **BEST (**

The Sandy River flows from Mount Hood and tumbles down a rocky bed. It's not filled with sand, though early pioneers thought it was. Actually, the milky color of many young mountain rivers is due to glacial silt.

This fine loop travels upstream to Ramona Falls, a 120-foot drop in a lovely fern-draped glen of columnar basalt. If the bridge is out when you visit (as it has been in the past), you will have to ford the Sandy River; this is easiest and safest late in the summer, when the water drops and exposes stones to cross over.

From the trailhead, head up the Sandy River 1.4 miles to a crossing. After fording the river, turn right on the PCT Horse Trail for 1.5 miles to a junction with the Pacific Crest Trail, and go left 0.5 mile to reach the falls on Ramona Creek. At the next junction just beyond the waterfall, continue left for 1.8 miles on the PCT, then take a left turn for 0.5 mile to return to the Sandy River crossing, fording it then going right the remaining 1.4 miles to the lot.

User Groups: Hikers, dogs, and horses. No mountain bikes allowed. No wheelchair facilities.

Permits: A free self-issue Wilderness Permit is required and is available at the trailhead. A federal Northwest Forest Pass is required to park here; the cost is $5 a day or $30 for an annual pass. You can buy a day pass at the trailhead, at ranger stations, or through private vendors.

Maps: For a map of the Mount Hood National Forest, contact Mount Hood National Forest Headquarters, 16400 Champion Way, Sandy, OR, 97055, 503/668-1700. A map of the Mount Hood Wilderness is available from Geo-Graphics. For a topographic map, ask the USGS for Bull Run Lake.

Directions: From Portland, drive U.S. 26 east toward Mount Hood 42 miles. At Zigzag, turn left onto East Lolo Pass Road and go 4.2 miles, then turn right on Road 1825. Drive 0.7 mile and turn right across the Sandy River. Continue 1.8 miles on Road 1825 and go left on Road 100 for 0.5 mile to a parking area at the end of the road.

Contact: Mount Hood National Forest, Zigzag Ranger District, 70220 East Highway 26, Zigzag, OR, 97049, 503/622-3191.

37 YOCUM RIDGE

16.2 mi/10.0 hr   👫5 ▲10

northeast of Zigzag in the Mount Hood
Wilderness

Map 3.2, page 126

The meadows on Yocum Ridge are the definition of "alpine country." Set beside the Sandy Glacier on the slopes of Mount Hood, the source of the Sandy River, this makes for one of the most spectacular views on the mountain. The ascent is as arduous as the scenery is spectacular: You'll need to climb 3,800 feet from the Sandy River to get to this lush viewpoint.

From the trailhead, head up the Sandy River 1.4 miles to a crossing. After fording the river, turn right on the PCT Horse Trail for 1.5 miles to a junction with the Pacific Crest Trail, and go left 0.5 mile to reach the falls on Ramona Creek. At the next junction just beyond the waterfall, turn right on the Timberline Trail. Follow this trail 0.6 mile to a right-hand junction up the Yocum Ridge for 4.7 miles.

User Groups: Hikers, dogs, and horses. No mountain bikes allowed. No wheelchair facilities.

Permits: A free self-issue Wilderness Permit is required and is available at the trailhead. A federal Northwest Forest Pass is required to park here; the cost is $5 a day or $30 for an annual pass. You can buy a day pass at the trailhead, at ranger stations, or through private vendors.

Maps: For a map of the Mount Hood National Forest, contact Mount Hood National Forest Headquarters, 16400 Champion Way, Sandy, OR, 97055, 503/668-1700. A map of the Mount Hood Wilderness is available from Geo-Graphics. For a topographic map, ask the USGS for Mount Hood North.

Directions: From Portland, drive U.S. 26 east toward Mount Hood 42 miles. At Zigzag, turn left onto East Lolo Pass Road and go 4.2 miles, then turn right on Road 1825. Drive 0.7 mile and turn right across the Sandy River. Continue 1.8 miles on Road 1825 and go left on Road 100 for 0.5 mile to a parking area at the end of the road.

Contact: Mount Hood National Forest, Zigzag Ranger District, 70220 East Highway 26, Zigzag, OR, 97049, 503/622-3191.

38 MCNEIL POINT

8.8 mi/5.0 hr   👫4 ▲10

northeast of Zigzag in the Mount Hood
Wilderness

Map 3.2, page 126   **BEST (**

In the 1930s, the Civilian Conservation Corps built a series of beautiful stone shelters encircling Mount Hood along the Timberline Trail. Only three remain, and the loftiest must surely be the one on McNeil Point, named for Portland newspaperman Fred McNeil. The climb to the towering plateau is every bit as amazing, circling Bald Mountain, ascending through thick huckleberry fields, and finally following a towering ridge to some alpine ponds and the 6,100-foot plateau edge. But be careful: The scenery here is so spectacular that you may want to move into the cabin like a modern-day Thoreau and never leave again.

Start by climbing on the Top Spur Trail up 0.5 mile to the Pacific Crest Trail, going right at a junction, then left at the next aside a big map board. Follow the Timberline Trail 2.3 miles, staying to the right on Timberline and hiking the ridge high above the roaring Muddy Fork. At 5,300 feet, you'll pass a faint side trail, but stay on the main Timberline Trail another 0.6 mile, passing a couple of ponds and the end of the Mazama Trail to a junction. Head up this trail to the right, following a ridge up a mile to the stone shelter high atop McNeil Point. Return the way you came.

User Groups: Hikers, dogs, and horses. No mountain bikes allowed. No wheelchair facilities.

Permits: A free self-issue Wilderness Permit is required and is available at the trailhead.

A federal Northwest Forest Pass is required to park here; the cost is $5 a day or $30 for an annual pass. You can buy a day pass at the trailhead, at ranger stations, or through private vendors.

Maps: For a map of the Mount Hood National Forest, contact Mount Hood National Forest Headquarters, 16400 Champion Way, Sandy, OR, 97055, 503/668-1700. A map of the Mount Hood Wilderness is available from Geo-Graphics. For a topographic map, ask the USGS for Mount Hood North.

Directions: From Portland, drive U.S. 26 east toward Mount Hood 42 miles. At Zigzag, turn left onto East Lolo Pass Road and go 4.2 miles, then turn right on Road 1825. In 0.7 mile, go straight on Road 1828 and follow signs for "Top Spur Trail" for 7.1 miles to a parking pullout on the gravel road.

Contact: Mount Hood National Forest, Zigzag Ranger District, 70220 East Highway 26, Zigzag, OR, 97049, 503/622-3191.

39 MAZAMA TRAIL TO CAIRN BASIN
8.6 mi/5.0 hr

northeast of Zigzag in the Mount Hood Wilderness

Map 3.2, page 126   **BEST (**

This difficult trail is maintained by the Mazamas, Portland's oldest outdoors club. In 1894, the Mazamas (155 men and 38 women in all) climbed this mountain to its peak to elect their first president. Now you can get a sense of what brought them here. The trail climbs massive Cathedral Ridge to the glassy tarns and wildflower meadows on Mount Hood. The stone shelter in Cairn Basin is a good destination—with views of the forests, meadows, and peak of Mount Hood. You can make this a short backpacking trip, too, by pitching your tent at Cairn Basin.

The path is straightforward, if steep. From the trailhead, climb the Mazama Trail one mile to the Mount Hood Wilderness sign atop

a series of switchbacks. Continue 2.7 miles to this trail's terminus with the Timberline Trail. To the right is a short walk to a couple mountain tarns. Continue to the left, where a right-hand junction leads to McNeil Point (see *McNeil Point,* previous listing), or continue on to the left to Cairn Basin, a total of 0.6 mile from the end of the Mazama Trail.

User Groups: Hikers and dogs. No horses or mountain bikes allowed. No wheelchair facilities.

Permits: A free self-issue Wilderness Permit is required and is available at the trailhead. Parking and access are free.

Maps: For a map of the Mount Hood National Forest, contact Mount Hood National Forest Headquarters, 16400 Champion Way, Sandy, OR, 97055, 503/668-1700. A map of the Mount Hood Wilderness is available from Geo-Graphics. For a topographic map, ask the USGS for Mount Hood North.

Directions: From Portland, drive U.S. 26 east toward Mount Hood 42 miles. At Zigzag, turn left onto East Lolo Pass Road and go 10.5 miles to Lolo Pass. Turn right on McGee Creek Road 1810 for 5.5 miles and turn right on gravel Road 1811 for 2.5 miles to a parking pullout.

Contact: Mount Hood National Forest, Hood River Ranger District, 6780 Highway 35, Parkdale, OR, 97041, 541/352-6002.

40 CAIRN BASIN VIA VISTA RIDGE
7.9 mi/4.0 hr

north of Hood River in the Mount Hood Wilderness

Map 3.2, page 126

The stone shelter at Cairn Basin is set among some towering old-growth trees, near meadows and picturesque views of Mount Hood's enormous peak and the Ladd Glacier. This loop trail also leads through two other mountain meadows: Wy'East Basin (an ancient Native American name for this iconic mountain)

© SEAN PATRICK HILL

view of Mount Hood from Eden Park

Forest, contact Mount Hood National Forest Headquarters, 16400 Champion Way, Sandy, OR, 97055, 503/668-1700. A map of the Mount Hood Wilderness is available from Geo-Graphics. For a topographic map, ask the USGS for Mount Hood North.

Directions: From Portland, drive U.S. 26 east toward Mount Hood 42 miles. At Zigzag, turn left onto East Lolo Pass Road and go 10.5 miles to Lolo Pass. Turn right on McGee Creek Road 1810 for 7.7 miles to Road 18. Continue on this paved road 3.2 miles and turn right on Road 16, then follow "Vista Ridge Trail" signs nine miles up Road 16 and Road 1650 to the trailhead.

Contact: Mount Hood National Forest, Hood River Ranger District, 6780 Highway 35, Parkdale, OR, 97041, 541/352-6002.

41 ELK COVE

8.0 mi/5.0 hr   3 9

north of Hood River in the Mount Hood Wilderness

Map 3.2, page 126

Elk Cove, a magnificent meadow on the slopes of Mount Hood, is not only an amazing destination for a day trip but a great spot to camp. Indeed, many people do spend the night here—such as ambitious backpackers who tackle the entire length of the Timberline Trail, which circles Mount Hood, visiting an array of unforgettable spots. The trail to Elk Cove starts fairly high up the mountain, making it one of the easier destinations on Mount Hood.

The popular hike to Elk Cove from the Cloud Cap Campground is officially closed due to massive flooding on the Timberline Trail. Check with the US Forest Service before attempting this route. The following description is another way to get to Elk Cove from the Vista Ridge Trail.

Start up the Vista Ridge Trail 0.4 mile, and keep right at a junction, climbing Vista Ridge for 2.1 miles. At the next junction, head to the

and Eden Park. You can easily get water from nearby Ladd Creek, making this a good destination for backpacking. Vista Ridge Trail is easier than the nearby Mazama Trail and has views to distant peaks to boot.

Start up the Vista Ridge Trail 0.4 mile, and keep right at a junction, climbing Vista Ridge for 2.1 miles. At the next junction, head to the left 0.3 mile to arrive at the edge of Wy'East Basin. Then go right on the Timberline Trail 1.1 rambling miles with excellent views to Cairn Basin. Just past the stone shelter, take a right-hand trail down a steep slope to Eden Park, continuing to the Vista Ridge Trail, a total of 1.5 miles. Then go left to return the way you came.

User Groups: Hikers and dogs. No horses or mountain bikes allowed. No wheelchair facilities.

Permits: A free self-issue Wilderness Permit is required and is available at the trailhead. Parking and access are free.

Maps: For a map of the Mount Hood National

left 0.3 mile to arrive at the edge of Wy'East Basin. Then go left on the Timberline Trail; in just under a mile, you'll reach Elk Cove's meadows and the junction with the Elk Cove Trail.

User Groups: Hikers and dogs. No horses or mountain bikes allowed. No wheelchair facilities.

Permits: A free self-issue Wilderness Permit is required and is available at the trailhead. A federal Northwest Forest Pass is required to park here; the cost is $5 a day or $30 for an annual pass. You can buy a day pass at the trailhead, at ranger stations, or through private vendors.

Maps: For a map of the Mount Hood National Forest, contact Mount Hood National Forest Headquarters, 16400 Champion Way, Sandy, OR, 97055, 503/668-1700. A map of the Mount Hood Wilderness is available from Geo-Graphics. For a topographic map, ask the USGS for Mount Hood North.

Directions: From Portland, drive U.S. 26 east toward Mount Hood 42 miles. At Zigzag, turn left onto East Lolo Pass Road and go 10.5 miles to Lolo Pass. Turn right on McGee Creek Road 1810 for 7.7 miles to Road 18. Continue on this paved road 3.2 miles and turn right on Road 16, then follow "Vista Ridge Trail" signs nine miles up Road 16 and Road 1650 to the trailhead.

Contact: Mount Hood National Forest, Hood River Ranger District, 6780 Highway 35, Parkdale, OR, 97041, 541/352-6002.

42 COOPER SPUR

6.8 mi/4.0 hr

north of Hood River in the Mount Hood Wilderness

Map 3.2, page 126

From Cloud Cap Campground, this trail climbs to one of three CCC-built stone shelters on the flanks of Mount Hood, this one on a windswept ridge populated by a few whitebark pines, the highest-growing tree in Oregon. But the fun has only started. A steady climb over the gravely ridge of the Cooper Spur leads to an impressive view of Mount Hood and the Eliot Glacier, which on a good summer day can be heard cracking and shifting under its own massive weight. Views extend far out to Mount Jefferson and north to the peaks of the Washington Cascades. Be sure to bring sunblock and a wide-brimmed hat; there's no protection up here from the relentless sun.

From the Cloud Cap Campground, head to the Timberline Trail and go left, following it up some small gorges 1.2 miles to a four-way junction. Go right onto the Cooper Spur Trail 0.1 mile to the Cooper Spur stone shelter. Continue on this trail 2.6 miles to get up the Cooper Spur to a saddle, where a rock is carved with a 1910 commemoration for a Japanese climbing party.

User Groups: Hikers and dogs. No horses or mountain bikes allowed. No wheelchair facilities.

Permits: A free self-issue Wilderness Permit is required and is available at the trailhead. A federal Northwest Forest Pass is required to park here; the cost is $5 a day or $30 for an annual pass. You can buy a day pass at the trailhead, at ranger stations, or through private vendors.

Maps: For a map of the Mount Hood National Forest, contact Mount Hood National Forest Headquarters, 16400 Champion Way, Sandy, OR, 97055, 503/668-1700. A map of the Mount Hood Wilderness is available from Geo-Graphics. For a topographic map, ask the USGS for Mount Hood North.

Directions: From Highway 35 on the east side of Mount Hood, between mileposts 73 and 74, go west on Cooper Spur Road for 3.3 miles to Tilly Jane Junction, and turn left on Road 3512 to go 10.3 miles to the Cloud Cap Campground.

Contact: Mount Hood National Forest, Hood River Ranger District, 6780 Highway 35, Parkdale, OR, 97041, 541/352-6002.

43 CLOUD CAP VIA POLALLIE RIDGE

6.0 mi/3.5 hr   🥾3 ⛰7

on the northeast slope of Mount Hood

Map 3.2, page 126

Atop a timbered knoll high on the flanks of Mount Hood is the Cloud Cap Inn, built in 1889 and listed on the National Register of Historic Places. Though the historic chalet is accessible by road, there's an old ski trail that leads there—making it that much more of a destination. Along the way, the trail passes the deep and scoured Polallie Canyon, with side trail options to the Cooper Spur and the stone shelter on its flanks (see *Cooper Spur,* previous listing). You'll also pass just behind the Tilly Jane Campground and its 1924 cookhouse and old amphitheater.

From the trailhead, hike 2.6 miles up Tilly Jane Ski Trail and along the Polallie Canyon to Tilly Jane Campground, then head to the right on a 0.5-mile spur trail to Cloud Cap Campground. From here, go to the road and follow it up a short distance to views from the old inn. Head back to Tilly Jane and follow the sign for "Tilly Jane #600A" to the Polallie Ridge Trail for a return loop.

User Groups: Hikers and dogs. No horses or mountain bikes allowed. No wheelchair facilities.

Permits: Permits are not required. Parking and access are free.

Maps: For a map of the Mount Hood National Forest, contact Mount Hood National Forest Headquarters, 16400 Champion Way, Sandy, OR, 97055, 503/668-1700. For a topographic map, ask the USGS for Mount Hood North.

Directions: From Highway 35 on the east side of Mount Hood, between mileposts 73 and 74, go west on Cooper Spur Road for 3.3 miles to Tilly Jane Junction, and turn left on Road 3512 to go 1.4 miles to a trail sign on the left.

Contact: Mount Hood National Forest, Hood River Ranger District, 6780 Highway 35, Parkdale, OR, 97041, 541/352-6002.

44 WILDCAT MOUNTAIN AND MCINTYRE RIDGE

10.0 mi/5.5 hr   🥾4 ⛰8

southeast of Sandy in Mount Hood National Forest

Map 3.2, page 126

The long McIntyre Ridge, alternately easy and steep, climbs to Wildcat Mountain and its overgrown former watchtower site. But the ridge has great views of the Mount Hood country from its meadows, looking over the Salmon-Huckleberry Wilderness and out to nearby Huckleberry Mountain.

From the McIntyre Ridge Trailhead, the path begins its climb through acres of huckleberry fields and forest 2.1 miles to the first clear viewpoint. Another 0.8 mile leads to a fine mountain meadow with awesome views, though the trails meander every which way here. The next 1.6 miles heads out into another large meadow to a junction with the Douglas Trail. Go left and up for 0.5 mile to the 4,480-foot summit of Wildcat Mountain.

User Groups: Hikers, dogs, and horses. No mountain bikes allowed. No wheelchair facilities.

Permits: A free self-issue Wilderness Permit is required and is available at the trailhead. Parking and access are free.

Maps: For a map of the Mount Hood National Forest and the Salmon-Huckleberry Wilderness, contact Mount Hood National Forest Headquarters, 16400 Champion Way, Sandy, OR, 97055, 503/668-1700. For a topographic map, ask the USGS for Wildcat Mountain.

Directions: From Portland, drive U.S. 26 toward Mount Hood. At 11 miles past Sandy, turn right onto East Wildcat Creek Road for 1.5 miles. Note that the BLM has closed the road to McIntyre Ridge from this point for the time being; contact the Forest Service for updates and for information on other access points. To hike into the trailhead from here, stay on the larger road at all forks for three miles. The McIntyre Ridge Trailhead is after the last stretch of deeply rutted road.

Contact: Mount Hood National Forest, Zigzag Ranger District, 70220 East Highway 26, Zigzag, OR, 97049, 503/622-3191.

45 WILDWOOD RECREATION SITE/BOULDER RIDGE/HUCKLEBERRY MOUNTAIN

1.5–11.6 mi/1.0–6.0 hr 🏃4 ⛰8

southeast of Sandy off U.S. 26

Map 3.2, page 126   **BEST (**

A network of trails here spans the Wildwood Recreation Site and the Salmon-Huckleberry Wilderness, located along the Wild and Scenic Salmon River. There's plenty to do here, including fishing, swimming, wildlife-watching, and a number of short loop trails. It's also the gateway to a challenging loop up Boulder Ridge to the summit of Huckleberry Mountain and back down again. If you're camping with a group of people and you have two cars, I recommend a shuttle to tackle Boulder Ridge; otherwise, the loop requires you to hike a long ways down roads and highways. If you try this loop, you'll follow the deep Cheeney Creek canyon and pass the abandoned shaft of the Bonanza Mine. If you have the kids, you can make it an easy day and stick to the easier Wildwood Trails.

The Wildwood loops are an easy 1.5 mile altogether and are all-accessible. To try the loops, or part of them, follow either the 0.7-mile Wetland Trail or the 0.8-mile Streamwatch Loop, which both begin at the trailhead parking area.

For a more challenging day, take the Wetland Trail loop 0.3 mile to the right to the Boulder Ridge Trail. This path climbs steeply up Boulder Ridge, passing two viewpoints 4.3 miles to a junction with the Plaza Trail. Turn right and go up another mile to a crest on Huckleberry Mountain. Another 0.5 mile follows the ridge to the Bonanza Trail. This, or any point before, would be a fine turn-around point.

If you've arranged for a shuttle, go left on the Bonanza Trail, following it down the mountain 2.4 miles to the mine shaft near a creek, and the remaining 2.7 miles to the end of the trail, fording a creek at the end.

User Groups: Hikers and dogs. No horses or mountain bikes allowed. Wildwood Trails are wheelchair accessible.

Permits: Permits are not required. The BLM charges a $5 parking fee at the site.

Maps: For a map of the Mount Hood National Forest and the Salmon-Huckleberry Wilderness, contact Mount Hood National Forest Headquarters, 16400 Champion Way, Sandy, OR, 97055, 503/668-1700. For a topographic map, ask the USGS for Rhododendron and Wildcat Mountain.

Directions: Follow U.S. 26 past Sandy 15.4 miles, and turn south into the Wildwood Recreation Site. To shuttle a car for the Bonanza Trail, drive U.S. 26 another mile east of Wildwood to a stoplight at Welches and turn right on Welches Road for 1.3 miles, staying left at a fork, and driving 0.7 mile to another junction, heading straight across a one-lane bridge. Take the second gravel street to the left and follow East Grove Lane to a fork. The road closed by a cable is the start of the Bonanza Trail. The Wildwood Trails begin in the Recreation Area.

Contact: Bureau of Land Management, Salem District Office, 1717 Fabry Road SE, Salem, OR, 97306, 503/375-5646, and Mount Hood National Forest, Zigzag Ranger District, 70220 East Highway 26, Zigzag, OR, 97049, 503/622-3191.

46 HUNCHBACK MOUNTAIN

4.2–9.0 mi/2.0–4.5 hr 🏃4 ⛰7

at Zigzag in the Salmon-Huckleberry Wilderness

Map 3.2, page 126

How did Hunchback Mountain get its name? I have two guesses: one is the general hunching shape of the mountain itself, easily discernable from the highway, and the other is the way you feel when you're going up this beast. Yes, Hunchback Mountain is steep, steep, steep, and coming down is no easier. The nine-mile round-trip out to the Great Pyramid is an ample day's journey. There are good viewpoints along the way, and once you're on top of the ridge things get a bit easier. A bit.

From the trailhead, climb on Hunchback Mountain Trail, a steep path, for 2.1 harsh, switchbacking miles to a viewpoint on some sheer rimrock just inside the wilderness boundary. In another 0.3 mile, a side trail leads to the big, jumbled "Viewpoint Rockpile"—another great view. Another 1.1 miles leads to the "Viewpoint Helispot 260," though as far as I know no helicopter has landed here in a long time. Another mile past that leads to a side trail by a junction leading out to a viewpoint on the 4,030-foot Great Pyramid, overlooking the Salmon River canyon. Though Devil's Peak is farther on, this is a good spot to turn around; the trail sharply drops in elevation after this, only to rise again later.

User Groups: Hikers and dogs. No mountain bikes or horses allowed. No wheelchair facilities.

Permits: A free self-issue Wilderness Permit is required and is available at the trailhead. Parking and access are free.

Maps: For a map of the Mount Hood National Forest and the Salmon-Huckleberry Wilderness, contact Mount Hood National Forest Headquarters, 16400 Champion Way, Sandy, OR, 97055, 503/668-1700. For a topographic map, ask the USGS for Rhododendron.

Directions: From Portland, drive 42 miles east on U.S. 26 to the Zigzag Ranger Station in Zigzag. Turn left into a large parking lot by the trailhead.

Contact: Mount Hood National Forest, Zigzag Ranger District, 70220 East Highway 26, Zigzag, OR, 97049, 503/622-3191.

47 CASTLE CANYON
1.8 mi/1.0 hr

north of Rhododendron in the Mount Hood Wilderness

Map 3.2, page 126

This fun trail leads to some colossal rock formations. You'll climb up about 800 feet in 0.9 mile to reach the jagged spires of Castle Canyon, and you'll have the opportunity to scramble up and play around on the peaks and ridges looking out far over the valleys below. But be careful: These cliffs are high. If you bring pets or children, be sure to keep them close.

User Groups: Hikers and dogs. No horses or mountain bikes. No wheelchair facilities.

Permits: Permits are not required. Parking and access are free.

Maps: For a map of the Mount Hood National Forest, contact Mount Hood National Forest Headquarters, 16400 Champion Way, Sandy, OR, 97055, 503/668-1700. A map of the Mount Hood Wilderness is available from Geo-Graphics. For a topographic map, ask the USGS for Rhododendron.

Directions: Drive east of Portland 44 miles on U.S. 26 to the village of Rhododendron, and turn left on East Littlebrook Lane. Keep left on the paved road 0.3 mile and turn left on the gravel road, following Barlow Road Route for 0.4 mile to a trailhead sign on the right. Park on the shoulder.

Contact: Mount Hood National Forest, Zigzag Ranger District, 70220 East Highway 26, Zigzag, OR, 97049, 503/622-3191.

48 HIDDEN LAKE
4.0 mi/2.0 hr

north of Government Camp in Mount Hood National Forest

Map 3.2, page 126

The name is appropriate enough, as this mountain lake is secreted on an access trail to the Mount Hood Wilderness. Though the lake has no views to speak of, it's circled with pink rhododendrons. Think of this easy-in, easy-out four-mile loop trail as a destination in and of itself, or as a way into the Zigzag Canyon and Paradise Park areas of the Mount Hood Wilderness. From the trailhead, follow the Hidden Lake Trail.

User Groups: Hikers, dogs, and horses. No mountain bikes allowed. No wheelchair facilities.

Permits: A free self-issue Wilderness Permit is required and is available at the trailhead. A federal Northwest Forest Pass is required to park here; the cost is $5 a day or $30 for an annual pass. You can buy a day pass at the trailhead, at ranger stations, or through private vendors.

Maps: For a map of the Mount Hood National Forest, contact Mount Hood National Forest Headquarters, 16400 Champion Way, Sandy, OR, 97055, 503/668-1700. A map of the Mount Hood Wilderness is available from Geo-Graphics. For a topographic map, ask the USGS for Mount Hood South and Government Camp.

Directions: From Portland, drive U.S. 26 toward Mount Hood. At 4.1 miles east of the town of Rhododendron, turn left on Road 2639 for two miles to the trailhead.

Contact: Mount Hood National Forest, Zigzag Ranger District, 70220 East Highway 26, Zigzag, OR, 97049, 503/622-3191.

49 ZIGZAG CANYON AND PARADISE PARK

4.4-12.3 mi/2.5-8.0 hr   🥾5   ⛰️10

from Timberline Lodge in the Mount Hood Wilderness

Map 3.2, page 126   BEST (

Some of the most dramatic alpine territory in the Pacific Northwest is easily accessible from the classic Timberline Lodge, a gem of a building on the slopes of Mount Hood. The Pacific Crest Trail passes by the lodge on its way around the mountain and on toward the

Paradise Park on Mount Hood

© SEAN PATRICK HILL

Columbia Gorge, and it is this access that opens up the high meadows of Paradise Park and the deep, glacier-carved gorge of Zigzag Canyon. This is some serious hiking: Take lots of water and stamina and be prepared for unforgettable mountain country. You can take the trail in bits or as a 12-plus mile-escapade; either way you'll be circling the mountain on one of the most famous trails in the country. Bring a camera.

From Timberline Lodge, you can either walk the road past the lodge, which turns to trail, or follow the PCT, which runs behind the lodge; either way, in 0.7 mile both paths meet beyond the last ski lift. From here, hike 1.5 miles down and out of the gravelly Little Zigzag Canyon and on to the lip of massive Zigzag Canyon, a good turnaround point for the less ambitious.

From here, it's a 1.5-mile crossing down and back up from the 700-foot-deep canyon, but it's a pleasure along the way—with wildflowers, shady woods, and a waterfall upstream from the crossing of the Zigzag River. Once out of the canyon, the loop begins through the meadows of Paradise Park. Go right on an uphill climb leading to the boulder-strewn meadows of this unparalleled scenic area, a 2.4-mile walk through heaven. After the trail slopes back down to the PCT, go left for 2.4 miles, passing lovely waterfalls along the way, to return to the beginning of the loop and the return trail.

User Groups: Hikers, dogs, and horses. No mountain bikes allowed. No wheelchair facilities.

Permits: A free self-issue Wilderness Permit is required and is available at the trailhead. Parking and access are free.

Maps: For a map of the Mount Hood National Forest, contact Mount Hood National Forest Headquarters, 16400 Champion Way, Sandy, OR, 97055, 503/668-1700. A map of the Mount Hood Wilderness is available from Geo-Graphics. For a topographic map, ask the USGS for Government Camp and Mount Hood South.

Directions: From Portland, drive U.S. 26 toward Mount Hood for 54 miles. Past Government Camp, turn left for six miles at the sign for Timberline Lodge. Park in the lot.

Contact: Mount Hood National Forest, Zigzag Ranger District, 70220 East Highway 26, Zigzag, OR, 97049, 503/622-3191.

50 SILCOX HUT
2.2 mi/2.0 hr   👫3 ⛰9

at Timberline Lodge on Mount Hood

Map 3.2, page 126

President Franklin D. Roosevelt showed up in 1937 for the dedication of Timberline Lodge, an incredible work of art that made use of some of the best Northwest artists and artisans. The building was a Works Progress Administration project during the Great Depression; it's received much care and attention over the years, leaving a legacy of beauty. These days you can visit, eat here, or even stay

overnight. Just above the lodge is the Silcox Hut, which was at the top of the Magic Mile Chairlift from 1939 to 1962, until it sat idle for 30 years. Today it operates in the style of a classic European chalet, and you can hike here for views extending south to Mount Jefferson and the Three Sisters.

Start by following the paved path along the right-hand side of Timberline Lodge and turn right on the Pacific Crest Trail, crossing a gully, then heading uphill 1,100 feet on the Mountaineer Trail to Silcox Hut—a total of one mile. Descend a different way by heading over to the top of the Magic Mile Chairlift and following the service road down 1.2 miles back to the lodge.

User Groups: Hikers and dogs. No horses or mountain bikes allowed. No wheelchair facilities.

Permits: Permits are not required. Parking and access are free.

Maps: For a map of the Mount Hood National Forest, contact Mount Hood National Forest Headquarters, 16400 Champion Way, Sandy, OR, 97055, 503/668-1700. For a topographic map, ask the USGS for Mount Hood South.

Directions: From Portland, drive U.S. 26 toward Mount Hood for 54 miles. Past Government Camp, turn left for six miles at the sign for Timberline Lodge. Park in the lot.

Contact: Mount Hood National Forest, Zigzag Ranger District, 70220 East Highway 26, Zigzag, OR, 97049, 503/622-3191.

51 TIMBERLINE TRAIL
40.7 mi/4-5 days   👫5 ⛰10

in the Mount Hood Wilderness

Map 3.2, page 126

Up for a backpacking adventure? Want to see the best that Mount Hood has to offer, including Zigzag Canyon, Paradise Park, Ramona Falls, Bald Mountain, Cairn Basin, Wy'East Basin, Elk Cove, and the Cooper Spur? The Timberline Trail circles Mount

Hood, almost completely in a wilderness area, with easy access from historic Timberline Lodge. Crossing meadows rich with wildflowers, gorges carved by prehistoric glaciers, mountain hemlock forests—and passing snowfields, waterfalls, and views in every direction—this is one of the most breathtaking trails in Oregon.

Due to a flood and landslide in 2006, a major crossing was swept away at the Eliot Branch of the Hood River, leaving behind an insurmountable gorge where the trail once was. The Forest Service has closed this portion of the trail and expressly forbids trying to cross it, though for the determined it is possible to circumvent the disaster by detouring on a number of trails between Elk Cove and Cloud Cap. Please use care, avoid the dangerous washout, and contact the Forest Service for updates on the condition of the trail.

There are numerous access points, the most popular being Timberline Lodge, Cairn Basin, the Mazama Trail, and Cloud Cap (see listings in this chapter).

User Groups: Hikers, dogs, and horses. No mountain bikes allowed. No wheelchair facilities.

Permits: A free self-issue Wilderness Permit is required and is available at the trailhead. Parking and access are free.

Maps: For a map of the Mount Hood National Forest, contact Mount Hood National Forest Headquarters, 16400 Champion Way, Sandy, OR, 97055, 503/668-1700. A map of the Mount Hood Wilderness is available from Geo-Graphics. For a topographic map, ask the USGS for Mount Hood North.

Directions: From Portland, drive U.S. 26 toward Mount Hood for 54 miles. Past Government Camp, turn left for six miles at the sign for Timberline Lodge. Park in the lot.

Contact: Mount Hood National Forest, Zigzag Ranger District, 70220 East Highway 26, Zigzag, OR, 97049, 503/622-3191, or Hood River Ranger District, 6780 Highway 35, Parkdale, OR, 97041, 541/352-6002.

52 ELK MEADOWS

6.8 mi/3.0 hr

north of Hood River in the Mount Hood Wilderness

Map 3.2, page 126

This unassuming entrance to the Mount Hood Wilderness leads to two of its most famous spots: the sweeping Elk Meadow, rimmed in by trees and shadowed by Mount Hood itself; and Gnarl Ridge, a deep canyon carved from the mountain's flanks. Though camping is prohibited within Elk Meadow in order to protect vegetation, there are camping spots back in the trees along a 1.2-mile perimeter trail, and there's a shelter used by cross-country skiers in the winter season.

From the trailhead, walk one mile on the Elk Meadows Trail to a junction, going to the right for 0.6 mile and entering the Mount Hood Wilderness. At a second junction, go straight and cross Newton Creek, then switchback up one mile to a four-way junction. Going to the right leads out to Elk Mountain; to the left, Lamberson Butte and Gnarl Ridge. Go straight a short 0.2 mile to the Elk Meadows perimeter trail, which you can hike clockwise or counterclockwise, avoiding the trails that radiate away from the meadow.

User Groups: Hikers, dogs, and horses. No mountain bikes allowed. No wheelchair facilities.

Permits: A free self-issue Wilderness Permit is required and is available at the trailhead. A federal Northwest Forest Pass is required to park here; the cost is $5 a day or $30 for an annual pass. You can buy a day pass at the trailhead, at ranger stations, or through private vendors.

Maps: For a map of the Mount Hood National Forest, contact Mount Hood National Forest Headquarters, 16400 Champion Way, Sandy, OR, 97055, 503/668-1700. A map of the Mount Hood Wilderness is available from Geo-Graphics. For a topographic map, ask the USGS for Badger Lake.

Directions: From Portland, drive U.S 26 to

Mount Hood and take Highway 35 toward Hood River for 8.3 miles. Go 1.5 miles past the Mount Hood Meadows turnoff and turn left on the Clark Creek Sno-Park loop for 0.3 mile to the second pullout.

Contact: Mount Hood National Forest, Hood River Ranger District, 6780 Highway 35, Parkdale, OR, 97041, 541/352-6002.

53 EAST FORK HOOD RIVER
4.6 mi/2.0 hr   🚶1 ⛰7

on the East Fork Hood River

Map 3.2, page 126

Portions of the East Fork Hood River Trail remain flood damaged from a massive landslide that occurred in November 2006, but this northernmost section is still fine. Just contact the US Forest Service before you go. This stretch of trail is quite popular with mountain bikers, who can make short work of it in only a few hours. But hikers are different, having a bit more length to deal with, but they get to glide along a riverbank that effectively drowns out any highway noise. The main access point is the Pollalie Trailhead; from here, going left leads 1.1 miles to a junction with the Tamanawas Trail, and going 0.6 miles further leads to a river crossing to the East Fork Trailhead, but the bridge was wiped out in a 2006 flood. Should the rest of the East Fork Trail reopen, it will continue to a lower trailhead and a sandy stretch near the defunct Robinhood Campground.

User Groups: Hikers, dogs, and mountain bikes. Horses not allowed. No wheelchair facilities.

Permits: A free self-issue Wilderness Permit is required and is available at the trailhead. A federal Northwest Forest Pass is required to park here; the cost is $5 a day or $30 for an annual pass. You can buy a day pass at the trailhead, at ranger stations, or through private vendors.

Maps: For a map of the Mount Hood National Forest, contact Mount Hood National Forest

Headquarters, 16400 Champion Way, Sandy, OR, 97055, 503/668-1700. For a topographic map, ask the USGS for Dog River and Badger Lake.

Directions: Drive Highway 35 on the east side of Mount Hood about 8.5 miles south from the junction with U.S. 26 to the Polallie Trailhead on the left.

Contact: Mount Hood National Forest, Hood River Ranger District, 6780 Highway 35, Parkdale, OR, 97041, 541/352-6002.

54 TAMANAWAS FALLS
5.6 mi/2.0 hr   🚶2 ⛰8

in the Mount Hood National Forest

Map 3.2, page 126

This 100-foot waterfall on the flanks of Mount Hood is named Tamanawas for the Chinook Indian word meaning "spiritual guardian." Cascading in a curtain over a water-carved grotto, these falls certainly are guarding the wilderness beyond. Hiking to this spot is easy and the walk along Cold Spring Creek makes it that much better. Making a loop of it won't add too much time and effort, and you'll be rewarded by the Polallie Overlook, which looks over a vast canyon carved by a 1980 flash flood that took out both the forest and the highway. Such is the power of Mother Nature in these mountains.

To get to the falls, cross the river and head right on the East Fork Trail for 0.6 mile, then left at a junction for 0.9 mile to a junction, which will be the start of the loop. Continue 0.4 mile, crossing the creek and arriving at the falls. Head back to the junction, this time going left if you want to try the loop. You'll go up and over a ridge and down 1.6 miles to a side trail on the left for the Polallie Overlook, then continue on to a junction at the Polallie Trailhead. Stay to the right, following the highway and the river 1.7 miles back to the trailhead.

User Groups: Hikers and dogs. No horses or mountain bikes allowed. No wheelchair facilities.

Permits: Permits are not required. A federal Northwest Forest Pass is required to park here; the cost is $5 a day or $30 for an annual pass. You can buy a day pass at the trailhead, at ranger stations, or through private vendors.

Maps: For a map of the Mount Hood National Forest, contact Mount Hood National Forest Headquarters, 16400 Champion Way, Sandy, OR, 97055, 503/668-1700. For a topographic map, ask the USGS for Dog River.

Directions: Drive Highway 35 on the east side of Mount Hood to the East Fork Trailhead near milepost 72.

Contact: Mount Hood National Forest, Hood River Ranger District, 6780 Highway 35, Parkdale, OR, 97041, 541/352-6002.

55 BADGER LAKE VIA GUMJUWAC SADDLE
5.4-11.5 mi/3.0-7.0 hr

east of Mount Hood in the Badger Creek Wilderness

Map 3.2, page 126

First of all, let it be said that not just any old car can make it to the Gumjuwac Saddle; only vehicles with clearance should attempt this. If you're driving one of those little economy cars, start at the Highway 35 trailhead instead, located between mileposts 68 and 69. Either way, the destination here is Badger Lake. But there are a myriad of ways to get here. You could take the easy route on the Divide Trail, which leads 2.5 miles straight from the Gumjuwac Saddle to the Badger Creek Trail; a left and a right on this trail will bring you to the shore and an old campground. And there are plenty more ways than that, including following Gumjuwac Creek and Badger Creek on a 6.7-mile loop, or the Gunsight Trail, passing Gunsight Butte on an 8.5-mile loop with the Divide Trail, or the big 11.5-mile difficult trek from Highway 35.

User Groups: Hikers, dogs, and horses. No mountain bikes allowed. No wheelchair facilities.

Permits: A free self-issue Wilderness Permit is required and is available at the trailhead. Parking and access are free.

Maps: For a map of the Mount Hood National Forest or the Badger Creek Wilderness, contact Mount Hood National Forest Headquarters, 16400 Champion Way, Sandy, OR, 97055, 503/668-1700. For a topographic map, ask the USGS for Badger Lake.

Directions: From Highway 35 on the east side of Mount Hood, between mileposts 70 and 71, go east on Dufur Mill Road 44 for 3.8 miles, then turn right on High Prairie Road 4410. Go 4.7 miles, staying always uphill, to a T-junction where the road goes from gravel to dirt. Go right on Bennett Pass Road 3550 for 1.9 very rugged miles to the trailhead by a large sign.

Contact: Mount Hood National Forest, Barlow Ranger District, 780 NE Court Street, Dufur, OR, 97021, 541/467-2291.

56 LOOKOUT MOUNTAIN
2.4 mi/1.0 hr

east of Mount Hood in Mount Hood National Forest

Map 3.2, page 126

Not nearly as well known as the nearby Mount Hood Wilderness, the Badger Creek Wilderness provides the same rugged country and sweeping views, especially from 6,525-foot Lookout Mountain, whose views encompass Mount Rainier to the Three Sisters. For the ambitious, this trail can be extended along the Divide Trail stretching along a row of craggy palisades with a side trail down to scenic Oval Lake.

The Lookout Mountain Trail begins on an old road through the sub-alpine meadows of High Prairie, heading across through wildflowers and up a long switchback to the Divide Trail. Go right to the summit, a 1.2-mile walk in all. To continue on the Divide Trail, go 1.4 mile to a junction. Going left and down 0.2 mile takes you to Oval Lake, but staying on the Divide Trail another 0.3 mile brings you to a viewpoint on Palisade Point.

User Groups: Hikers, dogs, and horses. No mountain bikes allowed. No wheelchair facilities.

Permits: A free self-issue Wilderness Permit is required and is available at the trailhead. A federal Northwest Forest Pass is required to park here; the cost is $5 a day or $30 for an annual pass. You can buy a day pass at the trailhead, at ranger stations, or through private vendors.

Maps: For a map of the Mount Hood National Forest or the Badger Creek Wilderness, contact Mount Hood National Forest Headquarters, 16400 Champion Way, Sandy, OR, 97055, 503/668-1700. For a topographic map, ask the USGS for Badger Lake.

Directions: From Highway 35 on the east side of Mount Hood, between mileposts 70 and 71, go east on Dufur Mill Road 44 for 3.8 miles, then turn right on High Prairie Road 4410. Go 4.7 miles, staying always uphill, to a T-junction where the road goes from gravel to dirt. Go left on High Prairie Road 200 yards and park at the trailhead on the right.

Contact: Mount Hood National Forest, Barlow Ranger District, 780 NE Court Street, Dufur, OR, 97021, 541/467-2291.

57 BALL POINT
2.0-7.0 mi/1.0-3.5 hr

east of Mount Hood in the Badger Creek Wilderness

Map 3.2, page 126

Heading east into the Badger Creek Wilderness, you begin to cross into another ecosystem and climate. Things here on the eastern slope of the Cascades are a bit drier, and you're more likely to find these pine-oak grasslands, where big showy balsamroots burst in summer. From

atop Ball Point, you'll overlook everything from Cascade peaks as far as Mount Jefferson and the Three Sisters to the distant farmlands of Eastern Oregon.

The School Canyon Trail to Ball Point is an easy one-mile climb to a saddle, but it's worth it while you're here to continue on another 2.6 miles to a viewpoint at a helispot with a camping spot nearby and a spring. Views overlook Little Badger Creek, and its namesake trail switchbacks steeply down to it, running four miles to Road 2710—along the way you'll pass an old mine. The School Canyon Trail continues on to Flag Point. If this is too far in its entirety, you can turn back at any time.

User Groups: Hikers, dogs, and horses. No mountain bikes allowed. No wheelchair facilities.

Permits: A free self-issue Wilderness Permit is required and is available at the trailhead. Parking and access are free.

Maps: For a map of the Mount Hood National Forest or the Badger Creek Wilderness, contact Mount Hood National Forest Headquarters, 16400 Champion Way, Sandy, OR, 97055, 503/668-1700. For a topographic map, ask the USGS for Flag Point and Friend.

Directions: From Portland, drive U.S. 26 beyond Mount Hood. After milepost 68, at a sign for Wamic, turn left on Road 43 and drive six miles. Turn right on Road 48 and go 15.2 miles, then turn left on Road 4810 and follow signs to Bonney Crossing Campground. After 0.2 mile, stay right on Road 4810 and go another 1.9 miles, then go right on Road 4811 for 1.2 miles, and turn right on the rough gravel road 2710 for 6.7 miles, going toward Tygh Valley. Turn left on Road 27 for 2.1 miles to a pullout and sign on the left for the School Canyon Trail.

Contact: Mount Hood National Forest, Barlow Ranger District, 780 NE Court Street, Dufur, OR, 97021, 541/467-2291.

58 DOUGLAS CABIN TRAIL
8.0 mi/4.5 hr

east of Mount Hood in the Badger Creek Wilderness

Map 3.2, page 126

The Douglas Cabin Trail traverses the Badger Creek Wilderness, offering access to a number of spots. The destination is the Flag Point Lookout, which—unlike other lookouts in this region—is sometimes staffed (when it's not, it's available for rental). You'll have to climb 1,200 feet to get to the lookout, and 60 more feet to get up to the top of the lookout itself, but the views of Mount Hood and the surrounding area are tremendous. Built in 1973, this observation cabin sits atop a timber pole tower that itself sits atop 5,650-foot Flag Point Butte. You can reach the cabin via a straight shot on the Douglas Cabin Trail, hitting 4,820-foot Gordon Butte along the way.

User Groups: Hikers, dogs, and horses. No mountain bikes allowed. No wheelchair facilities.

Permits: A free self-issue Wilderness Permit is required and is available at the trailhead. Parking and access are free.

Maps: For a map of the Mount Hood National Forest or the Badger Creek Wilderness, contact Mount Hood National Forest Headquarters, 16400 Champion Way, Sandy, OR, 97055, 503/668-1700. For a topographic map, ask the USGS for Flag Point.

Directions: From Portland, drive U.S. 26 beyond Mount Hood. After milepost 68, at a sign for Wamic, turn left on Road 43 and drive six miles. Turn right on Road 48 and go 15.2 miles, then turn left on Road 4810 and follow signs to Bonney Crossing Campground. After 0.2 mile, stay right on Road 4810 and go another 1.9 miles, then go right on Road 4811 for 1.2 miles, and turn right on the rough gravel road 2710 for 5.6 miles, and go left for 3.5 miles. (Note: The access road is gated October 1 to May 1.)

Contact: Mount Hood National Forest,

Barlow Ranger District, 780 NE Court Street, Dufur, OR, 97021, 541/467-2291.

59 BADGER CREEK
11.4-23.8 mi/6 hr-2 days

east of Mount Hood in the Badger Creek Wilderness

Map 3.2, page 126

By the time Badger Creek makes its way from the alpine forests of nearby Mount Hood to the sagebrush deserts of Eastern Oregon, it crosses a diverse array of landscapes with a variety of attendant plant life. At the beginning of the Wilderness area just above Bonney Crossing, the trail along Boulder Creek passes through an area of white oak, ponderosa pine, Western red cedar, and grand fir. Flowers along the way include the rare lady's slipper orchid, trilliums, balsamroot, larkspur, twinflowers, and white prairie stars—all in a gorgeous canyon with opportunities for long hikes all the way to Badger Lake.

The Badger Creek Trail sets out across the road from the Bonney Crossing Campground, heading in 5.7 miles to the confluence with Pine Creek, a good destination for the day. Return the way you came. If you're backpacking, consider going the rest of the way to Badger Lake, an additional 6.2 miles upstream (see *Badger Lake via Gumjuwac Saddle* listing in this chapter).

User Groups: Hikers, dogs, and horses. No mountain bikes allowed. No wheelchair facilities.

Permits: A free self-issue Wilderness Permit is required and is available at the trailhead. A federal Northwest Forest Pass is required to park here; the cost is $5 a day or $30 for an annual pass. You can buy a day pass at the trailhead, at ranger stations, or through private vendors.

Maps: For a map of the Mount Hood National Forest or the Badger Creek Wilderness, contact Mount Hood National Forest Headquarters, 16400 Champion Way, Sandy, OR, 97055,

503/668-1700. For a topographic map, ask the USGS for Flag Point.

Directions: From Portland, drive U.S. 26 beyond Mount Hood. After milepost 68, at a sign for Wamic, turn left on Road 43 and drive six miles. Turn right on Road 48 and go 15.2 miles, then turn left on Road 4810 and follow signs to Bonney Crossing Campground. After 0.2 mile, stay right on Road 4810 and go another 1.9 miles, then go right on Road 4811 for 1.2 miles, and turn right on the rough gravel road 2710 for 1.8 miles. The trail is on the left, but you will need to park in the lot along the entrance road to Bonney Crossing Campground and walk to the trailhead on Road 2710.

Contact: Mount Hood National Forest, Barlow Ranger District, 780 NE Court Street, Dufur, OR, 97021, 541/467-2291.

60 SALMON BUTTE
8.8 mi/5.0 hr

south of Zigzag in the Salmon-Huckleberry Wilderness

Map 3.2, page 126

Here's a straightforward trail whose view is anything but. From the peak of Salmon Butte, you'll look far out over the Salmon River Canyon to massive Mount Hood. Not only that, but you'll see Mount Jefferson and the Three Sisters on the Oregon side, and Mount Adams, Mount St. Helens, and Mount Rainier on the Washington side. No wonder they put a lookout here, though all that remains are bits and pieces.

From behind the gate, head up the Salmon Butte Trail 4.4 miles, connecting on the old road at the top and following it uphill to the summit. The trail is a single-shot with no junctions, up to the 4,900-foot peak and back.

User Groups: Hikers, dogs, and horses. No mountain bikes allowed. No wheelchair facilities.

Permits: A free self-issue Wilderness Permit is required and is available at the trailhead. A federal Northwest Forest Pass is required to park here; the cost is $5 a day or $30 for an annual pass. You can buy a day pass at the trailhead, at ranger stations, or through private vendors.

Maps: For a map of the Mount Hood National Forest and the Salmon-Huckleberry Wilderness, contact Mount Hood National Forest Headquarters, 16400 Champion Way, Sandy, OR, 97055, 503/668-1700. For a topographic map, ask the USGS for High Rock.

Directions: Drive east of Portland 42 miles on U.S. 26 to Zigzag. Turn south on Salmon River Road, following the paved road 4.9 miles to a bridge. Crossing the bridge, follow the gravel road 1.7 miles to a pullout on the left.

Contact: Mount Hood National Forest, Zigzag Ranger District, 70220 East Highway 26, Zigzag, OR, 97049, 503/622-3191.

61 SALMON RIVER TO DEVIL'S PEAK
15.7 mi one-way/1-2 days

south of Zigzag in the Salmon-Huckleberry Wilderness

Map 3.2, page 126

Just beyond civilization and a busy highway, the Salmon River extends into a deep wilderness area and roars beneath Hunchback Mountain through a canyon of its own making. The river rumbles far below the trail, and the view, once it opens up, is staggering. Atop Devil's Peak, rising off Hunchback, an old fire watchtower provides a good destination, not to mention a rugged climb. Hike the river or turn this one into a loop, but either way the route is good for backpacking.

From the trailhead, head into the old-growth forest following the Salmon River Trail for 3.6 miles, passing the primitive Rolling Riffle Camp, to arrive at a stupendous viewpoint high above the canyon and looking out over the mountains of the Salmon-Huckleberry Wilderness. Return as you came, or continue on another 2.5 miles, passing another campsite on Goat Creek, to a junction. Turn left and uphill for 2.0 miles on the Kinzel Lake Trail to reach a car campground on said lake. Continue to Road 2613, go left on the Hunchback Trail to arrive at Devil's Peak, a total of 1.6 miles. To complete a strenuous loop, continue on the Hunchback Trail another 2.4 miles and go left on the Green Canyon Way Trail, descending 3.3 miles back to the road. Go left 0.3 mile to return to your vehicle via the road.

User Groups: Hikers and dogs. No horses or mountain bikes allowed. No wheelchair facilities.

Permits: A free self-issue Wilderness Permit is required and is available at the trailhead. A federal Northwest Forest Pass is required to park here; the cost is $5 a day or $30 for an annual pass. You can buy a day pass at the trailhead, at ranger stations, or through private vendors.

Maps: For a map of the Mount Hood National Forest and the Salmon-Huckleberry Wilderness, contact Mount Hood National Forest Headquarters, 16400 Champion Way, Sandy, OR, 97055, 503/668-1700. For a topographic map, ask the USGS for Rhododendron, High Rock, and Wolf Peak.

Directions: Drive east of Portland 42 miles on U.S. 26 to Zigzag. Turn south on Salmon River Road, following the paved road 4.9 miles to a pullout on the left before a bridge.

Contact: Mount Hood National Forest, Zigzag Ranger District, 70220 East Highway 26, Zigzag, OR, 97049, 503/622-3191.

62 DEVIL'S PEAK LOOKOUT
8.2 mi/4.5 hr ⬚3 ⬚8

south of Zigzag in Mount Hood National Forest

Map 3.2, page 126

The use of airplanes largely made fire watchtowers irrelevant, so federal agencies removed most of them. Most, but not all. Some remain staffed year after year, and some remain as great rest stops for hikers—or even for camping. The Devil's Peak Lookout is kept unlocked for hikers. Volunteers keep it looking good, and will continue to do so if you do your

share. There is no outhouse here, so you'll have to make like you're backpacking, packing out all trash and toilet paper.

The trail is simple: a 4.1-mile climb up the Cool Creek Trail to a junction, meeting up with the Hunchback Trail (go right, then left at the next junction to the tower). Along the way there are some views to Mount Hood. Do this trail as an alternative to hiking in on the Salmon River Trail (previous listing).

User Groups: Hikers and dogs. No horses or mountain bikes allowed. No wheelchair facilities.

Permits: Permits are not required. Parking and access are free.

Maps: For a map of the Mount Hood National Forest, contact Mount Hood National Forest Headquarters, 16400 Champion Way, Sandy, OR, 97055, 503/668-1700. For a topographic map, ask the USGS for Government Camp.

Directions: Drive east of Portland 42 miles on U.S. 26 to Zigzag. Go 1.4 miles east of Zigzag and turn right on Still Creek Road, following this road 2.6 miles to the end of the pavement and an additional 0.3 mile on gravel to the crossing of Cool Creek. About 300 yards farther, watch on the right for a "Cool Creek Trail" sign and park here.

Contact: Mount Hood National Forest, Zigzag Ranger District, 70220 East Highway 26, Zigzag, OR, 97049, 503/622-3191.

63 LAUREL HILL
1.0-9.4 mi/0.5-4.0 hr ⬚2 ⬚7

west of Government Camp in Mount Hood National Forest

Map 3.2, page 126

In what seems like a distant past, Oregon Trail pioneers came trundling into Oregon in their covered wagons. For the longest time, all they could do on the last stretch was to raft the Columbia River, which then (before being dammed) was a rugged and dangerous roller-coaster ride. In 1845, Sam Barlow laid out his version of a new trail, which brought pioneers over Mount Hood to a nondescript knoll called Laurel Hill. Actually, it was anything but nondescript to the pioneers; on one cliff-edge, they had to lower their wagons down by a rope winched around the trees. Those trees still bear the burn marks, and you can see them for yourself, along with bits of the old wagon trail, on a series of trails around Laurel Hill. You can also hike an abandoned stretch of the old 1921 Mount Hood Highway, ducking through a tunnel on the way to Little Zigzag Falls.

The "wagon chute" is an easy one-mile round-trip walk from Highway 26 near a big historic marker sign just before milepost 51. Park along the highway and take the path to the top of the cliff, following the old Oregon Trail. You'll see quickly enough why the pioneers were so frustrated.

For a more extensive hike, start from the upper trailhead for the Pioneer Bridle Trail and follow the trail for 1.4 miles to the old tunnel, and turn right on the abandoned road. From here, it's 0.3 mile to the waterfall, following this road to the trail on the right. From the tunnel, you can continue on the Pioneer Bridle Trail another 0.4 mile to a junction that will lead you to the left and over busy Highway 26 to the Wagon Chute trail, and beyond this junction the trail continues another 2.3 miles.

User Groups: Hikers, dogs, and horses. No mountain bikes allowed. No wheelchair facilities.

Permits: Permits are not required. A pass is not required to park at the historic marker on U.S. 26, but for the Pioneer Brindle Trailhead a federal Northwest Forest Pass is required to park; the cost is $5 a day or $30 for an annual pass. You can buy a day pass at the trailhead, at ranger stations, or through private vendors.

Maps: For a map of the Mount Hood National Forest, contact Mount Hood National Forest Headquarters, 16400 Champion Way, Sandy, OR, 97055, 503/668-1700. For a topographic map, ask the USGS for Government Camp.

Directions: To reach the upper trailhead, drive

on U.S. 26 from Portland toward Mount Hood. Between mileposts 52 and 53, turn left off the highway onto Road 522 (across from the Mount Hood Ski Bowl entrance) for 0.2 mile to the lot for the Glacier View Sno-Park.

Contact: Mount Hood National Forest, Zigzag Ranger District, 70220 East Highway 26, Zigzag, OR, 97049, 503/622-3191.

64 MIRROR LAKE
3.2 mi/1.5 hr

west of Government Camp in Mount Hood National Forest

Map 3.2, page 126

It's easy to see how popular this trail is; its parking area is along the highway and it's always bursting at the seam. This trail ascends the oddly named Tom Dick & Harry Mountain to an amazing viewpoint of Mount Hood, the enormous Zigzag Valley, and little Mirror Lake, which you'll pass along the way named Mirror. Use is regulated at Mirror Lake, and only six designated campsites are available. From the peak, you'll be able to visit only one peak out of three; the other two are protected for peregrine falcons.

From the trailhead, cross Camp Creek above Yocum Falls and climb the Mirror Lake Trail 1.4 miles to Mirror Lake. A 0.4-mile loop trail circles the lake. If you're continuing to the 4,920-foot peak, stay right and climb another 1.8 miles to the viewpoint.

User Groups: Hikers and dogs only. No horses or mountain bikes allowed. No wheelchair facilities.

Permits: Permits are not required. A federal Northwest Forest Pass is required to park here; the cost is $5 a day or $30 for an annual pass. You can buy a day pass at the trailhead, at ranger stations, or through private vendors.

Maps: For a map of the Mount Hood National Forest, contact Mount Hood National Forest Headquarters, 16400 Champion Way, Sandy, OR, 97055, 503/668-1700. For a topographic map, ask the USGS for Government Camp.

Directions: From Portland, drive U.S. 26 towards Mount Hood. Between mileposts 51 and 52, park along the south shoulder of the highway at the trailhead.

Contact: Mount Hood National Forest, Zigzag Ranger District, 70220 East Highway 26, Zigzag, OR, 97049, 503/622-3191.

65 TWIN LAKES
5.0-9.1 mi/2.5-5.0 hr

south of Mount Hood in Mount Hood National Forest

Map 3.2, page 126

Just off the Wapinitia Pass, the Frog Lake Sno-Park offers wintry access to the Pacific Crest Trail where it curves near the old Barlow Road and a ridge and butte named for old Barlow, too. In a big glacial valley, a modern campground sits in for an old pioneer campground, and is still named Devil's Half Acre today. You can see these sites from Palmateer Point, a good destination on a fun loop that passes the two Twin Lakes, with options for swimming and exploring for all ages.

From the Frog Lake Sno-Park lot, follow the PCT 1.4 miles to a right-hand junction. Go right 0.7 mile to Lower Twin Lake, a good destination for a short walk. A 0.9-mile trail circles the lake. Continue beyond the lake another 1.4 miles on the Palmateer Point Trail, passing the smaller Upper Twin Lake and cliffs with views of Mount Hood. From here, continue 0.6 mile to the right and go right 0.3 mile to the Point. To complete the loop, return to the Palmateer Trail and continue to the right 0.9 mile to the junction with the PCT, and go left 3.5 miles back to the lot.

User Groups: Hikers, dogs, and horses. No mountain bikes allowed. No wheelchair facilities.

Permits: Permits are not required. A federal Northwest Forest Pass is required to park here; the cost is $5 a day or $30 for an annual pass. You can buy a day pass at the trailhead, at ranger stations, or through private vendors.

Maps: For a map of the Mount Hood National Forest, contact Mount Hood National Forest Headquarters, 16400 Champion Way, Sandy, OR, 97055, 503/668-1700. For a topographic map, ask the USGS for Mount Hood South.

Directions: From Government Camp, drive eight miles east on U.S. 26 to milepost 62, turning left into Frog Lake Sno-Park.

Contact: Mount Hood National Forest, Barlow Ranger District, 780 NE Court Street, Dufur, OR, 97021, 541/467-2291.

66 WHITE RIVER FALLS
0.6 mi/0.25 hr

north of Maupin on the White River

Map 3.2, page 126

By the time you're out roaming in the dry landscapes east of the Cascade Mountains, things get real distant from one another. You have to travel out quite a ways to get to a place like the small state park on the White River, but once you're there you'll find a lot to investigate. For one thing, you've got a three-tiered waterfall on the White River plunging over a basalt shelf into a canyon on its way to the Deschutes River. You'll also find an abandoned powerhouse that supplied Wasco and Sherman Counties with power from 1910 until 1960. There are also a couple beaches and an oak bench, but some of these areas should only be hunted by the most intrepid of explorers willing to endure poison oak and a rugged canyon mouth.

The trail from the parking lot is a simple 0.3-mile descent to a number of viewpoints and the old powerhouse. From there, you could go farther over the course of a mile through pungent sagebrush to a beach and oak grove. The trail to the mouth, however, is a fainter path yet, another 1.2 miles to a beach on the Deschutes beneath a railroad span.

User Groups: Hikers and dogs only. No mountain bikes or horses. Paved trails are wheelchair accessible.

Permits: Permits are not required. Parking and access are free.

Maps: For a topographic map, ask the USGS for Maupin.

Directions: From Highway 197 near milepost 34 between The Dalles and Maupin, go east on Highway 216 for four miles towards Sherars Bridge to the White River Falls State Park entrance on the right.

Contact: Oregon Parks and Recreation Department, 1115 Commercial Street NE, Salem, OR, 97301, 800/551-6949, www.oregonstateparks.org.

67 ROCK LAKES

7.7 mi/3.0 hr

southeast of Estacada in Mount Hood National Forest

Map 3.2, page 126

In the high country between the Roaring and Clackamas Rivers, these Ice Age–carved lakes glisten in the sun. Getting there is the hard part, as you'll have to endure some crummy roads; but once there you'll be privy to meadows, forested lakes, glacier-scoured country, and an impressive rock outcrop called High Rock.

From the Frazier Turnaround, head to the right-hand Serene Lake Trail and go 0.8 mile to a junction. A mere 0.2 mile to the left is Middle Rock Lake, and you can follow the shore back to a higher and smaller lake beyond. The main trail continues to the right and to Lower Rock Lake, with its sunken logs and tree-lined shores. Stay on the main trail another 2.1 miles to Serene Lake, a larger lake with cliffs diving into the water. To do the full loop, continue another 0.9 mile through woods and up to the plateau. Go left on the Grouse Point Trail for 1.8 miles past viewpoints to Cache Meadow, the remains of an old guard station, and a four-way junction. Stay left on the Grouse Point Trail at this and the next junction as you climb out of the bowl, the trail leveling out finally on the 2.1-mile return to the Frazier Turnaround.

User Groups: Hikers, dogs, horses, and mountain bikes. No wheelchair facilities.

Permits: Permits are not required. Parking and access are free.

Maps: For a map of the Mount Hood National Forest, contact Mount Hood National Forest Headquarters, 16400 Champion Way, Sandy, OR, 97055, 503/668-1700. For a topographic map, ask the USGS for High Rock.

Directions: From Oregon City on I-205, take Exit 12 and go 18 miles east toward Estacada. Go through Estacada and continue 26 miles on Highway 224 to the bridge at Ripplebrook. Go left on Road 57 toward Timothy Lake for 7.4 miles, then turn left on Road 58 for 6.9 miles toward High Rock, then left on Abbott Road 4610 for 1.3 miles. Go straight on the unmaintained dirt Road 240 at the sign for Frazier Fork for 4.4 miles, then keep left at a fork by Frazier Fork campground and go 0.2 mile to the end of the road.

Contact: Mount Hood National Forest, Clackamas River Ranger District, 595 NW Industrial Way, Estacada, OR, 97023, 503/630-6861.

68 TIMOTHY LAKE

12.0 mi/6.0 hr

south of Mount Hood in Mount Hood National Forest

Map 3.2, page 126   **BEST (**

The Pacific Crest Trail follows the eastern shoreline of this tremendous lake within eyeshot of Mount Hood. The 1,500-acre lake is maintained as parkland by Portland General Electric because of the PGE-run dam at its far end. There are a host of campgrounds around it, including a primitive spot to pitch a tent at Meditation Point, not to mention windsurfing and fishing. There's also plenty to see while hiking the loop around the lapping shores, making this an ideal outing for the family.

From Little Crater Campground, start off on the 0.3-mile connection trail to the PCT, passing Little Crater Lake. Go left on the PCT another 0.3 mile, following Crater Creek to the junction of the loop trail. To follow the PCT, head to the left 3.6 miles, passing views to the mountain. At the next junction, stay along the lakeshore for another thre miles, passing through the many campgrounds to a crossing of the lake's outlet on a log boom. Continue 1.2 miles along the shore to a 0.3-mile side trail out to Meditation Point, then the remaining three miles to the end of the loop.

User Groups: Hikers, dogs, horses, and mountain bikes. There are several wheelchair access points.

Permits: Permits are not required. Parking and access are free.

Maps: For a map of the Mount Hood National Forest, contact Mount Hood National Forest Headquarters, 16400 Champion Way, Sandy, OR, 97055, 503/668-1700. For a topographic map, ask the USGS for Timothy Lake.

Directions: From Portland, drive U.S. 26 toward Mount Hood. Drive past Wapinitia Pass 3.4 miles to a turnoff between mileposts 65 and 66. At a sign for Timothy Lake, turn onto Skyline Road 42 for four miles. Turn right on Abbott Road 58 for 1.4 miles to Little Crater Campground and park at the far end of the campground loop by the trail sign.

Contact: Mount Hood National Forest, Barlow Ranger District, 780 NE Court Street, Dufur, OR, 97021, 541/467-2291.

69 LOWER DESCHUTES RIVER

4.2-8.0 mi/2.0-4.0 hr

east of The Dalles in Deschutes River State Recreation Area

Map 3.3, page 127

An old railroad once ran along this penultimate stretch of the Deschutes River before it joins at last with the Columbia River at the easternmost edge of the Columbia River Gorge National Scenic Area. Now the railroad is gone, but the grade remains, and its path through this dry, rocky land is now a state park with many options for hiking, both easy and more challenging. Along the river, three rapids—Moody, Rattlesnake, and Colorado—tumble through this sagebrush-dotted canyon. For something a bit more wild, there are also a number of trails between the old railroad grade and the river. The bike path makes for good mountain biking, as well as easy hiking.

The railroad grade is the easiest, and makes for an eight-mile out-and-back trail to Gordon Canyon and an old corral. A loop trail up the bluff begins 1.4 miles out and heads up the canyon to a high viewpoint near Ferry Springs, then connects back down, about 2.5 miles in all. Other trails skirt the riverbank, some dropping down to beaches on the river and close-up views of the rapids.

User Groups: Hikers, dogs on leash only, horses, and mountain bikers. Limited wheelchair access.

Permits: Permits are not required. Parking and access are free.

Maps: For a free park brochure, call Oregon Parks and Recreation, 800/551-6949, or download a free map at www.oregonstateparks.org. For a topographic map, ask the USGS for Wishram and Emerson.

Directions: Drive past the Dalles Dam on I-84 to Exit 97 for Deschutes Park. Follow park signs two miles on Highway 206, and after crossing the Deschutes River turn right into the park. Park at the last lot.

Contact: Oregon Parks and Recreation Department, 1115 Commercial Street NE, Salem, OR, 97301, 800/551-6949, www.oregonstateparks.org.

70 TABLE ROCK

7.6 mi/3.5 hr

east of Salem in Table Rock Wilderness

Map 3.4, page 128

This small, seemingly insignificant wilderness area in the Cascade Mountains actually claims two formidable rock outcrops: Rooster

Rock and 4,881-foot Table Rock, which is entirely climbable and has views to spare. You'll see 10 full Cascade Peaks from here, and all you'll have to do is make it around a couple landslides. These woods are rich with Douglas fir and western hemlock and are home to two endangered plants: Oregon sullivantia and the Gorman's aster. You may even spot the elusive spotted owl.

Getting to the trailhead is part of the hike, as two landslides damaged the road quite a bit, making it impassable for all but on foot. Park before the first landslide and hike in 1.3 miles to the trailhead on the right. From there, climb 1.9 miles on the Table Rock Trail to a junction. To the left, 0.4 mile, is access to the peak of Table Rock, a good destination in and of itself with views north to Mount Rainier and west to the Willamette Valley. If you're up for more, go to the right after bagging the peak for 1.4 miles to view the sheer lava cliffs of Rooster Rock.

User Groups: Hikers, dogs, and horses. No mountain bikes. No wheelchair facilities.

Permits: A free self-issue Wilderness Permit is required and is available at the trailhead. Parking and access are free.

Maps: For a map of the Mount Hood National Forest, contact Mount Hood National Forest Headquarters, 16400 Champion Way, Sandy, OR, 97055, 503/668-1700. For a topographic map, ask the USGS for Rooster Rock.

Directions: From Molalla (east of I-5 at Woodburn), drive 0.5 mile on Highway 211 toward Estacada, and turn right on South Mathias Road for 0.3 mile, then left on South Feyrer Park Road for 1.6 miles, then right on South Dickey Prairie Road for 5.3 miles. At a junction with South Molalla Forest Road, turn right and cross the Molalla River and follow this paved road 12.8 miles to a fork, and go left on Middle Fork Road for 2.6 miles, then right at a sign for Table Rock Wilderness. After two miles, go left, following wilderness pointers. Go the last 2.4 miles to the landslide.

Contact: Bureau of Land Management, Salem District Office, 1717 Fabry Road SE, Salem, OR, 97306, 503/375-5646.

71 WHETSTONE MOUNTAIN

4.8 mi/2.5 hr   🏃2 ⛰8

southeast of Estacada in Bull of the Woods Wilderness

Map 3.4, page 128

Here's an easy way to get into the high country, overlooking the dense forests of the Opal Creek Wilderness and Bull of the Woods Wilderness. This moderately paced trail up Whetstone Mountain has views extending from Mount Rainier to the Three Sisters, with Mount Jefferson a prominent viewpoint. The mountain, like many others in the region, was a Native American site for vision quests. Find your own peace of mind here in this easy summit.

From the trailhead, head into the old-growth woods 1.3 miles on the Whetstone Mountain Trail, passing a little pond that is one of the sources for Whetstone Creek. At a junction, go right on a faint path for 1.1 miles, turning right at a signboard for the summit trail. You'll see the Bull of the Woods Lookout, and clear out over the Willamette Valley to the Coast Range.

User Groups: Hikers, dogs, and horses. No mountain bikes allowed. No wheelchair facilities.

Permits: A free self-issue Wilderness Permit is required and is available at the trailhead. Parking and access are free.

Maps: For a map of the Mount Hood National Forest, contact Mount Hood National Forest Headquarters, 16400 Champion Way, Sandy, OR, 97055, 503/668-1700. For a topographic map, ask the USGS for Battle Ax.

Directions: From I-205 near Oregon City, take Exit 12 and go east 18 miles to Estacada. Go through town and continue 26 miles on Highway 224 to the Ripplebrook bridge. Go straight on Road 46 for 3.6 miles, turn right on Road 63 for 3.5 miles, and turn right on

Road 70 for nine miles. Then follow signs for the Whetstone Mountain Trail, going left on Road 7030 for 5.6 miles, then right on Road 7020 for 0.7 mile. Just prior to the end of the road, turn left onto Road 028 to a parking area.

Contact: Mount Hood National Forest, Clackamas River Ranger District, 595 NW Industrial Way, Estacada, OR, 97023, 503/630-6861.

72 BAGBY HOT SPRINGS
3.0 mi/1.5 hr   🏃1 ⛰6

south of Estacada in Mount Hood National Forest

Map 3.4, page 128

The hike into Bagby Hot Springs is pleasant enough without its famous destination: a series of bathhouses that channel the thermal spring water down a series of flumes into cedar tubs. Really, it defies short explanation, and the trail in is a lovely walk through springtime rhododendron flowers and white trilliums along the Hot Springs Fork of the Collawash River. There's also a historic Guard Station being restored to its early 20th-century glory. From the trailhead, cross Nohorn Creek and follow the Bagby Trail into the woods 1.5 miles, crossing the Fork, and arriving at the hot springs complex. This trail continues into the Bull of the Woods Wilderness and its many destinations.

User Groups: Hikers and dogs. No horses or mountain bikes allowed. No wheelchair facilities.

Permits: Permits are not required. A federal Northwest Forest Pass is required to park here; the cost is $5 a day or $30 for an annual pass. You can buy a day pass at the trailhead, at ranger stations, or through private vendors.

Maps: For a map of the Mount Hood National Forest, contact Mount Hood National Forest Headquarters, 16400 Champion Way, Sandy, OR, 97055, 503/668-1700. For a topographic map, ask the USGS for Bagby Hot Springs.

Directions: From I-205 near Oregon City, take Exit 12 and go east 18 miles to Estacada. Go through town and continue 26 miles on Highway 224 to the Ripplebrook bridge. Go straight on Road 46 for 3.6 miles, turn right on Road 63 for 3.5 miles, and turn right on Road 70 for six miles to a parking lot on the left.

Contact: Mount Hood National Forest, Clackamas River Ranger District, 595 NW Industrial Way, Estacada, OR, 97023, 503/630-6861.

73 PANSY LAKE
2.3 mi/1.0 hr   🏃1 ⛰8

south of Estacada in Bull of the Woods Wilderness

Map 3.4, page 128

This easy exploration of the Bull of the Woods Wilderness visits green Pansy Lake, named for a nearby mining claim called the Pansy Blossom Mine, where Robert Bagby mined copper. Though the claim is a thing of the past, you can make a claim to a beautiful meadowed basin beneath Pansy Mountain, with options for camping and further hiking.

The easiest access is to follow the Pansy Lake Trail in from the road 0.9 mile to a junction. A right-hand trail goes into Pansy Basin on an abandoned trail. The left-hand trail goes promptly uphill to another junction; go straight 0.2 mile to Pansy Lake, where you can follow the trail to the right along the lakeshore.

User Groups: Hikers, dogs, and horses. No mountain bikes allowed. No wheelchair facilities.

Permits: A free self-issue Wilderness Permit is required and is available at the trailhead. Parking and access are free.

Maps: For a map of the Mount Hood National Forest, contact Mount Hood National Forest Headquarters, 16400 Champion Way, Sandy, OR, 97055, 503/668-1700. For a topographic map, ask the USGS for Bull of the Woods.

Directions: From I-205 near Oregon City, take Exit 12 and go east 18 miles to Estacada. Go through town and continue 26 miles on Highway 224 to the Ripplebrook bridge. Go straight on Road 46 for 3.6 miles, turn right on Road 63 for 5.6 miles, and turn right on Road 6340 for 7.8 miles, following signs for Pansy Basin Trail. Turn right on Road 6341 for 3.5 miles and park at a pullout on the right side. The trail begins across the road.

Contact: Mount Hood National Forest, Clackamas River Ranger District, 595 NW Industrial Way, Estacada, OR, 97023, 503/630-6861.

🟥 BULL OF THE WOODS LOOKOUT
6.4 mi/3.5 hr

south of Estacada in Bull of the Woods Wilderness

Map 3.4, page 128

This trail passes Pansy Lake (see previous listing) but continues up to the 1942 Bull of the Woods Lookout, which is sometimes staffed. It then follows a loop up and down a mountain cradling little Dickey Lake. Views extend out to Mount Jefferson, and to many more as well.

Follow the Pansy Lake Trail in from the road 0.9 mile to a junction. The right goes into Pansy Basin on an abandoned trail; take the left-hand trail, which goes promptly uphill to another junction. This time go straight 0.2 mile to Pansy Lake, taking the left-hand trail another 0.8 miles toward Twin Lakes. At the next junction, go uphill to the left on the Mother Lode Trail 1.9 miles, going left at a signed junction onto the Bull of the Woods Trail to the lookout tower. To complete the loop, continue past the tower 1.1 miles to a barely marked junction, then descend 1.3 miles on the Dickey Lake Trail, passing a short side trail to Dickey Lake, back to the Pansy Lake Trail, staying right at junctions back to the road.

User Groups: Hikers, dogs, and horses. No mountain bikes allowed. No wheelchair facilities.

Permits: A free self-issue Wilderness Permit is required and is available at the trailhead. Parking and access are free.

Maps: For a map of the Mount Hood National Forest, contact Mount Hood National Forest Headquarters, 16400 Champion Way, Sandy, OR, 97055, 503/668-1700. For a topographic map, ask the USGS for Bull of the Woods.

Directions: From I-205 near Oregon City, take Exit 12 and go east 18 miles to Estacada. Go through town and continue 26 miles on Highway 224 to the Ripplebrook bridge. Go straight on Road 46 for 3.6 miles, turn right on Road 63 for 5.6 miles, and turn right on Road 6340 for 7.8 miles, following signs for Pansy Basin Trail. Turn right on Road 6341 for 3.5 miles and park at a pullout on the right side. The trail begins across the road.

Contact: Mount Hood National Forest, Clackamas River Ranger District, 595 NW Industrial Way, Estacada, OR, 97023, 503/630-6861.

🟥 DICKEY CREEK
11.0 mi/5.5 hr

south of Estacada in Bull of the Woods Wilderness

Map 3.4, page 128

Want to visit an old-growth forest? Try the groves along the wilderness of Dickey Creek. To get here, you must hike *down* first, an unwelcome prospect for many. Still, the lakes you'll find back in these woods in the carved-out flanks of Big Slide Mountain make it worth the price of admission.

The Dickey Creek Trail begins as an old road then changes to trail, the first 0.8 mile heading down nearly 500 feet into an old-growth grove of Douglas fir. From here you'll pass a pond and follow Dickey Creek 2.1 miles to a crossing. Now you'll begin climbing nearly 1,400 feet in 2.6 miles to the shore of

Big Slide Lake, with the mountain looming above. There are campsites and a small island to explore, and the Bull of the Woods Lookout is on the ridge above.

User Groups: Hikers, dogs, and horses. No mountain bikes allowed. No wheelchair facilities.

Permits: A free self-issue Wilderness Permit is required and is available at the trailhead. Parking and access are free.

Maps: For a map of the Mount Hood National Forest, contact Mount Hood National Forest Headquarters, 16400 Champion Way, Sandy, OR, 97055, 503/668-1700. For a topographic map, ask the USGS for Bull of the Woods.

Directions: From I-205 near Oregon City, take Exit 12 and go east 18 miles to Estacada. Go through town and continue 26 miles on Highway 224 to the Ripplebrook bridge. Go straight on Road 46 for 3.6 miles, turn right on Road 63 for 5.6 miles, and turn right on Road 6340 for 2.8 miles following signs for Dickey Creek Trail. Turn left on Road 140 for one mile, and turn right at a T-junction 0.5 mile to the trailhead at road's end.

Contact: Mount Hood National Forest, Clackamas River Ranger District, 595 NW Industrial Way, Estacada, OR, 97023, 503/630-6861.

76 HAWK MOUNTAIN
10.4 mi/5.0 hr   3 ⛰8

south of Estacada in Mount Hood National Forest

Map 3.4, page 128

There is something romantic about a fire watchtower, with isolation and nature combining to form a kind of idyllic life. It took a certain kind of person to live alone on a mountaintop for a summer. There are many books written by authors who did this, from Jack Kerouac to Edward Abbey. With new

techniques for spotting fires, however, many of these lookouts have been abandoned and many of the original structures lost—this lonely cabin atop Hawk Mountain remains, however. Today you can visit this cabin, look out over Mount Jefferson, and get a sense of how lookouts lived. This trail up Rho Ridge (short for "Rhododendron") crosses two meadows and provides a first-hand look.

From the Graham Pass trailhead, follow the Rho Ridge Trail 1.1 miles, connecting with abandoned Road 33, to a junction with Road 270. Go right for one mile, staying right at a junction with Road 280 and left at a junction with Road 290. Take a right on the continuation of the trail along Rho Ridge for 2.7 miles, crossing another dirt road, to Round Meadow. A left-hand trail leads 0.4 mile to the old lookout cabin atop Hawk Mountain.

User Groups: Hikers, dogs, horses, and mountain bikes. No wheelchair facilities.

Permits: Permits are not required. Parking and access are free.

Maps: For a map of the Mount Hood National Forest, contact Mount Hood National Forest Headquarters, 16400 Champion Way, Sandy, OR, 97055, 503/668-1700. For a topographic map, ask the USGS for Breitenbush Hot Springs.

Directions: From I-205 near Oregon City, take Exit 12 and go east 18 miles to Estacada. Go through town and continue 26 miles on Highway 224 to the Ripplebrook bridge. Go straight on Road 46 for 3.6 miles, turn right on Road 63 for 8.8 miles. At a sign for Graham Pass, turn left on Road 6350 for 1.2 miles, then go right for 4.5 miles on the gravel road, then fork left staying on Road 6350. In one mile, park in a lot at a four-way junction.

Contact: Mount Hood National Forest, Clackamas River Ranger District, 595 NW Industrial Way, Estacada, OR, 97023, 503/630-6861.

⁷⁷ LITTLE NORTH SANTIAM RIVER

9.0 mi/4.0 mi

northeast of Mill City in Willamette National Forest

Map 3.4, page 128

Cascading through a boulder-lined bed, this tributary of the Santiam watershed flows through old-growth forests and over waterfalls squeezing between the lava canyon. The 4.5-mile Little North Santiam Trail, built by volunteers from Salem, sometimes scrambles down to swimming holes and beaches and ends at a campground upstream. Go as far as you like and return as you came; there's plenty to see.

From Elkhorn Road, start in 0.7 mile to a side trail down to a series of waterfalls. From here, a 2.6-mile stretch crosses Winter Creek and climbs to 1,800 feet and back down to a series of inaccessible pools and a beach. The final 1.2 miles crosses Cedar Creek and ends at the Shady Grove Campground.

User Groups: Hikers, dogs, and bicycles. No horses allowed. No wheelchair facilities.

Permits: Permits are not required. A federal Northwest Forest Pass is required to park here; the cost is $5 a day or $30 for an annual pass. You can buy a day pass at the trailhead, at ranger stations, or through private vendors.

Maps: For a map of the Willamette National Forest, contact Willamette National Forest Headquarters, 3106 Pierce Parkway, Suite D, Springfield, OR, 97477, 541/225-6300. For a topographic map, ask the USGS for Lyons.

Directions: Drive east from Salem on OR 22 for 23 miles to Mehama and turn left on Little North Fork Road for 14.5 miles. Beyond milepost 13, turn right on Elkhorn Drive, cross the river, and 0.4 mile later park on the left at a pullout.

Contact: Willamette National Forest, Detroit Ranger District, HC73, Box 320, Mill City, OR, 97360, 503/854-4239.

⁷⁸ HENLINE MOUNTAIN

5.6 mi/4.0 hr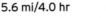

northeast of Mill City in Opal Creek Wilderness

Map 3.4, page 128

From the lookout site beneath Henline Mountain, the ridges and peaks of the Cascades ripple into the distance like frozen waves, their folded ridges flowing down to the Little North Santiam River. The lookout site is not on the peak of Henline, but who's counting? A 1.1-mile trail, rough as it is, continues past this lookout to the 4,650-foot peak, but the view from this destination is in itself worth the climb. This is also an initial foray into the Opal Creek Wilderness.

Prepare to climb steadily and steeply for the 2.8-mile trail to the old lookout point. You'll gain 2,200 feet in this short distance, so give yourself plenty of time.

User Groups: Hikers and dogs. No horses or mountain bikes allowed. No wheelchair facilities.

Permits: A free self-issue Wilderness Permit is required and is available at the trailhead. Parking and access are free.

Maps: For a map of the Willamette National Forest, contact Willamette National Forest Headquarters, 3106 Pierce Parkway, Suite D, Springfield, OR, 97477, 541/225-6300. For a topographic map, ask the USGS for Elkhorn.

Directions: Drive east from Salem on OR 22 for 23 miles to Mehama and turn left on Little North Fork Road for 16.3 miles to a fork. Go to the left on Road 2209 for one mile and park on the right near the trailhead.

Contact: Willamette National Forest, Detroit Ranger District, HC73, Box 320, Mill City, OR, 97360, 503/854-4239.

79 OPAL CREEK
7.1 mi/2.5 hr   👫2 ⛰8

northeast of Mill City in Opal Creek Wilderness
Map 3.4, page 128   **BEST (**

Let's just say the Opal Creek Wilderness is famous to some and infamous to others. Author David Seideman's 1993 book, *Showdown at Opal Creek: The Battle for America's Last Wilderness* amply details the 1980s controversy over the designation of this area as wilderness. What ensued here involved armed standoffs between federal agencies and the owners of the private land that stood between the National Forest and the proposed logging area, which houses some enormous stands of Douglas fir and Western red cedar. Senator Mark Hatfield stepped in to protect the area and it has now been preserved. The mining town back here called Jawbone Flats, where the owners made their stand, remains, and now that the furor is over ,the whole town has become the Opal Creek Ancient Forest Research Center. This trail follows the original road along the Little North Santiam River, passing an abandoned mill, slipping into the mining town, and setting off along Opal Creek towards the wilderness area.

From the locked gate, follow the old dirt road 3.5 miles. You'll scurry along some amazing half-bridges, where the road clings to the cliff-face, then arrive at the site of the Merton Mill and its hodgepodge of lumber bric-a-brac, and a side trail down to Sawmill Falls. You'll pass Slide Falls on the way, too. At Jawbone Flats, take a right-hand junction to a footbridge over heavily photographed Opal Pool. To return via a loop, go right for 1.4 miles back to a crossing over the river and return via the road. To extend your trip, however, you can go left on the Opal Creek Trail 1.5 miles to a stand of enormous red cedars that are staggering to see. The trail eventually reaches Beachie Creek and peters out.

User Groups: Hikers and dogs. No horses or mountain bikes allowed. No wheelchair facilities.

Permits: A free self-issue Wilderness Permit is required and is available at the trailhead. Parking and access are free.

Maps: An Opal Creek Wilderness map is available from Geo-Graphics. For a map of the Willamette National Forest, contact Willamette National Forest Headquarters, 3106 Pierce Parkway, Suite D, Springfield, OR, 97477, 541/225-6300. For a topographic map, ask the USGS for Battle Ax.

Directions: Drive east from Salem on OR 22 for 23 miles to Mehama and turn left on Little North Fork Road for 16.3 miles to a fork. Go to the left on Road 2209 for 4.2 miles and park on the shoulder at the locked gate.

Contact: Willamette National Forest, Detroit Ranger District, HC73, Box 320, Mill City, OR, 97360, 503/854-4239.

80 FRENCH CREEK RIDGE
8.2 mi/3.5 hr   👫2 ⛰8

north of Detroit in Opal Creek Wilderness
Map 3.4, page 128

This long ridge over the Opal Creek Wilderness passes a number of rock formations and peaks on its way to Mount Beachie, entering stands of rare Alaska cedar and offering views to Mount Jefferson, craggy Three-Fingered Jack, and the Three Sisters.

From the message board, start into the forest on the French Creek Ridge Trail, passing Marten Buttes, for 2.4 miles to a series of rock formations at a pass. Ignoring a side trail to the right, continue 1.7 miles past a pond and through a brush-lined path to the viewpoint on Mount Beachie.

User Groups: Hikers, dogs, and horses. No mountain bikes allowed. No wheelchair facilities.

Permits: A free self-issue Wilderness Permit is required and is available at the trailhead. Parking and access are free.

Maps: An Opal Creek Wilderness map is available from Geo-Graphics. For a map of the Willamette National Forest, contact

Willamette National Forest Headquarters, 3106 Pierce Parkway, Suite D, Springfield, OR, 97477, 541/225-6300. For a topographic map, ask the USGS for Battle Ax.

Directions: Drive 50 miles east of Salem on OR 22 to Detroit Lake. Just before the Breitenbush River turn left on French Creek Road 2223 and go 4.2 miles to a fork at pavement's end. Go right on Road 2207 for 3.7 miles and park at a large lot on the right.

Contact: Willamette National Forest, Detroit Ranger District, HC73, Box 320, Mill City, OR, 97360, 503/854-4239.

81 BATTLE AX
5.6–6.4 mi/3.0–3.5 hr

north of Detroit in Bull of the Woods Wilderness

Map 3.4, page 128

This mountain has such a rugged name, don't you think? Some say it's because of its sharp shape, others because of a brand of chewing tobacco around during the time of the gold prospectors. Either way, it's earned its moniker. This peak, the tallest in the Bull of the Woods Wilderness, has views extending as far as Diamond Peak in the southern Cascades and Mount Hood to the north. Beneath it, Elk Lake looks like a big puddle among the trees. Atop its rocky peak, a profusion of alpine flowers root down and thrive.

After parking at the fork in the road approaching Elk Lake Campground, walk the remaining 0.4 mile of road to the trailhead on the right. Strike out on the Bagby Hot Springs Trail for two miles, passing a number of ponds and steadily climbing to a junction. Go left 1.3 miles to the 5,558-foot peak of Battle Ax. To make a loop of this hike, continue forward and descend the mountain down a series of switchbacks 1.5 mile to the end of the road at Beachie Saddle. Walk the road back down 0.8 mile to the trailhead, then the remaining distance to your vehicle.

User Groups: Hikers, dogs, and horses. No mountain bikes allowed. No wheelchair facilities.

Permits: A free self-issue Wilderness Permit is required and is available at the trailhead. Parking and access are free.

Maps: An Opal Creek Wilderness map is available from Geo-Graphics. For a map of the Willamette National Forest, contact Willamette National Forest Headquarters, 3106 Pierce Parkway, Suite D, Springfield, OR, 97477, 541/225-6300. For a topographic map, ask the USGS for Battle Ax.

Directions: Drive 50 miles east of Salem on OR 22 to Detroit Lake. Cross the Breitenbush River and turn left on paved Road 46 for 4.4 miles to a sign for Elk Lake. Turn left on Road 4696 for 0.8 mile, then turn left onto Road 4697 and go 4.7 miles, then turn left yet again at a sign for Elk Lake. The next two miles are rough and difficult. At a fork for the Elk Lake Campground, passenger cars without clearance should park and hikers will need to continue on foot up the road another 0.4 mile to the trailhead. However, high-clearance vehicles can continue up the road and park on the shoulder.

Contact: Willamette National Forest, Detroit Ranger District, HC73, Box 320, Mill City, OR, 97360, 503/854-4239.

82 PHANTOM BRIDGE
4.6 mi/2.0 hr

north of Detroit in Willamette National Forest

Map 3.4, page 128

This rare and intimidating rock arch spans a 50-foot-deep gorge that will unnerve even the bravest. Maybe just a view of it is enough. The trail itself stretches away from French Creek Ridge, rounding Dog Rock and Cedar Lake before climbing to the arch. Below, the Opal Creek Wilderness drifts into the distance, with Opal Lake, source of the creek, within view.

Park in the lot at the end of Road 2223 and walk back down the road about 100 feet to the trailhead. In 1.3 miles you'll arrive at

Cedar Lake and a junction. Go left up the ridge another 0.7 mile to an old trailhead lot, then continue the remaining 0.3 mile to the Phantom Bridge.

User Groups: Hikers, dogs, horses, and mountain bikes. No wheelchair facilities.

Permits: Permits are not required. Parking and access are free.

Maps: For a map of the Willamette National Forest, contact Willamette National Forest Headquarters, 3106 Pierce Parkway, Suite D, Springfield, OR, 97477, 541/225-6300. For a topographic map, ask the USGS for Battle Ax.

Directions: Drive 50 miles east of Salem on OR 22 to Detroit Lake. Just before the Breitenbush River, turn left on French Creek Road 2223 and go 4.2 miles to a fork at pavement's end. Go right on Road 2207 for 3.7 miles and park at a large lot on the right.

Contact: Willamette National Forest, Detroit Ranger District, HC73, Box 320, Mill City, OR, 97360, 503/854-4239.

83 DOME ROCK AND TUMBLE LAKE
5.2 mi/2.5 hr

north of Detroit in Willamette National Forest

Map 3.4, page 128

From the edge of Detroit Reservoir, the Tumble Ridge Trail heads straight into the neighboring mountains, climbing steeply to the spire of Needle Rock and the vista of Dome Rock. Hidden up Tumble Creek is Tumble Lake, with a waterfall. Though you could hike in this way, there is an easier point of entry that makes for a quicker hike to these sights.

From the upper trailhead on Road 2223, go in 0.4 mile to a junction. To access Dome Rock, go left 0.5 mile to a second junction, then left another 0.5 mile to the 4,869-foot peak. To access Tumble Lake, go right at this first junction, crossing a meadow down into a gully for 1.2 miles to the shore. Follow the

shore to the left 0.3 mile to see the outlet creek and waterfall.

User Groups: Hikers, dogs, and mountain bikes. No horses allowed. No wheelchair facilities.

Permits: Permits are not required. Parking and access are free.

Maps: For a map of the Willamette National Forest, contact Willamette National Forest Headquarters, 3106 Pierce Parkway, Suite D, Springfield, OR, 97477, 541/225-6300. For a topographic map, ask the USGS for Battle Ax and Detroit.

Directions: Drive 50 miles east of Salem on OR 22 to Detroit Lake. Just before the Breitenbush River turn left on French Creek Road 2223 and go 4.2 miles to a fork at pavement's end. Fork left onto Road 2223 for 3.9 miles, watching carefully for a post on the left that marks the trailhead. Park on the right.

Contact: Willamette National Forest, Detroit Ranger District, HC73, Box 320, Mill City, OR, 97360, 503/854-4239.

84 STAHLMAN POINT
5.0 mi/2.5 hr

south of Detroit Reservoir in Willamette National Forest

Map 3.4, page 128

If you're in the area and looking for a quick view of the surrounding country, incorporating the Detroit Reservoir and Mount Jefferson, head up this fairly easy 2.5-mile trail that climbs 1,300 feet to an old lookout site. Below, sailboats drift on the massive lake and the mountain broods in the distance. Watch for fish-hunting osprey, which nest in the area.

User Groups: Hikers and dogs. No horses or mountain bikes allowed. No wheelchair facilities.

Permits: Permits are not required. Parking and access are free.

Maps: For a map of the Willamette National Forest, contact Willamette National Forest Headquarters, 3106 Pierce Parkway, Suite D,

Springfield, OR, 97477, 541/225-6300. For a topographic map, ask the USGS for Detroit.

Directions: Drive 50 miles east of Salem on OR 22 to the town of Detroit. Go 2.5 miles east of town, then turn right on Blowout Road 10 for 3.5 miles to the large parking area on the left side of the road.

Contact: Willamette National Forest, Detroit Ranger District, HC73, Box 320, Mill City, OR, 97360, 503/854-4239.

85 COFFIN MOUNTAIN LOOKOUT
3.0 mi/2.0 hr   🥾1 ⛰9

south of Detroit in Willamette National Forest
Map 3.4, page 128

From a distance, it's easy to see how Coffin Mountain got its name. This square and prominent peak atop a wall of cliffs certainly resembles a giant's final resting place, but those cliffs are deceptive; along the backside, an easy trail climbs to a staffed lookout tower—a 16-square-foot box that, if you're lucky, you may be able to visit. You'll see why these fire towers are still staffed on the way up: the trail passes through an old burn being repopulated by young noble fir and sub-alpine fir. From the trailhead, follow the old bulldozer road and finally trail up 1.5 miles to the peak.

User Groups: Hikers, dogs, and mountain bikes. No horses allowed. No wheelchair facilities.

Permits: Permits are not required. Parking and access are free.

Maps: For a map of the Willamette National Forest, contact Willamette National Forest Headquarters, 3106 Pierce Parkway, Suite D, Springfield, OR, 97477, 541/225-6300. For a topographic map, ask the USGS for Coffin Mountain.

Directions: Drive east of Salem 69 miles on OR 22. Beyond Marion Forks 2.9 miles, go right on Straight Creek Road for 4.2 miles to

a sign for Coffin Mountain Trailhead, and turn right for 3.8 miles on Road 1168 to the trailhead sign and parking area on the left.

Contact: Willamette National Forest, Detroit Ranger District, HC73, Box 320, Mill City, OR, 97360, 503/854-4239.

86 BACHELOR MOUNTAIN
3.8 mi/2.5 hr   🥾1 ⛰9

south of Detroit in Willamette National Forest
Map 3.4, page 128

Just beyond the towering cliffs of Coffin Mountain sits the slightly higher Bachelor Mountain. By coupling this trail with the Coffin Mountain Lookout hike (previous listing), both peaks are easy to bag in a single day (or even in a couple of hours). This trail traverses the Buck Mountain Burn, which in the 1970s reduced many of the trees to the white snags you see today.

From the trailhead, follow the ridge 1.2 miles to a junction with the Bruno Meadows Trail. Stay to the left and climb the final 0.7-mile rocky path up 500 feet to the peak.

User Groups: Hikers, dogs, horses, and mountain bikes. No wheelchair facilities.

Permits: Permits are not required. Parking and access are free.

Maps: For a map of the Willamette National Forest, contact Willamette National Forest Headquarters, 3106 Pierce Parkway, Suite D, Springfield, OR, 97477, 541/225-6300. For a topographic map, ask the USGS for Mount Bruno.

Directions: Drive east of Salem 69 miles on OR 22. Beyond Marion Forks 2.9 miles, go right on Straight Creek Road for 4.2 miles to a sign for Coffin Mountain Trailhead, and turn right for 4.5 miles on Road 1168 then turn left on Road 430, driving 0.5 mile to its end.

Contact: Willamette National Forest, Detroit Ranger District, HC73, Box 320, Mill City, OR, 97360, 503/854-4239.

87 OLALLIE LAKE AND POTATO BUTTE

7.2 mi/3.0 hr   🏃2 ⛰7

east of Detroit in Olallie Lakes Scenic Area

Map 3.5, page 129

A long stretch of power lines marks the boundary for the Olallie Lake Scenic Area, and the transformation to this lake-strewn plateau is abrupt. The Olallie Lake Scenic Area sits in the shadow of Mount Jefferson and offers many options for hiking. To start into the Scenic Area from the west, try this hike; it passes four big lakes and a couple smaller ones, finally topping it off with 5,280-foot Potato Butte, with views over the dense forest to the towering peak of Jefferson.

From the road, the Red Lake Trail crosses a clear-cut and joins a dirt road. Go left a short distance, then right on a spur road to find the continuation of the trail. Once you go under the power lines, you enter the Scenic Area. The first 1.6 miles of the trail reaches Red Lake. The next 1.3 miles passes Averill, Wall, and Sheep Lakes and arrives at a junction. Go left 0.7 mile past a few small ponds and up several steep switchbacks to the top of Potato Butte.

User Groups: Hikers, dogs, horses, and mountain bikes. No wheelchair facilities.

Permits: Permits are not required. Parking and access are free.

Maps: For a map of the Mount Hood National Forest, contact Mount Hood National Forest Headquarters, 16400 Champion Way, Sandy, OR, 97055, 503/668-1700. For a topographic map, ask the USGS for Olallie Butte.

Directions: From I-205 near Oregon City, take Exit 12 and go east 18 miles to Estacada. Go through town and continue 26 miles on Highway 224 to the Ripplebrook bridge. Go straight on Road 46 for 26.7 miles toward Detroit. Beyond the turnoff for Olallie Lake 4.9 miles, turn left on Road 380 for 0.9 mile to a point where the road becomes unmaintained. From Salem, follow OR 22 east to Detroit and go left on Breitenbush Road 46

for 18.2 miles to the right-hand turnoff for Road 380.

Contact: Mount Hood National Forest, Clackamas River Ranger District, 595 NW Industrial Way, Estacada, OR, 97023, 503/630-6861.

88 SOUTH BREITENBUSH GORGE

6.2 mi/2.0 hr   🏃2 ⛰8

east of Detroit on the South Breitenbush River

Map 3.5, page 129

The South Breitenbush River comes roaring down from the flanks of Mount Jefferson into this cool, green old-growth forest. Long ridges tower over the water, including nearby Devils Peak. At one point in the forest, the light pours down through a large swath of blowdown, the trees leveled by a 1990 windstorm. But the forest goes on, and in the midst of a particular glade the river squeezes into a 40-foot gorge running along for 100 yards. Fallen trees crisscross the lava walls, making for precarious bridges suitable, at best, for small mammals. The gorge is a perfect destination, though continuing onward will eventually bring you to Roaring Creek—another great turnaround point—and the slopes of Jefferson itself.

Begin at the site of an historic guard station, descending into the forest to the river, heading upstream for 1.2 miles, crossing the North Fork Breitenbush along the way, to a trail junction. Go straight along the river another 1.4 miles to a sign and spur trail on the right for "South Breitenbush Gorge." To continue on to Roaring Creek is only another 0.5 mile up the trail, and it's worth it for views of both the river and this lovely creek.

User Groups: Hikers and dogs. No horses or mountain bikes allowed. No wheelchair facilities.

Permits: Permits are not required. Parking and access are free.

Maps: For a map of the Willamette National Forest, contact Willamette National Forest

Headquarters, 3106 Pierce Parkway, Suite D, Springfield, OR, 97477, 541/225-6300. For a topographic map, ask the USGS for Breitenbush Hot Springs.

Directions: Drive 50 miles east of Salem on OR 22 to Detroit. Cross the Breitenbush River and turn left on Road 46 for 11.2 miles. Turn right on a gravel road and after 0.3 mile park on the left at the site of the old guard station.

Contact: Willamette National Forest, Detroit Ranger District, HC73, Box 320, Mill City, OR, 97360, 503/854-4239.

89 TOP LAKE AND DOUBLE PEAKS

5.3 mi/3.0 hr   🚶1 ⛰8

east of Detroit in Olallie Lakes Scenic Area

Map 3.5, page 129

The 6,000-year-old remnant of a glacier-carved plateau has left mile after mile of lakes scattered across the Olallie Lake Scenic Area like pearls from a broken necklace. To see for yourself, try this loop past several lakes to Double Peaks, a 5,998-foot summit towering above the lake basin and looking out to Olallie Butte and Mount Jefferson.

Follow the Red Lake Trail 1.1 miles through mountain hemlocks and lodgepole pines, keeping right at a junction to Timber Lake, to Top Lake and a three-way junction. Go left 0.4 mile, switchbacking up to the Pacific Crest Trail and then going left to Cigar Lake. At the next junction, leave the PCT and go right steeply up 0.8 mile to Double Peaks. To return via the loop, go back to the PCT, following it left 0.5 mile past Cigar Lake to a four-way junction with the Red Lake Trail. Stay straight on the PCT another 1.4 miles to the road at Head Lake, going right 0.3 mile back to the car.

User Groups: Hikers, dogs, and horses. No mountain bikes allowed. No wheelchair facilities.

Permits: Permits are not required. Parking and access are free.

Maps: For a map of the Mount Hood National Forest, contact Mount Hood National Forest Headquarters, 16400 Champion Way, Sandy, OR, 97055, 503/668-1700. For a topographic map, ask the USGS for Olallie Butte.

Directions: From I-205 near Oregon City, take Exit 12 and go east 18 miles to Estacada. Go through town and continue 26 miles on Highway 224 to the Ripplebrook bridge. Go straight on Road 46 for 21.8 miles toward Detroit. Turn left on Road 4690 at the Olallie Lake turnoff, following this road 8.1 miles, turning right on Road 4220 for 5.1 miles, turning right at an intersection with the Olallie Lake Resort. Go 0.3 mile to a message board on the right for the Red Lake Trail and park on the shoulder. From Salem, follow OR 22 east to Detroit and go left on Breitenbush Road 46 for 23.5 miles to the Olallie Turnoff.

Contact: Mount Hood National Forest, Clackamas River Ranger District, 595 NW Industrial Way, Estacada, OR, 97023, 503/630-6861.

90 MONON LAKE

3.9 mi/2.0 hr   🚶1 ⛰7

northeast of Detroit in Olallie Lakes Scenic Area

Map 3.5, page 129

Olallie Lake is a popular destination and rightfully so. With its big campgrounds and unparalleled view of nearby Olallie Butte, it makes for a great destination. But nearby Monon Lake, the second-biggest lake after Olallie, has its own beauty. Unfortunately, a 2001 fire blackened the shores of this scenic lake, but it is slowly recovering as the undergrowth begins its triumphant resurgence. These mountains, after all, evolved with forest fires, so you can get an edifying look at how a forest regenerates, even after such a devastating burn as this one.

From the campground, go 0.5 mile to the right along Olallie Lake to a junction with the Olallie Lake Trail, going right. You'll pass

Nep-Te-Pa and Mangriff Lakes and arrive at Monon Lake. Go right for a 2.9-mile loop around the lake, with 0.3 mile of it on the road, then rejoin the Olallie Trail. At the last junction, you can go left to return to the car or extend the day by going right 0.4 mile along Olallie Lake to another junction. Going left extends this trail another 0.9 mile to the Paul Dennis Campground; going right heads 0.4 mile into the Warm Springs Reservation to the shore of Long Lake.

User Groups: Hikers, dogs, horses, and mountain bikes. No wheelchair facilities.

Permits: Permits are not required. Parking and access are free.

Maps: For a map of the Mount Hood National Forest, contact Mount Hood National Forest Headquarters, 16400 Champion Way, Sandy, OR, 97055, 503/668-1700. For a topographic map, ask the USGS for Olallie Butte.

Directions: From I-205 near Oregon City, take Exit 12 and go east 18 miles to Estacada. Go through town and continue 26 miles on Highway 224 to the Ripplebrook bridge. Go straight on Road 46 for 21.8 miles toward Detroit. Turn left on Road 4690 at the Olallie Lake turnoff, following this road 8.1 miles, turning right on Road 4220 for seven miles, turning left at the Peninsula Campground entrance and following signs for the boat ramp. From Salem, follow OR 22 east to Detroit and go left on Breitenbush Road 46 for 23.5 miles to the Olallie Turnoff.

Contact: Mount Hood National Forest, Clackamas River Ranger District, 595 NW Industrial Way, Estacada, OR, 97023, 503/630-6861.

⑨⑪ PARK RIDGE

7.4 mi/5.0 hr

east of Detroit in Mount Jefferson Wilderness

Map 3.5, page 129

Jefferson Park is one of the most spectacular places in the Cascade Mountains. Don't let the word "Park" fool you though, for this is no city park with picnic tables. Rather, "Park" designates a mountain meadow, and this one is unsurpassed for its beauty, especially in early summer when the flower show begins. There are a number of ways in, and this one—despite the final two miles of rough roads—comes in from the north, up and over Park Ridge and down to Russell Lake and the jeweled expanse of lakes, alpine scenery, and islands of windswept trees. There's even a side trail to climb 6,095-foot Pyramid Butte on the way.

From the trailhead, follow the Pacific Crest Trail to the left for 0.6 mile to a junction. To continue to Jefferson Park, stay on the PCT for five miles to cross over Park Ridge and arrive at Russell Lake and the meadows. For a climb up Pyramid Butte, go right 1.1 miles, then right again to the peak. Coming back down, go one mile, staying right and rejoining the PCT.

User Groups: Hikers, dogs, and horses. No mountain bikes allowed. No wheelchair facilities.

Permits: A free self-issue Wilderness Permit is required and is available at the trailhead. Parking and access are free.

Maps: You can purchase a Mount Jefferson Wilderness Map from Geo-Graphics. For a map of the Mount Hood National Forest and the Mount Jefferson Wilderness, contact Mount Hood National Forest Headquarters, 16400 Champion Way, Sandy, OR, 97055, 503/668-1700. For a topographic map, ask the USGS for Olallie Butte Mount Jefferson.

Directions: From I-205 near Oregon City, take Exit 12 and go east 18 miles to Estacada. Go through town and continue 26 miles on Highway 224 to the Ripplebrook bridge. Go straight on Road 46 for 21.8 miles toward Detroit. Turn left on Road 4690 at the Olallie Lake turnoff, following this road 8.1 miles, turning right on Road 4220 for 10.5 miles, noting that the final two miles of this road are extremely rough and require high-clearance vehicles. Past Breitenbush Lake, turn left to the Pacific Crest Trail lot. From Salem, follow OR 22 east to Detroit and go left on

Breitenbush Road 46 for 23.5 miles to the Olallie turnoff.

Contact: Mount Hood National Forest, Clackamas River Ranger District, 595 NW Industrial Way, Estacada, OR, 97023, 503/630-6861.

92 TRIANGULATION PEAK
4.2 mi/2.0 hr   🏃1 ⛰9

east of Detroit in Mount Jefferson Wilderness

Map 3.5, page 129

A fitting name for a peak on which a fire watchtower once stood, Triangulation Peak offers an impressive view of Mount Jefferson not only from its peak, but from the mouth of a secret cave accessible by a cross-country scramble over the flanks of the peak. Along the way, the trail passes the towering monolith of Spire Rock and enters a series of alpine meadows covered with fish-filled lakes. For intrepid travelers, this trail also provides access deeper into Mount Jefferson Wilderness Area.

From the trailhead, start out 1.5 easy miles on the Triangulation Trail paralleling an old road and entering the Wilderness area. At a junction by Spire Rock's pillar, which rises from the trees and tempts rock climbers, go right to climb the remaining 500 feet and 0.6 mile. To find Boca Cave, beware of steep cliffs and watch your step. From the peak, hike down to a saddle and go right and cross-country to a second and lower peak. From here, a scramble trail descends along the right of a rock outcrop. The path ends at a cliff edge. Go to the right around the cliff and descend a steep forested slope to a 100-foot-deep cavern with a view of Mount Jefferson.

User Groups: Hikers, dogs, and horses. No mountain bikes allowed. No wheelchair facilities.

Permits: A free self-issue Wilderness Permit is required and is available at the trailhead. Parking and access are free.

Maps: You can purchase a Mount Jefferson Wilderness Map from Geo-Graphics. For a map of the Willamette National Forest and the Mount Jefferson Wilderness, contact Willamette National Forest Headquarters, 3106 Pierce Parkway, Suite D, Springfield, OR, 97477, 541/225-6300. For a topographic map, ask the USGS for Mount Bruno.

Directions: Drive 56 miles east of Salem on OR 22. One mile past Idanha, turn left on McCoy Creek Road 2233 for 9.2 miles. At a building, go right and continue 1.3 miles and park at spur Road 635. The trailhead is 100 feet down the spur road.

Contact: Willamette National Forest, Detroit Ranger District, HC73, Box 320, Mill City, OR, 97360, 503/854-4239.

93 JEFFERSON PARK
10.2 mi/5.0 hr   🏃3 ⛰10

south of Detroit in Mount Jefferson Wilderness

Map 3.5, page 129   **BEST (**

By far one of the most beloved places in Oregon, Jefferson Park is an alpine dream. Wildflowers dot the seemingly endless expanses of meadows, spotted here and there by mountain lakes and islands of wind-bent trees. Looming above it is Oregon's second-highest mountain, 10,497-foot Mount Jefferson. There are a number of ways into Jeff Park, as it's known, and this route is by far one of the most scenic. Climbing through an old-growth forest, the trail has expansive views of the mountain as it climbs and crosses the Sentinel Hills, passing rock fields where pikas dart in and out of their dens, and arriving at a virtual wonderland of lakes and undulating land.

The Whitewater Trail is easy to follow, climbing through the forest 1.5 miles to a junction. Go right along the Sentinel Hills 2.7 miles to a junction with the Pacific Crest Trail, then follow it 0.9 mile to the start of Jefferson Park. If you continue on the PCT another 0.7 mile, you'll come to Russell Lake, and side trails lead to other lakes: Scout, Rock, Bays, and Park.

User Groups: Hikers, dogs, and horses. No

mountain bikes allowed. No wheelchair facilities.

Permits: You can purchase a Mount Jefferson Wilderness Map from Geo-Graphics. A free self-issue Wilderness Permit is required and is available at the trailhead. A federal Northwest Forest Pass is required to park here; the cost is $5 a day or $30 for an annual pass. You can buy a day pass at the trailhead, at ranger stations, or through private vendors.

Maps: For a map of the Willamette National Forest and the Mount Jefferson Wilderness, contact Willamette National Forest Headquarters, 3106 Pierce Parkway, Suite D, Springfield, OR, 97477, 541/225-6300. For a topographic map, ask the USGS for Mount Jefferson.

Directions: Drive 61 miles east of Salem on OR 22. Beyond Detroit about 10 miles and between mileposts 60 and 61, turn left on Whitewater Road 2243 and drive 7.4 miles to its end at a parking area.

Contact: Willamette National Forest, Detroit Ranger District, HC73, Box 320, Mill City, OR, 97360, 503/854-4239.

94 PAMELIA LAKE AND GRIZZLY PEAK

10.0 mi/5.0 hr   🚶3 ⛰9

south of Detroit in Mount Jefferson Wilderness

Map 3.5, page 129

This popular trail has become, in the last umpteen years, too popular. What could it be? The stroll along Pamelia Creek? The shores of Pamelia Lake, with staggering Mount Jefferson reflected in its waters? Or possibly the side hike up domineering Grizzly Peak? Alas, it is all of these. To deal with the onslaught of hikers, the Forest Service requires hikers to obtain a free permit in advance. This helps to ease the congestion and allow for this fragile area, especially the lakeshore, to recover from overuse.

The first 2.2 miles of trail follow Pamelia Creek into the dense forest. At a junction you

have several options. Go straight to the lakeshore, and you can circle it to the right for a view of Mount Jefferson. Go right at the junction following a sign for Grizzly Peak to climb 2.8 miles to the 5,799-foot summit.

User Groups: Hikers, dogs, and horses. No mountain bikes allowed. No wheelchair facilities.

Permits: A free Limited Entry Permit is required for overnight and day visits to the Pamelia Lake area; contact the USFS for information. A federal Northwest Forest Pass is required to park here; the cost is $5 a day or $30 for an annual pass. You can buy a day pass at the trailhead, at ranger stations, or through private vendors.

Maps: You can purchase a Mount Jefferson Wilderness Map from Geo-Graphics. For a map of the Willamette National Forest and the Mount Jefferson Wilderness, contact Willamette National Forest Headquarters, 3106 Pierce Parkway, Suite D, Springfield, OR, 97477, 541/225-6300. For a topographic map, ask the USGS for Mount Jefferson.

Directions: Drive 62 miles east of Salem on OR 22. Beyond Detroit about 12 miles, between mileposts 62 and 63, turn left on Pamelia Road 2246 for 3.7 miles to the trailhead lot at the end of the road.

Contact: Willamette National Forest, Detroit Ranger District, HC73, Box 320, Mill City, OR, 97360, 503/854-4239.

95 MARION LAKE AND MARION MOUNTAIN

11.2 mi/5.5 hr   🚶3 ⛰8

east of Marion Forks in Mount Jefferson Wilderness

Map 3.5, page 129

Like nearby Pamelia Lake, this popular lake in the Mount Jefferson Wilderness shows obvious signs of overuse. The trail is well trammeled, and on a summer day you can expect to have company. None of this makes this big lake any less lovely. Anglers ply the waters, hikers climb over boulders to views of Three-Fingered Jack, and campers linger in the woods on cool mornings. Marion Lake isn't the only destination; you'll also see Marion Falls and Marion Mountain (did I mention this is Marion County?) along this hike. Granted, for some parts you will have to enter the notorious B&B Complex Burn, a devastating fire that roared through this wilderness in 2003, reducing much of it to ash.

The first 2.2 miles on the Marion Lake Trail are an easy walk through the forest, passing Lake Ann and its subterranean outlet. At a junction, go right on the Marion Lake Outlet Trail for 0.6 mile, watching on the right for the 0.2-mile side trail down to Marion Falls. At the next junction, you have a choice: left for a 0.7-mile trail along Marion Lake, which connects to a left-hand 0.3-mile trail back toward Lake Ann; or, if you're feeling sturdy, to the right, crossing Marion Creek and heading toward Marion Mountain on the Blue Lake Trail. The first mile enters the burn. At a pond-side junction, go right on the Pine Ridge Trail for 0.8 mile to a fork and a small sign for Marion Mountain. The remaining 0.8 mile climbs to the site of an old lookout with views to Three-Fingered Jack and Mount Jefferson.

User Groups: Hikers, dogs, and horses. No mountain bikes allowed. No wheelchair facilities.

Permits: A free self-issue Wilderness Permit is required and is available at the trailhead. A federal Northwest Forest Pass is required to park here; the cost is $5 a day or $30 for an annual pass. You can buy a day pass at the trailhead, at ranger stations, or through private vendors.

Maps: You can purchase a Mount Jefferson Wilderness Map from Geo-Graphics. For a map of the Willamette National Forest and the Mount Jefferson Wilderness, contact Willamette National Forest Headquarters, 3106 Pierce Parkway, Suite D, Springfield, OR, 97477, 541/225-6300. For a topographic map, ask the USGS for Marion Lake.

Directions: Drive 66 miles east of Salem on OR 22 to Marion Forks. Between mileposts 66 and 67 turn left on Marion Creek Road 2255 and drive 5.4 miles to the lot at road's end.

Contact: Willamette National Forest, Detroit Ranger District, HC73, Box 320, Mill City, OR, 97360, 503/854-4239.

96 CARL LAKE AND SOUTH CINDER PEAK
9.4-13.4 mi/4.5-6.0 hr

north of Sisters in Mount Jefferson Wilderness

Map 3.5, page 129

In 2003, the massive B&B Complex Fire (actually two forest fires that merged into one epic conflagration) swept through the Mount Jefferson Wilderness, torching many beloved places. Still, many areas were spared, including rock-rimmed Carl Lake. This camping-friendly lake also gives access to a number of great hikes, astonishing huckleberry fields, and a momentous view from the barren South Cinder Peak.

From the trailhead, march into the burned area which ends before the 1.9-mile walk to Cabot Lake and its side trail. From here the trail begins to switchback up into the high country, passing several ponds on the 2.8-mile walk to Carl Lake. Circle the lake for a variety of perspectives on the surrounding mountain country. The hike from here to South Cinder Peak is a challenge, requiring a 1.5-mile climb past Shirley Lake and along a deep valley to the Pacific Crest Trail. Go left on the PCT for 0.2 mile, then follow a path up the red cinder butte for views to Mount Jefferson and south to the Three Sisters.

User Groups: Hikers, dogs, and horses. No mountain bikes allowed. No wheelchair facilities.

Permits: A free self-issue Wilderness Permit is required and is available at the trailhead. A federal Northwest Forest Pass is required to park here; the cost is $5 a day or $30 for an annual pass. You can buy a day pass at the trailhead, at ranger stations, or through private vendors.

Maps: You can purchase a Mount Jefferson Wilderness Map from Geo-Graphics. For a map of the Deschutes National Forest and Mount Jefferson Wilderness, contact Deschutes National Forest Headquarters, 1001 SW Emkay Drive, Bend, OR, 97702, 541/383-5300.For a topographic map, ask the USGS for Marion Lake.

Directions: Drive 12 miles west of Sisters on U.S. 20 to a "Wilderness Trailheads" sign near milepost 88. Drive north on Jack Lake Road 12 for 4.4 miles and turn left on Road 1230 for 1.6 miles to pavement's end and seven miles on gravel to road's end at a large lot.

Contact: Deschutes National Forest, Sisters Ranger District, P.O. Box 249, Sisters, OR, 97759, 541/549-7700.

97 METOLIUS RIVER

5.4 mi/2.0 hr

north of Sisters in Deschutes National Forest

Map 3.5, page 129

The Metolius River rushes aboveground at 50,000 gallons a minute from an underground spring at the base of Black Butte. From there, the river makes a full display of itself with its ethereal blues and white water rushing through a forest of ponderosa pine and Douglas fir, where eagles wait in the branches for a chance at fish. This trail passes among songbirds amid some real scenery: islands of flowers entirely growing on fallen logs and a cascade of springs—including a waterfall splashing right out of the rock.

The easy West Metolius Trail is out-and-back from the Lower Canyon Creek Campground, heading 2.7 miles downstream to Wizard Falls and a fish hatchery. You can continue this hike as far downstream as far as you'd like, and can even cross the river and explore the opposite shore along a trail there, though there is no loop available in the form

of a second bridge to return you to the starting point.

User Groups: Hikers and dogs. No horses or mountain bikes allowed. No wheelchair facilities.

Permits: Permits are not required. Parking and access are free.

Maps: For a map of the Deschutes National Forest, contact Deschutes National Forest Headquarters, 1001 SW Emkay Drive, Bend, OR, 97702, 541/383-5300. For a topographic map, ask the USGS for Candle Creek.

Directions: Drive U.S. 20 west of Sisters nine miles, passing Black Butte. Near milepost 91, turn right at a sign for Metolius River and drive onto Road 1419 for 4.8 miles. At a stop sign, go straight on Road 1420 another 3.3 miles and turn right at a sign for Canyon Creek Campground, driving one mile to the end of the road.

Contact: Deschutes National Forest, Sisters Ranger District, P.O. Box 249, Sisters, OR, 97759, 541/549-7700.

98 COVE PALISADES STATE PARK

7.2 mi/2.5 hr

southwest of Madras in Cove Palisades State Park

Map 3.5, page 129   **BEST (**

In a dramatic canyon where three rivers—the Deschutes, the Crooked, and the Metolius—meet, an impressive array of cliff walls nestle the combined flow into the massive Lake Billy Chinook reservoir. One way to get the views of two arms of the canyon and The Island (actually a peninsula, whose towering plateau-expanse makes it the next best thing to an island) is to hike the Tam-A-Lau Trail to The Peninsula, a broad desert atop a plateau with views over Cove Palisades State Park. If you're lucky, you can spot the bald eagles that roost nearby, and on a clear day you'll certainly see Mount Jefferson on the horizon.

From the lot, follow the Tam-A-Lau Trail

0.5 mile through massive tumbled boulders, crossing the two entrance roads to a junction, going to the right. The next 1.3 miles climbs the canyon wall up a series of switchbacks to a junction with some old roads. Keep to the left and follow the trail along the lip of The Peninsula 1.2 miles to the tip above the strange formation of Steamboat Rock. For a longer loop, follow this trail around the plateau another 2.4 miles, returning to the Tam-A-Lau Trail.

User Groups: Hikers and dogs only. No wheelchair facilities.

Permits: Permits are not required. A $3 day-use fee is collected at the parking entrance, or you can get an annual Oregon Parks and Recreation pass for $25; contact Oregon Parks and Recreation, 800/551-6949.

Maps: For a free park brochure, call Oregon Parks and Recreation, 800/551-6949 or download a free map at www.oregonstateparks.org. For a topographic map, ask the USGS for Round Butte Dam.

Directions: Drive 15 miles north of Redmond on U.S. 97, going up and over Culver Butte, to a sign for The Cove State Park. Follow the Culver Highway and signs for the park into the canyon. Follow this road over a suspension bridge above the Crooked River, passing a turnout for the Crooked River Petroglyph, the park headquarters, and campgrounds. Turn right at a sign for the Tam-A-Lau Trail. Park in the big lot at the end of the road.

Contact: Oregon Parks and Recreation Department, 1115 Commercial Street NE, Salem, OR, 97301, 800/551-6949, www.oregonstateparks.org.

NORTHEASTERN OREGON

© SEAN PATRICK HILL

BEST HIKES

◖ **Desert Hiking**
Hells Canyon Reservoir, **page 232.**
Painted Hills, **page 233.**

◖ **Self-Guided Nature Walks**
Oregon Trail Interpretive Center, **page 257.**

◖ **Short Backpacking Trips**
North Fork John Day River, **page 240.**
Strawberry Lake and Little Strawberry Lake,
  page 253.

◖ **Non-Technical Summit Hikes**
Mirror Lake and Eagle Cap, **page 214.**
Onion Creek to Strawberry Mountain, **page 254.**

The Oregon Trail spans this area of the state,

crossing a rugged landscape of high deserts and mountains on its way to the paradise of the Willamette Valley. The Blue Mountains comprise several small ranges splayed across the region: the Wallowas, the Ochocos, and the Strawberries. Each differs in its flavor and coloring, but all are among the oldest ranges in the Western United States, having risen from the ocean floor millions upon millions of years ago. Over the top of this landscape are the massive Columbia River basalt lava flows that oozed from a giant crack in the earth, spreading across three states and all the way to the Pacific Ocean. This makes for a series of plateaus cut deep by the local rivers: the Walla Walla, the Umatilla, and the John Day.

A number of famed wilderness areas provide great hiking in north-eastern Oregon, including the Eagle Cap Wilderness, an island of granite rising above Hells Canyon, as well as the Strawberry Mountain Wilderness, a range of the Blue Mountains. Rivers get their due, too, including those in the North Fork Umatilla, Wenaha-Tucannon, and North Fork John Day Wildernesses. Though quickly accessible to the towns that dot this region, they are off the beaten path for residents of the major metropolitan areas of Western Oregon. Backpacks are a must.

There's plenty to love here: forests of western larch, golden in autumn; rivers where prospectors still pan for gold; Wallowa Lake, once home to the Nez Perce tribe; and Hell's Canyon, among the deepest ravines in the United States. Looking for solitude? Look no further: in northeastern Oregon, you'll have the chance for real seclusion. Watch for elk herds as you explore, and you'll see why many of the pioneers lay down their burdens in this region and called it home.

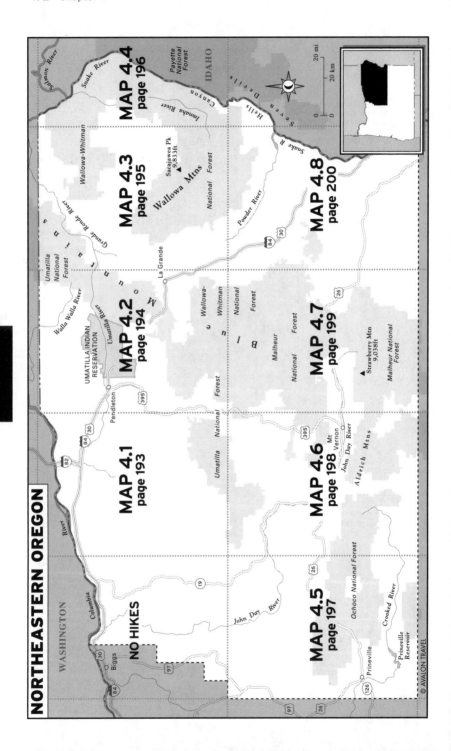

NORTHEASTERN OREGON

WASHINGTON

IDAHO

MAP 4.4
page 196

MAP 4.3
page 195

MAP 4.2
page 194

MAP 4.1
page 193

MAP 4.5
page 197

MAP 4.6
page 198

MAP 4.7
page 199

MAP 4.8
page 200

NO HIKES

Salmon River

Snake River

Imnaha River

Canyon

Payette National Forest

Seven Devils

Hells

Snake R

Wallowa-Whitman

Sacajawea Pk
9,833ft

Wallowa Mtns

National Forest

Powder River

Grande Ronde River

Umatilla National Forest

Walla Walla River

Umatilla River

UMATILLA INDIAN RESERVATION

Pendleton

La Grande

Wallowa-Whitman National Forest

Blue

Malheur National Forest

Strawberry Mtn
9,038ft

Malheur National Forest

Umatilla National Forest

Mt Vernon

John Day River

Aldrich Mtns

John Day River

Ochoco National Forest

Crooked River

Prineville

Prineville Reservoir

Columbia

River

Biggs

20 mi

20 km

© AVALON TRAVEL

Map 4.1

Hikes 1-3
Pages 201-202

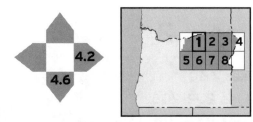

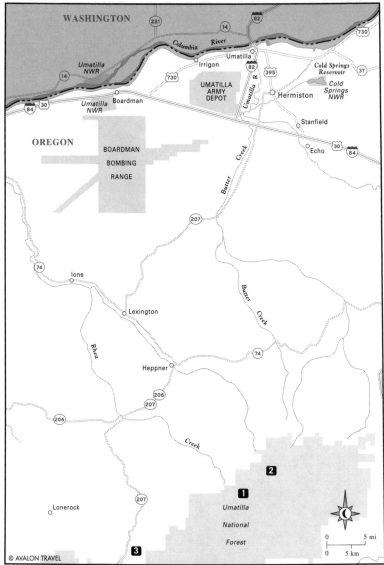

WASHINGTON

Columbia River

Umatilla
NWR

Umatilla
NWR

OREGON

BOARDMAN
BOMBING
RANGE

UMATILLA
ARMY
DEPOT

Boardman

Irrigon

Umatilla

Hermiston

Cold Springs
Reservoir

Cold
Springs
NWR

Stanfield

Echo

Butter Creek

Butter Creek

Ione

Lexington

Rhea

Heppner

Lonerock

Creek

Umatilla

National

Forest

0   5 mi
0   5 km

© AVALON TRAVEL

Map 4.2

Hikes 4-10
Pages 202-206

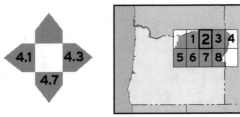

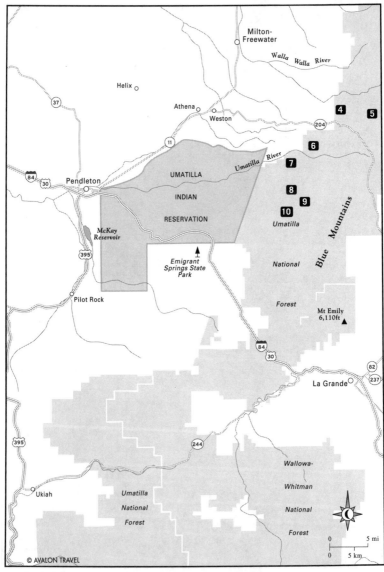

Map 4.3

Hikes 11-41
Pages 206-228

4.2   4.4

4.8

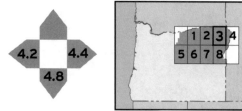

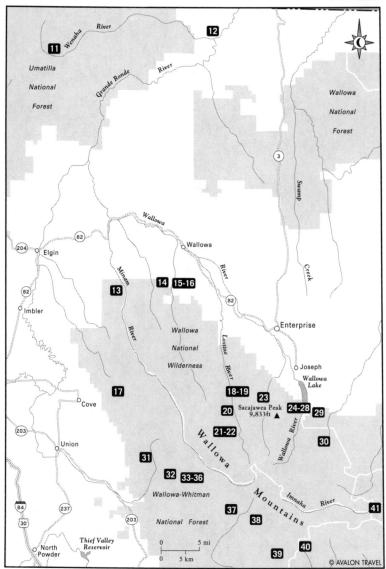

Map 4.4

Hikes 42-48
Pages 228-232

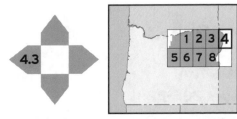

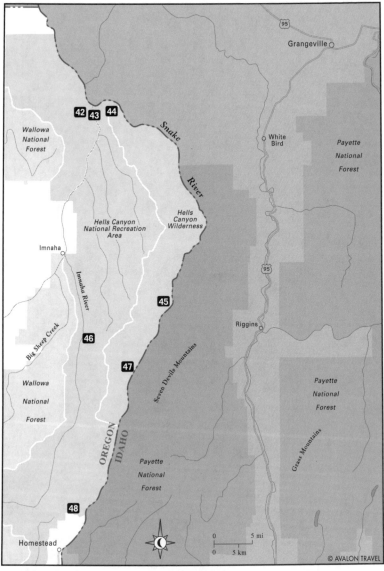

Map 4.5

Hikes 49-54
Pages 233-236

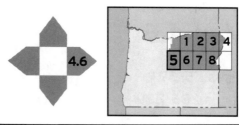

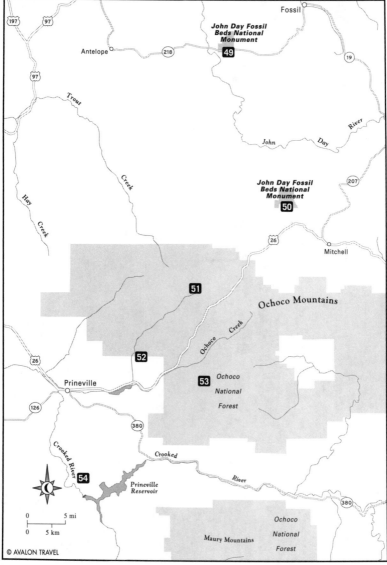

© AVALON TRAVEL

Map 4.6

Hikes 55-59
Pages 236-239

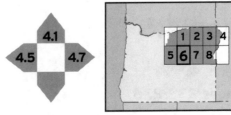

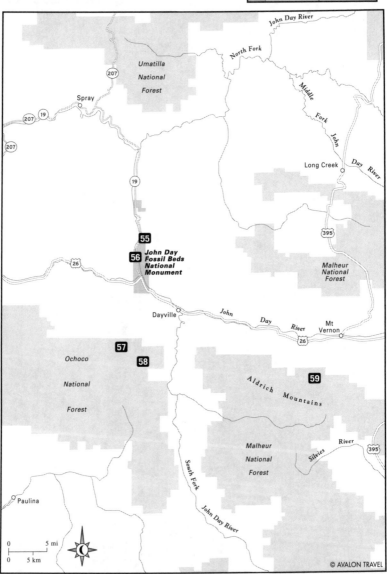

Map 4.7

Hikes 60-90
Pages 239-257

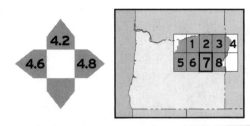

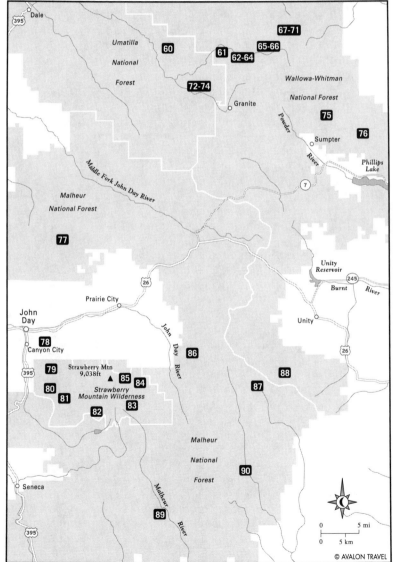

Map 4.8

Hike 91
Page 257

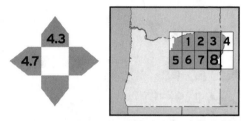

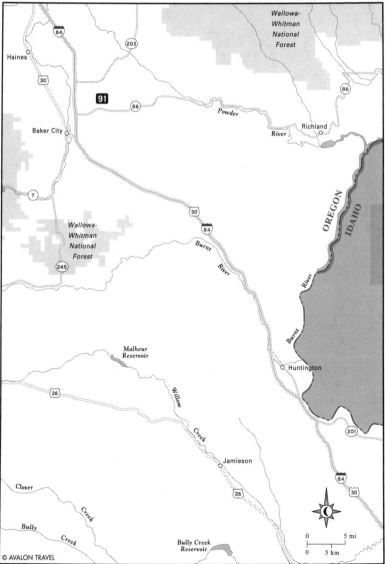

1 BALD MOUNTAIN

7.5 mi/3.0 hr

south of Heppner in Umatilla National Forest

Map 4.1, page 193

Morrow County, Oregon, may not strike anyone as a place to go hiking, but there's plenty of history (both natural and man-made) here. The Smith Ditch was built by the Civilian Conservation Corps in the 1930s as a way to bring irrigation to the area. The Gibson Cave's history goes back much further; Native Americans used the cave within the last thousand years, and a man named Gibson made this cave his home during the Great Depression, building a wall with a window at the mouth of the cave, and bringing in a cot, wood-burning stove, kerosene lamps, and other assorted furniture, some of which he built. You won't find anyone living there today, of course. This trail loops nicely, connecting with a few others in the area.

From the Coalmine Day Use Area, follow the Bald Mountain Trail 0.2 mile to the Smith Ditch. Another mile brings you to the Gibson Cave. Though the trail ends in a saddle between Little Bald Mountain and Bald Mountain, you can extend this trail to a loop by following the Hells Half Acre Trail 2.5 miles to Cutsforth Park, then taking the Willow Creek Trail 2.5 miles back to the Coalmine Day Use Area.

User Groups: Hikers, dogs, and horses or mountain bikes allowed. No wheelchair facilities.

Permits: Permits are not required. Parking and access are free.

Maps: For a map of the Umatilla National Forest, contact the Umatilla National Forest, 2517 SW Hailey Avenue, Pendleton, OR, 97801, 541/278-3716. For a topographic map, ask the USGS for Arbuckle.

Directions: From Heppner, drive one mile south on Highway 207 to Willow Creek Road. Follow Willow Creek Road 23 miles south to the Coalmine Day Use Area.

Contact: Umatilla National Forest, Heppner Ranger District, P.O. Box 7, Heppner, OR, 97836, 541/676-9187.

2 COPPLE BUTTE TRAIL

12.5 mi/6.5 hr

south of Heppner in Umatilla National Forest

Map 4.1, page 193

This trail makes an ideal mountain biking excursion, but there are opportunities for backpacking here, too—not to mention views of Mount Hood and Mount Adams from the eastern side of the Cascade Range. A profusion of trails reaches out from this area, making this a good entry point into the Blue Mountains of Morrow County. The elevation gain is nearly zero, following a ridgeline for 6.25 miles with views from Copple Butte, and nearby Texas Butte and the watchtower at Madison Butte. Hike bits of it, or make it a grand daylong excursion.

User Groups: Hikers, dogs, horses, and mountain bikes. No wheelchair facilities.

Permits: Permits are not required. Parking and access are free.

Maps: For a map of the Umatilla National Forest, contact the Umatilla National Forest, 2517 SW Hailey Avenue, Pendleton, OR, 97801, 541/278-3716. For a topographic map, ask the USGS for Madison Butte.

Directions: From Heppner, drive one mile south on Highway 207 to Willow Creek Road. Follow Willow Creek Road/County Road 678 for about 23 miles to FS Road 21. Follow FS Road 21 for 3.5 miles to Ditch Creek Guard Station and turn right on Road 050. Continue to the "Road Closure" sign at a corral, then go 1.25 miles across Martin Prairie to Texas Road 5350. Cross the road and follow a dirt road to a wooden gate. The trail begins here.

Contact: Umatilla National Forest, Heppner Ranger District, P.O. Box 7, Heppner, OR, 97836, 541/676-9187.

🛈 BULL PRAIRIE LAKE
0.5 mi/0.25 hr

south of Heppner in Umatilla National Forest

Map 4.1, page 193

This little lake in northeastern Oregon, 28 acres in all and 20 feet at its maximum depth, makes for a quiet day. No motorboats are allowed on the lake, but anglers cast from the docks for rainbow and brook trout. If you're camping here or doing some of the other trails in the area, consider this for an easy walk for the family in the cool shade of big pine trees.

User Groups: Hikers and dogs. No horses or mountain bikes. No wheelchair facilities.

Permits: Permits are not required. Parking and access are free.

Maps: For a map of the Umatilla National Forest, contact the Umatilla National Forest, 2517 SW Hailey Avenue, Pendleton, OR, 97801, 541/278-3716. For a topographic map, ask the USGS for Madison Butte.

Directions: From Heppner, drive 40 miles south on Highway 207. Turn left onto FS Road 2039 at a sign for Bull Prairie Recreation Area, driving one mile to the recreation area on the right. Access points are scattered around the lake.

Contact: Umatilla National Forest, Heppner Ranger District, P.O. Box 7, Heppner, OR, 97836, 541/676-9187.

🛈 SOUTH FORK WALLA WALLA RIVER
6.6-19.0 mi/3.0 hr-2 days

southeast of Milton-Freewater in Umatilla National Forest

Map 4.2, page 194

The Walla Walla River—its name means "little river"—slithers through its deep canyon (almost 2,000 feet in places) from a point high in the Blue Mountains. You can access the river from trailheads at its opposite ends, but the Rough Fork Trail descends roughly in the middle, allowing you to follow the river in either direction; if you go too far downstream, though, you'll quickly run into gas-powered motorbikes. It's more worth your while to stay in the more rugged middle point, where you can visit a box canyon and camping is possible.

From the Rough Fork Trailhead, descend into the canyon through forests and meadows for 3.3 miles to a footbridge over the South Fork Walla Walla. From here, you'll reach the junction with the South Fork Walla Walla Trail, a 19-mile trail. Return the way you came or continue on for a longer hike. Upstream the trail leads 7.5 miles to the Deduct Trailhead, and downstream continues 11.5 miles, passing Box Canyon, Bear Creek, and the Table Springs Trail before ending at a Forest Service road. Hike in either direction, and return via the Rough Fork Trail.

User Groups: Hikers, dogs, horses, and mountain bikes. No wheelchair facilities.

Permits: Permits are not required. Parking and access are free.

Maps: For a map of the Umatilla National Forest, contact the Umatilla National Forest, 2517 SW Hailey Avenue, Pendleton, OR, 97801, 541/278-3716. For a topographic map, ask the USGS for Jubilee Lake, Tollgate, and Bone Springs.

Directions: From I-84 at Pendleton, take Exit 210 and follow signs to Milton-Freewater on Highway 11 for 20.5 miles. After milepost 20, turn right at a sign for Elgin, then go left on Tollgate Road/Highway 204 for 19.9 miles. Turn left on Road 64 toward Jubilee Lake. Follow Road 64 north 13.5 miles to a fork, going left toward Walla Walla on Road 64. Go another 1.7 miles, then go left on Road 6403 (possibly unmarked) for 1.5 miles to a meadow at a junction. Fork right on an unmarked road 200 yards to a parking lot.

Contact: Umatilla National Forest, Walla Walla Ranger District, 1415 West Rose, Walla Walla, WA 99863, 509/522-6290.

5 JUBILEE LAKE NATIONAL RECREATION TRAIL

2.6 mi/1.0 hr 👥₁ ⛰₇

northeast of Tollgate in Umatilla National Forest

Map 4.2, page 194

Jubilee Lake was created by a dam in 1968, and the trail around it is designated a National Recreation Trail. It makes a good camping and fishing spot, certainly, but also a relatively wild hiking spot. You can make an easy day of it with the family if you're staying the night. The trail loops 2.6 miles around the lake, crossing the dam and sometimes making use of old dirt roads along the way; just stay along the lakeshore and you can't go wrong.

User Groups: Hikers and dogs only. No horses or mountain bikes allowed. The trail is designed for barrier-free access.

Permits: Permits are not required. There is a $5 day-use fee collected at the fee booth.

Maps: For a map of the Umatilla National Forest, contact the Umatilla National Forest, 2517 SW Hailey Avenue, Pendleton, OR, 97801, 541/278-3716. For a topographic map, ask the USGS for Jubilee Lake.

Directions: From I-84 at Pendleton, take Exit 210 and follow signs to Milton-Freewater on Highway 11 for 20.5 miles. After milepost 20, turn right at a sign for Elgin, then go left on Tollgate Road/Highway 204 for 19.9 miles. Turn left on Road 64 toward Jubilee Lake. Follow Road 64 north 11.5 miles and turn right into the Jubilee Campground for 0.6 mile to the fee booth, then 0.2 mile to the boat ramp parking. The trail begins at the parking lot.

Contact: Umatilla National Forest, Walla Walla Ranger District, 1415 West Rose, Walla Walla, WA 99863, 509/522-6290.

6 LICK CREEK TO GROUSE MOUNTAIN

7.8 mi/3.5 hr 👥₃ ⛰₇

southeast of Tollgate in North Fork Umatilla Wilderness

Map 4.2, page 194

Climbing a steep creek canyon into the North Fork Umatilla Wilderness, the Lick Creek Trail heads a mere 2.3 miles but climbs 1,800 feet through open stands of timber and native grasslands. Expect solitude. At a junction at the top of the ridge, the Lick Creek Trail continues its final mile to the right, but to the left a faint side trail leads 1.6 miles to a viewpoint at Grouse Mountain.

User Groups: Hikers, dogs, and horses. No mountain bikes allowed. No wheelchair facilities.

Permits: A free self-issue Wilderness Permit is required and is available at the trailhead. Parking and access are free.

Maps: For a map of the Umatilla National Forest and the North Fork Umatilla Wilderness, contact the Umatilla National Forest, 2517 SW Hailey Avenue, Pendleton, OR, 97801, 541/278-3716. For a topographic map, ask the USGS for Bingham Springs and Blalock Mountain.

Directions: To access the lower trailhead, take Exit 216 off I-84 south of Pendleton. Go north on Market Road/OR 331 for 1.9 miles to Mission-Cayuse Road, and go right for 1.6 miles, then go left on Cayuse Road for 11.2 miles. After milepost 15, turn right onto Bingham Road and follow it 14.7 miles. The trailhead is on the left.

Contact: Umatilla National Forest, Walla Walla Ranger District, 1415 West Rose, Walla Walla, WA 99863, 509/522-6290.

◼ NORTH FORK UMATILLA RIVER

9.1 mi one-way/1–2 days

east of Pendleton in North Fork Umatilla Wilderness

Map 4.2, page 194

Northeastern Oregon is a matter of lava, specifically the massive Columbia River basalt flows that poured out over this region over the course of millions of years. The Columbia Plateau was left behind, and rivers like the Umatilla slowly but surely carved their way, leaving steep canyons in the flat-as-a-pancake tablelands. For an exploration of one of these canyons, follow the North Fork Umatilla River into a wilderness area of cottonwood trees and red alders, which crowd the shores, and Douglas fir and Grand fir higher up. The lower part of the trail is popular and fairly easy, but it's the upper reaches where you'll find the most solitude, as well as exquisite views of the drainage.

From the trailhead, follow the North Fork Umatilla River and Trail 2.7 miles to a crossing of Coyote Creek and a campsite. Ignoring an unmaintained spur trail to the left, continue 1.6 miles along the river, then ascend Coyote Ridge over the next 2.8 miles. From a high point on the ridge, continue another two miles to an upper trailhead at Road 041, climbing 2,000 feet above the river.

User Groups: Hikers, dogs, and horses. No mountain bikes allowed. No wheelchair facilities.

Permits: A free self-issue Wilderness Permit is required and is available at the trailhead. Parking and access are free.

Maps: For a map of the Umatilla National Forest and the North Fork Umatilla Wilderness, contact the Umatilla National Forest, 2517 SW Hailey Avenue, Pendleton, OR, 97801, 541/278-3716. For a topographic map, ask the USGS for Bingham Springs.

Directions: To access the lower trailhead, take Exit 216 off I-84 south of Pendleton. Go north on Market Road/OR 331 for 1.9 miles to Mission-Cayuse Road, and go right for 1.6 miles, then go left on Cayuse Road for 11.2 miles. After milepost 15, turn right onto Bingham Road and follow it 15.7 miles. The trailhead is on the left. To reach the upper trailhead, drive west of Tollgate 1.2 miles on State Highway 204 and turn left on FS Road 3719. Follow this road about 1.5 miles and turn right on Road 040. After 0.6 mile, go right at a junction for 0.1 mile, then right 0.2 mile on Road 041 to road's end at the Coyote Ridge Trailhead.

Contact: Umatilla National Forest, Walla Walla Ranger District, 1415 West Rose, Walla Walla, WA 99863, 509/522-6290.

◼ NINEMILE RIDGE

6.8 mi one-way/4.0 hr

east of Pendleton in North Fork Umatilla Wilderness

Map 4.2, page 194

The North Fork Umatilla Wilderness has a quality of remoteness about it that draws people from the western part of the state, but for Eastern Oregonians, this may as well be their backyard. Ninemile Ridge rises above the Umatilla drainage enough so that the foliage changes dramatically from a deep fir forest to the sparse ponderosa pine stands and finally into grasslands and wildflower meadows. But it's a difficult climb, ascending more than 2,000 feet to a cairn at the summit, and ambling onward to an upper trailhead at Road 31. If you plan on backpacking, bring plenty of water, as there is no drinkable water along the way.

From the trailhead, go 200 feet to a four-way junction and take the left-hand Ninemile Ridge Trail, and in 0.1 mile go right toward the wilderness boundary. In two miles, the trail climbs out of the fir forests and into the pines, ascending nearly 1,200 feet to the start of the ridge. The next 1.6 miles climbs nearly 1,000 feet to the cairn marking the 4,568-foot summit. From here the trail continues along Ninemile Ridge 3.6 miles, joining the abandoned road that is the Umatilla Rim Trail for 0.7 mile to the upper trailhead at Road 31.

User Groups: Hikers, dogs, and horses. No mountain bikes allowed. No wheelchair facilities.

Permits: A free self-issue Wilderness Permit is required and is available at the trailhead. Parking and access are free.

Maps: For a map of the Umatilla National Forest and the North Fork Umatilla Wilderness, contact the Umatilla National Forest, 2517 SW Hailey Avenue, Pendleton, OR, 97801, 541/278-3716. For a topographic map, ask the USGS for Bingham Springs and Andies Prairie.

Directions: To access the lower trailhead, take Exit 216 off I-84 south of Pendleton. Go north on Market Road/OR 331 for 1.9 miles to Mission-Cayuse Road, and go right for 1.6 miles, then go left on Cayuse Road for 11.2 miles. After milepost 15, turn right onto Bingham Road and follow it 16.1 miles. Turn left on a rocky spur road 0.2 mile to a parking lot at road's end. For the upper trailhead, start from Tollgate and drive 8 miles south (or 14 miles north of Elgin) on State Highway 204 and turn west on FS Road 31. Go 2 miles and turn right on Road 3100-320 for 0.1 mile, then left on to Road 3100-330. After 2 miles, come to the end of the road at Shamrock Springs. The badly marked trail and trailhead are located 100 yards west of the springs.

Contact: Umatilla National Forest, Walla Walla Ranger District, 1415 West Rose, Walla Walla, WA 99863, 509/522-6290.

9 BUCK CREEK
5.5 mi/2.5 hr

east of Pendleton in North Fork Umatilla Wilderness

Map 4.2, page 194

The Buck Creek Trail certainly makes use of the creek, crossing and recrossing it up to 30 times along the way. Thus, you'll want to avoid this trail in the high spring runoff. But come summer, you'll be hopping the little creek easily, though you should wear a good pair of boots or shoes you can get wet. From the upper trailhead, it is possible to form a loop with the Buck Mountain Trail (see *Buck Mountain,* next listing) for a 12.2-mile loop. Note that the upper reaches of this trail cross clear-cuts and burned areas and may not make for the most scenic stretch.

From the trailhead, go 200 feet to a four-way junction and continue straight along Buck Creek. After three miles, the trail climbs 2.5 miles up a ridge and ends at the upper Lake Creek Trailhead at Road 3150.

User Groups: Hikers, dogs, and horses. No mountain bikes allowed. No wheelchair facilities.

Permits: A free self-issue Wilderness Permit is required and is available at the trailhead. Parking and access are free.

Maps: For a map of the Umatilla National Forest and the North Fork Umatilla Wilderness, contact the Umatilla National Forest, 2517 SW Hailey Avenue, Pendleton, OR, 97801, 541/278-3716. For a topographic map, ask the USGS for Bingham Springs.

Directions: To access the lower trailhead, take Exit 216 off I-84 south of Pendleton. Go north on Market Road/OR 331 for 1.9 miles to Mission-Cayuse Road, and go right for 1.6 miles, then go left on Cayuse Road for 11.2 miles. After milepost 15, turn right onto Bingham Road and follow it 16.1 miles. Turn left on a rocky spur road 0.2 mile to a parking lot at road's end. For the upper trailhead, from the town of Weston drive east on Highway 204 for 15.3 miles, turning right on McDougall Camp Road 3715 and driving 3.4 miles to its end at the trailhead.

Contact: Umatilla National Forest, Walla Walla Ranger District, 1415 West Rose, Walla Walla, WA 99863, 509/522-6290.

10 BUCK MOUNTAIN
6.5 mi/3.5 hr

east of Pendleton in North Fork Umatilla
Wilderness

Map 4.2, page 194

It is possible to make a loop of this trail with
the Buck Creek hike (see *Buck Creek,* previous
listing), though you'll have to cross a few logging roads and clear-cuts to do it. Nevertheless, you'll traverse the North Fork Umatilla
Wilderness and afford yourself some views of
this canyon country.

From the trailhead, hike in 200 feet to a four-
way junction and go right on the Buck Mountain
Trail. The trail climbs 2,100 feet in 2.2 miles
before leveling off along the rim and mountain
meadows for 4.3 miles to the upper trailhead
for Buck Creek. At the peak, you will have a
panoramic view of the surrounding country.

User Groups: Hikers, dogs, and horses. No
mountain bikes allowed. No wheelchair
facilities.

Permits: A free self-issue Wilderness Permit
is required and is available at the trailhead.
Parking and access are free.

Maps: For a map of the Umatilla National Forest and the North Fork Umatilla Wilderness,
contact the Umatilla National Forest, 2517
SW Hailey Avenue, Pendleton, OR, 97801,
541/278-3716. For a topographic map, ask
the USGS for Bingham Springs.

Directions: To access the lower trailhead, take
Exit 216 off I-84 south of Pendleton. Go north
on Market Road/OR 331 for 1.9 miles to Mission-Cayuse Road, and go right for 1.6 miles,
then go left on Cayuse Road for 11.2 miles. After
milepost 15, turn right onto Bingham Road and
follow it 16.1 miles. Turn left on a rocky spur
road 0.2 mile to a parking lot at road's end. For
the upper trailhead, from the town of Weston
drive east on Highway 204 for 15.3 miles, turning right on McDougall Camp Road 3715 and
driving 3.4 miles to its end at the trailhead.

Contact: Umatilla National Forest, Walla
Walla Ranger District, 1415 West Rose, Walla
Walla, WA 99863, 509/522-6290.

11 UPPER WENAHA RIVER
9.0 mi round-trip or 31.4 mi one-way/5.0 hr-6 days

east of Pendleton in Wenaha-Tucannon
Wilderness

Map 4.3, page 195

The Wenaha River covers quite a stretch of
this little corner of Oregon nestled up to
the Washington border. To do this river at a
stretch requires endurance and a love of getting wet since you'll have to ford the river and
side creeks at points. Then there are the rattlesnakes and high summer temperatures, but
after all, this is the high-and-dry country. On
the other hand, numerous bars along the river
afford good camping spots, and the canyon
itself is rugged and phenomenally beautiful,
particularly as it crosses the Wenaha-Tucannon Wilderness, with its western larch trees,
orchids, and wild mushrooms. This trail descends, so just remember that what goes down
must come back up.

From the historic guard station at Timothy
Springs, start out on the Wenaha Trail. In the
first two miles, the trail crosses two creeks and
follows the South Fork Wenaha River. At the
third creek crossing, look for a waterfall upstream from the crossing. After 0.3 mile, the
trail fords the 20-foot-wide river. If you decide
to cross, continue 2.2 miles up and down a cliff
face, crossing a small creek and reaching the
second major ford of Milk Creek, which makes
a good turnaround point. If you continue, the
trail goes on 5.7 miles to Wenaha Forks, 14.8
miles from there to Crooked Creek, then 4.1
miles to the National Forest boundary and 2.3
final miles to the town of Troy.

User Groups: Hikers, dogs, and horses. No
mountain bikes allowed. No wheelchair
facilities.

Permits: A free self-issue Wilderness Permit
is required and is available at the trailhead.
Parking and access are free.

Maps: For a map of the Umatilla National
Forest, contact the Umatilla National Forest, 2517 SW Hailey Avenue, Pendleton, OR,

97801, 541/278-3716. For a topographic map, ask the USGS for Wenaha Forks.

Directions: From I-84 at Pendleton, take Exit 210 and follow signs to Milton-Freewater on Highway 11 for 20.5 miles. After milepost 20, turn right at a sign for Elgin, then go left on Tollgate Road/Highway 204 for 19.9 miles. Turn left on Road 64 toward Jubilee Lake. Follow Road 64 north 13.5 miles. Two miles past Jubilee Lake, go right at a fork onto Road 6413 toward Troy, going 11.8 miles to a T-junction. Go left, staying on Road 6413 for 1.8 miles, then go left on Road 6415 for 6.9 miles to Timothy Springs Campground on the right. Turn right and stay on the middle road for 0.2 mile to a message board at the Wilderness boundary.

Opposite trailhead the same as Lower Wenaha River: From La Grande on I-84, take exit 261 and follow signs toward Enterprise, driving on Highway 82 for 65 miles. In Enterprise, turn left on First Street/Highway 3 for 35 miles to a sign for Flora, and turn left three miles to the ghost town of Flora, and continue 11.3 miles from paved road to a steep, one-lane gravel road and cross the Grande Ronde River. After the bridge, turn left for two miles to the town of Troy. Just before the downtown, turn right on Bartlett Road toward Pomeroy, going 0.4 mile to a pullout at a switchback. The trailhead is behind the message board.

Contact: Umatilla National Forest, Pomeroy Ranger District, 71 West Main Street, Pomeroy, WA 99347, 509/843-1891.

12 LOWER WENAHA RIVER
12.8 mi/6.5 hr 🏃3 ⛰7

west of Troy in Umatilla National Forest

Map 4.3, page 195

There are numerous access points to the Wenaha River, and the tiny town of Troy marks the lower stretch. From here, the trail heads into the whitewater canyon, passing ponderosa pine, mariposa lilies, and poison oak.

Undaunted, it follows the canyon walls into the Wenaha-Tucannon Wilderness, making for a long backpacking or horseback trip up to the historic guard station at Timothy Springs. For an easier day-hike, or a short backpacking trip, Crooked Creek makes a good destination point.

From the trailhead, hike the Wenaha Trail 2.3 miles upstream along the river to the National Forest boundary. From here, elevation gain is minimal. The next 4.1 miles continues to viewpoints and rimrock cliff overhangs to a junction; go left to a footbridge crossing of Crooked Creek and campsites. If you continue on, it is 14.8 miles to Wenaha Forks, and another 10.2 to Timothy Springs.

User Groups: Hikers, dogs, and horses. No mountain bikes allowed. No wheelchair facilities.

Permits: Permits are not required unless entering the wilderness area, where a free self-issue Wilderness Permit is required and is available on the trail. Parking and access are free.

Maps: For a map of the Umatilla National Forest, contact the Umatilla National Forest, 2517 SW Hailey Avenue, Pendleton, OR, 97801, 541/278-3716. For a topographic map, ask the USGS for Troy.

Directions: From La Grande on I-84, take exit 261 and follow signs toward Enterprise, driving on Highway 82 for 65 miles. In Enterprise, turn left on First Street/Highway 3 for 35 miles to a sign for Flora, and turn left three miles to the ghost town of Flora, and continue 11.3 miles from paved road to a steep, one-lane gravel road and cross the Grande Ronde River. After the bridge, turn left for two miles to the town of Troy. Just before the downtown, turn right on Bartlett Road toward Pomeroy, going 0.4 mile to a pullout at a switchback. The trailhead is behind the message board.

Opposite trailhead the same as Upper Wenaha Trail: From I-84 at Pendleton, take Exit 210 and follow signs to Milton-Freewater on Highway 11 for 20.5 miles. After milepost 20, turn right at a sign for Elgin, then go left on Tollgate Road/

Highway 204 for 19.9 miles. Turn left on Road 64 toward Jubilee Lake. Follow Road 64 north 13.5 miles. Two miles past Jubilee Lake, go right at a fork onto Road 6413 toward Troy, going 11.8 miles to a T-junction. Go left, staying on Road 6413 for 1.8 miles, then go left on Road 6415 for 6.9 miles to timothy Springs Campground on the right. Turn right and stay on the middle road for 0.2 mile to a message board at the Wilderness boundary.

Contact: Umatilla National Forest, Pomeroy Ranger District, 71 West Main Street, Pomeroy, WA 99347, 509/843-1891.

13 MINAM RIVER FROM ROCK SPRINGS TRAILHEAD
8.4 mi/4.0 hr   🏃2 ⛰7

northeast of La Grande in Eagle Cap Wilderness

Map 4.3, page 195

Making your way to the Minam River is difficult. No matter how you do it, you'll still have to descend into a 2,500-foot-deep canyon in the heart of the Eagle Cap Wilderness—and get back out. The Rock Springs Trail offers one of the most desirable entries to the canyon; it leads to the confluence of the mighty Minam River with the Little Minam River at a point where a few log cabin ruins mark an abandoned lodge. From the top of the canyon, the land stretches out like folds in a sleeve, but soon enough dives into the depths of the rimrock.

The trail almost immediately heads downhill into a forest of lodgepole pine, grand fir, subalpine fir, and western larch for 3.4 miles, coming to two good viewpoints of the canyon before dropping steeply into the final pitch of the canyon. Near the bottom, the trail comes to a junction; to the right is the Little Minam River Trail, which follows this river to the Moss Springs Trailhead 12 miles upstream (see *Little Minam River* in this chapter). To access the Minam River, go right past the abandoned lodge buildings, passing a more obvious trail on the right and continuing through the meadow. This path leads 0.8 mile along the river to a ford, far too cold and swift for hikers to attempt fording, so return as you came.

Otherwise, the nearest place to cross is to head 5.5 miles on the Little Minam River, then go right 1.1 miles to the old Reds Horse Ranch and cross to the other side there, from which you can follow the river upstream to Minam Lake.

User Groups: Hikers, dogs, and horses. No mountain bikes allowed. No wheelchair facilities.

Permits: A free self-issue Wilderness Permit is required and is available at the trailhead. Parking and access are free.

Maps: A contour map of the Wallowa Mountains is available from Imus Geographics. For a map of the Wallowa-Whitman National Forest, contact the Wallowa-Whitman National Forest Headquarters, P.O. Box 907, 1550 Dewey Avenue, Baker City, OR, 97814, 541/523-6391. For a topographic map, ask the USGS for Minam.

Directions: From the La Grande Exit 261 off I-84, follow Highway 82 toward Wallowa Lake for eight miles to Alicel. Turn right on Alicel Lane, and stay on this road through several turns and bends for four miles. Turn right on Gray's Corners Road for one mile and turn left on an unmarked gravel road that heads uphill. In 10.2 miles cross a bridge and turn left on Road 62, going 6.8 miles to a fork. Go right, continuing on Road 62 for three miles to the Rock Springs Trailhead. The trailhead is about 200 yards farther down the road.

Contact: Wallowa-Whitman National Forest, Eagle Cap Ranger District, 88401 Highway 82, Enterprise, OR, 97828, 541/426-5546.

14 STANDLEY CABIN
10.2 mi/4.5 hr   🏃3 ⛰6

south of Wallowa in Eagle Cap Wilderness

Map 4.3, page 195

The Standley Guard Station was used as the site for range studies in the early 1900s, and though it is not open for public use it is in remarkably good condition. The cabin is the destination on this hike along Standley Ridge, which passes through burned woods and fields of fireweed into the Eagle Cap Wilderness.

From the Bearwallow Trailhead, follow the Standley Trail along the ridge. In 0.8 mile, the trail passes Bald Knob, and 1.7 miles later moves into the burn, staying in the midst of the snags and fireweed for 1.6 miles to the Dobbins Creek Trail junction, which gives you the option of heading down four miles to the Bear Creek Guard Station (see *Bear Creek,* next listing). Instead, continue on: 0.9 mile past Dobbins Creek Trail junction, you'll reach the cabin and a spring. From the cabin, you'll have your pick of three different directions to hike into the wilderness for days of adventure.

User Groups: Hikers, dogs, and horses. No mountain bikes allowed. No wheelchair facilities.

Permits: A free self-issue Wilderness Permit is required and is available at the trailhead. Parking and access are free.

Maps: A contour map of the Wallowa Mountains is available from Imus Geographics. For a map of the Wallowa-Whitman National Forest, contact the Wallowa-Whitman National Forest Headquarters, P.O. Box 907, 1550 Dewey Avenue, Baker City, OR, 97814, 541/523-6391. For a topographic map, ask the USGS for Mount Moriah.

Directions: From the La Grande Exit 261 off I-84, follow Highway 82 toward Wallowa Lake for 35 miles. Turn right on Big Canyon Road 8270 for 10.8 miles, then go left on primitive Road 050 for 6.9 miles, staying on the main road at junctions. Park at the Bearwallow Trailhead at road's end.

Contact: Wallowa-Whitman National Forest, Eagle Cap Ranger District, 88401 Highway 82, Enterprise, OR, 97828, 541/426-5546.

15 BEAR CREEK
10.0 mi/4.5 hr

south of Wallowa in Eagle Cap Wilderness

Map 4.3, page 195

This fairly easy trail accesses the vast Eagle Cap Wilderness, with opportunities to connect to other trails in this wilderness area, or just to fish the stream. Bear Creek rolls through open country, pine stands, and dense fir forests. Cottonwood trees stand tall along the creek. Where Goat Creek joins Bear Creek, the historic Bear Creek Guard Station sits quietly in a meadow. Though locked to the public, there are plenty of campsites nearby. From there, the wilderness is at your fingertips.

From the trailhead and Boundary Campground, follow Bear Creek upstream 4.3 miles to the junction with the Goat Creek Trail. There are campsites in the woods here. Proceed on the Bear Creek Trail 0.7 mile to the cabin. In another 0.5 mile, another junction leads up 4.4 miles to Standley Ridge (see *Standley Cabin,* previous listing).

User Groups: Hikers, dogs, and horses. No mountain bikes allowed. No wheelchair facilities.

Permits: A free self-issue Wilderness Permit is required and is available at the trailhead. A federal Northwest Forest Pass is required to park here; the cost is $5 a day or $30 for an annual pass. You can buy a day pass at the trailhead, at ranger stations, or through private vendors.

Maps: A contour map of the Wallowa Mountains is available from Imus Geographics. For a map of the Wallowa-Whitman National Forest, contact the Wallowa-Whitman National Forest Headquarters, P.O. Box 907, 1550 Dewey Avenue, Baker City, OR, 97814, 541/523-6391. For a topographic map, ask the USGS for Fox Point.

Directions: From the La Grande Exit 261 off I-84, follow Highway 82 toward Wallowa Lake 46.5 miles to the town of Wallowa. Turn right toward North Bear Creek Road, which becomes Road 8250, for 8.2 miles. Go straight on Road 040, following signs for Boundary Campground, another 0.8 mile past the campground to the trailhead at road's end.

Contact: Wallowa-Whitman National Forest, Eagle Cap Ranger District, 88401 Highway 82, Enterprise, OR, 97828, 541/426-5546.

16 HUCKLEBERRY MOUNTAIN
3.8-16.0 mi/2.0 hr-2 days 🏃3 ⛰️7

south of Wallowa in Wallowa-Whitman National Forest

Map 4.3, page 195

This wonderfully rough trail, following an old cattle trail, arduously climbs to an old lookout site on Huckleberry Mountain, whose open grasslands fill with flowers in July and provide views down to the Lostine Canyon and Bear Creek. Although the trail crosses Little Bear Creek at the outset, water is scarce after that—unless you plan on following the trail six miles farther along the ridge to Little Storm Lake. You may find a good use here for your route-finding skills, as the trail is rougher than average and faint in places. Even the road to get there is a bit rough; with a high-clearance vehicle you can drive straight to the trailhead through a gate open July 15 through September 15. If you're not in the mood for busted shocks, simply park in Little Bear Saddle and walk in, adding one mile round-trip to your hike.

If need be, park at the intersection of Road 8250 and Road 160. Follow Road 160 by foot or vehicle up 0.5 mile to the trailhead on the left. The Huckleberry Mountain Trail climbs relentlessly from here 1.9 miles and 1,850 feet to the lookout site atop Huckleberry Mountain. This makes a good turnaround point. But the trail continues along the ridge and into the Eagle Cap Wilderness, where wilderness permits are required. Follow the trail six miles, dropping down to 7,200-foot elevation Little Storm Lake.

User Groups: Hikers, dogs, and horses. No

aspens in the Wallowa Mountains

© SEAN PATRICK HILL

mountain bikes allowed. No wheelchair facilities.

Permits: Permits are not required unless entering the Eagle Cap Wilderness, where a free permit can be filled out at the wilderness boundary. Parking and access are free.

Maps: A contour map of the Wallowa Mountains is available from Imus Geographics. For a map of the Wallowa-Whitman National Forest, contact the Wallowa-Whitman National Forest Headquarters, P.O. Box 907, 1550 Dewey Avenue, Baker City, OR, 97814, 541/523-6391. For a topographic map, ask the USGS for Lostine.

Directions: From the La Grande Exit 261 off I-84, follow Highway 82 toward Wallowa Lake 46.5 miles to the town of Wallowa. Turn right on North Bear Creek Road, which becomes Road 8250, for 8.2 miles. Go left, following signs for Huckleberry Trail, another 7.4 miles. At a fork in Little Bear Saddle, turn right on Road 160 for 0.5 mile to the trailhead. If the gate is closed or if you have a low-clearance vehicle, park at the intersection and follow the hiking directions in the hike description.

Contact: Wallowa-Whitman National Forest, Eagle Cap Ranger District, 88401 Highway 82, Enterprise, OR, 97828, 541/426-5546.

17 LITTLE MINAM RIVER
15.2 mi/2 days   🥾4 ⛺8

east of La Grande in Eagle Cap Wilderness

Map 4.3, page 195

Like the Rock Springs Trail to the Minam River, this trail along the Little Minam River drops into a canyon spiked with western larch, subalpine fir, and grand fir, and visits an unused lodge and the Reds Horse Ranch, a former dude ranch that is currently closed but maintained by volunteers. With camping available along the Minam River, and three creeks along the way for water, this makes a good overnighter.

From the trailhead lot, pass by the Lodgepole Trail and instead take the trail behind the message board, which immediately forks. Go left on the Horse Ranch Trail, gradually climbing down into the canyon. In 1.4 miles, the trail crosses Horseshoe Creek then begins following the Little Minam River for three miles to a bridge over the Little Minam. Stay left after the bridge, following the river then leaving it 2.1 miles to a pass. The trail to the left leads to the Rock Springs Trail; go straight 1.1 miles to the bridge over the Minam River and the old dude ranch.

User Groups: Hikers, dogs, and horses. No mountain bikes allowed. No wheelchair facilities.

Permits: A free self-issue Wilderness Permit is required and is available at the trailhead. A federal Northwest Forest Pass is required to park here; the cost is $5 a day or $30 for an annual pass. You can buy a day pass at the trailhead, at ranger stations, or through private vendors.

Maps: A contour map of the Wallowa Mountains is available from Imus Geographics. For a map of the Wallowa-Whitman National Forest, contact the Wallowa-Whitman National Forest Headquarters, P.O. Box 907, 1550 Dewey Avenue, Baker City, OR, 97814, 541/523-6391. For a topographic map, ask the USGS for Mount Moriah.

Directions: From the La Grande Exit 261 off I-84, follow Highway 82 toward Wallowa Lake for 1.8 miles, then go straight on East 1st Street, which becomes Highway 237, for 14 miles to the town of Cove. In Cove, follow the highway on Main Street to where it turns right, then go left on French Street, following signs for Moss Creek Campground. The road becomes Mill Creek Lane then Road 6220; follow this road 9.1 miles to the campground. The last seven miles of this road are steep and rough. Go right into the campground for 0.3 mile to the trailhead parking area at the end of a loop.

Contact: Wallowa-Whitman National Forest, Eagle Cap Ranger District, 88401 Highway 82, Enterprise, OR, 97828, 541/426-5546.

18 STEAMBOAT LAKE LOOP
29.3 mi/3 days   🥾5 ⛺10

south of Wallowa in Eagle Cap Wilderness

Map 4.3, page 195

If there is one thing the Eagle Cap Wilderness is famous for, it's lakes. In this corner of the wilderness, lakes abound, creeks tumble over the trails, and two major rivers, the Lostine and the Minam, have their headwaters here. This rough-and-tumble rocky mountain stretch makes for a mighty loop, backpacker and horse train worthy. Midweek, you may not see many people; there are far more popular areas in the wilderness, so you can really get away for days here. Along the way, you'll pass Chimney, John Henry, Steamboat, and Swamp Lakes—all camping friendly. Watch for elk, deer, and bear.

To hike the full loop, start at the Bowman Trailhead and climb into a forest of lodgepole pine, fir, and spruce 3.6 miles and 2,000 feet to a junction in Brownie Basin. Chimney Lake and the Laverty Lakes are 1.5 miles to the right and Hobo Lake is 1.6 mile farther on. For the loop, continue on the Bowman Trail 1.1 miles up to Wilson Pass, then switchback down 1.2 miles to a junction in Wilson Basin. John Henry Lake is 0.5 mile to the left and makes a good camping site for the first night.

From this junction, continue 1.2 mile over the Wilson Basin, then go left across a creek at a junction, continuing 2.5 miles to a three-way junction in North Minam Meadows. Go left toward Copper Creek, following the North Minam River 5.3 miles to Steamboat Lake, a good spot to camp for a second night; if not here, go 1.7 miles farther to Swamp Lake, passing a right-hand 1.8-mile spur trail to Long Lake. All three lakes are set in a granite basin.

Continue past Swamp Lake 1.7 miles to the uplands, then go left along the Copper Creek Trail 3.4 miles to a meadow, then 1.6 miles to a junction, staying left along the West Lostine River for 2.8 descending miles to the Two Pan Trailhead. From here, the walk back to the Bowman Trailhead is along the Lostine River Road 3.2 miles, but there are three developed campgrounds along the way, Shady Campground being the closest in 0.5 mile.

User Groups: Hikers, dogs, and horses. No mountain bikes allowed. No wheelchair facilities.

Permits: A free self-issue Wilderness Permit is required and is available at the trailhead. A federal Northwest Forest Pass is required to park here; the cost is $5 a day or $30 for an annual pass. You can buy a day pass at the trailhead, at ranger stations, or through private vendors.

Maps: A contour map of the Wallowa Mountains is available from Imus Geographics. For a map of the Wallowa-Whitman National Forest, contact the Wallowa-Whitman National Forest Headquarters, P.O. Box 907, 1550 Dewey Avenue, Baker City, OR, 97814, 541/523-6391. For a topographic map, ask the USGS for North Minam Meadows and Steamboat Lake.

Directions: From the La Grande Exit 261 off I-84, follow Highway 82 toward Wallowa Lake for 55 miles to Lostine. Where the highway turns left in town, go straight on Lostine River Road for 12.2 miles to the Lostine Guard Station, and continue on gravel another 2.9 miles to the Bowman Trailhead on the right. To find the Two Pan Trailhead, continue 3.2 miles on the Lostine River Road to road's end.

Contact: Wallowa-Whitman National Forest, Eagle Cap Ranger District, 88401 Highway 82, Enterprise, OR, 97828, 541/426-5546.

19 FRANCES LAKE
18.2 mi/2 days

south of Wallowa in Eagle Cap Wilderness

Map 4.3, page 195

The Frances Lake Trail offers some amazing views of Twin Peaks and Marble Point, and looks out over the Lostine Canyon to Chimney and Hobo Lakes (see *Steamboat Lake Loop* in this section). It's an arduous 3,300-foot climb to a high pass, then another nearly 1,000-foot drop to the lake itself. Climb switchback after switchback, following this trail 9.1 miles to the lake; be sure to carry adequate water. Because of the lack of water on the trail, the best place to camp is Frances Lake itself. Be sure to refill your bottles there.

User Groups: Hikers, dogs, and horses. No mountain bikes allowed. No wheelchair facilities.

Permits: A free self-issue Wilderness Permit is required and is available at the trailhead. A federal Northwest Forest Pass is required to park here; the cost is $5 a day or $30 for an annual pass. You can buy a day pass at the trailhead, at ranger stations, or through private vendors.

Maps: A contour map of the Wallowa Mountains is available from Imus Geographics. For a map of the Wallowa-Whitman National Forest, contact the Wallowa-Whitman National Forest Headquarters, P.O. Box 907, 1550 Dewey Avenue, Baker City, OR, 97814,

541/523-6391. For a topographic map, ask the USGS for North Minam Meadows and Chief Joseph Mountain.

Directions: From the La Grande Exit 261 off I-84, follow Highway 82 toward Wallowa Lake for 55 miles to Lostine. Where the highway turns left in town, go straight on Lostine River Road for 12.2 miles to the Lostine Guard Station, and continue on gravel another 2.9 miles to the Bowman Trailhead on the right.

Contact: Wallowa-Whitman National Forest, Eagle Cap Ranger District, 88401 Highway 82, Enterprise, OR, 97828, 541/426-5546.

20 MAXWELL LAKE
7.6 mi/4.5 hr   🥾3 ⛰️8

south of Wallowa in Eagle Cap Wilderness

Map 4.3, page 195

If the long hikes into the alpine wonder of the Eagle Cap Wilderness aren't your bag, consider the short—but by no means easy—trail to Maxwell Lake. Although some steepness will shorten your breath, Maxwell Lake itself will take your breath away. Nestled in a granite, glacier-carved basin above the Lostine River, the lake awaits at the end of the trail.

From the trailhead, descend to the river crossing and begin upward for 2.8 miles on the series of long, steady switchbacks known as the Maxwell Lake Trail. The next 0.8 mile climbs steeply to a pass, then descends 0.2 mile to the lakeshore and trail's end.

User Groups: Hikers, dogs, and horses. No mountain bikes allowed. No wheelchair facilities.

Permits: A free self-issue Wilderness Permit is required and is available at the trailhead. A federal Northwest Forest Pass is required to park here; the cost is $5 a day or $30 for an annual pass. You can buy a day pass at the trailhead, at ranger stations, or through private vendors.

Maps: A contour map of the Wallowa Mountains is available from Imus Geographics. For a map of the Wallowa-Whitman National

Forest, contact the Wallowa-Whitman National Forest Headquarters, P.O. Box 907, 1550 Dewey Avenue, Baker City, OR, 97814, 541/523-6391. For a topographic map, ask the USGS for North Minam Meadows.

Directions: From the La Grande Exit 261 off I-84, follow Highway 82 toward Wallowa Lake for 55 miles to Lostine. Where the highway turns left in town, go straight on Lostine River Road for 12.2 miles to the Lostine Guard Station, and continue on gravel another 5.6 miles to the Maxwell Lake Trailhead on the right.

Contact: Wallowa-Whitman National Forest, Eagle Cap Ranger District, 88401 Highway 82, Enterprise, OR, 97828, 541/426-5546.

21 MINAM AND MIRROR LAKES LOOP
11.6-17.7 mi/7.5 hr-2 days   🥾4 ⛰️9

south of Wallowa in Eagle Cap Wilderness

Map 4.3, page 195

The West Lostine River meanders through high mountain meadows between grassy banks, flanked by steep ridges and fed by Minam Lake. Less than a mile above that lake is little Blue Lake, walled in by stupendous cliffs. These two lakes make a good day trip, but if you're interested in a longer loop for backpacking you can continue over a high pass between two forks of the Lostine River to Mirror Lake, with the emblematic Eagle Cap peak towering above it, and return through some lovely meadows along the East Lostine River.

To head to Minam Lake, start off on the Minam Lake/West Fork Lostine River Trail (aka Two Pan Trail), keeping right at the first junction. Climb steadily 2.8 miles, keeping left at the Copper Creek junction. In another 1.5 miles, cross the river and continue 1.5 miles to the head of Minam Lake. In 0.8 mile the trail reaches the top of the lake at an earthen dam. To head to Blue Lake, follow the trail across the dam and climb 0.9 mile.

For a longer backpacking trip, start at the head of Minam Lake and follow a Lake Basin sign to the left and up 1.9 miles to the 8,560-foot Minam Pass, then down 1.3 miles on the far side. When you reach the two cairns marking a four-way junction, you can go straight on Trail 1661 to Mirror Lake. Going left follows the East Lostine River on the East Fork Trail through vibrant meadows 7.1 miles back to the Two Pan Trailhead (see *Mirror Lake and Eagle Cap,* next listing).

User Groups: Hikers, dogs, and horses. No mountain bikes allowed. No wheelchair facilities.

Permits: A free self-issue Wilderness Permit is required and is available at the trailhead. A federal Northwest Forest Pass is required to park here; the cost is $5 a day or $30 for an annual pass. You can buy a day pass at the trailhead, at ranger stations, or through private vendors.

Maps: A contour map of the Wallowa Mountains is available from Imus Geographics. For a map of the Wallowa-Whitman National Forest, contact the Wallowa-Whitman National Forest Headquarters, P.O. Box 907, 1550 Dewey Avenue, Baker City, OR, 97814, 541/523-6391. For a topographic map, ask the USGS for Steamboat Lake and Eagle Cap.

Directions: From the La Grande Exit 261 off I-84, follow Highway 82 toward Wallowa Lake for 55 miles to Lostine. Where the highway turns left in town, go straight on Lostine River Road for 12.2 miles to the Lostine Guard Station, and continue on gravel another 6.1 miles to the Two Pan Trailhead at road's end.

Contact: Wallowa-Whitman National Forest, Eagle Cap Ranger District, 88401 Highway 82, Enterprise, OR, 97828, 541/426-5546.

22 MIRROR LAKE AND EAGLE CAP

19.6 mi/1-2 days   🏃5 ⛰10

south of Wallowa in Eagle Cap Wilderness

Map 4.3, page 195   **BEST (**

From the Lostine River meadows, Eagle Cap looms. At 9,572 feet, it's the centerpiece of its namesake wilderness and dominates the skyline for this whole part of the Wallowa Mountains (though it's not the tallest peak in the area—that prize is reserved for Sacajawea, followed by the Matterhorn). What Eagle Cap has, though, is a 360-degree view of the surrounding range, down to lakes, ridges, and river valleys extending away from its point in all directions.

In one straight shot, this trail follows the East Lostine River to Mirror Lake, set beneath Eagle Cap's cliffs like an ornament. To climb Eagle Cap, plan this as a backpacking trip; you'll be grateful for the time and the rest required.

From the Two Pan Trailhead, follow the left-hand fork on the East Fork Lostine River Trail, passing a waterfall in 0.8 mile. In the next two miles, the trail switchbacks up over 1,000 feet to a series of ponds, then rolls along the Lostine Meadows nearly effortlessly for 2.3 miles to a river crossing, then climbs two miles across the meadows and up more switchbacks to a junction. To visit or camp at Mirror Lake, go left at the cairn 0.3 mile. To continue to Eagle Cap, go right at the cairn instead, then left at the next junction a short distance down the trail, then continue 2.7 miles, keeping left at every junction, climbing nearly 2,000 feet to the peak, where you'll find a summit register to leave your name.

User Groups: Hikers, dogs, and horses. No mountain bikes allowed. No wheelchair facilities.

Permits: A free self-issue Wilderness Permit is required and is available at the trailhead. A federal Northwest Forest Pass is required to park here; the cost is $5 a day or $30 for an annual pass. You can buy a day pass at the trailhead, at ranger stations, or through private vendors.

Maps: A contour map of the Wallowa Mountains is available from Imus Geographics. For a map of the Wallowa-Whitman National Forest, contact the Wallowa-Whitman National Forest Headquarters, P.O. Box 907, 1550 Dewey Avenue, Baker City, OR, 97814,

541/523-6391. For a topographic map, ask the USGS for Steamboat Lake and Eagle Cap.

Directions: From the La Grande Exit 261 off I-84, follow Highway 82 toward Wallowa Lake for 55 miles to Lostine. Where the highway turns left in town, go straight on Lostine River Road for 12.2 miles to the Lostine Guard Station, and continue on gravel another 6.1 miles to the Two Pan Trailhead at road's end.

Contact: Wallowa-Whitman National Forest, Eagle Cap Ranger District, 88401 Highway 82, Enterprise, OR, 97828, 541/426-5546.

23 HURRICANE CREEK AND ECHO LAKE

15.4 mi/8.0 hr

south of Enterprise in Eagle Cap Wilderness

Map 4.3, page 195

With plenty of water, spectacular views, and the chance to see bighorn sheep, mountain goats, and elk, plus side trips to a waterfall on Fall Creek and the cliff-rimmed Echo Lake, the Hurricane Creek entrance to the Eagle Cap Wilderness is one of the best. Views reach to the peaks of Eagle Cap, Matterhorn, and Sacajawea, and the trail follows in the shadow of massive granite and limestone cliffs clear down to wildflower meadows.

From the trailhead, follow Hurricane Creek 0.1 mile to a side-trail junction. A mere 0.2 mile up this trail is a viewpoint of Fall Creek Falls (this trail continues 3.8 difficult miles up the creek, almost 4,000 feet elevation gain, passing an old mine and fading out before Legore Lake beneath Twin Peaks). Follow Hurricane Creek 4.6 miles, crossing Slick Rock Creek Gorge after three miles. After Granite Creek, a side trail to the right climbs the canyon wall 1.9 miles up Granite Creek to the lip and a small pond. From here, cross the trailless meadow to find the trail, which continues 1.1 miles, climbing to Echo Lake.

To continue into the wilderness, stay on Hurricane Creek, fording Billy Jones Creek and Hurricane Creek, and follow trails

branching off to the Wallowa Lake Trailhead and the Two Pan Trailhead.

User Groups: Hikers, dogs, and horses. No mountain bikes allowed. No wheelchair facilities.

Permits: A free self-issue Wilderness Permit is required and is available at the trailhead. A federal Northwest Forest Pass is required to park here; the cost is $5 a day or $30 for an annual pass. You can buy a day pass at the trailhead, at ranger stations, or through private vendors.

Maps: A contour map of the Wallowa Mountains is available from Imus Geographics. For a map of the Wallowa-Whitman National Forest, contact the Wallowa-Whitman National Forest Headquarters, P.O. Box 907, 1550 Dewey Avenue, Baker City, OR, 97814, 541/523-6391. For a topographic map, ask the USGS for Chief Joseph Mountain and Eagle Cap.

Directions: From the La Grande Exit 261 off I-84, follow Highway 82 toward Wallowa Lake for 65 miles to Enterprise. Just past downtown, where the highway goes left toward Joseph, follow a Hurricane Creek sign onto Hurricane Creek Road 8205, following it 9.1 miles to the trailhead at road's end.

Contact: Wallowa-Whitman National Forest, Eagle Cap Ranger District, 88401 Highway 82, Enterprise, OR, 97828, 541/426-5546.

24 ICE LAKE AND THE MATTERHORN

15.0-18.8 mi/9.0 hr-2 days 🚶5 ⛰10

south of Joseph in Eagle Cap Wilderness

Map 4.3, page 195

High in the Eagle Cap Wilderness, sparkling Ice Lake lies in a basin beneath the Matterhorn, the Wallowa Mountain's second-highest peak. At 9,826 feet, it nearly commands the view here—but for nearby Sacajawea, which tops Matterhorn by just 12 feet. Getting there is the trick: you'll climb three sets of steep switchbacks just to get to the lake, following

Adam Creek as it tumbles over the ridges and two waterfalls on its way to the West Fork Wallowa River. The climb to the Matterhorn itself requires stamina, though this is certainly a non-technical climb, heading up 2,000 feet in 1.5 miles.

Begin at the Wallowa Lake Trailhead and follow the West Fork Wallowa River Trail 0.3 mile, then stay to the left and continue along the river 2.5 miles. Following a sign for Ice Lake, go right and begin the climb. The first 2.2 miles climbs over 1,100 feet up two sets of switchbacks to a viewpoint for an Adam Creek waterfall. The next 2.5 miles climbs 1,250 feet up the canyon wall past another waterfall and to the plateau of Ice Lake. A trail circles the lake for 1.7 miles.

To climb Matterhorn, stay to the right around the lake 0.4 mile to an inlet creek on the far side, and follow a faint trail up 1.5 miles to the peak on an obvious ridge.

User Groups: Hikers, dogs, and horses. No mountain bikes allowed. No wheelchair facilities.

Permits: A free self-issue Wilderness Permit is required and is available at the trailhead. Parking and access are free.

Maps: A contour map of the Wallowa Mountains is available from Imus Geographics. For a map of the Wallowa-Whitman National Forest, contact the Wallowa-Whitman National Forest Headquarters, P.O. Box 907, 1550 Dewey Avenue, Baker City, OR, 97814, 541/523-6391. For a topographic map, ask the USGS for Joseph, Aneroid Lake, and Eagle Cap.

Directions: From the La Grande Exit 261 off I-84, follow Highway 82 toward Wallowa Lake for 78 miles through Enterprise and on to Joseph. Go one mile along Wallowa Lake to the Wallowa Lake Trailhead at road's end.

Contact: Wallowa-Whitman National Forest, Eagle Cap Ranger District, 88401 Highway 82, Enterprise, OR, 97828, 541/426-5546.

25 LAKES BASIN LOOP
27.3 mi/2 days

south of Joseph in Eagle Cap Wilderness

Map 4.3, page 195

The Lakes Basin of the Eagle Cap Wilderness is the most famous spot in all this wilderness and as such is heavily used. Yet, with the amount of endurance it takes to get here, you can almost be assured that the difficulty will weed out the tenderfeet (but not the horses), leaving only sure-footed backpackers to lay claim to this area. High atop a plateau with views to Eagle Cap itself, six major lakes are within reach, though "within reach" depends on your stamina. This is a backpacker's dream, for certain. Choose a lake or two and continue on in any direction; from here, you can follow the West Fork Wallowa River, or head to Hurricane Creek, the Lostine River forks, and on to Eagle Cap itself.

From the Wallowa Lake Trailhead, follow the West Fork Wallowa River 6.1 miles to Sixmile Meadow, a possible camping spot, and a junction. To go on to the Lake Basin, go right, cross the river on a footbridge, and climb 3.1 miles to Horseshoe Lake. The trail splits here, and comes together again in one mile. If you go to the left, you'll follow Horseshoe Lake and pass little Lee Lake. At the end of the loop, go right 0.5 mile to Douglas Lake. Follow the left-hand trail two miles to Moccasin Lake, then go left again 2.7 miles, climbing up and over steep Glacier Pass, to cliff-rimmed Glacier Lake, high in an alpine bowl beneath Eagle Cap. Follow the trail down an outlet creek two miles to Frazier Lake, then stay to the left and follow it 1.8 miles, fording the Wallowa Fork, to the next junction, and keep left 2.2 miles to return to Sixmile Meadow.

User Groups: Hikers, dogs, and horses. No mountain bikes allowed. No wheelchair facilities.

Permits: A free self-issue Wilderness Permit is required and is available at the trailhead. Parking and access are free.

Maps: A contour map of the Wallowa

Mountains is available from Imus Geographics. For a map of the Wallowa-Whitman National Forest, contact the Wallowa-Whitman National Forest Headquarters, P.O. Box 907, 1550 Dewey Avenue, Baker City, OR, 97814, 541/523-6391. For a topographic map, ask the USGS for Joseph, Aneroid Lake, and Eagle Cap.

Directions: From the La Grande Exit 261 off I-84, follow Highway 82 toward Wallowa Lake for 78 miles through Enterprise and on to Joseph. Go one mile along Wallowa Lake to the Wallowa Lake Trailhead at road's end.

Contact: Wallowa-Whitman National Forest, Eagle Cap Ranger District, 88401 Highway 82, Enterprise, OR, 97828, 541/426-5546.

26 CHIEF JOSEPH MOUNTAIN
11.8-15 mi/6.0-8.0 hr   🏃‍♀️5 ⛰9

south of Joseph in Eagle Cap Wilderness

Map 4.3, page 195

The peak that towers above long and beautiful Wallowa Lake is named for the patriarch of the Nez Perce's Wallowa band. In 1877, chased by the U.S. Army, he led his people on a daring flight to Canada, a flight that eventually ended in surrender. The mountain stands as a monument to his endurance, and the sturdy hiker can climb to a knoll on the side of this rugged peak and look out over the lands once loved by the Nez Perce tribes. This is a steep and challenging climb, though there are opportunities to rest beside a few waterfalls and several viewpoints over Wallowa Lake. There are two ways to climb this trail: The first is from the Wallowa Lake Trailhead, which makes for a daunting 15-mile day. If you prefer to knock off three miles, opt instead to begin from the state park, climbing a steep 0.9 mile to join the main trail. (Note that a washout may have wrecked the trail at BC Creek; check with the Forest Service to see if the trail has been repaired. If not, head to the state park trailhead and start from there instead.)

From the Wallowa Lake Trailhead, start to the right for 0.3 mile, then go right on the Chief Joseph Mountain Trail for one mile to cross the West Fork Wallowa River's gorge and climb to a viewpoint of two falls on BC Creek. Continue along the edge of the mountain 1.2

Chief Joseph Mountain in the Wallowas

© SEAN PATRICK HILL

miles to where the State Park Trail joins from the left. The next 1.1 miles stays level, then climbs the remaining 3.9 miles through steep meadows beneath the mountain. Though there is no trail to the peak, you can climb atop a knoll near where the trail ends for a view of Mount Howard and the Wallowa country.

From Wallowa Lake State Park, find campsite B-25 and follow this trail 0.9 mile up to join the Chief Joseph Trail. Go left 1.2 miles to see the falls, or right to head to the mountain.

User Groups: Hikers, dogs, and horses. No mountain bikes allowed. No wheelchair facilities.

Permits: A free self-issue Wilderness Permit is required and is available at the trailhead. Parking and access are free.

Maps: A contour map of the Wallowa Mountains is available from Imus Geographics. For a map of the Wallowa-Whitman National Forest, contact the Wallowa-Whitman National Forest Headquarters, P.O. Box 907, 1550 Dewey Avenue, Baker City, OR, 97814, 541/523-6391. For a topographic map, ask the USGS for Chief Joseph Mountain.

Directions: From the La Grande Exit 261 off I-84, follow Highway 82 toward Wallowa Lake for 78 miles through Enterprise and on to Joseph. Go one mile along Wallowa Lake to the Wallowa Lake Trailhead at road's end. For the State Park trailhead, turn instead into the Wallowa Lake State Park entrance one mile before the end of the road, parking at the boat ramp lot.

Contact: Wallowa-Whitman National Forest, Eagle Cap Ranger District, 88401 Highway 82, Enterprise, OR, 97828, 541/426-5546.

27 WEST FORK WALLOWA RIVER TO HAWKINS PASS
24.0 mi/2 days 🥾5 ⛰10

south of Joseph in Eagle Cap Wilderness

Map 4.3, page 195

If you're in the mood to follow the West Fork Wallowa River as far as you can go, beyond even Ice Lake and the Lakes Basin, consider walking it all the way to its end at Hawkins Pass. Follow the river 10.1 miles to Frazier Lake, then go left the remaining 1.9 miles to Hawkins Pass. From there, you can fan out farther into the wilderness area at whim.

User Groups: Hikers, dogs, and horses. No mountain bikes allowed. No wheelchair facilities.

Permits: A free self-issue Wilderness Permit is required and is available at the trailhead. Parking and access are free.

Maps: A contour map of the Wallowa Mountains is available from Imus Geographics. For a map of the Wallowa-Whitman National Forest, contact the Wallowa-Whitman National Forest Headquarters, P.O. Box 907, 1550 Dewey Avenue, Baker City, OR, 97814, 541/523-6391. For a topographic map, ask the USGS for Joseph, Aneroid Lake, and Eagle Cap.

Directions: From the La Grande Exit 261 off I-84, follow Highway 82 toward Wallowa Lake for 78 miles through Enterprise and on to Joseph. Go one mile along Wallowa Lake to the Wallowa Lake Trailhead at road's end.

Contact: Wallowa-Whitman National Forest, Eagle Cap Ranger District, 88401 Highway 82, Enterprise, OR, 97828, 541/426-5546.

28 ANEROID LAKE
12.0 mi/7.0 hr 🥾4 ⛰9

south of Joseph in Eagle Cap Wilderness

Map 4.3, page 195

Two forks of the Wallowa River fall into big Wallowa Lake, and this trail follows the East Fork. Once the trail passes the wilderness boundary, the river deepens—and it even enters a gorge for a distance. Anglers ply the waters of Roger and Aneroid Lakes, beneath a range of mountains: Mount Howard, Bonneville Mountain, Aneroid Mountain, and East Peak. If you're curious as to what "aneroid" means, it's a kind of barometer, and one that a surveyor brought here in 1897 to measure the elevation. If you're backpacking, you can continue on this trail up and over Dollar Pass and visit the Bonny Lakes, or to Tenderfoot Pass to find the North Fork Imnaha River.

From the Wallowa Lake Trailhead, take the left-hand trail to the East Fork Wallowa River. Switchback up 0.8 miles, ignoring both a service road to the left and a horse trail to the right, then continue one mile up the river to a dam. Follow the river into the wilderness for 2.1 miles to a bridge crossing, and continue on the far side along a deep gorge and into meadows for 1.7 miles to Roger Lake. From here, Aneroid Lake is just ahead, and the trail rises 0.4 mile to overlook the lake.

User Groups: Hikers, dogs, and horses. No mountain bikes allowed. No wheelchair facilities.

Permits: A free self-issue Wilderness Permit is required and is available at the trailhead. Parking and access are free.

Maps: A contour map of the Wallowa Mountains is available from Imus Geographics. For a map of the Wallowa-Whitman National Forest, contact the Wallowa-Whitman National Forest Headquarters, P.O. Box 907, 1550 Dewey Avenue, Baker City, OR, 97814, 541/523-6391. For a topographic map, ask the USGS for Aneroid Lake.

Directions: From the La Grande Exit 261 off I-84, follow Highway 82 toward Wallowa Lake for 78 miles through Enterprise and on to Joseph. Go one mile along Wallowa Lake to the Wallowa Lake Trailhead at road's end.

Contact: Wallowa-Whitman National Forest, Eagle Cap Ranger District, 88401 Highway 82, Enterprise, OR, 97828, 541/426-5546.

29 MOUNT HOWARD
1.9–5.5 mi/1.0–2.5 hr

south of Joseph in Wallowa-Whitman National Forest

Map 4.3, page 195

The view from Mount Howard is amazing, for sure, but you have to be willing to pay to get to the top. What you get for your money is a 3,700-foot ride on a gondola to the grassy summits of this 8,241-foot peak. The gondola operates from mid-May to September 30, and takes 15 minutes to climb to its perch above long, blue Wallowa Lake. You can even have lunch at the Summit Grill. After that, strike out over the meadows for views of all the major peaks: Eagle Cap, the Matterhorn, and scores of others, including East Peak, which you can head towards on a trail that enters the Eagle Cap Wilderness.

From the tramway, hike clockwise around the trails to see the Valley Overlook, the Summit, and the Royal Purple Overlook, a 1.9-mile loop. For a longer hike, head south from the summit cross-country to a pass and an old trail that heads 0.8 mile over the ridge to a grassy saddle at the wilderness boundary. From there, follow cairns to rejoin the trail for one mile to its end at a spring.

User Groups: Hikers only. No dogs, horses, or mountain bikes allowed. The Wallowa Lake Tramway gondola is wheelchair accessible, though the summit trails are not maintained for wheelchairs.

Permits: Permits are not required. The Wallowa Lake Tramway costs $24 for adults, $21 for seniors, $18 for students, and $11 for children aged 4–11.

Maps: A contour map of the Wallowa Mountains is available from Imus Geographics. For a map of the Wallowa-Whitman National Forest, contact the Wallowa-Whitman National Forest Headquarters, P.O. Box 907, 1550 Dewey Avenue, Baker City, OR, 97814, 541/523-6391. For a topographic map, ask the USGS for Joseph.

Directions: Take exit 261 off I-84 in La Grande and follow Highway 82 for 77 miles to Joseph. Continue through town to Wallowa Lake, following it toward the state park. Go past the state park entrance 0.3 mile and park on the left at the Wallowa Lake Tramway.

Contact: Wallowa-Whitman National Forest, Eagle Cap Ranger District, 88401 Highway 82, Enterprise, OR, 97828, 541/426-5546; Wallowa Lake Tramway, 59919 Wallowa Lake Highway, Joseph, OR,541/432-5331.

30 BONNY LAKES AND IMNAHA DIVIDE
7.8-16.3 mi/4.0 hr-2 days 🏃4 ⛰️8

south of Joseph in Eagle Cap Wilderness

Map 4.3, page 195

The Tenderfoot Trailhead is underutilized and barely mentioned in hiking books, on outdoors websites, or even on the Forest Service's trail list. This should be a clue as to the relative use of this trail. Yet it provides access to the Big Sheep Basin, Tenderfoot Pass, the Imnaha Divide, and a set of three secret lakes: the two shallow but lovely Bonny Lakes and Dollar Lake, set on the high plateau of Dollar Pass. Granted, the trail sets off on a 1989 burn, but quickly enters into the high country of the Eagle Cap Wilderness through a huge valley along a fork of Big Sheep Creek. Though the lakes make good destinations, backpackers can make a loop of it by heading over two passes and following the Imnaha Divide. You really can't go wrong in this rugged and rocky landscape.

From the trailhead, cross the wilderness boundary and stay left at a junction, continuing 1.1 miles on the Tenderfoot Wagon Trail to a ford of Big Sheep Creek. Stay to the left and continue 1.2 miles to a junction with the Bonny Lakes Trail, the start of the loop. Go right up the valley 1.6 miles along the creek to reach the Bonny Lakes. In another 1.7 miles, the trail leaves the valley and climbs to Dollar Pass; if you head due south cross-country across the meadows for 0.3 mile you'll reach Dollar Lake.

To continue on the loop, stay on the main trail from Dollar Pass and continue 0.9 mile to a junction; to the right, Aneroid Lake is one mile away (see *Aneroid Lake* listing in this chapter). Go left 1.5 miles on the North Fork Imnaha Trail #1814, climbing 700 feet to Tenderfoot Pass and descending to another trail junction. Continue to the left on the North Fork Imnaha River Trail for 1.5 miles, then head left on the Tenderfoot Trail over the Imnaha Divide for 2.7 miles to a high pass. From here, the trail drops down 700 feet over 1.2 miles to complete the loop; go to the right, staying right at all junctions 2.3 miles back to the Tenderfoot Trailhead.

User Groups: Hikers, dogs, and horses. No mountain bikes allowed. No wheelchair facilities.

Permits: A free self-issue Wilderness Permit is required and is available at the trailhead. Parking and access are free.

Maps: A contour map of the Wallowa Mountains is available from Imus Geographics. For a map of the Wallowa-Whitman National Forest, contact the Wallowa-Whitman National Forest Headquarters, P.O. Box 907, 1550 Dewey Avenue, Baker City, OR, 97814, 541/523-6391. For a topographic map, ask the USGS for Aneroid Mountain.

Directions: From Joseph, head east on the Hells Canyon Byway and follow Imnaha Highway 8.3 miles to a sign for Salt Creek Summit, then go right on Wallowa Mountain Road 39 for 13 miles. After a creek crossing, turn right on Road 100 for 3.2 miles to the Tenderfoot Trailhead.

Contact: Wallowa-Whitman National Forest, Eagle Cap Ranger District, 88401 Highway 82, Enterprise, OR, 97828, 541/426-5546.

31 CATHERINE CREEK MEADOWS
8.6 mi/4.0 hr 🏃2 ⛰️7

east of La Grande in Eagle Cap Wilderness

Map 4.3, page 195

At some places in the Eagle Cap Wilderness, you may run into grazing sheep or cattle. Catherine Creek Meadows is one of those places, and you'll also be able to poke around a century-old log cabin with graffiti dating back at least to 1944. Backpackers, take note: From these meadows, you can head just about anywhere into the wilderness, as no less than six trails fan out in all directions from the creek.

The trail begins at the campground message board and follows North Fork Catherine Creek 3.8 miles upstream and into the Eagle Cap Wilderness. In the meadows, a rock cairn marks a faded trail to the right that climbs 2.8 miles to Meadow Mountain. In 0.3 mile, the trail forks; go to the right 200 yards to find the old cabin, or continue straight to cross the creek to a junction. Go right to continue up this creek another 3.9 miles to a junction with trails leading to Burger Pass and the Minam River; head left out of the canyon to access trails to Moss Springs Trailhead, the Jim White Trail, the Lodgepole Trail, and the Little Minam River.

User Groups: Hikers, dogs, and horses. No mountain bikes allowed. No wheelchair facilities.

Permits: A free self-issue Wilderness Permit is required and is available at the trailhead. A federal Northwest Forest Pass is required to park here; the cost is $5 a day or $30 for an annual pass. You can buy a day pass at the trailhead, at ranger stations, or through private vendors.

Maps: A contour map of the Wallowa Mountains is available from Imus Geographics. For a map of the Wallowa-Whitman National Forest, contact the Wallowa-Whitman National Forest Headquarters, P.O. Box 907, 1550 Dewey Avenue, Baker City, OR, 97814, 541/523-6391. For a topographic map, ask the USGS for China Cap.

Directions: From La Grande, go south on I-84 to Exit 265, going left on Highway 203 and following it 14 miles to Union. In Union, turn left on Beakman Street and follow Highway 203 for 11.4 miles. Turn left on Catherine Creek Lane/Road 7785 for 6.1 miles to the Catherine Creek Trailhead on the right.

Contact: Wallowa-Whitman National Forest, Eagle Cap Ranger District, 88401 Highway 82, Enterprise, OR, 97828, 541/426-5546.

32 BURGER PASS

8.8 mi/4.5 hr   🥾3 ⛺7

southeast of Union in Eagle Cap Wilderness

Map 4.3, page 195

A long ridge connects two distinctive high points in this dusty wilderness: Burger Butte and China Cap. Not only that, but it straddles two very different landscapes: one of granite and one a plateau of basalt lava. The trail that leads there is dusty with volcanic ash, the result of a long history of explosive eruptions that blanketed this former Pacific island worn down by glaciers. Yes, these mountains are really that old.

Follow the Elk Creek Alternate Trail from the message board 0.7 mile to a clear-cut and a junction with the Elk Creek Trail. Continue to the right on an ash-strewn trail 1.3 miles to a switchback, entering the granite landscape. Follow a plateau along a ridge 1.6 miles, crossing the Middle Fork Catherine Creek, to a junction with the China Ridge Trail. Go right along the base of China Cap, steadily climbing the ridge for 0.8 mile to Burger Pass. From here, the trail switchbacks down 300 feet to Burger Meadows in 0.6 mile at a junction. To the left, the trail leads to the Minam River and Tombstone Lake; to the right, Sand Pass and the Mule Peak Lookout.

User Groups: Hikers, dogs, and horses. No mountain bikes allowed. No wheelchair facilities.

Permits: A free self-issue Wilderness Permit is required and is available at the trailhead. A federal Northwest Forest Pass is required to park here; the cost is $5 a day or $30 for an annual pass. You can buy a day pass at the trailhead, at ranger stations, or through private vendors.

Maps: A contour map of the Wallowa Mountains is available from Imus Geographics. For a map of the Wallowa-Whitman National Forest, contact the Wallowa-Whitman National Forest Headquarters, P.O. Box 907, 1550 Dewey Avenue, Baker City, OR, 97814, 541/523-6391. For a topographic map, ask the USGS for China Cap.

Directions: From La Grande, go south on I-84 to Exit 265, going left on Highway 203 and following it 14 miles to Union. In Union, turn left on Beakman Street and follow Highway 203 for 11.4 miles. Turn left on Catherine Creek Lane/Road 7785 for 4.2 miles, then go right on Road 7787 for 3.9 miles, then left at a fork for 0.3 mile to the Buck Creek Trailhead on the right.

Contact: Wallowa-Whitman National Forest, Eagle Cap Ranger District, 88401 Highway 82, Enterprise, OR, 97828, 541/426-5546.

33 EAGLE CREEK TO TOMBSTONE AND DIAMOND LAKES

18.0 mi/2 days   🥾5 ⛰8

northeast of Baker City in Eagle Cap Wilderness

Map 4.3, page 195

More power to the backpackers, as this trail is anything but a day hike. The long route to Tombstone Lake is a relentless climb at points up long switchbacks into the Eagle Cap Wilderness, but that's no reason to turn back. Just beyond Tombstone is Diamond Lake. Pick a lake and drop the tent, and enjoy the walk along West Eagle Creek while it lasts, with its forest of rare Engelmann spruce and Wallowa-friendly western larch and grand fir.

The West Eagle Loop Trail starts out on an old road, but quickly becomes trail. Pass the meadows and enter the forest in 0.4 mile, coming to a junction with the Fake Creek Trail. Continue to the left on West Eagle Creek 0.7 mile and ford the creek. Continue 1.8 miles, fording the creek again and then climbing to a junction. Go left toward Tombstone Lake for 5.5 miles, switchbacking steeply up an 8,200-foot pass and dropping down 770 feet to the large lake. Just 0.5 mile beyond this and 0.2 mile to the right is Diamond Lake.

User Groups: Hikers, dogs, and horses. No mountain bikes allowed. No wheelchair facilities.

Permits: A free self-issue Wilderness Permit is required and is available at the trailhead. A federal Northwest Forest Pass is required to park here; the cost is $5 a day or $30 for an annual pass. You can buy a day pass at the trailhead, at ranger stations, or through private vendors.

Maps: A contour map of the Wallowa Mountains is available from Imus Geographics. For a map of the Wallowa-Whitman National Forest, contact the Wallowa-Whitman National Forest Headquarters, P.O. Box 907, 1550 Dewey Avenue, Baker City, OR, 97814, 541/523-6391. For a topographic map, ask the USGS for Bennet Peak.

Directions: From La Grande, go south on I-84 to Exit 265, going left on Highway 203 and following it 14 miles to Union. In Union, turn left on Beakman Street and follow Highway 203 for 14.2 miles. Following a sign for West Eagle, go left on increasingly rough Road 77 for 15.7 miles to the West Eagle Trailhead on the left.

Contact: Wallowa-Whitman National Forest, Eagle Cap Ranger District, 88401 Highway 82, Enterprise, OR, 97828, 541/426-5546.

34 ECHO AND TRAVERSE LAKES

13.2 mi/7.0 hr   🥾5 ⛰8

northeast of Baker City in Eagle Cap Wilderness

Map 4.3, page 195

Like the trail to Tombstone Lake, this trail follows West Eagle Creek into a forest of grand fir, western larch, and the rare Engelmann spruce. Only this trail stays on the creek, following it up nearly 2,300 feet to a pair of alpine lakes—Echo and Traverse—rimmed in by steep precipices and towering peaks and lined with blooms of phlox and mountain heather.

The West Eagle Loop Trail starts out on an old road, but quickly becomes trail. Pass the meadows and enter the forest in 0.4 mile, coming to a junction with the Fake Creek Trail. Continue to the left on West Eagle Creek 0.7 mile and ford the creek. Continue 1.8 miles, fording the creek again and then climbing to a junction. Continue to the right, climbing another 1,000 feet in 2.4 miles to Echo Lake, and another 500 feet in 1.3 miles to Traverse Lake. For the ambitious, the trail climbs another 700 feet to Wenker Pass, allowing for longer backpacking adventures.

User Groups: Hikers, dogs, and horses. No mountain bikes allowed. No wheelchair facilities.

Permits: A free self-issue Wilderness Permit is required and is available at the trailhead. A federal Northwest Forest Pass is required to park here; the cost is $5 a day or $30 for an annual pass. You can buy a day pass at the trailhead, at ranger stations, or through private vendors.

Maps: A contour map of the Wallowa Mountains is available from Imus Geographics. For a map of the Wallowa-Whitman National Forest, contact the Wallowa-Whitman National Forest Headquarters, P.O. Box 907, 1550 Dewey Avenue, Baker City, OR, 97814, 541/523-6391. For a topographic map, ask the USGS for Bennet Peak.

Directions: From La Grande, go south on I-84 to Exit 265, going left on Highway 203 and following it 14 miles to Union. In Union, turn left on Beakman Street and follow Highway 203 for 14.2 miles. Following a sign for West Eagle, go left on increasingly rough Road 77 for 15.7 miles to the West Eagle Trailhead on the left.

Contact: Wallowa-Whitman National Forest, Eagle Cap Ranger District, 88401 Highway 82, Enterprise, OR, 97828, 541/426-5546.

35 EAGLE CREEK LAKES LOOP
19.0 mi/2-3 days

northeast of Baker City in Eagle Cap Wilderness

Map 4.3, page 195

Backpackers can rejoice over Eagle Creek, as this loop—which follows two branches of the creek—visits not only waterfalls, but four or more lakes, depending on what you're up for (for side trips, see *Lookingglass and Bear Lakes,* next listing). This is a demanding loop, calling for over 4,000 feet of elevation gain in nearly 20 miles, but there's water and plenty of options for camping along the way, and a connection to trails leading to the Minam River and Traverse Lake. Enjoy the scenery as you walk in the glare of towering peaks along Eagle Creek.

Begin on the Main Eagle Trail, crossing a landslide and crossing the creek in 0.6 mile. In 1.9 miles, the trail crosses the creek again, and 0.5 mile later reaches a junction just beyond Copper Creek Falls, the start of the loop. Go left on the Bench Trail, which climbs steeply 1.5 miles, then crosses Bench Canyon Creek to the right and continues 0.8 mile to Arrow Lake (with Heart Lake to the right along the way, accessed by a cross-country jaunt). Continue above Arrow Lake over a 7,880-foot pass to a junction, keeping right. Go another 1.6 miles to a higher pass at 8,170 feet and descend 700 feet in two miles into the Eagle Creek Canyon and small Cached Lake. Descend further into meadows one mile to a junction; the left-hand trail climbs 350 feet in 1.1 miles to scenic Eagle Lake behind a dam. Return to the main trail and continue descending along Eagle Creek 1.8 miles to Eagle Creek meadow. At the next junction, stay to the right 1.4 miles, passing Bench Canyon Falls and completing the loop.

User Groups: Hikers, dogs, and horses. No mountain bikes allowed. No wheelchair facilities.

Permits: A free self-issue Wilderness Permit is required and is available at the trailhead. A federal Northwest Forest Pass is required to park here; the cost is $5 a day or $30 for an annual pass. You can buy a day pass at the trailhead, at ranger stations, or through private vendors.

Maps: A contour map of the Wallowa Mountains is available from Imus Geographics. For a map of the Wallowa-Whitman National Forest, contact the Wallowa-Whitman National Forest Headquarters, P.O. Box 907, 1550 Dewey Avenue, Baker City, OR, 97814, 541/523-6391. For a topographic map, ask the USGS for Eagle Cap.

Directions: From La Grande, go south on I-84

to Exit 265, going left on Highway 203 and following it 14 miles to Union. Turn left on Highway 203 for 21 miles to Medical Springs. Turn east on Eagle Creek Drive, following signs for Boulder Park for 1.6 miles, forking left on Big Creek Road 67. In 14.6 miles, go left on Road 77 for 0.8 mile, then straight on Road 7755 for 3.7 miles to road's end at the Main Eagle Trailhead.

Contact: Wallowa-Whitman National Forest, Eagle Cap Ranger District, 88401 Highway 82, Enterprise, OR, 97828, 541/426-5546.

36 LOOKINGGLASS AND BEAR LAKES
14.0 mi/7.0 hr 　　　🥾4 ⛰8

northeast of Baker City in Eagle Cap Wilderness

Map 4.3, page 195

If a long backpacking trip up the Eagle Creek and Bench Creek drainages (see previous listing) are too much for you, try a slightly easier route to a pair of alpine lakes high above Eagle Creek. With endurance, this hike can be done in a day—though it's also possible to backpack it. Lookingglass Lake is actually a reservoir, dammed for irrigation. Bear Lake remains in its pristine state. Both are accessible from the same trail, with two waterfalls and the gorgeous Eagle Creek Meadow along the way.

Begin on the Main Eagle Trail, crossing a landslide and crossing the creek in 0.6 mile. In 1.9 miles, the trail crosses the creek again, and 0.5 mile later reaches a junction just beyond Copper Creek Falls. Go right and stay on the Eagle Creek Trail another 1.4 miles, passing Bench Canyon Falls to the left and climbing steadily to Eagle Creek Meadow, hemmed in by stunning peaks. At a junction, go right on the Bear Lake Trail for one mile, fording Eagle Creek and climbing over 650 feet to a junction. To the right, a 1.7-mile trail crests a high point of 7,530 feet and descends 200 feet to Lookingglass Lake. To reach Bear Lake, continue straight 0.4 mile to Little Culver Lake, and finally 0.6 mile to Bear Lake.

User Groups: Hikers, dogs, and horses. No mountain bikes allowed. No wheelchair facilities.

Permits: A free self-issue Wilderness Permit is required and is available at the trailhead. A federal Northwest Forest Pass is required to park here; the cost is $5 a day or $30 for an annual pass. You can buy a day pass at the trailhead, at ranger stations, or through private vendors.

Maps: A contour map of the Wallowa Mountains is available from Imus Geographics. For a map of the Wallowa-Whitman National Forest, contact the Wallowa-Whitman National Forest Headquarters, P.O. Box 907, 1550 Dewey Avenue, Baker City, OR, 97814, 541/523-6391. For a topographic map, ask the USGS for Krag Peak.

Directions: From La Grande, go south on I-84 to Exit 265, going left on Highway 203 and following it 14 miles to Union. Turn left on Highway 203 for 21 miles to Medical Springs. Turn east on Eagle Creek Drive, following signs for Boulder Park for 1.6 miles, forking left on Big Creek Road 67. In 14.6 miles, go left on Road 77 for 0.8 mile, then straight on Road 7755 for 3.7 miles to road's end at the Main Eagle Trailhead.

Contact: Wallowa-Whitman National Forest, Eagle Cap Ranger District, 88401 Highway 82, Enterprise, OR, 97828, 541/426-5546.

37 HIDDEN LAKE
16.4 mi/2 days 　　　🥾4 ⛰8

northeast of Baker City in Eagle Cap Wilderness

Map 4.3, page 195

Glaciers, more than anything, scoured and shaped the Wallowa Mountains, creating stunning scenery. Hidden Lake is flanked by such rugged peaks, as is the entire hike along the East Fork Eagle Creek. This is a demanding day hike; backpackers may fare better.

From the gated road, follow the East Fork Eagle Creek into the canyon. In 2.5 miles, watch for a waterfall on the left. After gradually climbing four miles, the trail comes to a junction. Go left at a cairn, fording the creek and climbing nearly 1,000 feet in 1.7 miles to paradisiacal Hidden Lake, passing Little Moon Lake along the way.

Eagle Creek Trail continues up the creek another 0.9 mile to a junction. To the left, connector trails fan out to the Minam River, Minam Lake, and the Frazier Pass; to the right, the trail climbs 3.3 miles to Horton Pass, then splits—the left goes 1.3 mile to Mirror Lake, the right up 1.5 mile to the peak of Eagle Cap.

User Groups: Hikers, dogs, and horses. No mountain bikes allowed. No wheelchair facilities.

Permits: A free self-issue Wilderness Permit is required and is available at the trailhead. A federal Northwest Forest Pass is required to park here; the cost is $5 a day or $30 for an annual pass. You can buy a day pass at the trailhead, at ranger stations, or through private vendors.

Maps: A contour map of the Wallowa Mountains is available from Imus Geographics. For a map of the Wallowa-Whitman National Forest, contact the Wallowa-Whitman National Forest Headquarters, P.O. Box 907, 1550 Dewey Avenue, Baker City, OR, 97814, 541/523-6391. For a topographic map, ask the USGS for Bennet Peak.

Directions: Just north of Baker City on I-84, take exit 302 and follow Highway 86 east for 23.2 miles. At a sign for Sparta just beyond milepost 23, go left and uphill on Sparta Lane for 4.9 miles, then go left on East Eagle Creek Road for 5.8 miles to a five-way junction. Go left on Empire Gulch Road 7015 for 4.8 miles, cross a bridge, then go left on Road 77 for 2.8 miles. Fork right on East Eagle Road 7745 for 6.4 miles, passing the Eagle Creek Trailhead sign and continuing 0.8 mile to road's end at the East Eagle Trailhead.

Contact: Wallowa-Whitman National Forest, Eagle Cap Ranger District, 88401 Highway 82, Enterprise, OR, 97828, 541/426-5546.

38 CRATER LAKE
11.8 mi/7.0 hr

northeast of Baker City in Eagle Cap Wilderness

Map 4.3, page 195

Not to be confused with Crater Lake National Park in the southern Oregon Cascades, this lake is not set in a crater at all, but in a basin ground out by prehistoric glaciers. But the granite walls rising up around this clear lake will make you feel as if you've entered a crater.

From the turnaround parking loop, begin on the Little Kettle Creek Trail 0.1 mile, going left at a junction with the equestrian trail. The next 3.5 miles climbs thousands of feet to the lip of a ridge and crosses a creek. The trail then continues 2.3 miles through meadows, crossing a rockslide and passing smaller ponds, and finally arriving at Crater Lake. A 0.7-mile trail circles the lake and connects with a 0.3-mile spur trail to a junction with two trails, one leading to Tuck Pass, the other to Cliff Creek.

User Groups: Hikers, dogs, and horses. No mountain bikes allowed. No wheelchair facilities.

Permits: A free self-issue Wilderness Permit is required and is available at the trailhead. A federal Northwest Forest Pass is required to park here; the cost is $5 a day or $30 for an annual pass. You can buy a day pass at the trailhead, at ranger stations, or through private vendors.

Maps: A contour map of the Wallowa Mountains is available from Imus Geographics. For a map of the Wallowa-Whitman National Forest, contact the Wallowa-Whitman National Forest Headquarters, P.O. Box 907, 1550 Dewey Avenue, Baker City, OR, 97814, 541/523-6391. For a topographic map, ask the USGS for Krag Peak.

Directions: Just north of Baker City on I-84, take exit 302 and follow Highway 86 east for 23.2 miles. At a sign for Sparta just beyond milepost 23, go left and uphill on Sparta Lane for 4.9 miles, then go left on East Eagle Creek

Road for 5.8 miles to a five-way junction. Go left on Empire Gulch Road 7015 for 4.8 miles, cross a bridge, then go left on Road 77 for 2.8 miles. Fork right on East Eagle Road 7745 for 6.4 miles, passing the Eagle Creek Trailhead sign and continuing 0.8 mile to road's end at the East Eagle Trailhead.

Contact: Wallowa-Whitman National Forest, Eagle Cap Ranger District, 88401 Highway 82, Enterprise, OR, 97828, 541/426-5546.

39 SUMMIT POINT LOOKOUT
2.0 mi/1.0 hr 🥾1 ⛰8

northeast of Baker City in Wallowa-Whitman National Forest

Map 4.3, page 195

Set above the sagebrush meadows, this lookout tower affords views of the Elkhorn Range, the Wallowas, and the slopes falling down to Hell's Canyon. It's an easy hike, perhaps even a warm-up for the longer Pine Lakes tour described below. From the gate, follow the old road 0.7 mile, then go left 0.3 mile to the lookout on its 7,006-foot perch.

User Groups: Hikers, dogs, and horses. No mountain bikes allowed. No wheelchair facilities.

Permits: A free self-issue Wilderness Permit is required and is available at the trailhead. A federal Northwest Forest Pass is required to park here; the cost is $5 a day or $30 for an annual pass. You can buy a day pass at the trailhead, at ranger stations, or through private vendors.

Maps: A contour map of the Wallowa Mountains is available from Imus Geographics. For a map of the Wallowa-Whitman National Forest, contact the Wallowa-Whitman National Forest Headquarters, P.O. Box 907, 1550 Dewey Avenue, Baker City, OR, 97814, 541/523-6391. For a topographic map, ask the USGS for Jimtown.

Directions: Drive two miles north of Baker City on I-84 to Exit 302, and follow Highway 86 east toward Halfway for 49 miles.

Driving six miles beyond Richland, past milepost 48, go left on Road 77 following signs for Summit Point Lookout. In 11 miles, at a four-way junction, go right on the steep Road 7715 for 4.8 miles to the Summit Point Trailhead.

Contact: Wallowa-Whitman National Forest, Eagle Cap Ranger District, 88401 Highway 82, Enterprise, OR, 97828, 541/426-5546.

40 PINE LAKES
16.2-24.0 mi/2-4 days 🥾4 ⛰9

northeast of Baker City in Eagle Cap Wilderness

Map 4.3, page 195

Day hikers can head toward Pine Lakes, though the distance and nearly 3,000-foot elevation gain makes it a daunting day. There are easier destinations along the way: Little Eagle Meadows, for one, and a series of passes with views to 8,643-foot Cornucopia Peak to the east. Nip Pass or Tuck Pass are easy goals, but if you're headed for Pine Lakes, two lush lakes set beneath steep cliffs, you'd better pack some camping gear; you'll need to rest for the way back. On the other hand, why go back? The trail continues on in a number of directions to the Cornucopia Trailhead and Crater Lake. For a killer 24-mile loop, continue on along Pine Creek, visiting the ruins of an old gold-mining boomtown.

Behind the gate, follow the old road in 0.7 mile then stay left at a junction. Follow the Cliff Creek Trail 2.2 miles along the ridge and past a fence to reach Little Eagle Meadows. At a junction, go left along a steep slope 1.7 miles to Nip Pass, and another 0.5 mile to Tuck Pass and a junction. If you're going to Pine Lakes, go right here on the Pine Lakes Trail, climbing another 300 feet in 0.8 mile to a higher pass, then continue 2.2 miles past little Cirque Lake to the two Pine Lakes.

From here, you can continue on a long loop around Cornucopia Mountain, passing falls at the outlet of the Pine Lakes and switchbacking down to Pine Creek, going 5.3

miles to a bridge crossing, then 1.1 miles to another crossing, and the last mile to a road. Go 0.3 mile to the Cornucopia Trailhead, the end of the Pine Lakes Trail. Continue 0.9 mile down this road, then onto a dirt road to the right past the ruins of the boomtown. Turn right, following an old road 0.9 mile, then connecting with the trail to the left, going 3.5 miles and passing a cowboy cabin to return to Little Eagle Meadows and the Cliff Creek Trail.

User Groups: Hikers, dogs, and horses. No mountain bikes allowed. No wheelchair facilities.

Permits: A free self-issue Wilderness Permit is required and is available at the trailhead. A federal Northwest Forest Pass is required to park here; the cost is $5 a day or $30 for an annual pass. You can buy a day pass at the trailhead, at ranger stations, or through private vendors.

Maps: A contour map of the Wallowa Mountains is available from Imus Geographics. For a map of the Wallowa-Whitman National Forest, contact the Wallowa-Whitman National Forest Headquarters, P.O. Box 907, 1550 Dewey Avenue, Baker City, OR, 97814, 541/523-6391. For a topographic map, ask the USGS for Krag Lake.

Directions: Drive two miles north of Baker City on I-84 to Exit 302, then follow Highway 86 east toward Halfway for 49 miles. Driving six miles beyond Richland, past milepost 48, go left on Road 77 following signs for Summit Point Lookout. In 11 miles, at a four-way junction, go right on the steep Road 7715 for 4.8 miles to the Summit Point Trailhead.

Contact: Wallowa-Whitman National Forest, Eagle Cap Ranger District, 88401 Highway 82, Enterprise, OR, 97828, 541/426-5546.

41 SOUTH FORK IMNAHA RIVER

11.4-34.6 mi/7.0 hr-3 days 👥4 ⛰8

north of Richmond in Eagle Cap Wilderness

Map 4.3, page 195

The Imnaha River follows an old fault line; at a point, the fault opens up to allow the river to squeeze through a slot canyon. The result is the Blue Hole, 50 feet deep and emptying out onto a pebbled beach. Farther up the river is another gorge and Imnaha Falls. If it's a long trip you're looking for, this is as good an entry point as any to the Eagle Cap Wilderness and its many trails. The South Fork Imnaha Trail carries on farther to Hawkins Pass (see *West Fork Wallowa River to Hawkins Pass* listing in this chapter) near the river in a forest of Douglas fir and grand fir, but in 0.8 mile enters an old burn. In 1.2 miles the trail forks; go left to descend to the Blue Hole and its beach. Then continue upstream over a bluff; in 3.3 miles, you'll hear the water rushing through a second gorge. Continue 0.4 mile beyond and watch for a trail to the left that overlooks Imnaha Falls. This makes a good turnaround point for a day trip.

For a multi-day trip, you can head to either Tenderfoot of Hawkins Pass. After Imnaha Falls, continue 0.6 mile straight at a junction and go another 0.5 mile to a fork. To the right is the North Fork Imnaha Trail, which continues another 8.9 miles up to 8,500-foot Tenderfoot Pass; to the left, the South Fork continues another 10.5 miles to 8,330-foot Hawkins Pass.

User Groups: Hikers, dogs, and horses. No mountain bikes allowed. No wheelchair facilities.

Permits: A free self-issue Wilderness Permit is required and is available at the trailhead. A federal Northwest Forest Pass is required to park here; the cost is $5 a day or $30 for an annual pass. You can buy a day pass at the trailhead, at ranger stations, or through private vendors.

Maps: A contour map of the Wallowa

Mountains is available from Imus Geographics. For a map of the Wallowa-Whitman National Forest, contact the Wallowa-Whitman National Forest Headquarters, P.O. Box 907, 1550 Dewey Avenue, Baker City, OR, 97814, 541/523-6391. For a topographic map, ask the USGS for Deadman Point.

Directions: From Joseph, head east on the Hells Canyon Byway and follow Imnaha Highway 8.3 miles to a sign for Halfway, then go right on Wallowa Mountain Road 39 for 32 miles. Turn right on Road 3960 and go nine miles to the Indian Crossing Campground and park by the restroom on the right.

Contact: Wallowa-Whitman National Forest, Eagle Cap Ranger District, 88401 Highway 82, Enterprise, OR, 97828, 541/426-5546.

42 EUREKA VIEWPOINT
7.2-15.4 mi/4.0 hr-2 days 3 ⚠9

in Hells Canyon National Recreation Area

Map 4.4, page 196

From the historic Buckhorn Lookout, the land folds and ripples into the incredible distances of Hell's Canyon. The Snake River carves its way through this long furrow more than 4,000 feet below, making tangible the fact that Hells Canyon is deeper than the Grand Canyon. You can hike down into these depths—but be careful not to overtax your strength, keep track of your water, and avoid the high heat of summer. For backpackers, this is one way to get to the bottom and the Eureka Bar, though even that is a long, hard journey with poison oak along the way. For day hikers, it's best to climb down to a stunning viewpoint along the way, watching for the Imnaha River Canyon and Hat Point on the horizon.

You'll be amazed that people lived here and somehow managed to work the land. The trail follows the abandoned Eureka Wagon Road Trail, an old logging road that once supplied timber to a now defunct town in the bottom of the canyon. Along the descent, you'll pass the ruins of a cabin and an old mineshaft. At the Eureka Bar on the Snake River itself, you can see some of the ruins of that town, mainly the old Stamp Mill. Respect the history of the area and touch nothing.

From the parking area, walk back up Road 780 for 0.2 mile, then take the rough road to the right 1.2 miles to a gate (this road can be driven with a high-clearance vehicle). Follow the Cemetery Ridge Trail 0.5 mile through sparse trees and wildflowers to a fork at a saddle. Go right and follow the Eureka Wagon Road Trail 1.4 miles, staying to the left at a junction with the Tulley Creek Trail, down 750 feet to a wire fence in Spain Saddle. Cross the fence and continue 0.6 mile and another 350 feet down to a second fence and a viewpoint of the Snake River. To reach the Eureka Viewpoint, continue 1.1 miles and another 530 feet down to a rock cairn where the trail turns right. Head off-trail toward the lava formations and climb to the left to the ridgeline for views of the Snake River.

From here, the Eureka Bar still lies 2,500 feet below. Where the trail turned right at the cairn, it continues down 2.5 miles to Eureka Creek, and another 1.6 miles to the Snake River, an arduous journey not recommended for day hikes.

User Groups: Hikers, dogs, horses, and mountain bikes. No wheelchair facilities.

Permits: Permits are not required. Parking and access are free.

Maps: For a map of the Hells Canyon National Recreation Area, contact Wallowa Mountains Visitor Center, 88401 Highway 82, Enterprise, OR, 97828, 541/426-5546. For a topographic map, ask the USGS for Deadhorse Ridge.

Directions: From Enterprise, drive 3.5 miles east on Highway 82 and turn north at a sign for Buckhorn Spring onto Crow Creek Road for 1.2 miles, then go right and continue on Crow Creek Road for 4.2 miles. Go right on Zumwalt Road, which becomes Road 46, for 32.5 miles. At a sign for Buckhorn Overlook, go right on Road 780 for 0.3 mile to a junction, staying straight and to the right at the next two forks to road's end at the overlook parking area.

Contact: Hells Canyon National Recreation Area, 88401 Highway 82, Box A, Enterprise, OR, 97828, 541/523-1315.

43 EUREKA BAR
9.8 mi/4.0 hr

in Hells Canyon National Recreation Area

Map 4.4, page 196

Though the Eureka Bar can be reached by starting from the Buckhorn Overlook, it is a terribly arduous journey that makes more cause for misery than anything, despite the scenery. From the Imnaha River, though, it's an easier trail. But the road to get to the Cow Creek Bridge, where the trail begins, is what makes this trail a challenge. A long, hard drive down a rocky road makes this a true test of patience. Give yourself at least an hour for the 15-mile drive. It will make it all the more ludicrous to find the ruins of Eureka, an old mining town on the Snake River that didn't last much past its 1899 inception.

The trail begins at 1,200 feet elevation on the Imnaha River, descending the white-water river 4.2 miles to a cobble beach on the Snake River. Go to the left and downstream to visit the Stamp Mill ruins and old mineshaft. The trail along the river peters out after 0.7 mile at Eureka Creek.

User Groups: Hikers, dogs, horses, and mountain bikes. No wheelchair facilities.

Permits: Permits are not required. Parking and access are free.

Maps: For a map of the Hells Canyon National Recreation Area, contact Wallowa Mountains Visitor Center, 88401 Highway 82, Enterprise, OR, 97828, 541/426-5546. For a topographic map, ask the USGS for Deadhorse Ridge.

Directions: From downtown Joseph, follow the Imnaha Highway and signs for Hells Canyon Scenic Byway 29 miles to the town of Imnaha. Turn left on Lower Imnaha Road for 6.6 miles to Fence Creek, where pavement ends and the

rocky, rutted dirt road begins. Follow this road 15 miles to the Cow Creek Bridge over the Imnaha River. Turn left on a spur road to the parking area.

Contact: Hells Canyon National Recreation Area, 88401 Highway 82, Box A, Enterprise, OR, 97828, 541/523-1315.

44 SNAKE RIVER TRAIL VIA DUG BAR
8.6-48.0 mi/4.5 hr-6 days

in Hells Canyon Wilderness Area

Map 4.4, page 196

Once you are in depths of Hells Canyon, the rest seems easy by comparison. The Snake River Trail follows the canyon and the river through a designated wilderness area. With loop options and dispersed campsites along the river, it's a dream for backpackers and horseback riders. Wildflowers adorn the shores, and the rushing water follows the whole way, though the trail does at points leave the river to climb up and over the bluffs. Pay attention to water sources, rattlesnakes, poison ivy, and ticks along the way. Be sure to purchase a good map for the far-too-long-to-explain trail mileages here. A popular place to start is Dug Bar, since the trailhead itself is on the river and requires no climb in and out of the canyon—just prepare to allow two full hours to descend on the road into the canyon.

From Dug Bar, an easy day hike visits the mouths of Dug and Deep Creeks. From the parking lot, walk back up the road and turn left on the Snake River Trail, heading to a high viewpoint and continuing along a ridge 2.2 miles to Dug Creek. Head left, watching for poison oak, for 1 mile to the Snake River. If you're not winded yet, continue upstream 1.1 mile, passing good camping sites, to the mouth of Deep Creek. Return as you came.

User Groups: Hikers, dogs, and horses. No mountain bikes allowed. No wheelchair facilities.

Permits: A free self-issue Wilderness Permit is required and is available at the trailhead. Parking and access are free.

Maps: For a map of the Hells Canyon National Recreation Area, contact Wallowa Mountains Visitor Center, 88401 Highway 82, Enterprise, OR, 97828, 541/426-5546. For a topographic map, ask the USGS for Cactus Mountain.

Directions: From downtown Joseph, follow the Imnaha Highway and signs for Hells Canyon Scenic Byway 29 miles to the town of Imnaha. Turn left on Lower Imnaha Road for 6.6 miles to Fence Creek, where pavement ends and the rocky, rutted dirt road begins. Follow this road 25.4 miles to road's end at a boat launch and campground. Park beside the restroom. The trail begins back 150 feet on the road.

To begin the trail from the far opposite end, one must first climb into the canyon 10.1 miles from the Saddle Creek Trailhead. From downtown Joseph, follow the Imnaha Highway and signs for Hells Canyon Scenic Byway 29 miles to the town of Imnaha. Turn right on Upper Imnaha Road, following signs for Halfway. Drive 13 miles to a fork before a bridge and turn left on Road 4230. Drive 2.9 miles to the Saddle Creek Trailhead lot at road's end. Follow the Saddle Creek Trail to the Snake River, following the canyon downstream on the Snake River Trail toward Dug Bar.

Contact: Hells Canyon National Recreation Area, 88401 Highway 82, Box A, Enterprise, OR, 97828, 541/523-1315.

45 HAT POINT TO SNAKE RIVER

15.4 mi/10.0 hr-2 days   🥾5 ⛰9

in Hells Canyon National Recreation Area

Map 4.4, page 196

Atop a 6,910-foot ridge sits Hat Point lookout tower, a cabin atop a 90-foot tower that overlooks the magnificent Hells Canyon. A full 5,600 feet below lies the Snake River, carving its way through these canyonlands. Far down there lies the mouth of Saddle Creek, a destination for the most rugged hiker. If this hike sounds daunting, it is: For every one of those 5,600 feet you climb down, you will have to climb back up. Two days may be required for this one. Along the way, you'll find stunning viewpoints and an old cabin open to the public—as well as fields of poison oak.

Begin on the Hat Point Trail, going 0.2 mile across a meadow. Stay right and switchback down 3.5 miles through a Douglas fir forest, descending 2,200 feet to a junction. To the right on the High Trail lies the cabin. To continue down the canyon, go left at this junction and veer right at the next fork, following signs for Snake River. The next 0.3 mile follows a bench with views to Idaho's mountains, then begins to descend into Smooth Hollow. The next 1.2 miles drops 1,000 feet and peters out near an old corral. Go toward the cairn with a signpost in it, then head to the right, passing a viewpoint and switchbacking down 2.1 miles and 2,200 feet to the Snake River and Snake River Trail. To the right 0.4 mile is Saddle Creek.

User Groups: Hikers and dogs only. No horses or mountain bikes allowed. There are wheelchair facilities at the Hat Point Observation area.

Permits: A free self-issue Wilderness Permit is required and is available at the trailhead. A federal Northwest Forest Pass is required to park here; the cost is $5 a day or $30 for an annual pass. You can buy a day pass at the trailhead, at ranger stations, or through private vendors.

Maps: For a map of the Hells Canyon National Recreation Area, contact Wallowa Mountains Visitor Center, 88401 Highway 82, Enterprise, OR, 97828, 541/426-5546. For a topographic map, ask the USGS for Hat Point.

Directions: From downtown Joseph, follow the Imnaha Highway and signs for Hells Canyon Scenic Byway 29 miles to the town of Imnaha. Go straight through town onto Hat Point Road 4240. Climb steeply for five miles, then continue 17.6 miles to the parking area at Hat Point. Park at the first parking area at a sign for the trailhead.

Contact: Hells Canyon National Recreation Area, 88401 Highway 82, Box A, Enterprise, OR, 97828, 541/523-1315.

46 FREEZEOUT SADDLE
5.6-12.0 mi/4.0 hr-7.5 hr 🥾3 ⛰️8

in Hells Canyon National Recreation Area

Map 4.4, page 196

Hung above Hells Canyon and flanked by two ridges is Freezeout Saddle, named for the nearby creek that tumbles through the dark forests along its banks. But the trail itself sets out into ponderosa pine stands with views first out to the canyon walls of the Imnaha River, then to the Wallowas, and finally to the depths of Hell's Canyon and the Seven Devils Mountains in Idaho. For a longer hike, head up Summit Ridge into the Hells Canyon Wilderness, following it back to the trailhead on a meandering trip through wildflower meadows and past a cowboy camp.

The Saddle Creek Trail heads to the left from the lot on gentle switchbacks, climbing nearly 2,000 feet over 2.8 miles through meadows and ponderosa pines. At the four-way junction in Freezeout Saddle, go right for the loop. Hike 4.2 miles through meadows along Summit Ridge, then at a junction go right on an old road 0.4 mile, staying right at a fork, until the path peters out. Go downhill toward a rock cairn and signpost, and turn right on this trail. In 0.4 mile pass Marks Cabin, and in 0.2 mile stay left at a fork. The trail descends 2,200 feet down the ridge for 1.9 miles to a junction. Go right, descending another 1,000 feet in two miles to the trailhead.

User Groups: Hikers, dogs, and horses. No mountain bikes allowed. No wheelchair facilities.

Permits: Permits are not required. A federal Northwest Forest Pass is required to park here; the cost is $5 a day or $30 for an annual pass.

Hells Canyon from Freezeout Saddle

© SEAN PATRICK HILL

You can buy a day pass at the trailhead, at ranger stations, or through private vendors.

Maps: For a map of the Hells Canyon National Recreation Area, contact Wallowa Mountains Visitor Center, 88401 Highway 82, Enterprise, OR, 97828, 541/426-5546. For a topographic map, ask the USGS for Hat Point.

Directions: From downtown Joseph, follow the Imnaha Highway and signs for Hells Canyon Scenic Byway 29 miles to the town of Imnaha. Turn right on Upper Imnaha Road, following signs for halfway. Drive 13 miles to a fork before a bridge and turn left on Road 4230. Drive 2.9 miles to the Saddle Creek Trailhead lot at road's end.

Contact: Hells Canyon National Recreation Area, 88401 Highway 82, Box A, Enterprise, OR, 97828, 541/523-1315.

47 STUD CREEK
2.4 mi/1.0 hr

in Hells Canyon National Recreation Area

Map 4.4, page 196

The 330-foot-tall Hells Canyon Dam stands like a fortress on the Snake River, damming 20 miles of its flow into a giant reservoir. Just above the shores is the Hells Canyon Wilderness, some of the most rugged and wild terrain in the Northwest. This easy jaunt passes mock orange and sumac—not to mention poison ivy—from a visitors center to the mouth of Stud Creek, with views of the monolithic walls of Hells Canyon in all its natural glory along the way. You can visit an archeological site nearby, a shallow hole where a Native American pit house once stood. Don't plan on extending your trip: towering cliffs simply block any further opportunity to go forward. If you're looking for more, there is a 0.2-mile trail leading from the dam on the Idaho side down to Deep Creek and the dam's outlet tunnel.

From the visitors center, head to the boat dock and follow a walkway to the trail. In one mile you'll reach the cobble beach at the mouth of Stud Creek; the trail ends 0.2 mile later.

User Groups: Hikers and dogs only. No horses or mountain bikes allowed. No wheelchair facilities.

Permits: Permits are not required. Parking and access are free.

Maps: For a map of the Hells Canyon National Recreation Area, contact Wallowa Mountains Visitor Center, 88401 Highway 82, Enterprise, OR, 97828, 541/426-5546. For a topographic map, ask the USGS for Squirrel Prairie.

Directions: From Baker City, go north on I-84 to Exit 302. From the exit, drive Highway 86 east 65 miles to Oxbow. Follow Road 454 and signs to Hells Canyon Dam 23 miles. Cross the dam and drive 1.1 miles to the visitors center parking lot at road's end. The trail begins at the boat dock.

Contact: Hells Canyon National Recreation Area, 88401 Highway 82, Box A, Enterprise, OR, 97828, 541/523-1315.

48 HELLS CANYON RESERVOIR
8.6 mi/3.0 hr

in Hells Canyon National Recreation Area

Map 4.4, page 196   **BEST(**

Although this hike follows the Hells Canyon Reservoir, formed by the 330-foot dam downstream, it still makes for a rugged trip through the wilderness area. Side creeks pour in one after another and side trails roam deeper into the canyon's highlands. Some of those trails have been washed out, but the 32-Point Trail continues onward.

From road's end, start on the Hells Canyon Reservoir Trail by a message board. Cross Copper Creek, and continue 0.9 mile to cross Nelson Creek. In another 0.9 mile the trail crosses McGraw Creek; go left here 0.4 mile to a waterfall, but beyond this the trail is washed out and abandoned. Return to the main trail and continue 0.6 mile to the junction with the 32-Point Trail; long-distance backpackers can continue on this trail 8.2 miles to Buck Point Lookout and Road 3965. The Reservoir Trail goes beyond this junction 0.2 mile to Spring Creek, then is abandoned, though hikers with path-finding skills can continue 1.9 mile to its end at Leep Creek.

User Groups: Hikers, dogs, and horses. No mountain bikes allowed. No wheelchair facilities.

Permits: A free self-issue Wilderness Permit is required and is available at the trailhead. Parking and access are free.

Maps: For a map of the Hells Canyon National Recreation Area, contact Wallowa Mountains Visitor Center, 88401 Highway 82, Enterprise, OR, 97828, 541/426-5546. For a topographic map, ask the USGS for White Monument.

Directions: From Baker City, go north on I-84 to Exit 302. From the exit, drive Highway 86 east 65 miles to Oxbow. Go left onto Homestead Road and follow it nine miles to its end.

Contact: Hells Canyon National Recreation Area, 88401 Highway 82, Box A, Enterprise, OR, 97828, 541/523-1315.

49 CLARNO PALISADES
0.6 mi/0.5 hr   🏃1 △7

west of Fossil in the John Day Fossil Beds

Map 4.5, page 197

Prehistoric Oregon was not at all the place we see today. Before the Cascade Mountains rose, what is now Eastern Oregon went through several incarnations: marshy jungle, wild savanna. Some of the animals and plants that thrived here—including saber-toothed cats, miniature horses, and the dawn redwood—did so for a long time. But when the Cascade Mountains rose up in volcanic pyrotechnic displays of ash and fire, those living things were buried and fossilized. The John Day Fossil Beds is a great place to find fossils. At the Clarno Palisades, massive mudslides buried forests instantaneously, and you can see some of the fossilized trunks buried in the solidified mud and ash. Two trails, an easy 0.6-mile walk altogether, investigate the towering walls, all that remains of those prehistoric flows. A fossil loop invites you to explore the 44-million-year-old mud flows with branch and leaf fossils, and an uphill climb takes you to a viewpoint of an arch high on the rock wall. Remember to take nothing from the area!

User Groups: Hikers and dogs on leash only. No horses or mountain bikes allowed. No wheelchair facilities.

Permits: Permits are not required. Parking and access are free.

Maps: For a brochure, contact John Day Fossil Beds National Monument, 32651 Highway 19, Kimberly, OR, 97848, 541/987-2333. For a topographic map, ask the USGS for Clarno.

Directions: From The Dalles, drive I-84 east to Biggs (Exit 104) and turn south on U.S. 97 for 59 miles. When you reach Shaniko, turn left on Highway 218 for 26 miles, passing Antelope and Clarno. Cross the John Day River and continue three miles to a pullout on the left.

Contact: John Day Fossil Beds National Monument, 32651 Highway 19, Kimberly, OR, 97848, 541/987-2333.

50 PAINTED HILLS
2.6 mi/1.5 hr   🏃1 △8

northwest of Mitchell in the John Day Fossil Beds

Map 4.5, page 197   **BEST (**

In the distant past, 33-million-years-ago to be precise, powerful volcanoes forever changed the landscape of Eastern Oregon. The volcanic ash that fell here settled layer on layer, each with a different mineral content. After eons of erosion, what remains are the Painted Hills, eerily colorful mounds colored red, yellow, black—striped by manganese, iron, and other minerals. Four easy trails visit one of the most photographed places in Oregon, along with a few other interesting side trips to fossil-strewn mounds and mounds of claystone. Bring a camera, and choose a day with good light. But be sure to stay on all paths: these treasures are easily damaged.

All four trails in the Painted Hills Unit are close together and easy. The Painted Hills Overlook Trail is 0.3 mile, and the nearby Carroll Rim Trail climbs to a high viewpoint up 400 feet and 0.8 mile. Two other nearby trails, the Painted Cove Trail and the Leaf Hill Trail, are 0.2-mile loops.

User Groups: Hikers and dogs on leash only. No horses or mountain bikes allowed. The 0.2-mile Leaf Hill Loop is wheelchair accessible.

Permits: Permits are not required. Parking and access are free.

Maps: For a brochure, contact John Day Fossil Beds National Monument, 32651 Highway 19, Kimberly, OR, 97848, 541/987-2333. For a topographic map, ask the USGS for Painted Hills.

Directions: From the town of Mitchell on U.S. 26, drive four miles west to Burnt Ranch Road and turn right, going six miles to Bear Creek Road. Turn left on Bear Creek Road for 1.2 miles to the Painted Hills Overlook Area for the trailheads to Carroll rim and the Painted Hills. Continue another 0.7 mile on Bear Creek Road to a junction; the Leaf Hill Loop is 1.1 miles to the left, and the Painted Cove Trail is 0.5 mile to the right.

Painted Hills in the John Day Fossil Beds

Contact: John Day Fossil Beds National Monument, 32651 Highway 19, Kimberly, OR, 97848, 541/462-3961.

51 MILL CREEK WILDERNESS
16.8 mi/7.5 hr   👫 3   ⛰ 8

northeast of Prineville in Mill Creek Wilderness

Map 4.5, page 197

In 2000, a devastating fire roared through the Mill Creek Wilderness just north of the city of Prineville. Much of the forest has recovered, and now black morels sprout up among the snags and still-standing ponderosa pines. Twin Pillars Trail heads into a wilderness area, fording the creek 10 times on its way up to the Twin Pillars, a pair of distinctive rock formations towering above the creek. Watch for ticks along the way.

From the trailhead parking at Wildcat Campground, start on Twin Pillars Trail. The trail follows the creek 2.9 miles, fording it nine times, but watch for newer trails that avoid the fords. Stay to the left at a junction with the Belknap Trail. After the 10th ford, continue 2.6 miles and 1,400 feet up to a signed viewpoint of Twin Pillars. From here, the trail continues 2.6 miles farther to a junction with Road 27.

User Groups: Hikers, dogs, and horses. No mountain bikes allowed

Permits: A free self-issue Wilderness Permit is required and is available at the trailhead. Parking and access are free.

Maps: For a map of the Ochoco National Forest, contact Ochoco National Forest, 3160 NE 3rd Street, Prineville, OR, 97754, 541/416-6500. For a topographic map, ask the USGS for Steins Pillar.

Directions: From Prineville, drive 10 miles east on U.S. 26. Beyond milepost 28, turn left on Mill Creek Road and go 10.7 miles.

Contact: Ochoco National Forest, Lookout Mountain Ranger District, 3160 NE 3rd Street, Prineville, OR, 97754, 541/416-6500.

52 STEINS PILLAR

4.0 mi/2.0 hr

northeast of Prineville in Ochoco National Forest

Map 4.5, page 197

The Ochoco Mountains represent one of the westernmost terminuses of the Blue Mountain Range. This easy trail follows a ponderosa pine and bitterbrush slope to views of the Three Sisters, heading to 350-foot Steins Pillar, a rhyolitic ash column that hard-core rock climbers challenge themselves to top. For the hiker, there is an amazing rock outcrop beside the pillar to explore, and you can hike to the bottom of the pillar where the trail officially ends. From the trailhead, follow the one-way Steins Pillar Trail two miles to the base of Steins.

User Groups: Hikers, dogs, horses, and mountain bikes. No wheelchair facilities.

Permits: Permits are not required. Parking and access are free.

Maps: For a map of the Ochoco National Forest, contact Ochoco National Forest, 3160 NE 3rd Street, Prineville, OR, 97754, 541/416-6500. For a topographic map, ask the USGS for Steins Pillar.

Directions: From Prineville, drive 10 miles east on U.S. 26. Beyond milepost 28, turn left on Mill Creek Road and go 6.7 miles. At a sign for Steins Pillar Trailhead, go right across a bridge on Road 500 for two miles to a turnaround.

Contact: Ochoco National Forest, Lookout Mountain Ranger District, 3160 NE 3rd Street, Prineville, OR, 97754, 541/416-6500.

53 LOOKOUT MOUNTAIN

7.0 mi/3.0 hr

east of Prineville in the Ochoco National Forest

Map 4.5, page 197

Lookout Mountain earns its name in two ways: one, it was the site of a long-since removed fire lookout; two, the view is awesome.

From this peak, you'd think there was nothing but mountains, with the Three Sisters in the west, and the foothills of the Ochocos rolling away from the base of the colossal cliffs. Along the way, the trail passes stunning wildflower meadows with views to Big Summit Prairie, climbs a long slope to the lookout site, and finally descends to an abandoned cinnabar mine. Look at this mine from a distance, but don't go near it; old mines are dangerous.

If you parked at the lower lot, take the right-hand trail that goes up 0.9 mile to the upper trailhead. From the upper lot, start on the far-left Trail 808, which climbs through cool woods for one mile and tops the plateau. The next 3.2 miles travels through beautiful spring prairies, crosses Brush Creek, then begins the climb up the slope to the peak. Stay right at the junctions. From the 6,926-foot lookout site, the trail to the left goes 1.2 mile along the edge of the cliffs to a viewpoint. Otherwise, go straight on Trail 808, following it down 0.2 mile to a shelter, then stay left at a junction with Trail 808A for 2.6 miles, descending through deep woods to the Independent Mine and the lot.

User Groups: Hikers, dogs, horses, and mountain bikes. No wheelchair facilities.

Permits: Permits are not required. Parking and access are free.

Maps: For a map of the Ochoco National Forest, contact Ochoco National Forest, 3160 NE 3rd Street, Prineville, OR, 97754, 541/416-6500. For a topographic map, ask the USGS for Lookout Mountain.

Directions: From Prineville, drive 17 miles east on U.S. 26 then fork right on Ochoco Creek Road. Go 8.2 miles to the Ranger Station then right on Road 42 for 6.8 miles. Turn right on Road 4205 at a sign for Independent Mine. Go 100 yards to a parking area on the left for the Round Mountain Trail, or up 0.9 mile farther to an upper trailhead on Road 4205.

Contact: Ochoco National Forest, Lookout Mountain Ranger District, 3160 NE 3rd Street, Prineville, OR, 97754, 541/416-6500.

54 CHIMNEY ROCK
2.8 mi/1.0 hr   🏃1 ⛰7

south of Prineville on the Prineville Reservoir

Map 4.5, page 197

If you didn't know it was there, this fork of the Crooked River, snaking its way through a burnished desert canyon, would elude you. And many people don't know it's there, since it's far off the beaten path. The drive through the canyon alone is worth every minute; but for a bird's-eye view, the easy Rim Trail climbs a dry wash to a high bench and out to Chimney Rock, with its blooms of bitterroot and views to the Three Sisters in the west.

From the trailhead, walk into the dry gulch for 0.7 mile, then climb up to the head of a dry waterfall and continue 0.7 mile along the rimrock to the 40-foot-tall Chimney Rock, standing 500 feet over the river below.

User Groups: Hikers, dogs, horses, and mountain bikes. No wheelchair facilities.

Permits: Permits are not required. Parking and access are free.

Maps: For a brochure of the Lower Crooked Wild and Scenic River, contact the Bureau of Land Management, Prineville District, 3050 NE 3rd Street, Prineville, OR, 97754, 541/416-6700, or go to www.or.blm.gov/prineville. For a topographic map, ask the USGS for Stearns Butte.

Directions: From Prineville, head south on Main Street, which becomes Road 27 for 16.6 miles. At a sign for chimney Rock Recreation Site, park on the left side of the road at a sign for Rim Trail.

Contact: Bureau of Land Management, Prineville District, 3050 NE 3rd Street, Prineville, OR, 97754, 541/416-6700.

55 BLUE BASIN OVERLOOK
4.0 mi/2.0 hr   🏃1 ⛰8

northwest of Dayville in the John Day Fossil Beds

Map 4.6, page 198

Of all the strange formations left behind by the prehistoric volcanoes, mudslides, and ash deposits in what is now the John Day Fossil Beds, Blue Basin has to be the strangest. Blue Basin derives all its ghostly colors from colored ash. "Blue" may not be the best word to describe it; perhaps "Green Basin" would be better. Squabbling aside, what you'll find here is a box canyon entirely draped in blue-green ash deposits, like something from a fantasy film. Even the creek is a muddy green, as it slowly erodes the basin. Two great trails offer two ways to see it.

From the parking lot, follow the green creek on the Island in Time Trail leading to the right. In 0.2 mile, the trail splits; go left first, staying on the Island Trail 0.4 miles to see the interior of the basin and a few replicas of a fossilized saber-toothed cat and giant tortoise. Then return to the junction and go right, looping around the Overlook Trail for three miles to return to the lot.

User Groups: Hikers and dogs on leash only. No horses or mountain bikes allowed. No wheelchair facilities.

Permits: Permits are not required. Parking and access are free.

Maps: For a brochure, contact John Day Fossil Beds National Monument, 32651 Highway 19, Kimberly, OR, 97848, 541/987-2333. For a topographic map, ask the USGS for Picture Gorge West.

Directions: From the town of Mitchell on U.S. 26, drive 35 miles east into Picture Gorge, then turn left on Highway 19, going five miles to the Blue Basin parking lot on the right.

Contact: John Day Fossil Beds National Monument, 32651 Highway 19, Kimberly, OR, 97848, 541/987-2333.

56 SHEEP ROCK TRAILS
2.0 mi/1.0 hr   🏃1 ⛰7

northwest of Dayville in the John Day Fossil Beds

Map 4.6, page 198

The Sheep Rock unit of the John Day Fossil Beds has a number of impressive sights. If you're driving from Highway 26, east or west, you'll pass through Picture Gorge, a three-armed canyon where Native American petroglyphs are hidden on the high rocks. Sheep Rock is a story told in layers, as the John Day River carved through successive epochs of stone, leaving Sheep Rock a striped monument of different lava flows and formations. Located just above the historic James Cant Ranch, the 0.5-mile Sheep Rock Overlook Trail will give you a first-hand look, and the nearby 0.5-mile River Trail offers a view of the John Day River. Just across Highway 19, at the Condon Paleontology Center, a 0.5-mile trail leads to a view of the John Day River Valley.

Farther north on Highway 19, past the Island in Time Trail (see *Blue Basin Overlook,* previous listing), two more trails are worth a stop: the 0.25-mile Flood of Fire Trail, which crosses a ridge for a view of the basalt-rimmed John Day River Valley, and the 0.25-mile Story in Stone Trail, with its touchable exhibits along a basin of blue-green claystone.

User Groups: Hikers and dogs on leash only. No horses or mountain bikes allowed. The River Trail and Story in Stone Trail are wheelchair accessible.

Permits: Permits are not required. Parking and access are free.

Maps: For a brochure, contact John Day Fossil Beds National Monument, 32651 Highway 19, Kimberly, OR, 97848, 541/987-2333. For a topographic map, ask the USGS for Mount Misery.

Directions: From Dayville, drive five miles west on U.S. 26 to Highway 19. Turn right and go two miles to the John Day Fossil Beds National Monument sign at the James Cant Ranch and turn right and go to the parking lot and the trailheads for the River Trail and Sheep Rock Overlook, or to the left into the Thomas Condon Paleontology Center for the Condon Overlook Trail. Then go another seven miles north on Highway 19 for the Story in Stone and Flood of Fire Trails.

Contact: John Day Fossil Beds National Monument, 32651 Highway 19, Kimberly, OR, 97848, 541/987-2333.

57 ROCK CREEK TO SPANISH PEAK
16.0 mi/7.5 hr   🏃3 ⛰7

south of Dayville in Ochoco National Forest

Map 4.6, page 198

The Ochoco Mountains are one of the loneliest of mountain ranges. They sit just about in the middle of the state near Post, a little town that is the geographic center of Oregon. Rock Creek Trail is one of the few trails out this way, and you'll likely find solitude here to spare. Once you wander away from the road, you'll enter a wilderness that fits the definition if not the designation. Some of the people who found their way back here include those who built the Waterman Ditch, a late-1800s flume that supplied placer gold miners with water to wash gold from the hillsides. An abandoned cabin on Fir Tree Creek testifies to their presence, as well. The trail sets out in lodgepole pines, and if you go far enough you'll find stands of ponderosa pines at a saddle beneath Spanish Peak, crossing the imaginatively named First and Second Creeks. Climbing to the top of Spanish Peak is an option.

The Rock Creek Trail descends 500 feet and 2.4 miles from the trailhead to the start of the Waterman Ditch, then continues to follow it 1.4 level miles to the cabin ruins, crossing Fir Tree Creek. In 3.2 miles, the trail crosses Second Creek then First Creek and reaches the saddle beneath 6,871-foot Spanish Peak. The trail ends one mile ahead at the end of public land. The trail to the right begins a climb of Spanish Peak. To do that, follow this trail 4.5 miles, climbing 1,700 feet to a fork. Go left 0.8 mile, connecting with a road, and following it up to the peak.

User Groups: Hikers, dogs, and mountain bikes. No horses allowed. No wheelchair facilities.

Permits: Permits are not required. Parking and access are free.

Maps: For a map of the Ochoco National Forest, contact Ochoco National Forest, 3160 NE 3rd Street, Prineville, OR, 97754, 541/416-6500. For a topographic map, ask the USGS for Six Corners and Antone.

Directions: From Prineville, drive east on U.S. 26 for one mile and turn right on the Paulina Highway 59.5 miles east. Turn left on South Beaver Creek Road for 7.7 miles. At a sign for Wolf Creek Campground, go left on Road 42 for 1.5 miles, then go straight on Road 3810 for 3.2 miles, keeping right at a junction to stay on 3810 for 3.9 more miles, then right on Road 38 for 1.5 miles. At a junction, go straight on Road 38 for 1.7 miles to the Rock Creek Trailhead on the left.

Contact: Ochoco National Forest, Paulina Ranger District, 7803 Beaver Creek Road, Paulina, OR, 97751, 541/477-6900.

58 BLACK CANYON WILDERNESS
21.8 mi/2 days   🏃4 ⛰8

south of Dayville

Map 4.6, page 198

The Black Canyon Wilderness encompasses many different wilds, from the high meadows of the Ochoco Mountains to the sagebrush flats of the high desert. Because the lower end of this trail demands a ford of the South Fork John Day River, which is difficult, if not impossible at certain times of the year, another option is needed. Boeing Field, with its outrageous displays of big mules ear daisies, offers an easy 0.5-mile entry to the canyon itself. Along the way, backpackers will find ample opportunity to camp, and day hikers can take in the scenery, poke around a ruined cabin, and get their feet wet numerous times—almost too numerous to count. The crossings get more

difficult as the creek descends, getting deeper, until it at last reaches the John Day.

From Boeing Field, head down the trail 0.5 mile and cross Owl Creek. To the right, 1.5 miles upstream, is the Black Canyon Trail's official beginning at Road 5840, but go left two miles (the cabin is hidden in a series of meadows along the way to the left) to Black Creek. Cross the creek here and continue 1.4 miles to a second crossing. From here, the trail crosses and re-crosses the creek five more times in the next 0.9 mile. From there, the trail stays on the bank another 4.3 miles, then fords the by-now-deeper creek 10 times in 1.8 mile before arriving at the South Fork John Day River.

User Groups: Hikers, dogs, and horses. No mountain bikes allowed. No wheelchair facilities.

Permits: A free self-issue Wilderness Permit is required and is available at the trailhead. Parking and access are free.

Maps: For a map of the Ochoco National Forest, contact Ochoco National Forest, 3160 NE 3rd Street, Prineville, OR, 97754, 541/416-6500. For a topographic map, ask the USGS for Wolf Mountain.

Directions: From Prineville, drive east on U.S. 26 for one mile and turn right on the Paulina Highway 59.5 miles east. Turn left on South Beaver Creek Road for 7.7 miles, then fork right for 1.3 miles. Turn left on Road 5810 for 11.1 miles to a pullout on the left and the Boeing Field Trailhead.

Contact: Ochoco National Forest, Paulina Ranger District, 7803 Beaver Creek Road, Paulina, OR, 97751, 541/477-6900.

59 FIELDS PEAK AND MCCLELLAN MOUNTAIN
9.8 mi/5.0 hr   🏃3 ⛰8

southeast of Dayville in Malheur National Forest

Map 4.6, page 198

The largely barren Fields Peak has at least one thing going for it: set between the Strawberry

Mountains to the east and the Cascades to the west, it is the highest point between them. It takes in an enormous view. The trail up Fields Peak goes on to McClellan Mountain, a quiet and steady walk to another nearby peak, only 300 feet shorter, requiring an easy cross-country ramble up a grassy ridge. As there are no trees here to offer shade, be sure to bring ample water, sunblock, and a hat.

From the trailhead, climb 500 feet in 0.7 mile to Bitterroot Ridge, then continue uphill 600 feet and 0.8 mile to a junction. To climb Fields Peak, follow the wide path to the left 0.8 mile to the 7,362-foot peak. To continue to McClellan Mountain, return to the junction and follow the trail over a number of passes 2.2 miles to a meadow. Where the trail appears to end, follow the ridge east to the 7,043-foot peak of McClellan Mountain. The trail continues along the mountainside past meadows, leading 9.2 miles to the Riley Creek Trailhead.

User Groups: Hikers, dogs, horses, and mountain bikes. No wheelchair facilities.

Permits: Permits are not required. Parking and access are free.

Maps: For a map of the Malheur National Forest, contact Malheur National Forest, 431 Patterson Bridge Road, John Day, OR, 97845, 541/575-3000. For a topographic map, ask the USGS for Big Weasel Springs and McClellan Mountain.

Directions: From Dayville, drive east on U.S. 26 for 13 miles, then turn south on Fields Creek Road 21. Follow this road 8.6 miles to a sign for Fields Peak, and turn left on Road 115 for 0.4 mile, then turn right at a junction onto Road 2160 for 0.1 mile, then left on Road 041 for 1.2 miles to road's end at the McClellan Mountain Trailhead.

Contact: Malheur National Forest, Blue Mountain Ranger District, 431 Patterson Bridge Road, P.O. Box 909, John Day, OR, 97845, 541/575-3000.

60 WINOM CREEK
8.0-10.2 mi/4.0-5.0 hr

southeast of Ukiah in North Fork John Day Wilderness

Map 4.7, page 199

Comprising a massive part of the Blue Mountain range, the Winom Frazier OHV Complex has more than 140 miles of trail for off-road vehicles to roar into the forest. Just to the south, though, Winom Creek cascades through the North Fork John Day Wilderness, where all motorized vehicles are banned. Though a fire burned through here, the trail is well maintained and comprises a loop that returns via a nearby campground for a tour of the Blue Mountain region.

From the trailhead, the South Winom Trail heads out four miles and climbs 1,650 feet to its end along the creek, home to brook trout, redband trout, and bull trout. To make a slightly longer loop, turn left on the Big Creek Trail and go 4.5 miles to a tie trail on the left. Follow this 1.2 miles, then follow the campground road back 0.5 mile to the parking area.

User Groups: Hikers, dogs, and horses. No mountain bikes allowed. No wheelchair facilities.

Permits: A free self-issue Wilderness Permit is required and is available at the trailhead. Parking and access are free.

Maps: For a map of the Umatilla National Forest and the North Fork John Day Wilderness, contact Umatilla National Forest, 2517 SW Hailey Avenue, Pendleton, OR, 97801, 541/278-3716. For a topographic map, ask the USGS for Pearson Ridge and Kelsay Butte.

Directions: From Ukiah, drive 22.6 miles south on the Blue Mountain Scenic Byway/Road 52 and turn right on Road 440 for 0.7 mile. At a fork for South Winom Campground, go left 0.2 mile to a pullout on the right. The trailhead is across the road.

Contact: Umatilla National Forest, North Fork John Day Ranger District, P.O. Box 158, Ukiah, OR, 97880, 541/427-3231.

61 NORTH FORK JOHN DAY RIVER

5.2 mi–22.9 mi one-way/
2.0 hr–2 days 🚶2 ⛰8

northwest of Granite in North Fork John Day
Wilderness

Map 4.7, page 199 **BEST (**

In the riverbed of the North Fork John Day, mica sparkles and glistens like gold. No wonder so many miners have active claims here: watch for their tin signs nailed to the trees. Better yet, poke around some of the cabins, especially the "Bigfoot Hilton," a dilapidated miner's cabin that makes for a possible camp, though it may prove too rustic for some. Along the trail, western larches turn their own brand of gold in the autumn; it's the only conifer to lose its needles in winter. For an easy exploratory day trip or overnighter, consider fording the river at Crane Creek and returning via a loop. Otherwise, you can go on down the canyon as far as you like.

From the North Fork Trailhead, start off 0.1 mile then go to the right-hand trail. Cross Trail Creek and head into the canyon. In 2.5 miles, the trail comes to Trout Creek and the old miner's cabin on the right. Continue 4.0 miles down the river to the junction with the Crane Creek Trail. For a short loop, go left 0.2 mile to the river, fording it here. Then follow the Crane Creek Trail 4.1 miles to the Crane Creek Trailhead, then go left on the North Crane Trail back to the campground. For those wanting to continue on the North Fork John Day, continue on the remainder of this 22.9-mile trail to its end at the Big Creek Campground on dirt Road 5506.

User Groups: Hikers, dogs, and horses. No mountain bikes allowed. No wheelchair facilities.

Permits: A free self-issue Wilderness Permit is required and is available at the trailhead. A federal Northwest Forest Pass is required to park here; the cost is $5 a day or $30 for an annual pass. You can buy a day pass at the trailhead, at ranger stations, or through private vendors.

Maps: For a map of the Umatilla National Forest and the North Fork John Day Wilderness, contact Umatilla National Forest, 2517 SW Hailey Avenue, Pendleton, OR, 97801, 541/278-3716. For a topographic map, ask the USGS for Desolation Butte and Olive Lake.

Directions: From Baker City, go south on Main Street/Highway 7 toward John Day for 25 miles and turn right toward Sumpter on the Sumpter Valley Highway 220, continuing 20 miles to the town of Granite. Take Road 73 north nine miles to a stop sign, and turn left into the North Fork John Day Campground. Drive to the far end and the trailhead parking area.

To shuttle a car at Big Creek Campground, drive 14 miles south of Ukiah on U.S. 395 and go left on Road 55, following it for 5 miles. Go straight onto Road 5506, whose first 6.5 miles is gravel and remaining 6 miles is unmaintained dirt, to the trailhead at road's end.

Contact: Umatilla National Forest, North Fork John Day Ranger District, P.O. Box 158, Ukiah, OR, 97880, 541/427-3231.

62 BALDY LAKE

13.4 mi/7.0 hr 🚶3 ⛰7

west of Baker City in North Fork John Day
Wilderness

Map 4.7, page 199

This corner of the North Fork John Day Wilderness is hemmed in by granite cliffs, through which Baldy Creek makes its way to the North Fork John Day. At the head of one of those creek arms, fed by springs, Baldy Lake lies still and clear beneath Mount Ireland. The trail switchbacks up the path of an old power line that brought electricity to the gold miners working nearby.

Cross the North Fork John Day River and go 1.1 miles to a crossing of Baldy Creek. Ford Bull Creek and cross a patch of burned woods, then cross Baldy Creek again and head five miles up the canyon and 1,300 feet up in elevation to a junction. Stay right and go another 0.2 mile to Baldy Lake. Continue 0.4 mile around the lake to explore the shore and see the springs, but turn around from here; after this, the trail climbs a difficult one mile to its end at the upper Baldy Lake Trailhead, whose long and difficult drive doesn't make for a good shuttle.

User Groups: Hikers, dogs, and horses. No mountain bikes allowed. No wheelchair facilities.

Permits: A free self-issue Wilderness Permit is required and is available at the trailhead. Parking and access are free.

Maps: For a map of the Wallowa-Whitman National Forest and the North Fork John Day Wilderness, contact the Wallowa-Whitman National Forest Headquarters, P.O. Box 907, 1550 Dewey Avenue, Baker City, OR, 97814, 541/523-6391. For a topographic map, ask the USGS for Mount Ireland.

Directions: From Baker City, drive 19 miles north on I-84 to Exit 285. Following Anthony Lakes signs, go 3.9 miles west on North Powder River Lane, then left 0.7 mile on Ellis Road, then right 6.5 miles on Anthony Lakes Highway. Continue on Road 73 for 12.7 miles to a sign for the Baldy Creek Trail, turning left on Road 380 to its end at a parking area.

Contact: Wallowa-Whitman National Forest, Baker City Ranger District, 3165 10th Street, Baker City, OR, 97814, 541/523-4476.

63 MOUNT IRELAND AND DOWNIE LAKE
6.6–9.2 mi/3.0–4.0 hr 🏃3 ⛰7

west of Baker City in Wallowa-Whitman National Forest

Map 4.7, page 199

Perched on 8,321-foot Mount Ireland, a fire lookout tower (staffed in summer) peers over into a corner of the North Fork John Day Wilderness and the Baldy Lake basin, and as far out as the Elkhorn Range and Wallowa

Mountains. Along the way, a side trail leads to seldom-visited Downie Lake, a calm track of water bounded in buy subalpine fir and lodgepole pine.

Cross the berm and head up 0.2 mile on old Road 130 to a junction. Go left on Road 132 to find the Mount Ireland sign, then follow this old road 0.3 mile to where it becomes a trail. Continue 0.8 miles, cross Road 142, then climb 0.9 mile to a junction. To the left, the trail climbs 800 feet in 1.1 miles to the lookout at Mount Ireland.

Though this makes for a good hike in itself, it's worth it to extend the trip to visit Downie Lake. Coming back down from Mount Ireland to the junction, continue straight. The trail seems to disappear, but picks up 100 feet to the left and continues down 750 feet in elevation and 0.7 mile to a junction. Go left 0.1 miles at a sign for Downie Lake, then right 0.5 mile past two ponds to Downie Lake. Return as you came.

User Groups: Hikers, dogs, horses, and mountain bikes. No wheelchair facilities.

Permits: Permits are not required. Parking and access are free.

Maps: For a map of the Wallowa-Whitman National Forest and the North Fork John Day Wilderness, contact the Wallowa-Whitman National Forest Headquarters, P.O. Box 907, 1550 Dewey Avenue, Baker City, OR, 97814, 541/523-6391. For a topographic map, ask the USGS for Mount Ireland.

Directions: From Baker City, go south on Main Street/Highway 7 toward John Day for 25 miles and turn right toward Sumpter on the Sumpter Valley Highway 220, continuing 12.2 miles over the Grant County Line. Go right on bumpy Road 7370 at a sign for Mount Ireland LO for 0.6 mile, veering left to continue another 1.8 miles on this road, then left again for 0.6 mile to a fork with Road 100. Go right 0.3 mile and park at the "Mt Ireland LO Trail" sign.

Contact: Wallowa-Whitman National Forest, Baker City Ranger District, 3165 10th Street, Baker City, OR, 97814, 541/523-4476.

64 PEAVY TRAIL

7.2 mi/3.5 hr   🚶3 ⛰6

west of Baker City in North Fork John Day Wilderness

Map 4.7, page 199

The Peavy Cabin, which is available for rent, sits at a high pass on the Elkhorn Range—providing options to explore every which way on the Elkhorn Range, part of which lies in the North Fork John Day Wilderness. From the cabin, the Peavy Trail climbs 1,700 feet to the Elkhorn Crest Trail, connecting at Cracker Saddle. For a loop, follow the Crest Trail left 3.4 miles to Nip and Tuck Pass, then continue left one mile to the Cunningham Trail, going left 2.8 miles back to the cabin.

User Groups: Hikers, dogs, and horses. No mountain bikes allowed. No wheelchair facilities.

Permits: A free self-issue Wilderness Permit is required and is available at the trailhead. Parking and access are free.

Maps: For a map of the Wallowa-Whitman National Forest and the North Fork John Day Wilderness, contact the Wallowa-Whitman National Forest Headquarters, P.O. Box 907, 1550 Dewey Avenue, Baker City, OR, 97814, 541/523-6391. For a topographic map, ask the USGS for Crawfish Lake and Anthony Lakes.

Directions: From Baker City, drive 19 miles north on I-84 to Exit 285. Following Anthony Lakes signs, go 3.9 miles west on North Powder River Lane, then left 0.7 mile on Ellis Road, then right 6.5 miles on Anthony Lakes Highway. Continue on Road 73 22.2 miles, then turn left on Road 380 for three miles to its end.

Contact: Wallowa-Whitman National Forest, Baker City Ranger District, 3165 10th Street, Baker City, OR, 97814, 541/523-4476.

65 CRAWFISH LAKE

6.0 mi/2.5 hr   🚶1 ⛰7

west of Baker City in Wallowa-Whitman National Forest

Map 4.7, page 199

An easy hike into the North Fork John Day Wilderness follows the Crawfish Lake Trail through lodgepole pine woods to a pleasant lake beneath the Lakes Lookout. Though it crosses a 1989 burn in places, the trail also follows intact woods and meadows. Perfect for swimming, the lake also has a big granite outcrop for relaxing and taking in the view.

From the trailhead, follow the trail 1.4 miles to Crawfish Lake, passing through the burn along the way. The trail follows the lake 0.3 mile, then continues along an edge of the wilderness and finally along Crawfish Creek for 1.3 mile to a lower trailhead.

User Groups: Hikers, dogs, and horses. No mountain bikes allowed. No wheelchair access.

Permits: A free self-issue Wilderness Permit is required and is available at the trailhead. Parking and access are free.

Maps: For a map of the Wallowa-Whitman National Forest and the North Fork John Day Wilderness, contact the Wallowa-Whitman National Forest Headquarters, P.O. Box 907, 1550 Dewey Avenue, Baker City, OR, 97814, 541/523-6391. For a topographic map, ask the USGS for Crawfish Lake.

Directions: From Baker City, drive 19 miles north on I-84 to Exit 285. Following Anthony Lakes signs, go 3.9 miles west on North Powder River Lane, then left 0.7 mile on Ellis Road, then right 6.5 miles on Anthony Lakes Highway. Continue on Road 73 for 15 miles, and turn left on Road 216 at a sign for Crawfish Lake. Go 0.25 mile into a parking area.

Contact: Wallowa-Whitman National Forest, Baker City Ranger District, 3165 10th Street, Baker City, OR, 97814, 541/523-4476.

66 THE LAKES LOOKOUT

1.4 mi/1.0 hr

west of Baker City in Wallowa-Whitman
National Forest

Map 4.7, page 199

The Anthony Lakes area in the Blue Mountains has a plethora of hikes. Here's a start: a gentle climb to a viewpoint and the site of an old lookout tower, long gone. From the trailhead, climb an easy 0.7-mile trail, gaining 700 feet, to a view of the lake-strewn landscape below.

User Groups: Hikers and dogs. No horses or mountain bikes permitted. No wheelchair access.

Permits: Permits are not required. Parking and access are free.

Maps: For a map of the Wallowa-Whitman National Forest, contact the Wallowa-Whitman National Forest Headquarters, P.O. Box 907, 1550 Dewey Avenue, Baker City, OR, 97814, 541/523-6391. For a topographic map, ask the USGS for Anthony Lakes.

Directions: From Baker City, drive 19 miles north on I-84 to Exit 285. Following Anthony Lakes signs, go 3.9 miles west on North Powder River Lane, then left 0.7 mile on Ellis Road, then right 6.5 miles on Anthony Lakes Highway. Continue on Road 73 for 15.4 miles, and turn left on Road 210. Follow this rutted and rocky road 1.6 miles, then right 0.3 mile at a junction, then left to a parking area at the trailhead.

Contact: Wallowa-Whitman National Forest, Baker City Ranger District, 3165 10th Street, Baker City, OR, 97814, 541/523-4476.

67 ANTHONY LAKE TO HOFFER LAKES

3.0 mi/1.5 hr

west of Baker City in Wallowa-Whitman
National Forest

Map 4.7, page 199

Lying at the foot of the Elkhorn Range, Anthony Lake is a popular destination. With its historic guard station, its campgrounds, boat ramp, even a ski area, this is a well-known area to traverse, especially if you're going to circle the lake by foot. The lake is also an entryway to other lakes as well, including the two Hoffer Lakes, an easy distance away. Start by circling Anthony Lake, then strike out along Parker Creek to the two marshy lakes with their wildflower meadows.

Set out from the pavilion to Anthony Lake, and follow the lakeshore left 0.3 mile. Pass the boat ramp, and continue 0.3 mile to a junction. To visit Hoffer Lakes, go left along Parker Creek 0.6 mile to the first lake, where side trails lead to the second. To see the meadows, continue along the main trail 0.5 mile to an old service road. Return as you came to Anthony Lake, and continue left along its shore 0.4 mile back to the parking area.

User Groups: Hikers, dogs on leash only, and horses. No mountain bikes allowed. No wheelchair access.

Permits: Permits are not required. Parking and access are free.

Maps: For a map of the Wallowa-Whitman National Forest, contact the Wallowa-Whitman National Forest Headquarters, P.O. Box 907, 1550 Dewey Avenue, Baker City, OR, 97814, 541/523-6391. For a topographic map, ask the USGS for Crawfish Lake and Anthony Lakes.

Directions: From Baker City, drive 19 miles north on I-84 to Exit 285. Following Anthony Lakes signs, go 3.9 miles west on North Powder River Lane, then left 0.7 mile on Ellis Road, then right 6.5 miles on Anthony Lakes Highway. Continue on Road 73 for 10.2 miles to the Anthony Lake Campground on the left. Follow the entrance road, forking right then parking on the left at a picnic gazebo.

Contact: Wallowa-Whitman National Forest, Baker City Ranger District, 3165 10th Street, Baker City, OR, 97814, 541/523-4476.

68 DUTCH FLAT SADDLE LOOP
8.2 mi/4.0 hr   🥾2 ⛰8

west of Baker City in Wallowa-Whitman National Forest

Map 4.7, page 199

Anthony Lake is popular for camping, skiing, and boating, and is a haven for hiking. With its link to the Elkhorn Crest Trail and a section of the North Fork John Day Wilderness, this epic day-hike—or backpacking trip—circles around Angell Peak and Gunsight Mountain, with a passage above Crawfish Meadow and side-trip options to Dutch Flat Lake and Lost Lake.

Set out from the pavilion to Anthony Lake, and follow the lakeshore left 0.3 mile. At a boat ramp, take the Black Lake Trail on the left 0.5 mile past Lilypad Lake to the Elkhorn Crest Trail. Stay on the Elkhorn Crest Trail, keeping left at a junction to Black Lake itself, and continue 2.1 miles around Gunsight Mountain and Angell Peak, climbing 1,000 feet to Angell Pass. Enter the wilderness here, and in 0.6 mile the trail descends 300 feet to Dutch Flat Saddle and a junction. Go right on the Crawfish Basin Trail and continue through the wilderness and out again 2.5 miles to a road. Follow the road 0.1 mile, staying left at a junction and continuing 0.3 mile to a pass. Take an unmarked trail to the right 0.1 mile to another road, then go right on that road 0.3 mile to the Hoffer Lakes Trail. Follow the trail 1.1 miles back to Anthony Lake, then go left on the shore 0.4 mile back to the parking area.

User Groups: Hikers, dogs on leash only, and horses. No mountain bikes allowed. No wheelchair access.

Permits: A free self-issue Wilderness Permit is required and is available on the trail. Parking and access are free.

Maps: For a map of the Wallowa-Whitman National Forest, contact the Wallowa-Whitman National Forest Headquarters, P.O. Box 907, 1550 Dewey Avenue, Baker City, OR, 97814, 541/523-6391. For a topographic map, ask the USGS for Anthony Lakes.

Directions: From Baker City, drive 19 miles north on I-84 to Exit 285. Following Anthony Lakes signs, go 3.9 miles west on North Powder River Lane, then left 0.7 mile on Ellis Road, then right 6.5 miles on Anthony Lakes Highway. Continue on Road 73 for 10.2 miles to the Anthony Lake Campground on the left. Follow the entrance road, forking right then parking on the left at a picnic gazebo.

Contact: Wallowa-Whitman National Forest, Baker City Ranger District, 3165 10th Street, Baker City, OR, 97814, 541/523-4476.

69 BLACK LAKE
2.4 mi/1.0 hr   🥾1 ⛰7

west of Baker City in Wallowa-Whitman National Forest

Map 4.7, page 199

Lilypad and Black Lakes are set in the same forested landscape as big, popular Anthony Lake, but they don't get nearly the recognition. If you're camping up here with the kids, take this delightful day trip away from the crowds and the boats and head for some woodsy quiet.

Set out from the pavilion to Anthony Lake, and follow the lakeshore left 0.3 mile. At a boat ramp, take the Black Lake Trail on the left 0.5 mile past Lilypad Lake to the Elkhorn Crest Trail. Stay on the Elkhorn Crest Trail a short distance, then go right and climb 100 feet in 0.4 mile to Black Lake. To make a loop of it, return to the Elkhorn Trail and follow it to the left, staying on that trail 0.5 mile to a trailhead on Road 73. Take the next trail to the left back 0.3 mile to the campground and to the parking area.

User Groups: Hikers, dogs on leash only, and horses. No mountain bikes allowed. No wheelchair access.

Permits: Permits are not required. Parking and access are free.

Maps: For a map of the Wallowa-Whitman

National Forest, contact the Wallowa-Whitman National Forest Headquarters, P.O. Box 907, 1550 Dewey Avenue, Baker City, OR, 97814, 541/523-6391. For a topographic map, ask the USGS for Anthony Lakes.

Directions: From Baker City, drive 19 miles north on I-84 to Exit 285. Following Anthony Lakes signs, go 3.9 miles west on North Powder River Lane, then left 0.7 mile on Ellis Road, then right 6.5 miles on Anthony Lakes Highway. Continue on Road 73 for 10.2 miles to the Anthony Lake Campground on the left. Follow the entrance road, forking right then parking on the left at a picnic gazebo.

Contact: Wallowa-Whitman National Forest, Baker City Ranger District, 3165 10th Street, Baker City, OR, 97814, 541/523-4476.

70 ELKHORN CREST NATIONAL RECREATION TRAIL
22.8 mi one-way/2 days 🏃5 ⛰10

west of Baker City in Wallowa-Whitman National Forest

Map 4.7, page 199

The highest-elevation trail in the Blue Mountains runs north–south through the glaciated granite landscape of the Elkhorn Range. Lake after lake falls along the subalpine route, with views to the Blue Mountains and the Wallowas. Deer, elk, and mountain goats live in this high country, and much of the trail traverses the North Fork John Day Wilderness. The trail can be accessed from either end, or a shuttle can be arranged to make the whole run.

The northern end of the trail sets out from the trailhead on Road 73 near Anthony Lake, climbing 3.2 miles to Dutch Flat Saddle and into the wilderness, passing Black Lake and affording access to Dutch Flat Lake. In 1.9 miles, it reaches Nip and Tuck Pass, with access to Lost Lake and Meadow Lake. The next 3.4 miles rounds Mount Ruth and reaches Cracker Saddle, with access to Summit Lake (see *Elkhorn Crest Lakes,* next listing). The trail then leaves the wilderness and follows a long 9.5-mile slope, passing old mining prospects and rounding Rock Creek Butte. At the junction with Twin Lakes (see *Twin Lakes* listing in this chapter), the trail completes its traverse on an easy 3.8 miles to Marble Pass.

User Groups: Hikers, dogs, and horses. Mountain bikes not allowed in wilderness area. No wheelchair facilities.

Permits: A free self-issue Wilderness Permit is required and is available on the trail. A federal Northwest Forest Pass is required to park here; the cost is $5 a day or $30 for an annual pass. You can buy a day pass at the trailhead, at ranger stations, or through private vendors.

Maps: For a map of the Wallowa-Whitman National Forest, contact the Wallowa-Whitman National Forest Headquarters, P.O. Box 907, 1550 Dewey Avenue, Baker City, OR, 97814, 541/523-6391. For a topographic map, ask the USGS for Elkhorn Peak.

Directions: For the north access, begin in Baker City, driving 19 miles north on I-84 to Exit 285. Following Anthony Lakes signs, go 3.9 miles west on North Powder River Lane, then left 0.7 mile on Ellis Road, then right 6.5 miles on Anthony Lakes Highway. Continue on Road 73 for 9.9 miles to the Elkhorn Crest Trailhead on the left. For the south access, start in Baker City at exit 304 on I-84. Drive west on Campbell Street 1.5 miles, then turn right on 10th Street for 1.1 mile. At a flashing yellow light, turn left on Pocahontas Road for 7.6 miles, following signs for Marble Creek Picnic Area. Go straight on Marble Creek Road 8.1 miles to a pass and the Elkhorn Crest Trail. The final four miles of Marble Creek Road require vehicles with high clearance.

Contact: Wallowa-Whitman National Forest, Baker City Ranger District, 3165 10th Street, Baker City, OR, 97814, 541/523-4476.

71 ELKHORN CREST LAKES
24.8 mi/3 days   5 9

west of Baker City in Wallowa-Whitman
National Forest

Map 4.7, page 199

The northernmost section of the Elkhorn Crest National Recreation Trail has the most water. Along the way, spur trails lead to three subalpine lakes: Dutch Flat, Lost, and Summit. For backpackers, these three lakes offer great camping—the only catch is getting there. To reach the ultimate destination, the high-set Summit Lake, requires 2,600 feet of elevation gain. But the other two are along the way, easily accessible from trail passes.

The trail sets out from nearby Anthony Lake, climbing 3.2 miles and 750 feet to Dutch Flat Saddle and into the wilderness, passing Black Lake along the way (see *Black Lake* listing in this chapter). At the four-way junction of Dutch Flat Saddle, you'll see Dutch Flat Lake below to the east; take the left-hand trail down 1.1 miles to access it. Continue south on the Elkhorn Trail, passing the Cunningham Trail, for 1.9 miles to Nip and Tuck Pass. Just beyond this narrow slot in the rock, go left 1.3 miles to Lost Lake. For Summit Lake, the largest and prettiest, continue on the Elkhorn Trail 3.4 miles to Cracker Saddle, crossing an old ghost town dirt road, and go left 1.5 mile to Summit Lake.

User Groups: Hikers, dogs, and horses. No mountain bikes allowed. No wheelchair facilities.

Permits: A free self-issue Wilderness Permit is required and is available on the trail. A federal Northwest Forest Pass is required to park here; the cost is $5 a day or $30 for an annual pass. You can buy a day pass at the trailhead, at ranger stations, or through private vendors.

Maps: For a map of the Wallowa-Whitman National Forest, contact the Wallowa-Whitman National Forest Headquarters, P.O. Box 907, 1550 Dewey Avenue, Baker City, OR, 97814, 541/523-6391. For a topographic map, ask the USGS for Elkhorn Peak and Anthony Lakes.

Directions: Begin in Baker City, driving 19 miles north on I-84 to Exit 285. Following Anthony Lakes signs, go 3.9 miles west on North Powder River Lane, then left 0.7 mile on Ellis Road, then right 6.5 miles on Anthony Lakes Highway. Continue on Road 73 for 9.9 miles to the Elkhorn Crest Trailhead on the left.

Contact: Wallowa-Whitman National Forest, Baker City Ranger District, 3165 10th Street, Baker City, OR, 97814, 541/523-4476.

72 GRANITE CREEK
6.6 mi/2.5 hr   2 7

northwest of Granite in North Fork John Day
Wilderness

Map 4.7, page 199

For an introductory tour of gold mining country, look no further than Granite Creek. As in other areas in and around the North Fork John Day Wilderness, there are still active claims. The ponderosa pine–lined canyon leads down to the North Fork John Day River, where trails branch out in all directions into the wilderness. You'll pass a handy spring along the way, bubbling out of a pipe. Note the mica that sparkles in the riverbed like gold. For a tour of the devastation of mining, simply loop back on an old mining road that passes old ruins, active claims, and a few miners' shacks.

Follow the Granite Creek Trail 1.3 miles to a junction, staying to the right 0.6 mile to the first footbridge over Granite Creek. Continue 1.4 miles along Granite Creek to the John Day River, crossing Lake Creek and Snowshoe Spring on the way, and passing the Lake Creek Trail on the left. The John Day River makes a good turnaround point, but longer hikes can be extended along the John Day itself. The Granite Creek Trail ends at the North Fork John Day Trail, so you can return the way you came. To the right, the North Fork John Day Trail follows the river 13.6 miles to its end at the North Fork John Day Campground.

Across the river and to the left, the river trail ambles 11 miles to its opposite end.

User Groups: Hikers, dogs, and horses. No mountain bikes allowed. No wheelchair facilities.

Permits: A free self-issue Wilderness Permit is required and is available at the trailhead. A federal Northwest Forest Pass is required to park here; the cost is $5 a day or $30 for an annual pass. You can buy a day pass at the trailhead, at ranger stations, or through private vendors.

Maps: For a map of the Umatilla National Forest and the North Fork John Day Wilderness, contact Umatilla National Forest, 2517 SW Hailey Avenue, Pendleton, OR, 97801, 541/278-3716. For a topographic map, ask the USGS for Desolation Butte.

Directions: From Baker City, go south on Main Street/Highway 7 toward John Day for 25 miles and turn right toward Sumpter on the Sumpter Valley Highway 220, continuing 20 miles to the town of Granite. Go left on Road 10 for 1.5 miles, then right on Road 1035 for 4.6 miles, then left on Road 010 for 0.2 mile to the parking area before the gate. The trail begins behind the gate.

Contact: Umatilla National Forest, North Fork John Day Ranger District, P.O. Box 158, Ukiah, OR, 97880, 541/427-3231.

🞃 LOST CREEK AND SADDLE RIDGE

16.2 mi/8.0 hr

southeast of Dale in Umatilla National Forest

Map 4.7, page 199

Olive Lake is certainly popular, with its campground and boat ramp, but just beyond its shoreline lies a swath of the North Fork John Day Wilderness in a remote stretch of the Greenhorn Mountains. This big loop passes a marsh on Lake Creek, ambles along Saddle Ridge, then follows Lost Creek past Ben Harrison Peak through swales marked only by cairns. Along the way, the trail follows an old

redwood pipeline that once carried water to the nearby Fremont Powerhouse.

From Lost Creek Trailhead, go 0.2 mile to a junction and go right on the Saddle Camp Trail along an old pipeline. In 1.5 miles, cross a hill and arrive at a junction, going left. In 0.7 mile, the trail reaches the terminus of the Upper Reservoir marsh, and continues 1.9 miles and 800 feet up to Saddle Camp and a trail junction. Stay left for two miles along Saddle Ridge to Dupratt Spring Pass and a dirt road. Follow the Lost Creek Trail, an old roadbed 50 yards to the left of a cairn, 2.3 miles to another junction, staying left in the pass. Over the course of the next 2.7 miles the trail vanishes in a series of five meadows; watch for cairns and/or blazes along the way to find the trail again. At the final junction, go straight 0.2 mile to the trailhead.

User Groups: Hikers, dogs, and horses. No mountain bikes allowed. No wheelchair facilities.

Permits: A free self-issue Wilderness Permit is required and is available on the trail. A federal Northwest Forest Pass is required to park here; the cost is $5 a day or $30 for an annual pass. You can buy a day pass at the trailhead, at ranger stations, or through private vendors.

Maps: For a map of the Umatilla National Forest, contact Umatilla National Forest, 2517 SW Hailey Avenue, Pendleton, OR, 97801, 541/278-3716. For a topographic map, ask the USGS for Olive Lake.

Directions: From downtown Baker City, drive south on Main Street (which becomes Highway 7) for 25 miles. Turn right on Highway 220 toward Sumpter and go 20 miles to Granite. Turn left on Road 10 for 3.6 miles, then fork right on Road 10 where it becomes gravel. Go 8.1 miles to the Lost Creek Trailhead on the right.

Contact: Umatilla National Forest, North Fork John Day Ranger District, P.O. Box 158, Ukiah, OR, 97880, 541/427-3231.

74 OLIVE LAKE
2.7-6.5 mi/1.0-3.0 hr

southeast of Dale in Umatilla National Forest

Map 4.7, page 199

You could tour Olive Lake by starting at the campground on the lake itself, and if you're so inclined then follow the directions below to the Lake Creek Trailhead, but go 0.8 mile farther up Road 10 and go left on Road 480 to the lake. From here you can start at the boat ramp and take an easy 2.7-mile walk around the lake.

If you're in the mood for something longer, adding 3.8 miles to the trip, follow a wooded hike from a different trailhead. Start at the Lost Creek Trailhead, going 0.2 mile to a junction, then right on the Saddle Camp Trail along an old pipeline. In 1.5 miles, cross a hill and arrive at a junction, going right 0.2 mile to a road, then left on a short trail to the campground. Now follow the lakeshore in either direction for its 2.7-mile loop, quickly leaving the campground behind in favor of lodgepole pine woods. Make your way back to the start of the loop and return as you came to the Lost Creek Trailhead.

User Groups: Hikers, dogs, horses, and mountain bikes. No wheelchair facilities.

Permits: Permits are not required. A federal Northwest Forest Pass is required to park here; the cost is $5 a day or $30 for an annual pass. You can buy a day pass at the trailhead, at ranger stations, or through private vendors.

Maps: For a map of the Umatilla National Forest and the North Fork John Day Wilderness, contact Umatilla National Forest, 2517 SW Hailey Avenue, Pendleton, OR, 97801, 541/278-3716. For a topographic map, ask the USGS for Olive Lake.

Directions: From downtown Baker City, drive south on Main Street (which becomes Highway 7) for 25 miles. Turn right on Highway 220 toward Sumpter and go 20 miles to Granite. Turn left on Road 10 for 3.6 miles, then fork right on Road 10 where it becomes gravel. Go 8.1 miles to the Lost Creek Trailhead on the right.

Contact: Umatilla National Forest, North Fork John Day Ranger District, P.O. Box 158, Ukiah, OR, 97880, 541/427-3231.

75 SOUTH FORK DESOLATION CREEK
15.6 mi/7.5 hr

southeast of Dale in Umatilla National Forest

Map 4.7, page 199

South Fork Desolation Creek Trail is a good option for reaching Saddle Ridge (*Lost Creek and Saddle Ridge* is another way, see listing in this chapter) as well as entering the North Fork John Day Wilderness. This trail begins on Forest Service Road 45 and passes through the Vinegar Hill-Indian Rock Scenic Area, climbing 2,200 remote miles into the Greenhorn Range. From the trailhead, travel seven miles through a valley to the old Portland Mine. The trail completes its final 0.8 mile in the shadow of the Saddle Ridge, leading to Dupratt Spring Pass. From there, you arrive at a junction with the Blue Mountain Trail and the Lost Creek Trail, where you can head off along Lost Creek or up Saddle Ridge toward the junction to Olive Lake.

User Groups: Hikers, dogs, horses, and mountain bikes. No wheelchair facilities.

Permits: Permits are not required. A federal Northwest Forest Pass is required to park here; the cost is $5 a day or $30 for an annual pass. You can buy a day pass at the trailhead, at ranger stations, or through private vendors.

Maps: For a map of the Umatilla National Forest and the North Fork John Day Wilderness, contact Umatilla National Forest, 2517 SW Hailey Avenue, Pendleton, OR, 97801, 541/278-3716. For a topographic map, ask the USGS for Desolation Butte.

Directions: From downtown Baker City, drive south on Main Street (which becomes Highway 7) for 25 miles. Turn right on Highway 220 toward Sumpter and go 20 miles to Granite. Turn left on Road 10 for 3.6 miles, then fork right on Road 10 where it becomes gravel. Go 14.9 miles and turn left on Road 45 for one mile to the trailhead pullout on the right; the trail is on the left.

Contact: Umatilla National Forest, North Fork John Day Ranger District, P.O. Box 158, Ukiah, OR, 97880, 541/427-3231.

76 TWIN LAKES
6.2-10.2 mi/3.0-5.0 hr

west of Baker City in Wallowa-Whitman National Forest

Map 4.7, page 199

There are two ways to reach Twin Lakes: the southern access for the Elkhorn Crest Trail (see *Elkhorn Crest National Recreational Trail* listing in this chapter) or from this easier road, more suitable for your everyday car. The lakes themselves are cupped in an unbelievable bowl of rock, with the head of Rock Creek Butte— the highest point in the Blue Mountains at 9,106 feet—rising above it all, and equally dominating 8,931-foot Elkhorn Peak towering as well. Should you take the easier road in, you'll have a shorter hike but a steeper climb, but it's worth it to continue up and out of the valley to the Crest Trail, and amble along as long as you'd like. If you do, consider making this an excellent backpacking trip.

The Twin Lakes Trail climbs steeply for 3.1 miles along Lake Creek to Lower Twin Lake. At the far end, follow a user trail 0.2 mile to smaller Upper Twin Lake. Return as you came, or continue on the main trail one mile from Twin Lakes switchbacks up to a saddle on the Elkhorn Crest Trail.

From the junction with the Elkhorn Crest Trail, it's 3.8 miles to the right to trail's end at the Marble Pass Trailhead, and 1 mile to the left are viewpoints of Rock Creek Butte, which hovers above the Twin Lakes like a sentinel. Beyond this, the entire length of the trail stretches onward to Anthony Lake.

User Groups: Hikers, dogs, horses, and mountain bikes. No wheelchair facilities.

Permits: Permits are not required. Parking and access are free.

Maps: For a map of the Wallowa-Whitman National Forest, contact the Wallowa-Whitman National Forest Headquarters, P.O. Box 907, 1550 Dewey Avenue, Baker City, OR, 97814, 541/523-6391. For a topographic map, ask the USGS for Elkhorn Peak.

Directions: From downtown Baker City, drive east on Main Street, which becomes Highway 7, for 23.3 miles. Past Phillips Lake and between mileposts 28 and 29, go right on Deer Creek Road for 4.2 miles, then go straight on Road 030 for 3.8 miles to road's end at the trailhead.

Contact: Wallowa-Whitman National Forest, Baker City Ranger District, 3165 10th Street, Baker City, OR, 97814, 541/523-4476.

77 MAGONE LAKE AND MAGONE SLIDE
2.5 mi/1.5 hr

north of John Day in Malheur National Forest

Map 4.7, page 199

This pine-lined lake, popular with anglers, was born when an 1860s landslide apparently dammed up Lake Creek, creating this 5,000-foot elevation lake. Magone Lake is named for an Army major who stocked the lake by carrying buckets of fish on his shoulders. Rainbow and brook trout now feed in the lake, and bear, elk, deer, and cougar occasionally come to visit. The two-mile loop around Magone Lake makes for an easy walk; if you're up for more, cross the road to the trailhead for the Magone Slide, a 1.0-mile climb up and back down the landslide.

User Groups: Hikers and dogs only. No horses or mountain bikes. The hard-packed dirt trail around Magone Lake is wheelchair accessible in dry weather.

Permits: Permits are not required. Parking and access are free.

Maps: For a map of the Malheur National Forest, contact Malheur National Forest, 431

Patterson Bridge Road, John Day, OR, 97845, 541/575-3000. For a topographic map, ask the USGS for Magone Lake.

Directions: From John Day, drive U.S. 26 east 9.5 miles. Turn left on Road 18 for 13 miles, then turn left on Road 3620 for 1.2 miles, and right on road 3618 for 1.5 miles to the Magone Lake day-use area on the left.

Contact: Malheur National Forest, Blue Mountain Ranger District, P.O. Box 909, 431 Patterson Bridge Road, John Day, OR, 97845, 541/575-3000.

78 CANYON MOUNTAIN
11.4-29.0 mi/7.0 hr-2 days 🏃4 ⛰8

south of Canyon City in Strawberry Mountain Wilderness

Map 4.7, page 199

Driving the road into this trailhead, you'll wonder how Canyon City miners managed to get up here to mine the gold that was discovered here. The Strawberry Mountains are one of the farthest terminuses of gold in the Blue Mountain Range, but some 10,000 miners showed up here in 1862. Today, this part of Oregon is relatively quiet and rarely visited. It may even be possible to have this mountain to yourself.

From the trailhead, climb the Canyon Mountain Trail 750 feet and 1.6 miles to a crossing of Little Pine Creek, then gently climb 1.7 miles past a viewpoint in a high meadow with springs to Dog Creek, then another 2.2 miles to Dean Creek. This makes a good turnaround point, though the trail continues on 5.2 miles to the Joaquin Miller Trail and another 3.8 miles to the East Fork Canyon Creek Trail, where a backpacking spot is available at the Hotel De Bum Camp (see *East Fork Canyon Creek* hike in this chapter).

User Groups: Hikers, dogs, and horses. No mountain bikes. No wheelchair facilities.

Permits: Permits are not required. Parking and access are free.

Maps: For a map of the Malheur National

Forest and Strawberry Mountain Wilderness, contact Malheur National Forest, 431 Patterson Bridge Road, John Day, OR, 97845, 541/575-3000. For a topographic map, ask the USGS for Canyon Mountain.

Directions: From John Day, drive two miles south on U.S. 395 to Canyon City. Turn left on Main Street, which becomes Road 52, and drive 1.9 miles, then turn right on Gardner Road 77. In 0.3 mile, veer right. At the next fork, go straight onto the gravel road for 2.2 miles, which becomes very steep at times. Where the gravel ends in a saddle, go straight on a dirt road 200 feet to a pine tree with a blaze, then go left 300 feet to road's end at the trailhead for Canyon Mountain Trail.

Contact: Malheur National Forest, Blue Mountain Ranger District, P.O. Box 909, 431 Patterson Bridge Road, John Day, OR, 97845, 541/575-3000.

79 PINE CREEK
21.0 mi/2 days 🏃3 ⛰8

southeast of John Day in Strawberry Mountain Wilderness

Map 4.7, page 199

There are many entrances to the Strawberry Mountain Wilderness, a band of mountains that lifts from the prairies of Eastern Oregon like a great groundswell. This trail heads into the wilderness 10.5 miles, gaining a steady 800 feet in elevation. The trail heads to a spine of the wilderness, switchbacking up to a pass over Bald Mountain, then heads down to Wildcat Basin. Along the way, there is access to many trails: Canyon Mountain, East Fork Canyon Creek, Indian Creek, Onion Creek, and Buckhorn Meadows.

User Groups: Hikers, dogs, and horses. No mountain bikes allowed. No wheelchair facilities.

Permits: Permits are not required. Parking and access are free.

Maps: For a map of the Malheur National Forest and Strawberry Mountain Wilderness, contact Malheur National Forest, 431 Patterson Bridge Road, John Day, OR, 97845, 541/575-3000. For a topographic map, ask the USGS for Pine Creek Mountain.

Directions: From Prairie City, drive 6.5 miles west on U.S. 26 and turn left on Pine Creek Road/County Road 54. Follow this road 8.5 miles to road's end and the trailhead.

Contact: Malheur National Forest, Blue Mountain Ranger District, P.O. Box 909, 431 Patterson Bridge Road, John Day, OR, 97845, 541/575-3000.

80 JOAQUIN MILLER TRAIL
11.6 mi/8.0 hr   🏃4 ⛰8

south of Canyon City in Strawberry Mountain Wilderness

Map 4.7, page 199

Before setting out on this trail, it's good to get a sense of who Joaquin Miller was. A true man of the West, a former gold miner, Pony Express rider, and newspaper writer, he settled down to a law practice in nearby Canyon City in the 1860s, during the height of the gold rush, and eventually became a poet before moving on to Oakland, California. What's left of Miller is the cabin he built in town—now part of the Grant County Historical Museum—and this namesake trail, whose stately ponderosa pines are part of the Canyon Creek Natural Area. This steep and rugged trail, worthy of its name, climbs to a high crest and connects to three other trails in the wilderness. This trail climbs 3,250 dry feet, so bring plenty of water.

Start on the Joaquin Miller Trail, which reaches a fence and the wilderness boundary in 0.3 mile. Continue into the wilderness meadows and woods two miles to a junction with the Tamarack Creek Trail. Go left to stay on the Miller Trail and climb 2,000 feet to the Joaquin Miller Crest, passing Tamarack Creek itself, the only water source on this trail, in 1.8 miles. Continue 1.5 miles to a ridge crest. To see the view of the John Day Valley,

scramble 0.2 mile up this slope. This makes a good turnaround point, though the trail ends at the Canyon Mountain Trail only 0.7 mile farther up.

User Groups: Hikers, dogs, and horses. No mountain bikes. No wheelchair facilities.

Permits: Permits are not required. Parking and access are free.

Maps: For a map of the Malheur National Forest and Strawberry Mountain Wilderness, contact Malheur National Forest, 431 Patterson Bridge Road, John Day, OR, 97845, 541/575-3000. For a topographic map, ask the USGS for Canyon Mountain.

Directions: From John Day, drive south on U.S. 395 for 9.7 miles and turn left on County Road 65 for 2.9 miles. Turn left on Road 6510 and keep left on this road for five miles to the Joaquin Miller Trailhead.

Contact: Malheur National Forest, Blue Mountain Ranger District, P.O. Box 909, 431 Patterson Bridge Road, John Day, OR, 97845, 541/575-3000.

81 EAST FORK CANYON CREEK
4.4-20.3 mi/2.0 hr-2 days 🏃4 ⛰7

south of Canyon City in Strawberry Mountain Wilderness

Map 4.7, page 199

The Canyon Creek Natural Area features park-like stands of ponderosa pine, not to mention cottonwood and dogwood trees. A few creeks meander by, and camping spots crop up along the trail. For a day hike, head in as far as you like, or challenge yourself to hike the whole trail, even looping around Indian Creek Butte before returning. For backpackers, this is one of many entrances to the Strawberry Mountain Wilderness, following this deep gouge carved out by the East Fork of Canyon Creek.

From the trailhead, the East Fork Canyon Creek Trail climbs easily in 2.2 miles to the first camp at Yokum Corrals, to the right on a fork, and in another 0.3 mile connects to the

Tamarack Trail. Stay on the main trail 0.4 mile to ford Brookling Creek, then another 1.1 miles to Bingham Camp. The next 3.3 miles climb 1,200 feet to the Hotel de Bum Camp at the headwaters of the creek. The trail continues one mile to a junction that begins the loop. To climb gradually, go left 1.3 mile to the Canyon Mountain Trail, then right 0.9 mile around Indian Creek Butte, then right again for 0.9 mile to the Table Mountain Trail, then right 0.6 mile back to the East Fork Canyon Creek Trail.

User Groups: Hikers, dogs, and horses. No mountain bikes. No wheelchair facilities.

Permits: A free self-issue Wilderness Permit is required and is available at the trailhead. Parking and access are free.

Maps: For a map of the Malheur National Forest and Strawberry Mountain Wilderness, contact Malheur National Forest, 431 Patterson Bridge Road, John Day, OR, 97845, 541/575-3000. For a topographic map, ask the USGS for Canyon Mountain.

Directions: From John Day, drive south on U.S. 395 for 9.7 miles and turn left on County Road 65 for 2.9 miles. Turn left on Road 6510 and keep left on this road for 1.6 miles, then turn right on Road 812 for 2.8 miles to a parking lot at road's end.

Contact: Malheur National Forest, Blue Mountain Ranger District, P.O. Box 909, 431 Patterson Bridge Road, John Day, OR, 97845, 541/575-3000.

82 WILDCAT BASIN AND THE BADLANDS

6.9 mi/3.5 hr   🥾2 ⛰️8

south of Canyon City in Strawberry Mountain Wilderness

Map 4.7, page 199

The Roads End Trail begins where the road ends only for cars; for the hiker, the 1.5-mile trail is still an old road, though it leads to spectacular views of the Indian Creek Basin and also makes the shortest route to nearby Strawberry Mountain. It's also a quick way to get to some amazing alpine and wildflower territory. A 1996 fire cleared the forest but opened up sunlight for the wildflower gardens proliferating here. Erosion has cleared off the rock, too, exposing ash deposits left millions of years ago in two "badlands"—really, a series of striated outcrops set amidst pines and firs. This loop visits two ash badlands along the way.

Follow the Roads End Trail, actually an old roadbed, 1.2 miles to a junction. To the right, Strawberry Mountain is 2.4 miles away. Go left 0.3 mile to another junction. Go left 1.6 miles past a series of badlands to Wildcat Basin and its spring and campsites. At a junction, go right on the Pine Creek Trail one mile. Go right on the Indian Creek Trail 0.2 mile, then right 1.1 miles past another series of badlands to finish the loop. Then go left 0.3 mile and right on the Roads End Trail to return to the trailhead.

User Groups: Hikers, dogs, and horses. No mountain bikes. No wheelchair facilities.

Permits: A free self-issue Wilderness Permit is required and is available at the trailhead. Parking and access are free.

Maps: For a map of the Malheur National Forest and Strawberry Mountain Wilderness, contact Malheur National Forest, 431 Patterson Bridge Road, John Day, OR, 97845, 541/575-3000. For a topographic map, ask the USGS for Strawberry Mountain.

Directions: From John Day, drive south on U.S. 395 for 9.7 miles and turn left on County Road 65 for 13.6 miles. At a four-way intersection, go left on Road 16 for 2.5 miles, then left on Road 1640 for 9.6 miles and park near a switchback at a sign for the Roads End Trail.

Contact: Malheur National Forest, Blue Mountain Ranger District, P.O. Box 909, 431 Patterson Bridge Road, John Day, OR, 97845, 541/575-3000.

83 SKYLINE TRAIL
9.4 mi/5.0 hr

south of Prairie City in Strawberry Mountain Wilderness

Map 4.7, page 199

Potentially, there are three ways to get to the Skyline Trail; you connect to it from the Strawberry Campground, heading toward alpine Slide Lake, where you can continue with backpack on into the high country. Another, quicker route is from one of two trailheads, but it's the westernmost trailhead that leads to both Slide Lake and High Lake, which sits in a glaciated basin below Indian Spring Butte and the Rabbit Ears, a pair of prominent spires on a high ridge dividing this basin from the Strawberry Lakes.

The Skyline Trail descends 500 feet and 1.3 miles to High Lake, with a loop trail to campsites leading to the left. Continue past the Lake Creek Trail to the right and continue on the Skyline Trail 1.6 miles, climbing to a high pass. From here, descend 1.3 miles to a junction (note that this route can be covered with snow late into the summer). At the junction, go right to Slide Lake, with its one-mile loop around the shore. From here the Skyline Trail continues 0.5 mile to a junction that leads toward Strawberry Lake; go right to stay on the Skyline, which continues 12.3 miles to its end at Road 101.

User Groups: Hikers, dogs, and horses. No mountain bikes. No wheelchair facilities.

Permits: A free self-issue Wilderness Permit is required and is available at the trailhead. Parking and access are free.

Maps: For a map of the Malheur National Forest and Strawberry Mountain Wilderness, contact Malheur National Forest, 431 Patterson Bridge Road, John Day, OR, 97845, 541/575-3000. For a topographic map, ask the USGS for Roberts Creek and Logan Valley East.

Directions: From John Day, drive south on U.S. 395 for 9.7 miles and turn left on County Road 65 for 13.6 miles. At a four-way intersection, go left on Road 16 for 2.5 miles, then left on Road 1640 for 10 miles to the end of the road and the Skyline Trailhead.

Contact: Malheur National Forest, Prairie City Ranger District, P.O. Box 337, Prairie City, OR, 97869, 541/820-3800.

84 STRAWBERRY LAKE AND LITTLE STRAWBERRY LAKE
6.6 mi/3.0 hr

south of Prairie City in Strawberry Mountain Wilderness

Map 4.7, page 199   **BEST (**

As dry as the Strawberry Wilderness can be, it's amazing that there are such beautiful lakes—and a waterfall, too. A must-hike for day-hikers and backpackers alike, this trail heads in to two lakes, one large and one small, in a glaciated valley high in the Strawberry Mountain Wilderness. The bigger Strawberry Lake was formed by a thousand-year-old landslide, creating a perfect mirror of the rugged mountains surrounding it; the creek that feeds it runs mostly underground, hidden by the landslide.

From the parking area, head up the Strawberry Lake Trail one mile to a junction, go right 0.3 mile, then right again to Strawberry Lake. A trail loops around the lake; go right 0.9 mile along the west shore for views. At the far end, continue right 0.9 mile, climbing 600 feet to Strawberry Falls and a junction. Go left 0.4 mile to Little Strawberry Lake.

User Groups: Hikers, dogs, and horses. No mountain bikes. No wheelchair facilities.

Permits: A free self-issue Wilderness Permit is required and is available at the trailhead. Parking and access are free.

Maps: For a map of the Malheur National Forest and Strawberry Mountain Wilderness, contact Malheur National Forest, 431 Patterson Bridge Road, John Day, OR, 97845, 541/575-3000. For a topographic map, ask the USGS for Strawberry Mountain.

Directions: From U.S. 26 in Prairie City,

drive 0.5 mile south on South Bridge Street, then continue right on Bridge Street, which becomes County Road 60 and then FS Road 6001, for 10.7 miles to road's end at Strawberry Campground.

Contact: Malheur National Forest, Prairie City Ranger District, P.O. Box 337, Prairie City, OR, 97869, 541/820-3800.

85 ONION CREEK TO STRAWBERRY MOUNTAIN
7.2 mi/4.5 hr   🚶5 ⛰9

south of Prairie City in Strawberry Mountain Wilderness

Map 4.7, page 199   BEST (

The namesake of Strawberry Mountain Wilderness is a 9,038-foot brown peak surrounded by rugged, glacier-torn cirques and cliffs that fall down to a sagebrush plain stretching for miles. At that height, its no wonder the old lookout cabin blew away a piece at a time. Now it's inhabited only by wildflowers growing from the steep-pitched shale. A steep, relatively unused trail to the peak of Strawberry Mountain will cost you 10 miles round-trip and 4,000 feet elevation gain, but there is an easier way from a back route up the Onion Trail.

Follow the Roads End Trail, actually an old roadbed, 1.2 miles to a junction. Go right to the Onion Creek Trail 1.3 miles to a junction, continuing on the Onion Creek Trail to the left another 0.7 mile, climbing steadily up to a junction on the mountain itself, then climb to the left up the final 0.4 mile.

User Groups: Hikers, dogs, and horses. No mountain bikes. No wheelchair facilities.

Permits: A free self-issue Wilderness Permit is required and is available at the trailhead. Parking and access are free.

Maps: For a map of the Malheur National Forest and Strawberry Mountain Wilderness, contact Malheur National Forest, 431 Patterson Bridge Road, John Day, OR, 97845, 541/575-3000. For a topographic map, ask the USGS for Strawberry Mountain.

Directions: From John Day, drive south on U.S. 395 for 9.7 miles and turn left on County Road 65 for 13.6 miles. At a four-way intersection, go left on Road 16 for 2.5 miles, then left on Road 1640 for 9.6 miles and park near a switchback at a sign for the Roads End Trail.

Contact: Malheur National Forest, Prairie City Ranger District, P.O. Box 337, Prairie City, OR, 97869, 541/820-3800.

86 REYNOLDS CREEK
3.2 mi/1.5 hr   🚶1 ⛰6

south of Prairie City in Malheur National Forest

Map 4.7, page 199

This lower-elevation trail will allow for some spring hiking months before the rest of the Blue Mountains emerge from the snow. This easy hike follows Reynolds Creek into the Baldy Mountain Wildlife Emphasis Area and heads for a rock arch and mysterious petroglyphs. Simply follow this trail 1.4 miles to its end at a waterfall on Reynolds Creek and a dry side creek. You'll have to set out cross-country farther up the Reynolds Creek Canyon to find the arch 0.2 mile beyond.

User Groups: Hikers, dogs, horses, and mountain bikes. No wheelchair facilities.

Permits: Permits are not required. Parking and access are free.

Maps: For a map of the Malheur National Forest, contact Malheur National Forest, 431 Patterson Bridge Road, John Day, OR, 97845, 541/575-3000. For a topographic map, ask the USGS for Isham Creek and Bates.

Directions: From Prairie City, follow County Road 62 for 7.5 miles, then turn left on Road 2635 for 4.3 miles to the Reynolds Creek Trail parking area on the right.

Contact: Malheur National Forest, Prairie City Ranger District, P.O. Box 337, Prairie City, OR, 97869, 541/820-3800.

87 LITTLE MALHEUR RIVER
14.8 mi/7.5 hr

southwest of Unity in Monument Rock Wilderness

Map 4.7, page 199

The little-known Monument Rock Wilderness in the Blue Mountains is just wild enough to bring out the wildlife and make hiking a bit more adventurous. The trail along the headwaters of the Little Malheur River crosses the river on bridgeless fords seven times from end to end, a relatively short trail that can be done in a single day (or more if you're looking for escape from the crowds). Old-growth western larch grow along the trail, and meadows are filled with columbine and alders. When you find Lunch Creek, you can decide if it's the right spot to live up to its name.

The upper trailhead follows Elk Flat Creek 2.2 miles through meadows and stands of trees to a crossing of the Little Malheur. Over the next 2.6 miles, the trail fords the river four more times before fording South Bullrun Creek, then continues another 2.6 miles past two more crossings to its end at the lower trailhead.

User Groups: Hikers, dogs, and horses. No mountain bikes. No wheelchair facilities.

Permits: A free self-issue Wilderness Permit is required and is available at the trailhead. Parking and access are free.

Maps: For a map of the Malheur National Forest and Monument Rock Wilderness, contact Malheur National Forest, 431 Patterson Bridge Road, John Day, OR, 97845, 541/575-3000. For a topographic map, ask the USGS for Flag Prairie.

Directions: From Prairie City, follow County Road 62 for eight miles, then turn left on Road 13 for 11.7 miles. Next turn left on Road 1370 at a sign for Little Malheur River, keeping left for five miles to the parking area and trailhead sign.

Contact: Malheur National Forest, Prairie City Ranger District, P.O. Box 337, Prairie City, OR, 97869, 541/820-3800.

88 MONUMENT ROCK
5.6 mi/2 hr

southwest of Unity in Monument Rock Wilderness

Map 4.7, page 199

Monument Rock is a strange rock cairn that sits atop a 7,736-foot peak. No one knows who built it—probably not Native Americans, but perhaps miners or sheepherders. Regardless of its origin, you can find Monument Rock with a little bushwhacking into a wilderness that's home to deer, elk, badgers, and the rare wolverine. Though a fire passed through here in 1989, the area is recovering. Along this trail, there are opportunities to visit two viewpoints at the Table Rock Lookout and Bullrun Rock, as well as a trip to visit the mysterious cairn.

From the trailhead, enter the Monument Rock Wilderness by crossing the dirt berm to start out on an old road for 0.6 mile, keeping left at a junction and continuing another 1.1 miles to a junction marked by a post. To climb Bullrun Rock, go left 0.4 mile along the road to a wire fence, then climb to the left to the 7,873-foot peak.

To continue to Monument Rock, go right at the post instead, crossing a gate in the wire fence and continuing 0.2 mile to a small rock cairn at a junction in burned woods. Turn left on a faint path to a pass and follow the ridge to the right, climbing a steep slope and heading over a mountaintop to Monument Rock itself.

If you're up for adding another 1.6 mile to your day, then return to your car and walk the rest of the way up Road 1370, too steep and rugged for passenger cars, to the summer-staffed Table Rock Lookout.

User Groups: Hikers, dogs, and horses. No mountain bikes. No wheelchair facilities.

Permits: A free self-issue Wilderness Permit is required and is available at the trailhead. Parking and access are free.

Maps: For a map of the Malheur National Forest and Monument Rock Wilderness, contact Malheur National Forest, 431 Patterson Bridge Road, John Day, OR, 97845,

541/575-3000. For a topographic map, ask the USGS for Bullrun Rock.

Directions: From Prairie City, follow County Road 62 for eight miles, then turn left on Road 13 for 11.7 miles. Next turn left on Road 1370 at a sign for Little Malheur River, keeping left for 5.9 miles, then turn right at a sign for Table Rock Lookout, staying on Road 1370 for 0.2 mile to a fork. Take the rough and rocky left-hand fork for 3.8 slow miles to a message board and parking area along the road.

Contact: Malheur National Forest, Prairie City Ranger District, P.O. Box 337, Prairie City, OR, 97869, 541/820-3800.

89 MALHEUR RIVER NATIONAL RECREATION TRAIL

7.6 mi one-way/3.0 hr

southeast of Prairie City in Malheur National Forest

Map 4.7, page 199

The Malheur River carves its way through a gorge along this National Recreation Trail stretch from a sketchy road crossing at Malheur Ford to the meadows of Hog Flat, where it's possible to spot pronghorn antelope. Along the way, numerous creeks join the flow from rugged side canyons. Starting from the campground at Malheur Ford, follow the river downstream 7.6 miles to its end, where it leaves the river and climbs the canyon wall to Hog Flat and Road 142.

User Groups: Hikers, dogs, horses, and mountain bikes. No wheelchair facilities.

Permits: Permits are not required. Parking and access are free.

Maps: For a map of the Malheur National Forest, contact Malheur National Forest, 431 Patterson Bridge Road, John Day, OR, 97845, 541/575-3000. For a topographic map, ask the USGS for Dollar Basin.

Directions: From John Day, drive 9.7 miles south on U.S 395 and turn left on County Road 65, which becomes Road 15, for 13.6 miles to a four-way intersection. Turn left on

Road 16 for 5.3 miles, then turn right on Road 1643. Follow signs for Malheur River for nine miles to a fork and go left on Road 1651 for 1.3 miles to a parking area at Malheur Ford. For a shuttle, head back down 1.3 miles from Malheur Ford on Road 1651 and go left on Road 1653 for 6.5 miles, then left on Road 142 for 1.4 miles to its end.

Contact: Malheur National Forest, Prairie City Ranger District, P.O. Box 337, Prairie City, OR, 97869, 541/820-3800.

90 NORTH FORK MALHEUR RIVER AND CRANE CREEK

12.4-18.6 mi one-way/2 days

south of Prairie City in Strawberry Mountain Wilderness

Map 4.7, page 199

One of the first forty rivers in Oregon to be designated "Wild and Scenic," this 12-mile stretch of the North Fork Malheur is a scenic dream with old-growth ponderosa pine, rugged canyon walls, and steep talus slopes. This lightly used trail starts high and ends low, drinking in Crane Creek along the way. You'll cross the river immediately at the trailhead, then follow it down through a Wild and Scenic River stretch along the west side of the river, descending 850 feet and 12.4 miles to its end on private land. Access to this end of the trail is poor, and the Forest Service recommends beginning and ending at the main trailhead.

Another option for an extended hike begins at Crane Crossing. The Crane Creek Trail connects to the North Fork Malheur 2.8 miles down from the trailhead and climbs back into the mountains 1,100 feet and 6.5 miles up a woodsy valley, following the historic roadbed of the Dalles Military Road. This trail is also accessible from an upper trailhead.

User Groups: Hikers, dogs, and horses. No mountain bikes. No wheelchair facilities.

Permits: A free self-issue Wilderness Permit

is required and is available at the trailhead. Parking and access are free.

Maps: For a map of the Malheur National Forest and Strawberry Mountain Wilderness, contact Malheur National Forest, 431 Patterson Bridge Road, John Day, OR, 97845, 541/575-3000. For a topographic map, ask the USGS for Stemler Ridge.

Directions: For the North Fork Malheur Trail, start in Prairie City, follow County Road 62 for eight miles, then turn left on Road 13 for 16.2 miles, then right on Road 16 for 2.2 miles. Turn right on Road 1675 for four rough miles, passing the North Fork Campground, to the trailhead.

To start on the upper trailhead for Crane Creek, start in Prairie City and follow Road 62 south for 23 miles to Summit Prairie. Stay left on Road 16 another 4.5 miles, then turn right on Road 1663 for one mile to Crane Creek and go left to a gate, the start of the trail.

Contact: Malheur National Forest, Prairie City Ranger District, P.O. Box 337, Prairie City, OR, 97869, 541/820-3800.

91 OREGON TRAIL INTERPRETIVE CENTER
2.6 mi/1.0 hr   🏃1 ⛰7

east of Baker City off Highway 86

| Map 4.8, page 200 | BEST (|

Remarkably, some stretches of the Oregon Trail are preserved—nowhere better than the path below Flagstaff Hill at the Oregon Trail Interpretive Center. Paved paths, as well as a few unpaved stetches, make it easy year-round to visit an old mining site, Panorama Point, an old railroad grade, and finally down to the two ruts of the great Oregon Trail itself—complete with a covered wagon. You'll quickly see why many pioneers plopped down and said, this place will do: In the distance, the Blue Mountains rise as a formidable wall to any further progress. Baker City was founded this way, amidst the sagebrush desert of far Eastern Oregon.

After the short walk to the old Flagstaff Mine, continue one mile over Flagstaff Hill on the paved path to Panorama Point, then continue down 0.6 mile to a junction. Go straight to a bench and the covered wagon set down on the Oregon Trail. A 0.3-mile loop connects to the Eagle Valley Railroad Grade Loop Trail and continues across the paved trail on a 0.9-mile unpaved trail back to the interpretive center.

User Groups: Hikers only. No dogs, horses, or mountain bikes allowed. The 1.5-mile paved path to the Oregon Trail is wheelchair accessible.

Permits: Permits are not required. Entrance fees from April to October are $8 for two days, and $5 for two days from November to March ($4.50/$3.50 for seniors). Youth aged 15 and under are free.

Maps: A brochure map is available at the center. For a topographic map, ask the USGS for Virtue Flat.

Directions: Drive north of Baker City on I-84 to Exit 302 and drive five miles east on Highway 86 to the Oregon Trail Interpretive Center entrance road on the left.

Contact: National Historic Oregon Trail Interpretive Center, 22267 Highway 86, P.O. Box 987, Baker City, OR, 97814, 541/523-1843.

THE SOUTHERN CASCADES

© SEAN PATRICK HILL

BEST HIKES

❰ Desert Hiking
Smith Rock State Park, **page 288.**
Newberry Lava Tubes, **page 333.**

❰ Hikes for Kids
Shevlin Park, **page 301.**

❰ Hikes for Views
The Obsidian Trail, **page 293.**
Green Lakes via Fall Creek, **page 297.**
Mount Thielsen, **page 326.**
Mount Scott, **page 349.**
Pilot Rock, **page 364.**

❰ Hikes Through Old-Growth Forests
Lookout Creek Old-Growth Trail, **page 277.**

❰ Self-Guided Nature Walks
Lava Cast Forest, **page 335.**

❰ Short Backpacking Trips
Patjens Lakes, **page 286.**
Pacific Crest Trail to Matthieu Lakes, **page 290.**
Divide Lake, **page 314.**

❰ Non-Technical Summit Hikes
Black Crater, **page 290.**
South Sister Summit, **page 298.**
Mount Bailey, **page 327.**
Mount McLoughlin, **page 357.**

❰ Waterfall Hikes
Sahalie and Koosah Falls, **page 276.**
Proxy Falls/Linton Lake, **page 294.**
Tumalo Falls, **page 300.**
Salt Creek Falls and Vivian Lake, **page 311.**
Deschutes River Trail/Dillon and Benham Falls,
    page 332.

❰ Wheelchair-Accessible Trails
Natural Bridge and the Rogue Gorge, **page 347.**
OC&E Woods Line Linear State Park, **page 365.**

The Cascade Mountains, extending from British

Columbia to California, make their breathtaking sweep straight through the center of the state and are home to a series of fantastic volcanic peaks and dense, old-growth forests. Here you can hike along mountain rivers, visit fire watchtowers, or climb into alpine meadows lush with summer flowers. Reach some of the highest elevations in Oregon, including a non-technical – but difficult – climb of South Sister, Oregon's third-highest peak. Don't forget Crater Lake National Park, one of the prides of the state.

To the southwest, the Siskiyou Mountains feel more like California: Open forests of ponderosa pine, a rugged granite landscape, and whitewater stretches of the Rogue River lie in an entirely different and drier climate. In this billions-of-years-old landscape, you'll find rattlesnakes, mountain lions, and the California pitcher plant, a bug-devouring oddity found in these mountains.

In these two zones, you'll find the majority of Oregon's claim to the Pacific Crest Trail. This well-maintained path traverses the edge of the Siskiyou Mountains before cutting over to the Cascades, where it passes through a bevy of wilderness areas and the national park, and along innumerable streams and lakes. Many of the trails in this section use the PCT as an entry point or a destination in and of itself. And if you like mountains, the PCT brushes by all the biggies: Mount Jefferson, Three Fingered Jack, Mount Washington, the Three Sisters, Diamond Peak, Mount Thielsen, and Mount McLoughlin. You'll skirt Crater Lake, the Sky Lakes, Odell Lake, and Waldo Lake.

Just remember that weather is finicky in these mountains. Snow typically buries many of the trails from late November until as late as July, at least for high elevations. But there is plenty of surrounding area to explore, and year-round trails abound in the foothills both east and west of the divide.

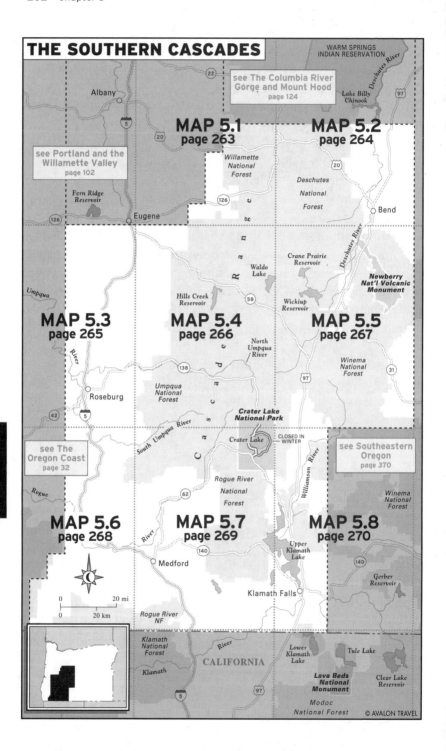

THE SOUTHERN CASCADES

see The Columbia River Gorge and Mount Hood
page 124

WARM SPRINGS
INDIAN RESERVATION

Deschutes River

Lake Billy
Chinook

Albany

MAP 5.1
page 263

MAP 5.2
page 264

see Portland and the
Willamette Valley
page 102

Willamette
National
Forest

Deschutes
National
Forest

Fern Ridge
Reservoir

Bend

Eugene

Umpqua

Crane Prairie
Reservoir

Waldo
Lake

**Newberry
Nat'l Volcanic
Monument**

Hills Creek
Reservoir

Wickiup
Reservoir

MAP 5.3
page 265

MAP 5.4
page 266

MAP 5.5
page 267

River

North
Umpqua
River

Winema
National
Forest

Roseburg

Umpqua
National
Forest

**Crater Lake
National Park**

see The
Oregon Coast
page 32

South Umpqua River

Crater Lake

CLOSED IN
WINTER

see Southeastern
Oregon
page 370

Rogue

Williamson River

Winema
National
Forest

MAP 5.6
page 268

Rogue River
National
Forest

MAP 5.7
page 269

MAP 5.8
page 270

River

Medford

Upper
Klamath
Lake

Gerber
Reservoir

0   20 mi

0   20 km

Klamath Falls

Rogue River
NF

Klamath
National
Forest

River

CALIFORNIA

Lower
Klamath
Lake

Tule Lake

Klamath

Clear Lake
Reservoir

**Lava Beds
National
Monument**

Modoc
National Forest

© AVALON TRAVEL

Map 5.1

Hikes 1-19
Pages 271-282

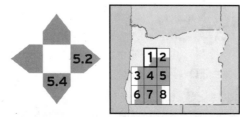

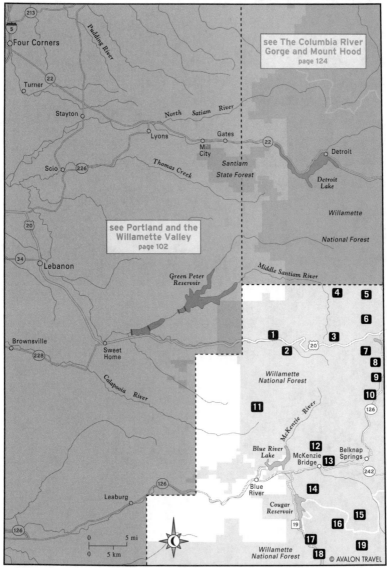

Map 5.2

Hikes 20-47
Pages 282-301

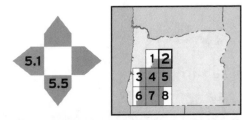

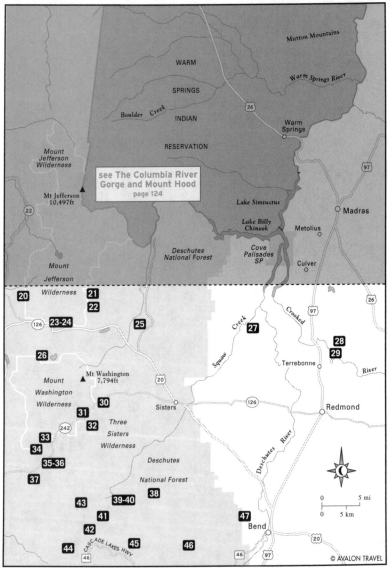

Map 5.3

Hike 48
Page 301

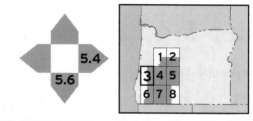

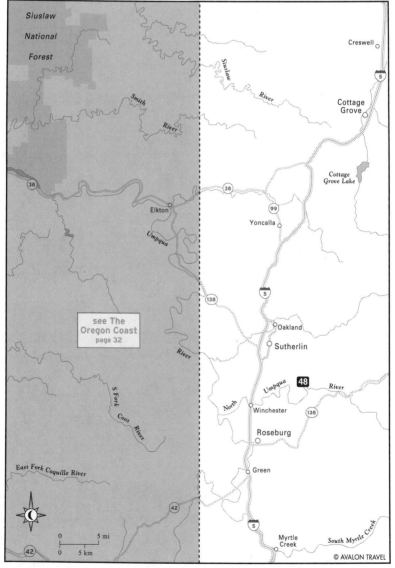

Map 5.4

Hikes 49-93
Pages 302-330

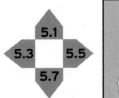

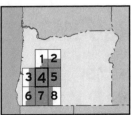

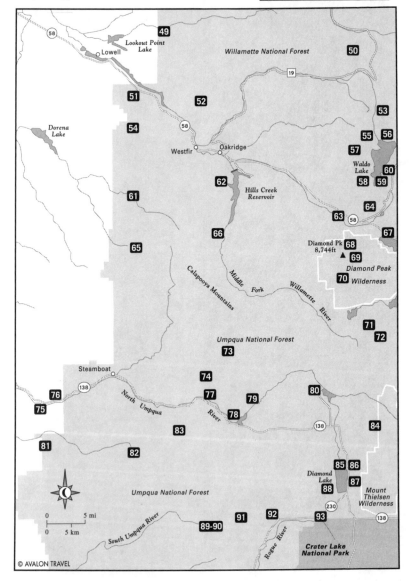

Map 5.5

Hikes 94-108
Pages 331-340

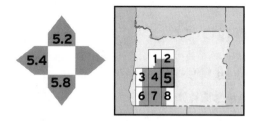

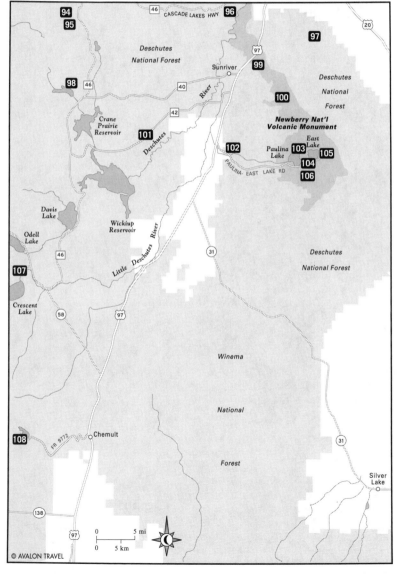

Map 5.6

Hikes 109-119
Pages 340-346

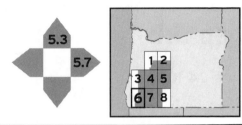

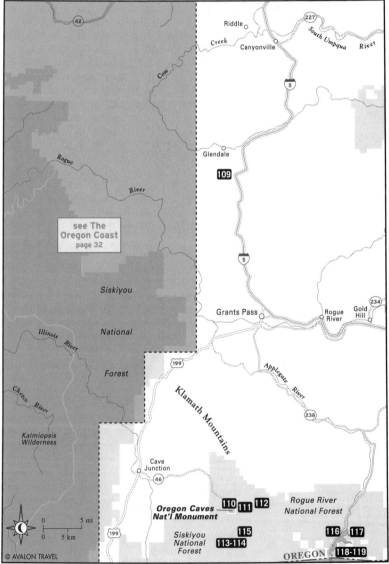

Map 5.7

Hikes 120-156
Pages 346-364

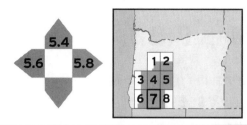

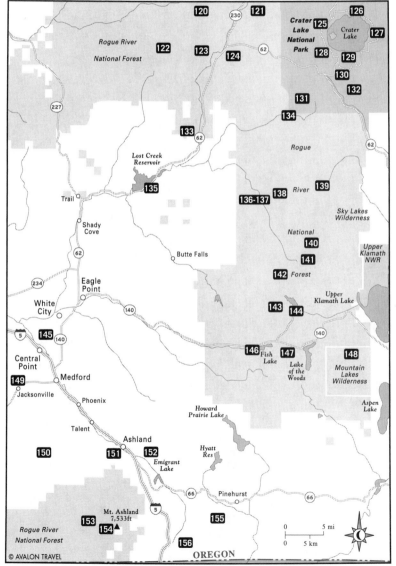

Map 5.8

Hikes 157-158
Pages 365-366

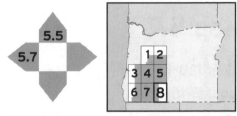

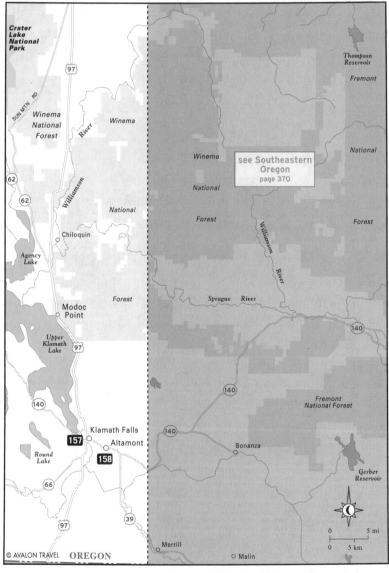

1 ROOSTER ROCK

4.2-6.6 mi/1.5-4.0 hr

west of Santiam Pass in Menagerie Wilderness

Map 5.1, page 263

This towering pillar of basalt and andesite is a popular destination for rock climbers, as are many of the spires in the Menagerie Wilderness: Rabbit Ears, Turkey Monster, Chicken Rock, The Eggs, The Siamese Twins, and the Royal Arch, to name a few. Each is a challenge in its own right. If you're not the mountain-climbing type but want to see what all the fuss is about, there are two ways in.

The shorter but harsher route is up the Rooster Rock Trailhead, climbing 1.6 miles up 1,500 feet to the junction with the Trout Creek Trail. From here, go right up 0.5 mile to a viewpoint near Rooster Rock.

The longer, but somewhat more gradual way, is from the Trout Creek Trailhead, climbing 1,600 feet over a distance of 2.8 miles to the Rooster Rock Trail, heading to the left and uphill the remaining 0.5 mile.

User Groups: Hikers and dogs. No horses or mountain bikes allowed. No wheelchair facilities.

Permits: A free self-issue Wilderness Permit is required and is available at both trailheads. Parking and access are free at the Rooster Rock Trailhead. A federal Northwest Forest Pass is required to park at the Trout Creek Trailhead; the cost is $5 a day or $30 for an annual pass. You can buy a day pass at the trailhead, at ranger stations, or through private vendors.

Maps: For a map of the Willamette National Forest and the Mount Jefferson Wilderness, contact Willamette National Forest Headquarters, 3106 Pierce Parkway, Suite D, Springfield, OR, 97477, 541/225-6300. For a topographic map, ask the USGS for Upper Soda.

Directions: From Sweet Home, go east on U.S. 20 for 21 miles just past Trout Creek Campground near milepost 49. Park at a pullout on the north side of the highway. The Rooster Rock Trailhead is 2.6 miles farther east on U.S. 20 at a pullout.

Contact: Willamette National Forest, Sweet Home Ranger District, 4431 Highway 20, Sweet Home, OR, 97386, 541/367-5168.

2 SANTIAM WAGON ROAD

4.8 mi round-trip or 19.5 mi one-way/2.5 hr-2 days

west of Santiam Pass in Willamette National Forest

Map 5.1, page 263

This stretch of the historic Santiam Wagon Road is famous not only for its history of travelers between the cattle farms of the Willamette Valley and the mining towns of Eastern Oregon, but also for a 1905 Trans-continental automobile race in which the new-fangled horseless carriages descended the steep mountains with trees tied to the autos to slow their descent of Sevenmile Hill. Some sections of the wagon trail are remarkably well preserved, while others become a jumble of logging roads. The trail can be taken in a series of segments, each with its own flavor. The entire stretch extends from the westernmost trailhead on U.S. 20 across from the Mountain House Restaurant to the easternmost trailhead at Fish Lake near the Santiam Pass, 19.5 miles in all.

The easiest and most historic route is from the trailhead across from the Mountain House Restaurant to House Rock, a 4.8-mile round-trip hike to a boulder that dwarfs everything around it and that served as shelter for entire pioneer families. Hike in 2.0 miles from Highway 20 along the most intact section of the old wagon road to the beginning of the loop, then head in either direction 0.8 mile around House Rock, located in the House Rock Campground.

To extend this segment to an 11.8-mile round-trip, continue from the loop on the Santiam Wagon Road to a viewpoint knoll atop Sevenmile Hill overlooking a canyon. Continue from the House Rock Campground 0.8 mile east to a gate, following the old wagon route. Go 0.3 mile to the left on Road 2044, cross the river, then turn right at the next gate to continue 2.3 mile to the knoll. If you continue one more mile, you will arrive at the Sevenmile Trailhead, where there are dispersed campsites. Otherwise, return as you came, bypassing the loop by staying to the left as you near the campground.

You could also start the hike by parking at the House Rock Campground, walking the 0.8-mile loop around House Rock and continuing on to the Sevenmile Knoll 3.4 miles past the loop, returning as you came.

Of course, you could continue further. The 4.2-mile stretch between Sevenmile Trailhead and Tombstone Pass has views to Iron Mountain, but the next 6.5-mile segment between Tombstone Pass and Hackleman Creek Road is not as interesting, as it follows newer roads that supplanted the original wagon road. The final 3.6-mile segment, however, follows an intact portion of the road to the trail's end at Fish Lake, where you'll find a historic guard station; note that parking is not allowed at Fish Lake, so park at the Hackleman Creek Road trailhead instead.

User Groups: Hikers, dogs, and horses. Mountain bikes allowed on some segments. No wheelchair facilities.

Permits: Permits are not required. Parking and access are free at the trailhead across from Mountain House Restaurant, House Rock Campground, and Hackleman Creek Road. A federal Northwest Forest Pass is required to park at the Sevenmile Trailhead; the cost is $5 a day or $30 for an annual pass. You can buy a day pass at the trailhead, at ranger stations, or through private vendors.

Maps: For a map of the Willamette National Forest and the Mount Jefferson Wilderness, contact Willamette National Forest Headquarters, 3106 Pierce Parkway, Suite D, Springfield, OR, 97477, 541/225-6300. For a topographic map, ask the USGS for Harter Mountain and Echo Mountain.

Directions: To begin the hike at Mountain House Restaurant, drive east from Sweet Home about 23 miles to the old restaurant between mileposts 52 and 53, going just beyond it to a parking area by a green gate on the south shoulder. To begin at House Rock Campground, drive east of Sweet Home 25 miles on U.S. 20 and turn right at a sign for House Rock Campground for 0.2 mile, then right again at the campground entrance for 0.2 mile to the trailhead. To reach the Sevenmile Trailhead, drive east of Sweet Home about 30.3 miles on U.S. 20 and turn right on spur Road 024, driving to the trailhead at road's end. The easternmost trailhead is on Hackleman Creek Road 2672, about 40 miles east of Sweet Home on U.S. 20; turn right onto Road 2672 and follow signs to the trailhead on the left.

Contact: Willamette National Forest, Sweet Home Ranger District, 4431 Highway 20, Sweet Home, OR, 97386, 541/367-5168.

❸ IRON MOUNTAIN
3.4 mi/1.5 hr 👫2 ⛰9

west of Santiam Pass in Willamette National Forest

Map 5.1, page 263

Despite its sturdy name, Iron Mountain is most famous for its wildflowers. With more than 300 species of flowering plants—including steer's head, scarlet gilia, glacier lilies, and blue flax—this peak is a designated Special Interest Area. Much of the trail follows Cone Peak, which will amaze and delight you with its array of summer colors. Bring a camera. You can visit the staffed lookout tower atop Iron Mountain's dangerous peaks. Be careful! One staffer fell to his death, and the entire tower blew off once in a winter storm. Stay away from the edge and keep a close eye on kids and dogs.

For the full loop, start at the Tombstone Pass Trailhead and go toward the nature trail and follow this 0.6 mile, crossing the highway. From here, the trail climbs 800 feet through stands of rare Alaska cedar into the meadows for 1.8 miles. From the meadows, you'll see Iron Mountain. Continue 1.5 miles along the trail to a junction. Go left and uphill, a steep 650-foot climb in 0.7 mile to the watchtower. To return, go back down Iron Mountain and take two lefts, then continue down one mile, crossing the highway again, to the Santiam Wagon Road Trail, going left 0.3 mile back to the Tombstone lot.

User Groups: Hikers and dogs. No horses or mountain bikes allowed. No wheelchair facilities.

Permits: Permits are not required. A federal Northwest Forest Pass is required to park here; the cost is $5 a day or $30 for an annual pass. You can buy a day pass at the trailhead, at ranger stations, or through private vendors.

Maps: You can purchase a Middle Santiam Wilderness Map from Geo-Graphics. For a map of the Willamette National Forest and the Mount Jefferson Wilderness, contact Willamette National Forest Headquarters, 3106 Pierce Parkway, Suite D, Springfield, OR, 97477, 541/225-6300. For a topographic map, ask the USGS for Harter Mountain.

Directions: Drive east of Sweet Home 36 miles on U.S. 20, parking at Tombstone Pass between mileposts 63 and 64.

Contact: Willamette National Forest, Sweet Home Ranger District, 4431 Highway 20, Sweet Home, OR, 97386, 541/367-5168.

◄ MIDDLE SANTIAM RIVER
13.0 mi/7.0 hr   🚶3 ⛰7

northwest of Santiam Pass in Willamette National Forest

Map 5.1, page 263

Virtually hidden in the Cascade foothills beyond a maze of logging roads, the Middle Santiam Wilderness encompasses everything great about the Oregon Cascades. Of course, negotiating this area of rain-gorged creeks means several crossings without bridges. In low water, you may be able to cross on logs. If no logs are there to help, wading shoes

will help. Some of the road that skirts this wilderness area was utterly demolished in a series of landslides, extending your journey somewhat. Nevertheless, you could take this trail as far as you'd like: the Shedd Camp Shelter, Pyramid Creek, or distant Donaca Lake all make excellent destinations, depending on your endurance.

From the Chimney Peak Trailhead, it's an easy 0.7 mile to the shake-roofed shelter and the Middle Santiam River, with 20-foot Shelter Falls. From here you'll have to cross the river and continue 0.3 mile to a junction with the South Pyramid Creek Trail. Stay left another two miles to another crossing on Pyramid Creek. If you're going on, continue 0.8 mile and cross Road 2041, then head into the wilderness area for 2.7 miles to Donaca Lake, which was dammed long ago by a massive landslide—look for boulders and snags of dead trees in the lake. Return as you came.

User Groups: Hikers, dogs, and horses. No mountain bikes allowed. No wheelchair facilities.

Permits: A free self-issue Wilderness Permit is required and is available at the trailhead. Parking and access are free.

Maps: You can purchase a Middle Santiam Wilderness Map from Geo-Graphics. For a map of the Willamette National Forest and the Mount Jefferson Wilderness, contact Willamette National Forest Headquarters, 3106 Pierce Parkway, Suite D, Springfield, OR, 97477, 541/225-6300. For a topographic map, ask the USGS for Harter Mountain.

Directions: From Sweet Home, drive 24 miles east on U.S. 20. Just beyond milepost 52, turn left on Soda Fork Road 2041 and stay on this road for eight miles to a six-way junction. Go straight, staying on Road 2041 for another 4.5 miles to a three-way fork. Take the middle Road 646 for 0.6 mile to its end at a lot for the Chimney Peak Trail.

Contact: Willamette National Forest, Sweet Home Ranger District, 4431 Highway 20, Sweet Home, OR, 97386, 541/367-5168.

5 THE PYRAMIDS

4.0 mi/2.0 hr   🏃1 ⛰8

northwest of Santiam Pass in Willamette National Forest

Map 5.1, page 263

Why go to Egypt when you can just come visit Oregon's version of the pyramids? These glaciated peaks in the Old Cascades, a mountain range far younger than the bigger, snow-clad peaks, provide a view stretching from Mount Hood in the north to Diamond Peak in the south. The climb to Middle Pyramid crosses terrain ranging from woodland slopes to wildflower meadows. Vanilla leaf, bleeding hearts, columbine, and the tall white lily stalks of hellebore keep you company along the way.

From the trailhead, cross a creek to the Old Cascades Crest Trail and go right uphill for 1.8 miles, steeply climbing switchbacks near the end. At a saddle, head uphill on a fainter path 0.2 mile to the 5,618-foot peak and the site of an old watchtower. Straddled between North and South Pyramid, you'll have views of the whole countryside.

User Groups: Hikers and dogs. No horses or mountain bikes allowed. No wheelchair facilities.

Permits: Permits are not required. Parking and access are free.

Maps: For a map of the Willamette National Forest and the Mount Jefferson Wilderness, contact Willamette National Forest Headquarters, 3106 Pierce Parkway, Suite D, Springfield, OR, 97477, 541/225-6300. For a topographic map, ask the USGS for Coffin Mountain.

Directions: From Salem, drive 77 miles east on OR 22. Between mileposts 76 and 77, go right on Lava Lake Meadow Road 2067 and follow this route 1.9 miles. Cross Park Creek and turn right, following a sign for the Pyramids Trail. Follow Road 560 for 3.5 miles to its end at a parking lot.

Contact: Willamette National Forest, Sweet Home Ranger District, 4431 Highway 20, Sweet Home, OR, 97386, 541/367-5168.

6 CRESCENT MOUNTAIN

8.6 mi/4.5 hr   🏃3 ⛰9

west of Santiam Pass in Willamette National Forest

Map 5.1, page 263

This aptly named mountain is just what it says it is: an enormous crescent-shaped bowl rimmed by a mighty peak, cradling little Crescent Lake and its outlet creek. The views from up here encompass Three-Fingered Jack, Mount Washington, and the Three Sisters. To get to the peak, and the last remnants of a watchtower, you'll cross a broad meadow on the Old Cascades Crest Trail to the 5,750-foot summit.

Follow the Old Cascades Crest Trail 1.1 miles to a crossing of Maude Creek then begin to climb for the next 3.2 miles to Crescent Mountain's high point along a ridge of subalpine fir and mountain hemlock.

User Groups: Hikers, dogs, and horses. No mountain bikes allowed. No wheelchair facilities.

Permits: Permits are not required. Parking and access are free.

Maps: For a map of the Willamette National Forest and the Mount Jefferson Wilderness, contact Willamette National Forest Headquarters, 3106 Pierce Parkway, Suite D, Springfield, OR, 97477, 541/225-6300. For a topographic map, ask the USGS for Echo Mountain.

Directions: Drive east of Sweet Home 43 miles on U.S. 20. Near milepost 71, turn left on Lava Lake Road for one mile, then left on Road 508 for 0.7 mile to a trailhead lot.

Contact: Willamette National Forest, Sweet Home Ranger District, 4431 Highway 20, Sweet Home, OR, 97386, 541/367-5168.

7 BROWDER RIDGE

8.4 mi/5.0 hr   🏃3 ⛰9

west of Santiam Pass in Willamette National Forest

Map 5.1, page 263

Amazing views, mountain wildflower meadows, old-growth forests… why don't people come here more often? Why ask? This summit-topping trail commands views of the Southern Cascade peaks from Jefferson to the Three Sisters, and if you're lucky you might not see another soul.

From the Gate Creek Trailhead, climb 3.1 miles up nearly 1,600 feet to a junction. Go right here, up another 0.9 mile and 250 feet along Browder Ridge. A cross-country summit is possible by climbing the last 0.2 mile the remaining 300 feet to a summit.

User Groups: Hikers, dogs, and horses. No mountain bikes allowed. No wheelchair facilities.

Permits: Permits are not required. Parking and access are free.

Maps: For a map of the Willamette National Forest and the Mount Jefferson Wilderness, contact Willamette National Forest Headquarters, 3106 Pierce Parkway, Suite D, Springfield, OR, 97477, 541/225-6300. For a topographic map, ask the USGS for Tamolitch Falls.

Directions: Drive east of Sweet Home 41 miles on U.S. 20. Near milepost 68, go south on Hackelman Creek Road for 1.7 miles, then turn right on Road 1598 for 2.8 miles to the trailhead.

Contact: Willamette National Forest, Sweet Home Ranger District, 4431 Highway 20, Sweet Home, OR, 97386, 541/367-5168.

8 CLEAR LAKE

5.4 mi/2.5 hr   🏃1 ⛰8

southwest of Santiam Pass in Willamette National Forest

Map 5.1, page 263

The source of the wild McKenzie River is the cold Clear Lake, fed by a giant spring emerging from an ancient lava flow. The lake itself was once a forest: the lava flow dammed an ancient river and flooded this tree-filled hollow, creating a kind of ghost forest of preserved white snags beneath the calm water. This is also the topmost stretch of the McKenzie River Trail, but you can do it in a loop around the lake. You'll pass picturesque views of the lake and the mountains, and be able to spot a variety of wildflowers in the forest.

Start at the Clear Lake Resort, heading north on the trail. The first 1.5 miles curves around Ikenick Creek and meets with the sometimes dry Fish Lake Creek. In another 0.5 mile you'll come to the massive springs that feed the lake. The next 2.2 miles crosses the lava flows and passes the campground before reaching a junction. To the left, the McKenzie River Trail heads to the waterfalls, but to continue the loop go right the last 1.2 miles to the lot, watching for views to the Three Sisters and Mount Washington.

User Groups: Hikers, dogs, and bicycles. No horses allowed. No wheelchair facilities.

Permits: Permits are not required. Parking and access are free.

Maps: For a map of the Willamette National Forest, contact Willamette National Forest Headquarters, 3106 Pierce Parkway, Suite D, Springfield, OR, 97477, 541/225-6300. For a topographic map, ask the USGS for Tamolitch Falls.

Directions: Drive east on OR 126 from McKenzie Bridge 20 miles. Between mileposts 3 and 4, turn east at the Clear Lake Resort sign, driving the paved loop road 0.4 mile to the parking lot.

Contact: Willamette National Forest, McKenzie River Ranger District, 57600 McKenzie Highway, McKenzie Bridge, OR, 97413, 541/822-3381.

9 SAHALIE AND KOOSAH FALLS
2.6 mi/1.0 hr   👫1 ⛰9

south of Clear Lake on the McKenzie River

Map 5.1, page 263   **BEST (**

In the Chinook language, a Native American trade jargon that gives many local places their colorful names, both "Sahalie" and "Koosah" mean sky or heaven—which makes these two dramatic waterfalls aptly named, as they are without a doubt two of the most beautiful waterfalls in all of Oregon. What formed them is a series of lava flows from the nearby Cascades, over which the river plunges twice before it slows behind the dam at the Carmen Reservoir. The convenient pullout and viewpoint at Sahalie Falls offers access to an excellent loop around both falls, so you can see them from opposite sides of the river. You'll also see the forest, lava outcrops, and spring trilliums and calypso orchids along the way.

From the lot, walk down to the viewpoint of double-plumed Sahalie Falls, then head downstream to the left, descending easily to sheer Koosah Falls in 0.5 mile. Keep going another 0.4 mile to the road, cross the bridge to the right, and head to the right again on the spur trail, arriving at the junction with the McKenzie River Trail. The next 1.3 miles passes the waterfalls again before arriving at an upper footbridge. Go right over the bridge, then right again for the 0.4-mile return to the pullout.

User Groups: Hikers, dogs, and bicycles. No horses allowed. There is wheelchair access to the overlook at Sahalie Falls.

Permits: Permits are not required. Parking and access are free.

Maps: For a map of the Willamette National Forest, contact Willamette National Forest

Koosah Falls on the McKenzie River

Headquarters, 3106 Pierce Parkway, Suite D, Springfield, OR, 97477, 541/225-6300. For a topographic map, ask the USGS for Tamolitch Falls.

Directions: Drive 19 miles east of McKenzie Bridge on OR 126. Near milepost 5, go left into the Sahalie Falls Overlook parking area.

Contact: Willamette National Forest, McKenzie River Ranger District, 57600 McKenzie Highway, McKenzie Bridge, OR, 97413, 541/822-3381.

10 TAMOLITCH POOL
4.2 mi/2.0 hr   👫1 ⛰8

north of McKenzie Bridge on the McKenzie River

Map 5.1, page 263

The upper reaches of the McKenzie River were shaped by a series of 6,000-year-old lava flows that poured down from the area around Mount

Washington, shifting, damming, and even covering the river. In the stretch above Tamolitch Pool—a Chinook word for "bucket"—the McKenzie River actually runs underground for three miles, ending at this strangely empty waterfall. At the base of the seeming invisible falls, a pool composed of colors simply unimaginable lies still as the sky, a haunting blue and emerald green. At the edge of this silent pool, the river roars to life, cascading on its long journey from the mountains. A beautiful walk in a rugged canyon, this is an excellent hike for kids you want to impress.

From the Trail Bridge Reservoir road 655, head north on the McKenzie River Trail for 2.1 miles to reach the viewpoint of Tamolitch Pool, then return as you came.

User Groups: Hikers, dogs, and bicycles. No horses allowed. No wheelchair facilities.

Permits: Permits are not required. Parking and access are free.

Maps: For a map of the Willamette National Forest, contact Willamette National Forest Headquarters, 3106 Pierce Parkway, Suite D, Springfield, OR, 97477, 541/225-6300. For a topographic map, ask the USGS for Tamolitch Falls.

Directions: Drive 14 miles east of McKenzie Bridge on OR 126 to Trailbridge Reservoir, and turn left at a sign for the Trailbridge Campground. Cross the bridge and turn right on Road 655. After 0.3 mile, park at a trailhead sign.

Contact: Willamette National Forest, McKenzie River Ranger District, 57600 McKenzie Highway, McKenzie Bridge, OR, 97413, 541/822-3381.

Valley, even a close-up view of one of Tidbits' two peaks. Old-growth forests line the trail, as do flowering rhododendrons and beargrass, a type of lily, and big Cascade lilies. On top, the trail passes the ruins of an old Forest Service shelter and the remains of a stairway that you won't need to get to the top.

From the trailhead, the Tidbits Mountain Trail climbs steadily 1.3 miles to a saddle with both the shelter ruins and a trail junction. Continue to the left 0.5 mile, nearly circling Tidbits Mountain, to a four-way junction. Go left and climb 0.2 mile to the summit. You can explore around the peak a bit, too.

User Groups: Hikers, dogs, horses, and mountain bikes. No wheelchair facilities.

Permits: Permits are not required. Parking and access are free.

Maps: For a map of the Willamette National Forest, contact Willamette National Forest Headquarters, 3106 Pierce Parkway, Suite D, Springfield, OR, 97477, 541/225-6300. For a topographic map, ask the USGS for Tidbits Mountain.

Directions: From Springfield, drive 44 miles east on OR 126, passing Blue River. Near milepost 44, turn left onto Road 15, following signs for Blue River Reservoir and going 4.8 miles. At pavement's end, continue on Road 1509 for 8 miles, passing a water tank, then go left on steep Road 877 for 0.2 mile to a left-hand spur parking area.

Contact: Willamette National Forest, McKenzie River Ranger District, 57600 McKenzie Highway, McKenzie Bridge, OR, 97413, 541/822-3381.

11 TIDBITS MOUNTAIN
4.0 mi/2.0 hr   👣2 ⛰8

north of Blue River in Willamette National Forest

Map 5.1, page 263

You couldn't ask much more of a hike: views to the snow-capped peaks of the Three Sisters and all the way down to the Willamette

12 LOOKOUT CREEK OLD-GROWTH TRAIL
7.0 mi/3.5 hr   👣2 ⛰6

north of McKenzie Bridge in Willamette National Forest

Map 5.1, page 263   BEST (

The H. J. Andrews Experimental Forest in the Blue River drainage is part of an ecological research program of Oregon State University and the National Science Foundation. This rugged trail enters a forest of old-growth Douglas fir, red cedar, and Pacific yew. Feel blessed that Oregon has preserved places like this for future generations; indeed, this is the whole purpose of the Experimental Forest.

Cross Lookout Creek and head into the woods. If you're looking for a turnaround point, a 3,000-foot rock pinnacle marks the 1.6-mile mark. Otherwise, it's another 1.9 miles to the end of the trail at an upper trailhead on the 1506 road.

User Groups: Hikers and dogs. No horses or mountain bikes allowed. No wheelchair access.

Permits: Permits are not required. Parking and access are free.

Maps: For a map of the Willamette National Forest, contact Willamette National Forest Headquarters, 3106 Pierce Parkway, Suite D, Springfield, OR, 97477, 541/225-6300. For a topographic map, ask the USGS for Tamolitch Falls.

Directions: From Eugene, drive 40 miles east on OR 126 to Blue River, then go beyond town three miles to FS Road 15. Turn left and go four miles to Lookout Creek Road 1506, turning right and driving seven miles to the parking area.

Contact: Willamette National Forest, McKenzie River Ranger District, 57600 McKenzie Highway, McKenzie Bridge, OR, 97413, 541/822-3381.

13 MCKENZIE RIVER NATIONAL RECREATION TRAIL

26.5 mi one-way/2 days   🏃3 ⛰9

between Clear Lake and McKenzie Bridge in Willamette National Forest

Map 5.1, page 263

Backpackers rejoice! This amazing stretch of the Wild and Scenic McKenzie River is brimming with not only day trips, but excellent opportunities for extended hikes. With maintained campgrounds along the way—and more primitive spots, if you can find them—it's tempting to do the whole trail. Along the way you'll find white-water rapids, hot springs, waterfalls, and lava fields culminating in the river's source at lovely Clear Lake. Access points abound along the way (see *Clear Lake, Sahalie and Koosah Falls,* and *Tamolitch Pool* listings in this chapter) and you're never too far from the road, though once you set out you'll find yourself worlds away.

Some basic mileage numbers: From the start of the trail to the McKenzie Ranger Station, a route paralleling the highway, is one mile. From the Ranger Station to Belknap Hot Springs, a private resort where you can pay to swim, is 3.9 miles, with Paradise Campground in-between. From Belknap to the natural hot springs at Deer Creek is five miles; you'll cross the river on a road and arrive at Deer Creek Road. From Deer Creek to the campground at Trail Bridge Reservoir is 3.3 miles. From Trail Bridge to Tamolitch Pool is 3.9 miles. From Tamolitch to Carmen Reservoir is 3.4 miles (along this stretch the river runs underground). From Carmen to the crossing of Highway 126, passing both Sahalie and Koosah Falls is two miles. From the highway to the upper trailhead, passing Clear Lake and Coldwater Cover Campground is four miles.

User Groups: Hikers, dogs, and bicycles. No horses allowed. No wheelchair facilities.

Permits: Permits are not required. Parking and access are free.

Maps: For a map of the Willamette National Forest, contact Willamette National Forest Headquarters, 3106 Pierce Parkway, Suite D, Springfield, OR, 97477, 541/225-6300. For a topographic map, ask the USGS for Tamolitch Falls.

Directions: To get to the lower trailhead at McKenzie Ranger Station, go 2.2 miles east of McKenzie Bridge on OR 126 and park at the station. To get to the upper trailhead, drive east on OR 126 from McKenzie Bridge about 21 miles, passing the entrance for Clear Lake Resort to the well-marked trailhead on the right.

Contact: Willamette National Forest, McKenzie River Ranger District, 57600 McKenzie Highway, McKenzie Bridge, OR, 97413, 541/822-3381.

14 CASTLE ROCK
2.0-11.4 mi/1.0-6.0 hr

south of Blue River in Willamette National Forest

Map 5.1, page 263

There are two main ways to climb Castle Rock: the easy way and the hard way. It's a matter of both distance and elevation gain, but the end point is the same: an excellent view down to the McKenzie River canyon and east to the Three Sisters. The peak itself, the remnant of a long-extinct volcano, has sheer cliffs at the summit, and you can look down into the peaks of the Douglas fir trees. To try the easy hike, follow the driving directions and head up the trail a mere mile to the summit.

For the difficult hike, you'll start at a lower trailhead. Once on Kings Road, instead of turning onto Road 480, continue 1.3 miles past it to the trailhead on the right. From here, the King Castle Trail sets off four miles, crosses Road 480, continues up 0.7 mile through a clear-cut, then arrives at the upper trailhead, with its remaining mile to the top.

User Groups: Hikers, dogs, horses, and mountain bikes. No wheelchair facilities.

Permits: Permits are not required. Parking and access are free.

Maps: For a map of the Willamette National Forest, contact Willamette National Forest Headquarters, 3106 Pierce Parkway, Suite D, Springfield, OR, 97477, 541/225-6300. For a topographic map, ask the USGS for McKenzie Bridge.

Directions: From Springfield, drive 45 miles east on OR 126 and turn right onto the Aufderheide Road 19. At the next fork in 0.5 mile, stay straight onto Road 410, and in another 0.4 mile go left onto Kings Road 2639 for 0.5

mile. Turn right on Road 480 and continue uphill 5.8 miles to road's end at the upper trailhead.

Contact: Willamette National Forest, McKenzie River Ranger District, 57600 McKenzie Highway, McKenzie Bridge, OR, 97413, 541/822-3381.

15 OLALLIE MOUNTAIN/ OLALLIE RIDGE
7.2-12.2 mi/4.0-6.0 hr

south of McKenzie Bridge in Three Sisters Wilderness

Map 5.1, page 263

When all is said and done, the Olallie Trail stretches 9.7 miles end to end, making this a great option for backpackers (another trailhead is located 6.0 miles away at Horsepasture Saddle; see *Horsepasture Mountain and Olallie Ridge* listing in this chapter). From this trail, you can bushwhack to a hidden lake, find the remains of an old guard station in Olallie Meadows, and climb to one of only two lookouts left in this wilderness, a 14-square-foot cabin with stunning views. Not only that, but the door is usually unlocked, opening it up for backpackers. You'll find the big metal fire locator still there, and the panoramic view is unequalled.

From Pat Saddle Trailhead, enter the Three Sisters Wilderness on the Olallie Trail. In 0.5 mile, cross Mosquito Creek (heading off-trail and upstream 0.2 mile leads to Wolverine Lake, but use your route-finding skills). Continue on the Olallie Trail 1.6 miles to a pass and junction. Head right 1.5 miles and up 700 feet to the lookout for a 7.2 mile round-trip hike, returning as you came.

Other options for extended trips abound. From the lookout tower, return to the Olallie Trail junction. Going right 0.9 mile farther leads to the guard station ruins in Olallie Meadows. In another 0.6 mile past the meadows, a left-hand junction goes 10.2 miles to Horse Lake, and the Bear Flat Trail heads to the right, making for a potential loop around Olallie Mountain by following it 6.9 miles to a junction with the French Pete Creek Trail, then heading right 2.9 mile back to the Pat Saddle Trailhead.

User Groups: Hikers, dogs, and horses. No mountain bikes allowed. No wheelchair facilities.

Permits: A free self-issue Wilderness Permit is required and is available at the trailhead. Parking and access are free.

Maps: A map of the Three Sisters Wilderness is available for purchase from Geo-Graphics. For a map of the Willamette National Forest, contact Willamette National Forest Headquarters, 3106 Pierce Parkway, Suite D, Springfield, OR, 97477, 541/225-6300. For a topographic map, ask the USGS for French Mountain.

Directions: From Springfield, drive 45 miles east on OR 126 and turn right onto the Aufderheide Road 19. At the next fork in 0.5 mile, go right on Road 19 for 10 miles to the French Pete Trailhead on the left. To begin at the top, start at the Pat Saddle Trailhead: From Springfield, drive 45 miles east on OR 126 and turn right onto the Aufderheide Road 19. At the next fork in 0.5 mile, go right on Road 19 for 2.8 miles to the reservoir. Turn left across the Cougar Dam on Road 1993 for 2.6 miles, then fork left and stay on Road 1993 another 11.3 miles to the Pat Saddle Trailhead on the left.

Contact: Willamette National Forest, McKenzie River Ranger District, 57600 McKenzie Highway, McKenzie Bridge, OR, 97413, 541/822-3381.

just before Olallie Mountain. Only the mountain retains the name Horsepasture—named because horseback wilderness rangers once camped here. The camp is long gone, though huckleberries—once harvested by Native Americans in the area—remain. Olallie, in fact, is a Chinook word for "berry."

For views as far as Mount Jefferson and Mount Hood, go left from the trailhead up 1.4 miles to the 5,660-foot summit. This easy hike also offers access to the Olallie Trail, which extends six miles from the Horsepasture Saddle to the Pat Saddle Trailhead.

User Groups: Hikers, dogs, horses, and mountain bikes. No wheelchair facilities.

Permits: Permits are not required. Parking and access are free.

Maps: A map of the Three Sisters Wilderness is available for purchase from Geo-Graphics. For a map of the Willamette National Forest, contact Willamette National Forest Headquarters, 3106 Pierce Parkway, Suite D, Springfield, OR, 97477, 541/225-6300. For a topographic map, ask the USGS for French Mountain.

Directions: From Springfield, drive 50 miles east on OR 126 to McKenzie Bridge. Cross the river and turn right on Horse Creek Road 2638 for 1.7 miles. Turn right on Road 1993 for 8.6 miles and park at the Horsepasture Trailhead on the right.

Contact: Willamette National Forest, McKenzie River Ranger District, 57600 McKenzie Highway, McKenzie Bridge, OR, 97413, 541/822-3381.

16 HORSEPASTURE MOUNTAIN AND OLALLIE RIDGE

2.8 mi/1.0 hr   👥1 ▲8

south of McKenzie Bridge in Willamette National Forest

Map 5.1, page 263

One entry to the Three Sisters Wilderness is Olallie Ridge, which leads up to the boundary

17 FRENCH PETE CREEK

9.8 mi one-way/4.0 hr   👥3 ▲7

south of Cougar Reservoir in Three Sisters Wilderness

Map 5.1, page 263

This lovely mountain creek makes a good day hike and provides entrance to the high country. In 1.7 miles, the French Pete Trail reaches the first ford. The next 1.3 miles runs along the opposite shore to a second ford. Beyond this the trail is not maintained, but runs another 1.8 miles to the five-mile marker. From here, continue another 4.8 miles to the Pat Saddle Trailhead, following Pat Creek rather than French Pete.

User Groups: Hikers, dogs, and horses. No mountain bikes allowed. No wheelchair facilities.

Permits: A free self-issue Wilderness Permit is required and is available at the trailhead. Parking and access are free.

Maps: A map of the Three Sisters Wilderness is available for purchase from Geo-Graphics. For a map of the Willamette National Forest, contact Willamette National Forest Headquarters, 3106 Pierce Parkway, Suite D, Springfield, OR, 97477, 541/225-6300. For a topographic map, ask the USGS for Cougar Reservoir.

Directions: From Springfield, drive 45 miles east on OR 126 and turn right onto the Aufderheide Road 19. At the next fork in 0.5 mile, go right on Road 19 for 10 miles to the French Pete Trailhead on the left.

Contact: Willamette National Forest, McKenzie River Ranger District, 57600 McKenzie Highway, McKenzie Bridge, OR, 97413, 541/822-3381.

🔟 REBEL ROCK

12.3 mi/7.0 hr   🥾4 ⛰️8

south of Cougar Reservoir in Three Sisters Wilderness

Map 5.1, page 263

One of two lookouts left in the Three Sisters Wilderness (the other is on Olallie Mountain), Rebel Rock Lookout is perched on a 5,000-foot promontory overlooking Mount Bachelor. You won't spot this from the wooded trail, however, so you'll have to be alert for its spur trail. This loop as a whole is a great entrance to the Three Sisters country, with a trail veering off at Rebel Rock (which is not

where the tower is, actually) into the deeper wilderness. This loop, though, is nothing to sneeze at: it will require some fortitude, as it travels more than 12 miles and climbs 3,300 feet along the way.

Start on the Rebel Creek Trail to the left at the trailhead, crossing two bridges and a true old-growth forest in the first 1.1 miles. The next 4.6 miles climbs away from the creek and up the canyon slope and into hemlock woods to a junction. Go right on the Rebel Rock Trail for 1.8 miles, watching to the left for the pillar of Rebel Rock. Watch for four rock cairns on the left and a faint path; follow this a short distance to the lookout. Continue on the main trail 0.5 mile to a viewpoint of the Three Sisters and Mount Jefferson. The trail descends to a meadow and continues the remaining 4.3 miles following Trail Creek back to the trailhead.

User Groups: Hikers, dogs, and horses. No mountain bikes allowed. No wheelchair facilities.

Permits: A free self-issue Wilderness Permit is required and is available at the trailhead. Parking and access are free.

Maps: A map of the Three Sisters Wilderness is available for purchase from Geo-Graphics. For a map of the Willamette National Forest, contact Willamette National Forest Headquarters, 3106 Pierce Parkway, Suite D, Springfield, OR, 97477, 541/225-6300. For a topographic map, ask the USGS for Chucksney Mountain and Grasshopper Mountain.

Directions: From Springfield, drive 45 miles east on OR 126 and turn right onto the Aufderheide Road 19. At the next fork in 0.5 mile, go right on Road 19 for 13 miles to the Rebel Creek Trailhead on the left.

Contact: Willamette National Forest, McKenzie River Ranger District, 57600 McKenzie Highway, McKenzie Bridge, OR, 97413, 541/822-3381.

19 LOWDER MOUNTAIN

5.6 mi/3.0 hr   🚶2 ⛰8

south of McKenzie Bridge in Three Sisters
Wilderness

Map 5.1, page 263

From the summit of Lowder Mountain, you
will see mountains from the Three Sisters to
Mount Hood. You can camp on the plains
atop the peak, with its sheer drop over the
cliffs down to inaccessible Karl and Ruth
Lakes, nearly 2,000 feet below. If you choose
to camp here, be sure to bring enough water.

From the trailhead, head to the left on the
Lowder Mountain Trail (the right-hand trail
goes to a quaking aspen swamp) and go uphill,
passing through three view-laden meadows in
the first two miles. At a junction, go left and
climb steeply up a series of switchbacks for 0.5
mile. When you reach the plain, go another
0.3 mile, almost to the forest, then turn uphill
0.2 mile to the cliffs.

User Groups: Hikers, dogs, and horses. No
mountain bikes allowed. No wheelchair
facilities.

Permits: A free self-issue Wilderness Permit
is required and is available at the trailhead.
Parking and access are free.

Maps: A map of the Three Sisters Wilderness is
available for purchase from Geo-Graphics. For
a map of the Willamette National Forest, contact Willamette National Forest Headquarters,
3106 Pierce Parkway, Suite D, Springfield,
OR, 97477, 541/225-6300. For a topographic
map, ask the USGS for French Mountain.

Directions: From Springfield, drive 45 miles
east on OR 126 and turn right onto the Aufderheide Road 19. At the next fork in 0.5 mile,
go right on Road 19 for 2.8 miles to the reservoir. Turn left across the Cougar Dam on
Road 1993 for 2.6 miles, then fork left and
stay on Road 1993 another 9.2 miles to the
Lowder Mountain Trailhead on the right.

Contact: Willamette National Forest, McK-
enzie River Ranger District, 57600 McKenzie Highway, McKenzie Bridge, OR, 97413,
541/822-3381.

20 DUFFY AND MOWICH LAKES

8.8-11.8 mi/4.5-6.0 hr   🚶2 ⛰8

west of Three Fingered Jack in Mount
Jefferson Wilderness

Map 5.2, page 264

Like all the Cascade Mountain wilderness
areas, Mount Jefferson's flanks are studded
with beautiful mountain lakes of all shapes
and sizes. In 2003, the unfortunate B&B
Complex Fire roared through this area, reducing much of the forest to snags and ash. Don't
let that stop you: This area is still untouched
in places, and the lakes are as cool and clear
as ever. Two lakes lie along this entrance to
backpacking adventures: Duffy Lake, below
the pointed peak of Duffy Butte, and Mowich
Lake, with one side untouched by fire. From
little Alice Lake you can climb Red Butte and
continue on to the Eight Lakes Basin. Or, you
can head to nearby Santiam Lake for a stunning view of Three Fingered Jack.

From the trailhead, follow the Duffy Trail
along the North Santiam River bed up 3.3
miles, staying left at a junction, to Duffy
Lake. From here, continue along Duffy Lake,
keeping to the left 1.1 miles to Mowich Lake,
then another mile to Alice Lake. An obvious
cross-country path climbs 0.5 mile up Red
Butte here. From there, the Blue Lake Trail
continues on to Eight Lakes Basin.

For a look at the alpine meadows around
Santiam Lake, source of the North Santiam
River, start from the outlet of Duffy Lake and
go 0.2 mile to a spur trail on the right, following it one mile to Santiam Lake at the bottom
of Three Fingered Jack's long slope from its
craggy heights.

User Groups: Hikers, dogs, and horses. No
mountain bikes allowed. No wheelchair
facilities.

Permits: A free self-issue Wilderness Permit
is required and is available at the trailhead.
Parking and access are free.

Maps: You can purchase a Mount Jefferson
Wilderness Map from Geo-Graphics. For a

map of the Willamette National Forest and the Mount Jefferson Wilderness, contact Willamette National Forest Headquarters, 3106 Pierce Parkway, Suite D, Springfield, OR, 97477, 541/225-6300. For a topographic map, ask the USGS for Santiam Junction.

Directions: From Salem, drive 76 miles east on OR 22. Near milepost 76, turn east on Big Meadows Road 2267 for three miles to road's end.

Contact: Willamette National Forest, Detroit Ranger District, HC73, Box 320, Mill City, OR, 97360, 503/854-4239.

21 ROCKPILE LAKE
10.8-13.2 mi/4.0-6.0 hr

north of Three Fingered Jack in Mount Jefferson Wilderness

Map 5.2, page 264

The 2003 B&B Complex Fire truly devastated this area, so you'll need to confirm trail conditions before hiking in these parts. Rockpile Lake Trail follows the massive Bear Valley steadily up to the Pacific Crest Trail and little Rockpile Lake, with access in either direction to great views along the Cascade Crest. If trails are in working order, it is possible to do a great loop around Bear Valley, stopping by little Minto Lake along the way.

From the trailhead follow the Rockpile Lake Trail to the right. In 0.3 mile, stay left at a junction, then stay left again in another 2.3 mile. From the second junction, climb steadily for 2.8 miles up 1,000 feet to the Pacific Crest Trail and Rockpile Lake to the right. Return as you came.

If the loop trail is open, and if you'd like to follow some stunning vistas along this high ridge, head south on the PCT for 3.4 miles to Minto Lake on the right. To the left, the Bear Valley Trail descends 4.4 miles into huckleberry groves and past Bear Valley Lake to the trailhead.

User Groups: Hikers, dogs, and horses. No mountain bikes allowed. No wheelchair facilities.

Permits: A free self-issue Wilderness Permit is required and is available at the trailhead. Parking and access are free.

Maps: You can purchase a Mount Jefferson Wilderness Map from Geo-Graphics. For a map of the Deschutes National Forest and the Mount Jefferson Wilderness, contact Deschutes National Forest Headquarters, 1001 SW Emkay Drive, Bend, OR, 97702, 541/383-5300. For a topographic map, ask the USGS for Marion Lake.

Directions: From Sisters, drive 12 miles west on U.S. 20 to about milepost 88. Turn right on Road 12 at a sign for Mount Jefferson Wilderness Trailheads. Drive north 3.7 miles on Road 12 and continue straight on Road 1230 for 1.5 miles, then turn left on Road 1234 for 0.8 mile. Turn right on Road 1235 for 3.9 miles to road's end.

Contact: Deschutes National Forest, Sisters Ranger District, P.O. Box 249, Sisters, OR, 97759, 541/549-7700.

22 CANYON CREEK MEADOWS
7.5 mi/4.0 hr

east of Three Fingered Jack in Mount Jefferson Wilderness

Map 5.2, page 264

For a worthy alpine meadow experience, and to get a look at a glacial-silt lake among an array of wildflowers, the Canyon Creek Meadows is it. By the grace of nature, the meadows were spared by the 2003 fire that decimated other parts of the wilderness, including the area around Jack Lake and the trailhead here. Did I mention you will also be standing beneath the towering crags of Three Fingered Jack? The creek begins in a cirque in the bowl of the mountain, surrounded by gravel walls. This trail, going from burn to forest to meadow to alpine rockfall, even a pitch to a saddle with a view over the mountain range to the south, allows you to visit just about every kind of ecosystem in this range. The meadows, too, are suitable for backpacking.

From Jack Lake, head up the Wasco Lake Trail 0.4 mile to a junction. Here the trail splits into the Canyon Creek Meadows Loop, and the USFS asks that you go to the left first, and return on the opposite loop. So go left 1.7 miles, leaving the burn and reaching the lower meadow. Go left another 1.5 miles, reaching the upper meadow and an alpine wonderland. If you follow the trail to the end, you'll climb a ridge above the meadows, climbing steeply to the saddle on the shoulder of the mountain. When you return, go left at the loop junction. Head 0.9 mile along the creek to a junction. If you'd like to visit Wasco Lake, go left 0.7 mile, watching for the waterfalls off the trail. Then return to this junction and go right 1.5 miles back to Jack Lake.

User Groups: Hikers, dogs, and horses. No mountain bikes allowed. No wheelchair facilities.

Permits: A free self-issue Wilderness Permit is required and is available at the trailhead. A federal Northwest Forest Pass is required to park here; the cost is $5 a day or $30 for an annual pass. You can buy a day pass at the trailhead, at ranger stations, or through private vendors.

Maps: You can purchase a Mount Jefferson Wilderness Map from Geo-Graphics. For a map of the Deschutes National Forest and the Mount Jefferson Wilderness, contact Deschutes National Forest Headquarters, 1001 SW Emkay Drive, Bend, OR, 97702, 541/383-5300. For a topographic map, ask the USGS for Three Fingered Jack.

Directions: From Sisters, drive 12 miles west on U.S. 20 to about milepost 88. Turn right on Road 12 at a sign for Mount Jefferson Wilderness Trailheads. Drive north 3.7 miles on Road 12 and continue straight on Road 1230 for 1.5 miles, then turn left on Road 1234 and going five miles to the trailhead at Jack Lake Campground.

Contact: Deschutes National Forest, Sisters Ranger District, P.O. Box 249, Sisters, OR, 97759, 541/549-7700.

23 PACIFIC CREST TRAIL TO THREE FINGERED JACK

10.5 mi/5.5 hr   🏃3 ⛰8

south of Three Fingered Jack in Mount Jefferson Wilderness

Map 5.2, page 264

Three Fingered Jack is a dark-hued volcanic core that resembles a frightening fortress. It rises abruptly from the surrounding mountains and practically begs rock climbers to try their luck. Most likely, one look will make you lose all nerve. Instead, this Pacific Crest Trail stretch offers a commanding look at this massive peak, and an entrance to the Mount Jefferson Wilderness. The forest was burned here in a 2003 fire, but that opened up the views as this trail follows the ridgeline. From the PCT trailhead, follow the PCT north 5.2 miles to a close-up viewpoint of the mountain. From there, you can return the way you came—or continue on as far as you like.

User Groups: Hikers, dogs, and horses. No mountain bikes allowed. No wheelchair facilities.

Permits: A free self-issue Wilderness Permit is required and is available at the trailhead. A federal Northwest Forest Pass is required to park here; the cost is $5 a day or $30 for an annual pass. You can buy a day pass at the trailhead, at ranger stations, or through private vendors.

Maps: You purchase a Mount Jefferson Wilderness Map from Geo-Graphics. For a map of the Willamette National Forest and the Mount Jefferson Wilderness, contact Willamette National Forest Headquarters, 3106 Pierce Parkway, Suite D, Springfield, OR, 97477, 541/225-6300. For a topographic map, ask the USGS for Three Fingered Jack.

Directions: The trailhead is located 20 miles west of Sisters on U.S. 20 at the Santiam Pass, accessible from either Sisters to the east or Eugene/Springfield/OR 126 or OR 22/Salem to the east.

Contact: Willamette National Forest, Detroit Ranger District, HC73, Box 320, Mill City, OR, 97360, 503/854-4239.

24 BERLEY AND SANTIAM LAKES
10.2 mi/4.5 hr   🏃2 △8

south of Three Fingered Jack in Mount Jefferson Wilderness

Map 5.2, page 264

The original trail to these lakes, which began at the ruins of the abandoned Santiam Lodge, was permanently closed after the 2003 wildfire that decimated this section of the Mount Jefferson Wilderness. There is another way to get to the two rock-rimmed tarns known as the Berley Lakes and to picturesque Santiam Lake at the base of Three Fingered Jack. This trail runs along a section of the Skyline Trail.

From the PCT trailhead on U.S. 20, go north 1.2 miles to a left-hand junction and go left 0.5 mile on this connector trail. Then go right 1.5 miles on the Santiam Lake Trail and watch for an unmarked turnoff to the left heading 0.3 mile to and along the lower and larger Berley Lake; follow this trail to another side trail and find the upper lake. Return to the Santiam Trail and go left another 1.9 miles to a right-hand turnoff for Santiam Lake.

User Groups: Hikers, dogs, and horses. No mountain bikes allowed. No wheelchair facilities.

Permits: A free self-issue Wilderness Permit is required and is available at the trailhead. A federal Northwest Forest Pass is required to park here; the cost is $5 a day or $30 for an annual pass. You can buy a day pass at the trailhead, at ranger stations, or through private vendors.

Maps: You can purchase a Mount Jefferson Wilderness Map from Geo-Graphics. For a map of the Willamette National Forest and the Mount Jefferson Wilderness, contact Willamette National Forest Headquarters, 3106 Pierce Parkway, Suite D, Springfield, OR, 97477, 541/225-6300. For a topographic map, ask the USGS for Santiam Lake.

Directions: The trailhead is located 20 miles west of Sisters on U.S. 20 at the Santiam Pass, accessible from either Sisters to the east or Eugene/Springfield/OR 126 or OR 22/Salem to the east.

Contact: Willamette National Forest, Detroit Ranger District, HC73, Box 320, Mill City, OR, 97360, 503/854-4239.

25 BLACK BUTTE
3.8 mi/2.5 hr   🏃3 △8

north of Sisters in Deschutes National Forest

Map 5.2, page 264

Set aside to the east of the bulk of the Cascades, Black Butte seems an oddball mountain. For one thing, this dominant 6,436-foot butte retains its perfectly symmetrical shape, a huge rounded mound set near peaks far more eroded than its stern face. This has less to do with age than with weather: the peaks to the west create a rainshadow that has largely kept this mountain from being weathered. This makes for a fairly easy climb, which explains why Black Butte hosts one of the few surviving fire watchtowers in the Cascade Mountains, with a view worth a summer spent spotting fires. Atop Black Butte, you can check out the old cupola-style lookout and get a glimpse of the new one. A second lookout built by the Civilian Conservation Corps in 1934 was destroyed in a storm. Beyond the edges of the peak, you'll have an expansive view of the Cascades, Green Ridge, and the Metolius River far below.

The trail is a straightforward lunge for the peak up 1.9 miles of trail that climbs steadily, even steeply at times. Follow it through the ponderosa pine forests onto the open prairies of wildflowers.

User Groups: Hikers, dogs, and horses. No mountain bikes allowed. No wheelchair facilities.

Permits: A federal Northwest Forest Pass is

historic Black Butte lookout

required to park here; the cost is $5 a day or $30 for an annual pass. You can buy a day pass at the trailhead, at ranger stations, or through private vendors.

Maps: For a map of the Deschutes National Forest contact Deschutes National Forest Headquarters, 1001 SW Emkay Drive, Bend, OR, 97702, 541/383-5300. For a topographic map, ask the USGS for Black Butte.

Directions: From Sisters, drive 5.5 miles west on U.S. 20 to Green Ridge Road 11. Turn right and follow this road north 3.8 miles, then turn left on Road 1110, following it 5.1 miles uphill to the parking area at road's end.

Contact: Deschutes National Forest, Sisters Ranger District, P.O. Box 249, Sisters, OR, 97759, 541/549-7700.

26 PATJENS LAKES
6.0 mi/3.0 hr   🥾2 ⛺8

at Big Lake in Mount Washington Wilderness

Map 5.2, page 264   BEST (

Big Lake earns its name and makes for a destination for car campers and, in the winter,

cross-country skiers. For hikers, adventure lies beyond the big lake in the Mount Washington Wilderness, with meadows, ponds, slopes of bracken ferns, and the Patjens Lakes hidden nicely back in Hidden Valley, with its view of Mount Washington's spire. The Patjens Lake Loop Trail follows the shore of Big Lake too, past a beach and towards views of broad and flat-topped Hayrick Butte. For backpackers, this makes a good entry into this little-explored wilderness.

From the trailhead, follow signs for Patjens Lakes, staying right at the first junction and left at the second for 1.8 miles to a saddle. Continue 1.7 miles into the midst of the lakes, the third of four being a perfect place to stop and eat. Continue 1.5 miles through Hidden Valley to a beach on Big Lake, going left along the shore one mile back to the trailhead.

User Groups: Hikers, dogs, and horses. No mountain bikes allowed. No wheelchair facilities.

Permits: A free self-issue Wilderness Permit is required and is available at the trailhead. Parking and access are free.

Maps: For a map of the Willamette National

Forest and the Mount Washington Wilderness, contact Willamette National Forest Headquarters, 3106 Pierce Parkway, Suite D, Springfield, OR, 97477, 541/225-6300. For a topographic map, ask the USGS for Clear Lake.

Directions: Drive U.S. 20 to the Santiam Pass and turn south on Big Lake Road four miles to a trailhead on the right.

Contact: Willamette National Forest, McKenzie River Ranger District, 57600 McKenzie Highway, McKenzie Bridge, OR, 97413, 541/822-3381.

Maps: For a topographic map, ask the USGS for Steelhead Falls.

Directions: From Sisters, drive east on U.S. 20 and veer left on OR 126 toward Redmond. Go 4.6 miles and turn left on Goodrich Road for 8.1 miles. At milepost 7, go left on Road 6360 through a green gate (remember to close the gate behind you). Go 4.1 miles and turn right at an Alder Springs sign, going 0.8 mile to road's end.

Contact: Crooked River National Grassland, 813 SW Highway 97, Madras, OR, 97741, 541/475-9272.

27 ALDER SPRINGS
6.0 mi/2.5 hr

northeast of Sisters in Crooked River National Grassland

Map 5.2, page 264

The creek formerly known as "Squaw Creek" is now called "Whychus Creek," derived from a Sahaptin word meaning "the place we cross the water." It's a fitting name for this hike, since you'll have to ford the creek to travel this trail in a remote canyon down to its confluence with the Deschutes River. Along the way the trail passes a dry waterfall and a massive spring that flows out of a cliff and down through a grove of alder into the main creek. At the confluence, note the incredible rock formations high on the canyon walls, and watch for more springs.

From the trailhead, go downhill on the Alder Springs Trail to a junction in 0.2 mile, continuing to the right for 1.2 miles along the canyon rim and finally down to the creek itself. Ford the creek and continue 1.6 miles downstream on the opposite shore to the confluence of the Deschutes and its massive, water-smoothed boulders.

User Groups: Hikers and dogs on leash only. No horses or mountain bikes. No wheelchair facilities.

Permits: Permits are not required. Parking and access are free.

28 GRAY BUTTE
4.8-7.1 mi/2.5-3.0 hr

north of Redmond in Crooked River National Grassland

Map 5.2, page 264

The lopsided pyramid that looms behind the crags of Smith Rock State Park is Gray Butte, and this not-well-known trailhead offers a free entrance to Smith Rock State Park (see next listing). From the saddle between the butte and the ridge that gently slopes down to the Crooked River canyon, this vista-rich trail looks out over the desert and Cascade Mountains and crosses a pass where you can find rare bitterroot flowers in spring. The root of these tiny flowers provided Native Americans with a valuable food.

From the Gray Butte Saddle Trailhead, follow the trail away from Gray Butte 1.4 miles to a pass. Pass by the dirt roads and continue one mile to the dirt Burma Road. You can continue on an unofficial trail to a viewpoint and along the ridge into Smith Rock, a 1.5-mile walk to the Crooked River.

A longer tour, perhaps better for mountain bikes, especially in summer, loops for a 7.1-mile ride around Gray Butte itself. From the Gray Butte Saddle Trailhead, go back to the four-way junction and go straight on a dirt road. The trail crosses this road, circling the butte. The longest stretch of walking trail goes 3.4 mile to the left, ending at the McCoin Orchard Trailhead. From here follow Road 57 down 0.7 mile, veering right on Road 5710 for 1.4 miles, then going right again on Road 5720 over the cattle guard and veering off on the trail to the right for the remaining 1.6 miles.

User Groups: Hikers, dogs, horses, and mountain bikes. No wheelchair facilities.

Permits: Permits are not required. Parking and access are free.

Maps: For a topographic map, ask the USGS for Gray Butte.

Directions: From Redmond, drive six miles north on U.S. 97 to Terrebonne and a sign for Smith Rock State Park. Turn east on Smith Rock Way for 5.9 miles to a junction, and go left on Lone Pine Road for 3.4 miles. At a sign for Gray Butte Trailhead go left on Road 5720 for 1.6 miles to a four-way junction. Turn left and park on the right by the trailhead.

Contact: Crooked River National Grassland, 813 SW Highway 97, Madras, OR, 97741, 541/475-9272.

29 SMITH ROCK STATE PARK
3.7–6.3 mi/1.5–3.5 hr   🏃3 ⛰9

north of Redmond

Map 5.2, page 264   **BEST (**

In a state rich with state parks, Smith Rock ranks in the upper echelon. Simply put, this is one of Oregon's most magnificent parks, an intense land of river canyon, rock formations, wildlife, and ponderosa pines. What makes it famous is its allure to rock climbers, and on any given spring, summer, or fall day—sometimes even winter, one of the best times to hike here—you're sure to see climbers on the many dizzying walls. The kingpin of these climbs is the welded tuff ash formation known as Monkey Face, which, from the right angle, resembles exactly that. Within view of all the climbing, aeries of golden eagles nestle in the cliff faces. Deer wander here, as do coyote and other animals. And arcing gracefully through it all is the Crooked River, oxbowing around this one-of-a-kind rock formation. You can easily spend a full day here, or two, and a walk-in campground for backpackers and climbers makes that a temptation. Two hikes crown the

Smith Rock State Park

park and visit everything you could want to see. Just be aware of the dangers here; people have died in this park by falling from the cliffs. Play it safe and stay on the trail.

To climb over Misery Ridge and visit Monkey Face close up, start from the parking area and descend 0.4 mile into the canyon and cross the footbridge. Continue to the left and up the Misery Ridge Trail 0.5 mile up staircases and a steep trail to the crest. Follow the trail to a junction, where a left-hand user trail goes down a ridge to a view of Monkey Face. You should not attempt this if you are afraid of heights. Continue on the Misery Ridge Trail down the opposite side of the ridge on a long series of steep switchbacks, then along the cliffs above the river to a junction with the river trail, 0.7 mile in all. From here you can explore at whim; going left along the river 1.7 miles will bring you back to the footbridge and the remaining 0.4 mile to the lot.

For a longer walk, hike 0.4 mile to the footbridge and follow the river downstream 2.2 miles, passing the climbing walls and huge boulders. Past Monkey Face and at a huge boulder, turn right up a path climbing a steep gully, following it 1.5 miles up and along the ridge to the Burma Road. From the road, going straight leads to Gray Butte (see listing in this chapter). For the loop, go right on Burma Road and descend back into the canyon 0.7 mile to the trail junction on the right, and follow this trail 1.1 mile back to the footbridge and the remaining 0.4 mile back to the parking lot.

User Groups: Hikers and dogs on leash only. No horses or mountain bikes. No wheelchair facilities.

Permits: Permits are not required. A $3 day-use fee is collected at a self-serve kiosk, or you can get an annual Oregon Parks and Recreation pass for $25; contact Oregon Parks and Recreation, 800/551-6949.

Maps: For a free park brochure, call Oregon Parks and Recreation, 800/551-6949, or download a free map at www.oregonstateparks.org. For a topographic map, ask the USGS for Gray Butte.

Directions: From Redmond, drive six miles north on U.S. 97 to Terrebonne and a sign for Smith Rock State Park. Turn east on Smith Rock Way and follow signs 3.3 miles to the parking area.

Contact: Oregon Parks and Recreation Department, 1115 Commercial Street Northeast, Salem, OR, 97301, 800/551-6949, www.oregonstateparks.org.

30 PACIFIC CREST TRAIL TO LITTLE BELKNAP CRATER

5.2 mi/2.5 hr   👥2 ⛰9

in the McKenzie Pass in Mount Washington Wilderness

Map 5.2, page 264

If you want to get a sense of what walking on a barren planet like, say, Mars is like (especially after the photographs from that red planet), all you have to do is walk onto the McKenzie Pass. At first view of these lava fields, it's hard not to be shocked. You'll feel a certain awe here, as the size of these flows staggers the imagination. You'll have a whole new respect for those that built the Pacific Crest Trail, carving its route over the black, jumbled basalt. You'll also get a sense of what volcanics really look like up close. An easy tour heads out onto the flow toward the Little Belknap Crater. Atop its knob, a series of lava caves plunge into the peak, and the views extend to far bigger Belknap Crater and Mount Washington and the Sisters. With a sharp eye you can spot "lava bombs"—which solidified in the shapes of tears as they were hurled through the air. Bring plenty of sunblock and water on this trail, especially in summer.

From the PCT trailhead, head north. The trail begins at the foot of a forested island in the lava, then crosses a second island, the trail heading 2.4 miles to the Little Belknap Crater. A cairn marks the right-hand side trail that climbs 0.2 mile up the crater. The PCT continues on along the base of Mount Washington and rises to the Santiam Pass.

User Groups: Hikers, dogs, and horses. No mountain bikes allowed. No wheelchair facilities.

Permits: A free self-issue Wilderness Permit is required and is available at the trailhead. A federal Northwest Forest Pass is required to park here; the cost is $5 a day or $30 for an annual pass. You can buy a day pass at the trailhead, at ranger stations, or through private vendors.

Maps: For a map of the Deschutes National Forest and the Mount Washington Wilderness, contact Deschutes National Forest Headquarters, 1001 SW Emkay Drive, Bend, OR, 97702, 541/383-5300. For a topographic map, ask the USGS for Mount Washington.

Directions: From McKenzie Bridge, drive east on OR 126 to the McKenzie Pass Highway 242. Follow the highway to a trailhead sign near milepost 77. From Sisters, drive OR 242 west 0.5 mile beyond the McKenzie Pass.

Contact: Deschutes National Forest, Sisters Ranger District, P.O. Box 249, Sisters, OR, 97759, 541/549-7700.

31 BLACK CRATER
7.4 mi/4.0 hr   👥4 ⛰9

in the McKenzie Pass in Three Sisters Wilderness

Map 5.2, page 264   **BEST (**

From the town of Sisters, the massive silhouette of Black Crater is imposing and dominant on the skyline. This monumental volcanic peak, carved into 500-foot-cliffs atop its peak by Ice Age glaciers, is a killer climb. From the top, you'll secure a view extending from Mount Hood to the Three Sisters atop a windswept peak of stunted, whitebark pine—one of the best views of the High Cascades anywhere.

The Black Crater Trail climbs 2,500 feet in 3.7 miles, crossing a glacier-carved valley on the crater's flank then climbing steeply up switchbacks to the craggy peak.

User Groups: Hikers, dogs, and horses. No mountain bikes allowed. No wheelchair facilities.

Permits: A free self-issue Wilderness Permit is required and is available at the trailhead. A federal Northwest Forest Pass is required to park here; the cost is $5 a day or $30 for an annual pass. You can buy a day pass at the trailhead, at ranger stations, or through private vendors.

Maps: A map of the Three Sisters Wilderness is available for purchase from Geo-Graphics. For a map of the Deschutes National Forest and the Three Sisters Wilderness, contact Deschutes National Forest Headquarters, 1001 SW Emkay Drive, Bend, OR, 97702, 541/383-5300. For a topographic map, ask the USGS for Black Crater.

Directions: From Sisters, drive west on the McKenzie Pass Highway 242. Between mileposts 80 and 81, turn left into the Black Crater Trailhead parking area.

Contact: Deschutes National Forest, Sisters Ranger District, P.O. Box 249, Sisters, OR, 97759, 541/549-7700.

32 PACIFIC CREST TRAIL TO MATTHIEU LAKES
6.0 mi/3.0 hr   👥2 ⛰7

in the McKenzie Pass in Three Sisters Wilderness

Map 5.2, page 264   **BEST (**

Although you could enter the Three Sisters Wilderness at the McKenzie Pass trailhead for the Pacific Crest Trail, that would result in a longer walk over black, jagged lava. A closer trailhead reaches the PCT quickly and sets out north for a loop around the two Matthieu Lakes. The northern lake is set in a deep forest, but the southern lake, the smaller one, is set high in Scott Pass with views to North Sister. Both of these lakes make for good camps (though regulations require that camps be 250 feet from the shore), and the swimming here is exquisite. It also makes for a launching point to other explorations including the Scott Trail and the mountains themselves.

From the Lava Camp Trailhead, set out toward the PCT for 0.2 mile and go left. Follow the PCT 0.7 mile to a junction. Get the high ground out of the way and go to the left on the PCT for 2.1 miles, with views down to North Matthieu Lake. At the next junction, go left on the PCT toward Scott Pass and South Matthieu Lake. To continue farther, note that the next junction splits; to the left, access to distant Green Lakes, and to the right the PCT continues toward Yapoah Crater and the Scott Trail. To return, go back to the junction before South Matthieu and go left 0.7 mile on the North Matthieu Lake Trail to reach the lower lake. Continue 1.4 miles to return to the PCT and the 0.9 mile back to the trailhead.

User Groups: Hikers, dogs, and horses. No mountain bikes allowed. No wheelchair facilities.

Permits: A free self-issue Wilderness Permit is required and is available at the trailhead. A federal Northwest Forest Pass is required to park here; the cost is $5 a day or $30 for an annual pass. You can buy a day pass at the trailhead, at ranger stations, or through private vendors.

Maps: A map of the Three Sisters Wilderness is available for purchase from Geo-Graphics. For a map of the Deschutes National Forest and the Three Sisters Wilderness, contact Deschutes National Forest Headquarters, 1001 SW Emkay Drive, Bend, OR, 97702, 541/383-5300. For a topographic map, ask the USGS for North Sister.

Directions: From Sisters, drive west on the McKenzie Pass Highway 242. Near milepost 78, turn left at a sign for Lava Lake Camp and follow Road 900 for 0.3 mile, then turn right for the PCT parking.

Contact: Deschutes National Forest, Sisters Ranger District, P.O. Box 249, Sisters, OR, 97759, 541/549-7700.

33 HAND LAKE AND OLD MCKENZIE WAGON ROAD

2.6 mi/1.0 hr   👫1 ⛰7

in the McKenzie Pass in Mount Washington Wilderness

Map 5.2, page 264

Though you can visit Hand Lake via the Benson Trail (see *Benson Lake and Scott Mountain,* next listing), it's easy to get there from the highway trailhead. This way you can spend a little time here exploring this strange lake that pools up against a rugged lava flow, and a piece of the old McKenzie Wagon Road chipped through that same flow by John Craig in 1871, meant to be a shortcut. You'll have to go off trail to find it, but with a landmark as substantial as this lava flow it presents no problem.

The stretch of hike goes an easy 0.5 mile along the Hand Lake Trail into the wilderness to the Hand Lake Shelter, with its view of Hand Lake and two of the Three Sisters. At a junction, go right (the left leads to Scott Lake and its campground) and walk 0.6 mile along the lake and lava flow. Watch for a series of rock cairns and the 15-foot-wide berth in the flow to the right. Cross on this old wagon road then follow the flow to the right, eventually finding Hand Lake again in one mile. Return the 0.5 mile to the trailhead.

User Groups: Hikers, dogs, and horses. No mountain bikes allowed. No wheelchair facilities.

Permits: A free self-issue Wilderness Permit is required and is available at the trailhead. Parking and access are free.

Maps: For a map of the Willamette National Forest and the Mount Washington Wilderness, contact Willamette National Forest Headquarters, 3106 Pierce Parkway, Suite D, Springfield, OR, 97477, 541/225-6300. For a topographic map, ask the USGS for North Sister.

Directions: From McKenzie Bridge, drive east on OR 126 to the McKenzie Pass Highway 242. Follow the highway to a trailhead sign between mileposts 72 and 73. From Sisters, drive OR 242 west 4.5 miles beyond the McKenzie Pass.

Contact: Willamette National Forest, McKenzie River Ranger District, 57600 McKenzie Highway, McKenzie Bridge, OR, 97413, 541/822-3381.

34 BENSON LAKE AND SCOTT MOUNTAIN
8.2–9.7 mi/4.0–4.5 hr 🏃3 ⛰9

in the McKenzie Pass in Mount Washington Wilderness

Map 5.2, page 264

When summer in the Central Oregon desert heats up, it's good to know that easy respite lies in any one of the mountain lakes strewn over the Cascade Crest. Benson Lake, for one, is a swimmer's dream: cold, clear, and deep. Beyond Benson Lake are even more lakes, the congregation of little pools known as the Tenas Lakes, set atop a plateau with a view out over the western range. If that's not enough of a day, try climbing Scott Mountain for an amazing view over the lava-rubble fields of the McKenzie Pass, with a perfect view of six Cascade peaks. To lengthen the trail even further, you can link to a loop past Hand Lake (see *Hand Lake and Old McKenzie Wagon Road,* previous listing) for a 9.7-mile jaunt that's great for backpacking.

Start out from the lot at Scott Lake and follow the Benson Trail straight for 1.4 miles to broad Benson Lake. In another 1.1 miles, the trail reaches a left-hand spur to the Tenas Lakes, a series of lovely rock bowls. To climb Scott Mountain, continue on 0.9 mile, staying right at a junction leading to The Knobs, to another junction on Scott Mountain itself. From here, go left and up 300 feet and 0.7 mile to the peak. This makes a fine turn-around point for the 8.2-mile hike, but you could continue on the Benson Trail another 1.8 miles to a junction, then go right 1.6 miles to Hand Lake, and continue to the right past

the shelter for the remaining 1.5 miles to Scott Lake, making for a 9.7-mile loop.

User Groups: Hikers, dogs, and horses. No mountain bikes allowed. No wheelchair facilities.

Permits: A free self-issue Wilderness Permit is required and is available at the trailhead. A federal Northwest Forest Pass is required to park here; the cost is $5 a day or $30 for an annual pass. You can buy a day pass at the trailhead, at ranger stations, or through private vendors.

Maps: For a map of the Willamette National Forest and the Mount Washington Wilderness, contact Willamette National Forest Headquarters, 3106 Pierce Parkway, Suite D, Springfield, OR, 97477, 541/225-6300. For a topographic map, ask the USGS for Linton Lake.

Directions: From McKenzie Bridge, drive east on OR 126 to the McKenzie Pass Highway 242. Follow the highway to a sign for Scott Lake between mileposts 71 and 72 and turn left, following Road 260 for 1.5 miles to its end. From Sisters, drive OR 242 west 5.6 miles beyond the McKenzie Pass.

Contact: Willamette National Forest, McKenzie River Ranger District, 57600 McKenzie Highway, McKenzie Bridge, OR, 97413, 541/822-3381.

35 SCOTT TRAIL TO FOUR-IN-ONE CONE
9.0 mi/5.0 mi 🏃3 ⛰8

in the McKenzie Pass in Three Sisters Wilderness

Map 5.2, page 264

The Scott Trail was blazed by Captain Felix Scott, who arduously led a wagon train across this volcanic landscape in 1862. This modern hiking trail follows his route and leads backpackers into the Three Sisters Wilderness, opening up their own world of exploration. Hike across a lava flow erupted from the Four-in-One Cone, four cinder cones with a view of North and Middle Sister and the surrounding

© SEAN PATRICK HILL

Sunshine Meadows in the Three Sisters Wilderness

volcanic landscape. You can also go farther and connect to the Pacific Crest Trail. Keep in mind that this trail is largely exposed to the sun—bring adequate water, headgear, and sunblock.

From the trailhead, cross the McKenzie Pass Highway and start on the Scott Trail, staying left at the first junction (the right leads to the Obsidian Trailhead and Frog Camp) and continue 2.7 miles. The next 1.4 miles crosses a rugged lava flow and the forested island in its midst, then arrives at a cairn beside the cinder cones. Climb to the left for a view of the mountains, 0.4 mile along the Four-in-One Cone's rim. From the cairn, it is another 0.8 mile up the Scott Trail to its junction with the PCT.

User Groups: Hikers, dogs, and horses. No mountain bikes allowed. No wheelchair facilities.

Permits: A free self-issue Wilderness Permit is required and is available at the trailhead. Parking and access are free.

Maps: A map of the Three Sisters Wilderness is available for purchase from Geo-Graphics. For a map of the Willamette National Forest and the Three Sisters Wilderness, contact Willamette National Forest Headquarters, 3106 Pierce Parkway, Suite D, Springfield, OR, 97477, 541/225-6300. For a topographic map, ask the USGS for North Sister.

Directions: From McKenzie Bridge, drive east on OR 126 to the McKenzie Pass Highway 242. Follow the highway to a sign for Scott Lake between mileposts 71 and 72 and turn left, then right into a parking area. From Sisters, drive OR 242 west 5.6 miles beyond the McKenzie Pass.

Contact: Willamette National Forest, McKenzie River Ranger District, 57600 McKenzie Highway, McKenzie Bridge, OR, 97413, 541/822-3381.

36 THE OBSIDIAN TRAIL

12.0 mi/6.0 hr   🥾3 ⛰10

west of McKenzie Pass in Three Sisters Wilderness

Map 5.2, page 264   **BEST (**

The Obsidian Trail in the Three Sisters Wilderness sees a multitude of visitors—including those who come to climb 10,047-foot Middle Sister, Oregon's fourth-highest mountain. Because of the trail's popularity, the Forest Service requires a special permit that can be attained in advance from the McKenzie Ranger Station. What makes it such a desirable destination are the meadows known as Sunshine, which offer some of the rarest landscape to be found anywhere. The trail passes 4.1 miles through deep forests and over jagged rivers of lava fields that poured down from nearby Collier Cone. Volcanic black glass abounds here, making it obvious how this trail acquired its name. Atop the Obsidian Cliffs, the alpine plateau sparkles with acres of glittering chips. You'll pass 20-foot Obsidian Falls tumbling into a forest that by late summer is full of the mop-head blooms of western pasque flower, known as "old man of the mountain." From the Sunshine Meadows around Glacier Creek, climbers ascend to summit Middle Sister. Backpacking and camping affords many opportunities for day trips. To the south lie the Linton Meadows, the Wickiup Plain, and South Sister. To the north, the PCT crosses the ridge of Little Brother and deep lava flows to the volcanic moonscape beneath North Sister and a steep climb up the Collier Cone.

Starting from the McKenzie Pass Highway, go 4.1 miles on the Obsidian Trail through forests and over lava fields. Immediately after crossing the White Branch Creek, take a right at a junction, staying on the Obsidian Trail for 1.7 miles. Once on the PCT, turn left for 1.4 miles to continue to Sunshine. A 0.7-mile spur trail heading downhill along Glacier Creek completes the loop, returning to the last 4.1-mile stretch of the Obsidian Trail back to the trailhead.

User Groups: Hikers, dogs, and horses. No mountain bikes allowed. No wheelchair facilities.

Permits: A Limited Entry Permit is required for overnight and day visits to the Pamelia Lake area; contact the USFS for information. A federal Northwest Forest Pass is required to park here; the cost is $5 a day or $30 for an annual pass. You can buy a day pass at the trailhead, at ranger stations, or through private vendors.

Maps: A map of the Three Sisters Wilderness is available for purchase from Geo-Graphics. For a map of the Willamette National Forest and the Three Sisters Wilderness, contact Willamette National Forest Headquarters, 3106 Pierce Parkway, Suite D, Springfield, OR, 97477, 541/225-6300. For a topographic map, ask the USGS for North Sister.

Directions: From McKenzie Bridge, drive east on OR 126 to the McKenzie Pass Highway 242. Follow the highway to a sign for the Obsidian Trail between mileposts 70 and 71 and turn right 0.4 mile into a parking area. From Sisters, drive OR 242 west 6.2 miles beyond the McKenzie Pass.

Contact: Willamette National Forest, McKenzie River Ranger District, 57600 McKenzie Highway, McKenzie Bridge, OR, 97413, 541/822-3381.

☷ PROXY FALLS/ LINTON LAKE
4.8 mi/2.5 hr 🏃1 ⛰8

west of McKenzie Pass in Three Sisters Wilderness

Map 5.2, page 264   **BEST (**

There's a reason you may have trouble finding parking here. These two easy hikes into the Three Sisters Wilderness are located just off the beautiful and heavily traveled McKenzie Pass Highway (a gateway to many fantastic hikes). That's no reason to pass up these two hikes, though, and their relative brevity makes it a good idea to do both.

The one-mile Proxy Falls loop should be hiked counterclockwise, as per Forest Service request; the loop visits Lower Proxy Falls, a tall cascade over a lava wall, and Upper Proxy Falls, which ends abruptly in a pool without a visible outlet (the water travels underground from here).

The Linton Lake Trail enters the woods and heads 1.4 miles to the edge of the lake at an ancient lava flow. You can continue 0.5 mile farther along the lakeshore to a beach. In the distance you can hear Linton Falls tumbling out of the hills.

User Groups: Hikers and dogs. No horses or mountain bikes. No wheelchair facilities.

Permits: A free self-issue Wilderness Permit is required and is available at the trailhead. A federal Northwest Forest Pass is required to park here; the cost is $5 a day or $30 for an annual pass. You can buy a day pass at the trailhead, at ranger stations, or through private vendors.

Maps: A map of the Three Sisters Wilderness is available for purchase from Geo-Graphics. For a map of the Willamette National Forest and the Three Sisters Wilderness, contact

Willamette National Forest Headquarters, 3106 Pierce Parkway, Suite D, Springfield, OR, 97477, 541/225-6300. For a topographic map, ask the USGS for Linton Lake.

Directions: From McKenzie Bridge, drive east on OR 126 to the McKenzie Pass Highway 242. For the Proxy Falls Trailhead follow this highway nine miles, and park on the roadside between mileposts 64 and 65. For the Linton Lake Trailhead, drive another 1.6 miles past Proxy Falls and park on the left. From Sisters, drive OR 242 west 13.5 miles beyond the McKenzie Pass.

Contact: Willamette National Forest, McKenzie River Ranger District, 57600 McKenzie Highway, McKenzie Bridge, OR, 97413, 541/822-3381.

38 CAMP LAKE AND CHAMBERS LAKES
14.2 mi/7.0 hr

southwest of Sisters in Three Sisters Wilderness

Map 5.2, page 264

Although this trail starts out hot and dry in a viewless, lodgepole pine forest, all that quickly changes. Soon enough the trail traverses one of the most stunning landscapes in the state, ambling along beneath North and Middle Sister, with views to South Sister and Broken Top. The heights are breathtaking, and the destination of Camp Lake, set in the alpine saddle between Middle and South Sister, is almost too beautiful to bear. It's hard to exaggerate this place's wonder—and to know that you could go even farther into the wilderness (with a map and compass, of course), and head for the trail-less Chambers Lakes higher in the saddle, makes this a true wilderness destination.

Start on the Pole Creek Trail, going 1.4 miles to a junction that heads to Scott Pass. Stay left and continue 0.6 mile to Soap Creek. At the junction here, go right (the left heads for Green Lakes) another 2.6 miles. At this point, a side trail to the left leads 0.8 mile

down to Demaris Lake, a possible side trip. Otherwise, continue 2.5 miles to trail's end at Camp Lake. To find the Chambers Lakes, watch for user trails and consult your map.

User Groups: Hikers, dogs, and horses. No mountain bikes allowed. No wheelchair facilities.

Permits: A free self-issue Wilderness Permit is required and is available at the trailhead. Parking and access are free.

Maps: A map of the Three Sisters Wilderness is available for purchase from Geo-Graphics. For a map of the Deschutes National Forest and the Three Sisters Wilderness, contact Deschutes National Forest Headquarters, 1001 SW Emkay Drive, Bend, OR, 97702, 541/383-5300. For a topographic map, ask the USGS for North Sister.

Directions: From Sisters, drive 1.4 miles west of Sisters on Highway 242 then turn left on Road 15 for 10.5 miles, following signs for the Pole Creek Trailhead.

Contact: Deschutes National Forest, Sisters Ranger District, P.O. Box 249, Sisters, OR, 97759, 541/549-7700.

39 PARK MEADOW
7.6 mi/4.0 hr

southwest of Sisters in Three Sisters Wilderness

Map 5.2, page 264

This unassuming trail beneath the Tam McArthur Rim is a back door to the very popular Green Lakes area (see *Green Lakes via Broken Top Trail* and *Green Lakes via Fall Creek* listings in this chapter). Park Meadow lies in the midst of thick woods with views to the nearby mountains. But the trail continues on, and with some path-finding skills you may be able to find nearly invisible Golden Lake nearly a mile off the trail, and could follow a series of tarns on the flanks of Broken Top.

The beginning of the Park Meadow Trail follows an old road 1.1 miles along the Snow Creek Ditch. Once the trail proper begins, it descends 2.7 miles to Whychus Creek (stay straight at a four-way intersection along the way). From here it's 1.1 miles to Park Meadow, fed by Park Creek, which is fed, in turn, by the Bend Glacier on Broken Top. From here the trail continues to Green Lakes, and following it you could wander off trail to the south to find Golden Lake with its impressive views, a waterfall, and sky-reflecting tarns high on the mountain.

User Groups: Hikers, dogs, and horses. No mountain bikes allowed. No wheelchair facilities.

Permits: A free self-issue Wilderness Permit is required and is available at the trailhead. Parking and access are free.

Maps: A map of the Three Sisters Wilderness is available for purchase from Geo-Graphics. For a map of the Deschutes National Forest and the Three Sisters Wilderness, contact Deschutes National Forest Headquarters, 1001 SW Emkay Drive, Bend, OR, 97702, 541/383-5300. For a topographic map, ask the USGS for Broken Top.

Directions: From Sisters, go south on Elm Street, which becomes Road 16, for 14.3 mostly paved miles to the Park Meadow Trailhead.

Contact: Deschutes National Forest, Sisters Ranger District, P.O. Box 249, Sisters, OR, 97759, 541/549-7700.

40 TAM MCARTHUR RIM
9.4 mi/4.0 hr   👥3 ⛰9

southwest of Sisters in Three Sisters Wilderness

Map 5.2, page 264

Tam McArthur Rim is the rim of a massive, long-dead volcano. It's far higher than most mountains in the state, making this is one of the best viewpoints in Oregon, with vistas as far as Mount Adams in Washington State—and everything in between. The rim itself drops impressively over 500-foot cliffs to the lakes below, and at the far end of the ridge lies Broken Top. With care, you can extend this hike along that ridge, which gets narrower

North Sister from the Tam McArthur Rim

as you go, to a hidden lake beneath the steep slope of craggy Broken Top.

From the trailhead, climb the Tam McArthur Rim Trail steadily through the woods nearly 600 feet and 0.7 mile to the rim. Continue 1.8 miles to a right-hand junction, which leads to an overlook on a long tongue of lava. From here, continue 2.2 miles, the trail becoming increasingly faint, to the lava plug of Broken Hand. The trail traverses the left side and continues on to the mountain itself, but only the sure-footed should attempt it.

User Groups: Hikers, dogs, and horses. No mountain bikes allowed. No wheelchair facilities.

Permits: A free self-issue Wilderness Permit is required and is available at the trailhead. A federal Northwest Forest Pass is required to park here; the cost is $5 a day or $30 for an annual pass. You can buy a day pass at the trailhead, at ranger stations, or through private vendors.

Maps: A map of the Three Sisters Wilderness is available for purchase from Geo-Graphics. For a map of the Deschutes National Forest and the Three Sisters Wilderness, contact Deschutes National Forest Headquarters, 1001 SW Emkay Drive, Bend, OR, 97702, 541/383-5300. For a topographic map, ask the USGS for Broken Top.

Directions: From Sisters, go south on Elm Street, which becomes Road 16, for 15.7 mostly paved miles to the trailhead on the left.

Contact: Deschutes National Forest, Sisters Ranger District, P.O. Box 249, Sisters, OR, 97759, 541/549-7700.

41 GREEN LAKES VIA BROKEN TOP TRAIL

9.6 mi/5.5 hr   🥾3 ⛰9

west of Bend in the Three Sisters Wilderness

Map 5.2, page 264

Getting to this trailhead requires one of the worst drives possible. Since you'll have to contend with badly rutted and steep dirt roads, washouts, shock-busting potholes, you'll want to drive something with clearance and you'll want to take it slow. The Broken Top Trail passes before the colossal crater of its namesake mountain, a desolate and rocky castle surrounded by meadows of wildflowers so intense you'd never think the two belonged together. Larkspur, columbine, and other varieties dot these high alpine meadows. Views extend out to Mount Bachelor and more distant peaks.

From the trailhead, follow the Broken Top Trail, not taking any side trails, until you reach Green Lakes in 4.8 miles. Watch for the Cayuse Crater along the way, a cinder vent along the trail at the end of a long ridge. Return as you came.

User Groups: Hikers, dogs on leash only, and horses. No mountain bikes allowed. No wheelchair facilities.

Permits: A free self-issue Wilderness Permit is required and is available at the trailhead.

A federal Northwest Forest Pass is required to park here; the cost is $5 a day or $30 for an annual pass. You can buy a day pass at the trailhead, at ranger stations, or through private vendors.

Maps: A map of the Three Sisters Wilderness is available for purchase from Geo-Graphics. For a map of the Deschutes National Forest and the Three Sisters Wilderness, contact Deschutes National Forest Headquarters, 1001 SW Emkay Drive, Bend, OR, 97702, 541/383-5300. For a topographic map, ask the USGS for Broken Top.

Directions: From Bend, drive 23.7 miles west on the Cascade Lakes Highway and turn right at a sign for Todd Lake onto Road 370. After 0.5 mile, continue on Road 370 (the gate stays closed most of the year) for 3.5 terrible miles to Road 380, going left on this road 1.3 miles to its end at the Broken Top Trailhead.

Contact: Deschutes National Forest, Bend-Fort Rock Ranger District, 1230 NE 3rd Street, Suite A-262, Bend, OR, 97701, 541/383-4000.

42 GREEN LAKES VIA FALL CREEK

8.4-11.4 mi/4.5-6.0 hr   🥾3 ⛰10

west of Mount Bachelor in Three Sisters Wilderness

Map 5.2, page 264   **BEST (**

Whereas other areas of the Three Sisters Wilderness are virtually empty, this trail—leading to what has to be one of the most beautiful places in the world—almost never is. The three Green Lakes lie in a valley between South Sister and Broken Top, with unparalleled views of both. To get there, you'll follow the loud and vivacious Fall Creek, which tumbles and tumbles on its way down, almost an endless waterfall; when it does level out, you'll pass a massive obsidian flow that glows in the sun. No wonder it's so popular.

This area has seen a lot of visitor damage over the years, so make sure you camp at a designated area marked by a post and stick to marked trails. You could do this trip in an out-and-back fashion, or make a loop of it using the Broken Top and Soda Creek Trails (recommended if you're backpacking).

From the trailhead, follow the Fall Creek Trail two miles, stay straight at a junction, and continue 2.2 miles to the next junction. Crest a rise and you'll see the Green Lakes, which you can visit by continuing another 1.2 miles. Return to the junction with the Broken Top Trail. You can return as you came or go left toward Broken Top for 2.7 miles, then right at a sign for Fall Creek Trailhead for 0.8 mile, then follow the Soda Creek Trail to the right down 3.7 miles to the lot.

User Groups: Hikers, dogs on leash only, and horses. No mountain bikes allowed. No wheelchair facilities.

Permits: A free self-issue Wilderness Permit is required and is available at the trailhead. A federal Northwest Forest Pass is required to park here; the cost is $5 a day or $30 for an annual pass. You can buy a day pass at the trailhead, at ranger stations, or through private vendors.

Maps: A map of the Three Sisters Wilderness is available for purchase from Geo-Graphics. For a map of the Deschutes National Forest and the Three Sisters Wilderness, contact Deschutes National Forest Headquarters, 1001 SW Emkay Drive, Bend, OR, 97702, 541/383-5300. For a topographic map, ask the USGS for Trout Creek Butte and Broken Top.

Directions: From Bend, drive 26.4 miles west on the Cascade Lakes Highway and turn right at a Green Lakes Trailhead sign to a parking area.

Contact: Deschutes National Forest, Bend-Fort Rock Ranger District, 1230 NE 3rd Street, Suite A-262, Bend, OR, 97701, 541/383-4000.

43 SOUTH SISTER SUMMIT
11.0-12.6 mi/1-2 days   👥5   ⛰10

west of Mount Bachelor in Three Sisters Wilderness

Map 5.2, page 264	

Of all the alpine climbs you could do in Oregon, and of all the peaks you could bag without needing equipment or real mountaineering expertise, South Sister is king. At the same time, you must make serious considerations and take precautions. Altitude sickness affects some more than others, and this trail will lift you 10,358 feet into the atmosphere on Oregon's third-highest mountain. You'll need all day to do it, too; starting early is never a bad idea. The most direct route—and most challenging—begins at the Devil's Lake Trailhead. It's easy to turn this into a backpacking multi-day pitch simply by securing a campsite near Moraine Lake, a little lake with a big view of South Sister and nearby Broken Top. Hike up, pitch a tent, and gather your strength: You'll need it. Be safe and check the weather before attempting an ascent. Any clouds are usually bad clouds. Also, a note on dogs: Because cinders are sharp and can badly cut a dog's paws, it's best to spare them this climb.

From the Devil's Lake Trailhead, climb 1.5 miles on the South Sister climbing trail, heading up a gully, gradually growing steeper, to a four-way junction at the first view of South Sister. To the right, the 0.8-mile side trail leads down to Moraine Lake, where camping is regulated (choose a spot marked with a post). To continue on the climb, go forward up the climber's trail 1.8 miles to the head of the canyon on the right. The next 1.1 miles climbs steeply up the mountain before arriving at a lake beneath the Lewis Glacier. The final grinding slog is up 0.7 mile of sliding cinder to the rim. Once at the top, follow the rim counter-clockwise 0.4 mile to the summit. From here, you'll see half the state of Oregon and, in the crater, Teardrop Pool—the highest lake in Oregon.

User Groups: Hikers, dogs on leash only, and horses. No mountain bikes allowed. No wheelchair facilities.

Permits: A free self-issue Wilderness Permit is required and is available at the trailhead. A federal Northwest Forest Pass is required to park here; the cost is $5 a day or $30 for an annual pass. You can buy a day pass at the trailhead, at ranger stations, or through private vendors.

Maps: A map of the Three Sisters Wilderness is available for purchase from Geo-Graphics. For a map of the Deschutes National Forest and the Three Sisters Wilderness, contact Deschutes National Forest Headquarters, 1001 SW Emkay Drive, Bend, OR, 97702, 541/383-5300. For a topographic map, ask the USGS for South Sister.

Directions: From Bend, drive 28.5 miles west on the Cascade Lakes Highway and turn left at a Devil's Lake Trailhead sign to a parking area.

Contact: Deschutes National Forest, Bend-Fort Rock Ranger District, 1230 NE 3rd Street, Suite A-262, Bend, OR, 97701, 541/383-4000.

44 SISTERS MIRROR LAKE AND WICKIUP PLAIN
8.3-11.3 mi/4.0-5.0 hr

west of Mount Bachelor in the Three Sisters Wilderness

Map 5.2, page 264

The Pacific Crest Trail passes breathtakingly close to South Sister, the third-highest mountain in Oregon, via the broad Wickiup Plain. In this alpine wonderland, you'll see expansive lava flows, smaller peaks, craters, and rolling meadows. It is strange, really, to find this corner of the Three Sisters Wilderness so bereft of crowds. This loop trail leads to backpacking sites near a bundle of lakes, the most well known of which is Sisters Mirror Lake; it somewhat reflects nearby South Sister, whose rounded crown peeks over the tree line. A small peninsula juts out into the lake, but camping is banned in this one spot. Instead, poke around some of the side trails to find plenty of other spots nearby.

From the trailhead, go 0.4 mile on the Mirror Lakes Trail to a four-way junction, staying straight for 2.7 miles to the PCT. The trail crosses Sink Creek and passes several ponds and Kokostick Butte. At the PCT, go left 0.2 mile along Sisters Mirror Lake. To find the other lakes, Lancelot and Denude, go back to the north shore and follow a user trail 0.4 mile. To make a loop from the Wickiup Plain, return to the four-way junction just north of Mirror Lake and continue north on the PCT. In 0.2 mile, you have a choice. For the shorter loop along the edge of the plain, go right here for 1.4 miles to the Wickiup Plains Trail, right at the next junction for one mile, then right again for 1.6 miles along the Elk-Devils Trail to the first four-way junction; go left 0.4 mile back to the lot. For a longer hike, continue on the PCT another 1.6 miles into the Wickiup meadows toward Le Conte Crater, beside the shimmering lava rock mesa. At a junction, go right towards Devil's Lake for 1.1 miles, then straight on the Wickiup Plains Trail for 0.5 mile, continuing left on this path for one mile. Now follow signs for Elk Lake to the right for 1.6 miles, and finally take the final left to return to the Mirror Lakes Trailhead.

User Groups: Hikers, dogs, and horses. No mountain bikes allowed. No wheelchair facilities.

Permits: A free self-issue Wilderness Permit is required and is available at the trailhead. A federal Northwest Forest Pass is required to park here; the cost is $5 a day or $30 for an annual pass. You can buy a day pass at the trailhead, at ranger stations, or through private vendors.

Maps: A map of the Three Sisters Wilderness is available for purchase from Geo-Graphics. For a map of the Deschutes National Forest and the Three Sisters Wilderness, contact Deschutes National Forest Headquarters, 1001 SW Emkay Drive, Bend, OR, 97702, 541/383-5300. For a topographic map, ask the USGS for South Sister.

Directions: From Bend, drive 29.8 miles west

on the Cascade Lakes Highway and turn right at a Trailhead sign to a parking area.

Contact: Deschutes National Forest, Bend-Fort Rock Ranger District, 1230 NE 3rd Street, Suite A-262, Bend, OR, 97701, 541/383-4000.

45 TUMALO MOUNTAIN
3.6 mi/2.5 hr   🥾 3 ⛰ 9

west of Bend in Deschutes National Forest

Map 5.2, page 264

This fairly straightforward climb offers views of surrounding peaks, but is far easier to climb than the others—though it is a 1,200-foot gain in elevation in less than two miles. The view down into Tumalo's eroded crater makes it worth it. From the Sno-Park, follow the Tumalo Mountain Trail up 1.8 miles to the peak.

User Groups: Hikers and dogs only. No horses or mountain bikes allowed. No wheelchair facilities.

Permits: No permits are required. Parking and access are free.

Maps: For a map of the Deschutes National Forest, contact Deschutes National Forest Headquarters, 1001 SW Emkay Drive, Bend, OR, 97702, 541/383-5300. For a topographic map, ask the USGS for Broken Top.

Directions: From Bend, drive 21.7 miles west on the Cascade Lakes Highway and turn right at the Dutchman Flat parking area.

Contact: Deschutes National Forest, Bend-Fort Rock Ranger District, 1230 NE 3rd Street, Suite A-262, Bend, OR, 97701, 541/383-4000.

46 TUMALO FALLS
6.8 mi/3.5 hr   🥾 2 ⛰ 8

west of Bend in Deschutes National Forest

Map 5.2, page 264   **BEST (**

The people who call Bend home are lucky to live such a short distance from such incredible beauty. Here, for instance, at the end of a long paved road into the forest is not one, but several waterfalls on Tumalo Creek, which flows all the way down to Bend, passing through Shevlin Park. In 1979, a wildfire started by a campfire burned off six-square-miles of stately trees. It's amazing how much the forest has recovered, and this hike doesn't stay long in the burn before getting into the good high-country forests.

Follow the South Fork Trail 0.2 mile to the right to find the top of 97-foot Tumalo Falls. Continue along the creek another 3.2 miles, passing four sets of waterfalls along the way. At a junction, go left on the Swampy Lakes Trail 2.1 miles on a high ridge (note that this trail enters the Bend Watershed, and that animals and mountain bikes are not allowed). Then follow the Bridge Creek Trail to the left 1.3 miles back to the lot.

User Groups: Hikers, dogs, horses, and mountain bikes. No mountain bikes or animals allowed in the Bend Watershed. There is a wheelchair-accessible trail to an overlook of Tumalo Falls.

Permits: A federal Northwest Forest Pass is required to park here; the cost is $5 a day or $30 for an annual pass. You can buy a day pass at the trailhead, at ranger stations, or through private vendors.

Maps: For a map of the Deschutes National Forest, contact Deschutes National Forest Headquarters, 1001 SW Emkay Drive, Bend, OR, 97702, 541/383-5300. For a topographic map, ask the USGS for Tumalo Falls.

Directions: From the west side of Bend, follow Skyliner Road 9.8 miles to its end at the OMSI camp, and turn right on dirt Road 4603 for 3.4 miles to the picnic area and trailhead.

Contact: Deschutes National Forest, Bend-Fort Rock Ranger District, 1230 NE 3rd Street, Suite A-262, Bend, OR, 97701, 541/383-4000.

47 SHEVLIN PARK

4.7-5.0 mi/2.0-2.5 hr

west of Bend

Map 5.2, page 264   **BEST** (

Suffice it to say that this has to be one of the country's best city parks—and it's not even in the city. Instead, it stretches out in a canyon along Tumalo Creek, a cold mountain river that passes under stately ponderosa pine, quaking aspen, Douglas fir, and Engelmann spruce. In spring and summer, wildflowers abound here, and you could spend all day trying out side trails, looking up gulches, and exploring farther up Tumalo Creek, where a biking trail leads all the way to Tumalo Falls. But for an easy start, try this loop trail that follows the canyon rim in a scenic loop around all the park's perks. The burn the trail passes over is the result of a 1990 forest fire that just missed destroying the forested canyon. Already, trees are growing back strong.

From the lot, head toward the creek on the Shevlin Loop Trail along the stand of aspen trees, crossing the creek on a footbridge and climbing the ridge to the burn. After the first 0.9 mile, the trail meets an old road. Follow this road a bit, then head back onto trail for one mile, dropping down into the canyon to a side creek flowing past enormous boulders. Cross the creek and continue 0.6 mile through denser woods of Douglas fir to a crossing of Tumalo Creek. Continue over the old road (though going left follows the creek back a ways into National Forest land) and follow this trail along the opposite side of the canyon 1.5 miles to the top of Red Tuff Gulch and a supply yard. Then walk the final 0.7 mile back to your vehicle.

For another walk, this one along the creek, follow the 2.5-mile Tumalo Creek Trail out-and-back; it passes footbridges connecting to the Loop Trail, a covered bridge, and historic Fremont Meadows before launching into the National Forest.

User Groups: Hikers, dogs on leash only, and mountain bikes. No horses allowed.

Paved portions of the park are wheelchair accessible.

Permits: No permits are required. Parking and access are free.

Maps: For a downloadable map, go to www.bendparksandrec.org. For a topographic map, ask the USGS for Shevlin Park.

Directions: From downtown Bend, follow Newport Avenue (which becomes Shevlin Park Road) 3.9 miles. Just after crossing Tumalo Creek, turn left at a bend in the road and park in the first lot.

Contact: Bend Parks and Recreation, 200 NW Pacific Park Lane, Bend, OR, 97701, 541/389-7275.

48 NORTH BANK DEER PRESERVE

6.9 mi/3.5 hr

north of Roseburg on the North Umpqua River

Map 5.3, page 265

The Columbia white-tailed deer once roamed widely in Western Oregon, but by the 1970s populations had dwindled to two pockets: one on the Columbia River, and the other along this bend of the Umpqua River. This 10,000-acre former ranch is now a wildlife preserve where you can certainly see wildlife, not to mention an assortment of landscapes from rolling forests and oak savannah to giant madrone trees and creek-carved chasms. The trail rises and falls, climbing two knobs high above the preserve. Watch for pennyroyal, blue-eyed grass, mariposa lilies, and cat's ear. Note that chiggers are a problem here, so wear long pants.

From the west access, hike straight onto an old road and up 1.8 miles to the 1,480-foot peak of South Knob. A right-hand trail leads to Whistler's Overlook over the Umpqua River, a good place to spot osprey, and will add three miles round-trip to your hike. From South Knob continue 1.5 miles over Middle Ridge to 1,816-foot Middle Knob. Keep going another 0.5 mile, sticking to the left, to a saddle. From here, go left for 2.3 miles through woods along Chasm Creek to a road. Turn left on the road for 0.8 mile back to the car, going to the left of the gate for the last stretch of trail.

User Groups: Hikers, horses, and bicycles. Dogs are discouraged. No wheelchair facilities.

Permits: Permits are not required. Parking and access are free.

Maps: For a topographic map, ask the USGS for Winchester and Oak Creek Valley.

Directions: From Roseburg, drive I-5 north four miles to Winchester (Exit 129). Turn left toward Wilbur for two miles, then turn right on North Bank Road for 5.5 miles. Beyond a gated road on the left, watch for a gravel lot on the left.

Contact: Bureau of Land Management, Roseburg District, 777 NW Garden Valley Boulevard, Roseburg, OR, 97471, 541/440-4930.

49 FALL CREEK NATIONAL RECREATION TRAIL
9.0-13.7 mi one-way/3.0 hr-2 days
🥾 2 ⛰ 7

southeast of Eugene in Willamette National Forest

Map 5.4, page 266

Open all year, this forested hike follows Fall Creek through a lush riparian zone, passing side streams and a small cave once used by Native Americans. A good beginning is to hike a nine-mile section of the trail to what was formerly a 90-foot log bridge, now gone. There is a primitive campsite about halfway out, which could make for a good backpacking spot. There are many access points along the way, but a good stretch begins at the westernmost point in an old-growth forest, and soon traverses out over a 2003 burn on its way upstream. With the bridge out about 9.5 miles upstream, it is possible to access the higher trailhead from the upper stretches of Road 18, hiking downstream to an old-growth grove on Marine Creek.

From the trailhead at the Dolly Varden Campground, follow the creek 2.9 miles through an old-growth forest of ferns and firs along the forested bank to a footbridge at Timber Creek. Along the way, the trail sometimes drops to gravel beaches and to a swimming hole two miles in. After the footbridge, the trail enters the burn from the 2003 Clark Fire, continuing another 0.6 mile to Road 18. Go left across the bridge, and continue upstream on the trail on the far side. In 1.1 miles, the trail passes the cave on Slick Creek and a possible camping area. Continuing another 0.4 mile, the trail forks; to the right is the Bedrock Campground, but the bridge to it is gone. Stay left, going 0.7 mile up a series of switchbacks to a junction with the Jones Creek Trail on the left, closed due to fire damage. The Fall Creek Trail exits the burn, staying high above the creek for one mile, then descending to the creekside again for 3.3 miles to gravel road 1828. This makes the best turnaround point, though continuing 0.5 mile on the trail will bring you to the spot the bridge once spanned, but the bridge being out and the creek being unfordable here makes this a fine ending.

The final 4.2 miles of trail beyond the missing bridge can be reached from Road 1833.

User Groups: Hikers and dogs only. No horses or mountain bikes allowed. No wheelchair facilities.

Permits: Permits are not required. Parking and access are free.

Maps: For a map of the Willamette National Forest, contact Willamette National Forest Headquarters, 3106 Pierce Parkway, Suite D, Springfield, OR, 97477, 541/225-6300. For a topographic map, ask the USGS for Saddleblanket Mountain.

Directions: From Eugene, drive east on Highway 58 for 14 miles and turn left across Dexter Reservoir at the covered bridge. Take Jasper-Lowell Road 2.8 miles through Lowell, following signs for Fall Creek. Turn right on Big Fall Creek Road for 10.3 miles, parking at a trail sign on the right just before the Dolly Varden Campground. To shuttle this as a 9-mile one-way walk, continue past the Dolly Varden Campground 8 miles and turn left on Road 1828 to the trailhead.

To reach the uppermost trailhead, follow Road 18 past Dolly Varden Campground another 12 miles, turn right on Road 1833 and cross a bridge. The trailhead is on the left.

Contact: Willamette National Forest, Middle Fork Ranger District, 46375 Highway 58, Westfir, OR, 97492, 541/782-2283.

50 CHUCKSNEY MOUNTAIN
10.3 mi/5.5 hr   👥3 ⛰8

northeast of Oakridge in Willamette National Forest

Map 5.4, page 266

From the peak of Chucksney Mountain, views extend to the Three Sisters, Broken Top, and Mount Bachelor in the east. The meadows atop the peak are home to wildflowers such as pearly everlasting, coneflower, and larkspur. You'll work for this peak, though, as you climb 2,000 feet in less than five miles, but on the way down the trail visits the headwaters of Box Canyon Creek and follows the stream down.

From the horse camp trailhead, follow the trail in 0.3 mile, keeping right at all junctions until you reach the Chucksney Mountain Loop Trail. Go right on this trail for 2.4 miles to a side trail on the right with views of the eastern peaks. Continue 0.6 mile to a crest, then switchback down into a large cirque and back out again for 1.7 miles to the 5,600-foot summit. Continue across the meadowed ridge 1.4 miles to the Grasshopper Trail. Go left for one mile to the meadows at the headwaters of Box Canyon Creek, then another 2.6 miles back down to the end of the loop, turning right 0.3 mile back to the horse camp.

User Groups: Hikers, dogs, horses, and mountain bikes. No wheelchair facilities.

Permits: Permits are not required. Parking and access are free.

Maps: For a map of the Willamette National

Forest, contact Willamette National Forest Headquarters, 3106 Pierce Parkway, Suite D, Springfield, OR, 97477, 541/225-6300. For a topographic map, ask the USGS for Chucksney Mountain.

Directions: From Blue River, drive four miles east on OR 126 to Road 19 and turn south for 25.5 miles to Box Canyon Horse Camp. From Westfir, drive 32 miles north on Road 19 to Box Canyon Horse Camp.

Contact: Willamette National Forest, McKenzie River Ranger District, 57600 McKenzie Highway, McKenzie Bridge, OR, 97413, 541/822-3381.

51 GOODMAN CREEK AND EAGLE'S REST
13.4 mi/6.0 hr   👥3 ⛰7

south of Lookout Point Reservoir in Willamette National Forest

Map 5.4, page 266

This popular trail is popular for several reasons: It's easily accessible from the Eugene/Springfield area, it's an easy hike for families, and it passes through an old-growth forest along Goodman Creek to a pretty waterfall and swimming hole. Continuing beyond the lower part of the trail on to Eagles Rest, passing a marshy swale of skunk cabbage and a shelter, you'll leave the crowds behind and make for a view over the Lost Creek Valley, standing high above the Lookout Point Reservoir.

From the trailhead, stick to the right-hand junction after 0.2 mile and follow the Goodman Creek arm of the Lookout Point Reservoir. In 1.8 miles, watch for an unmarked trail to the left leading to the waterfall and swimming hole. To continue on to Eagles Rest stay on the Goodman Trail, crossing the creek and continuing 1.2 miles along the creek, then crossing a side creek and climbing the next mile to a road crossing and the Eagles Rest Trailhead. Climb 700 feet over 1.5 miles of second-growth woods to the Ash Swale Shelter by its boggy marsh. Continue 0.3 mile up, cross another road, then ascend the final 0.7 mile to the rocky peak of Eagles Rest.

User Groups: Hikers, dogs, horses, and mountain bikes. No wheelchair facilities.

Permits: Permits are not required. Parking and access are free.

Maps: For a map of the Willamette National Forest, contact Willamette National Forest Headquarters, 3106 Pierce Parkway, Suite D, Springfield, OR, 97477, 541/225-6300. For a topographic map, ask the USGS for Mount June.

Directions: From Eugene, follow Highway 58 east to milepost 21, and park on the right at a trailhead sign.

Contact: Willamette National Forest, Middle Fork Ranger District, 46375 Highway 58, Westfir, OR, 97492, 541/782-2283.

52 TIRE MOUNTAIN
7.6 mi/3.0 hr

north of Oakridge in Willamette National Forest

Map 5.4, page 266

On the large, flat top of Tire Mountain a fire watchtower once stood atop a platform on a topped tree. The mountain itself is named for a nearby creek, which in turn was named for a wagon wheel someone left there. Today the trail accessing this mountain is part of the Eugene to Pacific Crest Trail system, which quite handily connects that nearby city to the mountains. Along this trail, wildflower meadows spread out over the ridge and views open to the distant Cascade peaks.

From the left side of the road, start up the Alpine Trail, going 1.2 miles into an old-growth forest then a meadow at 4,000 feet with views to the Three Sisters, Mount Bachelor, and Diamond Peak. At the junction, go right on the easy and level Tire Mountain Trail for two miles, crossing another steep mountainside meadow and two smaller meadows

on the way to the peak. A side trail to the left leads 0.6 mile to the 4,329-foot summit.

User Groups: Hikers, dogs, horses, and mountain bikes. No wheelchair facilities.

Permits: Permits are not required. Parking and access are free.

Maps: For a map of the Willamette National Forest, contact Willamette National Forest Headquarters, 3106 Pierce Parkway, Suite D, Springfield, OR, 97477, 541/225-6300. For a topographic map, ask the USGS for Westfir East and West.

Directions: From Eugene, follow Highway 58 east 30 miles then go left toward Westfir for 0.3 mile. At a three-way junction, go left 1.8 miles toward Westfir to a red covered bridge and go straight on Road 19 for 4.5 miles. Turn left on Road 1912 for 6.8 miles to Windy Pass, going straight onto Road 1910 for 0.3 mile, then right on Road 1911 for 0.4 mile to the Alpine Trail on the left.

Contact: Willamette National Forest, Middle Fork Ranger District, 46375 Highway 58, Westfir, OR, 97492, 541/782-2283.

53 ERMA BELL LAKES
8.4 mi/4.5 hr

northeast of Oakridge in Three Sisters Wilderness

Map 5.4, page 266

This trail has every right to be heavily used: Located just inside the Three Sisters Wilderness, the trail crosses Skookum Creek (Chinook for "powerful"), and loops around five major lakes, including the three Erma Bell Lakes, the lower and middle of which are joined by a waterfall falling over a rock ledge. As for the lakes themselves, they are wonderfully wild and without the usual trampling of shoreline trails. This doesn't mean there's no camping to be had, though it is prohibited on Lower Erma Bell Lake. Respect the rules and stay at least 200 yards away from lakeshores when pitching a tent.

From the Skookum Creek Campground, cross the creek and head into the wilderness on the Erma Bell Lake Trail 0.6 mile to a junction. Follow the right-hand main trail 1.1 miles to Lower Erma Bell Lake, another 0.4 mile past the waterfall to Middle Erma Bell Lake, and another 0.7 mile to Upper Erma Bell Lake on the right. Continue 0.7 mile to a junction, staying left on the Erma Bell Trail (the right-hand trail goes less than a mile past Mud Lake and Edna Lake to the Taylor Burn Campground). In another 0.7 mile, begin the loop by staying left on the Williams Lake Trail, then go 0.4 mile to Williams Lake. From here the trail gradually descends 2.4 miles through forest to the Irish Mountain Trail junction. Stay to the left another 0.3 mile to Otter Lake, then finish the loop in 0.3 mile. Return to Skookum Creek by going right 0.6 mile.

User Groups: Hikers, dogs, and horses. No mountain bikes allowed. The trail to Lower Erma Bell Lake is wheelchair accessible.

Permits: A free self-issue Wilderness Permit is required and is available at the trailhead. A federal Northwest Forest Pass is required to park here; the cost is $5 a day or $30 for an annual pass. You can buy a day pass at the trailhead, at ranger stations, or through private vendors.

Maps: A map of the Three Sisters Wilderness is available for purchase from Geo-Graphics. For a map of the Willamette National Forest and Three Sisters Wilderness, contact Willamette National Forest Headquarters, 3106 Pierce Parkway, Suite D, Springfield, OR, 97477, 541/225-6300. For a topographic map, ask the USGS for Waldo Mountain.

Directions: From McKenzie Highway 126, turn south on Road 19 toward the Cougar Reservoir for 25.6 miles. Pass Box Canyon Guard Station and go left on Road 1957 to Skookum Campground. The trail begins from the campground parking lot.

Contact: Willamette National Forest, Middle Fork Ranger District, 46375 Highway 58, Westfir, OR, 97492, 541/782-2283.

54 MOUNT JUNE AND HARDESTY MOUNTAIN

9.6-10.0 mi/5.0 hr   3   8

south of Lookout Point Reservoir in Willamette National Forest

Map 5.4, page 266

The name Hardesty Mountain has a certain ring to it, mostly because you have to be pretty hardy to attempt this steep climb. Eugene hikers slog up Hardesty Mountain Trail when they need a real bout of exercise. You'll find, though, that Hardesty has no views, the old lookout site being overgrown with trees. If you begin at Mount June, though, you'll traverse from one peak to the next and passing the 50-foot block of Sawtooth Rock with its shallow cave.

To climb Hardesty Mountain the tough way, start at the Highway 58 trailhead, keeping to the left at the junction in 0.2 mile. This Hardesty Mountain Trail climbs 3,300 feet in 4.8 miles to the summit, passing the Eula Ridge Trail on the left near the top. The final 0.2 mile goes to the left where the trail meets the Cutoff Trail on the right. Return as you came.

To start from Mount June, follow the Mount June Trail 0.7 mile. At a junction, climb 0.5 mile to the left to top 4,618-foot Mount June, which has views extending as far as Mount Hood. Return to the main trail and continue to the right another 0.7 mile on the Sawtooth Trail. Go right one mile through a wildflower meadow past the spire to another junction after some switchbacks, and stay left on the Sawtooth Trail another 2.2 miles to a three-way junction. From here, it is possible to do a short loop around the peak of Hardesty Mountain, going left 0.2 mile on the Hardesty Cutoff Trail, then right over the peak, then right another 0.2 mile back to the Sawtooth Trail. Return as you came.

User Groups: Hikers, dogs, and horses. No mountain bikes allowed. No wheelchair facilities.

Permits: Permits are not required. Parking and access are free.

Maps: For a map of the Umpqua National Forest, contact Umpqua National Forest, 2900 NW Stewart Parkway, Roseburg, OR, 97470, 541/672-6601; for a map of the Willamette National Forest, contact Willamette National Forest Headquarters, 3106 Pierce Parkway, Suite D, Springfield, OR, 97477, 541/225-6300. For a topographic map, ask the USGS for Mount June.

Directions: For the lower trailhead to Hardesty Mountain, start from Eugene and follow Highway 58 east to milepost 21, and park on the right at a trailhead sign. For the upper trailhead to Mount June, follow Highway 58 east from Eugene 11.4 miles to the Dexter Dam and turn right toward Lost Creek. After 3.7 miles, keep left onto Eagles Rest Road, following this road 7.8 miles to a fork. Keep left on Road 20-1-14 for 6.1 miles and turn left on Road 1721 for 0.1 mile, then left on Road 941 for 0.4 mile to the trailhead sign on the right.

Contact: Umpqua National Forest, Cottage Grove Ranger District, 78405 Cedar Park Road, Cottage Grove, OR, 97424, 541/767-5000; Willamette National Forest, Middle Fork Ranger District, 46375 Highway 58, Westfir, OR, 97492, 541/782-2283.

55 EDDEELEO LAKES
9.2-16 mi/4.0 hr-2 days

north of Waldo Lake in Waldo Lake Wilderness

Map 5.4, page 266

The strange name of these lakes is not so strange when you separate the syllables into three names: Ed, Dee, and Leo. These were three Forest Service workers who carried in fish to these lakes to stock them. The two lakes that carry their names are still being fished today. Lined up along the base of long Winchester Ridge, along with three other lakes, these lakes are jewels along a stone wall. Extending this trip makes for a good backpacking jaunt to Waldo Lake, the very large namesake of this wilderness area.

To begin, follow the Winchester Trail 0.8 mile, then take a left turn at a junction for 0.3 mile, then go right at the Blair Lake Trail junction for 1.1 miles to reach Lower Quinn Lake and another junction leading to Taylor Burn Campground. Stay right on the Six Lakes Trail to visit the lakes. The first mile passes a loop on the right to Upper Quinn Lake and arrives at the head of aptly named Long Lake. Follow this lake for most of the next 1.4 miles to the edge of Lower Eddeeleo Lake, and another 1.5 miles to Upper Eddeeleo. This can serve as a turnaround point.

If you're backpacking, continue 2.7 miles to the Waldo Shore Trail, then go south to Elbow Lake for 2.4 miles. At Elbow Lake, turn right on Trail 3585 for 0.8 mile, then right at the next junction on a cutoff trail for 300 yards, then left toward Waldo Mountain for 0.5 mile, then right on the Winchester Ridge Trail for 5.7 miles back to the Winchester Trail junction, then left 0.8 mile back to the trailhead.

User Groups: Hikers, dogs, and horses. No mountain bikes allowed. No wheelchair facilities.

Permits: A free self-issue Wilderness Permit is required and is available at the trailhead. Parking and access are free.

Maps: For a map of the Willamette National Forest and Waldo Lake Wilderness, contact Willamette National Forest Headquarters, 3106 Pierce Parkway, Suite D, Springfield, OR, 97477, 541/225-6300. For a topographic map, ask the USGS for Waldo Mountain.

Directions: From Highway 58 at Oakridge, turn north on Crestview Street for 0.2 mile to East 1st Street, going right. Follow this road, which becomes Salmon Creek Road 24, for 11 miles, then veer left on Road 2417 for 10.9 miles. Turn left at Road 254 for 0.3 mile, following signs for Winchester Trail. Park on the right at a parking lot.

Contact: Willamette National Forest, Middle Fork Ranger District, 46375 Highway 58, Westfir, OR, 97492, 541/782-2283.

56 RIGDON LAKES
8.0 mi/4.0 hr

north of Waldo Lake in Waldo Lake Wilderness

Map 5.4, page 266

Though the 1996 fires that burned through the north shore of Waldo Lake made the area a ghostly version of a forest, it does not follow that the area is off-limits. Burns have their own beauty and after time manage to regenerate. To access the Rigdon Lakes, you'll follow the 10-square-mile Waldo Lake, nearly surrounded by wilderness, on your way to Rigdon Butte and the lakes in its shadow. As long as you're here, why not make a loop of it? Visit Lake Kiwa and return on the far side of the butte, to the lake's outlet, the headwaters of the North Fork Middle Fork Willamette River—a mouthful, I know.

From the North Waldo Trailhead head west, ignoring a horse trail on the right, but noting instead a one-mile shoreline trail on the left that rejoins the main trail 0.7 mile later on the North Waldo Trail. Continue on this easy shoreline walk one mile past numerous ponds to the Rigdon Lakes Trail on the left. Go left 0.7 mile to Upper Rigdon Lake, circled on the far side by a user trail connecting to a 0.6-mile climb of Rigdon Butte. The final 1.3 miles of the Rigdon Lakes Trail passes Lower Rigdon Lake, Lake Kiwa, and little Ernie Lake before joining the Wahanna Trail. Go left at this junction 1.3 miles through the burned woods to a junction; go straight to the head of this fork of the Willamette. Otherwise, turn left and go 1.3 miles back along Waldo Lake to the beginning of the loop, then 1.7 miles back to the campground.

User Groups: Hikers, dogs, and horses. No mountain bikes allowed. No wheelchair facilities.

Permits: A free self-issue Wilderness Permit is required and is available at the trailhead. A federal Northwest Forest Pass is required to park here; the cost is $5 a day or $30 for an annual pass. You can buy a day pass at the trailhead, at ranger stations, or through private vendors.

Maps: For a map of the Willamette National Forest and Waldo Lake Wilderness, contact Willamette National Forest Headquarters, 3106 Pierce Parkway, Suite D, Springfield, OR, 97477, 541/225-6300. For a topographic map, ask the USGS for Waldo Mountain.

Directions: From Highway 58 go three miles west of the Willamette Pass and turn north on Road 5897 toward Waldo Lake for 13 miles to the North Waldo Campground. Park at a sign for the Waldo Lake Trail.

Contact: Willamette National Forest, Middle Fork Ranger District, 46375 Highway 58, Westfir, OR, 97492, 541/782-2283.

57 WALDO MOUNTAIN LOOKOUT
7.9-8.8 mi/4.0-5.0 hr

northwest of Waldo Lake in Waldo Lake Wilderness

Map 5.4, page 266

Waldo Lake, at 10 square miles, is so large that it's hard to get a sense of scale when you're standing on the shoreline. From the lookout atop Waldo Mountain, though, you'll have clear view down to the sparkling water and nearby peaks, including The Twins, Maiden Peak, Fuji Mountain, Diamond Peak, and the distant Three Sisters. The 1957 cabin, staffed in summer, is listed on the National Historic Lookout Register. A figure eight of trails on this mountain's flanks passes through a wildflower meadow, with a side trip to the pair of Salmon Lakes and a 20-foot waterfall. A number of loops are possible, so a map is essential in this wilderness area.

From the trailhead, enter the forest of big grand fir and hemlock for 200 yards to a junction, staying left on the Waldo Mountain Trail. The trail climbs gradually 1.9 miles up through beargrass plumes and sub-alpine trees to a T-junction, where you'll continue up one mile and almost 600 feet to the 6,357-foot summit. From here there are two ways to get down and form one of two loops.

The first way down is to return down the peak the way you came for one mile, keeping left at the next two junctions for 1.2 miles to Waldo Meadows and a T-junction. To return to the car, go right 2.5 miles on the Waldo Meadows Trail back to the trailhead. To find Upper and Lower Salmon Lakes, go left 100 feet to a signed trail on the right, going down 0.5 mile to the Upper Lake.

The second way down from the mountain, a longer loop, requires you to continue up and over the far side of the peak, descending 1.4 miles to a junction (ignore the left-hand Winchester Ridge Trail along the way). At the intersection, with Lake Chetco nearby to the left, instead go right 1.7 miles to Waldo Meadows, staying right at junctions to Elbow Lake and the Salmon Lakes, then continuing as above 2.5 miles back to the trailhead.

User Groups: Hikers, dogs, and horses. No mountain bikes allowed. No wheelchair facilities.

Permits: A free self-issue Wilderness Permit is required and is available at the trailhead. Parking and access are free.

Maps: For a map of the Willamette National Forest and Waldo Lake Wilderness, contact Willamette National Forest Headquarters, 3106 Pierce Parkway, Suite D, Springfield, OR, 97477, 541/225-6300. For a topographic map, ask the USGS for Waldo Mountain.

Directions: From Highway 58 at Oakridge, turn north on Crestview Street for 0.2 mile to East 1st Street, going right. Follow this road, which becomes Salmon Creek Road 24, for 11 miles, then veer left on Road 2417 for six miles. Turn right on Road 2424 and go 3.7 miles to the trailhead.

Contact: Willamette National Forest, Middle Fork Ranger District, 46375 Highway 58, Westfir, OR, 97492, 541/782-2283.

58 LILLIAN FALLS AND KLOVDAHL BAY

7.6 mi/4.5 hr   🏃2 ⛰7

west of Waldo Lake in Waldo Lake Wilderness

Map 5.4, page 266

Access to the western shore of Waldo Lake can be a long journey if you start from the eastern shore, where the road and campgrounds are. A backdoor entrance along Black Creek is just as easy, and opens up the network of trails inside the wilderness area bordering the shoreline. A short, easy jaunt leads to Lillian Falls, and a longer more rugged hike climbs to Klovdahl Bay on the eastern shore. Oddly, neither Black Creek, Nettle Creek, nor Klovdahl Creek are outlets for Waldo Lake—it has only one outlet in its northwestern corner; the creeks in this area slip away, fed instead by winter snows. But one Simon Klovdahl tried in 1912 to dynamite a tunnel from Waldo to the Black Creek Canyon, an irrigation and hydroelectric power scheme that failed.

Start out on the trail along Black Creek, climbing easily for 1.2 miles to the base of Lillian Falls. From here the trail switchbacks up 0.7 mile and begins to climb more fiercely, leveling off in a valley along Nettle Creek then climbing again to Klovdahl Creek and above the Waldo shore for 1.9 miles before descending to the Waldo Lake Trail and Klovdahl Bay.

User Groups: Hikers, dogs, and horses. No mountain bikes all owed. No wheelchair facilities.

Permits: A free self-issue Wilderness Permit is required and is available at the trailhead. Parking and access are free.

Maps: For a map of the Willamette National Forest and Waldo Lake Wilderness, contact Willamette National Forest Headquarters, 3106 Pierce Parkway, Suite D, Springfield, OR, 97477, 541/225-6300. For a topographic map, ask the USGS for Waldo Lake.

Directions: From Highway 58 at Oakridge, turn north on Crestview Street for 0.2 mile to East 1st Street, going right. Follow this road, which becomes Salmon Creek Road 24, for 11 miles, keeping right at a Y-junction and staying on Road 24 for another 3.2 miles, then going straight on Road 2421 for 8.2 miles to road's end.

Contact: Willamette National Forest, Middle Fork Ranger District, 46375 Highway 58, Westfir, OR, 97492, 541/782-2283.

59 WALDO LAKE SHORE
21.5 mi/2-3 days 👣4 ⛰8

on Waldo Lake north of Willamette Pass

Map 5.4, page 266

The best way to circumnavigate huge Waldo Lake, the second-largest freshwater lake in Oregon, is by mountain bike, and many do attempt its single-track challenge. The 21-plus-mile Jim Weaver Loop Trail mostly follows the lakeshore, though for a substantial portion it ducks a bit away from the lake into deep woods that are heavy with huckleberries in the late summer. This is also a backpacker's dream; there are camps aplenty dispersed along the shore, as well as secluded beaches reachable only by foot or boat. On top of that, the side trails radiate out from the northern, western, and southern shore into the Waldo Lake Wilderness, a maze of peaks and lakes good for extended trips. The Jim Weaver Trail is best accessed from either the Shadow Bay Campground or North Waldo Campground. Watch for bikes along the way!

User Groups: Hikers, dogs, horses, and mountain bikes. No wheelchair facilities.

Permits: Permits are not required. A federal Northwest Forest Pass is required to park here; the cost is $5 a day or $30 for an annual pass. You can buy a day pass at the trailhead, at ranger stations, or through private vendors.

Maps: For a map of the Willamette National Forest and Waldo Lake Wilderness, contact Willamette National Forest Headquarters, 3106 Pierce Parkway, Suite D, Springfield, OR, 97477, 541/225-6300. For a topographic map, ask the USGS for Waldo Lake.

Directions: To find the Shadow Bay Trailhead, drive Highway 58 three miles west of the Willamette Pass to milepost 59 and turn on Road 5897 for 6.7 miles, following signs for Waldo Lake. Turn left into the Shadow Bay Campground, continuing two miles to the boat ramp parking. To find the North Waldo Trailhead, continue 6.3 miles farther on Road 5897 to the North Waldo Campground and park at the Waldo Lake Trailhead.

Contact: Willamette National Forest, Middle Fork Ranger District, 46375 Highway 58, Westfir, OR, 97492, 541/782-2283.

60 THE TWINS
6.6 mi/3.0 hr 👣2 ⛰9

east of Waldo Lake in Willamette National Forest

Map 5.4, page 266

The peak of The Twins, with its distinct dual volcanic flanks and crater, is easy enough to spot from the east or west. Accessible from the Pacific Crest Trail, this 7,360-foot peak offers an outstanding view of Waldo Lake to the west, the Three Sisters to the north, and Diamond Peak to the south. The trail is an easy one-shot climb from the trailhead: Ascend the first 450 feet through lodgepole pine and mountain hemlock forest in 1.6 miles to the PCT junction, and continue straight 1.7 miles and 1,160 feet to the north summit. With a bit of path-finding, you can explore the crater and top the south summit as well.

User Groups: Hikers, dogs, horses, and mountain bikes. No wheelchair facilities.

Permits: Permits are not required. A federal Northwest Forest Pass is required to park here; the cost is $5 a day or $30 for an annual pass. You can buy a day pass at the trailhead, at ranger stations, or through private vendors.

Maps: For a map of the Willamette National Forest, contact Willamette National Forest Headquarters, 3106 Pierce Parkway, Suite D, Springfield, OR, 97477, 541/225-6300. For a topographic map, ask the USGS for The Twins.

Directions: Drive Highway 58 three miles past the Willamette Pass to milepost 59 and turn on Road 5897 for 6.2 miles, following signs for Waldo Lake. Park at the Twin Peaks Trailhead on the right.

Contact: Willamette National Forest, Middle Fork Ranger District, 46375 Highway 58, Westfir, OR, 97492, 541/782-2283.

61 BRICE CREEK
5.5-7.5 mi one-way/2.5-3.5 hr
🏃2 ⛰7

east of Cottage Grove in Umpqua National Forest

Map 5.4, page 266

In the Cascade Mountains above Cottage Grove, this lovely rushing creek bounds out of the forest in a forested canyon. Rain or shine, this trail is accessible all year, and it even has some primitive campsites along Road 22, not to mention bigger campgrounds and a backpacking spot along the far side of the creek. The trail stays on the far side of the creek away from the road, making for a quiet hike. There is also the option at the upper reach of the trail to loop around the two Trestle Creek Falls, adding two miles to the trip.

From the lower trailhead, follow the creek upstream 1.5 miles along the canyon and into old-growth forest. Ignore a side trail over the creek that goes to the Cedar Creek Campground, and continue 2.6 miles, passing a series of waterfalls over a rock shelf and the primitive Boy Scout Camp to another bridge crossing to the Lund Park Campground. The trail continues upstream 0.6 mile to the beginning of the loop. Going straight along the creek another 0.5 mile leads to Trestle Creek (for an interesting side-trip, follow a left-hand trail up 0.3 mile to a view of the lower falls). Continue another 0.3 mile up the Brice Creek Trail to its end at the upper trailhead.

A loop option leading to two waterfalls is also available at Trestle Creek. From the upper trailhead, this 3.4-mile loop makes for an easier trip that can be coupled with

a longer excursion downstream on the Brice Creek Trail. At the end of the Brice Creek Trail at the upper trailhead, note the side trail going uphill. Following this steep trail up nearly 1,000 feet you'll reach the Upper Trestle Creek Falls, pass behind them, and descend another mile to the Brice Creek Trail. Go left to return to the upper trailhead, passing the side trail to the lower waterfall, or go right for any length along the remaining 4.7 miles of the Brice Creek Trail.

User Groups: Hikers, dogs, and horses. No mountain bikes allowed. No wheelchair facilities.

Permits: Permits are not required. Parking and access are free.

Maps: For a map of the Umpqua National Forest, contact Umpqua National Forest, 2900 NW Stewart Parkway, Roseburg, OR, 97470, 541/672-6601. For a topographic map, ask the USGS for Rose Hill.

Directions: To find the lower trailhead, drive I-5 south of Eugene to Cottage Grove (exit 174), and follow signs east to Dorena Lake on Row River Road, which becomes Road 22, for 21.7 miles to a parking lot on the right. For the upper trailhead at the Trestle Creek Falls Loop, continue past the lower trailhead on Road 22 for another 5.5 miles to the next bridge and parking for the trailhead.

Contact: Umpqua National Forest, Cottage Grove Ranger District, 78405 Cedar Park Road, Cottage Grove, OR, 97424, 541/767-5000.

62 LARISON CREEK
12.6 mi/6.0 hr
🏃3 ⛰7

on Hills Creek Reservoir in Willamette National Forest

Map 5.4, page 266

This easy trail up Larison Creek weaves its way into some pretty stunning old-growth above the Hills Creek Reservoir. Douglas fir, red cedar, and the fabled yew trees—which Native Americans used for bows—all grow here.

You'll find a primitive campsite and a waterfall as you enter this deep, green canyon.

The trail begins along Larison Cove, an arm of the Hills Creek Reservoir; hillsides here are livid with poison oak. After 1.5 miles, the Larison Creek Trail reaches the end of the cove and a camping and picnic area. The trail then climbs gradually another 1.5 miles to a small waterfall and pool on the left. The next 2.2 miles leaves the creek and crosses a clear-cut before returning to the creek, crossing it near a creek fork. The last 1.1 miles climbs steeply up to trail's end at a dirt road. Return as you came.

User Groups: Hikers, dogs, horses, and mountain bikes. No wheelchair facilities.

Permits: Permits are not required. A federal Northwest Forest Pass is required to park here; the cost is $5 a day or $30 for an annual pass. You can buy a day pass at the trailhead, at ranger stations, or through private vendors.

Maps: For a map of the Willamette National Forest, contact Willamette National Forest Headquarters, 3106 Pierce Parkway, Suite D, Springfield, OR, 97477, 541/225-6300. For a topographic map, ask the USGS for Oakridge.

Directions: From Oakridge, drive 1.8 miles east on Highway 58. Between mileposts 37 and 38, turn south toward Hills Creek Dam on Road 23. In 0.5 mile, turn right on Road 21 for 3.3 miles to the trailhead on the right.

Contact: Willamette National Forest, Middle Fork Ranger District, 46375 Highway 58, Westfir, OR, 97492, 541/782-2283.

63 SALT CREEK FALLS AND VIVIAN LAKE
8.0 mi/4.0 hr   🥾3 ⛺9

in the Willamette Pass in Diamond Peak Wilderness

Map 5.4, page 266   **BEST (**

Fall Creek, Diamond Creek, and Salt Creek—talk about waterfalls. Salt Creek Falls, showering over a basalt flow 286 feet into the canyon below,

Vivian Lake in Diamond Peak Wilderness

© SEAN PATRICK HILL

are the second highest in Oregon. Diamond Creek Falls and the double-tiered Fall Creek Falls also grace this trail into Diamond Peak Wilderness. At the top lies muddy-bottomed Vivian Lake, with its towering white pine trees and view of nearby Mount Yoran, a volcanic plug dominating the skyline. Besides flowering rhododendrons, huckleberries grow in such profusion along this trail that it's doubtful you'll get anywhere quickly, but watch out as you're stumbling through the bushes like a hungry bear—ground wasps call this area home, and I can attest that they pack quite a sting.

From the lot for Salt Creek Falls, take a quick tour of the observation trail on the north side of the creek. Then go upstream and cross a footbridge. At a junction, go right on the Diamond Creek Falls Trail for 1.8 miles along the canyon rim, passing strangely named Too Much Bear Lake and a viewpoint of a tall waterfall streaming into Salt Creek's canyon. To see Diamond Creek Falls, take a right-hand signed side trail down 0.2 mile to see the 100-

foot fan-shaped falls. Return to the main trail and keep to the right, switchbacking up to a junction. Go right and begin steadily climbing along Fall Creek on the Vivian Lake Trail. In 1.3 miles, the trail reaches two viewpoints of Fall Creek Falls. The next mile is a more gradual grade, coming to a side trail on the right leading to Vivian Lake. From here, backpackers can continue on to Notch Lake and other trail connections into Diamond Peak Wilderness. For a return loop, return on the Vivian Lake Trail down 2.3 miles to the junction, this time going right 1.2 miles back to Salt Creek.

User Groups: Hikers, dogs, and horses. No mountain bikes allowed. No wheelchair facilities.

Permits: A free self-issue Wilderness Permit is required and is available at the trailhead. A federal Northwest Forest Pass is required to park here; the cost is $5 a day or $30 for an annual pass. You can buy a day pass at the trailhead, at ranger stations, or through private vendors.

Maps: For a map of the Willamette National Forest, contact Willamette National Forest Headquarters, 3106 Pierce Parkway, Suite D, Springfield, OR, 97477, 541/225-6300. For a topographic map, ask the USGS for Diamond Peak.

Directions: From Oakridge, drive Highway 58 east to milepost 57 and turn right at a sign for Salt Creek Falls. Follow this paved road to the parking lot at its end.

Contact: Willamette National Forest, Middle Fork Ranger District, 46375 Highway 58, Westfir, OR, 97492, 541/782-2283.

64 FUJI MOUNTAIN
3.0–11.2 mi/1.5–4.0 hr

south of Waldo Lake in Waldo Lake Wilderness

Map 5.4, page 266

The dominant peak of Fuji Mountain has a lot going for it. At 7,144 feet, it towers above the surrounding countryside, and with its 360-degree view of the surrounding Cascade Mountains, it has quite the stupendous view, reaching as far as the peak of Mount Hood in the north to Mount Thielsen in the south. The view also extends clear across monumental Waldo Lake, the reason this made a great lookout point long ago.

For the easier trailhead off Road 5883, follow the trail into the forest 0.3 mile to a junction and turn left on the Fuji Mountain Trail. The trail gets gradually steeper, climbing 1.2 miles to the peak.

For the more difficult climb, start from the trailhead on Road 5897, climbing one mile on the Fuji Mountain Trail to the forested plateau. In another two miles, the trail reaches Birthday Lake (warm in summer and a great place for a cool-down swim on the way down the mountain). In another 0.4 mile, it passes little Verde Lake on the left and comes to a junction. Go left 100 feet to a second junction, going right one mile and climbing to the junction with the Road 5883 spur trail. Keep right, and continue 1.2 miles to the top.

User Groups: Hikers, dogs, and horses. No mountain bikes allowed. No wheelchair facilities.

Permits: A federal Northwest Forest Pass is required to park here; the cost is $5 a day or $30 for an annual pass. You can buy a day pass at the trailhead, at ranger stations, or through private vendors.

Maps: For a map of the Willamette National Forest, contact Willamette National Forest Headquarters, 3106 Pierce Parkway, Suite D, Springfield, OR, 97477, 541/225-6300. For a topographic map, ask the USGS for Waldo Lake.

Directions: To find the shorter trail, begin in Oakridge and drive 15 miles east on Highway 58 to Eagle Creek Road 5883, between mileposts 50 and 51. Turn left on Road 5897 for 10.3 miles to the trailhead on the left. For the more difficult trail, continue on Highway 58 to milepost 59, and turn left on Road 5897, following signs for Waldo Lake. In two miles, park on the left at the trailhead.

Contact: Willamette National Forest, Middle Fork Ranger District, 46375 Highway 58, Westfir, OR, 97492, 541/782-2283.

65 BOHEMIA MOUNTAIN
1.6 mi/1.0 hr　　　　　🏃1 ⛰8

east of Cottage Grove in Umpqua National Forest

Map 5.4, page 266

If you think the road to Bohemia Mountain is long and rough, imagine what it must have been like for the miners who once lived in Bohemia City. This old mining town, now one of Oregon's many ghost towns, sits at the base of its namesake mountain. Residents drilled the Musick Mine looking for gold, which was discovered here by a Czech immigrant in 1863. Only one building remains: the old post office, visible from the peak. You can make your way to it, being careful not to cross any private land, by bushwhacking down a hillside and heading for the last remnant of a town that operated from 1880 to 1930.

Follow the Bohemia Mountain Trail up 0.8 mile and 700 feet to the peak, where views stretch from Mount Shasta in the south to Mount Hood in the north. If this isn't enough for you, you can return to the Bohemia Saddle and follow the road one mile up to the watchtower on Fairview Peak.

User Groups: Hikers and dogs only. No horses or mountain bikes allowed. No wheelchair facilities.

Permits: Permits are not required. Parking and access are free.

Maps: For a map of the Umpqua National Forest, contact Umpqua National Forest, 2900 NW Stewart Parkway, Roseburg, OR, 97470, 541/672-6601. For a topographic map, ask the USGS for Fairview Peak.

Directions: Drive I-5 south of Eugene to Cottage Grove (Exit 174) and follow signs east to Dorena Lake on Row River Road, which becomes Road 22, for 30.5 miles. Turn right on Road 2212 at a sign for Fairview Peak and go 8.4 miles to Champion Saddle, then turn left on Road 2460. Follow this steep and rough road 1.1 miles to a junction in Bohemia Saddle. Park at the saddle and walk 100 yards to the left to the Bohemia Mountain Trail.

Contact: Umpqua National Forest, Cottage Grove Ranger District, 78405 Cedar Park Road, Cottage Grove, OR, 97424, 541/767-5000.

66 MIDDLE FORK WILLAMETTE RIVER
33.1 mi one-way/3 days　　🏃5 ⛰8

south of Hills Creek Reservoir in Willamette National Forest

Map 5.4, page 266

The Hills Creek Reservoir catches all of the Middle Fork Willamette River, the main branch of this colossal and important Oregon river. With plenty of established campgrounds along the way, it's possible to spend days here exploring the trail in segments. Backpackers may be tempted to try it in longer stretches along any of the points between the reservoir and Timpanogas Lake, the river's headwaters. Along the way are a series of springs—Chuckle Springs and Indigo Springs—that add to the river's bulk. With all the mixed stands of conifers, wildflowers, and waterfalls, there's plenty to see and explore. The total elevation gain for the trail is 4,000 feet, so plan ahead with a map.

The trail segments are as follows: Sand Prairie to Road 2127, 5.1 miles; Road 2127 to Road 2133, 5.2 miles; Road 2133 to 2143, 4.7 miles; Road 2143 to Indigo Springs, three miles; Indigo Springs to 2153, including Chuckle Springs, 6.8 miles; Road 2153 to Road 2154, 7.1 miles; Road 2154 to Timpanogas Lake, 0.3 mile; from Timpanogas Lake to the Pacific Crest Trail, 4.5 miles.

User Groups: Hikers, dogs, and horses. No mountain bikes allowed in wilderness area. No wheelchair facilities.

Permits: A free self-issue Wilderness Permit is required to enter the uppermost section in Waldo Lake Wilderness and is available at the trailhead; otherwise, permits are not required. Parking and access are free.

Maps: For a map of the Willamette National Forest, contact Willamette National Forest Headquarters, 3106 Pierce Parkway, Suite D, Springfield, OR, 97477, 541/225-6300. For a topographic map, ask the USGS for Rigdon Point.

Directions: To find the lower trailhead from Oakridge, drive 1.8 miles east on Highway 58. Between mileposts 37 and 38, turn south toward Hills Creek Dam on Road 23. In 0.5 mile, turn right on Road 21 for 11 miles to the Sand Prairie Campground access. Along this route are many trailheads for the Middle Fork Willamette River Trail, including points at Roads 2120, 2127, 2133, 2143, 2153, and Timpanogas Lake. The uppermost trailhead is found at the Timpanogas Campground: From the lower trailhead, continue on Road 21 another 2.5 miles and turn left on Timpanogas Road 2154, following signs for Timpanogas Lake for 9.3 miles to the campground and a trailhead parking area on the right.

Contact: Willamette National Forest, Middle Fork Ranger District, 46375 Highway 58, Westfir, OR, 97492, 541/782-2283.

67 ROSARY LAKES AND MAIDEN PEAK

5.4–19.0 mi/2.0 hr-2 days 👣5 ⛰9

in the Willamette Pass in Willamette National Forest

Map 5.4, page 266

Of all the peaks in the Waldo Lake area, none stands higher than 7,818-foot Maiden Peak, easily visible from afar for its long, sloping sides and prominent spire near the summit. Looming above Odell Lake, it seems a daunting climb, yet a number of trails crisscross its flanks, including the Pacific Crest Trail, the main access point. Along the way, the trail passes the picturesque Rosary Lakes, a shelter, and little Maiden Lake.

Start by going north on the PCT for 2.7

gradual miles to Rosary Lakes, switchbacking up just before the lakes. Pass the three lakes over 1.4 miles, then keep straight on the PCT, climbing to Maiden Saddle. Keep right on the PCT and continue 1.8 miles to the log cabin Maiden Peak Shelter, built by the Eugene Nordic Club and Forest Service crews during the 1990s. Continue another 0.7 mile on the PCT to a junction. To climb Maiden Peak, turn right here on the Maiden Peak Trail, which climbs 1,700 feet in 2.7 miles to a left-hand, 0.3-mile summit trail climbing the final 300 feet to the crater. Return to the Maiden Peak Trail and continue forward on it to make a loop, descending 1,200 feet in 1.7 miles to a junction, going right toward Maiden Lake. After 0.6 mile, pass the lake and continue 2.3 miles back to the PCT. Go left to return to the highway and parking lot.

User Groups: Hikers, dogs, and horses. No mountain bikes allowed. No wheelchair facilities.

Permits: Permits are not required. Parking and access are free.

Maps: For a map of the Willamette National Forest, contact Willamette National Forest Headquarters, 3106 Pierce Parkway, Suite D, Springfield, OR, 97477, 541/225-6300. For a topographic map, ask the USGS for Willamette Pass and Odell Lake.

Directions: From Oakridge, drive east on Highway 58 to the Pacific Crest Trail lot 0.3 mile east of the Willamette Pass Ski Area.

Contact: Deschutes National Forest, Crescent Ranger District, 136471 Highway 97 North, P.O. Box 208, Crescent, OR, 97733, 541/433-3200.

68 DIVIDE LAKE

8.0 mi/4.0 hr 👣3 ⛰8

southeast of Hills Creek Reservoir in Diamond Peak Wilderness

Map 5.4, page 266   **BEST (**

It's hard to say if Divide Lake is a secret, but not many people seem to go there. For

© SEAN PATRICK HILL

Mount Yoran and Divide Lake

here, the trail switchbacks 0.8 mile up and over the Cascade Divide to meet the PCT.

User Groups: Hikers, dogs, and horses. No mountain bikes allowed. No wheelchair facilities.

Permits: A free self-issue Wilderness Permit is required and is available at the trailhead. Parking and access are free.

Maps: For a map of the Willamette National Forest, contact Willamette National Forest Headquarters, 3106 Pierce Parkway, Suite D, Springfield, OR, 97477, 541/225-6300. For a topographic map, ask the USGS for Diamond Peak.

Directions: To find the lower trailhead from Oakridge, drive 1.8 miles east on Highway 58. Between mileposts 37 and 38, turn south toward Hills Creek Dam on Road 23. Stay on Road 23 for 19.5 miles to a pass at Hemlock Butte. Turn left on a spur road to the trailhead parking area.

Contact: Willamette National Forest, Middle Fork Ranger District, 46375 Highway 58, Westfir, OR, 97492, 541/782-2283.

69 YORAN LAKE

12.0 mi/6.0 hr   👣3 ⛰8

south of Odell Lake in Diamond Peak Wilderness

Map 5.4, page 266

For travelers on Highway 58, one of the most beautiful sights is the view of Diamond Peak rising above enormous Odell Lake. Here's a chance at a much closer view, with long, red Diamond Peak lifting above clear and glassy, tree-rimmed Yoran Lake, a clear and glassy lake. There are plenty of opportunities here for backpackers to take a load off for the night—and there's more than one lake to choose from. Scattered along the Pacific Crest Trail are a bevy of beautiful lakes, each with its own personality: Midnight, Arrowhead, Hidden, and Lils, and a number of small ponds to boot. If you come in via the Pacific Crest Trail, you'll have to bushwhack your way a few hundred yards to big Yoran Lake,

through-hikers on the Pacific Crest Trail, it lies hidden behind the long wall of the Cascade Divide. The Divide Lake Trail itself is somewhat remote, lying west of Diamond Peak at the far end of a long, lonely drive. The trailhead, awash in huckleberries, seems a good sign that this is something special. And it is. The views of Diamond Peak, so close it's startling, provide ever-present company, and views extend to the north out to the Three Sisters. At the end of the trail, huddled beneath the massive volcanic plug of Mount Yoran, is Divide Lake, a perfect pond for camping and swimming. You can continue up the trail and climb out on the Cascade Divide, a wall that abruptly ends at a steep precipice where you can stand with a foot in two watersheds.

Start on the Vivian Lake Trail, going 0.8 mile to Notch Lake, a lovely series of ponds rimmed with mountain heather. Just 0.2 mile past these lakes, go right on the Mount Yoran Trail for three miles (steep at times) to Divide Lake, perfect for a backpacking camp. From where you can continue on a loop past very lovely Karen Lake, then descend along Trapper Creek through thick woods of white pine, Douglas fir, and rhododendron.

The trail begins at Pengra Pass on the Pacific Crest Trail. Go toward Midnight Lake, 1.4 miles into the woods. Continue on the PCT a steady 3.2 miles past Arrowhead Lake on the right and Hidden Lake on the left, with views of Diamond Peak ahead. When you reach Lils Lake, go just beyond it and point your compass true south, passing the lake and a small pond, crest a rise, cross a meadow, and then find the lakeshore of Yoran Lake. Follow the left side of the lake past some campsites to its far end and the Yoran Lake Trail. Head left on the trail to stop by Karen Lake, continuing 4.3 miles to a junction. Go left one mile, eventually joining the dirt road back to Pengra Pass.

User Groups: Hikers, dogs, and horses. No mountain bikes allowed. No wheelchair facilities.

Permits: A free self-issue Wilderness Permit is required and is available at the trailhead. Parking and access are free.

Maps: For a map of the Deschutes National Forest, contact Deschutes National Forest Headquarters, 1001 SW Emkay Drive, Bend, OR, 97702, 541/383-5300. For a topographic map, ask the USGS for Willamette Pass.

Directions: From Oakridge, drive east on Highway 58. West of Willamette Pass 0.5 mile, turn right at a sign for Gold Lake Sno-Park onto Abernethy Road for one mile. Fork left on Road 300, and in another 0.2 mile fork left on a dirt road and park 200 yards down this road at a sign for Midnight Lake.

Contact: Deschutes National Forest, Crescent Ranger District, 136471 Highway 97 North, P.O. Box 208, Crescent, OR, 97733, 541/433-3200.

70 DIAMOND PEAK

12.0 mi/1 day

south of Hills Creek Reservoir in Diamond Peak Wilderness

Map 5.4, page 266

Of all the peaks in the Central Oregon Cascades, Diamond Peak seems the most unassuming. Due to its relative anonymity and distance from major urban areas, this wilderness area does not see the crowds that other areas of the forest do. This is to the benefit of not only the area, but also the hiker and backpacker who comes here. There is much to love about Diamond Peak Wilderness: quiet lakes, stately forests, and, of course, the long and graceful peak that sits in the center of it all. What's more, you can summit 8,744-foot Diamond Peak via a little known climber's trail on its south ridge. Along the way, there are opportunities for resting at two lovely and untrammeled lakes. If you do choose to climb the mountain, come prepared with a map, compass, and path-finding skills. What you'll find on top are views over Waldo Lake, the Three Sisters, Mount Jefferson, and far off, the tip of Mount Hood.

Start off on the Rockpile Trail 1.3 miles to a four-way junction, continuing straight another 1.2 miles, passing the Diamond Rockpile ridge on the left. At the next intersection, either way leads to a lake; to the left 0.2 mile is the larger Marie Lake, and to the right, the main trail continues to a right-hand side trail to little Rockpile Lake. Continue on the main trail 0.5 mile to reach the Pacific Crest Trail. Go left for 1.2 miles to a sharp right-hand turn on a corner atop an open ridge—if you have a GPS device, mark this spot. A series of rock cairns guides climbers up to tree line, then follow the ridge up and over the false summit one mile from the PCT. The next section follows a hogback and is sketchy—be careful. This route arrives at the true summit in 0.4 mile. Return as you came. For those not at ease with the climb, you can continue hiking along the PCT along the slope of Diamond Peak.

User Groups: Hikers, dogs, and horses. No mountain bikes allowed. No wheelchair facilities.

Permits: A free self-issue Wilderness Permit is required and is available at the trailhead. Parking and access are free.

Maps: For a map of the Willamette National Forest, contact Willamette National Forest Headquarters, 3106 Pierce Parkway, Suite D, Springfield, OR, 97477, 541/225-6300. For a topographic map, ask the USGS for Diamond Peak.

Directions: To find the lower trailhead from Oakridge, drive 1.8 miles east on Highway 58. Between mileposts 37 and 38, turn south toward Hills Creek Dam on Road 23. In 0.5 mile go right on Road 21, staying on this route for 29.2 miles. In 0.4 mile past Indigo Springs Campground, go left on Pioneer Gulch Road 2149 for 3.5 miles, then right on Rockpile Road 2160 for 2.3 miles to a sign for the Rockpile Trail, parking beyond the trailhead on the right shoulder.

Contact: Willamette National Forest, Middle Fork Ranger District, 46375 Highway 58, Westfir, OR, 97492, 541/782-2283.

71 WINDY LAKES
11.2 mi/5.0 hr

south of Crescent Lake in Oregon Cascades Recreation Area

Map 5.4, page 266

Just south of Diamond Peak Wilderness is the largely unknown Oregon Cascades Recreation Area. You'd be hard pressed to find any other area in these mountains with so many lakes and ponds. The real jewels are at the end of the trail, where the Windy Lakes fan out below the massive wall of Cowhorn Mountain. Many of these lakes are deep, great for swimming, and certainly make great camping spots. Just be aware that early summer brings mosquitoes.

Begin on the Meek Lake Trail, crossing Summit Creek in 0.2 mile and arriving at Meek Lake in another 0.3 mile. From there the

trail ambles into a pond-strewn forest for most of the next 2.4 miles. At a junction, go left to continue toward Windy Lakes (the right-hand junction heads to Summit Lake). After 1.6 miles the trail reaches North Windy Lake, and a right-hand side trail leads down to East Windy Lake. At the intersection with the Crescent Lake Trail, go right toward South Windy Lake. In 0.9 mile the trail skirts East Windy, passes another lake, then reaches its end at South Windy Lake. Return as you came.

User Groups: Hikers, dogs, horses, and mountain bikes.

Permits: Permits are not required. Parking and access are free.

Maps: For a map of the Deschutes National Forest, contact Deschutes National Forest Headquarters, 1001 SW Emkay Drive, Bend, OR, 97702, 541/383-5300. For a topographic map, ask the USGS for Cowhorn Mountain.

Directions: Drive Highway 58, going seven miles east of the Willamette Pass to Crescent Junction, turning right on Road 60 for 2.2 miles. At an intersection, turn right to stay on this road for another five miles. Turn right on dirt Road 6010 to Summit Lake. Follow this road 3.9 miles to the Meek Lake Trail on the left.

Contact: Deschutes National Forest, Crescent Ranger District, 136471 Highway 97 North, P.O. Box 208, Crescent, OR, 97733, 541/433-3200.

72 COWHORN MOUNTAIN LOOP
11.9 mi/6.0 hr

south of Hills Creek Reservoir in Willamette National Forest

Map 5.4, page 266

Two mountain peaks, worn down by time, stand sentry over the source of the Middle Fork Willamette River. In their shadow, Timpanogas and Indigo Lakes glisten in the light. Sawtooth Mountain stands more than 1,000 feet above Indigo Lake, but the goal here is

Cowhorn Mountain, which once really did have a horn (it fell off in a 1911 storm). A magnificent loop climbs to the Pacific Crest Trail and scrambles to the 7,664 peak of Cowhorn with its amazing view north to the Three Sisters and south to Crater Lake.

Begin by following the Indigo Lake Trail 0.7 mile to a junction, staying to the left another 1.2 miles to Indigo, where a one-mile trail circles the lake. Continue on the main trail up a series of steady-climbing switchbacks 1.7 miles to a pass. To the right, a climber's trail heads up two miles and 600 feet to Sawtooth Mountain. Go left on the Windy Pass Trail 2.1 miles to a junction; to climb to the peak of Cowhorn go right 0.3 mile to the Pacific Crest Trail, then right on the PCT 0.3 mile to a scramble trail by a rock cairn following a ridge up the steep climb 0.4 mile. To descend on the loop, return to the Windy Pass Trail and go right and down 2.7 miles to a junction, and turn left toward Timpanogas Lake for 1.1 miles. At the lake, go right 0.4 mile back to the campground.

User Groups: Hikers, dogs, and mountain bikes. No horses allowed. No wheelchair facilities.

Permits: Permits are not required. Parking and access are free.

Maps: For a map of the Willamette National Forest, contact Willamette National Forest Headquarters, 3106 Pierce Parkway, Suite D, Springfield, OR, 97477, 541/225-6300. For a topographic map, ask the USGS for Cowhorn Mountain.

Directions: To find the lower trailhead from Oakridge, drive 1.8 miles east on Highway 58. Between mileposts 37 and 38, turn south toward Hills Creek Dam on Road 23. In 0.5 mile, turn right on Road 21 for 31.2 miles. Turn right on Timpanogas Road 2154, going 9.3 miles to the Timpanogas Campground on the left. Drive into the campground and watch for the trailhead sign on the right.

Contact: Willamette National Forest, Middle Fork Ranger District, 46375 Highway 58, Westfir, OR, 97492, 541/782-2283.

73 BULLPUP LAKE AND BULLDOG ROCK

1.4-7.0 mi/1.0-3.5 hr

north of North Umpqua River in Umpqua National Forest

Map 5.4, page 266

The Calapooya Mountains form a high divide between the watershed of the North Umpqua and the Willamette Rivers. One entry point to this heavily eroded lava mountain range is via Bullpup Lake, an easy destination in itself, with a shake-roofed shelter on the shore and towering andesite cliffs above it. Top that slope and the views quickly extend out to the Cascade Range, and you can go on farther to the Bear Camp Shelter, passing Bulldog Rock along the way.

The initial hike extends only 0.4 mile to Bullpup Lake and the shelter, and you can circle the lake on a 0.6-mile loop. At the far end of that loop (going left is the shortest, at 0.2-mile) you can continue up the slope and on the Bulldog Rock Trail 2.8 miles to a view of Bulldog Rock, and another 2.2 miles beyond that to the Bear Camp Shelter.

User Groups: Hikers, dogs, horses, and mountain bikes. No wheelchair facilities.

Permits: Permits are not required. Parking and access are free.

Maps: For a map of the Umpqua National Forest, contact Umpqua National Forest, 2900 NW Stewart Parkway, Roseburg, OR, 97470, 541/672-6601. For a topographic map, ask the USGS for Chiltcoot Mountain and Reynolds Ridge.

Directions: From Roseburg, drive east on OR 138 for 38.4 miles and turn left on Steamboat Creek Road for 10.4 miles to a fork. Go right on Bend Creek-Washboard Road 3817 for 2.2 miles, then right on Road 3850 for 5.6 miles, then left on Road 200 for 0.1 mile, and finally left on Road 300 for four miles to the trail parking area on the right.

Contact: Umpqua National Forest, North Umpqua Ranger District, 18782 North Umpqua Highway, Glide, OR, 97443, 541/496-3532.

74 ILLAHEE ROCK LOOKOUT
1.4 mi/1.0 hr   🏃1 ⛰8

north of Boulder Creek Wilderness in Umpqua
National Forest

Map 5.4, page 266

Not one, but two fire lookout towers are set
atop 5,382-foot Illahee Rock. The newer one
was built in 1958, and its 40-foot-high lookout
is staffed each summer. The older one is a
cupola-style lookout building, built in 1925
and housed in a lightning cage. This easy 1.4-
mile round-trip climbs 500 feet to the towers,
with high-point views extending out over a
number of Cascade peaks.

User Groups: Hikers, dogs, horses, and mountain bikes. No wheelchair facilities.

Permits: Permits are not required. Parking
and access are free.

Maps: For a map of the Umpqua National
Forest, contact Umpqua National Forest, 2900
NW Stewart Parkway, Roseburg, OR, 97470,
541/672-6601. For a topographic map, ask the
USGS for Illahee Rock.

Directions: From Roseburg, drive 47 miles on
OR 138 and turn left on Illahee Road 4760 for
eight miles. Go straight on Road 100 for 1.3
miles, then left on the steep and rocky Road
104 to its end.

Contact: Umpqua National Forest, North
Umpqua Ranger District, 18782 North Umpqua Highway, Glide, OR, 97443, 541/496-
3532.

75 NORTH UMPQUA NATIONAL RECREATION TRAIL
3.5-79.0 mi/1-10 days   🏃5 ⛰8

east of Roseburg on the North Umpqua River

Map 5.4, page 266

Just past Idleyld Park in the canyon of the
North Umpqua River begins a trail and
backpacking adventure. The North Umpqua National Recreation Trail follows the
river 79 miles, passing waterfalls, rapids, and

Toketee Falls on the North Umpqua River

© SEAN PATRICK HILL

gorges, crossing creeks, and meeting up with
several side trails leading to old homesteads
and shelters. You can even access hot springs
along the way. The trail follows the river up
to its headwaters at Maidu Lake high in the
Cascades, with many access points along the
good steady trip. You'll pass through unique
forests of sugar pine, Shasta red fir, and incense cedar. Be sure to contact the USFS and
BLM about trail conditions; at the time of
this writing, the Calf Segment is closed due
to unsafe conditions.

The Umpqua Trail is segmented into sections suitable for day hikes or backpacking
trips. The Swiftwater Trailhead accesses the
15.5-mile Tioga section along the south bank
of the river, ending at the Wright Creek Trailhead. From here, it's 5.5 miles to the Mott
Trailhead, then 5.0 miles to the Panther Trailhead. The next 3.7-mile section to Calf Creek
Trailhead is closed as of now. The 3.6-mile
section to Marsters Trailhead is open, however.
From here, the trail follows the north bank of

the river 4.1 miles through the Jessie Wright section to the Soda Springs Trailhead, then the longer 9.6-mile Deer Leap section to the Toketee Lake Trailhead. From here the trail leaves Highway 138, going 3.5 miles to the Hot Springs Trailhead, and on 13.0 miles into the strangely named Dread and Terror Section to the White Mule Trailhead, another 6.3 miles through the Lemolo section to the Kelsay Valley Trailhead, and finally 9.0 miles through the Maidu segment to the Digit Point Trailhead and the end of the trail.

User Groups: Hikers, dogs, horses, and mountain bikes. No wheelchair facilities.

Permits: Permits are not required. Parking and access are free for most trailheads, excepting Umpqua Hot Springs.

Maps: For a map of the Umpqua National Forest, contact Umpqua National Forest, 2900 NW Stewart Parkway, Roseburg, OR, 97470, 541/672-6601. For a topographic map, ask the USGS for Old Fairview, Mace Mountain, Steamboat, Illahee Rock, Toketee Falls, Lemolo Lake, Tolo Mountain, and Burn Butte.

Directions: To access the Tioga Trailhead, the westernmost entry for the North Umpqua Trail, follow OR 138 east from Roseburg 22 miles. One mile past Idleyld Park, turn right at a "Swiftwater Park" sign, cross the river, and park at the Tioga Trailhead. Trailheads are numerous along Highway 138 and Forest Service Road 3401.

Contact: Bureau of Land Management, Roseburg District, 777 NW Garden Valley Boulevard, Roseburg, OR, 97471, 541/440-4930, or Umpqua National Forest, 2900 NW Stewart Parkway, Roseburg, OR, 97470, 541/672-6601.

76 SUSAN CREEK FALLS AND FALL CREEK FALLS

3.8 mi/1.5 hr   🥾1 △7

east of Roseburg on the North Umpqua River

Map 5.4, page 266

If you're in the area of the North Umpqua River and looking for a place to stretch your legs or just take in the fresh air, try these two waterfalls just off Highway 138. The 70-foot Susan Creek Falls tumble over the canyon wall, on top of which is a fenced area of Indian mounds, where tribes reputedly held vision quests for their youth. A bit further east is Fall Creek Falls, with a side trail leading to a columnar basalt outcrop called Jobs Garden. Both trails are easily hiked together, though from two different trailheads.

The Susan Creek Falls Trail sets out 0.7 mile up to a viewpoint of the trail, and continues 0.3 mile to the top of the canyon and the Indian mounds. The Fall Creek Falls Trail climbs 0.9 mile to the top of the falls, with a side trail to Jobs Garden at the 0.3-mile mark.

User Groups: Hikers and dogs only. No horses or mountain bikes. Susan Creek Falls is wheelchair accessible.

Permits: Permits are not required. Parking and access are free.

Maps: For a topographic map, ask the USGS for Old Fairview and Mace Mountain.

Directions: To access Susan Creek Falls, drive east of Roseburg 28.3 miles on OR 138 to the Susan Creek Recreation Area lot on the right. To access Fall Creek Falls, drive another 3.9 miles east of Susan Creek on OR 138 and park at a trailhead sign on the left.

Contact: Bureau of Land Management, Roseburg District, 777 NW Garden Valley Boulevard, Roseburg, OR, 97471, 541/440-4930, or Umpqua National Forest, North Umpqua Ranger District, 18782 North Umpqua Highway, Glide, OR, 97443, 541/496-3532.

77 BOULDER CREEK

8.0-21.6 mi/3.0 hr-2 days   🥾3 △7

north of the North Umpqua River in Boulder Creek Wilderness

Map 5.4, page 266

Above the North Umpqua River, this low-elevation wilderness area is open year-round and makes for excellent backpacking. There is camping available on a plateau of ponderosa pines at the top of the Boulder Creek canyon. From this plateau, trails radiate in all directions; hike into this area to get a taste of what these mountains offer.

Go under the giant pipe and head up the Pine Bench Trail 0.4 mile, then go left 1.5 miles to top Pine Bench. Once you reach another trail junction, go right 0.4 mile to a viewpoint with a spring and camping area. Continue on 1.7 miles to a crossing of Boulder Creek, a good turnaround point. Backpackers can follow the Boulder Creek Trail another 6.8 miles, fording the creek three times then grinding uphill on a series of switchbacks to its end. Return as you came.

User Groups: Hikers, dogs, and horses. No mountain bikes allowed. No wheelchair facilities.

Permits: A free self-issue Wilderness Permit is required and is available at the trailhead. Parking and access are free.

Maps: For a map of the Umpqua National Forest and Boulder Creek Wilderness, contact Umpqua National Forest, 2900 NW Stewart Parkway, Roseburg, OR, 97470, 541/672-6601. For a topographic map, ask the USGS for Illahee Rock.

Directions: From Roseburg, drive 54.7 miles east on OR 138. Between mileposts 54 and 55, turn left at a sign for Spring Creek then immediately left on Soda Springs Road, following this gravel road 1.4 miles to a trailhead parking area on the left.

Contact: Umpqua National Forest, Diamond Lake Ranger District, 2020 Toketee Ranger Station Road, Idleyld Park, OR, 97477, 541/498-2531.

78 TOKETEE AND WATSON FALLS
1.4 mi/0.5 hr 👥1 ⛰8

west of Toketee Ranger Station in Umpqua National Forest

Map 5.4, page 266

These two easy trails head to two of the Umpqua Canyon's most famous falls. Toketee Falls is a heavily photographed (and heavily visited) plunge along the North Umpqua River, the water spills in two tiers, one falling 40 feet into a bowl and the other 80 feet over a notch in some of the most beautiful examples of hexagonal columnar basalt anywhere. From the trailhead, you'll head 0.8 mile out and back to a viewpoint overlooking this deep gorge.

You'll see Watson Falls, the highest in southwest Oregon, not from the top but from the bottom of the 272-foot plunge. Watson makes a fun 0.6-mile loop and passes a viewpoint at the base of the falls.

User Groups: Hikers and dogs only. No wheelchair facilities.

Permits: Permits are not required. Parking and access are free.

Maps: For a map of the Umpqua National Forest and Boulder Creek Wilderness, contact Umpqua National Forest, 2900 NW Stewart Parkway, Roseburg, OR, 97470, 541/672-6601. For a topographic map, ask the USGS for Illahee Rock.

Directions: To access Toketee Falls, drive 58.6 miles east of Roseburg on OR 138 and turn north on Toketee-Rigdon Road 34. Turn left at each junction for 0.4 mile to a parking area. To access Watson Falls, drive 60.9 miles east of Roseburg on OR 138 and turn south on Fish Creek Road 37 to a lot on the right.

Contact: Umpqua National Forest, Diamond Lake Ranger District, 2020 Toketee Ranger Station Road, Idleyld Park, OR, 97477, 541/498-2531.

79 UMPQUA HOT SPRINGS
0.6 mi/0.25 hr 🥾1 ⛰7

north of Toketee Ranger Station in Umpqua National Forest

Map 5.4, page 266

Along this stretch of the North Umpqua River Trail, a spur heads off to one of the most famous hot springs in Oregon: the sheltered pool of Umpqua Hot Springs. A number of pools have been dug into the orange travertine deposits that form this cascading cliff down to the North Umpqua River and its old-growth forests. Recently, the bridge has been removed over the river, but by the time of this publication it may have already been replaced. If not, you can hike in from a trailhead on Road 3401 just before the road crosses the river, which adds 1.6 miles to the hike but also adds a profusion of spring-flowering rhododendron bushes.

From the lot, follow the trail toward the river to a crossing and up the hill for 0.1 mile. At the junction, go right 0.2 mile to the shelter atop the cliff and the hot springs. The hot springs are clothing-optional.

User Groups: Hikers only. No wheelchair facilities.

Permits: Permits are not required. A federal Northwest Forest Pass is required to park here; the cost is $5 a day or $30 for an annual pass. You can buy a day pass at the trailhead, at ranger stations, or through private vendors.

Maps: For a map of the Umpqua National Forest and Boulder Creek Wilderness, contact Umpqua National Forest, 2900 NW Stewart Parkway, Roseburg, OR, 97470, 541/672-6601. For a topographic map, ask the USGS for Illahee Rock.

Directions: Drive 58.6 miles east of Roseburg on OR 138 and turn north on Toketee-Rigdon Road 34. Keep left along the lake and continue two miles, forking right on Thorn Prairie Road to a large lot on the left.

Contact: Umpqua National Forest, Diamond Lake Ranger District, 2020 Toketee Ranger Station Road, Idleyld Park, OR, 97477, 541/498-2531.

80 LEMOLO FALLS
3.4 mi/1.5 hr 🥾1 ⛰7

north of Toketee Ranger Station in Umpqua National Forest

Map 5.4, page 266

On this upper reach of the North Umpqua Trail, near the oddly named Dread and Terror Ridge, the river plunges over 100-foot Lemolo Falls and into a canyon. This woodsy hike begins at the spot the trail crosses Road 2610. Start the section of trail south of the road, crossing a canal. In 1.7 miles you'll reach a viewpoint of the falls, then continue another 0.7 mile to a footbridge crossing of the river. From here, the trail continues on another 10 miles towards the Umpqua Hot Springs.

User Groups: Hikers, dogs, horses, and mountain bikes. No wheelchair facilities.

Permits: Permits are not required. Parking and access are free.

Maps: For a map of the Umpqua National Forest, contact Umpqua National Forest, 2900 NW Stewart Parkway, Roseburg, OR, 97470, 541/672-6601. For a topographic map, ask the USGS for Lemolo Lake.

Directions: Drive east of Roseburg 70 miles on OR 138 and turn north on Road 2610 towards Lemolo Lake Recreation Area. After five miles cross the dam and go left on Road 2610 for 0.6 mile to a parking area.

Contact: Umpqua National Forest, Diamond Lake Ranger District, 2020 Toketee Ranger Station Road, Idleyld Park, OR, 97477, 541/498-2531.

81 WOLF CREEK FALLS
2.6 mi/1.0 hr 🥾1 ⛰7

southeast of Glide on the Little River

Map 5.4, page 266

The so-called "Land of Umpqua" (as the tourism advertisements like to call it) is, above all, a land of waterfalls. There are so many waterfalls feeding the North Umpqua River Canyon that it would be quite impossible to do them all even in a week's time. But here and there, you can catch some of the finest. The 70-foot Wolf Creek Falls feeds the Little River and makes for a good 2.6-mile in-and-out hike from the trailhead. In the rainy season, the falls really pound, but in the dryer months you'll get a chance to see some of the carved-out bedrock beneath the plunge.

User Groups: Hikers and dogs only. No wheel-chair facilities.

Permits: Permits are not required. Parking and access are free.

Maps: For a topographic map, ask the USGS for Red Butte.

Directions: From Roseburg, drive east on OR 138 toward Glide. At milepost 16, go right on Little River Road for 10.4 miles and park at the Wolf Creek Trail parking on the right.

Contact: Bureau of Land Management, Rose-burg District, 777 NW Garden Valley Boule-vard, Roseburg, OR, 97471, 541/440-4930.

82 HEMLOCK LAKE
7.2 mi/3.5 hr

southeast of Glide in Umpqua National Forest

Map 5.4, page 266

Beyond the reservoir of Hemlock Lake lie some of the most beautiful alpine meadows in this part of the world. Hellebore, also known as corn lily, bloom their tall sprouts in a series of meadows dotted by Douglas fir and Shasta red fir. In the Yellow Jacket Glade you'll find shooting stars (the flower, not the falling stardust) and trilliums, and in other sections you'll see marsh marigolds, yellow fawn lilies, bunchberry, and violets.

Starting on the Hemlock Creek Trail you'll quickly come to a junction; go right then left on the Yellow Jacket Loop Trail for a 1.1-mile tour of Hemlock Meadows. At a junction, it's worth it to go right up 0.8 mile to 5,310-foot Flat Rock with its views of the rim of Crater Lake, Diamond Peak, Mount Thielsen, and Mount Bailey. Head back to Yellow Jacket and go right at the junction through Yellowjacket

Glade, continuing 2.9 miles along a viewpoint ridge and paralleling Road 625 to the next junction, heading left on the faint path and passing Dead Cow Lake. Stay left at the next two junctions for 1.6 miles, reaching the shore of Hemlock Lake and returning to the park-ing area.

User Groups: Hikers, dogs, horses, and moun-tain bikes. No wheelchair facilities.

Permits: Permits are not required. Parking and access are free.

Maps: For a map of the Umpqua National Forest, contact Umpqua National Forest, 2900 NW Stewart Parkway, Roseburg, OR, 97470, 541/672-6601. For a topographic map, ask the USGS for Quartz Mountain.

Directions: Drive east of Roseburg on OR 138 to milepost 16 and turn right on Little River Road, which becomes Road 27. Follow this road 18.8 miles on pavement and 11.5 miles on gravel to Hemlock Lake, crossing the dam to an intersection and the trailhead.

Contact: Umpqua National Forest, North Umpqua Ranger District, 18782 North Um-pqua Highway, Glide, OR, 97443, 541/496-3532.

83 TWIN LAKES AND TWIN LAKES MOUNTAIN
3.2-5.4 mi/1.5-3.0 hr

south of the North Umpqua River in Umpqua National Forest

Map 5.4, page 266

If you are a novice backpacker, or just want a quick trip, or are camping with kids, make Twin Lakes your destination. Once you're settled in and the tent is pitched, you can ramble off on a couple side trails: Twin Lakes Mountain, for example, is a fairly easy climb to a viewpoint above the lakes that also looks out over the Cascade Mountains. You can also just circle the lakes to find a couple old shel-ters. Beyond lies the largely roadless Boulder Creek Wilderness.

From the trailhead, hike in 0.6 mile on

the Twin Lakes Trail to a junction, with a viewpoint of three Cascade peaks along the way. Turn right then a quick left for 0.3 mile to an old shelter. To the right at this junction are six campsites with picnic tables, and this Twin Lakes Loop Trail joins a loop around the larger of the two lakes, 0.7 mile in all. At the far end of the lake, a spur trail joins a 0.7-mile loop trail around the smaller lake, with another log shelter along the way.

To climb Twin Lakes Mountain head back from the old shelter on the larger lake toward the parking area. At the junction, go right and then stay right for 1.1 miles to a viewpoint. Another 0.6 mile and this trail ends at Road 530.

User Groups: Hikers, dogs, horses, and mountain bikes. No wheelchair facilities.

Permits: Permits are not required. Parking and access are free.

Maps: For a map of the Umpqua National Forest, contact Umpqua National Forest, 2900 NW Stewart Parkway, Roseburg, OR, 97470, 541/672-6601. For a topographic map, ask the USGS for Twin Lakes Mountain.

Directions: From Roseburg, drive 49 miles east on OR 138. Cross the North Umpqua River on Marsters Bridge and go right on Wilson Creek Road 4770, following this gravel road nine miles to the trailhead parking at road's end.

Contact: Umpqua National Forest, North Umpqua Ranger District, 18782 North Umpqua Highway, Glide, OR, 97443, 541/496-3532.

84 TIPSOO PEAK

6.2 mi/2.5 hr

northeast of Diamond Lake in Mount Thielsen Wilderness

Map 5.4, page 266

Nearby Crater Lake National Park and Diamond Lake attract a lot of tourists, but this alpine area begs for exploration. Just inside Mount Thielsen Wilderness is 8,034-foot Tipsoo Peak, a pretty substantial peak with the accompanying view it deserves. What's more, this trail leads right to its summit with a breathtaking view of the alpine territory around it, including the pumice plains dotted with clumps of trees, not to mention a view of peaks extending from Mount Shasta in California to the Three Sisters in Central Oregon, with Mount Thielsen's domineering spire clearly marking the centerpiece of this wilderness.

The Tipsoo Peak Trail itself is a single track heading up 3.1 miles to the summit. It is possible, with a compass, to hike cross-country across Tipsoo Meadow 0.5 mile to the Pacific Crest Trail. From there, Maidu and Miller Lakes are five miles to the north, Howlock Meadows only 1.6 miles south, and the access to the Mount Thielsen climbing trail five miles beyond that.

User Groups: Hikers, dogs, and horses. No mountain bikes allowed. No wheelchair facilities.

Permits: A free self-issue Wilderness Permit is required and is available at the trailhead. A federal Northwest Forest Pass is required to park here; the cost is $5 a day or $30 for an annual pass. You can buy a day pass at the trailhead, at ranger stations, or through private vendors.

Maps: For a map of the Umpqua National Forest and Mount Thielsen Wilderness, contact Umpqua National Forest, 2900 NW Stewart Parkway, Roseburg, OR, 97470, 541/672-6601. For a topographic map, ask the USGS for Mount Thielsen.

Directions: Drive east of Roseburg 75 miles on OR 138. Near milepost 75, turn east on Cinnamon Butte Road 4793 and go 1.7 miles. Go straight on Wits End Road 100 for 3.2 miles to a Tipsoo Trail sign on the right.

Contact: Umpqua National Forest, Diamond Lake Ranger District, 2020 Toketee Ranger Station Road, Idleyld Park, OR, 97477, 541/498-2531.

85 DIAMOND LAKE

11.5 mi/5.0 hr

on Diamond Lake in Umpqua National Forest

Map 5.4, page 266

It's easy to see why 3,015-acre Diamond Lake is one of the most popular destinations in the area, even more so than nearby Crater Lake National Park. Two mountains hover at opposite sides above the placid waters: Mount Thielsen and Mount Bailey. There are hundreds of campsites along the lake—well-established car campsites, needless to say—and picnic areas and boat ramps. There are, too, a few side trails to little Teal Lake and Horse Lake. All in all, the Diamond Lake Trail is a good trail if you're staying here. Plus, the entire route is paved, making it accessible to all and a good route for bikes. And if you're in the mood for a swim, Diamond Lake's 20-foot average depth means it warms up quickly, unlike so many of the other Cascade high-mountain lakes.

You can go either way along the loop trail. The east side follows routes through the large Diamond Lake Campground for most of its 3.8 miles to the South Shore Picnic Area. The south side continues 1.9 miles to a crossing of Road 4795, with side trails to two small lakes and along Silent Creek. The west side of the lakeshore is mostly private land, and the trail goes 2.9 miles above the road, but with views to Mount Thielsen. After crossing the road again near Thielsen View Campground and going another 1.2 miles to the road crossing at Lake Creek. The final uninterrupted stretch travels 1.7 miles along the north shore back to the lodge.

User Groups: Hikers, dogs, and mountain bikes. No horses allowed. The paved lakeshore loop is wheelchair accessible.

Permits: Permits are not required. Parking and access are free.

Maps: For a map of the Umpqua National Forest, contact Umpqua National Forest, 2900 NW Stewart Parkway, Roseburg, OR, 97470, 541/672-6601. For a topographic map, ask the USGS for Diamond Lake.

Directions: To find the Diamond Lake Lodge, drive east of Roseburg 78.6 miles east on OR 138 to a sign for Diamond Lake, and turn right on Road 6592, following signs for the Lodge, turning right and going past a boat ramp to the parking area.

Contact: Umpqua National Forest, Diamond Lake Ranger District, 2020 Toketee Ranger Station Road, Idleyld Park, OR, 97477, 541/498-2531.

86 THIELSEN CREEK AND HOWLOCK MOUNTAIN

11.4-15.7 mi/6.0-8.0 hr

northeast of Diamond Lake in Mount Thielsen Wilderness

Map 5.4, page 266

A series of meadows in the Mount Thielsen Wilderness lie strewn along Thielsen Creek and the Pacific Crest Trail, and the hardy hiker can visit one, two, or all three of them in a single hike. Along the way, there's plenty to see in this alpine country, including Mount Thielsen itself looming above this country like a church spire. The Howlock Mountain Trail provides the opportunity for a long loop, with extended opportunities for backpacking available, too.

The Howlock Mountain Trail starts at the trailhead, ducking through a tunnel under the highway, and continuing 1.1 miles to a junction with the Spruce Ridge Trail. Stay left on the Thielsen Creek Trail another 2.4 miles through a hot, dusty country of lodgepole pines and manzanita bushes to Timothy Meadows and Thielsen Creek. To continue on to Thielsen Meadow, go right 2.2 miles along Thielsen Creek to the junction of the Pacific Crest Trail.

From here, you can return as you came, or for an outstanding loop, go north and left on the PCT for three miles along the base of Howlock Mountain to Howlock Meadows, then left 3.5 miles back to Timothy Meadows.

User Groups: Hikers, dogs, and horses. No mountain bikes allowed. No wheelchair facilities.

Permits: A free self-issue Wilderness Permit is required and is available at the trailhead. A federal Northwest Forest Pass is required to park here; the cost is $5 a day or $30 for an annual pass. You can buy a day pass at the trailhead, at ranger stations, or through private vendors.

Maps: For a map of the Umpqua National Forest and Mount Thielsen Wilderness, contact Umpqua National Forest, 2900 NW Stewart Parkway, Roseburg, OR, 97470, 541/672-6601. For a topographic map, ask the USGS for Mount Thielsen.

Directions: From Roseburg, drive 78.6 miles east on OR 138 to a sign for Diamond Lake, and turn right on Road 6592 for 0.3 mile to a parking area on the left.

Contact: Umpqua National Forest, Diamond Lake Ranger District, 2020 Toketee Ranger Station Road, Idleyld Park, OR, 97477, 541/498-2531.

87 MOUNT THIELSEN
10.0 mi/6.0 hr   🏃5 ⛰10

northeast of Diamond Lake in Mount Thielsen Wilderness

Map 5.4, page 266   **BEST (**

Mount Thielsen's peak, a towering 9,182 feet in the sky, has earned the nickname "Lightning Rod of the Cascades" for no uncertain reason. What was once an 11,000-foot-high volcano has been whittled down by glaciers to its single lava plug, an andesite core left after 100,000 years. What you'll find on the peak are the lightning-melted spots of fulgurite, a re-crystalized glassy rock that pocks the summit boulders. Named for a pioneer railroad engineer, Thielsen is no climb for the weak-hearted. It demands endurance, stamina, sureness of hands, and outright skill; the final ascent is a dangerous technical climb that requires ropes and climbing partners to aid you.

Any ascent past the topmost ledge, a Class 4 rock climb, is done at your own risk. *Only experienced climbers should attempt this final pitch.* Should you make it, you'll find a canister summit register at the top.

From the Mount Thielsen Trailhead, climb 1.4 miles into the forest, staying right at a junction with the Spruce Ridge Trail, and continuing another 2.4 miles into the Wilderness Area to a junction with the PCT. To attempt the summit, continue straight up the ridge 1.2 miles on a climber's trail, spiraling to the right around the eastern ledge at the base of the 80-foot peak. The drop from this ledge to the east is thousands of feet, a dizzying view down to the deserts of Eastern Oregon. *Do not climb to the peak without rock climbing experience; rockfall and exposure make this pitch dangerous.* To ascend to the peak requires climbing up the series of cracks and fissures in the rock, wedging your way up to the peak. To be sure, the peak is an unnerving experience and only for the stout-hearted. The shoulder beneath the peak has expansive views across the Cascade Range, down into Crater Lake, and out and over Diamond Lake to the west.

User Groups: Hikers only. Dogs are not recommended. Horses can access the PCT from the nearby Howlock Mountain Trailhead. No mountain bikes allowed. No wheelchair facilities.

Permits: A free self-issue Wilderness Permit is required and is available at the trailhead. A federal Northwest Forest Pass is required to park here; the cost is $5 a day or $30 for an annual pass. You can buy a day pass at the trailhead, at ranger stations, or through private vendors.

Maps: For a map of the Umpqua National Forest and Mount Thielsen Wilderness, contact Umpqua National Forest, 2900 NW Stewart Parkway, Roseburg, OR, 97470, 541/672-6601. For a topographic map, ask the USGS for Mount Thielsen.

Directions: From Roseburg, drive 81.6 miles east on OR 138 to a large trailhead parking area on the left.

Contact: Umpqua National Forest, Diamond Lake Ranger District, 2020 Toketee Ranger Station Road, Idleyld Park, OR, 97477, 541/498-2531.

88 MOUNT BAILEY
9.8 mi/5.0 hr

west of Diamond Lake in Umpqua National Forest

Map 5.4, page 266	**BEST**

The Mount Bailey National Recreation Trail follows what in winter becomes a Nordic trail. Blue diamonds lead the way to some alpine ski runs on this dome-shaped mountain above Diamond Lake. But in summer, this mountain makes a fairly easy summit— no gear or technical expertise required. All you'll need is a little stamina to make it up the crater rim to an 8,368-foot view of the Cascade Mountains in all directions. From Road 300, the trail climbs steadily up 2.2 miles to cross another dirt road, then begins to really climb up the mountain's ridge for 2.7 miles and up 2,300 feet to the south summit with its small crater and finally the true summit.

User Groups: Hikers and dogs only. No wheelchair facilities.

Permits: Permits are not required. Parking and access are free.

Maps: For a map of the Umpqua National Forest, contact Umpqua National Forest, 2900 NW Stewart Parkway, Roseburg, OR, 97470, 541/672-6601. For a topographic map, ask the USGS for Diamond Lake.

Directions: Drive east of Roseburg 78.6 miles on OR 138 to a sign for Diamond Lake, and turn right on Road 6592, following this road to the South Shore Picnic Area. Turn right on Road 4795 for 1.7 miles and turn left on Road 300 for 0.4 mile to a parking area.

Contact: Umpqua National Forest, Diamond Lake Ranger District, 2020 Toketee Ranger Station Road, Idleyld Park, OR, 97477, 541/498-2531.

89 BUCKEYE AND CLIFF LAKES
3.4-8.9 mi/1.5-4.5 hr

in the Rogue-Umpqua Divide Wilderness

Map 5.4, page 266

In this 16- to 25-million-year-old mountain range, the forest has had time to get a foothold in this lovely bottom of high lakes. Even a massive landslide that befell this valley when Grasshopper Mountain collapsed 1,000 years ago has been repaired by the trees. Beneath what is left of that mountain, Buckeye and Cliff Lakes warm in the afternoon sun and invite backpackers. Being so close to Fish Lake (see next listing), you can easily turn this into a multi-day trip. For a different entry into the Rogue-Umpqua Divide Wilderness, try starting this trail from the Skimmerhorn Trailhead. You'll climb to a high meadow above the lakes.

To access the Lakes Trail from the Skimmerhorn Trailhead, hike in 0.2 mile and keep left at the first junction, going another 0.7 mile and keeping right at the next junction with the Indian Trail. After 0.1 mile go left at the next junction with the Acker Divide Trail for 0.4 mile, arriving at Buckeye Lake. In 0.3 mile arrive at Cliff Lake. From here, you can return as you came.

To continue on a longer loop to Grasshopper Mountain, continue another 0.3 mile past Cliff Lake to a junction. Now go right on the Grasshopper Trail and climb onto a high plateau of mixed conifer for one mile to Grasshopper Meadow. A right-hand junction leads 0.6 mile and 300 feet up to Grasshopper Mountain and good views. Going straight here leads to a junction with the Acker Divide Trail; go right on this trail and down 0.9 mile to a trailhead near Road 550 and go right, continuing on the Acker Divide Trail. In 0.4 mile find Mosquito Camp; continue on 1.7 miles, passing Little Fish Lake, and rejoining the Lakes Trail. Go left one mile to the trailhead.

User Groups: Hikers, dogs, and horses. No mountain bikes allowed. No wheelchair facilities.

Permits: A free self-issue Wilderness Permit is required and is available at the trailhead. Parking and access are free.

Maps: For a map of the Umpqua National Forest and Rogue-Umpqua Divide Wilderness, contact Umpqua National Forest, 2900 NW Stewart Parkway, Roseburg, OR, 97470, 541/672-6601. For a topographic map, ask the USGS for Buckeye Lake.

Directions: From Roseburg, drive 25 miles north on I-5 to the Canyonville exit 98, following signs towards Crater Lake. In Canyonville, turn east on 3rd Street and follow this road, which becomes the Tiller-Trail Highway, 23.3 miles to Tiller. Go through town and turn left on Road 46 for 24.2 miles, then go right on Road 2823. Follow Skimmerhorn Trailhead signs for 2.4 miles to a right turn on Road 2830 and go 3.9 miles. Turn left on Road 600 for 1.8 miles to road's end at the trailhead.

Contact: Umpqua National Forest, Tiller Ranger District, 27812 Tiller Trail Highway, Tiller, OR, 97484, 541/825-3201.

90 FISH LAKE
12.6 mi/7.0 hr   🏃3 ⛰9

in the Rogue-Umpqua Divide Wilderness

Map 5.4, page 266

This loop serves as an introduction to the Rogue-Umpqua Divide Wilderness, following a rugged landscape where the key word is "Highrock"—as in Highrock Creek, Highrock Meadow, and Highrock Mountain. Fish Lake, true to its name in regards to the fish, is a good destination for backpackers, as there are several camping sites along the lake, and access to a multitude of lakes and trails beyond. Take this trail up the dramatic andesite cliff-strewn backbone of Rocky Ridge for a peak experience.

From the Beaver Swamp Trailhead take the right-hand Beaver Swamp Trail in 1.5 miles to Fish Lake, staying left at a junction. When you reach the lake, go left around the lake and continue on the Fish Lake Trail past camping spots 1.3 miles

to a junction, staying left again for another three miles to the lovely Highrock Meadows beneath Highrock Mountain. At the next junction, go left on the Rogue Umpqua Divide Trail toward Rocky Ridge, staying left at a junction in 0.4 mile and continuing up the steep climb for 3.2 miles, over Standoff Point and several viewpoints. Keep left at the next junction and descend past more viewpoints 3.2 miles to the trailhead

User Groups: Hikers, dogs, and horses. No mountain bikes allowed. No wheelchair facilities.

Permits: A free self-issue Wilderness Permit is required and is available at the trailhead. Parking and access are free.

Maps: For a map of the Umpqua National Forest and Rogue-Umpqua Divide Wilderness, contact Umpqua National Forest, 2900 NW Stewart Parkway, Roseburg, OR, 97470, 541/672-6601. For a topographic map, ask the USGS for Buckeye Lake.

Directions: From Roseburg, drive 25 miles north on I-5 to the Canyonville exit (Exit 98), following signs towards Crater Lake. In Canyonville, turn east on 3rd Street and follow this road, which becomes the Tiller-Trail Highway, 23.3 miles to Tiller. Go through town and turn left on Road 46 for 24.2 miles, then go right on Road 2823. Follow Fish Lake Trailhead signs for 2.4 miles to a right turn on Road 2830 and go 3.9 miles, then go left on Road 2840 for 0.5 mile. Continue past the Fish Lake Trailhead another 4.6 miles to the Beaver Swamp Trailhead.

Contact: Umpqua National Forest, Tiller Ranger District, 27812 Tiller Trail Highway, Tiller, OR, 97484, 541/825-3201.

91 RATTLESNAKE MOUNTAIN
5.2-5.6 mi/3.0 hr   🏃2 ⛰9

in the Rogue-Umpqua Divide Wilderness

Map 5.4, page 266

In the heart of the Rogue-Umpqua Divide Wilderness, the wildflowers of Fish Creek

Valley see few visitors, which is fortunate for the intrepid explorer looking for a little quiet time. The meadows along Fish Creek are only the beginning; above them, a loop trail reaches Windy Gap and its awesome views, and a side trail climbs Rattlesnake Mountain, second highest in the Rogue Umpqua Divide Wilderness, with views out to nearby Mount Thielsen, Mount Scott, Mount Bailey, and Mount McLoughlin.

From the Happy Camp Trailhead, follow Fish Creek 0.7 mile along the Rogue Umpqua Divide Trail to a junction and go left on the Whitehorse Meadow Trail, climbing along a creek one mile to Windy Gap and a four-way junction. The right-hand Rattlesnake Way Trail (also known as the Rattlesnake Mountain Trail) climbs one mile and 1,000 feet to a viewpoint on Rattlesnake Mountain. Return as you came, for 5.6 miles in all.

For a loop option, which turns out to be 0.4 mile shorter, go back to Windy Gap and take the Castle Creek Trail, which heads along the ridge 0.4 mile to a junction. Go left, staying on Trail 1576, to descend 1.1 miles back to Happy Camp.

User Groups: Hikers, dogs, and horses. No mountain bikes allowed. No wheelchair facilities.

Permits: A free self-issue Wilderness Permit is required and is available at the trailhead. Parking and access are free.

Maps: For a map of the Umpqua National Forest and Rogue-Umpqua Divide Wilderness, contact Umpqua National Forest, 2900 NW Stewart Parkway, Roseburg, OR, 97470, 541/672-6601. For a topographic map, ask the USGS for Fish Mountain.

Directions: From Roseburg, drive east on OR 138, and between mileposts 60 and 61 turn right on Fish Creek Road 37 for 13 miles. Turn right on Incense Cedar Loop Road 800 for 3.5 miles, then right on Fish Creek Valley Road 870 for 4.2 miles to a "Rogue-Umpqua Trail" sign on the right. Park 100 yards farther down the road.

Contact: Umpqua National Forest, Diamond Lake Ranger District, 2020 Toketee Ranger Station Road, Idleyld Park, OR, 97477, 541/498-2531.

92 MUIR CREEK TO BUCK CANYON

15.0-22.8 mi/7.0 hr-2 days

🏃3 ⛰8

in the Rogue-Umpqua Divide Wilderness

Map 5.4, page 266

The relatively uncrowded Rogue-Umpqua Divide Wilderness is a must-do for the backpacking crowd. About the only visitors this area sees in the summer are the cows that are allowed to graze here. But don't let that dissuade you: This trail up Muir Creek and into Buck Canyon opens a door to numerous backpacking sites, beautiful meadows, and Buck Canyon. From here you can traverse out to other areas like Rattlesnake Mountain and Hershberger Mountain. This trail system begins within a stone's throw of a paved highway, yet you'd never know it was there. With some path-finding skills, you can make your way in a loop around theis wilderness and bushwhack a bit back to your car.

Starting from the highway, follow the Muir Creek Trail 2.7 miles to an overlook of Muir Falls, then continue one mile, keeping left at a junction, then 1.4 miles, keeping left at another trailhead junction. From here hike 1.6 miles into Buck Canyon and Hummingbird Meadows. The next junction has a right-hand turn to cross the creek and pass Wiley Camp; from here the main trail continues to follow Muir Creek another 0.8 mile past some falls, the crumbling Devil's Slide, and an upper meadow. For a day's exploration, this is adequate. Backpackers can continue on another 3.9 miles for three more camps and the Alkali Meadows and connections to trails fanning out from there.

User Groups: Hikers, dogs, and horses. No mountain bikes allowed. No wheelchair facilities.

Permits: A free self-issue Wilderness Permit is required and is available at the trailhead. Parking and access are free.

Maps: For a map of the Rogue River National Forest and the Rogue-Umpqua Divide Wilderness, contact the Rogue River-Siskiyou National Forest, 3040 Biddle Road, Medford, OR, 97504, 541/618-2200. For a topographic map, ask the USGS for Fish Mountain.

Directions: From Medford, drive 57 miles east on OR 62, going left onto Highway 230 for 10.3 miles. Just before the Muir Creek Bridge, park in a lot on the left.

Contact: Rogue River National Forest, Prospect Ranger District, 47201 Highway 62, Prospect, OR, 97536, 541/560-3400.

93 BOUNDARY SPRINGS AND UPPER ROGUE RIVER TRAIL

5.0-18.6 mi/2.0 hr-1 day

on the Upper Rogue River and in Crater Lake National Park

Map 5.4, page 266

From a massive series of springs just inside the boundary of Crater Lake National Park, the Rogue River begins its journey through the southern Cascade Mountains. Almost immediately, the river sets out into a forested canyon, plunging over Rough Rider Falls and No Name Falls. From there, the trail goes on and on, allowing for a long backpacking adventure along several access points. For a sampling of the Rogue's wonders, start from the easy pullout at the head of the canyon. Then you can plan out a longer trip along the Upper Rogue River Trail, following this Wild and Scenic River from the Crater Rim to the town of Prospect.

To see the Boundary Springs, follow the Upper Rogue River Trail in from the Crater Rim Viewpoint lot 0.5 mile to a junction. Go left on the Boundary Springs Trail 1.9 miles to the springs. Return as you came, or continue on to the viewpoint.

To descend instead into the Rogue Canyon and hike the uppermost segment of this famous trail, begin from the same trailhead, following the Upper Rogue Trail, and go to the right from this first junction. In 4.2 miles you'll march along the canyon rim and reach Rough Rider Falls, and in another 2.2 you'll go into the canyon itself to see No Name Falls. A final stretch of the trail continues through the forest another 1.7 miles to a lower trailhead at the Hamaker Campground.

The entire length of the Upper Rogue River Trail is 47.9 miles, with numerous access points along the way. Contact the Rogue River-Siskiyou National Forest (www.fs.fed.us/r6/rogue-siskiyou) for maps and information.

User Groups: Hikers and dogs only. No horses or mountain bikes allowed. No wheelchair facilities.

Permits: Permits are not required. Parking and access are free.

Maps: For a map of the Rogue River National Forest, contact the Rogue River-Siskiyou National Forest, 3040 Biddle Road, Medford, OR, 97504, 541/618-2200. For a topographic map, ask the USGS for Pumice Desert West and Hamaker Butte.

Directions: To reach the upper trailhead, start from Medford, drive 57 miles on OR 62 and continue on Highway 230 for 18.6 miles to the Crater Rim Viewpoint on the right. For the lower trailhead, go north on 230 approximately 14 miles from the junction with Highway 62. Turn right on Road 6530, and follow it one mile to Road 900. Continue 0.5 mile on Road 900. The trail begins east of the Hamaker Campground.

Contact: Rogue River National Forest, Prospect Ranger District, 47201 Highway 62, Prospect, OR, 97536, 541/560-3400.

94 HORSE LAKE
7.2-8.8 mi/4.0-4.5 hr

west of Mount Bachelor in the Three Sisters Wilderness

Map 5.5, page 267

In the stretches of the Three Sisters Wilderness south of the peaks themselves, the landscape is a dense forest punctuated by lakes. No wonder they call the main access road the Cascade Lakes Highway; this entire area east of the Cascade Divide is rife with ponds and lakes, many suitable for swimming. Starting from big Elk Lake, a superb loop trail passes through the forests to visit Horse Lake with its rocky peninsula, then returning past two smaller lakes, Colt and Sunset. Be prepared to walk through a burn, resulting from fire that torched this area in 1999.

From the trailhead, start on the right-hand Horse Lake Trail, immediately entering the wilderness area. In 1.3 miles, the trail crosses the Pacific Crest Trail. Continue straight on the Horse Lake Trail two miles to a T-junction with a sign for Horse Lake. After viewing the lake, you have a choice; to continue on the loop, go south from this junction toward Dumbbell Lake 0.1 mile, stay left at the next junction, and continue 0.3 mile to another junction, going to the left toward Sunset Lake.

To circle Horse Lake on a loop, however, go forward to the lake and to the right instead and watch for a side trail which circles the lake over 1.7 miles, keeping left at a junction 0.3 mile after the peninsula until you reach another junction. Go right toward Dumbbell Lake 0.3 mile, then go left away from Dumbbell Lake, going toward Sunset Lake instead.

Both options bring you to the same place. Now, to continue from either of these two options, start down the trail toward Sunset Lake, watching on the left for a faint trail to Colt Lake, and just beyond a trail to the right for Sunset Lake. Stay on this main trail 1.3 miles to a junction with the PCT. Go left on the PCT for 1.2 miles, then right on the Island Meadow Trail one mile back to the trailhead.

User Groups: Hikers, dogs, and horses. No mountain bikes allowed. No wheelchair facilities.

Permits: A free self-issue Wilderness Permit is required and is available at the trailhead. A federal Northwest Forest Pass is required to park here; the cost is $5 a day or $30 for an annual pass. You can buy a day pass at the trailhead, at ranger stations, or through private vendors.

Maps: A map of the Three Sisters Wilderness is available for purchase from Geo-Graphics. For a map of the Deschutes National Forest and the Three Sisters Wilderness, contact Deschutes National Forest Headquarters, 1001 SW Emkay Drive, Bend, OR, 97702, 541/383-5300. For a topographic map, ask the USGS for South Sister.

Directions: From Bend, drive the Cascades Lake Highway 32.7 miles west to the Elk Lake Trailhead on the right, following the 0.3-mile spur road to the parking area.

Contact: Deschutes National Forest, Bend-Fort Rock Ranger District, 1230 NE 3rd Street, Suite A-262, Bend, OR, 97701, 541/383-4000.

95 SIX LAKES TRAIL
2.0-19.0 mi/1.0 hr-1 day

southwest of Mount Bachelor in the Three Sisters Wilderness

Map 5.5, page 267

There are so many lakes along the Six Lakes Trail that it's hard to say which six give the trail its name. You'll pass two big ones, Blow and Doris, right off, then continue into a virtual maze of lakes both big and small. Bring a map and a backpack, and have your pick. Two other obvious goals are Cliff Lake and Mink Lake, both with rustic shelters. The Pacific Crest Trail curves right through this basin, allowing access to other hikes in the area, including Horse Lake and Sisters Mirror Lake to the north. Consider this hike either as a straight in-and-out, or with the possibility for a number of loops.

From the Six Lakes Trailhead, follow the trail one mile to Blow Lake, and another 1.4 miles to Doris Lake. In another 0.9 mile, stay right at a junction, climb a pass and descend to the PCT in 2.1 miles. Go left on the PCT 1.6 miles to an unmarked side trail on the left to Cliff Lake's shelter, just before a junction to Porky Lake. To continue to Mink Lake, leave the PCT and go right toward Porky Lake 1.6 miles, then left to Mink Lake's old shelter. A loop trail around Mink Lake is 2.6 miles.

From here, possibilities for loops can be done a number of ways. From Mink Lake, go right away from Porky Lake, then stay left on the main trail 1.2 miles to the PCT. Go left on the PCT 2.2 miles, passing five lakes to return to Cliff Lake. Another way is to leave Mink Lake towards Porky Lake, then go left 1.2 miles to Goose Lake, then right for 2.2 miles past smaller lakes to the PCT. Go straight to return to the trailhead.

User Groups: Hikers, dogs, and horses. No mountain bikes allowed. No wheelchair facilities.

Permits: A free self-issue Wilderness Permit is required and is available at the trailhead. A federal Northwest Forest Pass is required to park here; the cost is $5 a day or $30 for an annual pass. You can buy a day pass at the trailhead, at ranger stations, or through private vendors.

Maps: A map of the Three Sisters Wilderness is available for purchase from Geo-Graphics. For a map of the Deschutes National Forest and the Three Sisters Wilderness, contact Deschutes National Forest Headquarters, 1001 SW Emkay Drive, Bend, OR, 97702, 541/383-5300. For a topographic map, ask the USGS for Elk Lake and Packsaddle Mountain.

Directions: From Bend, drive the Cascades Lake Highway 34.7 miles west to the Six Lakes Trailhead on the right, following the spur road to the parking area.

Contact: Deschutes National Forest, Bend-Fort Rock Ranger District, 1230 NE 3rd Street, Suite A-262, Bend, OR, 97701, 541/383-4000.

96 DESCHUTES RIVER TRAIL/DILLON AND BENHAM FALLS

4.4-17.4 mi/2.0 hr-1 day   🏃3 ⛰9

southwest of Bend in the Deschutes National Forest

Map 5.5, page 267   **BEST (**

The city of Bend is blessed to have this Upper Deschutes River Trail. From here, the river makes its way to the center of town, languidly flowing behind a dam, creating Mirror Pond, but in the ponderosa pine forests of the lower Cascades, the river is a pounding cataract of falls and eddies, and at other times gentle as a pond. The landscape is one of lava flows, which constantly force the river into its shapes and drops—the remnants of a massive flow from nearby Lava Butte. It is possible to do the trail up and down in a day, and shuttling is easy enough; along the way, too, are a number of access points, making for combinations of hikes leading to the best points: Lava Island Falls and the Lava Island Cave, Dillon Falls and Ryan Ranch Meadow, and the absolutely beautiful Benham Falls.

From the Meadow picnic area, climb 0.5 mile on the Deschutes River Trail to a slough, keeping left along the river 0.6 mile to the cave and Lava Island Falls. Continue 1.1 woodsy miles to a view of Big Eddy Rapids, and another 1.1 miles to the Aspen Picnic Area. The next 0.9 mile enters pine woods and climbs to a viewpoint of Dillon Falls' long cascade. Follow the road to Ryan Ranch Meadows, with views to the lava on the opposite shore, and continue 2.3 miles to the Slough Day-Use Area. The next 1.5 miles climbs into cooler, denser woods and arrives at Benham Falls overlook. From here, the trail follows an old logging railroad grade 0.7 mile to a crossing of the Deschutes, arriving at the Benham West Day-Use Area, with a few more loop trails angling into the woods to an old mill site.

User Groups: Hikers, dogs on leash only, horses, and mountain bikes uphill only. The

Big Eddy Rapids, Dillon Falls, and Benham Falls West Area are wheelchair accessible.

Permits: Permits are not required. A federal Northwest Forest Pass is required to park here; the cost is $5 a day or $30 for an annual pass. You can buy a day pass at the trailhead, at ranger stations, or through private vendors.

Maps: For a map of the Deschutes National Forest, contact Deschutes National Forest Headquarters, 1001 SW Emkay Drive, Bend, OR, 97702, 541/383-5300. For a topographic map, ask the USGS for Benham Falls.

Directions: From Bend, take the Cascades Lake Highway 6.2 miles west to a sign for Meadow Day Use Area and turn left on gravel FS Road 100 for 1.3 miles to the road's end for the lower trailhead. To access other sites, continue another 1.6 mile on Cascade Lakes Highway then turn left on Conklin Road/Road 41. Go 2.6 miles and turn left on Road 4120 for 0.5 mile, then right on Road 4120 for 3.1 miles to the trailhead at road's end.

Contact: Deschutes National Forest, Bend-Fort Rock Ranger District, 1230 NE 3rd Street, Suite A-262, Bend, OR, 97701, 541/383-4000.

97 NEWBERRY LAVA TUBES
0.4-1.2 mi/1.0-2.0 hr   🏃2 ⛰8

east of Bend in the Deschutes National Forest

Map 5.5, page 267   BEST (

These trails require hiking underground. "Spelunking" gives an impression of clambering around in chambers, but that's not what Central Oregon caves are about—although you can do that too. These volcanic-formed caves are "lava tubes," formed when rivers of lava from nearby Newberry Caldera cooled on top, but left the lava flowing underneath. In time, the lava drained and left these rounded wormholes descending under the basalt roofs. Three caves along China Hat Road in the dry, burned forests east of Bend are open for walking—come prepared with warm clothes and a flashlight with plenty of batteries. Boyd Cave is shortest, Skeleton Cave a little longer. The Wind Cave is most difficult, but has a skylight, which is how the bats enter—thus, Wind Cave is closed from November to late April to protect their habitat.

The Boyd Cave is the easiest at 0.2 mile. Simply descend the stairs and follow the broad cave back to its low ceiling. The Skeleton Cave is more ambitious; go down the stairs and hike in 0.4 mile to a junction. The left tunnel peters out in a short distance, though you can get on your belly and go farther. The right path continues another 0.2 mile to its end. Wind Cave is most difficult of all, requiring climbing and descending massive jumbles of boulders 0.1 mile to the skylight room, and continuing 0.5 mile to its end.

User Groups: Hikers only. No dogs, horses, or mountain bikes allowed. No wheelchair facilities.

Permits: Permits are not required. Parking and access are free.

Maps: For a map of the Deschutes National Forest, contact Deschutes National Forest Headquarters, 1001 SW Emkay Drive, Bend, OR, 97702, 541/383-5300. For a topographic map, ask the USGS for Kelsey Butte.

Directions: Drive four miles south of Bend on U.S. 97 and turn left on China Hat Road 18. In nine miles, turn left at a sign for Boyd Cave. Another 0.5 mile beyond this turn, go left on Road 1819 for 1.6 miles to the Skeleton Cave. Another two miles east on China Hat, turn left at a sign for Wind Cave and park at the lot.

Contact: Deschutes National Forest, Bend-Fort Rock Ranger District, 1230 NE 3rd Street, Suite A-262, Bend, OR, 97701, 541/383-4000.

98 MUSKRAT LAKE CABIN
10.0-11.2 mi/3.5-4.0 hr 🏃2 ⛰7

north of Cultus Lake in Three Sisters Wilderness

Map 5.5, page 267

At this southeastern corner of the Three Sisters Wilderness, you'll be lucky to see anyone. Sure, it's far from the peaks, but close as it is to popular Cultus Lake, a wind-whipped lake high on the divide, visitors just don't seem to wander down here. The Winopee Trail follows the shore of this massive lake for a stretch, with possibilities for backpacking, then dives into the wilderness to access a number of lakes. The two large Teddy Lakes are an easy side trip, but the goal is a decrepit cabin on Muskrat Lake; it once was suitable for camping—with a stove, a loft, windows, and cupboards—but vandals have rendered unusable. It's worth a visit though, as this corner of the wilderness is quiet and deep.

Follow the Winopee Trail 2.9 miles along the shore of Cultus Lake, keeping left at the first junction to Corral Lakes, then heading right toward Winopee Lake 0.7 mile to a junction. To the right, two Teddy Lakes lie along a 0.6-mile trail. Continue left 1.4 miles to reach the cabin at Muskrat Lake.

User Groups: Hikers, dogs, and horses. No mountain bikes allowed. No wheelchair facilities.

Permits: A free self-issue Wilderness Permit is required and is available at the trailhead. A federal Northwest Forest Pass is required to park here; the cost is $5 a day or $30 for an annual pass. You can buy a day pass at the trailhead, at ranger stations, or through private vendors.

Maps: A map of the Three Sisters Wilderness is available for purchase from Geo-Graphics. For a map of the Deschutes National Forest and the Three Sisters Wilderness, contact Deschutes National Forest Headquarters, 1001 SW Emkay Drive, Bend, OR, 97702, 541/383-5300. For a topographic map, ask the USGS for Irish Mountain.

Directions: From Bend, drive the Cascades Lake Highway 44 miles west to the Cultus Lake Resort on the right. Turn right on Road 4635 for 1.8 miles, then go right on Road 100 toward the campground, keeping right on a Dead End road and parking at the trailhead in 0.5 mile.

Contact: Deschutes National Forest, Bend-Fort Rock Ranger District, 1230 NE 3rd Street, Suite A-262, Bend, OR, 97701, 541/383-4000.

99 LAVA RIVER CAVE
2.2 mi/1.5 hr 🏃2 ⛰9

southeast of Bend in the Newberry National Volcanic Monument

Map 5.5, page 267

Like Boyd, Skeleton, and Wind Caves (see *Newberry Lava Tubes* listing in this chapter), the Lava River Cave is a lava tube, only this one is the queen bee. A full 1.1 miles long, it actually goes beneath Highway 97, and features a double-tiered cave and strange formations of the Sand Garden that form castles on the floor as Mount Mazama ash leaks in from above. You may find crowds here visiting such notable places as Echo Hall and Low Bridge Lane, but it's worth joining the fray to see one of Oregon's treasures. The cave makes for an easy excursions, and guided tours are available.

User Groups: Hikers only. No dogs, horses, or mountain bikes. No wheelchair facilities.

Permits: Permits are not required. A federal Northwest Forest Pass is required to park here; the cost is $5 a day or $30 for an annual pass. You can buy a day pass at the trailhead, at ranger stations, or through private vendors. Lanterns can be rented for $2.

Maps: For a map of the Deschutes National Forest, contact Deschutes National Forest Headquarters, 1001 SW Emkay Drive, Bend, OR, 97702, 541/383-5300. For a topographic map, ask the USGS for Lava Butte.

Directions: From Bend, drive 11 miles south on U.S. 97 and turn left at a sign for Lava

River Cave. Between May and October, you can drive 0.3 mile to the fee booth; the rest of the year the road is gated, but you can walk it.

Contact: Deschutes National Forest, Bend-Fort Rock Ranger District, 1230 NE 3rd Street, Suite A-262, Bend, OR, 97701, 541/383-4000.

100 LAVA CAST FOREST

1.0 mi/1.0 hr

southeast of Bend in the Newberry National Volcanic Monument

Map 5.5, page 267   **BEST (**

Make this a destination if you're touring the entire Lava Lands complex. Lava Cast Forest makes an interesting educational outing with the kids, or if you're looking to entertain visitor—if they can stand the awful washboard gravel road to get there. This easy, paved one-mile loop crosses the lava landscape of the Newberry Caldera's eruption, with views to that great shield volcano itself. The "lava casts" are actually stone cast of ancient trees—when the lava pooled around them and cooled, the tree it embraced burned and left perfect casts, some wells in the ground deep enough to stand in up to your chest, or in some cases knocked them over, leaving tubes and tunnels you can look through horizontally.

User Groups: Hikers and dogs. No horses or mountain bikes allowed. The entire trail is wheelchair accessible.

Permits: Permits are not required. A federal Northwest Forest Pass is required to park here; the cost is $5 a day or $30 for an annual pass. You can buy a day pass at the trailhead, at ranger stations, or through private vendors.

Maps: For a map of the Deschutes National Forest, contact Deschutes National Forest Headquarters, 1001 SW Emkay Drive, Bend, OR, 97702, 541/383-5300. For a topographic map, ask the USGS for Lava Cast Forest.

Directions: From Bend, drive 13.2 miles south on U.S. 97 and turn left on Road 9720,

following this miserable road nine miles to its end at the trailhead.

Contact: Deschutes National Forest, Bend-Fort Rock Ranger District, 1230 NE 3rd Street, Suite A-262, Bend, OR, 97701, 541/383-4000.

101 FALL RIVER

7.0 mi/3.0 hr

southwest of Sunriver in the Deschutes National Forest

Map 5.5, page 267

Fall River is amazingly quiet and absolutely lovely. It seems only anglers appreciate its charm, but bird-lovers and hikers should, too. This easy hike follows the river up and down along its bends and riffles, right up to the point where the river emerges from the ground in its entirety. Just above this massive spring sits the quiet Fall River Guard Station (another possible place to begin the hike, though you'll be following old user trails to get to the main trail). Near the campground, a footbridge crosses a deep pool and leads to a reflective spot at a bench, a good place to admire the pines and listen to the water birds.

The main trail begins behind campsite #8, ambling 2.4 miles downstream for a stretch following an old road, before petering out near private land. From the picnic area of the campground, hike down to the footbridge. On the opposite side, go left 0.4 mile to the viewpoint. Cross the bridge once more, and set out upstream to the left to make your way 0.7 mile to the springs behind the guard station.

User Groups: Hikers, dogs, horses, and mountain bikes. No wheelchair facilities.

Permits: Permits are not required. Parking and access are free.

Maps: For a map of the Deschutes National Forest, contact Deschutes National Forest Headquarters, 1001 SW Emkay Drive, Bend, OR, 97702, 541/383-5300. For a topographic map, ask the USGS for Pistol Butte.

Directions: From Bend, drive 16 miles south

on U.S. 97 and turn right on Vandevert Road, following signs for Fall River. In one mile, turn left on South Century Drive for 0.9 mile, then right on Road 42 for 9.7 miles. Just before milepost 13, turn left and park in the Fall River Campground.

Contact: Deschutes National Forest, Bend-Fort Rock Ranger District, 1230 NE 3rd Street, Suite A-262, Bend, OR, 97701, 541/383-4000.

102 PAULINA CREEK TRAIL
9.2-17.0 mi/5.0 hr-2 days 🏃3 ⛰8

east of LaPine in the Deschutes National Forest
Map 5.5, page 267

Paulina Creek, fed by Paulina Lake in the collapsed volcano of the Newberry Caldera, falls in a double plume over the lip of the crater and begins a long descent down to the Deschutes River. A trail follows it through burned woods and out to a viewpoint of not only the uppermost falls, but two others as well. At the right time of year, expect to see salmon meandering beneath those massive top falls, thick enough you'd think you could walk over them. Two trailheads give access to the whole stretch—one going up, and one coming down. A shuttle is easy enough, as both trailheads start of the main road. If you do shuttle, you could easily start from the top and make your way to the bottom.

From the Paulina Falls Picnic Area, take the left trail and follow it 0.2 mile to a viewpoint. After this great view of the double falls, return to the junction and head upstream 0.3 mile to a road at the mouth of Paulina Lake. Go left, crossing the bridge, then go left to access the creek trail. In 3.3 miles you'll reach a lower falls, and in another 2.4 miles reach the falls at McKay Crossing with a campground to the right down the road. The last 2.8 miles continues to a crossing, joins an old road, and ends at the Ogden Trailhead.

From the Ogden Trailhead, a loop option is available. From the Ogden Camp, head back up trail and take a short spur trail to the right, then follow gravel road 2120 for 2.8 miles upstream. Cross a road and continue 5.0 miles on what is now trail. Watch for mountain bikes! This trail returns to the lot at the Paulina Creek Falls Overlook.

User Groups: Hikers, dogs, horses, and mountain bikes. No wheelchair facilities.

Permits: Permits are not required. Parking and access are free from the Ogden Camp Trailhead, but a federal Northwest Forest Pass is required to park at the Paulina Falls Trailhead; the cost is $5 a day or $30 for an annual pass. You can buy a day pass at the trailhead, at ranger stations, or through private vendors.

Maps: For a map of the Deschutes National Forest, contact Deschutes National Forest Headquarters, 1001 SW Emkay Drive, Bend, OR, 97702, 541/383-5300. For a topographic map, ask the USGS for Paulina Peak and Anns Butte.

Directions: From Bend, drive 22 miles south on U.S. 97 and turn left on Road 21 toward the Newberry Caldera. For the Ogden Trailhead, follow Road 21 for 2.8 miles and turn left at the Ogden Group Camp and park at the lot for the Peter Skene Ogden Trail. For the Paulina Falls Viewpoint, continue on Road 21 for 9.4 miles and turn left into the Paulina Falls Picnic Area.

Contact: Deschutes National Forest, Bend-Fort Rock Ranger District, 1230 NE 3rd Street, Suite A-262, Bend, OR, 97701, 541/383-4000.

103 PAULINA LAKE
8.6 mi/3.0 hr 🏃2 ⛰8

in the Newberry National Volcanic Monument
Map 5.5, page 267

The Newberry Caldera is rather like a small Crater Lake, though Newberry's crater is filled with not one but two lakes: Paulina and East. Paulina Lake has a trail around it, and it's quite a walk. The trail passes a smaller crater, a pumice cone, an obsidian flow, and a lakeside hot spring. For pretty much the whole hike, Paulina Peak is a massive presence at the south side of the water. This leisurely hike is the longest in the Newberry Caldera National Volcanic Monument, and is a must-do for day-hikers, campers, and even backpackers.

From the trailhead, set out along the lake-shore to the left. In 1.2 miles the trail crosses an obsidian lava flow and comes to a camping area on the right. In another 1.4 miles the trail passes more camping sites and a beach where hot springs bubble. The next 1.7 miles follows the lakeshore through the woods before arriving at the Paulina Lake Lodge. Continue on the trail, crossing the bridge over Paulina Creek, then continuing along the lakeshore 2.4 miles, passing two campgrounds. The trail crosses the entrance road to Little Crater Campground and climbs to the peak of Little Crater, then descends 1.9 miles back to the trailhead.

User Groups: Hikers and dogs. No horses or mountain bikes allowed. No wheelchair access.

Permits: Permits are not required. A federal Northwest Forest Pass is required to park here; the cost is $5 a day or $30 for an annual pass. You can buy a day pass at the trailhead, at ranger stations, or through private vendors.

Maps: For a map of the Deschutes National Forest, contact Deschutes National Forest Headquarters, 1001 SW Emkay Drive, Bend, OR, 97702, 541/383-5300. For a topographic map, ask the USGS for Paulina Peak.

Directions: From Bend, drive 22 miles south on U.S. 97 and turn left on Road 21 toward the Newberry Caldera. Follow Road 21 for 14.5 miles and turn left at the Little Crater Campground and follow this road 0.9 mile to the trailhead at road's end.

Contact: Deschutes National Forest, Bend-Fort Rock Ranger District, 1230 NE 3rd Street, Suite A-262, Bend, OR, 97701, 541/383-4000.

104 BIG OBSIDIAN FLOW

0.8 mi/0.5 hr   🥾1 ⛰8

in the Newberry National Volcanic Monument

Map 5.5, page 267

Breathtakingly short but nonetheless breath-taking, this terribly easy 0.8-mile trails loops into Oregon's most recent volcanic eruption, a sweeping and swirling flow of obsidian, a black volcanic glass that shines in the sun. When doing any of the other hikes in the Newberry Volcanic National Monument, make sure to include this one.

User Groups: Hikers only. No dogs, horses, or mountain bikes. No wheelchair facilities.

Permits: Permits are not required. A federal Northwest Forest Pass is required to park here; the cost is $5 a day or $30 for an annual pass. You can buy a day pass at the trailhead, at ranger stations, or through private vendors.

Maps: For a map of the Deschutes National Forest, contact Deschutes National Forest Headquarters, 1001 SW Emkay Drive, Bend, OR, 97702, 541/383-5300. For a topographic map, ask the USGS for East Lake.

Directions: From Bend, drive 22 miles south on U.S. 97 and turn left on Road 21 toward the Newberry Caldera. Follow Road 21 for 14.8 miles and turn right into the Obsidian Trail parking lot.

Contact: Deschutes National Forest, Bend-Fort Rock Ranger District, 1230 NE 3rd Street, Suite A-262, Bend, OR, 97701, 541/383-4000.

105 CINDER HILL AND THE DOME

1.4-7.2 mi/0.5-3.5 hr   🥾2 ⛰8

in the Newberry National Volcanic Monument

Map 5.5, page 267

The Newberry Caldera—a National Volcanic Monument—is well worth exploring. It's also a great place to camp. Whether you're here overnight or just for the day, make it a big day and hike as much of it as you can. There are plenty of short trails, and the trail to The Dome ranks high up there: the easy 0.7 mile climbs up to its crater rim with views to the Cascade peaks and Fort Rock Valley.

For a longer hike, climb to Cinder Hill, following its trail up 900 feet in 1.8 miles to the Crater Rim Trail, a long, hot, and dusty trail used primarily by mountain bikers. Go right 1.1 miles to Cinder Hill's peak, with its view to the Cascade Mountains and down to East Lake.

User Groups: Hikers and dogs. No horses allowed. Mountain bikes allowed only on the Crater Rim Trail. No wheelchair facilities.

Permits: Permits are not required. A federal Northwest Forest Pass is required to park here; the cost is $5 a day or $30 for an annual pass. You can buy a day pass at the trailhead, at ranger stations, or through private vendors.

Maps: For a map of the Deschutes National Forest, contact Deschutes National Forest Headquarters, 1001 SW Emkay Drive, Bend, OR, 97702, 541/383-5300. For a topographic map, ask the USGS for East Lake.

Directions: From Bend, drive 22 miles south on U.S. 97 and turn left on Road 21 toward the Newberry Caldera. Follow Road 21 for 17.4 miles to a junction. To go to The Dome, go right following Road 21 for 2.5 miles, and park on the right at The Dome Trailhead. To go to Cinder Hill, turn left at the junction 1.8 miles to Cinder Hill Campground. Continue 0.3 mile to the trailhead at road's end, or if the gate is closed park there and walk.

Contact: Deschutes National Forest, Bend-Fort Rock Ranger District, 1230 NE 3rd Street, Suite A-262, Bend, OR, 97701, 541/383-4000.

106 PAULINA PEAK

6.0 mi/4.0 hr

in the Newberry National Volcanic Monument

Map 5.5, page 267

At 7,984 feet, Paulina Peak is not only the highest point on the rim of the Newberry Caldera, but it's pretty much the highest point in the entire area. Thus, views extend from the Fort Rock Valley to the Cascade peaks, with the entire caldera below it, including the pudding-like surface of the Big Obsidian Flow, and the shimmering Paulina and East Lakes. Thing is, the road goes right to the top for this stunning view, so most people drive up. But you can climb it on foot, if you're up for a trail with an 8 percent grade that climbs 1,500 feet in only two miles. You'll feel, if not whipped, victorious at having achieved a view stretching from Mount Adams in Washington State to Mount Shasta in California on your own merits and heels.

Beginning at the Paulina Peak Trailhead, start out on the Crater Rim Trail. At the 2.7-mile mark, continue straight on the main trail. In 0.3 mile past this junction, the trail reaches the peak and overlook.

User Groups: Hikers, dogs, and horses. No mountain bikes allowed. No wheelchair facilities.

Permits: Permits are not required. A federal Northwest Forest Pass is required to park here; the cost is $5 a day or $30 for an annual pass. You can buy a day pass at the trailhead, at ranger stations, or through private vendors.

Maps: For a map of the Deschutes National Forest, contact Deschutes National Forest Headquarters, 1001 SW Emkay Drive, Bend, OR, 97702, 541/383-5300. For a topographic map, ask the USGS for Paulina Peak.

Directions: From Bend, drive 22 miles south on U.S. 97 and turn left on Road 21 toward the Newberry Caldera. Follow Road 21 for 13.2 miles and turn right at the visitors center. The trailhead is 50 feet before the vistors center on the right side of the road.

Contact: Deschutes National Forest, Bend-Fort Rock Ranger District, 1230 NE 3rd Street, Suite A-262, Bend, OR, 97701, 541/383-4000.

107 FAWN LAKE, PRETTY LAKE, AND STAG LAKE

6.8-7.3 mi/3.0-4.0 hr

north of Crescent Lake in Diamond Peak Wilderness

Map 5.5, page 267

Many of the stretches in the Diamond Peak Wilderness are dominated by dry, lodgepole pine forests, but there are points of beauty. In view of the nearly 7,000-foot Redtop Mountain, and slightly higher Lakeview Mountain, Fawn Lake is a jewel in this wilderness, though its popularity shows on the dusty, well-trodden path. For more seclusion, continue on the Pretty Lake, or take any number of side trails on your map to nearby Saddle and Stag Lakes, or even to big Odell Lake.

Start on the Fawn Lake Trail, crossing Road 60 and a horse trail, continuing straight 3.4 miles to Fawn Lake. At the lake, go left along the shore and continue 0.6 mile to Pretty Lake on the left. From here, the trail is not maintained; it descends into confusing woods 2.5 miles back to the Fawn Lake Trail. To visit Stag Lake, go back to Fawn Lake then continue around the lake, staying left past the Fawn Lake Trail, then left again 0.2 mile beyond that. Climb gradually for one mile, then go right 0.4 mile to this trail's end at Stag Lake beneath Lakeview Mountain.

User Groups: Hikers, dogs, and horses. No mountain bikes allowed. No wheelchair facilities.

Permits: A free self-issue Wilderness Permit is required and is available at the trailhead. Parking and access are free.

Maps: For a map of the Deschutes National Forest, contact Deschutes National Forest Headquarters, 1001 SW Emkay Drive, Bend, OR, 97702, 541/383-5300. For a topographic map, ask the USGS for Odell Lake.

Directions: From Crescent Junction on OR 58, go west on Road 60 for 2.2 miles, then turn right toward the campgrounds for 0.3 mile to Crescent Lake Campground. Turn left into the campground and then right into a lot at the Fawn Lake Trailhead.

Contact: Deschutes National Forest, Crescent Ranger District, 136471 Highway 97 North, P.O. Box 208, Crescent, OR, 97733, 541/433-3200.

108 MILLER AND MAIDU LAKES

5.1-8.4 mi/1.5-4.0 hr

at Miller Lake and in the Mount Thielsen Wilderness

Map 5.5, page 267

Two lakes are the goal of this hike, one inside and one outside the Mount Thielsen Wilderness. The Pacific Crest Trail intersects the trail and opens up routes farther into the wilderness area and also along the beginning of the North Umpqua Trail. Broad Miller Lake is a world apart from little Maidu Lake, where the Forest Service removed a shelter to help protect the area.

From Digit Point Campground, you can circle Miller Lake in either direction, a total of 5.1 miles. At the western end of the lake, by Evening Creek, a side trail launches up a cliff 2.1 miles to the PCT junction, continuing on as the North Umpqua Trail 0.8 mile to Maidu Lake, headwaters of the North Umpqua, at which point there is a one-mile loop around the lake.

If you feel like going farther, continue on the North Umpqua Trail another 1.2 miles to a junction. Take the trail to the left, a 0.7-mile loop around Lucile Lake.

User Groups: Hikers, dogs, and horses. Mountain bikes allowed around Miller Lake only. No wheelchair facilities.

Permits: A free self-issue Wilderness Permit is required and is available at the trailhead. Parking and access are free.

Maps: For a map of the Umpqua National Forest and Mount Thielsen Wilderness, contact Umpqua National Forest, 2900 NW Stewart Parkway, Roseburg, OR, 97470, 541/672-6601. For a topographic map, ask the USGS for Worden and Burn Butte.

Directions: From Bend, drive 65 miles south on U.S. 97 to the town of Chemult. Between mileposts 202 and 203, go west on Road 9772, following signs for Chemult Recreation Site. Go 12.5 miles to road's end at Digit Point Campground and park at the picnic loop.

Contact: Umpqua National Forest, Diamond Lake Ranger District, 2020 Toketee Ranger Station Road, Idleyld Park, OR, 97477, 541/498-2531.

109 WOLF CREEK PARK
3.8 mi/2.0 hr   🏃1 ⛰6

northwest of Grants Pass

Map 5.6, page 268

If you've driven the long stretch of I-5 through southern Oregon, you'll know that breaks are few and far between. If you *really* want to get out and move, Josephine County's Wolf Creek Park is located so close to the interstate you'll be amazed you never knew it was there. By stretching your legs, I mean stretching them up Jack London Peak to a 2,800-foot viewpoint. You've got to hand it to those who name things: West Coast writer Jack London would have appreciated this rugged climb above the little stagecoach town of Wolf Creek, where he once spent the night.

After walking across the dam, start climbing steadily up 1.9 miles to the highest viewpoint. From there, you could walk the rest of the trail as desired 0.6 mile to its end at a dirt road.

User Groups: Hikers and dogs. No horses or mountain bikes allowed. No wheelchair facilities.

Permits: Permits are not required. A $2-per-car day-use pass is required, or you can purchase a $25 annual pass.

Maps: For a topographic map, ask the USGS for Glendale.

Directions: From I-5, 18 miles north of Grants Pass, take Wolf Creek Exit 76 and drive 0.9 mile to the park at the end of Main Street.

Contact: Josephine County Parks, 125 Ringuette Street, Grants Pass, OR, 97527, 541/474-5285.

110 OREGON CAVES NATIONAL MONUMENT
1.0-9.3 mi/1.0-3.5 hr   🏃2 ⛰8

east of Cave Junction in the Siskiyou National Forest

Map 5.6, page 268

Established as a National Monument in 1909, the Oregon Caves are certainly one of the state's treasures. A one-mile tour of the caves (fee required) visits what was originally an island reef scraped up from the ocean floor by the advancing North American Plate. What is left is a series of marble rooms and calcite drippings forming stalagmites and stalactites. Just outside, a 3.8-mile loop trail heads through a Siskiyou Mountains forest to one of Oregon's largest Douglas fir trees. Other trails head out to No Name Creek and along Cave Creek, adding a total of 5.5 miles to the hikes you can do here in a day.

User Groups: Hikers only. Dogs are not allowed. No wheelchair facilities.

Permits: Permits are not required. There is a fee to enter the caves. Parking and access are otherwise free.

Maps: For a topographic map, ask the USGS for Oregon Caves.

Directions: From Grants Pass, drive U.S. 199 south 29 miles to Cave Junction and follow Oregon Caves signs east on Highway 46 for 20 miles to the turnaround lot.

Contact: Oregon Caves National Monument, 19000 Caves Highway, Cave Junction, OR, 97523, 541/592-2100, ext. 262.

111 STURGIS FORK/ BOUNDARY TRAIL
4.8 mi/3.5 hr

east of Oregon Caves in the Rogue River National Forest

Map 5.6, page 268

This simple but beautiful hike offers access to a number of backpacking areas: Grayback Mountain, the Oregon Caves National Monument, and the Red Buttes Wilderness. The trail passes through groves of Grand fir and meadows of blooming corn lily, rising to a 6,420-foot viewpoint over the Siskiyou Mountains. From here, the Boundary Trail continues on three miles to Grayback Mountain. From the Sturgis Fork Trail, you could also head 5.7 miles to Sucker Creek Gap.

From the trailhead go in 0.7 mile along the Sturgis Fork, keeping right at a junction and going 0.3 mile on the Boundary Trail to the next junction, again staying right on the Boundary Trail and climbing 0.8 mile through a lush meadow to a pass. From here, it's a 500-foot climb up 0.6 mile to a viewpoint, the turnaround point for this hike. The trail continues three miles to Grayback Mountain (see next listing). Head back to the Sturgis Fork Trail junction to return; from here, the Boundary Trail continues 5.7 miles to Sucker Creek Gap (see *Sucker Creek and Swan Mountain* listing in this chapter).

User Groups: Hikers, dogs, horses, and mountain bikes. No wheelchair facilities.

Permits: Permits are not required. A federal Northwest Forest Pass is required to park here; the cost is $5 a day or $30 for an annual pass. You can buy a day pass at the trailhead, at ranger stations, or through private vendors.

Maps: For a map of the Rogue River National Forest, contact the Rogue River-Siskiyou National Forest, 3040 Biddle Road, Medford, OR, 97504, 541/618-2200. For a topographic map, ask the USGS for Carberry Creek.

Directions: From Grants Pass follow signs to Murphy south for 6.5 miles, continuing on Highway 238 for 11.5 miles to milepost 18.

At the Applegate Bridge, go south on Thompson Creek Road for 11.9 miles. Turn right on Road 1020 for 3.7 miles, then fork right on rocky Road 600 for 0.6 mile, then fork left and uphill for 0.1 mile to the trailhead at road's end.

Contact: Rogue River-Siskiyou National Forest, Applegate Ranger District, 6941 Upper Applegate Road, Jacksonville, OR, 97530, 541/899-3800.

112 GRAYBACK MOUNTAIN
4.8 mi/3.0 hr

east of Oregon Caves in the Rogue River National Forest

Map 5.6, page 268

Like the nearby Sturgis Fork hike (see previous listing), the Boundary Trail passes right through this region of meadows and mountains. Hovering above these tree-edged meadows is the 7,048-foot peak of Grayback Mountain, with its panoramic view from the Pacific Ocean to Mount Shasta, and from Mount McLoughlin to the Illinois River Valley. At the base of the mountain, a historic cabin and a rustic snow shelter sit in the meadows at the head of O'Brien Creek. The trail is easy enough, and the meadows make for good camping, but for a real adventure you can go cross-country and scramble your way to the top.

From the Upper O'Brien Creek Trailhead, climb nearly 1,000 feet in only one mile, following O'Brien Creek. At the first junction, you can go in two directions: 0.3 mile to the left is the Grayback Snow Shelter and the Krause Log Cabin, and above them the Grayback Meadows; to the right, the trail climbs another mile to the Boundary Trail. Both routes can get you to Grayback Mountain: from the Krause Cabin, head cross-country through the meadows 0.4 mile to the Boundary Trail, then head up the mountain for 0.7 mile; from the junction of the O'Brien Trail and the Boundary Trail, jog a bit to the left then head up the mountain on an unofficial path.

User Groups: Hikers, dogs, horses, and mountain bikes. No wheelchair facilities.

Permits: Permits are not required. Parking and access are free.

Maps: For a map of the Rogue River National Forest, contact the Rogue River-Siskiyou National Forest, 3040 Biddle Road, Medford, OR, 97504, 541/618-2200. For a topographic map, ask the USGS for Grayback Mountain.

Directions: From Grants Pass, follow signs to Murphy south for 6.5 miles and continue on Highway 238 another 11.5 miles to the bridge at Applegate. Turn south on Thompson Creek Road for 11.9 miles, and at a pass turn right at a sign for O'Brien Creek Trail onto Road 1005, following this road 2.3 miles to road's end at the trailhead.

Contact: Rogue River-Siskiyou National Forest, Applegate Ranger District, 6941 Upper Applegate Road, Jacksonville, OR, 97530, 541/899-3800.

113 BOLAN MOUNTAIN
3.4 mi/2.0 hr

south of Oregon Caves in the Siskiyou National Forest

Map 5.6, page 268

A perfect place for a lookout, Bolan Mountain has a view of the surrounding Siskiyou Mountains and Mount Shasta, as well as a view down to the Illinois Valley and even the Pacific Ocean. Starting from a campground on Bolan Lake, the trail climbs over 800 feet to the rentable Bolan Mountain Lookout.

From the campground, climb 500 feet in one mile on the Bolan Lake Trail to a junction. Go left an easy 0.5 mile to the lookout road, heading left up the final 0.2 mile.

User Groups: Hikers, dogs, and horses. No wheelchair facilities.

Permits: Permits are not required. Parking and access are free.

Maps: For a map of the Rogue River National Forest, contact the Rogue River-Siskiyou National Forest, 3040 Biddle Road, Medford, OR, 97504, 541/618-2200. For a topographic map, ask the USGS for Oregon Caves.

Directions: Drive 35.5 miles south of Grants Pass on U.S. 199. Between mileposts 35 and 36 turn east on Waldo Road, going five miles then straight onto Happy Camp Road for 12.5 miles to a pass, turning left at a sign for Bolan Lake. At the next two junctions fork uphill, and at the 1.8-mile mark fork downhill to the right. After another 2.4 miles go left onto Road 040 and down 1.8 miles to the campground. Park at the trailhead message board.

Contact: Rogue River-Siskiyou National Forest, Wild Rivers Ranger District, 2164 NE Spalding Avenue, Grants Pass, OR, 97526, 541/471-6500.

114 TANNEN LAKES AND TANNEN MOUNTAIN
2.6-8.3 mi/1.0-4.5 hr

south of Oregon Caves in Red Buttes Wilderness

Map 5.6, page 268

Two lakes lie in cliff-rimmed cirques beneath Tannen Mountain and the beginning of the Boundary Trail, all of it in the Red Buttes Wilderness. It's so easy to get to Tannen Lake, you'll want to keep going to East Tannen Lake. From there the wilderness opens up, and the possibilities await. The forest you'll pass through gives rise to Douglas fir, tanoak native to these southern mountains, and incense cedar.

From the Tannen Lake Trailhead hike in 0.4 mile to Tannen Lake. Go left another 0.9 mile to East Tannen Lake, a good turnaround point. Or continue 0.6 mile, passing a left-hand trail to another trailhead, and continue 1.5 miles to the Boundary Trail (and passing the left-hand trail to Sucker Creek). Go to the right on the Boundary Trail 1.1 miles, climbing steeply to the meadows of Tannen Mountain. Head right up to the summit and its amazing views over the Klamath Mountains and ocean, and all the way to Mount Shasta. To make this a loop using roads and a compass, continue 0.5 mile to trail's end at Road 570. Go right 0.9 mile to the Sundown Gap pullout and follow an abandoned road into the meadows, then head due east through both meadows and woods to Tannen Lake and the return trail.

User Groups: Hikers, dogs, and horses. No mountain bikes allowed. No wheelchair facilities.

Permits: A free self-issue Wilderness Permit is required and is available at the trailhead. Parking and access are free.

Maps: For a map of the Rogue River National Forest and the Red Buttes Wilderness, contact the Rogue River-Siskiyou National Forest, 3040 Biddle Road, Medford, OR, 97504, 541/618-2200. For a topographic map, ask the USGS for Oregon Caves.

Directions: Drive 35.5 miles south of Grants Pass on U.S. 199. Between mileposts 35 and 36 turn east on Waldo Road, going five miles then straight onto Happy Camp Road for 12.5 miles to a pass, and turn left at a sign for Tannen Lakes. At the next two junctions fork uphill, and at the 1.8-mile mark fork downhill to the right. After another 2.4 miles go right 3.3 miles to a fork and keep left for 1.4 miles. Watch for the trailhead sign and park 100 yards farther down the road.

Contact: Rogue River-Siskiyou National Forest, Wild Rivers Ranger District, 2164 NE Spalding Avenue, Grants Pass, OR, 97526, 541/471-6500.

115 SUCKER CREEK AND SWAN MOUNTAIN

6.4-9.8 mi/3.0-5.0 hr 🏃3 ⛰8

south of Oregon Caves in Red Buttes Wilderness

Map 5.6, page 268

The Red Buttes Wilderness draws right up to the boundary of California, making this one of the southernmost hikes in Oregon. In fact, from here you could well hike right into the next state. But before you leave, why not backpack into the Sucker Creek Shelter? From here you can visit a little cirque lake and follow the Boundary Trail up to the shoulder of Swan Mountain, making your way up its manzanita-strewn ridge to the 6,272-foot peak.

From the trailhead, follow Sucker Creek up 1.7 miles to a junction, staying to the right another 1.2 miles to a spring and the Sucker Creek Shelter. At the junction with the Boundary Trail, you have two options. You could go straight another 0.2 mile, then right along a faint path to visit Cirque Lake. Or you could go left on the Boundary Trail, climbing 500 feet to a pass, then making your way up the ridge to the left to the peak of Swan Mountain.

User Groups: Hikers, dogs, and horses. No mountain bikes allowed. No wheelchair facilities.

Permits: A free self-issue Wilderness Permit is required and is available at the trailhead. Parking and access are free.

Maps: For a map of the Rogue River National Forest and the Red Buttes Wilderness, contact the Rogue River-Siskiyou National Forest, 3040 Biddle Road, Medford, OR, 97504, 541/618-2200. For a topographic map, ask the USGS for Oregon Caves.

Directions: From Grants Pass, drive U.S. 199 south 29 miles to Cave Junction and follow Oregon Caves signs east on Highway 46 for 13.3 miles. Where the highway switchbacks left, turn right on Road 4612. Follow Road 4612 for 9.9 miles, forking right at the first two forks, then going straight on Road 098. In another 3.6 miles pass a left-hand fork and park 0.1 mile farther at a trail sign on the right.

Contact: Rogue River-Siskiyou National Forest, Wild Rivers Ranger District, 2164 NE Spalding Avenue, Grants Pass, OR, 97526, 541/471-6500.

116 MILLER LAKE

3.9 mi/2.0 hr 　　　　　🥾1 ⛰7

east of Oregon Caves in Rogue River National
Forest

Map 5.6, page 268

With Grayback Mountain looming in the distance, this lonely trail runs all by its lonesome over a remote section of the Siskiyous. That being said, there's plenty here to see, including two lakes, a stand of Brewer's weeping spruce, and a view to Mount Shasta from a high pass. You'll also find old-growth Douglas fir, Shasta red fir, and huckleberries.

From the trailhead, follow the new Miller Lake Trail in 0.7 mile to the cliff-rimmed Miller Lake. Go to the right over an earthen dam to follow the trail to the right into the forest, passing the spruce stand and continuing up to Upper Miller Lake and the viewpoint. Then descend 1.1 miles to the shore of Miller Lake, and return as you came.

User Groups: Hikers, dogs, and horses. No mountain bikes allowed. No wheelchair facilities.

Permits: Permits are not required. Parking and access are free.

Maps: For a map of the Rogue River National Forest, contact the Rogue River-Siskiyou National Forest, 3040 Biddle Road, Medford, OR, 97504, 541/618-2200. For a topographic map, ask the USGS for Grayback Mountain.

Directions: From Grants Pass, follow signs to Murphy 6.5 miles and continue on Highway 238 another 11.5 miles to the bridge at Applegate. Turn south on Thompson Creek Road for 11.9 miles, and at a pass turn right at a sign for Miller Lake onto Road 1020 for 4.5 miles. At the next junction, go straight onto Road 400 for 3.5 miles to road's end.

Contact: Rogue River-Siskiyou National Forest, Applegate Ranger District, 6941 Upper Applegate Road, Jacksonville, OR, 97530, 541/899-3800.

117 COLLINGS MOUNTAIN

10.3 mi/5.0 hr 　　　　🥾3 ⛰7

on Applegate Lake in Rogue River National
Forest

Map 5.6, page 268

If there is one famous resident of Oregon, it must be Bigfoot. He (or she) is such a local icon around the Northwest that it's not uncommon to hear a few jokes passed around here and there, even some serious discussion about where the famed hairy Sasquatch may be. The first sighting in the Siskiyous was reported in 1895, and in 1975 a research group built a Bigfoot Trap here above Applegate Lake. Though the trap is somewhat overgrown in poison oak and the caretaker's cabin worn down by time, the trail to Collings Mountain, passing an old mine, is steady as ever. Looping up and around the mountain's summit and descending down to a run along Applegate Lake, this makes for a fine excursion through woods of scrub oak, madrone, and white pine.

From Hart-Tish Park, head uphill and across the road 0.6 mile on the Collings Mountain Trail to the weird Bigfoot Trap with its steel door and thick cell. The next 3.4 miles passes an old prospector's test prospect shaft and ambles along the mountain before arriving at the 3,625-foot summit at a grassy peak. Then descend 2.9 miles to the Watkins Campground and follow the Da-Ku-Be-Te-De Trail along the shore of Applegate Lake for 3.4 miles back to Hart-Tish.

User Groups: Hikers, dogs, horses, and mountain bikes. No wheelchair facilities.

Permits: Permits are not required. Parking and access are free.

Maps: For a map of the Rogue River National Forest, contact the Rogue River-Siskiyou National Forest, 3040 Biddle Road, Medford, OR, 97504, 541/618-2200. For a topographic map, ask the USGS for Carberry Creek.

Directions: From Jacksonville, head west on Highway 238 for eight miles to Ruch, then turn south following Upper Applegate signs for 15.9 miles. At one mile past the Applegate

Dam, turn right into Hart-Tish Recreation Area and park in the lot on the right.

Contact: Rogue River-Siskiyou National Forest, Applegate Ranger District, 6941 Upper Applegate Road, Jacksonville, OR, 97530, 541/899-3800.

118 APPLEGATE LAKE
17.8 mi/2 days

west of Ashland in Rogue River National Forest

Map 5.6, page 268

Though this "lake" is actually a reservoir, its position in the fir, pine, and madrone forests of the Siskiyou Mountains affords it respect. Plus, with the lake being the size it is, you can spend an entire day exploring its shoreline. The trail makes for a good bike ride, too, and some of it follows paved roads. Watch for fish-hunting osprey and three-leafed poison oak. Primitive campsites along the way make this a good backpacking trek.

From French Gulch, head out for a 4.7-mile excursion around a peninsula on the Payette Trail. After jostling along some old mining prospect roads for part of this stretch, continue on the Payette Trail another 4.5 miles along the lake, passing two primitive camps at Harr Point and Tipsu Tyee before arriving at the Manzanita Trailhead. From here, follow a dirt road 1.7 miles to the Seattle Bar picnic area, then continue around the lake on the paved road 1.4 miles to the Watkins Campground. Head into the campground and connect with the Da-Ku-Be-Te-De Trail for 4.3 miles along the shore to the dam. Cross the dam and follow the paved road 1.2 miles back to French Gulch.

User Groups: Hikers, dogs, and mountain bikes. No horses allowed. No wheelchair facilities.

Permits: Permits are not required. Parking and access are free.

Maps: For a map of the Rogue River National Forest or a brochure for Applegate Lake, contact the Rogue River-Siskiyou National Forest,

3040 Biddle Road, Medford, OR, 97504, 541/618-2200. For a topographic map, ask the USGS for Squaw Lakes.

Directions: From Jacksonville, head west on Highway 238 for eight miles to Ruch, then turn south following Upper Applegate signs for 14.9 miles. Turn left over the dam for 1.2 miles and park at the French Gulch Trailhead lot on the right.

Contact: Rogue River-Siskiyou National Forest, Applegate Ranger District, 6941 Upper Applegate Road, Jacksonville, OR, 97530, 541/899-3800.

119 STEIN BUTTE
9.4 mi/5.5 hr

east of Applegate Lake in Rogue River National Forest

Map 5.6, page 268

From this motorcycle trail, which climbs steadily, even relentlessly, toward a lookout site on Stein Butte, you will see over the border and into California. By the time you've come this far south into Oregon, you're practically in another kind of region matching California anyway: the Oregon state tree of Douglas fir begins to blend in with California natives black oak, canyon live oak, madrone, knob-cone pine, and Jeffrey pine. The lookout that the Civilian Conservation Corps built in 1936 is gone, but despite the towering manzanita bushes on the ridge, the view to Mount Shasta and Mount McLoughlin is unimpeded.

From the Seattle Bar Trailhead, you will climb the Stein Butte Trail 2,400 feet in 4.7 miles to the 4,400-foot peak of Stein Butte. Take in the views of Applegate Lake, then return as you came.

User Groups: Hikers, dogs, horses, and mountain bikes. No wheelchair facilities.

Permits: Permits are not required. Parking and access are free.

Maps: For a map of the Rogue River National Forest, contact the Rogue River-Siskiyou National Forest, 3040 Biddle Road, Medford,

OR, 97504, 541/618-2200. For a topographic map, ask the USGS for Squaw Lakes.

Directions: From Jacksonville, head west on Highway 238 for eight miles to Ruch, then turn south following Upper Applegate signs for 18.8 miles. At a junction past the Watkins Campground, go left 0.9 mile to the Seattle Bar Trailhead parking area.

Contact: Rogue River-Siskiyou National Forest, Applegate Ranger District, 6941 Upper Applegate Road, Jacksonville, OR, 97530, 541/899-3800.

120 HERSHBERGER MOUNTAIN AND CRIPPLE CAMP

5.8–13.4 mi/3.0 hr–2 days 👥2 ⛰7

in the Rogue-Umpqua Divide Wilderness

Map 5.7, page 269

From Pup Prairie in the Rogue-Umpqua Divide Wilderness, the backpacker and day tripper both can find their way into the marshes and mountains, with trails leading out in all directions. In the distance, Highrock Mountain rises into the thin air, and atop Hershberger Mountain an old fire watchtower, listed on the National Register of Historic Places, looks out as far as the snow-topped Cascade peaks, and nearby the towering spires of the Rabbit Ears. For a start, you can visit the lookout one of two ways: by driving or hiking 0.5 mile to the end of Road 530. From there, a metal staircase and trail lead to the cupola-style lookout.

To hike into the wilderness, start from the road's switchback following the Acker Divide Trail to the left, descending through woods to the meadows of columbine, larkspur, coneflower, paintbrush, and bluebells. After 1.6 miles the trail meets up with the Rogue-Umpqua Divide Trail. Go right another 0.8 mile into aptly named Toad Marsh to the Cripple Camp and the 1937 shelter amidst incense cedars and tiger lilies. From here, it is possible to backpack farther to Buckeye Lake,

Fish Lake, and the Highrock Meadows for a 13.4-mile loop that returns to the Hershberger Mountain Trailhead.

User Groups: Hikers, dogs, and horses. No mountain bikes allowed. No wheelchair facilities.

Permits: A free self-issue Wilderness Permit is required and is available at the trailhead. Parking and access are free.

Maps: For a map of the Rogue River National Forest and the Rogue-Umpqua Divide Wilderness, contact the Rogue River-Siskiyou National Forest, 3040 Biddle Road, Medford, OR, 97504, 541/618-2200. For a topographic map, ask the USGS for Fish Mountain.

Directions: From Medford, drive 57 miles east on OR 62, going left onto Highway 230 for 0.9 mile, then turning left across the Rogue River onto Road 6510 for 6.2 miles. Next, turn right on Road 6515 for 9.2 miles, then turn left on Road 530 for 1.8 miles and park at a switchback.

Contact: Rogue River National Forest, Prospect Ranger District, 47201 Highway 62, Prospect, OR, 97536, 541/560-3400.

121 NATIONAL CREEK FALLS

0.8 mi/0.5 hr 👥1 ⛰7

west of Crater Lake in Rogue River National Forest

Map 5.7, page 269

Traveling through the mountains between Medford and Crater Lake? Why not stop and see an impressive waterfall that drops in two 80-foot drops over a basalt ledge in a deep green forest? People have been stopping here for years—as far back as the 1860s, when the gold miners dropped in for a rest. From the trailhead, it's an easy 0.4-mile walk through grand fir, white pine, and hemlock to the base of the falls on National Creek.

User Groups: Hikers and dogs only. No wheelchair facilities.

Permits: Permits are not required. Parking and access are free.

Maps: For a map of the Rogue River National Forest, contact the Rogue River-Siskiyou National Forest, 3040 Biddle Road, Medford, OR, 97504, 541/618-2200. For a topographic map, ask the USGS for Hamaker Butte.

Directions: From Medford, drive 57 miles east on OR 62 and then go left on Highway 230. After six miles, go right on Road 6530 for 3.7 miles, then right on Road 300 to road's end.

Contact: Rogue River National Forest, Prospect Ranger District, 47201 Highway 62, Prospect, OR, 97536, 541/560-3400.

122 ABBOTT BUTTE
7.2 mi/4.0 hr   🏃3 ⛺8

in the Rogue-Umpqua Divide Wilderness

Map 5.7, page 269

From this entry into the Rogue-Umpqua Divide Wilderness, the backpacking choices seem unlimited. Start by exploring the abandoned lookout on Abbott Butte and the enormous rock formation of the Elephant Head, a good destination for that first backpacking camp. In summer, expect to see plumes of beargrass lilies, balsamroot, and monkeyflower.

The Rogue Umpqua Divide Trail sets out around Quartz Mountain, paralleling the abandoned road to the lookout. In 1.4 miles, it reaches Windy Gap, and in 1.3 miles crosses the service road to Abbott Butte. At this point and to the right, up one mile and a little over 300 feet, is the lookout, whose tower shelters its little cabin. Continue 0.3 mile on the Rogue Umpqua Divide Trail and go 1.6 miles to Elephant Head Pond, bypassing a Cougar Butte Trail junction, and the towering Elephant Head. Just 0.3 mile beyond the pond is Saddle Camp, a good place to pitch a tent. From there, the Divide Trail continues into the wilderness area.

User Groups: Hikers, dogs, and horses. No mountain bikes allowed. No wheelchair facilities.

Permits: A free self-issue Wilderness Permit

is required and is available at the trailhead. Parking and access are free.

Maps: For a map of the Rogue River National Forest and the Rogue-Umpqua Divide Wilderness, contact the Rogue River-Siskiyou National Forest, 3040 Biddle Road, Medford, OR, 97504, 541/618-2200. For a topographic map, ask the USGS for Abbott Butte.

Directions: From Medford, drive east on OR 62, and between mileposts 51 and 52 turn left on Woodruff Meadows Road 68, staying on this road at all junctions for 4.9 miles of pavement and 7.4 miles of gravel. At the pass by a large national forest sign, park on the right for the Rogue-Umpqua Divide Trail.

Contact: Umpqua National Forest, Tiller Ranger District, 27812 Tiller Trail Highway, Tiller, OR, 97484, 541/825-3201.

123 NATURAL BRIDGE AND THE ROGUE GORGE
2.4-8.2 mi/1.0-3.0 hr   🏃2 ⛺8

on the Rogue River in Rogue River National Forest

Map 5.7, page 269   BEST (

As the Rogue River plunges through its canyon, it sometimes squeezes itself into some pretty tight spaces. The Rogue Gorge is one such place, with deep, fern-draped cliffs dropping 100 feet to the river. Even stranger is the Natural Bridge, where the river goes underground, or more precisely, beneath an ancient lava flow for a distance of 200 feet, with the water spouting out of blowholes along the way. You can easily see both sights from near the parking area, but why not make a longer hike out of it? This is, after all, the Upper Rogue River Trail, and it's worth exploring at length.

From the Natural Bridge viewpoint, head on the left-hand trail to a crossing. Follow this trail to a viewpoint of the Natural Bridge— you can even walk out on the sturdy flow itself. From here, you can continue on the trail to a second footbridge, crossing it and going right back to the car to make a 2.4-mile loop. But if you are ready for a longer hike, go left after the footbridge instead, reaching the Union Creek Campground in 1.7 miles and the Gorge viewpoint in 1.2 miles. The trail continues another 0.4 mile to a campground and ends. Return as you came.

User Groups: Hikers and dogs. No horses or mountain bikes allowed. Paved viewpoints are wheelchair accessible.

Permits: Permits are not required. Parking and access are free.

Maps: For a map of the Rogue River National Forest, contact the Rogue River-Siskiyou National Forest, 3040 Biddle Road, Medford, OR, 97504, 541/618-2200. For a topographic map, ask the USGS for Union Creek.

Directions: Drive OR 62 east of Medford 55 miles and turn left at a sign for Natural Bridge Campground. Keep left for 0.7 mile to the parking area.

Contact: Rogue River National Forest, Prospect Ranger District, 47201 Highway 62, Prospect, OR, 97536, 541/560-3400.

124 UNION CREEK
8.2 mi/3.5 hr

west of Crater Lake in Rogue River National Forest

Map 5.7, page 269

Near the Union Creek Resort, which was used in the past by Jack London and Herbert Hoover, this woodsy trail of old-growth fir and Pacific yew heads up nearby Union Creek to a pair of small waterfalls. Start out east on the Union Creek Trail for 3.3 miles to reach the first waterfall, an eight-foot drop, then continue 0.8 mile to 10-foot Union Creek Falls.

User Groups: Hikers and dogs. No horses or mountain bikes allowed. No wheelchair facilities.

Permits: Permits are not required. Parking and access are free.

Maps: For a map of the Rogue River National Forest, contact the Rogue River-Siskiyou

National Forest, 3040 Biddle Road, Medford, OR, 97504, 541/618-2200. For a topographic map, ask the USGS for Hamaker Butte.

Directions: From Medford, drive OR 62 east 56 miles to Union Creek and park on the right at a pullout by the trailhead.

Contact: Rogue River National Forest, Prospect Ranger District, 47201 Highway 62, Prospect, OR, 97536, 541/560-3400.

125 THE WATCHMAN AND THE DEVIL'S BACKBONE
5.6 mi/2.0 hr

in Crater Lake National Park

Map 5.7, page 269

Two hikes fan out along the Crater Lake rim to two distinctive viewpoints. One climbs to the Watchman Lookout with its views over the caldera, and the other circles Hillman Peak to viewpoints of the Devil's Backbone, a volcanic dike left when magma seeped into a crack in ancient Mount Mazama.

From the pullout, go right to climb to The Watchman. Take the trail 0.4 mile to a junction, then to the left and up 0.4 mile to the 8,013-foot peak. For the Devil's Backbone viewpoint, go left from the trailhead and circle Hillman Peak following a two-mile trail to two viewpoints over sparkling Crater Lake below.

User Groups: Hikers only. No dogs, horses, or mountain bikes allowed. No wheelchair facilities.

Permits: Permits are not required unless backcountry camping. A $10 fee, good for seven days, is collected at the entrance stations.

Maps: For a map of Crater Lake National Park, contact Crater Lake National Park, P.O. Box 7, Crater Lake, OR, 97604, 541/594-3000, or for a free downloadable map go to www.nps.gov/crla. For a topographic map, ask the USGS for Crater Lake West.

Directions: Drive four miles north on Rim Drive from Rim Village, or 2.2 miles south of the junction with the north entrance road to the pullout parking area.

Contact: Crater Lake National Park, P.O. Box 7, Crater Lake, OR, 97604, 541/594-3000.

126 CLEETWOOD COVE/ WIZARD ISLAND
4.7 mi/2.0–4.0 hr

in Crater Lake National Park

Map 5.7, page 269

Welcome to Crater Lake, one of the most incredible places in the country. This is Oregon's sole National Park, and a stunning one at that. The remnant of a massive volcanic blast, this collapsed caldera slowly filled with abundant snowfall and rain to form this 1,943-foot-deep shimmering lake that casts a ghostly blue hue into the deep. The Cleetwood Cove Trail is the only trail to access the lake itself, but from here you can take a private boat on a 45-minute tour out to Wizard Island to continue your hike; you'll pay $26 for adults and $15.50 for kids to get there, and more if you're dropped off.

From the rim, hike down the switchbacking 1.1-mile trail to Cleetwood Cove and catch the boat to Wizard Island. On Wizard Island, two trails explore this cinder cone: a 0.4-mile trail heads to the left to a lava flow and Fumarole Bay, and a 1.1-mile trail climbs to the crater, with a 0.3-mile loop around the peak.

User Groups: Hikers only. No dogs, horses, or mountain bikes allowed. No wheelchair facilities.

Permits: Permits are not required unless backcountry camping. A $10 fee, good for seven days, is collected at the entrance stations.

Maps: For a map of Crater Lake National Park, contact Crater Lake National Park, P.O. Box 7, Crater Lake, OR, 97604, 541/594-3000, or for a free downloadable map go to www. nps.gov/crla. For a topographic map, ask the USGS for Crater Lake East and West.

Directions: From Rim Village, drive clockwise on Rim Drive 10.6 miles to the trailhead. From the north entrance, go left at Rim Drive 4.6 miles.

Contact: Crater Lake National Park, P.O. Box 7, Crater Lake, OR, 97604, 541/594-3000.

127 MOUNT SCOTT
5.0 mi/3.5 hr

in Crater Lake National Park

Map 5.7, page 269   **BEST (**

When Mount Mazama blew its top 7,700 years ago, it decimated the surrounding landscape and left the massive crater that is Crater Lake. The highest point remaining is Mount Scott, Oregon's 10th-tallest mountain. The hike to this peak is actually quite easy. The goal is a fire watchtower that overlooks the whole panoramic scope of the National Park and beyond.

From the trailhead, this well-graded trail sets out 2.5 miles up Mount Scott, climbing 1,000 feet to the peak. From the peak, look for Klamath Lake, Mount Shasta, Mount McLoughlin, Mount Thielsen, and the Three Sisters.

User Groups: Hikers only. No dogs, horses, or mountain bikes allowed. No wheelchair facilities.

Permits: Permits are not required unless backcountry camping. A $10 fee, good for seven days, is collected at the entrance stations.

Maps: For a map of Crater Lake National Park, contact Crater Lake National Park, P.O. Box 7, Crater Lake, OR, 97604, 541/594-3000, or for a free downloadable map go to www. nps.gov/crla. For a topographic map, ask the USGS for Crater Lake East.

Directions: From Rim Village, drive counterclockwise on Rim Drive 11 miles to a parking pullout. From the north entrance, go left on East Rim Drive 13 miles to the trailhead.

Contact: Crater Lake National Park, P.O. Box 7, Crater Lake, OR, 97604, 541/594-3000.

128 LIGHTNING SPRING/ DISCOVERY POINT/ DUTTON CREEK LOOP

13.1 mi/7.0 hr

in Crater Lake National Park

Map 5.7, page 269

Though the Pacific Crest Trail has some of the most scenic views in the Cascade Mountains, its path through Crater Lake National Park is quite hidden. It passes a few miles away from the rim, thus missing Discovery Point, where it is believed that the Hillman prospecting party first saw the lake in 1853. This strenuous hike goes from the rim to the PCT, connecting with a few campsites at Lightning Spring and along Dutton Creek, passing Discovery Point on the very lip of the volcano itself.

From Rim Village, set out north along the rim for 1.3 miles to Discovery Point and continue 1.2 miles to the third pullout. Cross the road and head to the Lightning Springs Trailhead. In 0.8 mile, you'll reach a series of backcountry campsites. Continue 3.2 miles to the PCT and go left 4.2 miles through a lodgepole forest to a junction on Dutton Creek. Turn left to go 2.4 miles back to the Rim Village.

User Groups: Hikers only. Horses allowed on the PCT only. No dogs or mountain bikes allowed. No wheelchair facilities.

Permits: Permits are not required unless backcountry camping. A $10 fee, good for seven days, is collected at the entrance stations.

Maps: For a map of Crater Lake National Park, contact Crater Lake National Park, P.O. Box 7, Crater Lake, OR, 97604, 541/594-3000, or for a free downloadable map go to www. nps.gov/crla. For a topographic map, ask the USGS for Crater Lake West.

Directions: The trail begins in the large parking lot in Rim Village.

Contact: Crater Lake National Park, P.O. Box 7, Crater Lake, OR, 97604, 541/594-3000.

129 GARFIELD PEAK

3.4 mi/1.5 hr

in Crater Lake National Park

Map 5.7, page 269

Named for Teddy Roosevelt's Secretary of the Interior, who created this National Park in 1902, this 8,054-foot peak set high on Castle Crest overlooks a series of pretty meadows and the Phantom Ship, a rock formation forever adrift in Crater Lake. From the visitors center, set out east toward Crater Lake Lodge for 0.2 mile, then continue up Castle Crest for 1.5 miles to the peak.

User Groups: Hikers only. No dogs, horses, or mountain bikes allowed. No wheelchair facilities.

Permits: Permits are not required unless backcountry camping. A $10 fee, good for seven days, is collected at the entrance stations.

Maps: For a map of Crater Lake National Park, contact Crater Lake National Park, P.O. Box 7, Crater Lake, OR, 97604, 541/594-3000, or for a free downloadable map go to www. nps.gov/crla. For a topographic map, ask the USGS for Crater Lake East and West.

Directions: The trail begins in the large parking lot in Rim Village.

Contact: Crater Lake National Park, P.O. Box 7, Crater Lake, OR, 97604, 541/594-3000.

130 ANNIE CREEK AND GODFREY GLEN

2.7 mi/1.0 hr

in Crater Lake National Park

Map 5.7, page 269

Two easy hikes explore canyons carved out of the flank of Crater Lake's massive volcano. Since they're located close to one another, it's worth it to hike both. Annie Creek's 1.7-mile loop follows a glacier-carved canyon with a series of ash pinnacles left over from the 7,700-year-old eruption. Godfrey Glen's one-mile loop looks over Munson Creek's canyon and its haunting pillars of solidified ash.

User Groups: Hikers only. No dogs, horses, or mountain bikes allowed. No wheelchair facilities.

Permits: Permits are not required unless back-country camping. A $10 fee, good for seven days, is collected at the entrance stations.

Maps: For a map of Crater Lake National Park, contact Crater Lake National Park, P.O. Box 7, Crater Lake, OR, 97604, 541/594-3000, or for a free downloadable map go to www. nps.gov/crla. For a topographic map, ask the USGS for Union Peak.

Directions: To see Annie Creek, start from the park entrance on OR 62, driving 0.3 mile toward Rim Village and turning right at a sign for Mazama Campground. Park at the store and walk to camping area C; the trailhead begins behind site C-11. To see the Godfrey Glen, go past the Mazama Campground and drive toward Rim Village an additional 2.1 miles, turning right at a sign for Godfrey Glen Nature Loop.

Contact: Crater Lake National Park, P.O. Box 7, Crater Lake, OR, 97604, 541/594-3000.

131 UNION PEAK
11.0 mi/6.0 hr

in Crater Lake National Park

Map 5.7, page 269

This trail heads to 7,709-foot Union Peak, making this the most challenging hike in Crater Lake National Park. Union Peak is the oldest mountain in the park; it's a heavily eroded volcanic plug rising above forests of lodgepole pine and mountain hemlock growing from deep layers of pumice. This hike is bit off the beaten path, and it makes use of the Pacific Crest Trail. Note that there is no water on this trail, so bring plenty to cover this long trip.

Set out on the PCT for 2.9 miles along an old fire road. In a pumice plain, go right on the Union Peak Trail 2.6 miles to the peak, switchbacking steeply at the end.

User Groups: Hikers only. Horses allowed on

the PCT only. No dogs or mountain bikes allowed. No wheelchair facilities.

Permits: Permits are not required unless back-country camping. A $10 fee, good for seven days, is collected at the entrance stations.

Maps: For a map of Crater Lake National Park, contact Crater Lake National Park, P.O. Box 7, Crater Lake, OR, 97604, 541/594-3000, or for a free downloadable map go to www. nps.gov/crla. For a topographic map, ask the USGS for Union Peak.

Directions: Drive 72 miles east of Medford on OR 62 to a summit about one mile west of Mazama Village. Park at a Pacific Crest Trail side road on the right.

Contact: Crater Lake National Park, P.O. Box 7, Crater Lake, OR, 97604, 541/594-3000.

132 CRATER PEAK
6.2 mi/3.0 hr

in Crater Lake National Park

Map 5.7, page 269

High above the Sun Notch, and with views extending to a host of Cascade peaks and Klamath Lake, Crater Peak is host to high meadows of summer lupine where elk browse in summer. Atop the peak is a volcanic crater filled in with the pumice and ash left from Mazama's violent explosion. From the Vidae Falls Picnic Area, the trail climbs 1,000 feet up 3.1 miles to the crater atop this overlook peak. Once atop the volcanic crater, you can loop 0.4 mile to inspect this long-dead peak.

User Groups: Hikers only. No dogs, horses, or mountain bikes allowed. No wheelchair facilities.

Permits: Permits are not required unless back-country camping. A $10 fee, good for seven days, is collected at the entrance stations.

Maps: For a map of Crater Lake National Park, contact Crater Lake National Park, P.O. Box 7, Crater Lake, OR, 97604, 541/594-3000, or for a free downloadable map go to www.nps.gov/crla. For a topographic map, ask the USGS for Crater Lake East and Maklaks Crater.

Directions: From Rim Village, follow Rim Drive East 2.9 miles to the Vidae Falls Picnic Area on the right.

Contact: Crater Lake National Park, P.O. Box 7, Crater Lake, OR, 97604, 541-594-3000.

133 TAKELMA GORGE
5.2 mi/2.0 hr   🚶1 ⛰8

on the Rogue River in Rogue River National Forest

Map 5.7, page 269

If you don't have the time to hike large stretches of the Upper Rogue River, but prefer something shorter, a walk where a fanny pack would be enough for an outing, try the Takelma Gorge. This mile-long surge through a 150-foot-deep lava slot comes close to the final stretch of this long trail, and provides an exciting series of views into the Rogue's chasm.

From the Woodruff Bridge picnic area, go downstream 1.6 miles to the beginning of the chasm, then continue one mile farther along the stunning viewpoints to a switchback down to a beach on a much calmer section. This makes a good turnaround point, but beyond that, the river trail continues about 8.5 miles to its end at North Fork Park.

User Groups: Hikers and dogs. No horses or mountain bikes allowed. No wheelchair facilities.

Permits: Permits are not required. Parking and access are free.

Maps: For a map of the Rogue River National Forest, contact the Rogue River-Siskiyou National Forest, 3040 Biddle Road, Medford, OR, 97504, 541-618-2200. For a topographic map, ask the USGS for Hamaker Butte.

Directions: Drive east of Medford on OR 62 and between mileposts 51 and 52 turn left on Woodruff Meadows Road for 1.7 miles. Turn left into the Woodruff Bridge picnic area.

Contact: Rogue River National Forest, Prospect Ranger District, 47201 Highway 62, Prospect, OR, 97536, 541-560-3400.

134 RED BLANKET FALLS AND STUART FALLS
10.0 mi/4.5 hr   🚶3 ⛰7

south of Crater Lake in Sky Lakes Wilderness

Map 5.7, page 269

At the southern border of Crater Lake National Park lies the Sky Lakes Wilderness, with three major basins of lakes and the peak of Mount McLoughlin to claim as its territory. At the northwestern corner, this trail enters in so close to the national park that you'll pass a 1902 corner marker; after that, you'll follow Red Blanket Creek into its canyon, reaching two waterfalls and a lush huckleberry meadow. From there, the trail heads in two directions to the Pacific Crest Trail, with access to Crater Lake and the Sky Lakes.

The first 2.9 miles of the trail follows Red Blanket Creek to Red Blanket Falls and a junction. To head to Stuart Falls, go left up one mile to another junction, then left again another 0.4 mile. From this point, it is 2.8 miles to the PCT. Return 0.4 mile to the junction and this time go left 0.8 mile on the Stuart Falls Trail to the next junction. Staying to the left heads 2.7 miles to the PCT; go right for a 1.6-mile loop through Lucky Meadow. This Lucky Camp Trail returns to Red Blanket Falls.

User Groups: Hikers, dogs, and horses. No mountain bikes allowed. No wheelchair facilities.

Permits: A free self-issue Wilderness Permit is required and is available at the trailhead. Parking and access are free.

Maps: For a map of the Rogue River National Forest and Sky Lakes Wilderness, contact the Rogue River-Siskiyou National Forest, 3040 Biddle Road, Medford, OR, 97504, 541-618-2200. For a topographic map, ask the USGS for Union Peak.

Directions: Drive east of Medford 45 miles on OR 62 and turn right toward Prospect for 0.7 mile. In town, turn left on Butte Falls Road for one mile, then left on Red Blanket Road for 0.4 mile. At a fork, go left on Road 6205 for 11.4 miles to road's end at a parking area.

Contact: Rogue River National Forest, Prospect Ranger District, 47201 Highway 62, Prospect, OR, 97536, 541/560-3400.

135 LOST CREEK LAKE
5.0–18.7 mi/2.0 hr–2 days 👥3 ▲7

on the Rogue River in Stewart State Park

Map 5.7, page 269

Stewart State Park is a busy park with lots of visitors and lots of things to do: biking, camping, swimming, boating, you name it. It so happens that the majority of the nearby Lost Creek Lake Reservoir is not only quieter, but provides opportunities for backpacking, making use of three remote camping spots. The Grotto makes an easy destination from Lewis Road, and is actually quite a sight: This box canyon of basalt and green ash left over from the volcanic explosion of Crater Lake is an easy side excursion.

To begin, set out from Lewis Road on the trail. In 0.9 mile you'll reach the first primitive camp, Fire Glen Camp. Another 1.5 miles leads to a right-hand side trail up 0.1 mile to the Grotto overlook. The next 3.4 miles heads to a crossing of Lost Creek, passing Sugar Pine Camp along the way. The next 3.8 miles starts around the opposite shore, passing Four Corners Camp and arriving at a boat ramp at Takelma Park. Here the trail continues 1.4 miles, crossing the dam. The next 2.8 miles heads to the state park, passing through it for 3.6 miles. The final stretch is all on paved roads, following Highway 62 to the left over Peyton Bridge 0.3 mile, then going left on Lewis Road for the last mile.

User Groups: Hikers and dogs. No horses allowed. Trails in Stewart State Park are wheelchair accessible and suitable for mountain biking.

Permits: Permits are not required. Parking and access are free.

Maps: For a topographic map, ask the USGS for McLeod and Cascade Gorge.

Directions: Drive east of Medford 35.5 miles on OR 62. After crossing a bridge over Lost Creek Lake turn left on Lewis Road for one mile to the Lewis Road Trailhead on the left.

Contact: Oregon Parks and Recreation Department, 1115 Commercial Street Northeast, Salem, OR, 97301, 800/551-6949, www.oregonstateparks.org.

136 UPPER SOUTH FORK ROGUE RIVER
12.0 mi/6.0 hr 👥3 ▲7

southeast of Prospect in Rogue River National Forest

Map 5.7, page 269

The South Fork of the Rogue River is a young river, not as wide as you might suspect, but this section of trail follows it through some substantial trees and large logs along the shore, plus a few gravel bars thrown in for good measure. You'll also find Pacific yew, which Native Americans used for bows because of its flexibility. Along this trail you'll cross several creeks, as well.

From the trailhead, start out upriver on the South Fork Trail, a primitive and seldom-maintained trail. In 0.7 mile you'll cross Big Ben Creek; avoid the side trail on the left leading to a campground. Continue on 4.4 miles, crossing Sam Creek, Wickiup Creek, and Little Billie Creek to a crossing of Road 800. The last 0.9 mile of trail continues to an upper trailhead on Road 37. From here, backpackers can follow nearby Road 720 southeast one mile to the trailhead for the Blue Lake Trail and the Sky Lakes Wilderness.

User Groups: Hikers and dogs. No horses or mountain bikes allowed. No wheelchair facilities.

Permits: Permits are not required. Parking and access are free.

Maps: For a map of the Rogue River National Forest and Sky Lakes Wilderness, contact the Rogue River-Siskiyou National Forest, 3040 Biddle Road, Medford, OR, 97504,

541/618-2200. For a topographic map, ask the USGS for Cascade Gorge.

Directions: From Medford, drive 14.5 miles east on OR 62 and turn right on the Butte Falls Highway for 15 miles to the town of Butte Falls. Go straight one mile then left at a sign for Prospect for nine miles. Turn right on Lodgepole Road for 8.5 miles. Go past South Fork Campground 0.5 mile to a parking area on the right.

Contact: Rogue River National Forest, Butte Falls Ranger District, 47201 Highway 62, Prospect, OR, 97536, 541/865-2700.

137 LOWER SOUTH FORK ROGUE RIVER

13.6-14.0 mi/6.0-7.0 hr   🏃3   ⛰7

southeast of Prospect in Rogue River National Forest

Map 5.7, page 269

The lower stretch of trail on the South Fork of the Rogue River is accessible to mountain bikes. It also provides a glimpse of many sugar pine trees, including one particularly large one on a short side trail. This section of trail ambles over creeks and through woods down to its end at a diversion dam.

Cross the road from the parking area and take the South Fork Trail along the river 1.6 miles to the left-hand side trail; a short 0.2-mile walk crosses Road 3775 and visits the giant sugar pine. The remaining 5.2 miles follows the river down to the dam.

User Groups: Hikers, dogs, and mountain bikes. No horses allowed. No wheelchair facilities.

Permits: Permits are not required. Parking and access are free.

Maps: For a map of the Rogue River National Forest and Sky Lakes Wilderness, contact the Rogue River-Siskiyou National Forest, 3040 Biddle Road, Medford, OR, 97504, 541/618-2200. For a topographic map, ask the USGS for Cascade Gorge.

Directions: From Medford, drive 14.5 miles east on OR 62 and turn right on the Butte Falls Highway for 15 miles to the town of Butte Falls. go straight one mile then left at a sign for Prospect for nine miles. Turn right on Lodgepole Road for 8.5 miles. Go past South Fork Campground 0.5 mile to a parking area on the right.

Contact: Rogue River National Forest, Butte Falls Ranger District, 47201 Highway 62, Prospect, OR, 97536, 541/865-2700.

138 SEVEN LAKES TRAIL

8.4-10.4 mi/3.5-5.0 hr   🏃4   ⛰9

east of Prospect in Sky Lakes Wilderness

Map 5.7, page 269

The Sky Lakes Wilderness is heaven for backpackers and horses, with many opportunities to camp throughout the area. The Seven Lakes Basin, one of the more popular spots, has camps aplenty—just as long as you camp where the USFS asks you to, which means paying attention to posted camp spots. Horses are required to camp at designated areas, are banned from grazing, and are not allowed within 200 feet of lakeshores, unless on trails or near designated watering spots. If this sounds like a lot of information, don't let it dissuade you. It's only to keep the area as pristine as possible. To enter from the west, the Seven Lakes Trail climbs over a pass into a water-dotted landscape that is best viewed from nearby Devils Peak, accessible from the Pacific Crest Trail.

The Seven Lakes Trail sets out from behind a guardrail into the wilderness. At 0.7 mile, go right and continue 2.8 miles, passing Frog Lake, to a pass. Here the trail splits: Take the left trail down 0.2 mile to the basin. At the next junction, going left on the Alta Lake Trail leads to half-mile-long Alta Lake with its campsites. Going straight passes South Lake and Cliff Lake in 1.5 miles; another left-hand trail connects to three more lakes. Continue 0.4 mile to the PCT. For a climb up Devils Peak, turn right on the PCT for 2.5 miles, then heading right up the peak. Head back down and continue on the PCT another 0.6 mile to a junction. Go right on a 1.3-mile spur trail to return to the pass over Seven Lakes.

User Groups: Hikers, dogs, and horses. No mountain bikes allowed. No wheelchair facilities.

Permits: A free self-issue Wilderness Permit is required and is available at the trailhead. Parking and access are free.

Maps: For a map of the Rogue River National Forest and Sky Lakes Wilderness, contact the Rogue River-Siskiyou National Forest, 3040 Biddle Road, Medford, OR, 97504, 541/618-2200. For a topographic map, ask the USGS for Devil's Peak.

Directions: From Medford, drive 14.5 miles east on OR 62 and turn right on Butte Falls Highway for 15 miles to the town of Butte Falls. Go straight one mile and turn left toward Prospect for nine miles, then right on Lodgepole Road 34 for 8.5 miles. Continue straight on Road 37 for 0.4 mile, then go right on Road 3780 for 4.1 miles to a parking area on the left.

Contact: Rogue River National Forest, Butte Falls Ranger District, 47201 Highway 62, Prospect, OR, 97536, 541/865-2700.

139 SEVEN LAKES BASIN VIA SEVENMILE/PCT
11.4-17.3 mi/6.0-9.0 hr   4 ⛰9

east of Prospect in Sky Lakes Wilderness

Map 5.7, page 269

The eastern entrance to this mythic landscape of lakes visits the same area as the Seven Lakes Trail (see previous listing) but is both longer and easier. For one, you won't have the elevation gain. Plus, you'll be in the headwaters of the Middle Fork Rogue River, including Sevenmile Marsh. From here, you can also walk the shore of Cliff Lake with its views to Devils Peak, and you can climb Devils Peak for a world-class view of the lake country.

Start on the Sevenmile Trail for 1.8 miles,

and go right on the Pacific Crest Trail for 2.7 miles. At the next junction, you can create a 2.4-mile loop past Grass Lake, Middle Lake, and Cliff Lake by going right then staying left for the next three junctions. To climb Devils Peak stay on the PCT another 3.2 miles up to a high pass, climbing the peak to the right. If you want to expand this loop to a 17-plus-mile hike, continue on the PCT 0.6 mile to a junction and go right 1.3 miles on a spur trail to a second pass, connecting with the Seven Lakes Trail. Then go right and stay on this trail for 1.7 miles back to the PCT.

User Groups: Hikers, dogs, and horses. No mountain bikes allowed. No wheelchair facilities.

Permits: A free self-issue Wilderness Permit is required and is available at the trailhead. Parking and access are free.

Maps: For a map of the Rogue River National Forest and Sky Lakes Wilderness, contact the Fremont-Winema National Forest, 1301 South G Street, Lakeview, OR, 97630, 541/947-2151. For a topographic map, ask the USGS for Devils Peak.

Directions: Drive north from Klamath Falls on OR 62 to Fort Klamath, near milepost 90. Turn west on Nicholson Road and go straight 3.9 miles. Go left on Road 3300 at a sign for Sevenmile Trailhead for 0.4 mile, then go right on Road 3334 to road's end.

Contact: Winema National Forest, Klamath Falls Ranger District, 2819 Dahlia Street, Klamath Falls, OR, 97601, 541/883-6714.

140 SKY LAKES FROM NANNIE CREEK TRAIL
12.8-16.7 mi/6.0-8.0 hr   ⛰5 ⛰9

west of Klamath Lake in Sky Lakes Wilderness

Map 5.7, page 269

The Sky Lakes Basin has a challenging side, and this trail is it. This section of lakes huddles around imposing Luther Mountain like jewels flung across the forest. The Nannie Creek Trail will get you there, but once you're there it's up to you to wander around and lose yourself in the landscape. Here are a couple of hikes, both rigorous, to get you warmed up.

The Nannie Creek Trail heads out on a ridge for 2.4 miles to Puck Lakes on the right, and another 1.9 miles to a junction with the Snow Lakes Trail. To hit the main course, go left 1.4 miles passing numerous ponds to a junction. Here you can go 0.5 mile to the right to Marguerette Lake, then form a loop: go left 0.2 mile to Trapper Lake, then left at the junction of the Cherry Creek Trail 0.7 mile to Donna and Deep lakes to complete the loop.

For a climb around Luther Mountain, instead go right at Marguerette Lake, climbing heartily up 2.8 miles to the PCT. Go right on the PCT for 1.1 miles, then right on the Snow Lakes Trail 2.3 miles back to the Nannie Creek Trail, passing little tarns along the way. Return on the Nannie Creek Trail.

User Groups: Hikers, dogs, and horses. No mountain bikes allowed. No wheelchair facilities.

Permits: A free self-issue Wilderness Permit is required and is available at the trailhead. Parking and access are free.

Maps: For a map of the Rogue River National Forest and Sky Lakes Wilderness, contact the Fremont-Winema National Forest, 1301 South G Street, Lakeview, OR, 97630, 541/947-2151. For a topographic map, ask the USGS for for Pelican Butte.

Directions: From Klamath Falls, go west on Highway 140 for 25 miles. Between mileposts 43 and 44, go north on Westside Road for 12.2 miles, then left on Road 3484 for 5.2 miles to road's end.

Contact: Winema National Forest, Klamath Falls Ranger District, 2819 Dahlia Street, Klamath Falls, OR, 97601, 541/883-6714.

141 SKY LAKES FROM COLD SPRINGS TRAILHEAD
6.9 mi/3.0 hr   🚶3 ⛺8

west of Klamath Lake in Sky Lakes Wilderness

Map 5.7, page 269

The Sky Lakes Basin is a picture-perfect mesh of ponds and lakes. For an easy entrance into its wonders—visiting Heavenly Twin Lakes, with its view of Luther Mountain, and Isherwood Lake, as well as Lakes Florence, Liza, Elizabeth, and Notasha—try this easy loop.

From the Cold Springs Trailhead, head in 0.6 mile to a junction. For the quickest walk through the lodgepole and hemlock woods, go right on the South Rock Creek Trail for 1.8 miles to the next junction. To the left, a 0.3-mile spur connects to a shorter loop with the cold Springs Trail and runs between the heavenly Twin Lakes. For a longer loop among far more lakes, go right 0.4 mile along the lakeshore to the Sky Lakes Trail, then left at the next junction 0.8 mile past the rest of the lovely lakes. At the next junction, go right 0.3 mile, then left on the Cold Springs Trail 2.4 miles back to the car.

User Groups: Hikers, dogs, and horses. No mountain bikes allowed. No wheelchair facilities.

Permits: A free self-issue Wilderness Permit is required and is available at the trailhead. Parking and access are free.

Maps: For a map of the Rogue River National Forest and Sky Lakes Wilderness, contact the Fremont-Winema National Forest, 1301 South G Street, Lakeview, OR, 97630, 541/947-2151. For a topographic map, ask the USGS for for Pelican Butte.

Directions: From Medford, drive east 6 miles on OR 62, then right on Highway 140 to milepost 41, and turn north on Road 3651; watch for Cold Springs Trailhead sign. Go 10.1 miles to its end at the Cold Springs Trailhead.

Contact: Winema National Forest, Klamath Falls Ranger District, 2819 Dahlia Street, Klamath Falls, OR, 97601, 541/883-6714.

142 BLUE LAKE BASIN
7.4-11.0 miles/3.0-6.0 hr   3   ▲8

north of Mount McLoughlin in Sky Lakes Wilderness

Map 5.7, page 269

Sky Lakes seems a fitting name for a wilderness that hosts lakes so pure they seem to hold their own sky. From some of the shores of these lakes, the true sky seems magnificently large, endless, spanning from one horizon to another. Perhaps this is what Judge John Waldo thought as he passed through here with a horse party in 1888. He left his mark carved into a large Shasta red fir on the shore of Island Lake, a spot you can visit on this fabulous hike.

Take the Blue Canyon Trail 2.3 miles, passing Round Lake, to Blue Lake. Go right at the junction with the South Fork Trail and continue 0.3 mile to the next junction (with a horse camp on the left). Go left and continue 2.9 miles on the Blue Canyon Trail, passing access points to large Horseshoe Lake and Pear Lake, then watching for an unmarked side trail to the left, leading to Waldo's signature and the shore of Island Lake. Another 0.4 mile beyond this trail is the junction with the Badger Lake Trail, and a right turn there leads 0.2 mile to the Pacific Crest Trail.

User Groups: Hikers, dogs, and horses. No mountain bikes allowed. No wheelchair facilities.

Permits: A free self-issue Wilderness Permit is required and is available at the trailhead. Parking and access are free.

Maps: For a map of the Rogue River National Forest and Sky Lakes Wilderness, contact the Rogue River-Siskiyou National Forest, 3040 Biddle Road, Medford, OR, 97504, 541/618-2200. For a topographic map, ask the USGS for Pelican Butte.

Directions: From Medford, drive 14.5 miles east on OR 62 and turn right on Butte Falls Highway for 15 miles to the town of Butte Falls. Go straight one mile and turn left toward Prospect for nine miles, then right on Lodgepole Road 34 for 8.5 miles. Continue straight on Road 37 for 7.4 miles, then turn left on Road 3770 for 5.3 miles to a pullout on the right.

Contact: Rogue River National Forest, Butte Falls Ranger District, 47201 Highway 62, Prospect, OR, 97536, 541/865-2700.

143 MOUNT MCLOUGHLIN
10.6 mi/6.0 hr   5   ▲10

west of Klamath Lake in Sky Lakes Wilderness

Map 5.7, page 269   **BEST (**

After years of having hikers climb helter-skelter to this 9,495-foot peak, the Forest Service finally laid out a trail. Bring plenty of water and sunscreen and prepare for a rugged, demanding climb, but also a view of half the state of Oregon, and far into California. Named for the Hudson Bay Company leader at Fort Vancouver, this mountain is one of the best non-technical climbs in the state. Just be sure to stay on the trail—even with such a view of the surrounding area, it's easy to get lost.

Cross the Cascade Canal and climb one mile to the Pacific Crest Trail. Follow the PCT uphill and to the right for 0.4 mile, passing a right-hand side trail to Freye Lake, then leaving the PCT on the climber's route to the left. For 1.5 miles the trail is steady before it hurtles upwards the remaining 2.4 miles, heading above tree line, with the final half gaining 1,300 feet.

User Groups: Hikers, dogs, and horses. No mountain bikes allowed. No wheelchair facilities.

Permits: A free self-issue Wilderness Permit is required and is available at the trailhead. A federal Northwest Forest Pass is required to park at the Trout Creek Trailhead; the cost is $5 a day or $30 for an annual pass. You can buy a day pass at the trailhead, at ranger stations, or through private vendors.

Maps: For a map of the Rogue River National Forest and Sky Lakes Wilderness, contact the Fremont-Winema National Forest, 1301 South G Street, Lakeview, OR, 97630, 541/947-2151.

For a topographic map, ask the USGS for Mount McLoughlin.

Directions: From Klamath Falls, go west on Highway 140 to milepost 36, and just beyond it turn right on Road 3661 for 2.9 miles, then left on Road 3650 for 0.2 mile to a parking lot.

Contact: Winema National Forest, Klamath Falls Ranger District, 2819 Dahlia Street, Klamath Falls, OR, 97601, 541/883-6714.

144 FOURMILE LAKE TO LONG LAKE
9.0-14.0 mi/4.0-7.0 hr   🏃3 ⛰7

west of Klamath Lake in Sky Lakes Wilderness

Map 5.7, page 269

Fourmile Lake is bordered on nearly every side by the Sky Lakes Wilderness, through which the Pacific Crest Trail glides by on a relatively level trail. This large lake, with its view of the pyramid-like Mount McLoughlin, offers access to a number of lakes in the Wilderness Area. The route can be extended to a 14-mile loop, though much of it passes through viewless woods and leaves the lakes behind for quite a while.

From the Fourmile Trailhead, head left for 0.8 mile, crossing Road 3661, then left on the Badger Lake Trail, which crosses the Cascade Canal. Now the trail heads into the Wilderness Area, arriving at Badger Lake in 1.8 miles and Long Lake in another 1.9 miles, passing Horse Creek Meadow along the way. This is the last of the lakes this trail sees, but to continue on a wide loop, head farther down the trail 1.6 miles to the PCT, going left. Follow the PCT 5.4 miles, then turn left on the Twin Ponds Trail for 2.5 miles, passing one last lake, and arriving back at the Fourmile Trailhead.

User Groups: Hikers, dogs, and horses. No mountain bikes allowed. No wheelchair facilities.

Permits: A free self-issue Wilderness Permit is required and is available at the trailhead. Parking and access are free.

Maps: For a map of the Rogue River National Forest and Sky Lakes Wilderness, contact the Fremont-Winema National Forest, 1301 South G Street, Lakeview, OR, 97630, 541/947-2151. For a topographic map, ask the USGS for Lake of the Woods North.

Directions: From Klamath Falls, go west on Highway 140 to milepost 36, and just beyond it turn right on Road 3661 for 5.7 miles to Fourmile Campground. Follow signs for the trailhead.

Contact: Winema National Forest, Klamath Falls Ranger District, 2819 Dahlia Street, Klamath Falls, OR, 97601, 541/883-6714.

145 TABLE ROCKS
2.8-5.4 mi/1.0-2.5 hr   🏃1 ⛰8

north of Medford

Map 5.7, page 269

The two formations known as the Table Rocks, rising like fortresses above the Rogue River, seem out of place in this valley. They were, in fact, used as fortresses by the Takelma tribe against the U.S. Army, which came for them when they attacked settlers and gold miners in 1853. These mesas are the remnants of a 9.6-million-year-old lava flow, standing 800-feet-high and capped with tough andesite. Atop the plateaus you'll find scrub oak grasslands and a profusion of wildflowers, which is why The Nature Conservancy built the trail on Lower Table Rock, now a nature preserve. In fact, a rare fairy shrimp—federally listed as threatened—is found in the vernal pools atop the mesa.

To climb Upper Table Rock, you need ascend only 720 feet up a 1.1-mile trail to the viewpoints. The trail to Lower Table Rock is longer; it sets off 1.6 miles across the valley floor, then goes up cliffs studded with black oak and madrone to the mesa. From there, you can hike out to two viewpoints: one just 0.4 mile to the left, and the other 1.1 miles down an old airstrip to a viewpoint. You'll catch views of the Crater Lake rim, Mount McLoughlin, and the Rogue River.

User Groups: Hikers. Dogs not allowed on Lower Table Rock. No horses or mountain bikes allowed. No wheelchair facilities.

Permits: Permits are not required. Parking and access are free.

Maps: For a topographic map, ask the USGS for Sams Valley.

Directions: For Lower Table Rock, return to Table Rock Road and turn right, continuing to milepost 10. Turn left on Wheeler Road 0.8 mile to a parking spur on the left. For Upper Table Rock, take the I-5 north of Medford to Exit 33 for Central Point, driving east on Biddle Road for one mile. Turn left on Table Rock Road for 5.2 miles and turn right on Modoc Road for 1.5 miles to the trailhead lot on the left.

Contact: Bureau of Land Management, Medford Office, 3040 Biddle Road, Medford, OR, 97504, 541/618-2200.

146 FISH LAKE AND THE HIGH LAKES TRAIL
12.7 mi one-way/7.0 hr

south of Mount McLoughlin in Rogue River National Forest

Map 5.7, page 269

This fairly new trail makes for a great bike ride or an extended hike. Of course, it can be broken up into segments starting from either Fish Lake or Lake of the Woods. The trail crosses the Cascade Crest and largely follows a massive lava flow erupted from Brown Mountain, which occupies the horizon here like a sentry. An easy 6.6-mile round-trip hike follows the shore of Fish Lake and joins the High Lakes Trail at its far end, and it's here that this description begins.

From the Fish Lake Trailhead, walk in 0.6 mile to a junction near the Fish Lake Dam. Go left and follow the main trail 3.7 miles through an old clear-cut, crossing a road and passing the Fish Lake Resort, and following the Fish Lake shore to the Fish Lake Campground and the start of the High Lakes Trail.

In one mile the trail crosses the Pacific Crest Trail. From here, it's 4.8 miles to Lake of the Woods, following the edge of the Brown Mountain Lava Flow (see next listing) to a visitors center. The trail continues along the edge of the lake for 0.8 mile to the Aspen Point Picnic Area, and continues across a big meadow 1.8 miles to the upper trailhead at the Great Meadow Recreation Site.

User Groups: Hikers, dogs, and bicycles. No horses allowed. No wheelchair facilities.

Permits: Permits are not required. Parking and access are free.

Maps: For a map of the Rogue River National Forest and Sky Lakes Wilderness, contact the Rogue River-Siskiyou National Forest, 3040 Biddle Road, Medford, OR, 97504, 541/618-2200. For a topographic map, ask the USGS for Mount McLoughlin.

Directions: To access the Fish Lake Trailhead, drive east of Medford 35 miles on Highway 140. Between mileposts 28 and 29, turn south on Road 37. In 0.5 mile turn left at the trailhead parking. To access the Lake of the Woods Trailhead, park in a lot on Highway 140 between mileposts 37 and 38.

Contact: Rogue River-Siskiyou National Forest, Ashland Ranger District, 645 Washington Street, Ashland, OR, 97520, 541/552-2900.

147 BROWN MOUNTAIN
5.8 mi/2.0 hr

south of Mount McLoughlin in Rogue River National Forest

Map 5.7, page 269

The Brown Mountain Lava Flow spilled quite a mess here, and the builders of the Pacific Crest Trail, which crosses it, had to dynamite their way through. Now the rugged landscape is being pioneered by chinkapin oak and a variety of lichens. Bring water, as summer sun can make a lava field a simmering experience.

From the trailhead, hike in 0.2 mile and go left on the Pacific Crest Trail. In 0.4 mile cross Highway 140 and continue 0.2 mile to a junction with the High Lakes Trail, going straight. Within the next two miles, you will cross the largest part of the flow and arrive at a high point, with views to Mount McLoughlin along the way. If you continue on, you can travel 5.8 miles to the Brown Mountain Trail, which does not climb the mountain but rather goes around it.

User Groups: Hikers, dogs, and horses. No mountain bikes allowed. No wheelchair facilities.

Permits: Permits are not required. Parking and access are free.

Maps: For a map of the Rogue River National Forest and Sky Lakes Wilderness, contact the Rogue River-Siskiyou National Forest, 3040 Biddle Road, Medford, OR, 97504, 541/618-2200. For a topographic map, ask the USGS for Brown Mountain.

Directions: From Medford, drive Highway 140 to a pullout on the left between mileposts 32 and 33, at a sign for Summit Sno-Park. The trail starts at this parking area.

Contact: Rogue River-Siskiyou National Forest, Ashland Ranger District, 645 Washington Street, Ashland, OR, 97520, 541/552-2900.

148 MOUNTAIN LAKES WILDERNESS LOOP

17.1 mi/1-2 days

west of Klamath Lake in the Mountain Lakes Wilderness

Map 5.7, page 269

At only six square miles, the exact size of a township, this is surely one of the smallest wilderness areas there is. This pocket remains as it was since 1964: a stunning terrain of mountainous country hovering over Upper Klamath Lake. Glaciers have carved this area, a collapsed volcano not unlike that of Crater Lake, into towering cliffs, lake basins, and eroded volcanic cones. Piercing a lateral moraine, the grit swept to the sides by glaciers, the trail follows a path of ponderosa pine, Shasta red fir, and white fir into an alpine landscape that just

begs for a backpacker or two—but no more than 10 at a time, according to regulations. Even though this is one of the first designated Wilderness Areas in the country, it remains quite a secret to the public.

Follow the Varney Creek Trail 4.4 miles, with views of Mount Harriman, to a fork at the beginning of the loop. If you're backpacking, go left on the Mountain Lakes Loop Trail to the lakes. You'll reach Lake Como in 0.7 mile, and larger Lake Harriette 1.2 miles beyond that; both are suitable for camping. From Lake Harriette, continue 1.5 miles up to a high pass and go right (the left trail dead-ends at South Pass Lake). In 0.4 mile you'll pass a side route up Aspen Butte, a one-mile cross-country climb to an old lookout site at 8,208 feet. Continuing on the loop, stay straight on the main trail for 2.7 miles to a pass on Whiteface Peak, passing both an unmaintained trail and the Clover Creek Trail on the left. At the peak, go right (the other path leads to Road 3660 on the Mountain Lakes Trail, descending 2,000 feet and past Lake Waban) to finish the loop, heading 1.4 miles down to Zeb and Eb Lakes. In another 0.4 mile, you'll meet with the Varney Creek Trail; go left to return to the trailhead.

User Groups: Hikers, dogs, and horses. No mountain bikes allowed. No wheelchair facilities.

Permits: A free self-issue Wilderness Permit is required and is available at the trailhead. Parking and access are free.

Maps: For a map of the Rogue River National Forest and Sky Lakes Wilderness, contact the Fremont-Winema National Forest, 1301 South G Street, Lakeview, OR, 97630, 541/947-2151. For a topographic map, ask the USGS for Lake of the Woods North.

Directions: From Klamath Falls, drive 21 miles west on Highway 140. Between mileposts 46 and 47, turn south on Road 3637 at a Varney Creek Trailhead sign, following this road 1.8 miles. Turn left on Road 3664 for 1.9 miles to its end.

Contact: Winema National Forest, Klamath

Falls Ranger District, 2819 Dahlia Street, Klamath Falls, OR, 97601, 541/883-6714.

149 JACKSONVILLE WOODLANDS
1.0-8.0 mi/1.0-2.5 hr

in Jacksonville

Map 5.7, page 269

The little city of Jacksonville is designated a National Historic Landmark, a true distinction here in Oregon. This former mining town at the foot of the Siskiyous is charming in its own right, and retains much of its 1886 allure, a leftover from when the railroad abandoned this area and the gold ran out. The woodlands that lie just outside it add to the ambiance. In 1989, citizens of this little red-brick town rallied to preserve the area, and the result is this 20-parcel forest intersected by eight miles of trail, following Jackson Creek, touring old mining ruins, and climbing to a 1,900-foot summit over the town.

From the lot set out 0.8 mile along Jackson Creek on the Zigler Trail. To climb to the summit of Panorama Point, head up 0.7 mile on the Jackson Forks and Rich Gulch Trails. After the viewpoint, the Rich Gulch Trail heads to Rich Gulch, where gold was discovered in 1852, passing some old mining tailings and a side trail to the Chinese Diggings, where the Chinese teams did some of the most extensive diggings. The trail ends at Oregon Street and heads 0.6 mile back to town. From here you can even tour the historic town itself, well worth the trip, then return along C Street to the lot.

User Groups: Hikers, dogs, and mountain bikes. No horses allowed. No wheelchair facilities.

Permits: Permits are not required. Parking and access are free.

Maps: Maps are available at the trailhead and online at www.jvwoodlands.org. For a topographic map, ask the USGS for Medford West.

Directions: From I-5, take the Medford exit (Exit 30) and follow signs seven miles west to Jacksonville on Highway 238. Turn right on C Street and go to its end at a visitors center lot.

Contact: Jacksonville Woodlands Association, P.O. Box 1210, Jacksonville, OR, 97530, info@jvwoodlands.org.

150 STERLING MINE DITCH
4.7 mi /2.0 hr

south of Jacksonville

Map 5.7, page 269

In 1854, just three years after gold was discovered at Jacksonville, miners struck it big at Sterling Creek. After panning gold from the creek, they went after the gold in the surrounding gravel slopes. To achieve this, Chinese laborers built a nearly 27-mile ditch to carry water from the Little Applegate River to these hills. The ditch remained in use from 1877 well into the 1930s. Now that the gold is gone, only the oak and pine forests and open grasslands are left, and a large segment of the ditch has been converted into a trail. Five trailheads—Little Applegate, Tunnel Ridge, Bear Gulch, Wolf Gap, and Deming Gulch—access the ditch trail, but Tunnel Ridge Trailhead offers the middle access with a short loop, and springtime offers a wildflower show to accompany the history. Of course, this trail can be taken for much longer journeys as well.

There are many entry points along Little Applegate Road, so why not start out easy? For an initial 4.7-mile loop, start at the Tunnel Ridge Trailhead and hike in one mile to the junction with the Sterling Mine Tunnel. From here, you could go right one-way for 5.1 miles to the Little Applegate Trailhead, another option. But head left, where you'll pass an old tunnel and continue 2.1 miles on the Sterling Ditch to a junction. Here you could go left 1.0 mile to the Bear Gulch Trailhead, then left along the road 0.6 mile to Tunnel Ridge Trailhead, completing the short 4.7-mile loop. To continue on the Ditch however, go right at this junction as far as you'd like. Another 1.6 miles leads to a junction, where going right leads 1.5 miles to the Wolf Gap Trailhead, and left heads the remaining 7.8 miles to the Deming Gulch Trailhead and the end of the trail.

User Groups: Hikers, dogs, horses, and mountain bikes. No wheelchair facilities.

Permits: Permits are not required. Parking and access are free.

Maps: For a topographic map, ask the USGS for Sterling Creek.

Directions: From Medford, follow Highway 238 through Jacksonville to the town of Ruch. Turn south at a sign for Upper Applegate and continue 2.9 miles and turn left on Little Applegate Road for 9.7 miles to the Tunnel Ridge Trailhead parking on the right.

Contact: Bureau of Land Management, Medford Office, 3040 Biddle Road, Medford, OR, 97504, 541/618-2200.

151 LITHIA PARK
2.8 mi/1.0 hr
🏃1 ⛰7

in Ashland

Map 5.7, page 269

Ashland's idyllic Lithia Park certainly ranks high among city parks. Once the site of a water-powered sawmill, this parkland now stretches along Ashland Creek through some fairly wild territory—just watch out for poison oak. There are spots to pause and reflect on stone beaches or footbridges, flowers to admire, and a sense of peace that radiates from this little town, home to the Oregon Shakespeare Festival, whose stages are nearby. If you dare, you can even take a drink from the fountains of bubbly Lithia Springs water, which is the other thing Ashland is famous for. The 2.8-mile loop follows both sides of the creek, intersecting along a series of footbridges, so you can go as far as you like. Along the way, you can circle little Meyer Lake and Black Swan Lake and follow the creek up as far as Reservoir Park.

User Groups: Hikers and dogs. No horses or mountain bikes allowed. Paved portions of the park are wheelchair accessible.

Permits: Permits are not required. Parking and access are free.

Maps: For a topographic map, ask the USGS for Ashland.

Directions: From I-5, take either Ashland exit (Exit 14 or 19) and follow signs for City Center and Lithia Park.

Contact: Ashland Parks and Recreation, 340 South Pioneer Street, Ashland, OR, 97520, 541/488-5340.

152 GRIZZLY PEAK
5.4 mi/2.0 hr
🏃1 ⛰7

east of Ashland

Map 5.7, page 269

Grizzly Peak broods over the town of Ashland and I-5 with views to the snowy cap of Mount Ashland from what was once a forested plateau until a 2002 fire swept over the western face. If anything, it opened up the view even more, and the Grizzly Peak Trail is still a fine walk along the edge to three excellent viewpoints of Mount Shasta, Pilot Rock, and Emigrant Lake.

Climb 1.2 miles to the junction, the beginning of the loop. Go left 0.3 mile to a side spur to the viewless summit and continue 0.8 mile out onto the burn to two viewpoints. Continue along the western face 0.7 mile to a view of Ashland, then return 1.2 miles to the first junction.

User Groups: Hikers, dogs, horses, and mountain bikes. No wheelchair facilities.

Permits: Permits are not required. Parking and access are free.

Maps: For a topographic map, ask the USGS for Grizzly Peak and Rio Canyon.

Directions: From I-5, take the southern Ashland exit (Exit 14) and go east on Highway 66 for 0.7 mile, then turn left on Dead Indian Memorial Highway for 6.7 miles. Turn left again on Shale City Road for three miles, then left on Road 38-2E-9.2 and after 0.8 mile go straight through a three-way junction, continuing 0.9 mile to road's end.

Contact: Bureau of Land Management, Medford Office, 3040 Biddle Road, Medford, OR, 97504, 541/618-2200.

153 WAGNER BUTTE
10.4 mi/6.0 hr

south of Ashland in Rogue River National Forest

Map 5.7, page 269

For panoramic views of the Rogue and Little Applegate Valleys and the mountains that surround them, try this mountain named for early settler Jacob Wagner, who operated a flour mill in nearby Ashland—which you'll get a view of, too. A few pieces remain of an old lookout tower on the 7,140-foot peak, which was intentionally burned down by smokejumpers in 1972. The trail passes the Sheep Creek Slide, where 400,000 tons of soil went crashing down four miles to the Little Applegate River in a 1983 thunderstorm. Now a wealth of wildflowers are pioneering the slopes.

The Wagner Butte Trail begins steep, then gets easier for the first 2.4 miles, crossing the slide along Sheep Creek. Then the trail climbs steeply through sagebrush, gaining nearly 500 feet in 0.9 mile to the Wagner Glade Gap. The final 1.9 miles passes through quaking aspen stands and mountain mahogany, and by a piped spring before its pitch over boulders to the summit.

User Groups: Hikers and dogs only. No horses or mountain bikes. No wheelchair facilities.

Permits: Permits are not required. Parking and access are free.

Maps: For a map of the Rogue River National Forest, contact the Rogue River-Siskiyou National Forest, 3040 Biddle Road, Medford, OR, 97504, 541/618-2200. For a topographic map, ask the USGS for Siskiyou Peak and Talent.

Directions: From I-5 take exit 21 for Talent and go 0.4 mile west on Valley View Drive

and turn left on Old Highway 99 for another 0.4 mile. Turn right on Rapp Road and go 1.1 miles to a stop sign, continuing straight on Wagner Creek Road for 6.5 miles, going from paved road to gravel. Go left on Road 22, heading 2 miles to the trailhead parking on the right.

Contact: Rogue River-Siskiyou National Forest, Ashland Ranger District, 645 Washington Street, Ashland, OR, 97520, 541/552-2900.

154 MOUNT ASHLAND MEADOWS AND GROUSE GAP
6.8 mi/3.0 hr

south of Ashland in Rogue River National Forest

Map 5.7, page 269

The tallest peak in the Siskiyou Range is also the most popular. Mount Ashland is the sole ski area in this part of the state, and winter finds Mount Ashland Meadows a destination for the downhill crowd. In summer, it's another story: The meadows are dominated by bursts of lupine, larkspur, sneezeweed, aster, yarrow, and paintbrush. Granite rock formations, stands of grand fir and Shasta red fir, and views to Mount Shasta itself on the California horizon make this stretch of the Pacific Crest Trail worth exploring. It's also part of the final stretch of the PCT before it enters California at the Siskiyou Gap. You can even climb Mount Ashland itself, but it's an easy and short hike up a dirt road.

At the trailhead, cross the road and head on the PCT into the forest for 0.5 mile to the beginning of the meadows. In another 1.1 miles the trail crosses a road and continues 1.8 miles to Grouse Gap and another road leading to a picnic shelter. Here you'll end this hike with a stunning view of Mount Shasta.

User Groups: Hikers, dogs, and horses. No mountain bikes allowed. No wheelchair facilities.

Permits: Permits are not required. Parking and access are free.

Maps: For a map of the Rogue River National Forest, contact the Rogue River-Siskiyou National Forest, 3040 Biddle Road, Medford, OR, 97504, 541/618-2200. For a topographic map, ask the USGS for Mount Ashland.

Directions: From I-5, take Ashland Exit 6 and follow Mount Ashland Ski Area signs. After 0.7 mile, go right on Mount Ashland Road 20 for 7.2 miles and park at a pullout on the right.

Contact: Rogue River-Siskiyou National Forest, Ashland Ranger District, 645 Washington Street, Ashland, OR, 97520, 541/552-2900.

155 PILOT ROCK

1.2 mi/1.0 hr 🏃1 ⛰8

south of Ashland in Cascade Siskiyou National Monument

Map 5.7, page 269   **BEST (**

Pilot Rock is aptly named, as it's what pioneers steered by to cross the Siskiyou Pass between California and Oregon. This basalt remnant of a 30-million-year-old lava flow formed of weird, geometric pillars and columns is a destination for serious rock climbers. With the Pacific Crest Trail running just below it, hikers can get close to the rock as well—though climbing it is not recommended. Stay away from that tempting ledge, too—it ends at a cliff.

From the lot, cross the road and head east on the PCT 0.2 mile to a side trail, following this up 0.4 mile to Pilot Rock. For a longer hike, consider continuing on the PCT another 6.5 miles to Soda Mountain (see next listing).

User Groups: Hikers and dogs only. No horses or mountain bikes allowed. No wheelchair facilities.

Permits: Permits are not required. Parking and access are free.

Maps: For a topographic map, ask the USGS for Siskiyou Pass.

Directions: From I-5, take the Ashland Exit 6 and follow Mount Ashland signs along Highway 99, and in 0.7 mile go under the freeway and follow Highway 99 for 1.2 more miles. Turn left on Pilot Rock Road 40-2E-33 and go 2.8 miles to a parking area on the right.

Contact: Bureau of Land Management, Medford Office, 3040 Biddle Road, Medford, OR, 97504, 541/618-2200.

156 SODA MOUNTAIN

4.2 mi/2.5 hr 🏃1 ⛰8

south of Ashland in Cascade Siskiyou National Monument

Map 5.7, page 269

The Cascade-Siskiyou National Monument is a biologically diverse area that creates a kind of bridge between its two namesake mountain ranges. The trees create a strange mix of white oak, cedar, and grand fir, and the big sunflower-like arrowleaf balsamroots thrive the slopes. Atop 6,089-foot Soda Mountain a staffed watchtower looks over Mount Shasta, the Klamath River Canyon, and the Trinity Alps.

Take the Pacific Crest Trail to the right toward Soda Mountain for 1.1 miles to a left-hand junction. Follow this spur 0.2 mile to a road, and go right 0.8 mile to the peak.

User Groups: Hikers, dogs, and horses. No mountain bikes allowed. No wheelchair facilities.

Permits: Permits are not required. Parking and access are free.

Maps: For a topographic map, ask the USGS for Soda Mountain.

Directions: From I-5, take the Ashland Exit 14 and go east on Highway 66 for 15 miles. Turn right on Soda Mountain Road 39-3E-32.3 and go 3.7 miles to a trailhead by power lines.

Contact: Bureau of Land Management, Medford Office, 3040 Biddle Road, Medford, OR, 97504, 541/618-2200.

157 LINK RIVER NATURE TRAIL

4.8 mi/2.0 hr   🏃1 ⛰6

in Klamath Falls

Map 5.8, page 270

Odd thing about Klamath Falls is that there aren't actually any waterfalls, at least not since the dam on the Link River silenced them. These falls once fell from the outlet of Upper Klamath Lake, the stupendously large inland lake where thousands of birds pass through on their migrations. Though the Link River is now itself a kind of lake, cormorants and pelicans still frequent the water, and this nature trail strides its length between Upper Klamath Lake and Lake Ewauna.

From the trailhead, follow the river through a canyon, crossing a canal and passing a steel staircase to a gauging station and the shore for 1.7 miles. Pass the power station and Favell Museum, go left on Main Street, then continue 0.4 mile to a 0.6-mile loop on the Wingwatchers Trail.

User Groups: Hikers and dogs on leash only. No horses or mountain bikes. The Wingwatchers Trail is wheelchair accessible.

Permits: Permits are not required. Parking and access are free.

Maps: For a topographic map, ask the USGS for Klamath Falls.

Directions: Drive U.S. 97 for one mile north of downtown Klamath Falls and take the Lakeshore Drive exit, following Nevada Avenue onto lakeshore Drive for 0.8 mile. Cross the Link River and turn left into a parking area for the Nature Trail.

Contact: Klamath County Department of Tourism, 1451 Main Street, Klamath Falls, OR, 97601, 541/884-0666.

158 OC&E WOODS LINE LINEAR STATE PARK

6.6-82.0 mi/2.0 hr-5 days 🏃2 ⛰7

east of Klamath Falls on Highway 140

Map 6.4, page 270   **BEST (**

In the great "Rails to Trails" movement, the OC&E Woods Line State Trail is a triumph. A full 82 miles long, this old logging railroad of the Oregon, California, and Eastern Line has been transformed into a linear park that has something for everybody. The first 7.1 miles are paved, and the rest lies a bit more rugged, passing the Sprague River, little towns, and ending at the Sycan Marsh, an avid spot for bird-watchers.

An easy introduction to the trail is the first 3.3-mile segment, which begins in Klamath Falls and ends at Highway 39. Because it is in town, this section is busy with bikers, joggers, and walkers. If you want a longer day on the paved portion, continue to the town of Olene 3.8 miles away, passing through countryside with views of Mount Shasta along the way.

Beyond Olene, the trail is less improved but enters the southern Oregon landscape in full force. The next 24.2 miles passes through old farming communities and juniper and sagebrush country. The end of this stretch reaches the Switchbacks Trailhead, where restrooms and camping are available. In the next 5.5 miles the trail reaches the Sprague River, following it 12.5 miles to the Sycan Siding Trailhead.

Here the trail splits. To the right, one path continues along the Sprague River 14 miles to the town of Bly, the official end of the trail. The left-hand trail crosses the river and heads out for 18.7 miles, following Five Mile Creek for a stretch, before arriving at the Horse Glade Trailhead, another spot to camp. The trail continues 14.2 miles, passing the 400-foot-long Merritt Creek Trestle to its end at Sycan Marsh, a spot renowned for waterfowl and wildlife.

User Groups: Hikers, dogs, horses, and mountain bikes. The eight-mile stretch from Klamath Falls to the town of Olene is paved and wheelchair accessible.

Permits: Permits are not required. Parking and access are free.

Maps: For a free park brochure, call Oregon Parks and Recreation, 800/551-6949, or download a free map at www.oregonstateparks.org. For a topographic map, ask the USGS for Klamath Falls, Altamont, Bonanza, Sprague River East, Beatty, Bly, Sycan Marsh, and Ferguson Mountain.

Directions: To get to the Klamath Falls paved trailhead, begin on Main Street in downtown Klamath Falls and go east on South 5th Street/OR 39, continuing onto South 6th Street, for 1.6 miles. Turn right on Washburne Way for 0.4 mile, then left on Crosby Avenue 0.2 mile to the trailhead.

For the Switchbacks Trailhead, drive north of Olene 12.5 miles to Bliss Road and go north 12.3 miles to the trailhead in the National Forest, to the left on Road 22. For the Sprague River Trailhead, continue 4.1 miles on Bliss Road to the town of Sprague River, then go left on Main Street less than a mile to the trailhead. For trail's end, drive 44.3 miles east on Highway 140 to the town of Bly. Go right 1.1 miles on Edler Street, left 0.5 mile on Gerber Ranch Road, and left 0.8 mile toward the OC&E State Trail.

Contact: Oregon Parks and Recreation Department, 1115 Commercial Street Northeast, Salem, OR, 97301, 800/551-6949, www.oregonstateparks.org.

SOUTHEASTERN OREGON

© SEAN PATRICK HILL

BEST HIKES

❰ Bird-Watching
Summer Lake Wildlife Refuge, **page 383.**

❰ Desert Hiking
Leslie Gulch, **page 381.**
Petroglyph Lake, **page 387.**
Steens Mountain Summit and Wildhorse Lake,
    page 393.

❰ Hikes for Views
Steens Mountain Summit and Wildhorse Lake,
    page 393.

❰ Short Backpacking Trips
Big Indian Gorge, **page 392.**

In the rugged and remote Oregon Outback, the

desert landscape dominates. The vast region of this seldom-traveled corner of the state is dominated by the high-desert landscape, a region of sagebrush steppes and western juniper stands carved through by prehistoric canyons, some dry and some still cradling their rivers. But don't let the word "desert" fool you; this landscape is anything but deserted. Pronghorn antelope wander the range of the Hart Mountain Wildlife Refuge, and bighorn sheep skirt the cliffs of Steens Mountain. Wildflowers spread for miles over the plateaus and golden eagles wheel in the skies. The farther you go, the more tremendous the scenery.

There are the occasional odd landscapes, too. The Newberry Caldera rises just south of Bend, a 60-mile wide shield volcano cupping two lakes, massive obsidian lava flows, and waterfalls. The Owyhee River carves its way through one of the deepest canyons in North America. With so much to see, it's essential to go prepared. Lots of water, a wide-brimmed hat, and plenty of sunscreen are essential for a good trip. Try to avoid the dead of summer and the hottest part of the day. Desert hikes can make for excellent fall, winter, and spring hikes as well, especially when the rest of the Oregon mountains are snowed in for most of the year. You'll also find access to colorful hot springs, one of the classic Oregon topographical features.

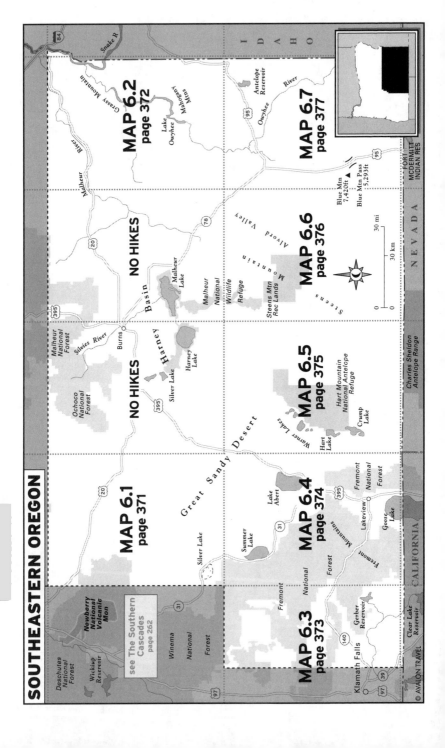

SOUTHEASTERN OREGON

MAP 6.1 page 371

MAP 6.2 page 372

MAP 6.3 page 373

MAP 6.4 page 374

MAP 6.5 page 375

MAP 6.6 page 376

MAP 6.7 page 377

NO HIKES

NO HIKES

see The Southern Cascades page 262

IDAHO

NEVADA

CALIFORNIA

FORT McDERMITT INDIAN RES

Deschutes National Forest

Wickiup Reservoir

Newberry National Volcanic Mon

Winema National Forest

Klamath Falls

Clear Lake Reservoir

Gerber Reservoir

Goose Lake

Lakeview

Fremont Mountains

Fremont National Forest

Summer Lake

Lake Abert

Silver Lake

Great Sandy Desert

Warner Lakes

Hart Lake

Crump Lake

Hart Mountain National Antelope Refuge

Charles Sheldon Antelope Range

Steens Mountain

Steens Mtn Rec Lands

Alvord Valley

Blue Mtn 7,420ft ▲
Blue Mtn Pass 5,293ft

Malheur National Wildlife Refuge

Malheur Lake

Harney Lake

Silver Lake

Harney Basin

Burns

Silvies River

Malheur National Forest

Ochoco National Forest

Malheur River

Grassy Mountain

Lake Owyhee

Mahogany Mtns

Owyhee River

Antelope Reservoir

Snake R

30 mi
30 km
0
0

© AVALON TRAVEL

Map 6.1

Hikes 1-5
Pages 378-381

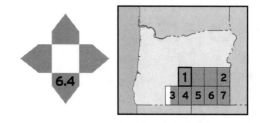

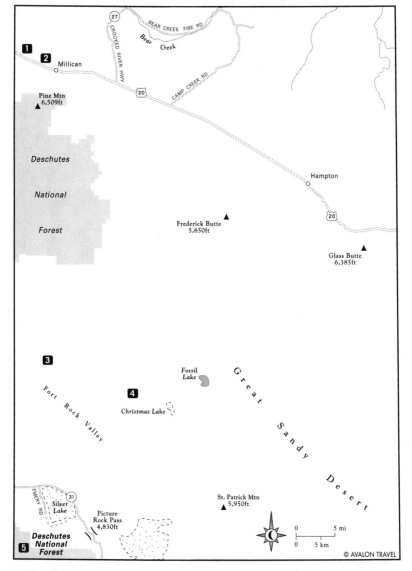

Map 6.2

Hikes 6-7
Pages 381-382

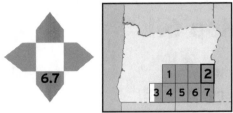

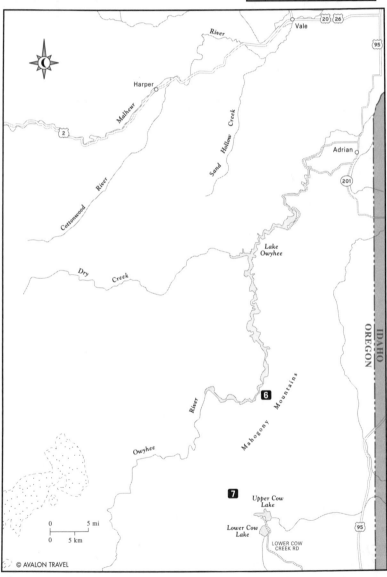

Map 6.3

Hikes 8-9
Pages 382-383

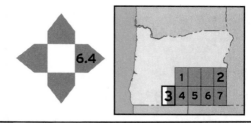

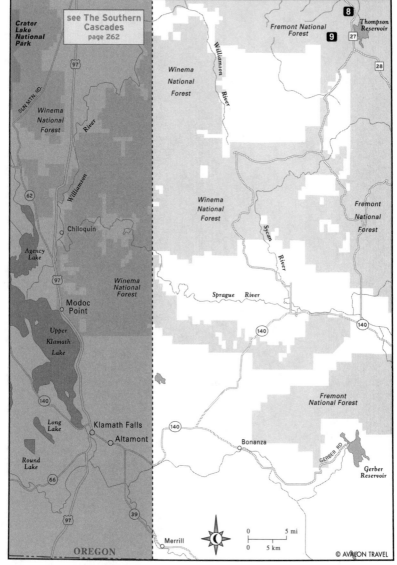

Map 6.4

Hikes 10-17
Pages 383-387

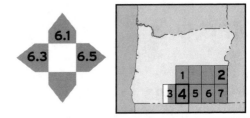

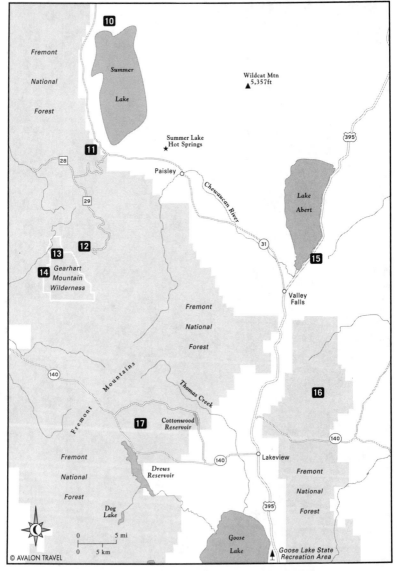

Map 6.5

Hikes 18-21
Pages 387-390

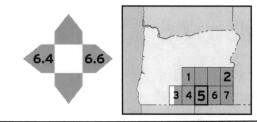

6.4 6.6

1 2
3 4 5 6 7

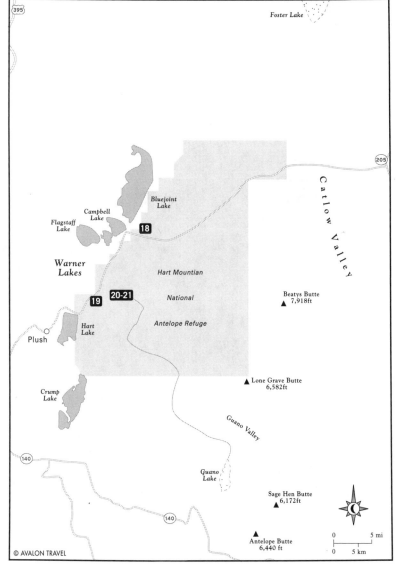

395

Foster Lake

205

Catlow Valley

Bluejoint
Lake

Campbell
Lake

Flagstaff
Lake

18

Warner
Lakes

Hart Mountian

20-21

National

19

Antelope Refuge

Plush

Hart
Lake

Beatys Butte
▲ 7,918ft

Lone Grave Butte
▲ 6,582ft

Crump
Lake

Guano Valley

140

Guano
Lake

Sage Hen Butte
▲ 6,172ft

N

0   5 mi
0   5 km

140

© AVALON TRAVEL

Antelope Butte
▲ 6,440 ft

Map 6.6

Hikes 22-28
Pages 390-395

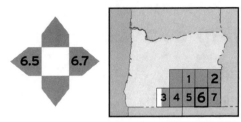

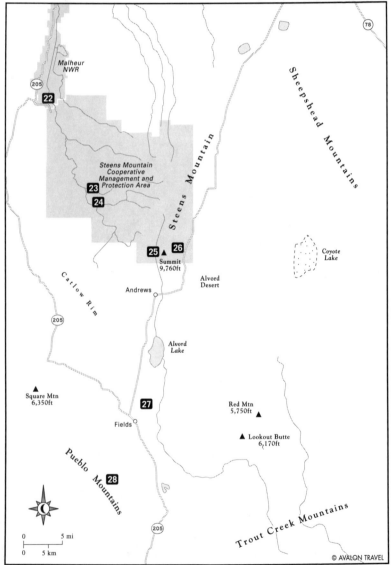

Map 6.7

Hike 29
Page 395

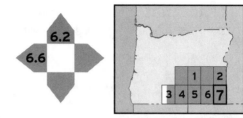

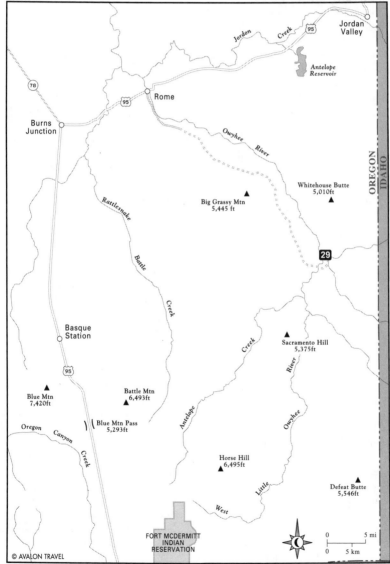

◻ THE BADLANDS
11.0–12.7 mi/3.5–4.0 hr

in the Badlands Wilderness Study Area southeast of Bend

Map 6.1, page 371

Just 12 miles southeast of Bend, the Badlands is a quiet refuge. In this wilderness study area, the largely flat sagebrush and juniper landscape has some strange formations that break up the seeming monotony. Flatiron Rock and Badlands Rock are outcrops of cracked rock, the remnants of "pressure ridges." The desert is home to an array of plants and flowers, as well as coyote, jackrabbits, raptors, and other animals. Note that Badlands Rock is closed from March through August to protect raptor nesting sites.

From the Flatiron Trailhead, take the right-hand Flatiron Trail 1.3 miles to a fork with the Homestead Trail. Keep left, then take a right at an intersection with the Ancient Juniper Trail. Turn left at a third intersection and continue on for 1.6 miles to Flatiron Rock. When you return 1.6 miles to the jumble of intersections, you can return as you came for a 5.8-mile round-trip. For a slightly longer hike, consider veering right on the Ancient Juniper Trail at the first intersection, which returns 2 miles to the trailhead for a 6.5-mile round-trip.

The second hike begins from the Badlands Rock Trailhead. Head 0.3 mile, passing the Homestead Trail on the left, to a fork, then keep left and continue 2.8 miles along this old road to the great gaping crater of Badlands Rock. Return as you came.

User Groups: Hikers, dogs, horses, and mountain bikes. No wheelchair facilities.

Permits: Permits are not required. Parking and access are free.

Maps: For a brochure and map of the Badlands Wilderness Study Area, contact Bureau of Land Management, Prineville District Office, 3050 NE Third Street, Prineville, OR, 97754, 541/416-6700, or go to www.blm.gov/or/districts/prineville. For a topographic map, ask the USGS for Horse Ridge and Alfalfa.

Directions: For the Flatiron Trail, drive east of Bend for 16 miles on U.S. 20 and park at the trailhead on the left. For the Badlands Rock Trailhead, continue east on U.S 20 for 1.5 miles. At the bottom of a long decline, turn left on a gravel road and cross a cattle guard. Go straight past the gravel piles on a paved road one mile, parking at a signboard for the Badlands Rock Trail on the left.

Contact: Bureau of Land Management, Prineville District Office, 3050 NE Third Street, Prineville, OR, 97754, 541/416-6700.

◻ DRY RIVER CANYON
6.0 mi/2.0 hr

in the Badlands Wilderness Study Area southeast of Bend

Map 6.1, page 371

It's hard to believe, but the vast deserts east of Horse Ridge were once the bed of a massive, inland lake. During the Ice Age, those shores lapped against the ridge and finally found a fault, and the entire lake drained through what is now Dry River Canyon, a slot where Native Americans once fished along the long-extinct river. Though Highway 20 follows the canyon up and over Horse Ridge with a pullout to view it, the only real way to experience it is to see it firsthand. As you walk the canyon, notice how it deepens, and how the walls change color with different lava flows and algae. Plowing through groves of sagebrush and mountain mahogany, the trail comes upon massive ponderosa pines, which seem somehow out of place here. There is also a lower segment of the canyon from a different trailhead, where the river dug a smaller canyon, but one with aged and barely perceptible petroglyphs. Take care not to touch anything, and be aware of the seasonal closure (Feb. 1– Aug. 31) for the upper canyon stretch to protect nesting raptors.

To hike the larger upper canyon, start from the parking area and follow the remaining dirt road to where it becomes trail. Follow the trail three miles to the top end of the canyon, where it ends at a fence marking private land. For the lower canyon, start from the Badlands Rock Trail and go 0.3 mile to a fork. Go right 0.9 mile along an old road. Where the road drops down to a series of big boulders, leave the road and go right into the canyon mouth, a 0.3-mile walk through the 40-foot-deep canyon.

User Groups: Hikers only. No dogs, horses, or mountain bikes allowed. No wheelchair facilities.

Permits: Permits are not required. Parking and access are free.

Maps: For a topographic map, ask the USGS for Horse Ridge.

Directions: Drive east of Bend for 17.6 miles on U.S. 20. At the bottom of a long decline, turn left on a gravel road and cross a cattle guard. For the upper canyon, turn right into a Highway Department gravel pile storage lot, go to the far side and follow the dirt road 0.8 mile toward the canyon to a fork and park on the right by the cliff. For the lower canyon, cross the cattle guard and go straight past the gravel piles on a paved road one mile, parking at a signboard for the Badlands Rock Trail on the left.

Contact: Bureau of Land Management, Prineville District Office, 3050 NE Third Street, Prineville, OR, 97754, 541/416-6700.

3 FORT ROCK

1.7 mi/1.0 hr   🏃1 ▲7

southeast of LaPine in Fort Rock State Park

Map 6.1, page 371

Once an inland lake, the Fort Rock Valley now is a stretch of desert wandering as far as you can see into the distances of vast tablelands. Evidence of this ancient lake can be seen on the wave-lapped stone of Fort Rock, the remnants of a massive volcano that later was transformed into an island. Ancient peoples used a nearby cave for shelter, where in 1938 archeologists unearthed a pair of sandals made of sagebrush bark, estimated at some 9,000 to 13,000 years old.

For a tour of Fort Rock, take the short paved route from the picnic area to a dirt path, 0.1 mile in all, to the cliff face. Follow an old road 0.6 mile through the interior of Fort Rock, keeping right at all junctions. At a four-way junction, an

Fort Rock State Park

easy 0.2-mile jog to the right leads to a viewpoint of the Fort Rock Cave. Returning to the junction, go straight 0.4 mile back to the lot.

User Groups: Hikers, dogs, horses, and mountain bikes.

Permits: Permits are not required. Parking and access are free.

Maps: For a topographic map, ask the USGS for Fort Rock.

Directions: From Bend, drive 29 miles south on U.S. 97 and turn left on OR 31. Follow this highway 29.2 miles and turn left on Fort Rock Road for 6.5 miles. At a sign for Fort Rock State Park, turn left on Cabin Lake Road/ County Road 5-11 for one mile, then left on Cow Cave Road/County Road 5-11A for 0.6 mile to the park entrance on the right.

Contact: Oregon Parks and Recreation Department, 1115 Commercial Street Northeast, Salem, OR, 97301, 800/551-6949, www.oregonstateparks.org.

4 CRACK-IN-THE-GROUND
1.0–2.0 mi/0.5–1.0 hr 🥾1 ⛰7

north of Christmas Valley

Map 6.1, page 371

Like nearby Fort Rock Valley, Oregon's Christmas Valley is a desert landscape of caves, lava flows, windswept sand dunes, and dry lakes. Just beyond the Four Craters lava flow, a strange shifting of the earth after the eruption created a long fissure aptly named Crack-in-the-Ground. Inside, it's easy to see how the crack formed, as the canyon walls are like puzzle pieces. You'll notice right away the temperature change, too; the crack stays amply cool even in summer, which is why homesteaders had picnics down here and made ice cream from the snow they found lingering here even in summer.

Follow the Crack-In-The-Ground Trail 0.2 mile to the beginning of the canyon. At a split in the trail, go right into the slot as far as you'd like. The other trail at the junction follows the crack from the rim, crossing it through a gap twice and continuing on the rim to its end.

User Groups: Hikers and dogs only. No horses or mountain bikes. No wheelchair facilities.

Permits: Permits are not required. Parking and access are free.

Maps: For a topographic map, ask the USGS for Crack-in-the-Ground.

Directions: From Bend, drive 29 miles south on U.S. 97 and turn left on OR 31. Follow this highway 29.2 miles and turn left on Fort Rock Road for 12.3 miles, following County Road 5-10 to the right another 10.2 miles. After the road twists through a couple turns, turn left on Christmas Valley Highway for 11 miles. Turn left at a sign for Crack-in-the-Ground and follow this gravel road 7.2 miles to a signed parking lot on the left. The trail begins across the road.

Contact: Bureau of Land Management, Lakeview District Office, 1301 South G Street, Lakeview, OR, 97630, 541/947-2177.

5 HAGER MOUNTAIN
8.0 mi/4.0 hr 🥾3 ⛰7

south of Silver Lake in Fremont National Forest

Map 6.1, page 371

Whereas other peaks crowned with fire lookouts get tons of visitors, this is not the case with the more remote Hager Mountain. You can ascend 7,185-foot Hager via the Fremont Trail in an eight-mile out-and-back hike, or choose from two other trailheads if you'd prefer a longer or shorter route. Along the way, ponderosa pines, big yellow balsamroots and Indian paintbrush line the path to the staffed lookout tower, which is rentable during the rest of the year. On a clear day, views reach from Mount Shasta in California to Mount Jefferson in the north.

From Road 28, begin gradually on the Fremont Trail 0.7 mile, crossing Road 012 at the second trailhead. The trail continues its steady climb 0.8 mile to a junction on the left to the third trailhead. Stay right and continue climbing on the Fremont Trail 1.1 miles and 650 feet to a junction. Go right 1.4 miles to the lookout.

User Groups: Hikers, dogs, horses, and mountain bikes. No wheelchair facilities.

Permits: Permits are not required. Parking and access are free.

Maps: For a map of the Fremont National Forest, contact Fremont-Winema National Forest Headquarters, 1301 South G Street, Lakeview, OR, 97630, 541/947-2151. For a topographic map, ask the USGS for Hager Mountain.

Directions: Drive 29 miles south from Bend on U.S. 97 and turn left onto OR 31. Go 47 miles and turn right on Road 28 for 9.3 miles to the Hager Mountain Trailhead pullout on the left. Park and walk back along the road to the trail. To find the higher trailhead, continue 0.2 mile on Road 28 and turn left on Road 012, going 1.2 miles to a trail sign, or even 0.8 mile farther to a parking area on the right. Each trailhead accesses the Fremont Trail directly.

Contact: Fremont National Forest, Silver Lake Ranger District, Highway 31, P.O. Box 129, Silver Lake, OR, 97638, 541/576-2107.

6 LESLIE GULCH
7.0 mi/2.5 hr

northwest of Jordan Valley on the Owyhee Reservoir

Map 6.2, page 372   **BEST (**

Bring your camera, as Leslie Gulch, an Oregon landmark, is one of the most spectacular areas of the state. Easily drivable, this narrow canyon of volcanic tuff formations, rare plants, and wildlife slips down to the Owyhee Reservoir and the Slocum Campground and makes for a good drive punctuated with several easy hikes. Whether you visit for the day or spend the night, these short hikes can be done in a single day. Drive down to the Slocum Campground to start the first hike, then backtrack up the canyon to each sight.

The honeycomb cliffs and gulches of Leslie Gulch are home to not only rare wildflowers found only in this canyon (Packard's blazing star and Etter's groundsel), but California bighorn

sheep, elk, bobcats, as well as birds like the rock wren and chukar. Each of these hikes offers an opportunity to spot something rare among the amazing geology of this ash-flow tuff.

From Slocum Campground, begin by following a primitive trail 1.3 miles up the Slocum Gulch, home to seasonal Slocum Creek, which flows in this ever-narrowing canyon. Then drive up Leslie Gulch 2.35 miles to an unmarked 0.6-mile trail on the left into Timber Gulch, with its scenic rock formations. Driving 1.25 miles beyond that, park on the left for the 0.8-mile Juniper Gulch Trail, which makes for an easy walk beneath overhanging cliffs—just don't go any further than is safe. Finally, drive one more mile up Leslie Gulch and park at a turnaround by a gate and follow this old road into Dago Gulch, a fortress of green ash and stone pillars, 0.8 mile to a gate, beyond which lies private land.

User Groups: Hikers and dogs only. No horses or mountain bikes allowed. No wheelchair facilities.

Permits: Permits are not required. Parking and access are free.

Maps: For a topographic map, ask the USGS for Rooster Comb.

Directions: From Jordan Valley, drive north on U.S. 95 for 27 miles and turn left on Succor Creek Road for 8.4 miles. At a junction, continue left on Succor Creek Road 1.8 miles, then go left on Leslie Gulch Road 14.5 miles. The Slocum Campground is at road's end at the Owyhee Reservoir.

Contact: Bureau of Land Management, Vale District Office, 100 Oregon Street, Vale, OR, 97918, 541/473-3144.

7 COFFEEPOT CRATER
1.0 mi/0.5 hr

northwest of Jordan Valley in the Jordan Craters Lava Beds

Map 6.2, page 372

Before you even think of coming here, check the weather. Wet weather makes many Eastern Oregon roads impassable, and both winter weather and the dead of summer can be inordinately harsh. If you make it, you'll find a 9,000-year-old eruption that leaked lava over 27 square miles. A row of "spatter cones," blocks of lava that acted as vents for hot gases, snake away from Coffeepot Crater and its easy loop trail overlooking the cracked and pitted lava flow. Dogs are not recommended as rough lava can severely hurt their paws.

From the lot, follow the trail to the right of the sign 0.3 mile up to the crater rim and a spur trail leading into the crater itself. Continue around the rim 0.2 mile back to the car, and take a side trail 0.2 mile out to the row of spatter cones.

User Groups: Hikers only. Dogs are not recommended. No horses or mountain bikes allowed. No wheelchair access.

Permits: Permits are not required. Parking and access are free.

Maps: For a topographic map, ask the USGS for Jordan Craters North.

Directions: From Jordan Valley, drive north 8.3 miles on U.S. 95. Turn west onto Cow Creek Road and go 11.4 miles to a fork, following signs for Jordan Craters. At a fork, go right 6.7 miles. At the next fork, go left on a bad road 5.9 miles to yet another fork. Fork left 1.5 miles, then fork left again 1.4 miles to the a parking lot at road's end.

Contact: Bureau of Land Management, Vale District Office, 100 Oregon Street, Vale, OR, 97918, 541/473-3144.

8 SILVER CREEK/ FREMONT TRAIL
4.4-18.1 mi/1.5-6.0 hr 🏃3 ⛰7

southwest of Silver Lake in Fremont National Forest

Map 6.3, page 373

The Fremont National Forest, named for explorer Captain John Fremont, who traversed this area in 1843, has only one trail, the Fremont Trail, though at 147 miles it is no mere footpath. It traverses this dry mountain

country, home to stands of ponderosa pine, topping peaks and following creeks along the way. For a shorter, or even longer stretch of the Fremont Trail, strike out along Silver Creek into an ash-strewn land dusted with the volcanic blasts of Mount Mazama nearly 8,000 years ago. Watch not only for spring wildflowers, but mosquitoes and ticks.

This section of the Fremont Trail begins near the campground entrance and crosses Road 27, then heads one mile to the creek. The next 1.2 miles follows the West Fork Silver Creek to a bridge near the North Fork, an easy day hike. To continue, cross the creek on another bridge and continue along the North Fork Silver Creek and leave the canyon behind, marching into lodgepole pine woods 2.6 miles on the Fremont Trail to a road crossing, then continuing another 3.2 miles to the Antler Trailhead.

User Groups: Hikers, dogs, horses, and mountain bikes. No wheelchair facilities.

Permits: Permits are not required. Parking and access are free.

Maps: For a map of the Fremont National Forest, contact Fremont-Winema National Forest Headquarters, 1301 South G Street, Lakeview, OR, 97630, 541/947-2151. For a topographic map, ask the USGS for Bridge Creek Draw and Partin Butte.

Directions: Drive 29 miles south from Bend on U.S. 97 and turn left onto OR 31. Go 46.6 miles and turn right on Road 27 for 10.4 miles to the Silver Creek Marsh Campground.

Contact: Fremont National Forest, Silver Lake Ranger District, Highway 31, P.O. Box 129, Silver Lake, OR, 97638, 541/576-2107.

9 YAMSAY MOUNTAIN/ FREMONT TRAIL
17.2 mi/1 day 🏃4 ⛰8

southwest of Silver Lake in Fremont National Forest

Map 6.3, page 373

Yamsay Mountain is the westernmost terminus of the 147-mile Fremont Trail. With views extending over the Fort Rock Valley, the peaks of the Cascades, and even as far as Mount Shasta in California, the 8,196-foot peak is a worthy goal. This is hot, dry country, so come prepared. Begin at the Antler Trailhead for a relatively easy approach. You can also take a short detour to see some volcanic rock pillars, adding only 0.5 mile to the overall hike.

To see the pillars, take the far right-hand trail from the lot, heading one mile to the rock pillars, and continuing 0.3 mile to the Fremont Trail. Go right, climbing 1,000 feet in 4.1 miles to Antler Springs and a four-way junction. Continue straight into mountain hemlock woods and then whitebark pine another 3.9 miles to the summit. To return, follow the Fremont Trail all the way back to the Antler Trailhead, turning left into the lot just before Road 038.

User Groups: Hikers, dogs, horses, and mountain bikes. No wheelchair facilities.

Permits: Permits are not required. Parking and access are free.

Maps: For a map of the Fremont National Forest, contact Fremont-Winema National Forest Headquarters, 1301 South G Street, Lakeview, OR, 97630, 541/947-2151. For a topographic map, ask the USGS for Yamsay Mountain.

Directions: Drive 29 miles south from Bend on U.S. 97 and turn left onto OR 31. Go 46.6 miles and turn right on Road 27 for 9.4 miles and turn right for 2.6 miles on Road 2804. Follow signs for the Antler Trailhead, and go left on Road 7645 for 4.8 miles, then left on Road 036, keeping right at all junctions, for 2.2 miles to the Antler Trailhead parking area on the right.

Contact: Fremont National Forest, Silver Lake Ranger District, Highway 31, P.O. Box 129, Silver Lake, OR, 97638, 541/576-2107.

🔟 SUMMER LAKE WILDLIFE REFUGE
9.2 mi/3.0 hr

east of Fremont National Forest on Summer Lake

Map 6.4, page 374   **BEST (**

When Captain John C. Fremont first spotted this lake from snowy Winter Ridge, he named it after the fact that it appeared a sunny oasis in December 1843. Beginning in 1944, Oregon Department of Fish and Wildlife bought more than 18,000 acres of this desert marshland—an important stopover for migratory birds on the Pacific flyway—to provide habitat for birds as diverse as pelicans, stilts, curlews, mallards, geese, and swans. The best time to come is from March to May, when those migratory birds come through. For a couple wildlife-viewing hikes, use the old dike roads that lead out on the marsh. Mosquitoes can be a problem here, to say the least.

From the Windbreak Campground, head out on the gated dike road for two miles, passing numerous viewpoints. At Summer Lake, the road turns right for 0.5 mile on the Gold Dike to trail's end. For a second hike, start from the Bullgate Campground and follow this dike road 2.1 miles to Summer Lake.

User Groups: Hikers, dogs on leash only, horses, and mountain bikes. The camping areas at Windbreak Dike and Bullgate Dike are wheelchair accessible.

Permits: Permits are not required. Parking and access are free.

Maps: For a downloadable map of Summer Lake Wildlife Area, go to www.dfw.state.or.us/resources/visitors/summer_lake_wildlife_area.asp. For a topographic map, ask the USGS for Summer Lake.

Directions: From Bend, drive south on U.S. 97 for 29 miles and turn left on OR 31 toward Silver Lake. Drive 70 miles to the town of Summer Lake, turning left into the wildlife refuge headquarters. Follow Wildlife Viewing Area signs to a gravel road, going 1.6 miles to a junction. To reach the Windbreak Dike, go right 0.9

mile to the Windbreak Campground. To go to the Bullgate Dike, go left 1.3 miles.

Contact: Oregon Department of Fish and Wildlife, Summer Lake Wildlife Area, 53447 Highway 31, Summer Lake, OR, 97640, 541/943-3152.

11 WINTER RIDGE/ FREMONT TRAIL

3.4-10.2 mi/1.0-3.5 hr 👣1 🔺8

north of Bly in Fremont National Forest

Map 6.4, page 374

First, don't be confused by the name. Though Captain John C. Fremont officially named this fault-block ridge "Winter Ridge," locals insist on calling it Winter Rim. Either way, you'll agree with both the locals and the explorers that this is something to see. Below the ridge, Summer Lake bakes in summer heat, with the occasional dust devil whipped up on the yellow alkaline flats. The trail along the ridge is part of the 147-mile Fremont Trail, which crosses the Fremont National Forest and connects to many trails in this section.

From the parking area, head toward the rim and follow the Fremont Trail north 1.7 miles through big pines and big stumps to a viewpoint accessible by going off-trail. In another 0.7 mile, take a detour left 0.3 mile through a meadow of quaking aspen and corn lily to Currier Spring. Continue on the main trail 1.4 miles; from here, it is not well marked, but you can continue out along the ridge another 0.7 mile to a viewpoint, and continue as far as you'd like. From the trailhead, it is also possible to follow the trail south along the rim.

User Groups: Hikers, dogs, horses, and mountain bikes. No wheelchair facilities.

Permits: Permits are not required. Parking and access are free.

Maps: For a map of the Fremont National Forest, contact Fremont-Winema National Forest Headquarters, 1301 South G Street, Lakeview, OR, 97630, 541/947-2151. For a topographic map, ask the USGS for Harvey Creek.

Directions: Drive 29 miles south from Bend on U.S. 97 and turn left onto OR 31. Go 82 miles and turn right on Road 29, continuing up 9.5 miles to a junction. Go right on Road 2901 and in 0.1 mile park on the right at a trailhead sign.

Contact: Fremont National Forest, Paisley Ranger District, Highway 31, P.O. Box 67, Paisley, OR, 97636, 541/943-3114.

12 CAMPBELL AND DEAD HORSE LAKES LOOP TRAIL

7.4 mi/3.0 hr 👣2 🔺7

south of Summer Lake in Fremont National Forest

Map 6.4, page 374

Set down in a lodgepole pine forest, these two lakes shimmer like mirrors in their alpine, glacier-carved basins. From the rims above, there are views extending out to the Winter Rim, Abert Rim, Hart Mountain, and even distant Steens Mountain. Below, the view reveals lakes bounded by thick trees. As with many trails in this area, you might not see anyone else on the trail with you.

Begin at Campbell Lake on the Lakes Loop Trail, passing a pond and going 0.2 mile to a junction. Go left 1.3 miles to begin the loop, climbing 500 feet up the Campbell Rim. At the next junction, go right along the rim 1.5 miles to another junction. For a short loop, go right here 1.9 miles back to Campbell Lake. For the full loop to Deadhorse Lake, continue forward one mile, then go right at the next junction and down 1.1 miles to Deadhorse. To avoid hiking through campgrounds and on the road, go left 0.6 mile along the lakeshore to an uphill junction on the left. Go up, cross the road, and continue 0.4 mile to a junction with the shorter loop spur, going left 1.3 miles back to Campbell Lake.

User Groups: Hikers, dogs, horses, and mountain bikes. No wheelchair facilities.

Permits: Permits are not required. Parking and access are free.

Maps: For a map of the Fremont National Forest, contact Fremont-Winema National Forest Headquarters, 1301 South G Street, Lakeview, OR, 97630, 541/947-2151. For a topographic map, ask the USGS for Lee Thomas Crossing.

Directions: From Bend, drive south on U.S. 97 for 29 miles and turn left on OR 31 toward Silver Lake. Drive 47 miles to Silver Lake and turn right on Road 28. Go 18 miles to a T-junction, and go left on Road 28 for 34 miles. Turn right on Road 033 for 1.9 miles and turn left into Campbell Lake Campground, driving 0.5 mile to the trailhead parking area on the left.

Contact: Fremont National Forest, Paisley Ranger District, Highway 31, P.O. Box 67, Paisley, OR, 97636, 541/943-3114.

Forest and the Gearhart Mountain Wilderness, contact Fremont-Winema National Forest Headquarters, 1301 South G Street, Lakeview, OR, 97630, 541/947-2151. For a topographic map, ask the USGS for Lee Thomas Crossing.

Directions: From Bend, drive south on U.S. 97 for 29 miles and turn left on OR 31 toward Silver Lake. Drive 47 miles to Silver Lake and turn right on Road 28. Go 18 miles to a T-junction, and go left on Road 28 for 36.2 miles. Turn left on Road 3411 for six miles, then left on Road 3372 for two miles, then right on Road 015 for 1.5 miles to the North Fork Sprague Trailhead.

Contact: Fremont National Forest, Bly Ranger District, Highway 140, P.O. Box 25, Bly, OR, 97622, 541/353-2427.

13 BLUE LAKE
5.6-12.8 mi/3.0-6.0 hr

north of Bly in Fremont National Forest

Map 6.4, page 374

This popular and pretty lake is also an entrance to the rarely visited Gearhart Mountain Wilderness. You can hike to 7,031-foot Blue Lake, or head up farther to The Notch, the gateway to the peak of Gearhart (see *Gearhart Mountain,* next listing). Thus, it is possible to make this lake a backpacking waystation for a summit of 8,370-foot Gearhart.

From the North Fork Sprague Trailhead, climb 700 feet up 2.4 miles on the Gearhart Mountain Trail to Blue Lake, then circle it on a 0.8-mile loop. The trail continues four miles to The Notch and continues 1.3 miles to a high saddle, from where it is possible to climb the mountain itself.

User Groups: Hikers, dogs, and horses. No mountain bikes allowed. No wheelchair facilities.

Permits: A free self-issue Wilderness Permit is required and is available at the trailhead. Parking and access are free.

Maps: For a map of the Fremont National

14 GEARHART MOUNTAIN
12.0 mi/7.0 hr

north of Bly in Gearhart Mountain Wilderness

Map 6.4, page 374

The Gearhart Mountain area is a landscape of lava. The mountain itself is a long outcrop of lava, and the trail spanning it passes a series of haunting pillars, a palisade of andesite pinnacles. Near the top, the trail enters a series of lovely meadows at the headwaters of Dairy Creek. Though the official trail doesn't reach the top, the ambitious can summit the mountain by trailblazing up to the ridge for views extending over handfuls of Cascade peaks.

From the parking area, follow the Gearhart Mountain Trail 0.7 mile into The Palisades. Continue into the forest of pine and white fir for four miles, passing The Dome and arriving at a saddle. The trail continues past a right-hand trail fork and below the peak and into the meadows 1.3 miles to The Notch, where the trail continues down to Blue Lake (see previous listing). If you're looking to climb the peak, be prepared to route-find and use your hands if necessary to make your way to the ridge. Return to the saddle, and head northwest 0.2 mile to the ridge, following it 1.3 miles to the summit.

User Groups: Hikers, dogs, and horses. No mountain bikes allowed. No wheelchair facilities.

Permits: A free self-issue Wilderness Permit is required and is available at the trailhead. Parking and access are free.

Maps: For a map of the Fremont National Forest and the Gearhart Mountain Wilderness, contact Fremont-Winema National Forest Headquarters, 1301 South G Street, Lakeview, OR, 97630, 541/947-2151. For a topographic map, ask the USGS for Lee Thomas Crossing.

Directions: From Bend, drive south on U.S. 97 for 29 miles and turn left on OR 31 toward Silver Lake. Drive 47 miles to Silver Lake and turn right on Road 28. Go 18 miles to a T-junction, and go left on Road 28 for 40 miles. Turn right on Road 34 for 10.4 miles, and turn right toward Corral Creek Campground on Road 012 for 1.5 increasingly rough miles to road's end at the Lookout Rock Trailhead.

Contact: Fremont National Forest, Bly Ranger District, Highway 140, P.O. Box 25, Bly, OR, 97622, 541/353-2427.

15 ABERT RIM
3.6 mi/3.0 hr   🏃4 ▲8

north of Lakeview on Lake Abert

Map 6.4, page 374

From Lake Abert, the great fault-block mountain of Abert Rim is absolutely imposing. The enormous fault scarp extends 30 miles along a lake teeming with wildlife. Despite its monstrous size, the Abert Rim is, in fact, climbable—though perhaps "scramble-able" is the word to use. This challenging climb hauls itself up 2,000 feet to a high promontory for outstanding views of the surrounding country.

From the Wildlife Viewing parking area, where you're sure to spot a plethora of waterfowl, cross the highway and head into the

sagebrush to find an old roadbed. Go left on it 0.1 mile to a rain tank. For the next 1.5 miles, you'll need to weave your way up the canyon of Juniper Creek through sagebrush, a meadow, a boulder field, and thick mountain mahogany. Near the top, keep to the right along the rimrock wall. When you reach a stand of ponderosas at the top, go right along the rim 0.2 mile to a viewpoint.

User Groups: Hikers only. Dogs not recommended. No mountain bikes or horses allowed. No wheelchair facilities.

Permits: Permits are not required. Parking and access are free.

Maps: For a topographic map, ask the USGS for Lake Abert South.

Directions: Drive north from Lakeview on U.S. 395 for 30 miles. Between mileposts 84 and 85, park at the Wildlife Viewing Area pullout.

Contact: Bureau of Land Management, Lakeview District Office, 1301 South G Street, Lakeview, OR, 97630, 541/947-2177.

16 CROOKED CREEK/ FREMONT TRAIL
8.2-13.8 mi/4.0-6.5 hr   🏃3 ▲7

north of Lakeview in Fremont National Forest

Map 6.4, page 374

The Fremont Trail, not entirely finished in places, nevertheless spans an ambitious 147 miles across the dry and rocky regions of Eastern Oregon. This section along Crooked Creek once had a lower trailhead, and still does despite the washed-out road. This higher trailhead has the benefit of sweeping views to Drake Peak, Light Peak, and Twelvemile Peak, as well as quaking aspen and ponderosa pine groves, but also follows a rugged canyon downhill—every bit down is another bit up. Be sure to keep this in mind!

From the trailhead, cross the road and start on the Fremont Trail. In 0.6 mile cross a road and continue on the Fremont Trail, crossing two forks of Crooked Creek, then starting down 1,000 feet into the canyon in two miles to a ford. For an easy 8.2-mile round trip, turn back here. Otherwise, do one of two things: Ford the creek to connect with an old road, or stay on this bank and bushwhack downstream 0.2 mile to meet the road. From here, the trail descends downstream along the old road 2.6 miles to the Mill Trailhead.

User Groups: Hikers, dogs, horses, and mountain bikes. No wheelchair facilities.

Permits: Permits are not required. Parking and access are free.

Maps: For a map of the Fremont National Forest, contact Fremont-Winema National Forest Headquarters, 1301 South G Street, Lakeview, OR, 97630, 541/947-2151. For a topographic map, ask the USGS for Crook Peak.

Directions: Drive north from Lakeview on U.S. 395 for five miles and go east on Highway 140 for 8.5 miles. Turn left on North Warner Road 3615 for 10.6 miles to the South Fork Crooked Creek Trailhead on the right.

Contact: Fremont National Forest, Lakeview Ranger District, 18049 Highway 395, Lakeview, OR, 97630, 541/947-3334.

🔳 COUGAR PEAK AND COTTONWOOD MEADOW LAKE

3.6-7.6 mi/1.0-4.0 hr

west of Lakeview in Fremont National Forest

Map 6.4, page 374

Cottonwood Meadow Lake, actually a reservoir, is circled by campgrounds and feeder creeks. A trail entirely circles it, making use of the roads at points. The trail also connects to a climb of Cougar Peak after a ramble along Cougar Creek on an abandoned road. The view from the old lookout site stretches right into California along massive Goose Lake and Mount Shasta. Circle the lake, climb the peak, or do both.

From the Cottonwood Trailhead, start one mile on the trail to an intersection with a road. The two hikes fan out from here. To circle the

lake, go straight over the road and continue on the trail uphill one mile and down to Cottonwood Creek and a junction. Go straight and continue another mile past the dam to a junction of roads. Go straight on Road 3870 to return 0.6 mile to the car.

To climb Cougar Peak, go left at the first junction along an old road-turned-trail 1.5 miles along Cougar Creek. Cross a road and start up an old, rough road 0.2 mile, then veer to the left on the hiker route for 1.1 miles to the 7,919-foot peak.

User Groups: Hikers, dogs, horses, and mountain bikes. No wheelchair facilities.

Permits: Permits are not required. Parking and access are free.

Maps: For a map of the Fremont National Forest, contact Fremont-Winema National Forest Headquarters, 1301 South G Street, Lakeview, OR, 97630, 541/947-2151. For a topographic map, ask the USGS for Cougar Peak.

Directions: Drive east of Klamath Falls on Highway 140 for 74 miles and turn left on Road 3870 toward Cottonwood Meadow for 6.1 miles. Where the pavement ends, turn left into the Cottonwood Trailhead lot.

Contact: Fremont National Forest, Lakeview Ranger District, 18049 Highway 395, Lakeview, OR, 97630, 541/947-3334.

🔳 PETROGLYPH LAKE

5.0 mi/2.5 hr   🧍2 ⛰8

in the Hart Mountain National Antelope Refuge

Map 6.5, page 375   **BEST (**

The area now designated as the Hart Mountain National Antelope Trail has been used by people for centuries, and you'll find remnants of those old cultures still. Mysterious petroglyphs dot the landscapes of Eastern Oregon, along with the occasional arrowhead and glittering piles of obsidian chippings left from their construction. Like many hikes in the Hart Mountain Refuge, the hike to Petroglyph Lake has no actual trail. It's a cross-country jaunt that leads up to a stunning viewpoint over the Warner lakes from Poker Jim Ridge, where on a good day, you may be able to spot bighorn sheep. Just below the crest of this ridge, partially hidden by a lava wall, is Petroglyph Lake, so named because its lava wall is painted with ancient rock drawings. Route-finding skills will come in handy, but the route is fairly straightforward.

From the parking area, cross the main road and head north and uphill toward the ridge for about one mile. When you reach the crest, continue north along the ridge 1.2 miles to a viewpoint on a knoll. Then look downhill to the east to spot two lakes; head for the one on the right. Proceed 0.8 mile downhill, working toward the left-hand shore. The lake will vanish into the desert as you approach. When you reach it, walk 0.5 mile along the long wall of drawings. At a dirt road, head back across the desert, southwest and toward the massive Warner Peak for 1.5 miles; you'll spot the road and your car as you get closer.

User Groups: Hikers and dogs on leash only. No horses or mountain bikes allowed. No wheelchair facilities.

Permits: Free self-issue permits are required only for backpackers, and are available at the visitors center. Parking and access are free.

Maps: For a brochure and map of the Hart Mountain Wildlife Refuge, contact Hart Mountain National Antelope Refuge, P.O. Box 111, Lakeview, OR, 97630, 541/947-2731, or download at www.fws.gov/sheldonhartmtn/Hart/index.html. For a topographic map, ask the USGS for Campbell Lake.

Directions: Drive north of Lakeview on U.S. 395 for five miles then turn east on Highway 140 for 16 miles. Go toward Plush, turning left on Road 3-13 for 20 miles to the town of Plush. Continue 0.8 mile through town and turn right on Road 3-12 toward Hart Mountain for 21.6 miles and park beside a right-hand dirt road with a sign for Hilltop Reservoir.

Contact: U.S. Fish and Wildlife Service, Hart Mountain National Antelope Refuge, P.O. Box 111, Lakeview, OR, 97630, 541/947-2731.

🔟 DEGARMO CANYON
1.4-9.4 mi/0.5-5.0 hr

in the Hart Mountain National Antelope Refuge

Map 6.5, page 375

On a high plateau rising above the Warner Lakes, the Hart Mountain Wildlife Refuge's high desert landscape is home to some serious wildlife, including the pronghorn antelope and bighorn sheep. Notched in the side of this colossal wall is DeGarmo Canyon, which climbs DeGarmo Creek past a waterfall and up to the vast steppe of the refuge. The canyon is surprisingly and refreshingly lush, and makes for a good introduction to desert ecology. Be aware that the upper stretches of the canyon don't have trails, but connect to other trails at the DeGarmo Notch.

Follow the trail into the canyon mouth past a small waterfall upstream to a shallow creek crossing, then continue 0.7 mile to trail's end at a far larger waterfall. Though you could return as you came, watch on the right just before the waterfall for a steep scramble route. Head up and around the waterfall cliffs, and past another lava flow 500 feet to an obvious trail. If you choose to loop back to the parking area, go left 0.9 mile along the canyon. The trail switchbacks down and becomes lost in sagebrush, but it's easy to spot your car and go cross-country.

If you choose to go farther up the canyon, go right on the upper trail instead for 1.8 miles to where the pine trees and the trail ends. But it's easy to cross the meadows, following the creek one mile to an old road on the left leading to Hart Mountain Hot Springs (3.4 miles) or another 0.6 mile farther to the DeGarmo Notch at a quaking aspen stand.

User Groups: Hikers, dogs on leash only. No horses or mountain bikes allowed. No wheelchair facilities.

Permits: Free self-issue permits are required only for backpackers, and are available at the visitors center. Parking and access are free.

Maps: For a brochure and map of the Hart Mountain Wildlife Refuge, contact Hart

Mountain National Antelope Refuge, P.O. Box 111, Lakeview, OR, 97630, 541/947-2731, or download at www.fws.gov/sheldonhartmtn/Hart/index.html. For a topographic map, ask the USGS for Hart Lake.

Directions: Drive north of Lakeview on U.S. 395 for five miles then turn east on Highway 140 for 16 miles. Go toward Plush, turning left on Road 3-13 for 20 miles to the town of Plush. Continue 0.8 mile through town and turn right on Road 3-12 toward Hart Mountain for 9.2 miles to just before a sign for DeGarmo Canyon, and turn right on a dirt road. Follow this road 0.5 mile, keeping right then left to stay on the main road. Park at road's end.

Contact: U.S. Fish and Wildlife Service, Hart Mountain National Antelope Refuge, P.O. Box 111, Lakeview, OR, 97630, 541/947-2731.

20 HART MOUNTAIN HOT SPRINGS TO WARNER PEAK

11.1 mi/6.0 hr   🏃3 ⛰8

in the Hart Mountain National Antelope Refuge

Map 6.5, page 375

Hart Mountain Hot Springs simmer up out of the ground at a comfortable temperature, a great dip on a chilly night if you're camping in the nearby campground—the only campground in the refuge. It's also a great place to start a hike. Looming above the hot springs and little oasis of trees that is the campground, 8,017-foot Warner Peak broods, sometimes holding snow in its lees well into summer. An absolute maze of trails leads to the radio tower on the peak, but easy routes abound if you utilize the old roads in this upper corner of the refuge.

From the springs, cross the meadow on an old road toward the campground, about 0.2 mile. When you come to the Barnhardi Road, go right 0.3 mile to a gate. Continue following the road one mile to a junction, keeping left. In another 0.9 mile, watch for the Barnhardi

Hart Mountain National Antelope Refuge

© SEAN PATRICK HILL

Cabin to the right up the creek. Head for the cabin, then follow the creek uphill 0.9 mile to the DeGarmo Notch. From here, head cross-country two miles to the left up the open ridge to Warner Peak's summit. Return as you came.

User Groups: Hikers, dogs on leash only, and horses. Mountain bikes allowed only on main roads only. No wheelchair facilities.

Permits: Free self-issue permits are required only for backpackers, and are available at the visitors center. Parking and access are free.

Maps: For a brochure and map of the Hart Mountain Wildlife Refuge, contact Hart Mountain National Antelope Refuge, P.O. Box 111, Lakeview, OR, 97630, 541/947-2731, or download at www.fws.gov/sheldonhartmtn/Hart/index.html. For a topographic map, ask the USGS for Warner Peak.

Directions: Drive north of Lakeview on U.S. 395 for five miles then turn east on Highway 140 for 16 miles. Go toward Plush, turning left on Road 3-13 for 20 miles to the town of

Plush. Continue 0.8 mile through town and turn right on Road 3-12 toward Hart Mountain for 24 miles to the refuge headquarters. Turn right on Blue Sky Road for 4.5 miles to a parking area to the right by the bathhouse.
Contact: U.S. Fish and Wildlife Service, Hart Mountain National Antelope Refuge, P.O. Box 111, Lakeview, OR, 97630, 541/947-2731.

21 DEGARMO NOTCH
7.7 mi/4.0 hr   👥2 ▲7

in the Hart Mountain National Antelope Refuge

Map 6.5, page 375

This trail follows DeGarmo Creek up to the DeGarmo Notch, a grassy saddle of aspen trees part way up a 2,000-foot wall. Day hikers can make a loop out of it, returning by a different route altogether. Backpackers can explore this stretch of the sagelands, hiking to the notch and then continuing into the canyon (see *DeGarmo Canyon* listing in this chapter). The trail to the DeGarmo Notch requires a bit of cross-country hiking, so route-finding skills will prove valuable.

From the hot springs, cross the meadow on an old road toward the campground, about 0.2 mile. When you come to the Barnhardi Road, go right 0.3 mile to a gate. Continue following the road one mile to a junction, keeping left. In another 0.9 mile, watch for the Barnhardi Cabin to the right up the creek. Head for the cabin, then follow the creek uphill 0.9 mile to the DeGarmo Notch. Follow the creek into the canyon 0.6 mile, and go right at a canyon fork on an old road. Follow this track 0.7 mile to a ridge crest, then descend to the right on a road 1.1 miles back to Barnhardi Road, then left 1.5 miles back to the hot springs.
User Groups: Hikers, dogs on leash only, and horses. Mountain bikes allowed only on main roads only. No wheelchair facilities.
Permits: Free self-issue permits are required only for backpackers, and are available at the visitors center. Parking and access are free.
Maps: For a brochure and map of the Hart

Mountain Wildlife Refuge, contact Hart Mountain National Antelope Refuge, P.O. Box 111, Lakeview, OR, 97630, 541/947-2731, or download at www.fws.gov/sheldonhartmtn/Hart/index.html. For a topographic map, ask the USGS for Hart Lake.
Directions: Drive north of Lakeview on U.S. 395 for five miles then turn east on Highway 140 for 16 miles. Go toward Plush, turning left on Road 3-13 for 20 miles to the town of Plush. Continue 0.8 mile through town and turn right on Road 3-12 toward Hart Mountain for 24 miles to the refuge headquarters. Turn right on Blue Sky Road for 4.5 miles to a parking area to the right by the bathhouse.
Contact: U.S. Fish and Wildlife Service, Hart Mountain National Antelope Refuge, P.O. Box 111, Lakeview, OR, 97630, 541/947-2731.

22 DONNER UND BLITZEN RIVER
2.8 mi/1.0 hr   👥1 ▲7

south of Burns on Steens Mountain Loop Road

Map 6.6, page 376

The Malheur Wildlife Refuge is fed by the lazy, marshy Donner und Blitzen River, which has its headwaters in the nearby Steens Mountain Wilderness Area. Mosquitoes are vicious in early summer, so be prepared. The river, whose name means "thunder and lightning" in German, was named by Army Colonel George Curry, who led battles in the Bannock Indian War in 1864—ultimately banishing the defeated tribes who once occupied this desert country to reservations in Burns and Yakima. Two short trails are accessible from a trailhead in the Page Springs Campground.

The easiest trail sets off to the right 0.7 mile along the Donner und Blitzen River. The second trail begins to the left at a Nature Trail sign, heading up a side canyon 0.5 mile, then turns left to the rim and descends 0.7 mile back to the campground. Walk the last 0.2 mile to the left to return to the trailhead.

User Groups: Hikers and dogs only. No horses or mountain bikes allowed. No wheelchair facilities.

Permits: Permits are not required. Parking and access are free.

Maps: For a topographic map, ask the USGS for Frenchglen and Page Springs.

Directions: From Burns, drive east on Highway 78 for 1.7 miles, then turn right on Highway 205 for 61 miles to Frenchglen. Turn left on Steens Mountain Loop for 2.9 miles, crossing the river, to a fork. Go right into the Page Springs Campground entrance, staying to the right for 0.6 mile to the trailhead.

Contact: Bureau of Land Management, Burns District Office, 28910 Highway 20 West, Hines, OR, 97738, 541/573-4400.

㉓ LITTLE BLITZEN RIVER
5.6-17.0 mi/2.0 hr-3 days 4 ▲9

southeast of Burns in Steens Mountain Wilderness

Map 6.6, page 376

Steens Mountain is open precious little time out of the year, and this road is usually gated from November to May. But when it's open, it's incredible. One of Oregon's newest designated wilderness areas, Steens Mountain offers plenty to explore. The fault-block mountain is sheared through by enormous glacier-carved gorges, one of them being the canyon of the Little Blitzen River, which feeds into the larger Donner und Blitzen River. If you're looking for a backpacking trip in the Steens, this is it: With the longest trek possible away from roads, you'll have the opportunity to camp in a deep river canyon. Day-hikers can sample two stretches, one a short walk to the Donner und Blitzen passing the historic Riddle Ranch. The longer hike is far more adventurous, requiring a creek crossing (best done in summer when the water is low), a mile of cross-country trekking, and a cumulative climb of 1,800 feet.

The trail to the Donner und Blitzen begins at the Riddle Ranch (though cars with low clearance will have to park down the road at the gate, and walk the remaining 1.3 miles). Cross the footbridge to the house, then take a trail behind an outhouse 1.5 miles to the river.

For the Little Blitzen Gorge Trail, cross the Steens Mountain Loop road from the trailhead and go 100 yards farther up the road to the trail on the left. Go one mile to a ford, and continue 2.1 miles into meadows and pools along the river. Continue one mile up the canyon to reach 4-Mile Camp. This makes a good turnaround, but hikers can continue 4.5 rougher miles, passing two waterfalls before the trail ends.

User Groups: Hikers, dogs, and horses. No mountain bikes allowed. No wheelchair facilities.

Permits: Permits are not required. Parking and access are free.

Maps: For a topographic map, ask the USGS for Tombstone Canyon and Fish Lake.

Directions: From Burns, drive east on Highway 78 for 1.7 miles, then turn right on Highway 205 for 61 miles to Frenchglen. Continue another 10 miles on this highway and turn left on Steens Mountain Loop Road. Drive 19.2 miles to a junction. To visit the Donner und Blitzen, follow a sign for Riddle Ranch and turn left 1.3 mile to a gate open Thursday through Sunday, mid-June through October. If your car has clearance, you can continue the last 1.3 miles to road's end at the ranch. For the Little Blitzen Canyon, continue 0.8 mile on the Steens Mountain Loop to the Little Blitzen Trailhead on the right.

Contact: Bureau of Land Management, Burns District Office, 28910 Highway 20 West, Hines, OR, 97738, 541/573-4400.

24 BIG INDIAN GORGE

8.2 mi/4.0 hr 🥾3 ⛺9

southeast of Burns in Steens Mountain Wilderness

Map 6.6, page 376 **BEST (**

A spectacular 2,000-foot gorge carved into the side of the Steens Mountain is the bed of Big Indian Creek, lined with quaking aspen and cottonwood trees, and excellent for camping. It is said that long after the Bannock Indian War of 1864, the local tribes still came to this canyon to camp and race horses. Now it is as quiet as anything you can imagine, with only the wind in the willow leaves and the swift creek following you. Though the approach is on an arid plain following a dirt road, even that has its share of views as far as Hart Mountain in the west. Once the canyon begins, it swallows you up.

From the South Steens Campground, follow the old road behind the gate 1.9 miles to a woodsy ford of Big Indian Creek. In another 0.2 mile, ford Little Indian Creek near a falls. Watch for a ruined cabin in another 0.4 mile, then continue into the gorge 0.6 mile to the final crossing of Big Indian Creek. In another mile, the trail curves with the canyon to a long stretch with views to the Steens summit. The trail continues another 2.4 miles to a camping spot before the trail peters out, though hiking is still entirely possible another 1.6 miles to a series of creek forks.

User Groups: Hikers, dogs, and horses. No mountain bikes allowed. No wheelchair facilities.

Permits: Permits are not required. Parking and access are free.

Maps: For a topographic map, ask the USGS for Fish Lake.

Directions: From Burns, drive east on Highway 78 for 1.7 miles, then turn right on Highway 205 for 61 miles to Frenchglen. Continue another 10 miles on this highway and turn left on Steens Mountain Loop Road. Drive 19.5 miles on the Steens Mountain Loop to the South Steens Campground on the right. Take the second entrance and drive all the way to the far end, parking at a gate.

Contact: Bureau of Land Management, Burns District Office, 28910 Highway 20 West, Hines, OR, 97738, 541/573-4400.

© SEAN PATRICK HILL

Big Indian Gorge in Steens Mountain Wilderness

25 STEENS MOUNTAIN SUMMIT AND WILDHORSE LAKE

2.4 mi/1.0 hr   👣1 ⛰9

southeast of Burns on Steens Mountain

Map 6.6, page 376   **BEST (**

Oregon's highest-elevation road drives nearly to the top of 9,733-foot Steens Mountain, and all around the roadbed lies the wilderness area designated by Congress in 2000. Late snows can keep the final pitch to the summit blocked well into July, so be sure to call ahead to confirm conditions. Along the way, the road passes viewpoints of the Kiger Gorge and East Rim, making this a dramatic drive. At the end, hike up an easy trail to the summit and down into a basin that holds Wildhorse Lake, one of Oregon's highest. The views from Steens reach as far as you can see, over the yellow alkali Alvord Basin and beyond.

To head to the summit, take the left trail up 0.4 mile to the radio buildings. To go to Wildhorse Lake, take the right-hand trail 1.2 miles and down 1,100 feet to the shore.

User Groups: Hikers, dogs, and horses. No mountain bikes allowed. No wheelchair facilities.

Permits: Permits are not required. Parking and access are free.

Maps: For a topographic map, ask the USGS for Wildhorse Lake.

Directions: From Burns, drive east on Highway 78 for 1.7 miles, then turn right on Highway 205 for 61 miles to Frenchglen. Turn left on Steens Mountain Loop for 24.5 miles to a four-way junction. Go left at a Wildhorse Lake for two rough miles to the trailhead at road's end.

Contact: Bureau of Land Management, Burns District Office, 28910 Highway 20 West, Hines, OR, 97738, 541/573-4400.

26 PIKE CREEK CANYON

5.4 mi/3.0 hr   👣2 ⛰8

north of Fields on the east face of Steens Mountain

Map 6.6, page 376

On the eastern side of Steens Mountain, you can truly get a sense of the desert. Spread out like a great yellow carpet, the Alvord Playa bakes in the sun to a cracked landscape where virtually nothing can grow. Even the creeks don't know what to do here; they just run down to the lip of this desert and disappear. Such is the fate of Pike Creek, but if you find the creek higher up, it's wonderfully cold and clear, and it has its own path into a steep and narrow canyon among the ruins of old mines.

From a giant boulder at the upper campground, cross the creek and follow an old mining road up and to the right. This path climbs one mile and nearly 500 feet to a second creek crossing, then climbs steeply 300 feet in 0.4 mile to the end of the road. From here, you can go to the road's highest point and follow a series of cairns and faint paths up another 1.3 miles and nearly 600 feet to the Pike Knob, which cleanly divides two forks of the creek.

User Groups: Hikers, dogs, and horses. No mountain bikes allowed. No wheelchair facilities.

Permits: Permits are not required. Parking and access are free.

Maps: For a topographic map, ask the USGS for Alvord Hot Springs.

Directions: From Fields, follow Highway 205 north 1.3 miles and continue to the right on gravel Fields-Follyfarm Road for 24 miles along the mountain, then turn left over a cattle guard on an unmarked dirt road. Park here unless you have a high-clearance vehicle, then continue 0.6 mile up this rough road to the camping area.

Contact: Bureau of Land Management, Burns District Office, 28910 Highway 20 West, Hines, OR, 97738, 541/573-4400.

27 BORAX HOT SPRINGS
3.0 mi/1.0 hr   🥾1 ⛰8

northeast of Fields

Map 6.6, page 376

Oregon is hot spring country, and the Steens Mountain area is particularly rife with hot water cauldrons. People swim in the Alvord Springs, and visit Mickey Springs, but the Borax Springs are something else altogether—far too hot to touch. Instead, they have an unmatched beauty due to the phenomenal colors that grow in the pools. This Nature Conservancy–protected area is also the site of Borax Lake, an ancient arsenic-laced pond that's home to the borax chub (an endangered species that lives nowhere else). The trail also passes huge, rusting boiling vats for a borax company that once mined the white alkaline soils all around. Stay away from the pools themselves! The edges can be dangerous and unstable, so keep children close at hand. You'll want to wear sunglasses here, since the ground can be so bright it can hurt your eyes.

Cross the wire gate and follow the road 0.4 mile past the Lower Borax Lake Reservoir to a junction, staying right another 0.5 mile past the rusting vats to Borax Lake. Continue to the left 0.6 mile past a series of the strange, boiling springs, the last two beyond a fence.

User Groups: Hikers only. No dogs, horses, or mountain bikes allowed. No wheelchair facilities.

Permits: Permits are not required. Parking and access are free.

Maps: For a topographic map, ask the USGS for Borax Lake.

Directions: From Fields, follow Highway 205 north 1.3 miles and continue to the right on gravel Fields-Follyfarm Road for 0.4 mile, then go right onto a dirt powerline road for 2.1 miles. Turn left at the first fork and go 1.8 miles to road's end at a wire gate. The trail starts behind the fence.

Contact: The Nature Conservancy, 821 SE 14th Avenue, Portland, OR, 97214, 503/802-8100.

28 PUEBLO MOUNTAINS
7.2 mi/3.0 hr   🥾3 ⛰8

south of Fields near the Nevada border

Map 6.6, page 376

There are people in this world known as desert rats. They enjoy seemingly stark landscapes with a lack of trees, trails, and water. If you're one of those, then this is the trail for you. Still, mule deer thrive here, and you'll come upon wildflowers and willows, with side trips to the Van Horn Basin and Pueblo Mountain in what is easily the most remote and least known range in Oregon. Part of a 2,000-mile desert trail, this stretch will test your endurance. Bring plenty of water and hike early in the day if you can.

From the trailhead at the first cairn, follow the old road 0.6 mile and veer into the left-hand valley. The "trail" is marked almost entirely by rock cairns, spaced within sight of each other. Continuing 1.0 mile past several cairns brings you to a 6,900-foot saddle. In two miles, the trail reaches a 7,790-foot high point before continuing on toward Nevada and the town of Denio, 13 miles away—but for the unprepared day-hiker, it's safest to turn back here.

User Groups: Hikers, dogs, and horses. No mountain bikes allowed. No wheelchair facilities.

Permits: Permits are not required. Parking and access are free.

Maps: For a Pueblo Mountains Desert Trail map, contact Bureau of Land Management, Burns District Office, 28910 Highway 20 West, Hines, OR, 97738, 541/573-4400, or contact the Desert Trail Association, P.O. Box 34, Madras, OR, 97741, www.thedeserttrail.org/index.html. For a topographic map, ask the USGS for Van Horn Basin.

Directions: From Fields, drive south on Highway 205 for 3.1 miles to a sign for Domingo Pass. Turn right here across a cattle guard onto a gravel road for 3.8 miles. At a fork, go right 0.5 mile. At the next fork, go left 0.2 mile, crossing another cattle guard. At the third fork go left and stay going straight for 0.9 mile to a 90-degree turn to the left. Turn left at this corner and go 1.25 miles to a rock cairn at a side road to the right.

Contact: Bureau of Land Management, Burns District Office, 28910 Highway 20 West, Hines, OR, 97738, 541/573-4400.

29 THREE FORKS HOT SPRINGS
4.2-7.2 mi/2.0-3.0 hr 🚶2 ⛰8

south of Rome in the Owyhee River Canyon

Map 6.7, page 377

Loneliest of all, the trail to Three Forks Hot Springs lies in the farthest and most remote corner of Oregon. Even the road there feels vast and never-ending. And the road down into the canyon is nothing to sneeze at either; it's a slow 1.5 miles over very primitive road to get to the Owyhee River and its fantastic canyon. If you come in spring, you may catch some boaters going by, as this is a popular rafting river. As summer progresses, though, the river drops dramatically; still, you'll have to wade a number of times to get to the hot spring pool fed by a pouring waterfall from a warm creek in a side canyon.

From the parking area, go to the boat ramp and walk to the left and upstream along the river, fording the North Fork Owyhee River. On the far side, stay along the shore and follow an old wagon road two miles along the river. After a few twists, you'll begin to see and smell the warm water flowing over the trail—look across to find the big springs. Where a road comes down to the shore, ford the river (sometimes knee-deep, sometimes ankle-deep) to a gravel bar on the far side, then follow the old road up to a bridgeless crossing to the hot springs.

User Groups: Hikers and dogs. No horses or mountain bikes allowed. No wheelchair facilities.

© SEAN PATRICK HILL

Three Forks Hot Springs on the Owyhee River

Permits: Permits are not required. Parking and access are free.

Maps: For a topographic map, ask the USGS for Three Forks.

Directions: From Burns, drive Highway 78 east 93 miles to Burns Junction and go left on U.S. 95 for 30.5 miles, passing the hamlet of Rome and crossing the Owyhee River. At a sign for Three Forks, turn right on Three Forks Road and go 27.6 miles to a T-junction. Go right 2.7 miles to an old corral and park here. If you have a vehicle with high clearance, continue down the canyon wall 1.4 miles to a junction, then go right 0.1 mile toward the lone outhouse.

Contact: Bureau of Land Management, Vale District Office, 100 Oregon Street, Vale, OR, 97918, 541/473-3144.

RESOURCES

NATIONAL FORESTS

United States Forest Service lands provide access to a great deal of Oregon's hikes, including everything from remote wilderness areas to public campgrounds. Camping is generally allowed anywhere unless specifically prohibited, as it is in sensitive wilderness areas or places where camping is restricted to preexisting sites. To escape the crowds, and to perhaps find real solitude, the national forests are your best bet.

Many Forest Service trails traverse areas with limited water, so always be sure to bring plenty if hiking in a dry area. Likewise, many remote Forest Service campgrounds have no water and no toilet facilities. For campgrounds like these, there is usually no fee or reservation required. For established campgrounds with drinking water and more elaborate facilities, there is nearly always a modest fee. Campgrounds at higher elevations are subject to closure during winter months.

Dogs are permitted in national forests, though it is strongly recommended that they be under total verbal control by the owner. The leading cause of lost pets in the wild is through chasing wildlife. In some places leashes on dogs are required.

Some areas require special permits, and wilderness areas are the main one. These free self-issue permits are usually obtainable at either the trailhead or the wilderness boundary. They are required between the Friday of Memorial Day weekend and October 31 for all groups that enter the wilderness. Limited Entry Permits are required for overnight and day visits to the Obsidian area in the Three Sisters Wilderness, issued only by the Sisters Ranger District or the McKenzie Ranger District, and the Pamelia area in Mount Jefferson Wilderness, issued only by the Detroit Ranger District.

Northwest Forest Pass

Many sites in the Deschutes, Fremont-Winema, Mount Hood, Siuslaw, Umpqua, and Willamette National Forests, as well as the Columbia River Gorge National Scenic Area, require a Northwest Forest Pass for each vehicle parked at a designated trailhead. Daily passes are $5; annual passes are available for $30. You can purchase the Northwest Forest Pass at any Forest Service ranger station or at many, but not all, of the trailheads. Retail outlets, especially outdoors stores, frequently carry them as well. For a list of businesses, go to www.fs.fed.us/r6/passespermits/vendors.php. You can also order passes online at www.naturenw.org. For phone orders, call 800/270-7504. Checks should be made payable to the USDA Forest Service.

Golden Eagle Passports will be honored in lieu of Northwest Forest Passes until they expire, and the Golden Age and Golden Access Passports are valid for the pass holder's lifetime. Parking is free in the national forests on two "free days": National Trails Day in June and Public Lands Day in September. A pass is not required on those days.

A current list of sites requiring the Northwest Forest Pass is online at www.fs.fed.us/r6/passespermits/sites.shtml. Recreation passes do not cover fees for winter Sno-Parks, cabin rentals, or developed campgrounds, and are not substitutes for climbing or wilderness permits. Recreation passes are not valid at concessionaire-operated day-use sites, though many honor passes through discounts at Forest Service campgrounds.

National Forest Reservations

Reservations at popular campgrounds, horse camps, and group camps are made by a reservation system. Reservations can be made online at www.recreation.com or by calling 877/444-6777. Individual campsites can be reserved up to 240 days in advance of arrival, and group sites up to 360 days in advance. There is a nonrefundable fee of $9 for reservations; major credit cards are accepted. Holders of Golden Age or Golden Access passports receive a 50 percent discount for single-family campsites. Some forests, such as the Deschutes National Forest, authorize private concessionaires by a Special Use Permit to manage campgrounds;

contact the national forest offices for details. Camping longer than 14 consecutive days at the same spot is generally not allowed.

National Forest Maps

National Forest maps detail access roads, hiking trails, campgrounds, and lakes, and are generally about $9. Orders can be placed by phone directly by calling the supervisor's office for each individual National Forest. You can also purchase select topographic wilderness maps from the Forest Service by contacting U.S. Forest Service, National Forest Store, P.O. Box 8268, Missoula, MT, 59807, 406/329-3024, fax 406/329-3030, www.nationalforeststore.com. You can also purchase maps from Discover Your Northwest at www.discovernw.org.

Forest Service Information

Forest Service personnel are helpful when it comes to trail and road information. Phone in advance of your trip for the best service, though you can also visit their offices during the week. For specific information on a particular national forest, contact the following offices:

USDA Forest Service

Pacific Northwest Region
333 SW 1st Street
P.O. Box 3623
Portland, OR 97208-3623
503/808-2468
fax 503/808-2210
www.fs.fed.us/r6

Columbia Gorge National Scenic Area

902 Wasco Avenue, Suite 200
Hood River, OR 97031
541/308-1700
www.fs.fed.us/r6/columbia

Crooked River National Grassland

813 SW Highway 97
Madras, OR 97741
541/475-9272
www.fs.fed.us/r6/centraloregon

Deschutes National Forest

1001 SW Emkay Drive
Bend, OR 97702
541/383-5300
www.fs.fed.us/r6/centraloregon

Fremont-Winema National Forest

1301 South G Street
Lakeview, OR 97630
541/947-2151
www.fs.fed.us/r6/frewin

Hells Canyon National Recreation Area

88401 Highway 82, Box A
Enterprise, OR 97828
541/523-1315
www.fs.fed.us/r6/w-w

Malheur National Forest

431 Patterson Bridge Road
John Day, OR 97845
541/575-3000
www.fs.fed.us/r6/malheur

Mount Hood National Forest

16400 Champion Way
Sandy, OR 97055
503/668-1700
www.fs.fed.us/r6/mthood

Newberry Volcanic National Monument

1001 SW Emkay Drive
Bend, OR 97702
541/383-5300
www.fs.fed.us/r6/centraloregon

Ochoco National Forest

3160 NE 3rd Street
Prineville, OR 97754
541/416-6500
www.fs.fed.us/r6/centraloregon

Oregon Dunes National Recreation Area
4077 SW Research Way
P.O. Box 1148
Corvallis, OR 97339
541/750-7000
www.fs.fed.us/r6/siuslaw

Rogue River-Siskiyou National Forest
3040 Biddle Road
Medford, OR 97504
541/618-2200
www.fs.fed.us/r6/rogue-siskiyou

Siuslaw National Forest
4077 SW Research Way
P.O. Box 1148
Corvallis, OR 97339
541/750-7000
www.fs.fed.us/r6/siuslaw

Umatilla National Forest
2517 SW Hailey Avenue
Pendleton, OR 97801
541/278-3716
www.fs.fed.us/r6/uma

Umpqua National Forest
2900 NW Stewart Parkway
Roseburg, OR 97470
541/672-6601
www.fs.fed.us/r6/umpqua

Wallowa-Whitman National Forest
P.O. Box 907
1550 Dewey Avenue
Baker City, OR 97814
541/523-6391
www.fs.fed.us/r6/w-w

Willamette National Forest
3106 Pierce Parkway, Suite D
Springfield OR, 97477
541/225-6300
www.fs.fed.us/r6/willamette

STATE PARKS

Oregon has one of the best state parks systems in the nation. From the coast to the mountains to the deserts, there are numerous day-use areas, campgrounds, and hiking trails. Many campgrounds offer drive-in campsites, showers and bathrooms, interpretive tours, even yurts. Reservations are always a good idea, especially in the high summer season.

If you're looking for a good camping spot, be sure to call ahead and make reservations, as Oregon State Park campgrounds are among the best in the state and go quickly months in advance. Fees are reasonable, and some state parks have walk-in camping for free.

State Park Reservations

Half of Oregon State Parks campgrounds accept campsite reservations, and the rest are first-come, first-serve. Reservations may be made from two days to nine months in advance. Reservations for Oregon State Parks are made through Reserve America by phone at 800/452-5687 or online at www.reserveamerica.com. A reservation fee of $8 is charged for a campsite. Major credit cards are accepted by phone and online, but generally not at the parks themselves. The charge is based on one vehicle, and additional vehicles are charged more.

For general information about Oregon State Parks, contact:

**Oregon Parks and
Recreation Department**
1115 Commercial Street NE
Salem, OR 97301
800/551-6949
www.oregon.gov/oprd/parks/index.shtml

NATIONAL PARKS

Oregon has one major National Park, the amazing Crater Lake. Though campgrounds are not as numerous as at other National Parks, there are spots available at Crater Lake Lodge and Mazama Village Motor Inn; reservations are strongly recommended and can be made through Xanterra Parks & Resorts at 541/830-8700. Half the campsites at Mazama Campground are on a reservation system and can be attained by calling 888/774-2728. Expect to pay an entrance fee of $10 per car, good for seven days. For an additional fee, a Golden Eagle sticker can be added to the National Parks Pass, which in turn eliminates fees for many sites managed by the Forest Service, U.S. Fish and Wildlife, and Bureau of Land Management. Discounts are available for holders of the Golden Age and Golden Access passports, including a 50 percent reduction of individual camping fees and a waiver of park entrance fees.

Oregon also has a number of National Historic Trails, National Monuments, and National Historic Parks.

National Park Service
Pacific West Region
One Jackson Center
1111 Jackson Street, Suite 700
Oakland, CA 94607
510/817-1304
www.nps.gov

Crater Lake National Park
P.O. Box 7
Crater Lake, OR 97604
541/594-3000
www.nps.gov/crla

John Day Fossil Beds National Monument
32651 Highway 19
Kimberly, OR 97848
541/987-2333
www.nps.gov/joda

Lewis and Clark National Historic Park
92343 Fort Clatsop Road
Astoria, OR 97103-9197
503/861-2471
www.nps.gov/lewi

Oregon Caves National Monument
19000 Caves Highway
Cave Junction, OR 97523
541/592-2100, ext. 262
www.nps.gov/orca

BUREAU OF LAND MANAGEMENT
The Bureau of Land Management (BLM) manages many trails and primitive campsites in Oregon, including forest and desert areas. The BLM is also the manager for the Steens Mountain Wilderness. For specific information on a particular area, contact the following offices:

Burns District Office
28910 Highway 20 West
Hines, OR 97738
541/573-4400
www.blm.gov/or/districts/burns

Coos Bay District
1300 Airport Lane
North Bend, OR 97459
541/756-0100
www.blm.gov/or/districts/coosbay

Eugene District Office
2890 Chad Drive
Eugene, OR 97440
541/683-6600
www.blm.gov/or/districts/eugene

Lakeview District Office
1301 South G Street
Lakeview, OR 97630
541/947-2177
www.blm.gov/or/districts/lakeview

Medford Office
3040 Biddle Road
Medford, OR 97504
541/618-2200
www.blm.gov/or/districts/medford

Prineville District
3050 NE 3rd Street
Prineville, OR 97754
541/416-6700
www.blm.gov/or/districts/prineville

Roseburg District
777 NW Garden Valley Boulevard
Roseburg, OR 97471
541/440-4930
www.blm.gov/or/districts/roseburg

Salem District Office
1717 Fabry Road SE
Salem, OR 97306
503/375-5646
www.blm.gov/or/districts/salem

Vale District Office
100 Oregon Street
Vale, OR 97918
541/473-3144
www.blm.gov/or/districts/vale

OTHER VALUABLE RESOURCES

State Forests
Oregon Department of Forestry
2600 State Street
Salem, OR 97310
503/945-7200
fax 503/945-7212
www.oregon.gov

Santiam State Forest
North Cascade Unit
22965 North Fork Road SE
Lyons, OR 97358
503/859-4344
fax 503/859-2158
www.oregon.gov

Tillamook State Forest
Forest Grove District Office
801 Gales Creek Road

Forest Grove, OR 97116
503/357-2191,
http://egov.oregon.gov

City/County/Regional Park Departments
Ashland Parks and Recreation
340 South Pioneer Street
Ashland, OR 97520
541/488-5340
www.ashland.or.us

City of Eugene Parks
99 W 10th Avenue, Suite 340
Eugene, OR 97401
541/682-5333
www.eugene-or.gov

Lane County Parks
90064 Coburg Road
Eugene, OR 97408
541/682-2000
www.lanecounty.org

Linn County Parks and Recreation
3010 SW Ferry Street
Albany, OR 97322
541/967-3917
www.co.linn.or.us

Josephine County Parks
125 Ringuette Street
Grants Pass, OR 97527
541/474-5285
www.co.josephine.or.us

North Clackamas Parks and Recreation District
9101 SE Sunnybrook Boulevard
Clackamas, OR 97015
503/794-8041
www.clackamas.us

Oregon Parks and Recreation Department
1115 Commercial Street NE
Salem, OR 97301
800/551-6949
www.oregonstateparks.org

Portland Parks and Recreation
1120 SW 5th Avenue, Suite 1302
Portland, OR 97204
503/823-PLAY (503/823-7529)
www.portlandonline.com/parks

**Washington County
Facilities Management**
169 North 1st Avenue, MS 42
Hillsboro, OR 97124
503/846-8715
www.co.washington.or.us

Regional, State, and Federal Offices
Metro Regional Center
600 NE Grand Avenue
Portland OR 97232
503/797-1700
www.oregonmetro.gov

Oregon Department of Fish and Wildlife
3406 Cherry Avenue NE
Salem, OR 97303
800/720-ODFW (800/720-6339)
  or 503/947-6000
www.dfw.state.or.us

U.S. Fish and Wildlife Service
1849 "C" Street NW
Washington, DC 20240
www.fws.gov

U.S. Geological Survey
Branch of Information Services
P.O. Box 25286, Bldg. 810, MS 306
Federal Center
Denver, CO 80225
888/ASK-USGS (888/275-8747)
  or 303/202-4700
www.usgs.gov

Information Services
Cape Perpetua Visitor Center
2400 Highway 101
Yachats, OR 97498
541/547-3289

**National Historic Oregon
Trail Interpretive Center**
22267 Highway 86
P.O. Box 987
Baker City, OR 97814
541/523-1843

**Oregon Dunes National
Recreation Area Visitors Center**
855 Highway Avenue
Reedsport, OR 97467
541/271-6019

MAP SOURCES
Geo-Graphics
18860 SW Alerwood Drive
Beaverton, OR 97006
503/591-7635
www.geo-graphicsmaps.com

Imus Geographics
P.O. Box 161
Eugene, OR 97440
www.imusgeographics.com

U.S. Forest Service
Attn: Map Sales
P.O. Box 8268
Missoula, MT 59807
406/329-3024
fax 406/329-3030
www.fs.fed.us

U.S. Geological Survey
Branch of Information Services
P.O. Box 25286, Federal Center
Denver, CO 80225
303/202-4700 or 888/ASK-USGS (888/275-8747)
fax 303/202-4693
www.usgs.gov

HIKING CLUBS AND GROUPS

Bergfreunde
10175 SW Barbur Boulevard, Suite 100-BB
Portland, OR 97219
503/245-8543
www.bergfreunde.org

Chemeketans
P.O. Box 864
Salem, OR 97308
www.chemeketans.org

Friends of the Columbia Gorge
522 SW 5th Avenue, Suite 720
Portland, OR 97204
503/241-3762
http://gorgefriends.org

Mazamas
527 SE 43rd Avenue
Portland, OR 97215
503/227-2345
www.mazamas.org

Obsidians
P.O. Box 322
Eugene, OR 97440
503/344-1775
www.obsidians.org

Oregon Sierra Club
1821 SE Ankeny Street
Portland, OR 97214
503/238-0442
http://oregon.sierraclub.org

Pacific Crest Trail Association
5250 Date Avenue, Suite L
Sacramento, CA 95841
916/349-2109
www.pcta.org

Trails Club of Oregon
P.O. Box 1243
Portland, OR 97207
503/233-2740
www.trailsclub.org

Index

A

Abbott Butte: 347
Abert Rim: 386
Agate Beach: 57
Alder Springs: 287
Alsea Falls: 60
Alsea River: 60
Aneroid Lake: 218
Angels Rest: 131
Ankeny Wildlife Refuge: 113
Annie Creek: 350
Anthony Lake: 243
Applegate Lake: 344–345
Ashland: 345, 362–364
Astoria: 38

B

Babyfoot Lake: 93
Bachelor Mountain: 180
Badger Creek: 165
Badger Creek Wilderness: 163–165
Badger Lake: 163
Badlands: 252, 378
Badlands Wilderness Study Area: 378
Bagby Hot Springs: 173
Baker Beach: 65
Baker City: 222–226, 240–246, 249, 257
Bald Butte: 148
Bald Mountain: 89, 201
Baldy Lake: 240
Ball Point: 164
Bandon: 76–77
Banks Vernonia Linear Park: 43
Banks-Vernonia Railroad: 43
Barklow Mountain: 79
Baskett Slough Refuge: 112
Battle Ax: 178
Bayocean Spit: 46
Bear Creek: 209
Bear Lake: 147, 224
Bend: 297, 300–301, 332–335, 378

Benham Falls: 332
Benson Lake: 292
Berley Lake: 285
Big Indian Gorge: 392
Big Lake: 286
Big Obsidian Flow: 337
Big Pine Interpretive Loop: 87
Black Butte: 285
Black Canyon Wilderness: 238
Black Crater: 290
Black Lake: 244
Blacklock Point: 78
Blue Basin Overlook: 236
Blue Lake: 385
Blue Lake Basin: 357
Blue River: 277, 279
Bly: 384–385
Boardman State Park: 95
Bohemia Mountain: 313
Bolan Mountain: 342
Bonny Lakes: 220
Borax Hot Springs: 394
Boulder Creek: 320
Boulder Creek Camp: 92
Boulder Creek Wilderness: 319–320
Boulder Ridge: 157
Boundary Springs: 330
Boundary Trail: 341
Brice Creek: 310
Briggs Creek: 88
Broken Top Trail: 297
Browder Ridge: 275
Brown Mountain: 359
Buck Canyon: 329
Buck Creek: 205
Buck Mountain: 206
Buckeye Lake: 327
Bull of the Woods Lookout: 174
Bull of the Woods Wilderness: 172–174, 178
Bull Prairie Lake: 202
Bullards Beach State Park: 77

Bulldog Rock: 318
Bullpup Lake: 318
Burger Pass: 221
Burns: 390–393
Burnt Lake: 150

C

Cairn Basin: 153
Camp Lake: 295
Campbell: 384
Cannon Beach: 39, 41–42
Canyon City: 250–252
Canyon Creek: 251
Canyon Creek Meadows: 283
Canyon Mountain: 250
Cape Arago: 74
Cape Blanco: 78
Cape Blanco State Park: 78
Cape Falcon: 41
Cape Lookout: 48
Cape Lookout State Park: 48
Cape Meares: 47
Cape Meares State Park: 46–47
Cape Mountain: 64
Cape Perpetua: 61–62
Cape Sebastian: 89
Cape Sebastian State Park: 89
Carl Lake: 186
Carl Washburne State Park: 63
Carter Lake Dunes: 70
Cascade Head: 51
Cascade Head Experimental Forest: 51
Cascade Head Inland Trail: 51
Cascade Head Nature Conservancy Trail: 52
Cascade Head Preserve: 52
Cascade Locks: 139–145
Cascade Siskiyou National Monument: 364
Cascadia State Park: 116

Castle Canyon: 158
Castle Rock: 279
Catherine Creek Meadows: 220
Cave Junction: 89, 92–93, 340
Chambers Lakes: 295
Champoeg State Park: 111
Chief Joseph Mountain: 217
Chimney Rock: 236
Christmas Valley: 380
Chucksney Mountain: 303
Cinder Hill: 337
Clackamas: 110
Clackamas River: 137
Clarno Palisades: 233
Clatsop Spit: 38
Clear Lake: 275–276, 278
Cleetwood Cove: 349
Cliff Lake: 327
Cloud Cap: 156
Coast Range: 54, 76
Coffeepot Crater: 381
Coffin Mountain Lookout: 180
Cold Springs Trailhead: 356
Collings Mountain: 344
Columbia Gorge: 130
Columbia River: 38
Columbia River Gorge: 130–132, 134, 139–146
Cooper Spur: 155
Coos Bay: 74–76
Copper Canyon: 84
Copple Butte Trail: 201
Coquille River Falls: 80
Corvallis: 114–115
Cottage Grove: 310, 313
Cottonwood Meadow Lake: 387
Cougar Peak: 387
Cougar Reservoir: 280–281
Council Crest: 107
Cove Palisades State Park: 187
Cowhorn Mountain Loop: 317
Crack-in-the-Ground: 380
Crane Creek: 256
Crater Lake: 225, 346, 348, 352

Crater Lake National Park: 330, 348–351
Crater Peak: 351
Crawfish Lake: 242
Crescent Lake: 317, 339
Crescent Mountain: 274
Cripple Camp: 346
Crooked Creek: 386
Crooked River National Grasslands: 287
Cultus Lake: 334
Cummins Creek: 62
Cummins Creek Wilderness: 63
Cummins Ridge: 63

D
Dale: 247–278
Dalles, The: 171
Dayville: 236–238
Dead Horse Lakes Loop Trail: 384
Degarmo Canyon: 388
Degarmo Notch: 390
Deschutes National Forest: 187, 285, 300, 332–333, 335–336
Deschutes River State Recreation Area: 171
Deschutes River Trail: 332
Detroit: 177–185
Detroit Reservoir: 179
Devil's Backbone, The: 348
Devil's Peak: 166
Devil's Peak Lookout: 167
Devils Punch Bowl: 55
Devils Punch Bowl State Natural Area: 55
Diamond Lake: 222, 324–327
Diamond Peak: 316
Diamond Peak Wilderness: 311, 314–316, 339
Dickey Creek: 174
Dillon Falls: 332
Discovery Point: 350
Divide Lake: 314
Doerner Fir: 76
Dome Rock: 179
Dome, The: 337

Donner und Blitzen River: 390
Double Peaks: 182
Douglas Cabin Trail: 165
Downie Lake: 241
Downtown Portland: 107
Drift Creek Falls: 53
Drift Creek Wilderness: 59
Dry Creek Falls: 142
Dry River Canyon: 378
Duffy Lake: 282
Dug Bar: 229
Dutch Flat Saddle Loop: 244
Dutton Creek Loop: 350

E
Eagle Cap: 214
Eagle Cap Wilderness: 208–209, 211–218, 220–227
Eagle Creek: 141, 222
Eagle Creek Lakes Loop: 223
Eagle's Rest: 303
Echo Lake: 215, 222
Ecola State Park: 39
Eddeeleo Lakes: 306
Elijah Bristow State Park: 120
Elk Cove: 154
Elk Creek Falls: 80
Elk Meadows: 161
Elk Mountain: 44
Elkhorn Crest Lakes: 246
Elkhorn Crest National Recreation Trail: 245
Elowah Falls: 139
Enchanted Valley: 66
Enterprise: 215
Erma Bell Lakes: 304
Estacada: 135–138, 170, 172–175
Eugene: 66–67, 117–120, 302
Eureka Bar: 229
Eureka Viewpoint: 228

F
Face Rock: 77
Face Rock Wayside: 77

Fall Creek: 297
Fall Creek Falls: 320
Fall Creek National Recreation Trail: 302
Fall River: 335
Falls City: 54
Fawn Lake: 339
Fields: 393–394
Fields Peak: 238
Finley Wildlife Refuge: 115
Fish Lake: 328, 359
Floras Lake State Natural Area: 78
Florence: 63–68
Forest Grove: 47
Forest Park: 106
Fort Rock: 379
Fort Rock State Park: 379
Fort Stevens State Park: 38
Fossil: 233
Four-in-One Cone: 292
Fourmile Lake: 358
Frances Lake: 212
Freezeout Saddle: 231
Fremont National Forest: 380–387
Fremont Trail: 382, 386
French Creek Ridge: 177
French Pete Creek: 280
From Timberline Lodge: 159
Fuji Mountain: 312

G

Gales Creek: 45
Garfield Peak: 350
Gearhart Mountain: 385
Gearhart Mountain Wilderness: 385
Gleneden Beach: 55
Glide: 322–323
Godfrey Glen: 350
Gold Beach: 79–86, 89
Golden Falls: 74
Goodman Creek: 303
Government Camp: 158, 167–168
Granite: 240, 246
Granite Creek: 246
Grants Pass: 85–88, 340
Grassy Knob: 79

Grassy Knob Wilderness: 79
Gray Butte: 287
Grayback Mountain: 341
Green Lakes: 297
Gresham: 130–133
Grizzly Peak: 185, 362
Grouse Gap: 363
Grouse Mountain: 203
Gumjuwac Saddle: 163
Gwynn Creek: 62

H

Hager Mountain: 380
Hagg Lake: 47
Hand Lake: 291
Hardesty Mountain: 305
Harris Ranch Trail: 59
Hart Mountain Hot Springs: 389
Hart Mountain National Antelope Refuge: 387–390
Harts Cove: 51
Hat Point: 230
Hatfield Wilderness: 147
Hawk Mountain: 175
Hawkins Pass: 218
Heceta Head: 63
Hells Canyon National Recreation Area: 228–232
Hells Canyon Wilderness Area: 229
Hemlock Lake: 323
Henline Mountain: 176
Heppner: 201–202
Herman Creek: 142
Hershberger Mountain: 346
Hidden Lake: 158, 224
High Lakes Trail: 359
Highway 140: 365
Hills Creek Reservoir: 310, 313–314, 316–317
Hoffer Lakes: 243
Honeyman State Park: 68
Honeyman State Park Dunes: 68
Hood River: 146–149, 153–155, 161–162
Horse Creek Trail: 59
Horse Lake: 331
Horsepasture Mountain: 280

Horsetail Falls: 132
Howard Buford Recreation Area: 118
Howlock Mountain: 325
Huckleberry Mountain: 157, 210
Hug Point: 41
Humbug Mountain: 82
Humbug Mountain State Park: 82
Hunchback Mountain: 157
Hurricane Creek: 215

I

Ice Lake: 215
Illahee Rock Lookout: 319
Illinois River: 85
Illinois River Falls: 92
Illinois River Trail: 89
Imnaha Divide: 220
Imnaha River: 227
Indian Mary Park: 85
Indian Point: 142
Iron Mountain: 272

JK

Jacksonville: 361
Jacksonville Woodlands: 361
Jefferson Park: 184
Joaquin Miller Trail: 251
John Day: 249–250
John Day Fossil Beds: 233, 236–237
Johnson Butte: 94
Jordan Craters Lava Beds: 381
Jordan Valley: 381
Joseph: 215–220
Jubilee Lake National Recreation Trail: 203
Kalmiopsis Wilderness: 89–94
Kentucky Falls: 67
Kings Mountain: 44
Kiwanda Beach: 50
Klamath Falls: 365
Klamath Lake: 355–358, 360
Klovdahl Bay: 308
Koosah Falls: 276

L

La Grande: 208, 211, 220
Lake Abert: 386
Lake Marie: 72
Lakes Basin Loop: 216
Lakes Lookout, The: 243
Lakeview: 386–387
Lapine: 336, 379
Larch Mountain Crater: 134
Larison Creek: 310
Latourell Falls: 130
Laurel Hill: 167
Lava Cast Forest: 335
Lava River Cave: 334
Lebanon: 116
Lemolo Falls: 322
Leslie Gulch: 381
Lewis and Clark Nature Trail: 130
Lewis and Clark State Park: 130
Lick Creek: 203
Lightning Spring: 350
Lillian Falls: 308
Lincoln City: 51–53
Link River Nature Trail: 365
Linton Lake: 294
Lithia Park: 362
Little Belknap Crater: 289
Little Blitzen River: 391
Little Malheur River: 255
Little Minam River: 211
Little North Santiam River: 176
Little River: 322
Little Strawberry Lake: 253
Long Lake: 358
Lookingglass Lake: 224
Lookout Creek Old-Growth Trail: 277
Lookout Mountain: 163, 235
Lookout Point Reservoir: 303, 305
Lost Creek: 247
Lost Creek Lake: 353
Lost Lake: 148
Lost Lake Butte: 149
Lowder Mountain: 282
Lower Deschutes River: 171
Lower Wenaha River: 207

M

Macleay Park: 107
Madras: 187
Magone Lake: 249
Magone Slide: 249
Maiden Peak: 314
Maidu Lake: 339
Malheur National Forest: 238, 249, 254, 256
Malheur River National Recreation Trail: 256
Manzanita: 42
Marion Forks: 185
Marion Lake: 185
Marion Mountain: 185
Marquam Gulch: 107
Marquam Nature Park: 107
Mary's Peak: 58
Matterhorn: 215
Matthieu Lakes: 290
Maupin: 169
Maxwell Lake: 213
Mazama Trail: 153
McClellan Mountain: 238
McDonald Research Forest: 114
McDowell Creek Falls: 116
McIntyre Ridge: 156
McKenzie Bridge: 276–280, 282
McKenzie Pass: 289–294
McKenzie River: 276
McKenzie River National Recreation Trail: 278
McNeil Point: 152
Medford: 358
Memaloose Lake: 137
Menagerie Wilderness: 271
Metolius River: 187
Middle Santiam River: 273
Mill City: 176–177
Mill Creek Wilderness: 234
Miller Lake: 339, 344
Milo McIver State Park: 135
Milton-Freewater: 202
Minam and Mirror Lakes Loop: 213
Minam River from Rock Springs Trailhead: 208
Mirror Lake: 168, 214

Mislatnah Peak: 91
Mislatnah Trail: 91
Mitchell: 233
Monon Lake: 182
Monument Rock: 255
Monument Rock Wilderness: 255
Mosier Twin Tunnels: 146
Mount Ashland Meadows: 363
Mount Bachelor: 297–299, 331
Mount Bailey: 327
Mount Bolivar: 82
Mount Defiance: 144, 147
Mount Hebo: 50
Mount Hood: 156, 160, 163–165, 169–170
Mount Hood National Forest: 135–138, 142, 148–149, 156, 158, 162–163, 167–170, 173, 175
Mount Hood Wilderness: 149–155, 158–161
Mount Howard: 219
Mount Ireland: 241
Mount Jefferson Wilderness: 183–186, 282–285
Mount June: 305
Mount McLoughlin: 357, 359
Mount Pisgah: 118
Mount Scott: 349
Mount Talbert: 110
Mount Talbert Natural Area: 110
Mount Thielsen: 326
Mount Thielsen Wilderness: 324–326, 339
Mount Washington Wilderness: 286, 289, 291–292
Mountain Lakes Wilderness: 360
Mountain Lakes Wilderness Loop: 360
Mowich Lakes: 282
Muir Creek: 329
Multnomah Falls: 132, 134
Munson Creek Falls: 49
Munson Creek State Natural Site: 49
Muskrat Lake Cabin: 334

N

Nannie Creek Trail: 355
National Creek Falls: 346
Natural Bridge: 347
Neahkahnie Mountain: 42
Nehalem Bay: 42
Nehalem Bay State Park: 42
Neskowin: 50
Nesmith Point: 139
Newberg: 111
Newberry Lava Tubes: 333
Newberry Volcanic National
    Monument: 334–338
Newport: 55–58
Niagara Falls: 49
Ninemile Ridge: 204
North Bank Deer Preserve:
    301
North Fork John Day River:
    240
North Fork John Day
    Wilderness: 239–240, 242,
    246
North Fork Malheur River:
    256
North Fork Umatilla River:
    204
North Fork Umatilla Wil-
    derness: 203–206
North Umpqua National
    Recreation Trail: 319
North Umpqua River: 301,
    318–320, 323
Nye Beach: 57

O

Oak Island: 105
Oakridge: 303–304
Oaks Bottom: 108
Oaks Bottom Wildlife
    Refuge: 108
Obsidian Trail: 293
OC&E Woods Line Linear
    State Park: 365
Ochoco National Forest:
    235, 237
Odell Lake: 315
Olallie Lake: 181
Olallie Lakes Scenic Area:
    181–182

Olallie Mountain: 279
Olallie Ridge: 279–280
Old Baldy: 135
Old McKenzie Wagon Road:
    291
Olive Lake: 248
Ona Beach State Park: 58
Oneonta Gorge: 132
Onion Creek: 254
Opal Creek: 177
Opal Creek Wilderness:
    176–177
Oregon Cascades Recreation
    Area: 317
Oregon Caves: 341–344
Oregon Caves National
    Monument: 340
Oregon Dunes National
    Recreation Area: 69–73
Oregon Dunes Overlook: 70
Oregon Trail Interpretive
    Center: 257
Oswald West State Park:
    41–42
Otter Point: 86
Owyhee Reservoir: 381
Owyhee River Canyon: 395
Oxbow Park: 133

P

Pacific City: 50
Pacific Crest Trail: 284,
    289–290, 355
Painted Hills: 233
Pamelia Lake: 185
Pansy Lake: 173
Panther Ridge: 81
Paradise Park: 159
Park Meadow: 295
Park Ridge: 183
Patjens Lakes: 286
Paulina Creek Trail: 336
Paulina Lake: 336
Paulina Peak: 338
Peavy Trail: 242
Pendleton: 204–206
Petroglyph Lake: 387
Phantom Bridge: 178
Philomath: 58
Pike Creek Canyon: 393

Pilot Rock: 364
Pine Creek: 250
Pine Lakes: 226
Polallie Ridge: 156
Port Orford: 78–79, 82
Porter Point: 50
Portland: 43, 105, 107–108,
    110
Potato Butte: 181
Powell Butte: 108
Powell Butte Nature Park: 108
Prairie City: 253–254, 256
Pretty Lake: 339
Prineville: 234–236
Prineville Reservoir: 236
Prospect: 353–355
Proxy Falls: 294
Pueblo Mountains: 394
Pyramids, The: 274

QR

Ramona Falls: 151
Rattlesnake Mountain: 328
Rebel Rock: 281
Red Blanket Falls: 352
Red Buttes Wilderness:
    342–343
Redmond: 287–288
Redwood Nature Trail: 96
Reedsport: 72
Reynolds Creek: 254
Rhododendron: 158
Richmond: 227
Ridgeline National Recre-
    ation Trail: 119
Rigdon Lakes: 307
Riverside National Recre-
    ation Trail: 138
Roads End Wayside: 53
Rock Creek: 237
Rock Lakes: 170
Rockpile Lake: 283
Rogue Gorge: 347, 352–354
Rogue River: 84–85
Rogue River National Forest:
    341, 344–348, 352–354,
    359, 363
Rogue River Trail: 83
Rogue-Umpqua Divide Wil-
    derness: 327–329, 346–347

Rome: 395
Rooster Rock: 271
Rosary Lakes: 314
Roseburg: 301, 319–320
Ruckel Ridge: 141
Ruth Bascom Riverside Path
    System: 117

S

Saddle Mountain: 40
Saddle Mountain State
    Natural Area: 40
Saddle Ridge: 247
Sahalie Falls: 276
Salem: 111–114, 171
Salishan Spit: 55
Salmon Butte: 166
Salmon River: 166
Salmon-Huckleberry Wil-
    derness: 157, 166
Salt Creek Falls: 311
Sandy: 156–157
Sandy River: 133
Santiam Lakes: 285
Santiam Pass: 271–275
Santiam State Forest: 114
Santiam Wagon Road: 271
Sauvie Island: 105
Scoggins Valley Park: 47
Scott Mountain: 292
Scott Trail: 292
Seal Rock: 58
Seaside: 40
Seven Devils Wayside: 76
Seven Lakes Basin: 355
Seven Lakes Trail: 354
Sevenmile: 355
Sheep Rock Trails: 237
Sheepshead Rock: 136
Shellburg Falls: 114
Shevlin Park: 301
Shore Acres State Parks: 74
Shotgun Creek Park: 117
Shotgun Creek Recreation
    Site: 117
Shrader Old-Growth Trail:
    86
Silcox Hut: 160
Siltcoos Lake: 69
Siltcoos River: 69

Silver Creek: 382
Silver Falls: 74
Silver Falls State Park: 74,
    112
Silver Lake: 380, 382
Siskiyou National Forest:
    79–80, 84–88, 90, 92–93,
    96, 340, 342
Sisters: 186–187, 285, 287,
    295–296
Sisters Mirror Lake: 299
Siuslaw National Forest:
    49–51, 53, 58, 64–67
Siuslaw Ridge: 66
Six Lakes Trail: 331
Sky Lakes: 355–356
Sky Lakes Wilderness: 352,
    354–358
Skyline Trail: 253
Smelt Sands Wayside: 61
Smith River: 67
Smith Rock State Park: 288
Snake River: 230
Snake River Trail: 229
Snow Camp Lookout: 90
Soda Mountain: 364
South Beach State Park: 57
South Breitenbush Gorge:
    181
South Breitenbush River:
    181
South Cinder Peak: 186
South Fork Desolation
    Creek: 248
South Fork Mountain: 137
South Jetty Trail: 57
South Santiam River: 116
South Sister Summit: 298
South Slough Estuary: 75
South Slough Reserve: 75
Southeast Portland: 108
Spanish Peak: 237
Spencer Butte: 118
Spencer Butte Park: 118
Springfield: 117
Stag Lake: 339
Stahlman Point: 179
Standley Cabin: 208
Starvation Creek Falls: 143
Starvation Ridge: 144

Steamboat Lake Loop: 211
Steens Mountain: 393
Steens Mountain Loop
    Road: 390
Steens Mountain Summit:
    393
Steens Mountain Wilder-
    ness: 391–392
Stein Butte: 345
Steins Pillar: 235
Sterling Mine Ditch: 361
Stewart State Park: 353
Strawberry Lake: 253
Strawberry Mountain: 254
Strawberry Mountain Wil-
    derness: 250–254, 256
Stuart Falls: 352
Stud Creek: 232
Sturgis Fork: 341
Sucker Creek: 343
Summer Lake: 383–384
Summer Lake Wildlife
    Refuge: 383
Summit Point Lookout: 226
Sunriver: 335
Sunset Bay: 74
Susan Creek Falls: 320
Sutton Creek Dunes: 65
Swan Mountain: 343
Sweet Creek Falls: 67
Sweet Home: 116

T

Table Rock: 171
Table Rock Wilderness: 171
Table Rocks: 358
Tahkenitch Creek: 71
Tahkenitch Dunes: 72
Takelma Gorge: 352
Tam McArthur Rim: 296
Tamanawas Falls: 162
Tamolitch Pool: 276
Tannen Lakes: 342
Tannen Mountain: 342
Taylor Creek: 87
Thielsen Creek: 325
Three Fingered Jack:
    282–285
Three Forks Hot Springs:
    395

Three Sisters Wilderness: 279–282, 290, 292–299, 304, 331, 334
Tidbits Mountain: 277
Tillamook: 44–49
Tillamook Head: 39
Tillamook State Forest: 44–45
Timberline Lodge: 160
Timberline Trail: 160
Timothy Lake: 170
Tincup Trail: 92
Tipsoo Peak: 324
Tire Mountain: 304
Toketee Falls: 321
Toketee Ranger Station: 321–322
Tollgate: 203
Tolovana Beach State Recreation Site: 41
Tom McCall Preserve: 146
Tombstone Lake: 222
Top Lake: 182
Traverse Lake: 222
Triangulation Peak: 184
Troy: 207
Tryon Creek State Park: 110
Tumala Mountain: 136
Tumalo Falls: 300
Tumalo Mountain: 300
Tumble Lake: 179
Twin Lakes: 169, 249, 323
Twin Lakes Mountain: 323
Twins, The: 309

UV
Ukiah: 239
Umatilla National Forest: 201–203, 207, 247–248
Umpqua Dunes: 73
Umpqua Hot Springs: 322
Umpqua Lighthouse State Park: 72
Umpqua National Forest: 310, 313, 318–319, 321–323, 325, 327
Union: 221
Union Creek: 348
Union Peak: 351
Unity: 255

University Falls: 45
Upper Rogue River: 330
Upper Rogue River Trail: 330
Upper Wenaha River: 206
Valley of the Giants: 54
Vista Ridge: 153
Vivian Lake: 311
Vulcan Lake: 94
Vulcan Peak: 93

W
Wagner Butte: 363
Wahclella Falls: 140
Wahkeena Falls Loop: 131
Wahtum Lake: 147
Waldo Lake: 306–309, 312
Waldo Lake Shore: 309
Waldo Lake Wilderness: 306–308, 312
Waldo Mountain Lookout: 307
Waldport: 59–60
Walla Walla River: 202
Wallowa: 208–214
Wallowa River: 218
Wallowa-Whitman National Forest: 210, 219, 226, 241–246, 249
Warner Peak: 389
Warrior Rock: 105
Washington Park: 106
Watchman: 348
Watson Falls: 321
Wauna Viewpoint: 140
Wenaha-Tucannon Wilderness: 206
Wheeler Creek Research Natural Area: 96
Wheeler Ridge: 96
Whetstone Mountain: 172
White River: 169
White River Falls: 169
Whittaker Creek Recreation Site: 66
Wickiup Plain: 299
Wild Rogue Wilderness: 81–83
Wildcat Basin: 252
Wildcat Mountain: 156

Wildhorse Lake: 393
Wildwood Recreation Site: 157
Wildwood Trail: 106
Willamette Mission State Park: 111
Willamette National Forest: 176, 178–180, 271–275, 277–280, 302–305, 309–310, 313–314, 317
Willamette Pass: 309, 311, 314
Willamette River: 111, 117, 313
Windy Lakes: 317
Windy Valley: 90
Winom Creek: 239
Winter Ridge/Fremont Trail: 384
Wizard Island: 349
Wolf Creek Falls: 322
Wolf Creek Park: 340
Wygant Peak: 145

XYZ
Yachats: 61–63
Yamsay Mountain: 382
Yaquina Head: 56
Yaquina Head Lighthouse: 56
Yocum Ridge: 152
Yoran Lake: 315
Zigzag: 149–153, 157, 166–167
Zigzag Canyon: 159
Zigzag Mountain: 149–150

www.moon.com

MOON.COM is ready to help plan your next trip! Filled with fresh trip ideas and strategies, author interviews, informative travel blogs, a detailed map library, and descriptions of all the Moon guidebooks, Moon.com is all you need to get out and explore the world—or even places in your own backyard. While at Moon.com, sign up for our monthly e-newsletter for updates on new releases, travel tips, and expert advice from our on-the-go Moon authors. As always, when you travel with Moon, expect an experience that is uncommon and truly unique.

MOON IS ON FACEBOOK—BECOME A FAN!
JOIN THE MOON PHOTO GROUP ON FLICKR

OUTDOORS

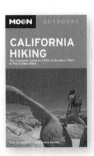

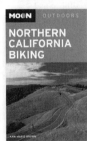

"Well written, thoroughly researched, and packed full of useful information and advice, these guides really do get you into the outdoors."

—GORP.COM

ALSO AVAILABLE AS FOGHORN OUTDOORS ACTIVITY GUIDES:

250 Great Hikes in
  California's National Parks
California Golf
California Waterfalls
California Wildlife
Camper's Companion
Easy Biking in Northern
  California

Easy Hiking in Northern
  California
Easy Hiking in Southern
  California
Georgia & Alabama Camping
Maine Hiking
Massachusetts Hiking
New England Cabins
  & Cottages

New England Camping
New Hampshire Hiking
Southern California
  Cabins & Cottages
Tom Stienstra's Bay Area
  Recreation
Vermont Hiking
Washington Boating
  & Water Sports

MOON OREGON HIKING

Avalon Travel
a member of the Perseus Books Group
1700 Fourth Street
Berkeley, CA 94710, USA
www.moon.com

Editor: Elizabeth Hollis Hansen
Series Manager: Sabrina Young
Copy Editor: Ellie Winters
Production and Graphics Coordinator:
   Domini Dragoone
Cover Designer: Domini Dragoone
Interior Designer: Darren Alessi
Map Editor: Albert Angulo
Cartographers: Kat Bennett, Brice Ticen

ISBN-13: 978-1-59880-098-2
ISSN: 1547-2949

Printing History
1st Edition – 2004
2nd Edition – May 2010
5 4 3

Text © 2010 by Sean Patrick Hill.
Maps© 2010 by Avalon Travel.
All rights reserved.

KEEPING CURRENT

We are committed to making this book the most accurate and enjoyable hiking guide to Oregon. You can rest assured that every trail in this book has been carefully reviewed in an effort to keep this book as up-to-date as possible. However, by the time you read this book, some of the fees listed herein may have changed and trails may have closed unexpectedly.

If you have a favorite gem you'd like to see included in the next edition, or see anything that needs updating, clarification, or correction, please drop us a line. Send your comments via email to feedback@moon.com, or use the address above.